Cirencester College Library
Fosse Way Campus
Stroud Road
Cirencester
GL7 1XA

936.11 wk

Our Changing Coast:
A survey of the intertidal archaeology of Langstone Harbour, Hampshire

02 06   This book is to be returned on or before
         the last date stamped below.

cirencester
college
a beacon college

D1145505

338501

Our Changing Coast:
A survey of the intertidal archaeology of Langstone Harbour, Hampshire

Michael J Allen and Julie Gardiner

with principal contributions from
Neil J Adam, Jon Adams, A M ApSimon, John M Bingeman,
Alan Clapham, Justin K Dix, Sarah Draper-Ali, Dominic Fontana,
Val Fontana, Rowena Gale, Michael Hughes, Arthur T Mack,
Lorraine Mepham, Jacqueline I McKinley, Garry Momber,
Paul Pettitt, Rob Scaife, and Rachael Seager Smith

illustrations by
S E James and the authors
(Digital Map data supplied by Dept of Geography, University of Portsmouth)

CBA Research Report 124
Council for British Archaeology
2000

Published 2000 by the Council for British Archaeology
Bowes Morrell House, 111 Walmgate, York YO1 9WA

Copyright Authors and Council for British Archaeology
All rights reserved

British Library Cataloguing in Publication Data
A catalogue for this book is available from the British Library

ISSN 0589–9036
ISBN 1 902771 14 1

Typeset by Archetype IT Ltd, Cheltenham, UK and Camplong d'Aude, France
Printed by Henry Ling Ltd, The Dorset Press, Dorchester, Dorset

The publishers acknowledge with gratitude a grant from
Hampshire County Council towards the publication of this report.

Cover photographs
Front cover, Augering in the mudflats off North Binness Island (Elaine A Wakefield)
Back cover: Top, Ditch 1711 on the foreshore of North Binness Island as first discovered, showing the spread
of artefacts and animal bone on the surface (Elaine A Wakefield)
Middle, The multidisciplinary team in action examining hearth 1702 (Elaine A Wakefield)
Bottom, Examining the cliff section at the west end of North Binness Island (Neil J Adam)

for
Richard Bradley and Arthur Mack,
professional and amateur alike
who have shown a passion for the past of Langstone Harbour

We hope that this survey will encourage others, as they have us,
to explore the archaeology of the Langstone area and to test, modify, improve,
and replace the interpretations we have presented here.

'Here civilization ends and Langston begins' (Scott Hughes 1956, 127)

Scott Hughes, J, 1956 *Harbours of the Solent*. London, Christopher Johnson

Contents

List of figures

List of plates

List of tables

Contributors' names and addresses

Neil J Adam: formerly Wessex Archaeology, Portway House, Old Sarum Park, Salisbury, Wilts, SP4 6EB

Jon Adams: Dept of Archaeology, University of Southampton, Highfield, Southampton, SO17 1BJ

Dr Michael J Allen: Wessex Archaeology, Portway House, Old Sarum Park, Salisbury, Wilts, SP4 6EB

A M ApSimon, FSA: Mansell Cottage, Swanmore Road, Swanmore, Hants, SO32 2QH

John M Bingeman: 5 Rumbolds Close, Chichester, West Sussex, PO19 2JJ

Dr Alan Clapham: MacDonald Institute, University of Cambridge, Cambridge, CB2 3JW

Prof Barry Cunliffe, FSA, FBA: Institute of Archaeology, University of Oxford, 36 Beaumont St, Oxford, OX1 2PG

Dr Justin K Dix: Dept of Archaeology, School of Ocean & Earth Science, University of Southampton, Highfield, Southampton, SO17 1BJ

Sarah Draper-Ali: formerly HWTMA, Southampton Oceonography Centre, University of Southampton, Empress Dock, Southampton, SO14 3ZH

Joy Ede: Farming and Rural Conservation Practice, Woodthorne, Wergs Road, Wolverhampton, WV6 8TQ

Dominic Fontana: Dept of Geography, University of Portsmouth, Lion Terrace, Portsmouth, PO1 3HE

V J L Fontana: 43, St David's Road, Southsea, Hampshire, PO5 1QJ

Rowena Gale: Folly Cottage, Chute Cadley, Andover, Hants, SP11 9EB

Dr Julie Gardiner, FSA: Wessex Archaeology, Portway House, Old Sarum Park, Salisbury, Wilts, SP4 6EB

Cathy Groves: Archaeological Research School, University of Sheffield, West Court, Mappin Street, Sheffield, S1 4DT

Michael Hughes, FSA: 5 Cyprus Road, Hatch Warren, Basingstoke, Hants, RG22 4UY

Andrew J Lawson, FSA: Wessex Archaeology, Portway House, Old Sarum Park, Salisbury, Wilts, SP4 6EB

Arthur T Mack: 95 Henderson Rd, Southsea, Hants, PO4 9JE

Lorraine Mepham: Wessex Archaeology, Portway House, Old Sarum Park, Salisbury, Wilts, SP4 6EB

S E James: Wessex Archaeology, Portway House, Old Sarum Park, Salisbury, Wilts, SP4 6EB

Jacqueline I McKinley: Wessex Archaeology, Portway House, Old Sarum Park, Salisbury, Wilts, SP4 6EB

Garry Momber: HWTMA, Southampton Oceanography Centre, University of Southampton, Empress Dock, Southampton, SO14 3ZH

Prof D P S Peacock: Dept of Archaeology, University of Southampton, Highfield, Southampton, SO17 1BJ

Dr Paul Pettitt: Oxford Radiocarbon Accelerator Unit, University of Oxford, 6 Keble Road, Oxford, OX1 3QJ

Dr Rob Scaife: Dept of Geography, University of Southampton, Highfield, Southampton, SO17 1BJ

Rachael Seager Smith: Wessex Archaeology, Portway House, Old Sarum Park, Salisbury, Wilts, SP4 6EB

Pippa Smith: Wessex Archaeology, Portway House, Old Sarum, Salisbury, Wilts, SP4 6EB

Grahame Soffe: Hayling Island Excavation Project, Dept of Archaeology, King Alfred's College, Winchester, Hants, SO22 4NR

Brian Sparks, OBE: HWTMA, Southampton Oceanography Centre, University of Southampton, Empress Dock, Southampton, SO14 3ZH

Kit Watson: formerly Wessex Archaeology, Portway House, Old Sarum Park, Salisbury, Wilts, SP4 6EB

Dr D F Williams: Dept of Archaeology, University of Southampton, Highfield, Southampton, SO17 1BJ

Elaine A Wakefield: Wessex Archaeology, Portway House, Old Sarum Park, Salisbury, Wilts, SP4 6EB

Sarah F Wyles: Wessex Archaeology, Portway House, Old Sarum Park, Salisbury, Wilts, SP4 6EB

Acknowledgements

This project was instigated by Michael Hughes, then County Archaeologist for Hampshire, who acted as team leader during the project and to whom due credit must be given for his foresight, and for securing funding from Hampshire County Council for the project. His monitoring role for the County Council was taken over by David Hopkins who was always very supportive. Funding of some of the post-excavation analysis was provided by Michael J Allen, and contributions towards radiocarbon dating were gratefully received from Hampshire County Council, Prehistoric Society Research Fund, Oxford University Radiocarbon Accelerator Unit, and the Hampshire and Wight Trust for Maritime Archaeology. The encouragement, support and advice of Prof Richard Bradley throughout the project is acknowledged.

The project was a collaborative one and involved the experience and expertise of two local fieldworkers, Arthur Mack and John Bingeman, without whom much would have been missed. Access to the more muddy extremes of the harbour would not have been as easy without Arthur's rowing skills. Permission from, and collaboration with, the local conservation and wildlife bodies was greatly welcomed and, in particular, help, advice and information were supplied by Andy Polkey and John Badley (RSPB, Langstone), and Bob Chapman (Hampshire Wildlife Trust). The safety aspects during fieldwork were paramount, and we thank Capt Hansen and the Langstone Harbour Board for their forbearance, the staff of Lee-on-Solent coastguard station and the Langstone mud-rescue team.

We gratefully acknowledge the advice and enthusiasm shown by our three referees, Richard Bradley, Leendert Louwe Kooijmans, and David Tomalin, whose wider view of the results was greatly appreciated, and prevented us from keeping our heads in the mud. Finally we thank the CBA for helping us get this into print; Kate Sleight who encouraged and guided us in the first instance, and especially to Jonathan Bateman for his careful and painstaking editorial work.

Wessex Archaeology would like to thank all those who participated in the strenuous fieldwork (especially Neil Adam, Vaughan Birbeck, Rod Brook, Gil Marshall, and Nick Wells). The initial stages of the project were overseen by Sue Davies for Wessex Archaeology. Illustrations from digital data were provided by Portsmouth University, and conventional drawings were largely prepared for publication by S E James. Figures 16, 17, and 18 were prepared from raw data for us by Rob Goller. Much advice on the digital preparation and execution of these figures was provided by Linda Coleman.

We received particular help and advice on the pottery from John Barrett, David Coombs, and David Tomalin, and are grateful to the staff at Portsmouth City Museum, and especially Jenny Stevens, for access to their collections. The harpoon was radiocarbon dated by Paul Pettitt, through the kind auspices of the Oxford University Radiocarbon Accelerator Unit and with permission of the owner, Eric McCleod. Advice on sea-level changes was given by Rob Scaife and Anthony Long. Details of the previous pollen work were provided by Keith Fowler (Portsmouth University). Jessica Winder provided advice and interpretation of the oyster structures and A J C Reger gave freely of his recent historical research on Hayling Island. The Langstone Harbour Board, through the kind offices of Capt Nigel Jardine, gave permission to reproduce their aerial photograph (Plate 41), which was facilitated through the offices of Niki Mein of Adams Hendry. Jessica Joslin and Josie Grant, while on work-placement from school, helped rationalise the errors in the County SMR and to compile a definitive record of the late Bronze Age vessels previously recorded in the harbour environs. The County Council's SMR officers fended off our continual enquiries in the latter stages of this project, so thanks especially to Bruce Howard and Anna Purdy for putting up with the disruption we caused. Discussions with Steve Rippon on the medieval use of saltmarshes elsewhere in the country were invaluable. We would like to thank Arthur ApSimon and Grahame Soffe for their reports and research on the previously unpublished sites so very late on in the reporting of this project.

Arthur ApSimon's grateful thanks, for information, help and advice, are due to Mr Russell Fox and Ms Jenny Stevens (Portsmouth City Museum), to Mr Noel Pycroft and Mr John Budden, to Dr David Williams, to Prof Barry Cunliffe and Prof Richard Bradley, and above all to Dr David Tomalin, for critical encouragment.

Grahame Soffe thanks Noel Pycroft, Nicholas Hall and Martin Williams for help with excavation and recording of the Langstone pit site, Valerie King for pottery drawing (Figure 34), Dr Hilary Howard and Elaine Morris for clay fabric analysis, Dr Justine Bayley (Ancient Monuments laboratory, English Heritage) for examining the cremation, and Prof Tony King (King Alfred's College, Winchester) for identifying the animal bones.

The Hampshire and Wight Trust for Maritime Archaeology would like to thank the Department for Culture, Media, and Sport (formerly Department of National Heritage), Hampshire County Council, SCOPAC, the Esmee Fairbairn Charitable Trust, the Inverforth Charitable Trust, the Garfield Weston Foundation, the Sir Jeremiah Colman Gift Trust, the Robert Kiln Charitable Trust, the Alan and Babette Sainsbury Charitable Fund, the John Coates Charitable Trust, and Lloyds TSB plc (formerly Lloyds Bank plc) for their support during the project.

The HWTMA's involvement in the Langstone project was led throughout by Brian Sparks with diving undertaken by Officers employed by the Trust and volunteers over the duration of the fieldwork, the majority of whom had undergone training with the Nautical Archaeology Society. A number of Masters students from the Department of Archaeology, Southampton University, under the guidance of Jon Adams and the HWTMA, served as a field team, and between them undertook the underwater excavation including that of the Sinah circle structure.

The team from University of Portsmouth, Department of Geography comprised an academic team of Peter Collier, Dominic Fontana, and Alastair Pearson with technical support from Paul Carter, Lawrence Dixon, David Payne, and Tremlett Stamp. The Portsmouth team would like to thank Simon Mears from Leica UK for GPS advice and Group Captain T F Cockerell of University of Cambridge Committee for Aerial Photography for air photographs of Langstone Harbour.

Langstone Project Team
Michael J Allen, Dominic Fontana, Julie Gardiner,
Michael Hughes, and Brian Sparks
December 1999

General notes

1 All radiocarbon results used in this volume have been calibrated with the 20 year atmospheric calibration curve using CALIB 2.0 using the maximum intercept method (Stuiver and Reimer 1986) with the datasets from Stuiver and Pearson (1986) and Pearson and Stuiver (1986). All calibrated date ranges are expressed at the 95% confidence level (at two standard deviations), with the end points rounded outwards to 10 years following the form recommended by Mook (1986).

2 The SMR (Sites and Monuments Record) is maintained by Hampshire County Council, and the information presented in Appendix 2 (the project sites and monuments archive) has been presented to the county's SMR office, and will in due course be included and allocated SMR ascriptions and numbers.

3 Abbreviations used in this report are:

Cal Lib Roll:	Calendar of Liberate Rolls
CSPD:	Calendar of State Papers Domestic
CTB&P:	Calendar of Treasury Books and Papers
DEM:	Digital Elevation Model
GIS:	Geographic Information System
GPS:	Global Positioning System
HCC:	Hampshire County Council
HRO:	Hampshire Record Office
HWMT:	High-water mark of Mean Tides
HWTMA:	Hampshire and Wight Trust for Maritime Archaeology
LNEBA:	Late Neolithic and Early Bronze Age
NAS:	Nautical Archaeology Society
PCM:	Portsmouth City Museum
PCRO:	Portsmouth City Records Office
PRO:	Public Record Office
PU:	Portsmouth University
RSL:	Relative Sea-Level
SMR:	Sites and Monuments Record
VCH:	Victoria County History

4 The Wessex Archaeology project archive is held in the Portsmouth City Museum. Wessex Archaeology recorded the project under the site code W622. Much of the material within the private collection of Arthur Mack has been be donated to the Portsmouth City Museum to be archived with material from this project and that found by previous workers (Chris Draper, Richard Bradley, and Barri Hooper, see bibliography for their fieldwork). Mr Mack, however, retains some of the diagnostic pieces.

Summary

The Langstone Harbour Archaeological Survey Project was a multidisciplinary study of the prehistoric to early-historic use and development of what is now a large, shallow, marine inlet on the south coast of England. Its main objectives were to survey and record the archaeology within the harbour itself and of its immediate hinterland and to determine its physical, environmental, and social development. The harbour was already well known for its archaeological content, and threats to the resource through erosion of the surviving islands and foreshores provided the stimulus for research.

The exposed terrestrial landscape and the intertidal and underwater zones were examined by a suite of 'seamless' fieldwork methods which sought to examine each part of the modern environment in a similar manner. The methodologies developed and employed in the survey are described and evaluated. Fieldwork involved large-scale 'fieldwalking' aimed at identifying, dating, and characterising artefact scatters, sub-surface features, and standing structures, underpinned by GPS survey; auger survey across all three main environments; limited exploratory excavation and test-pitting to examine sedimentary and stratigraphic sequences; underwater geophysical prospection where physical examination was impossible; and a review and reanalysis of previous finds. The report concentrates on the prehistoric and early-historic data which form the bulk of evidence recovered from the harbour itself but includes a brief historical summary of the later use of the area.

The survey recorded extensive flint and pottery distributions, mainly around four vestigial islands in the north of the harbour. Palaeolithic to late Bronze Age flintwork is present and analysis attempted to distinguish areas of specific activity. Only a handful of possible Palaeolithic flints are known, all from earlier research. Sporadic use of the area in the Mesolithic and Neolithic periods was followed by the establishment of a middle–late Bronze Age flat urnfield cemetery and several large cinerary urns and their contents were recovered. The archaeological data implies that the harbour had been dry-land until at least the middle Bronze Age. This was confirmed by palaeoenvironmental data, including pollen and molluscan sequences, and by the remains of two small relict submerged forests that provided radiocarbon dates of 3350–2910 cal BC and 2310–1950 cal BC. These indicate that Langstone Harbour was a low-lying basin with two deeply incised rivers flowing through it that was being exploited for essentially terrestrial rather than marine resources.

Re-examination of earlier collections showed that much of the material previously recorded as being of Iron Age date is, in fact, later Bronze Age. The Iron Age is actually poorly represented within the harbour itself though important late Iron Age sites are known on Hayling Island (a univallate hillfort and temple). From this time at least, Langstone was a tidal inlet and a principal activity around its margins was salt production. During the Roman period it seems to have been a shallow harbour used for salt manufacture and possibly brick making and oyster farming but was, essentially, undeveloped and certainly did not share in the importance of Chichester and Portsmouth Harbours to either side. A Roman road running to the north of Langstone sported a few minor villas but no development of the Roman waterfront could be identified.

Throughout the historic periods, even to the present day, Langstone Harbour has remained a quiet backwater with little urban or commercial development. Salt making, oyster farming, and fishing have been its main industries though it has played an important part in the defence of the south coast over at least the last three centuries. Its role in defending Portsmouth during the two World Wars has left tangible evidence while its contribution to the D-Day landings is both well documented and still visible through the remains of a Mulberry Harbour caisson which lies near the entrance to the harbour.

An analysis of erosion regimes is presented and an erosion model proposed to explain the movement of artefacts from terrestrial deposits to their eventual removal from the harbour. It is concluded that the archaeological resource is being rapidly lost as the context from which it derives is being eroded by wave action, largely because of the on-going dieback of *Spartina* grass which helps to consolidate the islands. The report concludes with statements on the significance and management of the archaeological resource, its inextricable link with ecological conservation issues and its implications, and a review of the methods adopted by the project and their applicability to other similar surveys.

Sommaire

Le Projet du Relevé Archéologique du Port de Langstone était une étude pluridisciplinaire sur l'utilisation et le développement, des temps préhistoriques au début de l'histoire, de ce qui est à l'heure actuelle un grand bras de mer peu profond de la côte sud de l'Angleterre. Ses principaux objectifs étaient de faire un relevé de l'archéologie dans le port lui-même et dans son arrière-pays proche, de noter les résultats, et de déterminer son développement tant sur le plan de l'environnement que sur le plan physique et social. Le port était déjà bien connu pour sa richesse archéologique et la menace que présentait pour cette ressource l'érosion des îles et des estrans qui restaient encore donnèrent la motivation nécessaire à la recherche.

Le paysage terrestre exposé, et les zones inter-cotidales et sous-marines, ont été examinés par une série de méthodes de travail 'intégrées' sur le terrain qui cherchaient à étudier chaque partie de l'environnement moderne de la même façon. Les méthodologies développées et utilisées pour le relevé sont décrites et évaluées. Le travail sur le terrain a entraîné un 'arpentage' à grande échelle dans le but d'identifier, de dater et de classifier les objets façonnés éparpillés, les particularités en dessous de la surface, et les structures verticales, appuyé par un relevé par GPS ; un sondage par auger dans les trois principaux environnements; des fouilles exploratoires et des sondages à petite échelle afin d'examiner les séquences sédiment-aires et stratigraphiques; la prospection géophysique sous-marine là où un examen physique était impossible; et une mise en revue et une nouvelle analyse des découvertes antérieures. Le rapport se focalise sur les données préhistoriques et celles du début de l'ère historique qui constituent la majeure partie des indices récupérés dans le port même mais il comprend également un court sommaire historique concernant l'utilisation ultérieure de cette zone.

Le relevé a indiqué d'importantes répartitions de silex et de poterie, principalement autour de quatre îles érodées dans la partie septentrionale du port. Il y avait du silex datant du paléolithique à la fin de l'âge de bronze et une analyse a cherché à établir une distinc-tion entre les zones d'activités précises. Seuls quelques silex paléolithiques possibles, provenant tous de recherches antérieures, sont connus. Une utilisation sporadique de cette zone pendant le mésolithique et le néolithique fut suivie de l'établissement d'un cimetière d'urnes plat datant du milieu à la fin de l'âge de bronze, et plusieurs grandes urnes cinéraires et leur contenu ont été récupérées. Les données archéologiques laissent supposer que le port était à l'intérieur des terres jusqu'au moins le milieu de l'âge de bronze. Ceci a été confirmé par les données paléologiques environne-mentales, y compris les séquences de mollusques et de pollen, et par les quelques vestiges de deux forêts submergées qui ont donné des dates au radiocarbone de 3350 à 2910 cal avant J.-C. et de 2310 à 1950 avant J.-C.. Elles indiquent que le Port de Langstone était un bassin à basse altitude, traversé par deux rivières qui l'érodaient profondément, et qui était exploité essentiellement pour ses ressources terrestres plutôt que maritimes.

Un nouvel examen des collections antérieures a montré que la majeure partie du matériel enregistré précédemment comme datant de l'âge de fer était en fait de la fin de l'âge de bronze. L'âge de fer est en fait mal représenté dans le port même bien qu'on connaisse d'importants sites de la fin de l'âge de fer dans l'île de Hayling (un temple et une place fortifiée en hauteur entourée d'un seul fossé). A partir de cette époque au moins, Langstone était un bras de mer qui avait des marées et la production du sel était une importante activité autour de ses côtes. A l'époque romaine, Langstone semble avoir été un port peu profond utilisé pour la production de sel, et peut-être la manufacture de briques et l'ostréiculture, mais il était essentielle-ment non développé et n'avait certainement pas l'importance des ports de Chichester et de Portsmouth tout proches. Quelques petites villas jouxtaient une route romaine qui passait au nord de Langstone mais aucun développement du front de mer romain n'a pu être identifié.

Au cours de toutes les périodes historiques, même jusqu'à l'heure actuelle, le port de Langstone est resté un petit endroit tranquille avec peu de développement urbain ou commercial. La production de sel, l'ostréi-culture et la pêche ont été ses principales industries, bien qu'il ait joué un rôle important dans la défense de la côte sud pendant au moins les trois derniers siècles. Il existe encore des indices tangibles de son rôle dans la défense de Portsmouth pendant les deux guerres mondiales et sa contribution au débarquement du Jour J est toujours visible à travers les vestiges d'un caisson du Mulberry Harbour [installation portuaire mobile temporaire, utilisée pour la préparation du débarque-ment], qui se trouve près de l'entrée du port.

Une analyse des régimes d'érosion est présentée et un modèle d'érosion est proposé pour expliquer le mouvement des objets façonnés, de leur déposition dans le sol jusqu'à leur éventuel enlèvement du port. On en conclut que la ressource archéologique disparaît rapidement car le contexte dont elle dépend est érodé par les vagues, à cause, en grande partie, du dépéris-sement continu de l'herbe *Spartina* qui contribue à consolider les îles. Le rapport se termine par des déclarations sur l'importance et la gestion de la ressource archéologique, sur ses liens inextricables avec les questions de conservation écologique et sur ses implications, et sur une mise en revue des méthodes adoptées par le projet et leur applicabilité à d'autres relevés similaires.

Zusammenfassung

Die multidisziplinäre archäologische Bestands-aufnahme des Hafengebietes von Langstone, das heute durch eine weitläufige, seichte Bucht an der englischen Südküste gekennzeichnet ist, umfasst die prähistorische bis frühe geschichtliche Epoche. Die Hauptziele waren in erster Linie die Untersuchung und Erfassung der archäologischen Funde im Hafengebiet selbst und dessen unmittelbaren Hinterland, aber auch die Dokumentation der morphologischen, sozialen und Umweltveränderungen. Die archäologische Bedeutung des Hafens war zwar schon gut bekannt, aber die Bedrohung der Ufer und rudimenären Inseln durch die fortschreitende Küstenerosion gaben den Anstoss für dieses Forschungsprojekt.

Der Übergang vom Festland über das Gezeitenübergangsgebiet zur Unterwasserzone wurde anhand nahtloser Geländearbeit untersucht, die zum Ziel hatte, jeden Teil der modernen Umgebung durch ähnliche Methoden zu untersuchen. Die Methoden, die in diesem Projekt entwickelt und angewandt wurden, sind beschrieben und kritisch ausgewertet. Untersuchungen vor Ort wurden mit Hilfe grossangelegter, systematischer 'Durch-kämmung' durchgeführt, die zum Ziel hatte die Ausbreitung von Fundstellen, Bodenumrisse und freistehende Strukturen zu charakterisieren, identifizieren, datieren und durch GPS Vermessung zu kartieren. Bohrkerne wurden von allen drei Zonen entnommen; Aufschlüsse ergaben eine Einsicht in die Schichtenfolge und stratigraphischen Zusammen-hänge; eine geophysische Untersuchung unter Wasser, wo eine direkte Bestandsaufnahme nicht möglich war; und eine Revision und Neuanalyse von Funden aus früheren Ausgrabungen. Die Haupt-bestandteile diese Berichts konzentrieren sich auf die prähistorischen Funde und Daten aus der frühen geschichtlichen Epoche, die den Hauptteil der Zeugnisse aus dem Hafen selbst ausmachen, der Bericht beinhaltet jedoch auch eine kurze Zusammen-fassung der geschichtlichen Nutzung dieses Gebietes.

Die Bestandsaufnahme hat Feuerstein- und Keramikfunde dokumentiert, hauptsächlich in der Nähe von vier rudimentären Inseln im Norden des Hafens. Steinfunde aus dem Paläolithikum und der späten Bronzezeit wurden geborgen und deren Analyse hatte zum Ziel spezielle Aktivitätsstätten zu differenzieren. Nur eine Handvoll von Stein-funden aus dem Paläolithikum sind bekannt und alle stammen aus früheren Ausgrabungen. Während des Mesolithikums und Neolithikums wurde dieses Gebiet nur sporadisch genutzt. In der mittleren bis späten Bronzezeit jedoch wurden Flachgräber angelegt, die mehrere grosse Urnen mit Brandbestattungen enthielten, und deren Inhalt geborgen wurde. Die archäologischen Funde bezeugen, dass der heutige Hafen bis mindestens in die späte Bronzezeit Festland war. Das wurde vor allem durch archäobotanische und archäo-zoologische Methoden bestätigt (hauptsächlich durch Analyse von Pollen und Mollusken), und den Überresten von zwei kleinen relikten 'ertrunkenen Wäldern' deren C14-Altersbestimmung Daten von 3350-2910 v. Chr. und 2310-1950 v. Chr. ergaben. Aufgrund dieser Daten konnte ermittelt werden, dass der Hafen von Langstone ein niedriges Becken war, dass von zwei tief eingeschnittenen Flüssen entwässert wurde und, im Gegensatz zu der späteren maritimen Nutzung, als Festland genutzt wurde.

Eine Neuuntersuchung von Sammlungen aus früh-eren Ausgrabungen hat ergeben, dass ein Grossteil der Funde, die zuvor der Eisenzeit zugeschrieben wurden, tatsächlich der Bronzezeit angehören. Die Eisenzeit ist im Hafen selbst nur spärlich vertreten, obwohl Siedlungen aus der späten Eisenzeit (eine Hügelfestung und Tempel) von der Insel Hayling bekannt sind. Ab diesem Zeitpunkt war Langstone eine Bucht, die dem Gezeitenwechsel Einlass erlaubte, und an deren Ufern sich die Salzproduktion als eine der wichtigsten Gewerbeaktivitäten entwickelte. Während der Römerzeit scheint es ein nur seichter Hafen gewesen zu sein, der zwar zur Salzproduktion genutzt wurde, und möglicherweise auch zur Man-ufaktur von Ziegeln und zum Austernfang, im wesentlichen allerdings unterentwickelt war und sich an Bedeutung nicht mit den benachbarten Häfen von Chichester und Portsmouth messen konnte. An der Römerstrasse, die nördlich von Langstone verlief, siedelten sich einige wenige Villas von geringer Bedeutung an, aber eine Erschliessung eines römischen Hafengebiets konnte nicht erwiesen werden.

Während der gesamten geschichtlichen Epoche, selbst bis heute, blieb der Hafen von Langstone ein stilles Wasser mit nur spärlicher städtischer und kommerzieller Entwicklung. Wahrend der letzten drei Jahrhunderte spielte er zwar eine wichtige Rolle in der Verteidigung der Südküste, aber die Salzproduktion, Austernfischerei, und Fischfang sind seit langem die wichtigsten ökonomischen Tätig-keiten. Seine Rolle in der Verteidigung von Ports-mouth in den letzten zwei Weltkriegen hinterliess sichtbare Spuren; der Beitrag zu den D-Day Landungen ist gut dokumentiert, und durch die Überreste des Schleusenponton des Mulberry Hafens ersichtlich, der in der Nähe des Hafen-eingangs liegt.

Anhand der Darstellung und Analyse der

Erosionsformen wurde ein Erosionsmodell entwickelt, um die Erosion der Artefakte aus den terrestrischen Ablagerungen und deren Entfernung aus dem Hafengebiet zu erklären. Daraus ergab sich, dass das reiche archäologische Erbe erschreckend rapide verloren geht, da die Kulturschichten aus denen die Funde stammen durch Wellentätigkeit erodiert werden, insbesondere wegen des fortschreitenden Absterbens des Spartina Gras, dass zur Stabilisation der Inselufer beiträgt. Am Schluss des Berichtes wird die Bedeutung der Archäologie und der Denkmalpflege hervorgehoben, deren enge Verflechtung mit dem Umweltschutz betont und dessen Auswirkungen diskutiert. Der Bericht schliesst mit einer Kritik der angewandten Methoden und deren Anwendbarkeit für ähnliche Untersuchungen.

Foreword *by Barry Cunliffe*

For those of us who grew up in Portsmouth the familiar green backdrop of Portsdown and the isolated expanse of Farlington Marsh spreading out at its foot provided welcome escapes from the, then, dreary and still bomb-scarred city sprawling over Portsea Island. For me, Farlington Marsh, with its remarkable saltmarsh flora and migrant bird life, became a haven but its fascination grew out of all proportion when one day a local amateur archaeologist, Chris Draper, brought a bag of flints, which he had found on the eroding foreshores of North Binness and Long Island, to one of the evening meetings of volunteers arranged in the local museum. It was in the company of Chris Draper, encouraged through treacherous knee-deep mud to reach North Binness, that I first experienced the excitement of field archaeology. A decade or so later another local lad, Richard Bradley, was to tramp the foreshores and islands in pursuit of eroding sites – and later to publish his results with customary efficiency (Bradley and Hooper 1973). The fieldwork of Chris Draper, Richard Bradley, and Bari Hooper, who worked with him, firmly established the archaeological potential of Langstone Harbour.

The 1970s were to see Hampshire County Council take the lead in developing a professional archaeological service, firmly embedding it within the infrastructure of local government. Hampshire was one of the first counties to appoint a full-time archaeological officer to its Planning Department charged, among many other duties, with the creation and maintenance of a Sites and Monuments Record. The County's first energetic, and persuasive, Archaeological Officer, Michael Hughes, soon made sure that archaeology earned a high profile within local government, and, as the awareness of the importance of the archaeological resource grew under his careful guidance, so the County authorities showed increasing willingness to back a more pro-active attitude towards archaeological evaluation. It was in this atmosphere that the Langstone Harbour Project was set up as a funded initiative of the County Council.

Langstone Harbour is a mysterious backwater – at high tide a great, almost land-locked lagoon of salt water, at low tide an expanse of grey mud. The urban conurbation all around turns its back on the harbour as though it does not wish to know. Unlike its neighbour, Portsmouth Harbour, there are no naval installations and little commercial development. Yet the demands of the urban population are now beginning to impinge on the harbour and its fringes, threatening to erode its natural beauty and its archaeology. To provide a framework within which informed planning decisions could be reached it became clear that a thorough evaluation of the archaeology had to be made. At the request of the County Council a research design was developed by Wessex Archaeology and Portsmouth University. It was comprehensive involving an impressive variety of survey and sampling methods, and paved the way for a programme of fieldwork which was carried out between 1993 and 1998. This volume outlines the research aims and methods and presents the results.

What has emerged is something of a surprise. The general view, before the fieldwork got under way, was that the harbour muds masked a drowned archaeological landscape. But not so. What has now become clear is that the present harbour is an eroded inland basin of which the islands at the north end are the last vestiges of the *in situ* archaeological deposit. The detailed studies have allowed an entirely new picture to be built up. The results of the survey have a pleasing completeness about them. They provide a context for understanding the quite considerable body of archaeological material collected over the years, and they create a firm framework of constraints for future planning decisions. Thus the two principal aims of the project are satisfied. But there is more. The carefully refined fieldwork procedures, thoroughly discussed in this report, provide a model for further projects working in these fragile and fascinating intertidal zones.

The Langstone Harbour survey offers a microcosm of all that is good about British archaeology – an energetic and responsible contribution by local amateur archaeologists built into a highly professional and innovative survey designed by professionals and supported financially by a farsighted local authority. All concerned can be justly proud of the result.

1 Introduction *by Michael J Allen and Julie Gardiner*

The potential of the seabed and intertidal zones for the preservation and recovery of organic archaeological material has long been recognised, as has the fact that such areas are often the location of submerged forests which have been of great antiquarian geological interest (eg Borlase 1753; 1757; 1758). Such areas are also known to contain deep and ancient sequences of Holocene sediment offering the opportunity to acquire detailed pollen evidence of past environmental changes (eg Southampton and Portsmouth Harbours; Everard 1954a; Godwin and Godwin 1940; Godwin 1945). Important archaeological resource-bases are to be found in these environments. These greatly expand the fragmentary information available from terrestrial sites and they are often capable of providing well preserved organic materials, extensive pollen records, and long sediment sequences, all of which are largely unobtainable from eroded dry-land locations. Thus coastlines with intertidal and estuarine deposits offer great potential for archaeological survival; they can also offer evidence of specialised human activity where past populations have been drawn to the natural resources offered by lowland saltmarsh and deeper marine environments of the coast.

The detailed, scientific, exploration of intertidal and underwater archaeological remains has a much more recent history than has dry-land archaeology (Tyson *et al* 1997), not least because of the physical difficulties of working in these environments using standard terrestrial techniques (*cf* Wilkinson and Murphy 1986). New methods have been developed comparatively recently for the accurate recording of underwater sites (Dean *et al* 1992) but intertidal zones present their own problems – effectively, they are neither land nor sea yet they may encompass a range of 'sites' and assemblages which offer enormous, largely untapped, potential for landscape survey and reconstruction.

Well preserved in these intertidal locations as they may be, these resources are both fragile and diminishing. Threats to preservation include changes in ecological equilibrium such as those resulting in dieback of *Spartina* grass and the loss of intertidal saltmarsh to the sea (Bird and Ranwell 1964; Haynes and Coulson 1982; May 1969). Physical erosion of the landscape by riverine and fluviatile action and tidal forces is a further cause of loss. All of these have been to a greater, or lesser, extent engendered by oscillation in sea-level throughout the Holocene period (eg Long and Roberts 1997). Equally important are the human threats induced by development and coastal improvement and the construction of coastal defences (eg Brean Down, Allen *et al* 1997; Allen and Ritchie in press 2000).

These activities not only directly affect archaeological remains but also may cause longer-term knock-on effects by altering hydrological and tidal regimes in adjacent areas of coastline. Questions of how to survey, record, manage, and legislate for the archaeological resources contained within the intertidal zone are part of an ongoing source of debate and concern (see, for instance, DoE 1993; Firth 1993; in press; Fulford *et al* 1997; Tomalin 1993) and provided one impetus for the Langstone Harbour Archaeological Survey Project which is the subject of this report.

The widespread adoption by local planning authorities of the Government's policies for archaeological remains on land, as defined in *Planning Policy Guidance Notes* (*PPG*) 15 and 16 (November 1990), has meant that conventional, terrestrial, archaeological sites now receive development control through the planning process. The limit of the Local Planning Authorities jurisdiction stops with the county boundaries which 'as a general rule' is the Mean Low Water Mark (PPG20, paragraph 1.6). This clearly anomalous situation in the planning process between terrestrial and intertidal and underwater archaeological remains led the former County Archaeological Officer for Hampshire, Michael Hughes, to draft a report in 1990 on the problems of maritime archaeology. In that report, 'maritime' archaeology was defined as including:

a) Archaeological sites that through changes in sea-level are now underwater or on the immediate shoreline
b) Underwater historic wrecks or those in tidal river estuaries

It was particularly pertinent that Michael Hughes should have taken the lead in producing such a report as it was he who, many years earlier, was involved in pioneering and implementing development control strategies for the protection and management of terrestrial sites in Hampshire. One of the most significant recommendations was for the establishment of a maritime archaeological record for Hampshire, and a Solent-based maritime archaeological trust. To its credit, Hampshire County Council took on board most of the report's recommendations and, in conjunction with the Isle of Wight County Council, the Hampshire and Wight Trust for Maritime Archaeology (hereafter HWTMA) was established. This superseded and subsumed the Isle of Wight Trust for Maritime Archaeology which had promoted similar objectives. Its primary objectives were to promote the education of the public in matters of maritime archaeological interest, to seek

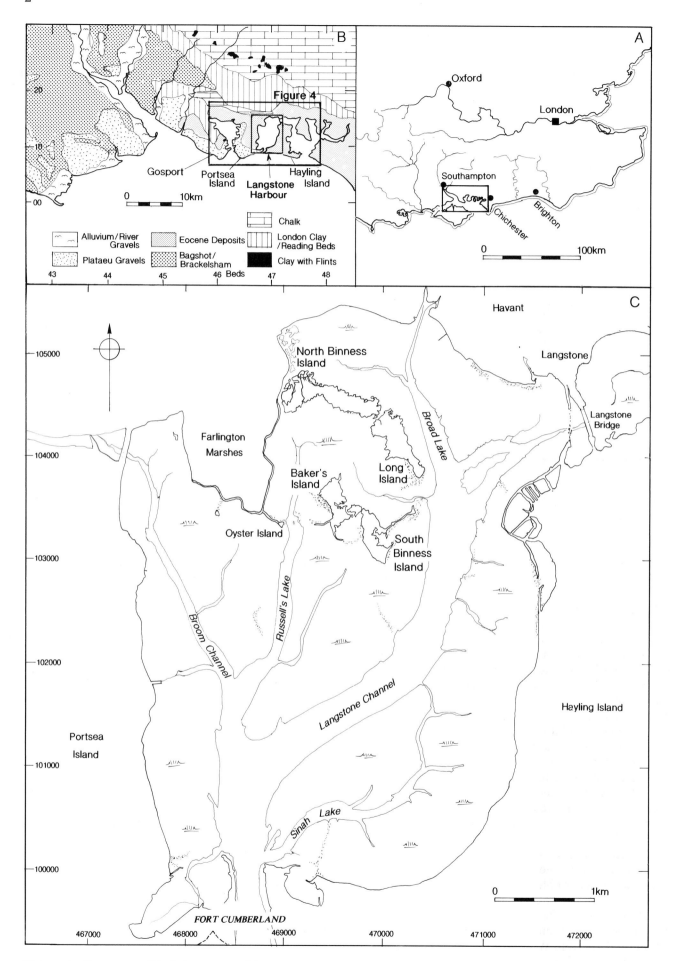

Figure 1   Langstone Harbour: general location and outline geology. Drawn by S E James

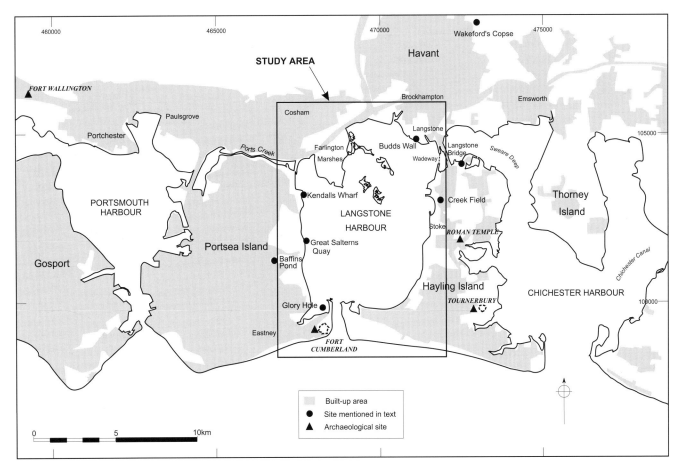

Figure 2   The Langstone Harbour area; places and known archaeological sites mentioned in text. Drawn by S E James

to preserve important maritime archaeological sites and artefacts, and to coordinate survey, recording, and conservation programmes.

Hughes's 1990 report was prescient indeed as, in 1992, *Planning Policy Guidance Note* 20: *Archaeology and Coastal Planning* was published, bringing the whole area of underwater and intertidal archaeology to the fore at last. Hughes set up a pilot study to examine and review the archaeological potential of a stretch of Hampshire's coastline and to test methods for the recovery of archaeological data both underwater, in the intertidal regions, and on the dry littoral, with a view to making recommendations for the future management and curation of the County's coastal resources. The Langstone Harbour Archaeological Survey Project was, therefore, a response to increasing concern regarding the impact of coastal erosion and coastal defence works upon archaeological remains.

Because of its archaeological potential and underdeveloped environment, Langstone Harbour was identified as a suitable area for study. Figuring least in the selection of this area was Michael Hughes' own familiarity with the region in general (eg Fort Wallington, Fareham, Hughes 1974; Hughes and ApSimon 1977, and Wallingford, Hughes 1977), and with Langstone Harbour specifically, having been a volunteer during Chris Draper's peremptory survey

of the harbour in the late 1950s (eg Draper 1958; 1961; 1963). He was also aware of Barri Hooper's more structured fieldwork in the same area (Bradley and Hooper 1973). A collaborative research design was prepared by Wessex Archaeology (archaeological aspects) and Portsmouth University (GPS mapping). The resultant document; *The Langstone Harbour Project; an integrated research design for the study, mapping and interpretation of the archaeological resource of an intertidal zone*, (University of Portsmouth and Wessex Archaeology 1993) formed the basis of the research project.

The research design recommended the recording and mapping of the present harbour and the employment of a seamless approach to devise, develop, and test a series of methodological approaches for the recording the archaeological and palaeoenvironmental evidence in the study area. This research was implemented collaboratively with Wessex Archaeology, Portsmouth University, Hampshire and Wight Trust for Maritime Archaeology, and subsequently Southampton University.

Langstone Harbour setting

Langstone Harbour encompasses some 23km² and lies between the harbours of Portsmouth and

Chichester and more specifically between Portsea Island (Portsmouth) and Hayling Island on the Solent coast of Hampshire (Figs 1 and 2). It is larger than its neighbouring inlet, Portsmouth Harbour (c 1:1.4) and is not so industrially developed. It has greater similarities in both morphology and archaeological evidence with Chichester Harbour (see Cartwright 1982), which is a low-lying 'drowned' inlet. Both Langstone and Chichester Harbours contain large expanses of intertidal mudflats and shingle banks with sand banks exposed at low tide. A drier saltmarsh survives on four main vestigial islands in the northern area, and in the north-west corner, on Farlington Marshes (Fig 1). The harbour is drained by one main and several subsidiary channels with fast running tides (Fig 3).

From an archaeological perspective Langstone Harbour is an area of considerable importance. The shores and islands have long been known for their archaeological content and important assemblages of finds had previously been recovered and reported from the harbour area by both professional and amateur archaeologists (eg Draper 1958; Bradley and Hooper 1973). Limited field investigations in the past around the shoreline and within the intertidal zone have indicated the presence of archaeological sites and finds of all periods, beginning with, at least, the later Mesolithic (6th–5th millennia BC), through to those of recent historic interest (see Fig 7, below). Large collections of flint and pottery artefacts reported from unsystematic collections by locals were also important; one, a fisherman, Arthur Mack, who discovered the *Invincible* in the Solent, had been collecting from the harbour for over 50 years, while John Bingeman, an amateur marine archaeologist, had worked on the *Mary Rose* and had previously played an important role in the identification and recording of the *Invincible*. Thus the archaeological significance of the locality had long been registered with the archaeological community and the County Archaeological Officer.

The shoreline of the harbour is not heavily developed and the northern half, at least, offers little in the way of tourist or leisure facilities. Much of the coastline itself is only easily accessible on foot. The generally quiet and undisturbed character, particularly of the islands, is reflected in the development of ecologically rich micro-environments which are of especial importance for wildfowl. Indeed, so important is Langstone for its itinerant bird population that it is designated a Site of Special Scientific Interest (SSSI), a Special Protection Area, an RSPB reserve, and a Ramsar site (Wetland of International Importance). Such designations afford considerable protection to the ecology of the harbour and, *inter alia*, its archaeology – from human intervention if not from natural interference. The 'contained' nature of the harbour, its variety of ecological zones and the protection afforded them by the various designations, its lack of major development, and its known archaeological importance, provided the ideal

setting for the pilot study and the ensuing four years of fieldwork.

Origins and aims of the project

Origins and development of the project

The origins of this project, therefore, lay in concerns about the condition and extent of the archaeological resource and associated palaeoenvironmental potential of Hampshire's coastline in general and of Langstone Harbour in particular, and a need for the understanding and interpretation of the deposits in order to implement proper curation and management strategies for that resource.

Pioneering archaeological work in intertidal zones that demonstrate the potential of these areas for landscape reconstruction include the extensive work by Peter Murphy and Tony Wilkinson on the Essex coast at Blackwater and Hullbridge (Wilkinson and Murphy 1995), and ongoing work in the Humberside wetlands (van de Noort and Davies 1993), Goldcliff, South Wales (Bell and Neumann 1996; 1997; Neumann and Bell 1997; Bell *et al* 2000), the Severn Estuary (Barnes 1993; Rippon 1997), Gwent Levels (Rippon 1996), Brean, Somerset (Allen *et al* 1997; Allen and Ritchie in press 2000) and Wootton-Quarr, Isle of Wight (see Bradley *et al* 1997; Tomalin 1993; Tomalin *et al* forthcoming). The importance and innovation of the Langstone Harbour Archaeological Survey Project lay in the fact that it was selected to be the test-bed for a project funded through a County Council in order both to meet academic criteria, through investigation of a known and documented archaeological resource, and also to address questions of management, curation, and development control of that archaeological resource which were of direct relevance to the planning department concerned. It was also intended that the archaeological survey should encompass a variety of ecological zones and test a suite of techniques for working in them, and operate in combination with a wide range of other geographical, ecological, and sedimentological studies to produce a comprehensive survey of the past and present landscape. This survey, initiated in 1993, was essentially the precursor of the now established English Heritage Rapid Coastal Zone Assessment Surveys (English Heritage 1999).

The project was conceived, at the outset, as a multidisciplinary survey of the archaeology of Langstone Harbour encompassing the intertidal and underwater zones of the harbour and limited areas of the dry hinterland fringe. Overriding logistical concerns resulting from the involvement in the project of a number of separate organisations and strict financial constraints had to be embraced. Nevertheless the principal project-wide concept – that of a *seamless* approach – was adopted (Allen *et al* 1993; 1994). The details of this approach and the nested survey strategy adopted to achieve it are presented below.

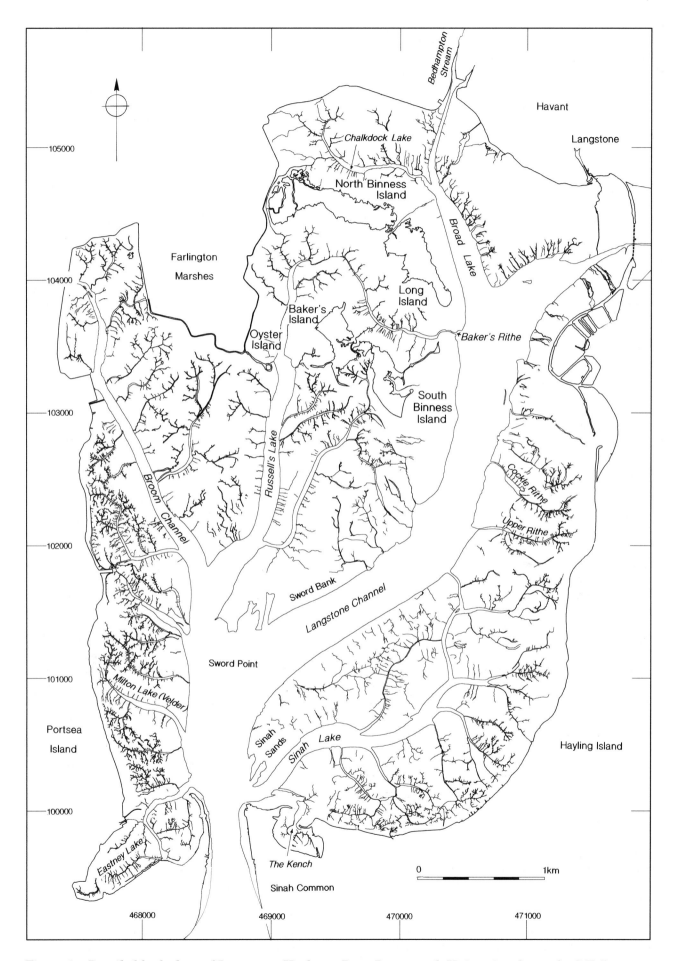

Figure 3   Detailed hydrology of Langstone Harbour. Data Portsmouth University, drawn by S E James

Factors influencing the development of the project design

It was recognised from the outset that the positions of identified archaeological assemblages of different date within the harbour could not be taken at face value since they had been subject to a range a depositional, post-depositional, and recovery factors. Among these were:

- ground conditions prevailing at the time when archaeologically recovery took place (ie permanently wet, dry, intertidal, mudflats, etc)
- nature of archaeological activity/site function
- durability of various archaeological materials (stone tools, pottery, wood, environmental data, etc) and their preservation under changing conditions, such as saline/brackish, intermittent wet and dry, permanently dry, or waterlogged conditions
- post-depositional changes in human utilisation of the harbour, including modern landfill
- post-depositional coastal change affecting preservation of material *in situ*
- movement of material due to post-depositional coastal erosion and subsequent redeposition
- nature and extent of archaeological exposure
- ground conditions at time of recovery
- variations in the aims, interests, abilities, and accuracy of field recording and identification of the various individuals recovering archaeological material
- likelihood of further archaeological areas not available for immediate inspection (ie underwater or sealed by alluvium) or remaining undetected

Any attempt to reconstruct the human use of the harbour and its littoral should also pay particular attention to its sedimentological, geological, and topographical history, from which its present configuration and nature could not be divorced. Research was directed towards the elucidation of the archaeological resource in relation to *processes* involved in the development and change of the present-day harbour landscape (eg zones effected by drying out, erosion, accretion, excavation, etc). It attempted to avoid the present-day configuration as a basis for interpreting the past. Within this document reference to Langstone Harbour includes all areas below the High Water Mark of Medium Tides (HWMT) and all areas of currently dry-land within 1km inland of that mark, south of gridline SU 06.

Aims and objectives

The aims of the project were explicitly given in the original research design (University of Portsmouth and Wessex Archaeology 1993) and published in the first assessment report (Allen *et al* 1994). These sought to describe and interpret:

A the development of the harbour and its surrounding landscape from the early postglacial period to the present
B human activity and utilisation of harbour and its littoral resources through time
C the impact of coastal change on archaeological distributions and the potential for future recovery

Clearly the aims revolved around several main themes. These are described in more detail below. The principal objectives for the fulfilment of the aims were to:

1 Establish and assess the nature, date, circumstances of recovery, and current whereabouts of all known archaeological data from Langstone Harbour and a limited hinterland of 1km dryland;
2 Establish and assess the relative and absolute, horizontal and vertical, positions (OD) of archaeological data in relation to observable past landforms and recent human activity;
3 Combine the results of archaeological research with that of topographical, sedimentological and cartographic research undertaken by the Department of Geography, Portsmouth University;
4 Provide an indication of relative and absolute sea-level OD change for dated (nominated) periods;
5 Map known potential archaeological and palaeo-environmental resources by period;
6 Undertake terrain modelling of archaeological distributions by period in conjunction with similar modelling of landform development, erosion, and deposition sequences;
7 Identify weaknesses inherent in both past recording and recovery strategies, and to identify the need for more detailed research to redress imbalances;
8 Undertake limited fieldwork and subsequent analysis to enhance the archaeological and associated environmental databases;
9 Assess and enhance terrain models;
10 Provide and then test predictive models of archaeological distributions;
11 Provide an interpretation of the archaeological and landform development of the harbour area with reference to the themes described below;
12 Assess the methodologies employed and their application to other intertidal areas.

Research themes

A series of research themes were identified before any fieldwork or desk based study was conducted. These themes determined the nature and direction of the fieldwork and survey, even though not all could be fully met in the conclusion of the project (see Chapters 7 and 8).

A Development of the harbour and its surrounding landscape from the early postglacial to the present

The physical, morphological, topographical, and sedimentological development of the harbour was seen to be paramount to both the development of human activity and the existence, preservation, and accessibility of surviving archaeological and palaeoenvironmental resources. The record of the sedimentary units and their relation to Ordnance Datum enabled comparison with the known general sea-level changes in southern England (Akeroyd 1966; 1972; and *cf* Thompson 1980) with the more relevant, specifically local, studies in the area (Western Yar, Isle of Wight and Solent) by Devoy (1982; 1987a; Sutherland 1984; L G Allen 1991; Allen and Gibbard 1994; Long and Tooley 1995; Long and Scaife 1996). It was considered that the record of local eustatic and sea-level changes and basic sediment patterns would enable the production of a regression model for the development of the harbour and an assessment of the effects of oscillating zones of high energy. This, in turn, would provide the basis for all predictive modelling of the archaeological resource which would be necessary for *analysis, interpretation,* and *management.* This data would therefore act as the basis for:

- predictive modelling of the changing archaeological and palaeoenvironmental resources within the harbour and its immediate hinterland. This would provide the necessary basis for the research presented in Theme B below
- potential preservation and survival of sedimentary units and their archaeological and palaeoenvironmental significance required for the research presented in Theme C

The sedimentary units could be dated by their association with recovered and recorded artefactual material. With the aid of palaeoenvironmental evidence won from, for instance, pollen analysis, a relative chronology might also be achieved. More detailed examination of the local palaeoenvironments and sedimentation regimes could be obtained by both interpretation of the sediment parcels (*cf* Needham 1992) and analytical work (eg pollen analysis). The resolution of this data, and all the predictive and regression modelling, was to be defined not only by precision in the mapping of data but, more significantly, by the chronological framework and absolute and relative dates obtained for specific identified events.

B Human activity and utilisation of littoral resources through time

Human activity within and around Langstone Harbour has been recorded for all periods since the early postglacial period and the identification and interpretation of the archaeological remains of these activities was the principal aim of the project.

At the outset of the project, Langstone Harbour was considered to have been a relatively shallow coastal inlet since at least the early postglacial. However, its morphology has not remained static during the last 10,000 or so years. Dynamic changes in geography, topography, and sedimentology have occurred both as gradual processes and episodically. Periods of increasing and decreasing salinity, inundation, erosion, and alluvial deposition will have affected comparatively large areas within the harbour at one time or another. Such natural factors affect potential food resources for human and faunal populations alike as well as affecting, for instance, the areas of dry-land available for use and the access to deeper water channels. They have also created, and destroyed, microenvironmental niches within the overall ecological milieu of the harbour. Although most of these changes have taken place within a height range of just a few metres they will undoubtedly have had a dramatic effect on both the natural environment (faunal and floral) and on the nature and extent of human activities in and around the harbour at different periods.

These activities are likely to have varied in nature through time and have resulted in different types of recoverable archaeological assemblages. To some extent the composition of these assemblages and any associated structures or archaeological deposits will reflect the functions of the sites to which they refer, but all archaeological assemblages are subject to preservational biases, especially in such a dynamic environment, limiting the scope for interpretation of individual assemblages or sites. Our understanding of the overall pattern of human utilisation at each period had therefore to be viewed against a range of biasing factors, outlined above, mitigation against which forms another aspect of the project's research strategy.

When interpreting the archaeological assemblages of the harbour, a major consideration must be the significance of its particular resources and the activities that these have attracted at different periods. These have included the exploitation of fish, shellfish, and birdlife, and the recovery of salt as well as the use of the creeks and channels as a place of safe anchorage.

In the former case the composition of these assemblages provides an important indicator and it was anticipated that associated structures might be identifiable (shell-middens, saltpans, staithes, wrecks etc). The period and extent of any past activities will be closely interlinked with, and dependent on, the natural environment of the harbour. Any rapid or extensive changes in that environment are likely to have led to the sudden cessation of those activities (or the commencement of others). The position of, for instance, a Roman road, medieval priory, or modern infrastructure development is less likely to be influenced directly by the harbour itself, though the harbour may have important effects upon it (drainage, land reclamation, coastal defences, harbour works, dredging etc), and upon the preservation of earlier archaeological deposits.

C   Impact of coastal change on the distribution of the archaeological resource and the potential for future recovery strategies

The significance of producing a predictive coastal and land change regression model is that this data can be used both to determine and predict the position of groups of artefacts of any period. It can also enhance our understanding of where such artefacts may be preserved under alluvial or marine sediments, or where they might be destroyed by marine-scaping or eradicated by erosion. An understanding of the biases within these distributions are a valuable aid to the management of this fragile and non-renewable resource.

The record of defined sediment 'parcels' (their location, fragility, and vulnerability) can be assessed with regard to their known, likely, or potential archaeological and palaeoenvironmental significance. This basic database can be visually presented as a series of maps showing the distribution of artefacts by period, and areas of potential archaeological importance. These should form the basis for guidelines for the future management of the archaeological resource.

It was essential that the potential impact of modern development, harbour-use, and dredging is archaeologically assessed, constrained, and monitored. This call for close liaison and cooperation between all regulating and operating bodies including those concerned with planning control at county and district levels and those responsible for the implementation of shoreline management plans and the management of coastal protection. Changes in the natural resources of the harbour, such as the de-stabilisation of sediment banks and the loss of *Spartina* colonies, may not be so readily managed or controlled. Through the production of regression maps of the development of the harbour combined with an understanding of present environmental (faunal, floral, and physical) conditions it was hoped to enable a crude predictive model of areas most susceptible to threat by further erosion, as well as areas which may become inundated, and thus less easily available for archaeological research.

It was considered that the interrogation and review of the methodologies adopted and attempted (as well as potential methodologies not employed) would enable the formulation of an integrated strategy for the identification (see Chapter 8 and Appendix 3), presentation, and interpretation of further archaeological material. An integrated strategy might combine a series of fieldwork methodologies (land- and sea-based), GIS recording of locational data, and terrain modelling. Such an approach would enhance the interpretative and analytical power, as well as the management potential of the database (Appendix 3). The review of

methodologies and proposed strategy may have application well beyond Langstone Harbour.

Location, geology, and topography
by Justin K Dix and Rob Scaife

Langstone Harbour is a tidal basin which lies on the current coastal margins of the Hampshire basin. Along with many of the harbours and inlets on the southern coast it is considered to be a drowned valley (Dyer 1975) with many small creeks. This structurally defined Hampshire basin represents an asymmetrical syncline with steeper inclined strata on the southern flanks of the basin and a gently dipping northern limb. The steeply dipping chalk of the Portsdown inlier means that the Langstone intertidal zone is physically very close to the Hampshire chalklands (Figs 1 and 4). In the Palaeogene period (Eocene and Oligocene) a wide variety of sediments accumulated in shallow seas, estuaries, lakes, and lagoons that developed within this basin. This sequence of Tertiary infilling exhibits cyclical sedimentation ranging from near-shore marine to freshwater facies. A subsequent long period of folding, uplift, and erosion, during the Neogene (Miocene and Pliocene *c* 6–2 Myr), created another series of axial parallel folds.

During the cold phases of the Pleistocene, river valleys were incised into this Tertiary landscape, to altitudes well below the present sea-level. This recurrent fluvial system was dominated by the 'Solent River', the major axial stream of the Hampshire Basin, which flowed eastwards across south-east Dorset and south Hampshire as an extension of the modern River Frome (Wymer 1999, 105). The channels of Langstone represented one of many northern tributary systems that fed the main channel. The lower course of this river system was drowned during the Flandrian Transgression, with the streams that had originally formed in broad unconfined valleys being transformed into the extensive complex of intertidal basins of the current Hampshire coastline.

The present harbour is drained by a main (Langstone) channel and a lesser (Broom) channel which are fed by an extensive network of minor tributaries. These are incised into extensive intertidal mudflats (Fig 3). The margins of the harbour are low-lying with relief ranging from less than +1m to +8m OD. To the north and west of the harbour, and on the intra-harbour islands, these margins consist of species-rich marshes. The islands are susceptible to continual erosion and as a result numerous small, unstable, and frequently shifting islets occur. Today the harbour supports important floral communities, notably on Farlington Marshes.

Pre-Pleistocene geology

The bedrock of Langstone Harbour represents a lithological sequence that dates from the Cretaceous

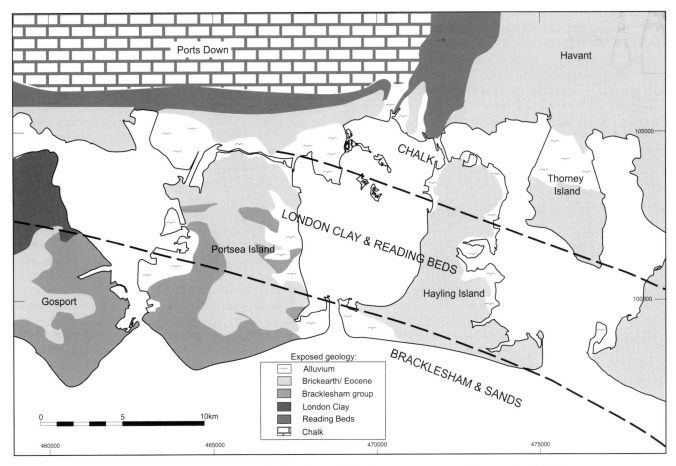

Figure 4   Drift geology and underlying solid geology of the Langstone area. Drawn by S E James

to the Middle Eocene. The oldest unit to outcrop in the harbour is the Campanian Upper Chalk. This occurs in the most northerly reaches (Melville and Freshney 1982). The Chalk is unconformably overlain by the Lower London Tertiary Group, the basal unit of which is the Reading Beds (Palaeocene – Sparnacian Stage). Bedrock outcrops are limited within the area so that the actual boundary between these two units is poorly understood. However, a high-resolution seismic (*Chirp*) survey of the harbour, undertaken for this project (see Chapter 2), tentatively locates this ESE–WNW trending boundary at *c* Northing GR 102000. The unconformable nature of this boundary is further emphasised by the downlapping geometry of the internal reflectors, identified from the *Chirp* profiles, within the Reading Beds onto the Upper Chalk surface.

The basement of the Reading Beds is a layer of large unworn flints with black/dark-green exteriors. These are embedded in *c* 3m of loamy glauconitic sand, resting directly on an eroded and piped Upper Chalk surface. Above this basement bed the strata are dominated by red-mottled plastic clays (West 1980). The Reading Beds range in thickness within the basin from 25–47m with the thickness of individual Tertiary units often increasing in a south-easterly direction (West 1980). Measurements on apparent dips taken from the *Chirp* profiles suggest a maximum thickness of the Reading Beds within

Langstone Harbour of *c* 44m, the unit dominating the bedrock stratigraphy of the central section of the harbour. Included within the Lower Tertiary Group is the London Clay Basement Bed (Palaeocene – Sparnacian Stage, *c* 65 Myr), a sandy and glauconitic unit, *c* 5m thick, resting with a sharp erosive junction on the Reading Beds.

The beds of the Lower London Tertiary Group are conformably overlain by those of the Upper London Tertiary Group. This lithological group is dominated by the Lower Eocene (Ypresian) 'London Clay above Basement Bed' (Melville and Freshney 1982). This is a homogeneous bluish clay with scattered septarian nodules that, in the Langstone area, reaches a thickness of between *c* 90m and 100m. Again on the basis of the *Chirp* survey, the ESE–WNW boundary between the two London Tertiary Groups has been tentatively placed at Northing GR 100075, immediately due north of the junction between the Langstone and Broom Channels

The 'London Clay above Basement Bed' is conformably overlain by the Bagshot Beds (Ypresian), a unit of yellow and white micaceous sands with seams of grey pipeclay and impersistent bands of flint pebbles. The Bagshot Beds extend in a very narrow belt westwards from Portsmouth so it is questionable if they actually reach their interpolated position at Lock Lake at the inner mouth of Langstone Harbour. There is no evidence from the seismic records in this area for the major acoustic boundary that would have been anticipated by the juxtaposition of a homogeneous clay and micaceous sands.

Finally, the outer parts of the harbour rest upon the basal members of the Lower to Middle Eocene Bracklesham Group. A composite section constructed from data collected from Gosport and Fawley gives a thickness of this unit of *c* 140m with a thin (0.25–0.45m) basal bed of rounded flints (Melville and Freshney 1982). In the outer part of Langstone Harbour the Bracklesham Group is probably represented by the Wittering Formation a variable including the Redend Sandstone, the Pipeclay Beds, and Agglestone Grits.

Pleistocene geology

The Pleistocene geology of the Hampshire Basin is dominated by sequential development of the major eastwardly flowing 'Solent River' system. The hypothesis of the 'Solent River' system dates back to Darwin-Fox in the mid-19th century (1862). However, the pioneering work on this feature was by Reid (1892; 1893; 1902; and 1903) who recognised that a series of widespread gravel deposits found throughout Hampshire represented fluvial deposition, in successive stages, over a long period of geological time. The turn of the century Geological Memoirs divided them into 'Plateau Gravels' and 'Valley Gravels' on the basis of height and position relative to the modern rivers. These include riverine deposits which relate to the Solent River system giving a broad west to east aggradation from *c* +123m OD down to sea-level (Everard 1954b; Wooldridge and Linton 1955)

Plateau and Valley Gravels are composed almost exclusively of flint with occasional pebbles of sarsen (silicified sandstone). They rarely exceed 5–6m in thickness (West 1980) and they are undisturbed by faulting or folding. These deposits lie on a series of terraces around the estuary and descend from levels of *c* +123m OD in the northern part of the Hampshire Basin (Allen and Gibbard 1994) down to –20m OD at the mouth of Southampton Water (Curry *et al* 1968). At this same locality the floor of the Solent River is identified at a depth of –24.4m OD. Seismic surveys within the East Solent (Dyer 1975) have been able to trace the submerged base of this river to a maximum incised depth of –46m OD east of the Nab Tower.

Dating of the variety of drift deposits in the region is difficult, particularly as the region lies beyond the conventionally accepted limits of the Pleistocene ice sheets in Britain. The numerous transgressive and regressive events provided many repetitions of the conditions under which each particular lithology accumulated.

Shingle deposits of Hoxnian age (*c* 400–360 Kyr) occur at +30m OD to the north of Chichester and Portsmouth Harbours and these are believed to be part of the Goodwood-Slindon-Wallington raised beach. Several interglacial marine beaches, each with lower gravels grading to them, are likely to be present in the region. Forming the lower ground around the estuaries are more extensive raised beach deposits. These are beds of pebbles and sands which lie on a wave cut platform between +1.8 and +5.6m OD (Hodgson 1964) and grade northeastwards into subangular river gravels. This lower beach has also been identified around Portsmouth where it has been named the '15ft beach' or 'Selsey Raised Beach'. It has since been divided into the Pagham raised beach and Norton raised beach (Wymer 1999, 147–153), the conventional view suggesting that this is of Ipswichian (*c* 110 Kyr) age (Wymer 1999, 147; West 1972). Mud deposits of limited distribution are found in channels beneath the Ipswichian raised beach or equivalent low-level gravels which are also attributed to Ipswichian age. The complexity of these interglacial deposits suggests that they may represent three separate interglacial events. Metamorphic and igneous erratics occur in both the low-level raised beach and finer channel deposits (Prestwich 1872; White 1913).

Overlying parts of the raised beach at Langstone are outcrops of coombe rock – chalk debris resulting from solifluction. It presumably formed when former periglacial conditions, during the Devensian, affected the Upper Chalk core of the Portsdown Anticline. The coombe rock grades southwards into a structureless brown silt, or brickearth, that is believed to be an aqueous deposit resting directly on the Pleistocene fluvial gravels. Similarly, gravels lie at appreciable depths under Langstone Harbour.

The distribution of the Pleistocene deposits is closely related to the positions of the modern rivers and estuaries of the Hampshire Basin. By the beginning of the Pleistocene the local rivers had already been established in approximately their present positions on a coastal plain (Wooldridge and Linton 1955). During periods of glacial advance and lower sea-levels the eastward flowing 'Solent River' complex developed, depositing sheets of Plateau and Valley Gravels in the East Solent. During the interglacials, sea-level rise flooded the lower parts of the river system to form broad estuaries in the Solent region. Early remnants are the raised beach deposits of the Goodwood-Slindon-Wallington line. After the Hoxnian Interglacial sea-level fell, the estuary disappeared, and some of the gravels below the shingle to the north of Chichester and Portsmouth (at +30m OD) were deposited. During the following Ipswichian interglacial a broad estuary developed as sea-level attained at least +7.6m OD and extensive marine erosion led to the formation of another set of raised beaches. Again the sea retreated during the Devensian, with the Solent River again extending through the area excavating a channel to even greater depths and connecting with the westward flowing extension of the River Seine. Borehole data suggests the old river channel of Southampton Water passed beneath Calshot Spit, continuing south-easterly under the Brambles bank before joining the main channel which descends eastwards through the Solent. The gravel on the central valley floors of the estuary was deposited during this final phase of the Pleistocene.

The palaeogeographical reconstructions of Allen and Gibbard (1994) suggest that the Solent River progressively migrated south throughout the Pleistocene, resulting in the preservation of terrace remnants only on the left bank of the Solent valley

Holocene geology (primarily related to the Flandrian Transgression)

Holocene deposits

During the early Flandrian (Holocene) the sea began to invade the eastern region of the Solent River at a relatively rapid rate. By Sub-boreal (Neolithic) times there was probably a standstill or even a temporary regression with sea-level occurring at –3m OD (see Long and Scaife 1996). This resulted in the spread of land vegetation over the saltmarshes and mudflats to form peats and submerged forests. It is also possible that during this period the majority of the shingle in the Spithead could have travelled by longshore drift along former beaches and spits. The transgression was resumed during the Bronze Age and by at least Romano-British times.

Flooding combined with wave erosion has occurred on shores facing open stretches of water, whilst areas sheltered from wave attack, particularly those driven by the prevailing south-westerly winds, are sites of organic-rich silty clay deposition forming tidal mudflats and saltmarshes. Often sedimentation has kept pace with rising sea-level and this has enabled the gradual increase and development of the very shallow areas and saltmarsh while the size of the estuary has also expanded.

Sea-level change (see also palaeoenvironmental background, below)

The importance of sea-level change cannot be overestimated, especially in a low-lying near-marine landscape such as Langstone Harbour. This is all the more significant when attempting to view change and development of human communities over the past nine millennia. During this period, significant changes have had a direct impact upon the physical and ecological nature of the study area.

The rate of Holocene sea-level change in England has varied considerably on both spatial and temporal scales. Both isostatic (land movements) or eustatic (oceanic) variables, as well as shoreline response to sea-level change, are specific to any individual locality and thus variable around the whole country's coastline (Long and Roberts 1997). Although some national and even regional trends can be discerned, the nature of sea-level rise and the shoreline response must be viewed at a local level.

The potential for palaeoenvironmental sequences to determine relative sea-level and landscape change is well attested in southern England (Devoy 1982 and 1990; Preece et al 1990). Particularly relevant are major sequences at Bracklesham Bay, Sussex (West et al 1984) and on coastal margins of, and offshore from, the Isle of Wight (Devoy 1987a). The analysis of marine sediments can provide detailed sea-level records from which local change can be mapped (cf Akeroyd 1966; 1972; Devoy 1982; 1987a; Churchill 1965). This evidence is of particular significance in determining the nature of past landscapes and the shape of contemporaneous coastlines. A number of postgraduate research theses have specifically concentrated on the marine sediments and the evolution of the Solent itself (L G Allen 1991) and south-east England in general (Sutherland 1984; Ackeroyd 1966).

Significant Holocene deposits and submerged peats have been recorded and analysed along the south coast over the past 50 years. The main sequences of recorded early-prehistoric peats are from Southampton Water (Everard 1954a; Godwin and Godwin 1940; Hodson and West 1972) and Portsmouth Harbour (Godwin 1945). Much of this work concerns submerged peat beds of Palaeolithic and early Mesolithic date in buried channels within the two harbours. The analysis was primarily concerned with the construction and dating of the regional postglacial vegetation history (cf Godwin and Switsur 1966; Godwin and Godwin 1940; Godwin 1945). More locally, the detailed analysis at Wootton-Quarr, Isle of Wight, on the opposite side of the Solent channel, provides a basis for comparison and analogy on the opposite side of the channel (Tomalin et al forthcoming), see palaeoenvironmental background, below.

In Langstone Harbour itself, Mottershead (1976) records appreciable, but relatively uniform, marine silts but Flandrian peat sequences have also been recorded. More significant, however, are the recent records of younger peats in channels in the northern margins of the harbour which on preliminary analysis, indicate peat formation during the Boreal and Atlantic periods (Scaife pers obs). The potential for detailed palynological and sedimentological analysis to define the broad palaeoenvironment, combined with the environmental data from archaeological contexts (cf Bradley and Hooper 1973) to provide an integrated interpretation of the development of both the landscape and land-use, is therefore high.

Summary of the present-day harbour

The coastal zone, that is Langstone Harbour including the intertidal mudflats, the littoral zone, and the terrestrial coastal margins (eg Figs 1 and 2; Plate 1), is flat and low-lying (below +5m OD). Much of the terrestrial coastal margins are developed but there remain undeveloped areas especially on Farlington Marshes and the intra-harbour islands themselves.

The Portsea Island coastline is largely developed

Plate 1 The foreshore at the north-western end of Baker's Island during fieldwork in 1994. Note the low cliff line with exposed planar clay surface above. World War II structures stand on the highest points beyond (Elaine A Wakefield)

Plate 2 Farlington Marshes, the seawall and the channel between Farlington and North Binness at low tide. A faint track mark across the channel in the middle distance marks one of very few places where it is safe to cross (Elaine A Wakefield)

or under grassland; the majority of this coastline is protected with a substantial sea wall. Only in the southern area, north of Fort Cumberland, is there an undefended coastline. The coast consists of firm shingle beach with some sand giving way to very soft muds. Farlington Marshes is a nature reserve of former marshland (Plate 2). Since the construction of a seawall in the 1970s this area has become low-lying pasture. At the foots of the seawall lie shingles and muds. On the eastern side, between Farlington Marshes and North Binness, the mud is especially deep and treacherous. The northern harbour shore is mostly comprised of shingle which contains a large quantity of modern debris including the remains of

relatively recent wooden revetments by Budds Farm (Wessex Archaeology 1999), see Figure 2.

The Hayling Island coast is a combination of shingle shore and intertidal muds, the latter particularly towards the south. It is, however, clear that the present nature of this shore, with its shingle cover, has changed within the past 40 years. During the 1960s, areas of soft muds were exposed here from which briquetage was recovered of prehistoric and Roman saltworkings (Bradley pers comm; Bradley and Hooper 1973). These locations now comprise shingle and modern debris. The coast and intertidal zone at the harbour mouth is either non-existent or largely inaccessible due to concrete harbour

Plate 3 Langstone Harbour saltmarshes at high tide (Elaine A Wakefield)

Plate 4 North Binness Island: typical condition of mudflats within the main bay of the island at or around low tide (Neil J Adam)

constructions. Sea defences, particularly on the Portsea and Hayling Island coasts, have fossilised the position of the coastline and, to a certain extent, any floral communities landward of that.

The mainland supports typical argillic brown earths of the Hamble 2 association and typical argillic gley soils of the Park Gate association on Hayling Island, with pelo-alluvial gley soils over the former marshes of Farlington Marshes (Jarvis *et al* 1984). The islands, however, support raw and unripened alluvial gley and humic alluvial gley soils (Avery 1990). Details of the soils and the soil profile on the islands is given in more detail in Chapter 3 (see North Binness Island).

The islands exist as oases of natural flora and

fauna with relatively little human interference; they are one of the few areas where no sea defences have been constructed or coastline modifications made. The islands and local marshes support *Spartina* grass (*Spartina townsendii*) (Plate 3), but this community is diminishing here as it is elsewhere in southern England (eg Haynes and Coulson 1982; Bird and Ranwell 1964; May 1969). The islands are also home to important wildlife, especially bird, colonies. North Binness and Long Island are accessible from Farlington Marshes, but Baker's Island and South Binness Island are generally only accessible by boat.

Farlington Marshes are now largely pasture, but prior to the sea defence construction they would have

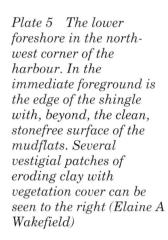

Plate 5 The lower foreshore in the north-west corner of the harbour. In the immediate foreground is the edge of the shingle with, beyond, the clean, stonefree surface of the mudflats. Several vestigial patches of eroding clay with vegetation cover can be seen to the right (Elaine A Wakefield)

supported a flora similar to that on the islands (Bryant 1967). During fieldwork a number of species was recorded and they compare well with Bryant's records (*op cit*). Woody and tree species only occur on North Binness Island, essentially as a small copse of oak, blackthorn, and gorse (Plate 4). On the drier parts of the islands (central part of North Binness and isolated parts of Long Island) a number of maritime grasses and Poaceae are present (including long-leaved scurvy grass, *Cochlearia anglica*, and danish scurvy grass, *Cochlearia danica*) and species such as slender tare (*Vicia tetrasperma*), hemlock water-dropwort (*Oenanthe crocata*), toadflax (*Linaria vulgaris*), seaside mayweed (*Triplespermum maritimum*), and sea couch (*Agrpyron pungens*).

In localised muddy areas on North Binness, Long Island, and South Binness Island, spartina (*Spartina townsendii*) and sea purslane (*Halimione portulaloides*) are present along with all of the following on one island or another: glassworts (*Salicornia* sp), sea arrowgrass (*Triglochin maritima*), sea aster (*Aster tripolium*), sea plantain (*Plantago maritima*), sea spurrey (*Spergula marina*), and larger sea spurrey (*S. media*). Less waterlogged locations around these, including ditches, were dominated by rush (*Juncus* sp) and sedge (*Carex* sp), with sea purslane, and a number of other species listed by Bryant (1967, 9).

The open muddy areas were not examined for the flora, but included algaes, *Spartina* and eel grasses (*Zostera marina*, *Z. angustiolia*, and *Z. noltii*). Eel grasses were mapped in the detailed archaeological study areas (see Figs 8 and 9) but very little was evident showing that this important food resource for the migrating bird population (see below) is also diminishing.

Sediments within the harbour mainly comprise fine silts and organic matter (Plate 5), accumulation having been locally assisted by the rapid growth of *Spartina* marshes since the late-19th century. However, over the surface of some mudflats, angular flint gravels occur and similar material outcrops along channel and creek beds and as beaches at high-water mark. There are probably extensive sub-surface spreads beneath the superficial muds (Tubbs 1980).

The harbour is part of what is essentially a single biological system (with Portsmouth and Chichester) comprising connected tidal basins that are drained at low water by systems of channels which unite to form common exits into the Solent (Tubbs 1980). The fragile nature of this resource (Bryant 1967) is emphasised not only by the physical erosion of the tidal margins (see for instance Perraton 1953; Bradley and Hooper 1973) but also by the decline in some of the floral communities, particularly the *Spartina* (Haynes and Coulson 1982; Bird and Ranwell 1964). Solent saltmarshes evidently developed during a period when the physical character of the Solent was different from today and the majority can therefore be regarded as relict features. Marshes terminate abruptly in mud cliffs up to 2 metres high and these are subject to active wave erosion at high water (Plate 6). Exceptions are in a few localities where more sheltered habitats occur where the marshes are abutted and and protected by more recently developed *Spartina* marsh which has developed at the lower level in the tidal range (J R L Allen 1991). The 48ha of saltmarsh that remain represent only a relict part of formerly extensive tracts, which at their greatest extent probably occupied the larger portion of the upper northern part of the harbour at least (Tubbs 1980). *Spartina* dieback has certainly occurred here, and although current theories are poorly developed, this has left areas of exposed mud which are not being successfully

*Plate 6   Cliff section on
North Binness Island
(Elaine A Wakefield)*

recolonised. These bare platforms of accreting mud are now subject to slumping and erosion by wave attack.

Whether the *Spartina* dieback is due to progressively poorer aeration associated with the decreasing particle size of the sediments accumulating around the plant base (Goodman 1959; Ranwell 1964), genetic changes in the *Spartina* population (Haynes and Coulson 1982), or physical erosion rather than plant dieback (Nyman *et al* 1994), what is clear is that exposed bare surfaces and low cliffs on the margins of islands are more susceptible to erosion. As a result, the exposure of archaeological artefacts by cliff retreat is much higher.

Coastal features of longshore sediment movement are common in the Solent area, with the majority of the estuaries having well developed spits primarily derived from material from local cliff erosion. The muds that dominate the harbour floor are predominantly of marine origin and have entered via estuarine circulation. At the mouth of Langstone Harbour the strong currents result from the inflow and exit of large volumes of water deflecting two spits into the harbour. Maximum surface currents of 1.5 ms^{-1} occur at the mouth of the harbour inlets (Dyer 1980). The tidal delta at the mouth of the harbour grades from coarse to fine sediment in both inward and outward directions. These spits are sand-dominated on the eastern side of the inlets with shingles on the west. These deposits are Sinah Sands and the Sword Bank in Langstone Harbour, which are sandy, and Mallard Sands, which is a sandy mud (Dunn 1972). Outside the harbour entrances there is a similar distribution of intertidal sand and shingle bars including the extensive offshore bank, the East Winner, at the mouth of Langstone and Chichester.

The term Plateau Gravels covers a wide range of gravel spreads; some of the highest 'appear' to mark outlines of the eastwardly flowing 'Solent River' while the lowest are related to the exisiting drainage pattern. 'Valley Gravels' largely consist of re-sorted Plateau Gravel material. They form terraces lining the valley sides up to 15m above the present valley floors. In addition, they underlie the alluvium of the major streams, which in their lower reaches, are further underlain by buried valleys at least 18m deep.

Sediments within the harbour mainly comprise fine silts and organic matter; accumulation has been locally assisted by the rapid growth of *Spartina* marshes since the late-19th century. However, over the surface of some mudflats, angular flint gravels occur and similar material also outcrops along channel and creek beds and as beaches along the high-water zone. These probably represent extensive subsurface spreads which are otherwise concealed beneath the superficial muds. The coastlines of the area are exposed to wave action which is generally from a south-west or south-east quarter due to the sheltering effect of the Isle of Wight.

Accretion has occurred on the western margin of the harbour entrance near the fortifications, while erosion is evident near the outfall at Eastney. At the latter a maximum loss of 30m is attested between the years 1870 and 1932. Tithe maps of 1838–43 show that the plots of land adjacent to the seawall were predominantly arable; this is indicative of several centuries of coastal stability within the harbour. Generally, in the Solent as a whole there has been abundant cartographic evidence to suggest considerable loss of intertidal sediments particularly since the 18th century (Tubbs 1980). This resulted in a narrowing of the intertidal zone, probably accompanied by a lowering of the profile of the remaining muds and possibly by a change from a generally convex to a generally concave section. A lowering of the intertidal profile would accentuate cliffing at the margins of mixed saltmarsh and *Spartina* marsh alike and this would increase their vulnerability to wave attack.

We can see a series of basic sediment distribution in the harbour which can be summarised as follows:

Unconsolidated muds	Located on shallow intertidal mudflats
Holocene sands	Aeolian sand at the east and west peripheries of the harbour entrance and marine sands in the deep channels within the harbour and forming sand banks outside the harbour entrance
Alluvial deposits	Modern river deposits (largely grey silts with seams of gravel and freshwater shells) associated with peats round Farlington Marshes
Gravels	Mainly in the deep channels within the harbour

Present-day harbour: national and international designations
by Julie Gardiner

Langstone supports a rich and varied ecology and its islands and saltmarshes are of particular importance for wildfowl. The whole harbour is designated a Site of Special Scientific Interest (SSSI) and a Special Protection Area (SPA) under the 1981 *Wildlife and Countryside Act* and the 1985 *Wildlife and Countryside Amendment Act*. Its status is further recognised by English Nature in its designation as a Ramsar Site, that is as a Wetland of International Importance in accordance with the *Convention on Wetlands of International Importance as Wildfowl Habitat* 1971. As in most harbours of the south coast there is a sizable resident bird population, but Langstone also supports, at various times of the year, some of the largest itinerant bird populations in the country. It is of particular importance for breeding colonies of seabirds such as various species of tern and provides a safe and well-stocked haven for many species of migrating birds, which gather here to 'fatten-up' before leaving Britain for their winter habitats and to refuel on their return. The harbour is a wardened RSPB reserve and is also partly managed by the Hampshire Wildlife Trust (HWT), which takes particular responsibility for Farlington Marshes.

Between them, the RSPB and HWT are responsible for managing and monitoring the ecological and conservation aspects of the SSSI and SPA. In administrative terms, however, Langstone is divided between the local authority juristriction of Portsmouth City Council and Havant Borough Council, the boundary running approximately through the centre of the harbour, north to south. In practical terms, much of the 'day-to-day' management of activity in and around the harbour is undertaken by the Langstone Harbour Board (a jointly run organisation which includes representatives from the two local authorities, the County Council, local amenity societies, and from the national and local wildlife conservation organisations) though, under the terms of the *Harbours Act* 1964, the main areas of responsibility for harbour authorities are in conservation and public access rather than development concerns. Thus, the choice of Langstone Harbour for this research project served also to highlight the complicated position of this and other coastal areas in terms of administrative responsibility and practical management. It is fortunate that all parties concerned with Langstone work well together in full collaboration to protect and conserve its natural beauty and ecological richness.

The various forms of statutory protection relating to Langstone impact upon the archaeology in several ways and it is important to make a few brief points here. First, it must be remembered that none of these designations takes any account of the archaeological resource, they are all concerned with ecology and, specifically, with the bird population. Any protection afforded the archaeology within the harbour is purely coincident on its position in relation to the designated areas. Conservation management issues are therefore inextricably linked with the archaeological resource but, in administrative terms, it is the nature conservation issues which may directly determine any change to the survival of the archaeology and not the other way round. Consequently, it was considered vital not only to the planning and operation of the project itself, but also for the development of any strategies for the future curation and management of the archaeological deposits contained within Langstone Harbour, that all the authorities with immediate responsibility for conservation management be brought on board.

In practical terms it would, in any case, have been impossible to run the project without the cooperation of these various bodies, all of whom, thankfully, were extremely interested in the project and only too eager to help. Without the permission and full cooperation of the RSPB warden (Andrew Polkey) and the HWT warden (Bob Chapman) it would not have been possible to gain access to the islands and Farlington Marshes in order to undertake the fieldwork. As it was, while limited recording by the team from Portsmouth University of survey points and structures on the harbour foreshore was possible at most times of the year, the main episodes of fieldwork had to be timed to suit the needs of the birds. Essentially, there was a small 'window of opportunity' available in August–September each year between the main breeding season and the gathering of roosting birds prior to migration. This window was only 3–4 weeks in duration and all the archaeological data collection, excavation, test-pitting, and recording had to be completed in that time. The practical constraints imposed on the fieldwork are discussed further below.

Methodological approach

Human activity within and around Langstone Harbour has been recorded for all periods since the early postglacial period and the identification and interpretation of the archaeological remains of these activities was the principal aim of the project. It is reasonable to assume that throughout the archaeological past, human activity would have extended down to any contemporary low tide mark. Utilisation of water would have extended beyond this, potentially leaving archaeologically recognisable traces. Therefore the study of human activity within Langstone cannot be complete without a study of submerged sites.

No systematic survey of the archaeological remains had previously been undertaken. Similarly, no systematic study had been made of the sedimentation history and physical development of the harbour. A staged approach to the collection of data was therefore proposed, with the each season's work building upon the results of previous years. This approach was flexible, allowing various methods of survey, mapping, and fieldwork to be tested and assessed for use in subsequent stages of the project.

The archaeological aims to meet the objectives and research themes of the project were to:

- Provide a full database of known archaeological sites within Langstone Harbour
- Map known archaeological resources by period
- Record the real and predicted biases in the database
- Assess the potential for the development of predictive models for the position and potential for future recovery of archaeological data for each period
- Provide the basis of a methodological statement for the future study and management of intertidal archaeological resources
- In order to achieve these aims a series of objectives were defined. These revolve around the exploration of three interrelated themes described below

Seamless concept

Techniques for archaeological recording and sampling on dry-land are well known, and an entirely separate suite of methods have developed from these principles for underwater archaeology (Dean *et al* 1992). The most difficult operation terrain is probably the intertidal zone which is neither wholly *terra*

firma, nor submarine. Not only is physical mobility difficult and restricted, but all aspects of fieldwork are compromised by the conditions, and the removal of heavy objects, such as waterlogged wooden artefacts and large bulk samples, often very difficult. Separate operational methodologies have been developed for these areas (see for example Wilkinson and Murphy 1986; Murphy and Wilkinson 1991), and for a seamless approach to be valid, *operational* variation between these zones is to be expected, but the basic methodological approach must remain constant.

One of the principal concerns with regard to the methods to be employed for the fieldwork was the need to devise a *seamless* strategy. This concept took as its basis that, despite the physical nature of the present-day environment, the same methodological approaches should be adopted whatever modern conditions prevailed, regardless of their relevance to those which prevailed in the past. In short, that which could be done on land would also be done in the intertidal zone and underwater so that the results of each would be directly comparable. The same methods of field investigation, data retrieval, recording, and high precision survey were employed regardless of terrain, ie terrestrial, intertidal, or submarine. This approach was considered essential to ensure compatibility of the results. Survey recording using a high precision Global Positioning System (see below) provided the control network accuracy necessary for the accurate surveying of the detailed search areas, and of significant find-spots so that this data could potentially be used in the compilation of computer based GIS maps. In turn they could be used in the subsequent interrogation of the archaeological and sedimentological data. This concept attempted to ensure that the results of fieldwork and survey from the different present-day environments were not heavily biased by the current environments encountered. In previous projects there has been a tendency to design individual methodologies for each of these different operational environments, potentially making the recorded information incompatible and non-comparable.

It is significant that, previously, the common concept of many field practitioners has been that the current environment (ie sea or coastal plain) is the same, or similar, to that which existed in the historic or archaeological past. This preconception is dangerous, and as we shall show from Langstone, can be far from the truth.

The integrated programme of study for the assessment comprised five main elements:

- archaeological and palaeoenvironmental desktop study
- mapping by collation and digitising of existing cartographic and aerial photographic information
- auger survey
- walkover and swimover survey
- detailed recording of selected artefact-rich areas (collection units)

Staged approach: a nested survey strategy

It was proposed that a formal integrated and staged approach to the research project be adopted (Portsmouth University and Wessex Archaeology 1993), progressing from a desktop study of the existing data to the production of thematic maps modelling the area by archaeological period. The details of the proposed stages of investigation were altered and developed through the course of the project. Only one of the major elements initially defined could not be carried through; that of developing specific fieldwork to test selected predicative models of site occurrence and of artefact movement (see Chapters 2, 4, and 6, below).

Four basic stages of investigation were undertaken:

Stage 1: Compilation of a project database and initial construction of the GIS

- archaeological and palaeoenvironmental desk-based study (largely presented below)
- digitisation of existing maps, design and initial construction of the GIS
- mapping of the known archaeology and incorporation in the GIS
- identification of potential areas for targeted, more detailed, archaeological investigations

Stage 2: Archaeological assessment and enhancement of the project database

- assessment and recording of existing artefacts in museum collections
- initial high-resolution photogrammetric survey and creation of 3D digital base map
- rapid archaeological assessment fieldwork to include:
  rapid walkover survey
  large-scale general auger survey
- evaluation of the potential of the archaeological resource including
  rapid assessment and scan of the archaeological artefacts
  rapid assessment of artefact assemblage character, location, and distribution
- testing and evaluation of the proposed methods
- isolation of specific areas for more detailed archaeological investigation

Stage 3: Detailed archaeological investigation

- high-resolution photogrammetric survey of targeted areas
- archaeological fieldwork in targeted areas, to include
  augering
  test-pitting (and reinstatement of the saltmarsh SSSI)
  excavation
  detailed gridded artefact collection
  coring for pollen
  sampling for palaeoenvironmental data

Stage 4: Analysis, interpretation, and dissemination

- analysis of the artefact and palaeoenvironmental data recovered
- preparation of basic data reports
- preparation of interpretative archaeological discussion (regression analysis and development of the use of the study area)
- suggest strategy for future research with, and archaeological resource management of, intertidal zone generally and Langstone Harbour specifically
- assess and review the methodological approach adopted and provide a proven archaeological methodological package for working in foreshore and intertidal locations

Constraints on fieldwork

This project was small-scale in comparison with others such that as at Goldcliff, Gwent (Bell and Neumann 1996; 1997; Bell *et al* 2000), Wooton-Quarr, Isle of Wight (Bradley *et al* 1997; Tomalin *et al* pers comm/forthcoming), the Thames foreshore project (Milne 1995; Milne *et al* 1997) and Humber wetlands (Davies and van der Noort 1993). Nevertheless, the array of data and information was impressive. Unlike these others, the Langstone Project was never intended as a long-term research project; it was conceived as a limited exercise to investigate specific problems and establish a fuller potential for future research and a framework for archaeological resource management. Apart from obvious constraints on resources there were a number of other physical and practical constraints within which the project had to operate. These are set out below as they are pertinent not only to this project but to other similar fieldwork exercises in other marginal intertidal environments.

Constraints on the timing and scale of fieldwork were defined by four factors and these were identified as follows:

- ecological constraints as a consequence of the importance of the harbour as a wildlife reserve limiting access to the islands to a short period of about three weeks during the summer between the main breeding season and the gathering of roosting birds prior to migration
- the physical nature and conditions of the Langstone Harbour environment in which part of survey was carried out
- the limitation upon available manpower and finance which only permitted a restricted programme of fieldwork and, more specifically, post-excavation analysis

and finally

- limitations set by the project at the outset largely as a programme of survey and assessment

Ecology and wildlife reserve

The importance of the ecology and its consequent national and international designations is outlined above. Consideration of these important ecological habitats and of the natural flora and fauna was respected at all times. The timing of the fieldwork season was defined for us by the RSPB, English Nature, and the Hampshire Wildlife Trust. Access, especially to the islands, was only allowed during a few weeks in August and September each year. Moreover, all archaeological fieldwork proposals by Wessex Archaeology were formulated in consultation with the local RSPB warden who submitted them to English Nature on our behalf to obtain consent (under the *Wildlife and Countryside Act* 1981) for the work to be undertaken within the designated areas (see above). Constant liaison was maintained with Andrew Polkey, the RSPB warden, and with Bob Chapman, the Hampshire Wildlife Trust warden for Farlington Marshes, and ensured the smooth running of the project with a minimum of disturbance to the local wildlife and floral communities. It also ensured that information was passed to local ornithologists who were quick to spot and report the presence of our field teams on the islands.

The physical environment and safety

Difficulties of working in intertidal areas have been well explored (see Murphy and Wilkinson 1991; Tyson *et al* 1997) and the conditions in Langstone Harbour are similar, but not identical, to many other areas. The physical conditions of Langstone Harbour with its deep muds, oscillating tides, and the need to carry all equipment and finds over sometimes considerable distances, placed often severe constraints and restrictions both on the archaeological work, and on the fieldworkers themselves; it made for a challenging and strenuous environment in which to work. Most of the foreshore of the harbour is relatively easy to access, by foot at least, but not necessarily to travel within. The islands within the harbour comprise fairly 'dry' upper saltmarsh, albeit with grasses sometimes up to waist height, which made moving across them difficult because of the many mud-filled creeks which dissect them; it was, for example, impossible to move in a straight line for any distance. The accreting muds in many areas of Langstone are potentially treacherous and team members frequently found themselves in some difficulty when attempting to cross innocuous looking areas of shallow mud only to find it topped their wellington boots as they sank with every step. Moreover, the distribution of soft mud over the hard clay surface was seen to change on a regular basis and the incoming tides tend to seep under the mudflats long before any water is visible (Bingeman and Mack pers comm and field team pers obs). Additional physical difficulties were encountered when trying to find and identify archaeological material. Often the mobile

shingle and modern detritus on the foreshores obstructed features and obscured archaeological artefacts, restricting the recovery and recording in some areas of the rapid walkover survey. Similarly, during the underwater survey, new and heavy growth of weed and mobile sediments often obscured the seabed which made the identification of possible archaeological features and artefacts difficult.

The division between those areas of the intertidal zone which were to be subjected to terrestrial-based fieldwork approaches, and the 'submarine' zone, which was surveyed through a wholly marine approach, is not as distinct is it might at first seem. Deep, soft intertidal muds which were only exposed at low tide were the most difficult to access from land. Turning of the tides limited the time available for any survey investigation. This was particularly acute for the farthest margins of the intertidal zone which are only exposed at low water on spring tides and pose the extremes of all physical and practical constraints. Potentially, therefore, these areas seemed more suited to swimover survey but the shallowness of the water, the strong tides and the mobile and easily disturbed nature of the sediments making very murky working conditions meant that only very limited diving could be carried out effectively. These fringing areas between high intertidal and deep marine conditions, therefore, pose the most severe problems for physical survey, but in retrospect they were of relatively little archaeological significance.

On a day-to-day basis, survey and fieldwork was conducted at the most favourable times, around the low tides when the largest area of the harbour was exposed. The teams therefore worked flexible hours, sometimes starting early (as early as 5:00am) or late (2:30pm) and working for up to eight hours in accordance with the local tides and available daylight. They were not permitted, on both safety grounds and because of the bird colonies, to remain on the islands during the high tide (or overnight!).

The most important constraint of all concerned the safety of the field teams. Members of the Portsmouth survey team were already familiar with conditions in Langstone but none of the archaeological team had worked in this kind of environment before. Langstone is a very beautiful place but its calm serenity masks a potentially very dangerous environment and, every year, people have to be rescued from the muds. Wessex Archaeology has a strict company Health and Safety Policy and, following a detailed risk assessment, the field team was issued with information about Langstone itself, tide tables, phone numbers of the local coastguard, the Harbour Master and the various wardens, and a set of safety instructions (see Appendix 3). A mobile telephone was carried at all times and the team communicated between themselves using mobile 'walkie-talkies'. When working in the intertidal zones fluorescent jackets were worn, ropes and distress flares carried, and team members were required to maintain visual or 'walkie-talkie' contact at all times. All transect survey work began at the furthest point from dry-land and worked back towards it. In the first season of work the team were required to ring the local coastguard every day both on arrival and on departure (failure to do the first but not the second would result in the rescue boat or helicopter being launched!) and ring Wessex Archaeology's main office once a day. In subsequent seasons, once they were familiar with the terrain and its idiosyncrasies, these last requirements were relaxed, though the coastguard and Harbour Master were informed of the dates of fieldwork and the Langstone mud rescue team kept an eye on proceedings. In one or two areas (notably the Portsea shore around Great Salterns) the muds proved to be too deep for safe working. As any surviving archaeological data in this area would have been completely masked by the muds anyway discretion was taken to be the better part of valour here!

A final hazard was the possibility of unexploded wartime shells and other ammunition. Total collection was deemed not to include unidentified metal objects, especially if they were khaki-coloured or ticking! Fortunately, with rare exceptions, no-one got stuck in the mud deeper than their wellingtons and no major problems were encountered. It is to the great credit of the field team that they were able to complete so much work over such short periods in exhausting conditions.

Workforce, finance, and practicalities

Hampshire County Council made a major financial contribution to the project for a three-year research programme of field survey and investigation (1993–5). The Department of National Heritage (now Department for Culture, Media, and Sport), also grant-aided the project indirectly through its funding of the HWTMA.

The archaeological fieldwork 'seasons' were essentially limited to two, or at most three, weeks each year with each task being carried out by small teams of only three or four people. Field investigation for the entire archaeological field investigation totalled fewer than 120 person days. The underwater survey was conducted on an *ad-hoc* basis with each dive generally undertaken by two members of the HWTMA on occasional days, rather than by sustained and continuous programme of underwater fieldwork. The more detailed survey of the Sinah circle structure was undertaken over a three-day period, whilst other more detailed underwater excavations and studies were only possible with the collaboration of Southampton University and the Nautical Archaeology Society.

Research and student input of both Portsmouth and Southampton Universities made a significant contribution to the project aiding the GPS survey and underwater investigations respectively. Whilst post-excavation analysis was funded by Hampshire County Council, many individual professionals also gave much of their own resources and time free, without which many of the analytical contributions reported here would not have been achieved. The total project budget and manpower was, therefore, substantial (but less than £60,000), but no individual task or activity was extensively funded. Comparison with the level of funding of other English wetland and intertidal projects enables some direct indication of their relative scale. Other wetland projects such as the North-West Wetlands and Humber Wetlands projects, each of which comprise six or seven internal projects, were grant aided by English Heritage at about £1.1M and £1.5M respectively. Recent intertidal projects have been less well-funded, and yet are more costly in manpower to conduct in the field. The Wootton-Quarr intertidal project on the Isle of Wight received direct grant aid from English Heritage in the region of £400,000 over 10 years. Excluded from this was the suite of 119 radiocarbon determinations (*c* £40,000) and a series of 40 dendrochronological determinations provided by English Heritage and staff time from the Isle of Wight Archaeological Committee. Significant and long term analysis in the Goldcliff intertidal region of the Severn Estuary, Gwent received direct grant aid of less than £140,000 (excluding pollen analysis and a radiocarbon dating programme of a similar scale to Wootton-Quarr) and the final conclusion of the project (Bell *et al* 2000) was only achieved through the ability of the universities to provide analyses and, like Langstone, through the dedication of the project staff.

The majority of the fieldwork at Langstone was conducted during three short, field seasons in 1993–5, with some additional survey and recovery subsequently. Despite the physical, fiscal, and practical limitations on fieldwork and the scope of the project, the collaborative effort of the several cooperating institutions and individuals provided an end product, in terms of data gathered alone, which was exceptionally cost-effective especially when compared to other larger-scale projects conducted in similar seaboard environments.

Project limitations

At the outset, although the overall project was ambitious, it was principally an archaeological survey and was never designed as a major analytical research project. It was an exploration of the archaeological and palaeoenvironmental potential of a known rich resource. Major sampling, coring, scientific analysis, radiocarbon dating programmes etc were not significant parts of the project, but the acquisition and record of basic fieldwork data was.

Therefore, despite the importance and significance of some of the finds and sites, detailed programmes of in-depth analysis were not possible, nor indeed warranted, within the overall tenor of the project. The combination of the constraints

Plate 7   The multidisciplinary team in action, examining hearth 1702. From left to right: Mike Allen (Wessex Archaeology), Michael Hughes (former County Archaeologist for Hampshire), Brian Sparks (Director, Hampshire and Wight Trust for Maritime Archaeology), Dominic Fontana (Portsmouth University) (Elaine A Wakefield)

outlined above set the parameters in which the project operated and the aim was to maximise the information within the resources available. This constituted an interesting logistical and management exercise in its own right.

Methods employed
by Neil J Adam, Jon Adams, Michael J Allen, Sarah Draper-Ali, Dominic Fontana, Julie Gardiner, Garry Momber, and Kit Watson

The methods employed during the Langstone Harbour Archaeological Survey Project consisted of a nested strategy of augering, walkover surveys, swimover surveys, site recording, test-pitting, and excavation. All of these methods were treated as experimental and were constantly monitored and reviewed in regard to their relative effectiveness or ineffectiveness in these terrains (see Review of methods, Chapter 8).

Areas of responsibility

The land-based fieldwork, augering, and recording were carried out by archaeologists from Wessex Archaeology; underwater fieldwork, including augering was the responsibility of the HWTMA with Department of Archaeology, University of Southampton, and underwater archaeologists from Wessex Archaeology, and the detailed survey and mapping were undertaken by the Department of Geography, University of Portsmouth (Plate 7). Further practical assistance in the field was provided by Arthur Mack, a local fisherman who had a detailed knowledge of the harbour itself and its archaeological distribution, and who also provided a boat which allowed much easier access to the islands when the timing of the tides was awkward. Assistance was also provided by John Bingeman (a local amateur marine archaeologist) who assisted in the diving and recording of underwater structures. The local knowledge of these two individuals was of great assistance. During this work other specific specialist services were engaged (eg Dr Rob Scaife, who undertook palaeoenvironmental sampling and analysis and text on sea-level, Justin Dix from the Department for Oceanography, Southampton University, who carried out a series of underwater geophysical surveys, and Dr Anthony Long from Department of Geography, University of Durham, who aided with the analysis of the former sea-level). Research of the historical activities in and around the harbour is ongoing by Val Fontana but only a summary of this work was available for inclusion in this volume. The overall project was coordinated, as County Archaeologist and then Project Leader, by Michael Hughes, and subsequently David Hopkins.

The analytical tasks were largely conducted by the bodies generating the data, but more detailed liaison was obviously required at the interrogation and interpretation stages which have been undertaken initially at a more communal level.

1   Creation of a database

Archaeological and palaeoenvironmental desktop study

Past archaeological research within the harbour is known to have been sporadic and largely unsystematic and the areas which have been explored dictated either by their position on dry-land or by their accessibility at low tide. Published archaeological accounts are few, the most important being those by Jacobi (1981), Bradley and Hooper (1973), and Bradley (1992). Material included in these reports and other published information has been reported to the Hampshire Sites and Monuments Record (SMR). Additional relevant archaeological and palaeoenvironmental data has been recorded from Portsmouth and Chichester Harbours, some of which is published (*ibid*) and has provided good background data.

The compilation of the database of known archaeological data was undertaken which included the interrogation of the SMR and a wider documentary search of published and unpublished accounts for material of all periods. The findspots of archaeological data recovered during this project were established by the GPS as accurately as possible (horizontally and vertically) and further information collected wherever possible. This information includes: nature and extent of archaeological exposure (eg artefacts eroding out of shingle bank) ground conditions at time of recovery and known aims, interests, abilities, and accuracy in recording and identification of individuals recovering archaeological material. The desktop study collated in some detail the available information on known archaeological sites and finds and palaeoenvironmental data from the harbour and dry-land areas within 1km of its shores, together with background information from a wider region to provide a broader context for the data (Wessex Archaeology 1994a, see Archaeological and palaeoenvironmental background, below) and produced a gazetteer of nearly 100 known records (Appendix 2). This data allowed a review of the distribution of sites and finds providing the archaeological and palaeoenvironmental background to the project and is presented below.

Museum recording

A record of the archived artefacts (largely flint and pottery collections) from the study area and held by Portsmouth City Museum was made by relevant project specialists (Gardiner and Seager Smith); some of this material had already been briefly looked at in 1981 by one of the project team as part of a wider research project (Gardiner 1988). Examination of the archived artefacts from previous fieldwork was undertaken specifically to:

i   augment the information provided by the desk based study and obtain information not recorded in the county's SMR
ii provide project consistent artefact type descriptions
iii reassess artefacts described by Bradley and Hooper
iv produce a single uniform database of all the artefactual information

The artefacts were recorded by the project specialists using the same methods and format as those from the field survey and entered onto the relevant archaeological databases. This information was then accessible for full reassessment and integration into the project reporting.

Digitisation, photogrammetry, and the creation of the project GIS
by Dominic Fontana

Achieving an effective integration of the interdisciplinary data collected by survey and research was seen to be an important aid to the success of the venture. The method adopted to address this challenge was to use the spatial location (geography) of each aspect of the various studies as their common linkage. To this end a geographic information system (GIS) was begun which allowed for the building of an extensive and integrated database. It was envisaged that this database could then be accessed through the spatial location of a find, sample, or structure and allow the plotting of archaeological information from the project in relation to other datasets such as historical mapping or aerial photographs.

Essentially, the approach is straightforward, aiming to collect a wide variety of data from several different disciplines, bringing it together into one system and thereby allowing the data to be viewed, investigated and analysed as a whole. Each set of data within the system therefore provides part of the story itself whilst adding to the information richness of the whole.

The GIS was constructed at the University of Portsmouth, using software packages considered most appropriate in the first instance, for the input, interpretation, and display of the geographical information (survey data, photogrammetry, aerial photography etc) to underpin the archaeological survey. The archaeological survey data was collected using traditional field techniques and recording systems supplemented by spot data recording points. With hindsight, in order for the archaeological and geographical datasets to have been more effectively interpreted, the field recording methods should have included a stronger locational component in recording spot data with a higher degree of detail and precision (the practical limitations on this aspect are discussed in Chapter 8).

GPS survey and the survey control network

All detailed survey work for the GIS database was undertaken by the University of Portsmouth. High precision Global Positioning System (GPS) equipment was used to provide an accurate survey control network for the photogrammetric digital mapping of the harbour. The accuracy of this base mapping was critical. The control network was fitted to a single OS Trigangulation Pillar to ensure that any positional inaccuracy in the survey fit to the National Grid could be rectified by applying a global correction factor, ie the survey was very precise within itself and was fitted into the OS grid only through the Eastern Road Triangulation Pillar (SU 4673 1037).

All archaeological points such as auger holes, survey grids, and recorded cliff section points were surveyed either by GPS or Total Station survey, extended from the GPS derived control network to ensure precise compatibility of the survey data. The archaeological field team placed tagged canes at all significant points requiring surveying so that, should weather or other conditions preclude completion of the survey while fieldwork was in progress,

Plate 8   The Trimble GPS being used to record an auger transect point off North Binness (Dominic Fontana)

the points could be identified and recorded at a later date (Plate 8). Where excavation or test-pitting was being undertaken, this had the added advantage that the archaeological work could be concluded without having to wait for the survey team, thus maximising the available fieldwork time. Underwater survey points were also recorded in a similar manner. All this data, as well as historic maps, various sets of air photographs and other datasets which provide a wealth of contextual support, was intended to be entered into the developing GIS databases so that the information could be displayed in the context of the photogrammetrically-derived digital map and digital elevation model (digital terrain model) which underpins the GIS.

The harbour survey and GIS

The digitising of existing cartographic and aerial photographic information provided some of the backdrop for the plotting of archaeological data and introduces some time-depth to, at least, post-medieval developments in the harbour's morphology. Clearly, much of this historical map information cannot be considered spatially accurate in its provenance by the standards required for the collection of the field archaeological evidence from this particular study. However, the relative lack of metrical accuracy contained in these maps does not detract from their usefulness as illustrations providing historical context to the archaeological data when viewed within the GIS. Clearly, these maps were not made with the needs of a modern archaeological survey in mind, but it is important that their lack of metrical accuracy is not used as an excuse for the collection of new archaeological evidence at anything less than the best spatial recording that can be achieved in the particular conditions that prevail at that point and

time. In other words, that the historical maps do not give a precise line which defines the position of a coastline or feature does not really matter provided that the new archaeological evidence is surveyed with an appropriate degree of precision relating to what and where it is. The known level of accuracy for the newly collected archaeological evidence will allow that evidence to support a researcher's interpretation of the historical mapping. A historical map suggests the morphology of the past landscape and the newly collected archaeology may be used to support or refute that suggestion.

The base mapping   Central to the development of both the project background map and any GIS is the quality of the digital map base upon which it is built. This must be of a sufficiently high resolution for the scale at which it is to be used and of a high enough precision to represent reality reasonably accurately. The usual source of base mapping in the UK is the Ordnance Survey. The OS have surveyed the area to only 1:2500. The specification of these 1:2500 maps is not intended for such an exacting use, and as they provide very little height data they were not suitable as the base mapping for this project. It was, therefore, necessary to create an appropriate base map of the harbour on which to build the GIS.

Constraints on the mapping   Langstone Harbour consists of a very large expanse of tidal mudflats. These are inaccessible at high tide and both difficult and dangerous to cross when the tide is low. Additionally the mud is a fragile ecosystem which may be damaged by walking in it. Furthermore, any archaeological material within the mud may also be disturbed by the process of surveying. The methods of surveying need to encounter a minimum of interference with the 'site' itself to minimise damage. Several options for the 'remote sensing' of the harbour presented themselves – principally by the use of satellite images or air photographs. A satellite option had the advantage of being readily available and cheap but had a resolution of only 20m. The air photographs allowed many more possibilities for interpretation and repeated analysis and because a photograph represents a single moment in time, monitoring of change through time. However, the significant drawback to air photographs is that they are not an orthogonal view of the ground. This requires specialist, and expensive, equipment to extract the accurate data that was needed for the mapping.

Photogrammetry   The method adopted was the use of the photogrammetric facilities available in the Department of Geography at the University of Portsmouth. These facilities allowed the very precise mapping of the harbour from air photographs using equipment similar to that used by the OS. The harbour was photographed by the University of Cambridge in July 1992 at very low tide using a specialist metric camera. These colour photographs, at a scale of 1:5000, allowed the accurate mapping to a planimetric scale of around 1:500 when plotted in a Leica DSR 14 analytical photogrammetric plotter. The output from this device is in digital form which is ideally suited to the development of the GIS map.

Ground Control Collection by Global Positioning System   Before it was possible to collect the map data from the photographs it was necessary to triangulate the separate photographs into strips, to scale the resultant photogrammetric model, and to orient this to the ground and to the OS National Grid. To achieve this a control network of very accurately surveyed points, visible in the photographs, was constructed. This was effected by a differential global positioning system borrowed from Leica UK which fixes positions from US Military Navstar Satellites to an accuracy of 5mm ± 1ppm (see Plate 8).

Once the control network had been constructed the photogrammetric plotting of the map data could proceed. This was carried out using the data specification, outlined in the research design, with a 20m grid of spot heights being collected for the whole harbour and a 10m grid being applied over the initial area of interest, North Binness Island. In addition to the grid data, hard features and breaks of curve were collected to assist with the Digital Terrain Modelling (DTM) from which the contours for the mapping were to be interpolated. The photogrammetric plotting was carried out at the Department of Geography, University of Portsmouth.

Map data processing   Initially the data from the photogrammetry was processed in the GIS Arc/Info using the Arc/Tin module to create a triangulation network DTM of the whole harbour at a nominal 1:10,000 scale. The mapping from this model was then further developed and the technique extended to create the larger scale mapping. As the project

developed alternative models were made from the original photogrammetric data using newer pieces of software to create polygons (regions) of height zones in the MapInfo GIS software system. Primarily, this was achieved using Vertical Mapper V1.5 from Northwood Geoscience.

Archaeological data processing   The data from the archaeological survey and sample collection exercise was compiled and processed by Wessex Archaeology. These data were tabulated or collected into a text database and then processed further by the Portsmouth team to create a GIS enabling the interrogation of the collected data through the specific geographical location of an archaeological find or sample.

2   Archaeological assessment and database enhancement

Walkover and swimover surveys

Walkover survey

A rapid and almost complete walkover survey was carried out on the foreshore areas of the harbour and islands down to the low-water mark where accessible (see Figs 8 and 9, below). The aim of the walkover survey was to enhance the SMR, provide further information on artefact scatters in the area and to locate areas of interest for further work (Plate 9). It provided a rapid, relatively systematic, search of the exposed and accessible foreshore and intertidal zones, and the exposed 'cliff' sections on the islands (Plate 10). Investigations were confined to those parts of the harbour where the chances of exposed archaeological material were at their highest and where archaeological finds had been reported in the past, ie the islands, their foreshores and the intertidal mudflats between them, the coastline of the harbour itself up to about the HWMT, and the intertidal mudflats beyond. For practical reasons, permanently submerged areas of the harbour were not surveyed, along with many areas on the landward side of the high-water mark. The systematic search was undertaken by a team of between two and four experienced archaeologists with the aid of Arthur Mack (see Areas covered, Chapter 2), and was intended to record artefact scatters, indentify diagnostic artefacts and the presence of topographical or archaeological features and organic remains, and collect a representative sample of artefacts to help characterise the assemblages (see Table 1).

In addition to this controlled walkover survey were added artefacts collected in a more casual manner by local enthusiasts and fishermen (J M Bingeman and A Mack in particular) over a period of more than 50 years. The results here do not provide a definitive record of all that has been found in the harbour, but has provided a substantial database with which to make some interpretation of the

Plate 9   Methods: walkover survey, flint scatters on Baker's Island (Neil J Adam)

Plate 10   Methods: examining the cliff section at the west end of North Binness. Note the clear band of artefacts and height of the cliff (Neil J Adam)

nature of prehistoric and early historic settlement and activity in this location, now called Langstone Harbour.

The walkover survey therefore aimed to isolate the main concentrations and scatters of artefacts and not to record a comprehensive record of all the artefacts within the harbour. In the intertidal zone more time was spent on the higher intertidal areas over firm clay, not just because these areas afforded easier access, but because they were obviously more artefact rich. The very soft muds further from the shore were not thoroughly searched, but rapid examination showed that these areas contained very few stones let alone artefacts. Areas where no or few finds were recorded can therefore confidently be

isolated as areas with no significant artefact scatters exposed at the time of fieldwork.

For ease of reference the entire harbour was nominally subdivided into smaller units or Areas and each was characterised by the nature of the sediments, ground conditions (eg extent of seaweed cover), and the archaeological deposits it contained (see Fig 8, below). In this way, those areas of highest current archaeological potential could be identified together with any features or structures; other areas eliminated from further work; and a fairly comprehensive record made of the current, surface, sediment patterns and an assessment made of their effect on any possible surviving archaeological remains, whether currently visible or not. Access to

Table 1 Summary of collection strategies and correlation with collection areas

Collection strategy	Aim	Remit	Areas	Figure
Major Walkover Areas	SMR enhancement, survey and search. Isolation of main artefact concentrations, identification of features/ sites	The entire study area was apportioned into large areas for rapid walkover survey. Recovery of diagnostic and representative material only. Large areas were subdivided (see *Walkover Areas*), and more detailed localised collection strategies implemented within these areas	8 – 13 (see Appendix 1)	Figures 8 and 9
Walkover Areas/ Collection Areas	Closer definition within Major Walkover Areas	Sub-divisions of the main Walkover Areas provided more spatial and locational control over general artefact scatters and of the location of features	14–26, 77/0– 77/6	Figures 9, 26, 29, 30 & 31
Total Collection Units	Collection of representative artefact sample of larger scatters	Small 2m^2 total collections units were placed within large artefacts scatters to provide a controlled and representative collection to help characterise the assemblages	numerous	Figures 9, 26 & 29
Total Gridded Artefact Collections	Total collection over larger artefacts scatters to define, characterise and examine spatial component of the distributions. Principally, though not exclusively, on the islands	Important artefact scatters identified during the walkover survey were gridded into 2m squares for controlled total artefact recovery to provide controlled collections of larger scatters	1, 3 & 4	Figures 26, 29, 30 & 31

South Binness was severely restricted throughout the project and so the southern and eastern shorelines of this island were, therefore, walked more thoroughly in *c* 50m strips running from the edge of the saltmarsh to the low-water mark, and a sample of finds recovered from each strip. The northern and western shores were more rapidly searched, any concentrations of material noted and, again, representative artefact samples taken.

Baker's Island could not be included in the survey until the third season of work (1995). The whole island and its foreshore was subdivided into smaller areas for rapid walkover and sample artefact recovery conducted.

Swimover surveys
by Sarah Draper-Ali, Garry Momber, and
Michael J Allen

The aim of all swimover surveys and searches was to extend the walkover and site surveys on land into the subtidal areas. Unfortunately the underwater visibility in Langstone Harbour averages about 3m. Only a small section of seabed can be seen at a time which makes detailed investigation very time consuming. Temporary loss of orientation of divers

undertaking a visual search in an area, or of an object, in low visibility is inevitable. Consequently, the need for strictly controlled search and survey methods are essential.

The underwater area of the harbour is vast so a realistic sampling policy was required. In part, the auger transects sampled this area linking the stratigraphy to those areas not submerged (see below). As it was impossible to cover the entire submarine bed by systematic search, a programme of controlled swimover transects augmenting the swimover searches with underwater spot surveys was undertaken by HWTMA divers with assistance from NAS trained volunteers and Wessex Archaeology. Fourteen separate dive tasks were completed with eight locations investigated.

Specific spot surveys were conducted at sites where anomalies were suspected or known to exist. Where anomalies of particular interest were discovered, further, more detailed survey was carried out. A selection of search methods was employed, including circular, snagline, swimline, corridor, and contour searches.

Swimline transects In the first instance a small team of 'walkers' in 'buddy' pairs and using scuba equipment, swam across an area in a systematic manner, examining the harbour floor. This provided general background information from which smaller, more detailed samples of the larger areas were tested. These comprised a series of sample transects (swimlines) perpendicular to the slope of the seabed to enable controlled observation, navigation and data recovery. Each transect was located by the Total Station which had been based on one of the control network points on North Binness Island, and aimed to build on information retrieved in the walk-over survey.

The intention of the swimover survey was therefore to extend the walkover survey into areas currently underwater and inaccessible to it. A rapid swimover survey around the island margins, recording artefacts in convenient unit areas, was intended to record the archaeological resource to the same level as the walkover survey. However, because of the overall size of the harbour and undoubted scouring effect of the tides in the main channels at least, the controlled swimover was restricted mainly to the south shores of North Binness and Long Islands, though other underwater spot surveys were conducted (see below). These swimover transects were specifically located to test areas of known archaeological artefact distributions, and swim from as far inshore as possible out into the sea towards the centre of the deeper marine river channels, over the inaccessible muds and subtidal surfaces.

Each transect was measured from the shore with 50m tapes, and divers swam at high tides along submerged tape measures recording the nature of the seabed and collecting samples of both sediment and potential artefacts and their position recorded. The transects were kept true by using shore based ranging rods.

Four transects of between 100 and 150m were swum; two off the south of North Binness Island, and two from the south and east of Long Island. Small areas to the south of North Binness and Long Islands were investigated at high tide specifically to investigate whether archaeological features or artefact scatters recognised on the intertidal foreshore could be identified on the harbour floor, even in those areas which are permanently underwater.

A general low level of artefacts encountered meant that a total recovery policy along the swimlines was actually undertaken. The paucity of finds may have been genuine but recording proved to be very difficult for the divers because of the flourishing growth of green algae (eg *Enteromorpa* spp and *Ulva*) and poor visibility resulting from the suspension of loose sediments in the warm, shallow water.

Other searches As it was impossible to cover the entire submarine bed by systematic search, the HWTMA divers augmented the controlled swimover survey with less systematic underwater spot surveys. These spot surveys consisted of a number of selected searches conducted during the fieldwork season at known points within the harbour using similar methods to those described above.

Circular searches (akin to Boismier's 'dog-leash' fieldwalking methods – Boismier in Fasham *et al* 1980) are relatively quick and useful when searching for objects in a known area. A swimline tape was attached to a fixed datum to establish a series of circles which are swum and searched using the taught tape to prescribe the circumference. The datum was buoyed to the surface which was used for accurate positioning. The radii of the circles were varied by extending the swimline tape distance, and the area covered was dependent upon visibility and coverage required. Objects were located in the survey by recording the bearing and distance from the datum. A variant of this technique was the circular snagline search which was ideal for the low visibility conditions in Langstone. The diver swims at the extremity of the tape and rather than using visual inspection, detection relies on obtrusive objects within the circle becoming snagged by the tape.

A final survey was the contour search which utilised the current seabed topography as the basis for searching. Searches were conducted at pre-defined depths along submerged inclines for set distances. At the end of each 'transect', a new depth was defined for the next bottom search. When objects were found, the depth, time, and distance along the search line was recorded. Record of the time was necessary to calculate the depth relative to the state of the tide.

Auger surveys (land and sea based)

Two auger surveys were conducted. The first consisted of a series of large transects across the entire harbour, including the islands, foreshores, and harbour bed, at about 50m intervals, to establish the basic Holocene sediment sequence (see Fig 8, below). The second involved more specific augering within the walkover, detailed study, and excavation areas to characterise the nature of the sediments. Augering was conducted to depths of c 3.5m until gravels or chalky deposits were reached, or until it became physically impossible to continue (see Plate 14, Chapter 2, below). In all cases augering was conducted using a 30mm diameter gouge auger with a 1m sample chamber. The sediments were recorded and logged in the field and voucher samples taken for description verification. Each auger point was marked and surveyed using the GPS to ensure accurate locational and ordnance datum data was established.

Boreholes in permanently flooded areas, ie submarine or marine augering, were undertaken by HWTMA. Exactly the same equipment and methods were deployed by the diving team as by the land-based survey. For submarine augering a small working boat was used as a diving platform with a larger supporting vessel (*MV Viney Peglar*) acting as a working station for describing and recording the

Plate 11   Methods: recording sediments obtained by underwater augering (Dominic Fontana)

Plate 12   Methods: Searching for artefacts in detailed collection units on Long Island (near feature 305, see Figure 29), during the walkover survey (Vaughan Birbeck)

sediment sequence and taking any voucher samples. Two divers undertook the submarine augering (Plate 11). A 6m pole was placed on the auger point, with the Total Station's reflector mounted to top, extending above the water. Its location was recorded using a Total Station based on shore and its position included in the project GIS.

Chirp survey

A marine seismic prospection survey (*Chirp*) was conducted within the harbour and on the adjacent Solent coastline. It surveyed the harbour entrance and the main Langstone and Broom Channels to define the nature of their infill stratigraphy and profile. In addition, the record of any anomalous

target (site or finds) could be investigated by the underwater archaeological team.

3   Detailed archaeological investigation

Intertidal archaeological survey areas and total gridded artefact collections

On the basis of the desk-based study and the walkover survey a series of specific locations were selected for more detailed and controlled archaeological investigation and more rigorous artefact collection (Plate 12). Archaeological survey involved the planning of all archaeological features (and sediment units) at a scale of 1:20 with archaeological features being recorded at 1:10 where necessary. Photographic and other records were made following

Plate 13   Methods: underwater recording (Jon Adams)

Wessex Archaeology's standard archaeological practice.

The main areas for detailed survey were on the islands. On North Binness and Long Islands total collection grids were established in three areas where artefacts were particularly concentrated and, in two cases, where features were encountered. All surface artefacts were collected from 2 × 2m units. Areas 1 (40 × 50m = 500 units) and 4 (30 × 50m = 375 units) were located on the south shore of North Binness Island towards its western and eastern ends respectively, and Area 3 (40 × 50m) was on the north-western headland of Long Island (see Fig 9, below). Further areas along the shores of both islands supported smaller concentrations of artefacts and, in these locations, individual 2 × 2m total collection units were established. On Baker's Island 32 individual collection units were established and, in a single day's visit to South Binness, three collection units were used to investigate small concentrations observed in the northern part of the island.

At least two coordinates at the corners of the three main grids and the south-west coordinate for every individual collection unit were surveyed in for the GIS using the Total Station electronic theodolite. These positions were used to construct maps of the survey areas and the distributions of finds.

Archaeological excavation

Local excavations were undertaken to recover individual artefacts such as whole pots sunk into the foreshore muds, or small isolated features such as hearths. Excavation and sectioning of other features, almost exclusively within the detailed survey areas, was also conducted. Such excavations followed standard methods and practice, and where appropriate full three-dimensional records were made of all artefacts recovered.

Underwater excavation
by Jon Adams

A small scaffold frame was assembled around any area chosen to be excavated. In the case of the Sinah circle excavation it was firmly bedded on sandbags placed on the seabed thus obviating the need to drive vertical grid posts into the sediment and possibly damage hidden, unexcavated, material. Elsewhere, in less archaeologically sensitive areas, scaffold poles were driven into the sediments. Excavation was carried out with the tools familiar on land: trowels, and for more delicate work around organic material, paintbrushes. Spoil was removed with an airlift. In this method of excavation the excavator rests on the scaffold framework rather than on the excavation. The aim is that neither the excavator nor the spoil removing equipment actually touches the deposit, only the chosen tool of excavation. In this way a controlled dissection of less consolidated marine deposits is achieved with no loss of visibility (which would occur if the excavator was lying on the sediment) and no damage or disturbance to fragile materials lying just below the surface (Fig 5). The excavation area was first trowelled down to remove loose, mobile upper sediments, before recording of the more undisturbed sediments, artefacts and features could begin (Plate 13). The waters in Langstone Harbour are very murky, and this prevents publication of photographs of the archaeological work and finds – Figure 5 is drawn from a photograph of the excavation of the Sinah structure.

Test-pit excavation

In some specific areas keyhole test-pit transects were hand excavated through the saltmarsh to identify, in plan, the archaeological contexts which are being lost on the foreshore to erosion. As stated, full cooperation

Figure 5   Using an airlift during the excavation of the Sinah Circle structure, drawn from a photograph by J Adams

and liaison with the RSPB and Hampshire Wildlife Trust was maintained through the formulation of the excavation strategies and acquiring formal consent. Test-pits were excavated in transects perpendicular to the shoreline at 20 or 25m intervals on Baker's Island and individual test-pits excavated on North Binness Island (inland from the foreshore area where ditches were recorded). Test-pits of 1.5 × 1.5m were carefully excavated by hand and all artefacts recorded in three dimensions, related to recorded datum height. All other recording (context and artefacts) followed standard procedures.

Because of the ecological importance of the saltmarsh communities, square turves were carefully cut and stacked. The spoil was retained in spit or context order and each test-pit was carefully back-filled within 24 hours of excavation; every attempt was made to layer the horizons as recovered. Finally the saltmarsh turf was carefully reinstated to the satisfaction of the RSPB.

Wreck surveys
by Garry Momber

A number of wreck sites are recorded in Langstone Harbour in the Hampshire County Council SMR and

the Royal Commission on the Historic Monuments of England NMR (see below) but their current state of preservation is unknown. As part of the Langstone Harbour Archaeological Survey Project, the HWTMA located some of the sites (with the aid of Arthur Mack and John Bingeman) and limited surveys were conducted by field officers of HWTMA and NAS trained volunteers, to address this discrepancy. The object was to qualify the existing records and assess the time and resources required to obtain key measurements required.

The investigations began with a visual survey of the wrecks to assess their major characteristics and layout, followed by a rapid tape measurement survey. Survey methods deployed to record the wrecks varied at each site, dependent on the nature of the wreck, and were formulated following a reconnaissance dive. Measurements were taken using tape measures and the Sonardyne Homer acoustic measuring system. Direct tape measurements were made either using the trilateration method, where positions were fixed by measuring them to known datum points, or offset measurements where right angled distances were taken from a baseline, or a combination of both was used.

The Sonardyne Homer is an underwater acoustic measuring system consisting of transponders beacons and a hand held unit. The hand held unit interrogates each beacon in turn with an acoustic signal. The beacons reply with signals at set frequencies in the 40kHz band. The return time for the signals to pass between the hand unit and the transponder is measured and the distances through water are calculated. These units are positioned on the seabed at appropriate locations to enable survey of the wreck parameters.

Survey of wooden structures
by Dominic Fontana, Kit Watson, and Jon Adams

Survey of harbour-edge timber structures and features

The visible timber structures in the harbour, most of which survive around the coastal margins, were surveyed into the control network using a Total Station electronic theodolite to establish their positions in three dimensions. These surveys conducted by Portsmouth University were confined to single data points rather than an archaeological graphic record of the harbour-edge wooden structures. One further timber structure was recorded in 1999 by Wessex Archaeology.

Sinah stake circle

Metrical survey methodology 1993–94: The initial underwater survey of a timber circle, discovered by Arthur Mack in the south-eastern part of the harbour, was undertaken by John Bingeman to provided a basic sketch plan of the general layout and

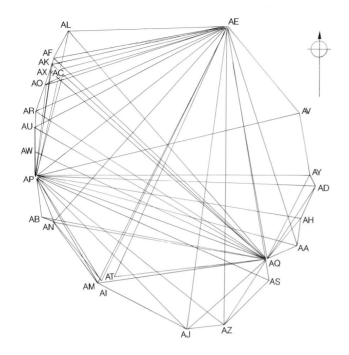

Figure 6   Web for Windows survey of the Sinah circle. Drawn by S E James based on data from J Adams

topography of the surviving structure with a measured sketch of each timber. The development of a more detailed, measured plan was required before other options, including excavation, could be considered. A more detailed metrical survey directed by Jon Adams was, therefore, undertaken (see Plate 11, above). All stable timbers were tagged with a copper nail and a coded identity tag. The inter-distances and three-dimensional positions of these 'site points' could then be established. The inter-distances between the stakes were measured with tape measures to build up a 'web' of measurements.

A computer program was used to establish the 3D positions of each nail (*Web for Windows*, developed for underwater recording on the *Mary Rose* project by Nick Rule). Initially the timber coordinates were related to an arbitrary site zero but, as this survey process gave positions of the timbers relative to each other to a high degree of precision but did not fix their positions to the National Grid, three of the timbers were then surveyed using a shore-based total station, with a prism fixed on a 6m pole (as had been used in the underwater sections of the auger transect). This allowed them to be related to the OS grid and to the Langstone GIS. The coordinates were fed into the *Web* programme and used to adjust the coordinates of the other timbers accordingly (Fig 6). The accuracy of the plan is indicated by the average residual of distance and relative depth measurements, which was < 5mm. By digitising the relative positions derived from the *Web for Windows* programme and assigning the measured National Grid and OD heights to the three measured timbers, it was possible to arrive at good coordinates for each of the extant timbers.

The finished 'web' is a three-dimensional plot of

where the datums are in 3D space, in this case accurate to 3mm. The positions are expressed as Cartesian coordinates and can be used to control the generation of any other type of survey, from conventional drawings, topographic modelling, or photogrammetry. It had been intended to produce a photo-mosaic, but on subsequent visits to the site equipment problems or low visibility has prevented this. A further topographical survey was also undertaken by Kit Watson of Wessex Archaeology, and the data manipulated in Excel and AutoCAD to generate a figure of the site as a terrain model (eg Adam *et al* 1995, fig 3), the spikes being the timbers which could be related to observed differences in surface sediment.

Photographs of the timbers were taken from above to construct a photo-mosaic in which each photograph records at least two known locations (tagged timbers). Underwater visibility to date has hindered the completion of the photo-mosaic survey.

Archaeological survey: As a part of the 1994 season's work an archaeological plan of the stake circle and associated deposits was undertaken by HWTMA with Kit Watson over three days. This recorded the visible archaeological material and provided a survey of the sea-bed around it.

Archaeological and palaeoenvironmental background
by Julie Gardiner, Michael J Allen, Rob Scaife, and Justin K Dix

The full archaeological survey of the harbour was preceded by an initial period of field and desk-based assessment. The latter (Wessex Archaeology 1994a) aimed to compile as much information as possible about previous archaeological finds and palaeo-environmental data obtained from the harbour and its immediate hinterland, together with any relevant published material relating to Portsmouth and Chichester Harbours in particular and the Solent coast in general. That desk-based assessment (Wessex Archaeology 1994a) is essentially presented below. The main thrust of the project was to examine in detail the harbour itself and its physical archaeology with only a limited dry-land area around the margins. For this reason detailed research into the medieval history of Portsea and Hayling Islands and the coastal plain to the north was not undertaken as part of the initial assessment. Similarly, full details of the industrial archaeology of the harbour were not sought, nor of the harbour works themselves or coastal defences. Settlement is attested, and is clearly demonstrable, in all these areas throughout the historic periods, from at least the later Saxon period, but such detailed research was considered to be beyond the scope of the initial assessment. For the historic periods, attention focused, therefore, on information pertaining directly to the harbour and its shorelines.

Palaeoenvironmental background

by Rob Scaife, Michael J Allen, and Justin K Dix

Few palaeoenvironmental analyses from archaeological sites have been conducted within the study area, despite the relative wealth of archaeological evidence (see below). One exception to this is the Wootton-Quarr project, Isle of Wight (Tomalin *et al* forthcoming). Nevertheless, a number of more traditional earlier palaeogeographical studies had aimed at examining long sequences of vegetation and climate change. The coastal plain and intertidal zones had specifically been isolated as areas of archaeological resource potential in Hampshire (Allen 1996). As a consequence this section concentrates principally upon the evidence for sea-level change in the Holocene which can be related to human activity in the harbour, and on palaeoenvironmental data from archaeological deposits.

Evidence of the former sea-level

The importance of sea-level change to the landscape development cannot be overestimated in the low-lying, near marine landscape of Langstone Harbour. Studies of relative sea-level are crucial when attempting to view change and development of human communities which occupied this region over the past nine millennia. During this time significant changes have had a direct impact upon both the physical and ecological nature of the defined study area. The potential for major palaeoenvironmental sequences to reveal such changes in sea-level and landscape is well attested in other areas of southern England (Long 1992; Long and Tooley 1995; Devoy 1982; 1990; Preece *et al* 1990; Allen and Gibbard 1994).

Holocene sea-level change can be viewed at global and regional scales and at a more local level. In the former, postglacial sea-level rise from *c* –27m OD at *c* 10,000 BP was consequent upon the melting of Devensian ice caps. A sharp increase in sea-levels occurred during the early Holocene (Flandrian I) so that by the start of the middle Holocene (Flandrian II), at *c* 7000 BP, this had led relative sea-level to rise to *c* –10m OD (based on Long and Tooley 1995 for southern England). Subsequent relative rise was gradual with levels of –3 to –4m OD at *c* 3000–4000 BP. Superimposed on this change were the effects of isostatic rebound and other local tectonic activity. Changes also occurred in palaeotidal range (Shennan 1989; Long and Shennan 1993) and local patterns of sedimentation and erosion (Long and Scaife 1996). Thus, regional variation in patterns of marine inundation and even regression have occurred which have prompted studies in regional and local eustatic change (Long and Roberts 1997). A number of southern English and south coast sea-level altitude/time record models have now been proposed and these allow broad palaeogeographic reconstructions to be made of the inundated coastal landscape of the coastline of south-east England. Holocene relative sea-level (RSL) graphs have been generated for a number of areas in southern England including the Thames (Devoy 1979), East Kent (Long 1992), Romney Marshes and East Sussex (Long and Innes 1993), and south-west England (Heyworth and Kidson 1982). Comparison of these graphs reveals important differences between areas, largely attributed to differential crustal movements or changes in palaeotidal range (eg Shennan 1989; Long and Shennan 1993; Long and Tooley, 1995).

Relative sea-level studies which relate to the Solent have focused on the extensive submerged and intertidal peat and sediment sequences. This significance of these has been recognised since the last century (eg Clement Reid 1893; James 1847) but they have remained little studied. Early pollen analyses were carried out on low-level peat deposits in Southampton Water (Godwin and Godwin 1940) and Portsmouth (Godwin 1945). These provided information on local vegetation changes which formed part of Godwin's postglacial zonation scheme. Studies of the regional palaeodrainage system were also carried out. Everard's concept of the Solent River System (Everard 1954b), Allen and Gibbard's (1994) recent examination of this model, and Dyer's work on the submerged palaeochannels of the Solent (Dyer 1975) are of particular note.

Despite the abundant potential of the Solent region for sea-level studies (eg Hodson and West 1972; Long and Tooley 1995), systematic research in this area has been limited and it has lagged behind that in other areas of southern England. For over twenty years just four dates from Fawley provided the only absolute chronology for coastal sedimentation in the Solent. During this time the Holocene relative sea-level (RSL) record from the Solent mainland was one characterised by much speculation but little data. Although the coastal sediments had been studied for over a century (James 1847; Shore 1893; 1905; Shore and Elwes 1889; Hooley 1905; Anderson 1933; Godwin and Godwin 1940; Everard 1954a; Hodson and West 1972; Nicholls and Clarke 1986), most of these previous studies were completed in a haphazard manner, taking opportunist advantage of sections as and when they became exposed during excavations. Only three studies (Hodson and West 1972; Long and Scaife 1996; Long and Tooley 1995) have sought to use a combination of litho-, bio-, and chronostratigraphic data to reconstruct environments of deposition.

Hodson and West (1972) described a sequence of unconsolidated Holocene deposits up to 21m thick west of Langstone Harbour on the shores of Southampton Water (at Fawley and Hythe). One main peat bed was recorded between –5.00 and 0m OD, the base and top of which was dated to 2130–1560 cal BC and 2410–1740 cal BC respectively. Two samples of organic sediments infilling a channel at –7.63m and –7.33m OD were also dated to 5500–4960 cal BC and 5570–5040 cal BC (Godwin and Switsur 1966).

A series of six radiocarbon determinations was described by Long and Tooley (1995) from Holocene sediments at Stansore Point on the north side of the Solent between Calshot Spit and the Beaulieu River and date the three peat horizons. One prominent peat bed (between c –3.5m and –0.5m OD) is recorded, together with an additional peat recorded above and below this main deposit. The three peats formed at c 4800 cal BC, between 4540–3700 cal BC and 2470–1880 cal BC, and at c 770–200 cal BC respectively. Long and Tooley (1995) compared the ages and altitudes of these index points with others collected from sites in southern England. The mid-Holocene Solent dates plotted between 1–2m above those of similar age to the east (eg the Thames Estuary).

Recently, Long and Scaife (1996) reported further stratigraphic, radiocarbon, pollen, and diatom data from three additional sites in Southampton Water (Hythe, Bury Farm, and the Hamble Estuary). Peats at all three sites occur at depths below c –1m OD, above which silts, clays, and thin saltmarsh deposits are to be found. The end of the main phase of peat formation has been dated in the Hamble Estuary to 3330–2890 cal BC (–2.33m OD), and at Bury Farm to 1450–1110 cal BC (–0.11m OD). Long and Scaife (1996) report two further dates from the Hythe Marshes, one from the base of a peat (4330–3890 cal BC) and a second from the top of a thin peat which formed in a small valley draining onto Hythe Marshes behind a gravel bar (cal AD 670–940).

In summary, the available radiocarbon dates from the Solent are few compared with those from other areas in southern England. Prior to the 1980s most work had been completed in an unsystematic manner, and no attempt was made to link graphs of RSL to the history of human activity in the region during the prehistoric period. The temptation to over-interpret the limited available data should be resisted, but the stratigraphy and radiocarbon dates indicate widespread peat accumulation in the Solent region between c 4000 and 1500 cal BC. The age for the end of peat accumulation is diachronous within the region and there is no evidence for synchronous episodes of peat formation. Lithostratigraphic data from other sites in the Solent region support the contention that peat-forming communities were more widespread during the mid-Holocene than during the late-Holocene. For example, Everard (1954a) reveals thick peats extending across part or all of the River Itchen between c –6 and 0m OD (estimated ages 5000–0 cal BC). Similar thicknesses of peat are recorded by Godwin and Godwin (1940) from the Southampton Dock excavations. This widespread occurrence of peats led Nicholls and Clark (1986) to suggest a regional fall in RSL during the mid to late Holocene.

In Langstone Harbour itself Mottershead (1976) records intertidal Holocene peat deposits at the base of the present main channels (Broom Channel and Langstone Channel). These are sealed below about 13m of blue-grey silty clays at –11.9 and –10.75m OD respectively (Wimpey 1962). Despite the presence of these deposits and their potential, they have remained little studied.

The most significant work in the region is the major programme of analysis in Wooton-Quarr, Isle of Wight, which provides a detailed and systematic study of coastal change. That research has shown that RSL at 8000 cal BC in the English Channel was below –30m OD (Long and Scaife 1996; Tomalin et al forthcoming) and that the contemporary Solent coastline lay some distance south of the Isle of Wight, although tidal influence may have penetrated someway inland along the former course of the River Solent (probably not as far as Southampton Water itself). Stratigraphic and pollen data suggest that widespread freshwater peats formed in Southampton Water at this time (Godwin and Godwin 1940; Long and Scaife 1996). RSL rose rapidly during the early and mid Holocene (being at c –9m OD at 5300 cal BC to –2.5m OD by 3000 cal BC after which the rate of rise fell), inundating the outer portions of Southampton Water by c 7000 cal BC. RSL continued to rise progressively inundating extensive areas of alder-dominated woodland in Southampton Water. By c 1500 cal BC, most peat-forming communities had been drowned and mineral rich sedimentation persisted until changes occurred in the Spartina cover during the last 100 years or so. By c cal AD 0 most freshwater peat-forming communities were severely restricted and minerogenic mudflat and saltmarsh sedimentation has characterised patterns of coastal evolution since this time. This model, showing an expansion of mid-Holocene peat-forming communities and their progressive inundation, provides the simplest explanation for the data currently available.

Archaeologically derived palaeoenvironmental data

Most of the known archaeological evidence from the environs of Langstone is a result of surface collection and spot finds. Consequently there has been little opportunity to recover environmental information from bones, carbonised plant remains, land molluscs, or pollen sequences from sealed contexts. Few excavations have been conducted to modern fieldwork standards within the area (see previous fieldwork, below) and most of these did not recover environmental material or, where such data exist, have yet to be comprehensively published. The only published environmental programme from any earlier excavations concerns the processing of a bulk soil sample from a pit containing Grooved Ware pottery at Wallington. This sample was processed for carbonised plant remains but unfortunately contained none (Hughes 1977). A large faunal assemblage was recovered from both Iron Age and Roman phases of the excavations at Hayling Island temple (A King pers comm) and this provides information particularly associated with the Iron Age building. This assemblage was dominated by sheep and pig but is, as King and Soffe (1994, 115) acknowledge, 'unlike contemporary local settlement sites'. The same is true of the Roman assemblage but as the activity was demonstrably associated with the temple, this material probably contributes little to our understanding of 'normal' Roman farming practice in the local area.

Despite the paucity of palaeoenvironmental data within the Langstone environs the *potential* for the recovery of environmental information concerning both the terrestrial landscape and the natural resource of that landscape available for exploitation by past communities is extremely high because of the diverse micro-habitats which exist. The most obvious palaeoenvironmental component is waterlogged material such as preserved wood. Although submerged 'forests' are recorded in Southampton Water (Godwin and Godwin 1940), relatively little in the way of preserved wooden artefacts has been recorded, neither has preserved wooden fish traps or other structures well attested elsewhere (*cf* Salisbury 1991). However, preserved wooden timbers of a late Bronze Age structure were recorded on the Hayling Island coast at the Wadeway, the pre-19th century low-water horse road to the mainland (Williams and Soffe 1987) and many undated, and hitherto unsystematically examined, wooden structures survive in the intertidal muds around much of the harbour foreshore. The level of potential environmental data from the Langstone environs is nevertheless high. This contrasts markedly with the adjacent gravels, which offer few preservational opportunities, or even the Chalk which, although it has the capacity to preserve land snails and bone, does not offer the opportunity to preserve pollen and the organic artefacts which more readily survive in waterlogged contexts.

Archaeological background
by Julie Gardiner

Sporadic work in the harbour area in the past has revealed the presence of considerable archaeological material. Much of this information remains unpublished, or inadequately so. No systematic survey has been undertaken, however the quantity and range of finds reported to the County Sites and Monuments Record (SMR) over the years indicate that the harbour area, in particular, is potentially very rich in archaeological finds (Fig 7). The islands within the northern part of the harbour, in particular, are known to have produced much prehistoric and Roman material.

The principal data source for the desk-based assessment (1993) of the known archaeology of Langstone Harbour was the County Sites and Monuments Record (SMR). Most of the records in the SMR are of chance finds not recovered during deliberate archaeological investigation. Secondary sources

consulted included a range of published and unpublished works available in the libraries of Southampton and Reading Universities and Wessex Archaeology, and Ordnance Survey maps at various scales and of various dates on which archaeological sites and finds are occasionally marked. The search for information was not exhaustive but aimed to provide as comprehensive a background database as available time and resources would permit. Later in the project archaeological finds extant in Portsmouth City Museum were checked for identification and against the SMR records (see Chapter 4, below). In the discussion which follows, project numbers are allocated for those sites and finds in the immediate area (eg BI.26, see Appendix 2, where the SMR number is also given) and elsewhere SMR references are provided where appropriate (eg SU70SW 61) but it should be noted that some of the identifications of material provided under these references within the SMR have proved erroneous.

There are a number of known archaeological 'sites' and monuments within the immediate hinterland of the harbour but only a relatively small number of excavations are recorded or published (Fig 7). Excavation of a Roman 'villa' at Havant (Ha89a) is recorded by F Warren (1926–30) and recently published (Gilkes 1998), a site which also produced Neolithic flintwork and other finds. Elisabeth Lewis excavated a site at Wakeford's Copse, also at Havant (SU 7278 0914; Bradley and Lewis 1974) which produced late Mesolithic, late Neolithic, and later Bronze Age material.

A Bronze Age round barrow (Windmill Hill) comprised of burnt flint, at Pound Field to the north of Tournerbury on Hayling Island, was 'excavated', but can more readily be described as a burnt mound (Bradley pers comm). A 'tree-trunk coffin burial, burnt or decayed' was recorded beneath it and flint scrapers and 'arrowheads' (Trigg 1892; Williams-Freeman 1919). Richard Bradley, on behalf of Margaret Rule, excavated part of a middle Iron Age saltworking site on North Hayling brickfield (Creek Field, note the SMR incorrectly refers to this as Crake Field) with flues, saltern troughs, and briquetage with a firepit and associated typical saucepan forms of middle/late Iron Age pottery (Bradley pers comm, see Bradley 1992). Richard Bradley and Mike Fulford undertook small-scale excavation at the Iron Age earthwork of Tournerbury Camp (SZ 732 999; Bradley and Fulford 1975) to re-examine a section through the rampart made by J R Boyden in 1959. The largest excavation in the area was that of the Hayling Island Iron Age and Roman temple, which still awaits full publication (Downey *et al* 1979; King and Soffe 1994; 1998). This site was previously investigated and is summarily reported by Ely (1904; 1908). Slightly further afield a Mesolithic flint scatter was exposed during stripping for construction of the M27 near Fort Wallington, Fareham in 1972 and investigated (Hughes and ApSimon 1977). In the same year an Iron Age site was excavated on the line of the Wallington military

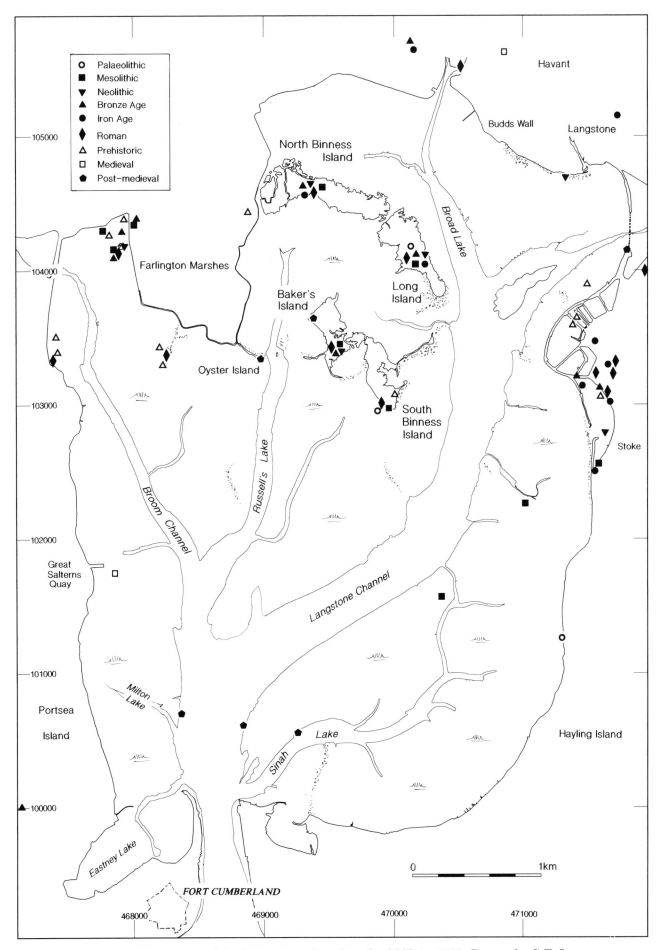

Legend:
- ○ Palaeolithic
- ■ Mesolithic
- ▼ Neolithic
- ▲ Bronze Age
- ● Iron Age
- ◆ Roman
- △ Prehistoric
- □ Medieval
- ⬟ Post-medieval

North Binness Island

Havant

Budds Wall

Langstone

Farlington Marshes

Baker's Island

Long Island

Broad Lake

Oyster Island

South Binness Island

Russell's Lake

Stoke

Broom Channel

Langstone Channel

Great Salterns Quay

Portsea Island

Milton Lake

Hayling Island

Sinah Lake

Eastney Lake

FORT CUMBERLAND

0   1km

Figure 7   Summary of the sites and finds locations listed in the SMR in 1993. Drawn by S E James

road by Michael Hughes (1974). These sites are discussed in more detail below.

Surface collection

Most archaeological finds from within the harbour have been recovered as surface finds, either during episodes of deliberate 'fieldwalking' or as chance finds made by locals, particularly fishermen. Archaeological investigation of the islands and intertidal zones has always been difficult as a result of their general inaccessibility on foot except around low tide and the depth of mud in many places. Most finds seem to be the product of a number of brief forays, principally in pursuit of prehistoric flintwork.

The SMR records a number of Mesolithic flints and flintwork generally from South Binness Island recovered by A J Seagrave in 1975–7 but the majority of collection on the islands was by Chris Draper and by Bari Hooper and Richard Bradley. The first of these, a keen and very knowledgeable local amateur archaeologist from Fareham, visited the islands on a number of occasions in the late 1950s and early 1960s and remarked on their continued erosion. Most of his finds, which included Palaeolithic, Mesolithic, and later flintwork as well as fragments of saddle quern and several Bronze Age urns, came from the southern foreshores of the four main islands (Draper 1958; 1961; 1963; Wymer 1977, 114–8; Jacobi 1981).

Bradley and, in particular, Hooper also collected mainly from the foreshores during the early 1960s where they record finding Mesolithic and later flintwork, Bronze Age, Iron Age, and Roman pottery, and Roman tiles and brick (Bradley and Hooper 1973; Wymer 1977, 118). A major difficulty with all finds from the islands is the lack of accurate maps available to the collectors and the shifting nature of the islands themselves. Bradley and Hooper at least tended to assign all finds from one island to a generalised, approximate, grid reference (Bradley pers comm).

All three of these individuals also walked areas of the intertidal zone and saltmarshes of Farlington Marshes and a number of small, unstable islands to its south, some of which no longer exist. Hooper recorded finds of abraded early Roman pottery, briquetage, burnt and worked flint, and a possible hearth from one of these. A pit 'exposed' (presumably eroding out of the cliff) on Farlington in 1979 was observed by Hooper who noted 25 pieces of Deverel-Rimbury pottery representing at least three vessels.

The western shore of Hayling Island was also investigated by Richard Bradley who recorded numerous concentrations of Iron Age and Roman pottery, briquetage, bricks, hearths, and possible kiln sites, all below the then HWMT in areas which have since been made-up. The Portsea side of the harbour does not appear to have been systematically investigated at any time.

Palaeolithic

Three Palaeolithic flints were recorded by Draper (1961; Wymer 1977, 426) as coming from Long Island. These were a shouldered point found on the south-west shoreline in 1960, a scraper-knife with inverse retouch from the south-east shore in 1958, and a graver from mudflats roughly halfway between the other two in 1959. A blade knife, nearly 4¾ inches (95mm) in length, was picked up on Baker's Island some years previously. A further piece is recorded in the SMR as having come from the centre of Long Island in 1973 (LI.1). A 'Levallois' type core was picked up by Richard Bradley on the northwest shore of Hayling Island (pers comm), but whether it was a true (middle Palaeolithic) example or a late Neolithic one is not clear (the piece has not been seen by the present author).

Two handaxes have been recovered from Hayling Island. One was recovered from intertidal mudflats in 1981 (HI.2) and another from Fleet (Wessex Archaeology 1994b, gazetteer no SXRB–3, no 13). A third handaxe came from a garden on the Chalk or the Bagshot Sands at Havant in 1984 (Ha.3). Several others are reported from Portsmouth and around the northern part of Portsmouth Harbour (Wessex Archaeology 1994b).

The coastal plain generally has produced a great number of Palaeolithic flints, mostly handaxes, from alluvial and gravel deposits. Particular concentrations occur around Fareham, on Selsey, around Chichester, and on the Sussex raised beaches around Slindon. The gravel and sand quarries at Boxgrove, West Sussex have produced an important Acheulian flint industry with associated faunal and exceptionally early hominid remains (this information summarised most recently in Wessex Archaeology 1993; 1994b; Roberts and Parfitt 1999; Wymer 1999).

Mesolithic

Mesolithic flintwork is recorded from all the islands in the harbour (Draper 1958; 1963; Wymer 1977, 114–18; Jacobi 1981). Most of it seems to come from the southern foreshores and mudflats. The material includes scrapers, flakes, blades, cores, at least one tranchet adze from Baker's Island (BI.12), and picks from South Binness (SB.6) and Baker's Islands (BI.12).

The foreshore distribution continues around Farlington Marshes and into the north-west corner of the harbour. In the intertidal zone and on several former small islands to the south of Farlington a Mesolithic core, blade, and a saw were recovered by Hooper (FM.8). Draper records a microlith from the shore to the east of Eastern Road, Portsea Island (FM.7) – one of only four microliths recorded from the harbour area (Draper 1958; Wymer 1977, 118) – with another example, together with a core, blades, flakes, a saw, and pick from a small island to the south-west of the marshes (FM.11). Portsmouth Museum contains a collection of material from Farlington Marshes, of which that mentioned above presumably forms part, which comprises 289 flakes and blades, 58 retouched blades, one blade core and a core rejuvenation flake, a pick, eleven scrapers, and three microliths (Gardiner 1988, cat no H277). The stray find of a tranchet adze is recorded from Hayling Island (SU 72 00, Gardiner 1988, cat no 866) and of a pebble macehead with an hourglass perforation from Hillsea (PI.9).

One Mesolithic assemblage has been excavated, at Wakeford's Copse, Havant (Bradley and Lewis 1974). Here, six shallow and one deep pit were excavated, lying close to a possible flint knapping floor. Stakeholes were possibly recorded partly enclosing these hollows and which might indicate the presence of actual structures (Jacobi 1981, 19). A total of 429 struck flints was recovered, including two simple rod microliths, two tranchet adzes, two more sharpening flakes and several microburins. The assemblage is late Mesolithic in character, probably of the 6th millennium BC.

Mesolithic flints are also known from various locations around both Portsmouth and Chichester Harbours, most notably at Cams, Fareham (SU 587 056, Wymer 1977, 113; Jacobi 1981; Gardiner 1988, cat no H028); Rainbow Bar (SU 530 022, Draper 1963; Wymer 1977, 113; Jacobi 1981; Gardiner 1988, cat no H311); and Apuldram (SU 840 030, Pitts 1980; Wymer 1977, 291; Gardiner 1988, cat no S245). Excavation of the flint scatter exposed during construction of the M27 at Fort Wallington, Fareham (Hughes and ApSimon 1977) also revealed part of the assemblage to have slumped into two deep solution hollows which occurred at the junction between the Chalk and the raised beach gravels. Some of the material had been carried down as much as 6m into the pipes. The assemblage included fifteen axes and 21 sharpening flakes, seven microliths, three picks, and a variety of other tools together with nearly 3000 waste flakes and blades, and 108 cores.

A number of tranchet adzes are also known from the coastal plain between Southampton Water and Chichester, including a massive (300mm plus in length) example from Fishbourne (SU 845 045, Gardiner 1988, cat no 668, Chichester Museum).

Neolithic

The distribution of Mesolithic flintwork within the harbour is reflected by that of Neolithic assemblages which are mostly recorded from the islands and shorelines of the north-west part of the harbour, principally by Draper, and Bradley and Hooper. These include plano-convex knives, three leaf-shaped and one triangular arrowhead, fabricators, knives, polished and unpolished axe fragments, and scrapers from around 0m OD on Long Island (LI.21 and LI.48 = SU70SW 66, recorded as Bronze Age but personally examined by JPG: Bradley and Hooper

1973; Gardiner 1988, cat no H122); scrapers and flakes from South Binness (SB.22); scrapers, polished axe and adze fragments (NB.27), scrapers, flakes, and an awl (NB.59b), and Neolithic scrapers 'in situ' associated with Roman finds (NB.27) from North Binness. Fragments of a saddle quern of probable Neolithic–Bronze Age date were recovered from Baker's Island in 1958 and Draper found fragments of another in approximately the same place in 1969 (BI.26).

A crouched inhumation of an elderly woman was found by Richard Bradley in mudflats off the south coast of North Binness Island. It is reported (Bradley and Hooper 1973, 24) as being Neolithic in date but there was no dating evidence associated with the body (*ibid*, and confirmed by Bradley pers comm). 'Iron Age' pottery was found not far away (NB.73).

The distribution of finds again seems to extend into Farlington Marshes and the mudflats around it. Bari Hooper recorded burnt flints apparently associated with a hearth and flint implements on one of the small islands (FM.30) and other Neolithic artefacts on the mud-banks to the south of the marshes (FM.31). One of the small islands visited by Draper produced a broken leaf-shaped arrowhead and other flints (FM.25). A tanged arrowhead, over 100 scrapers, and various other tools from Farlington are extant in Portsmouth Museum (Gardiner 1988, cat no H067).

Foreshore areas of the north-eastern harbour coast have also produced Neolithic flints. Nine Neolithic flints, all apparently retouched and including two scrapers, were found in 1991 on intertidal mudflats to the west of Langstone Bridge (Ha.20), and a quantity of struck flakes, scrapers, and blades are recorded as having been found on the foreshore at Warblington Bay, at a height of 2m OD, which may have derived from 'eroding soil overlying the Coombe Rock' (Ha.102).

Neolithic finds from the dry-land margins of the harbour are not common. Unstratified finds from Wakeford's Copse (Bradley and Lewis 1974) included a few sherds of Peterborough Ware and a small amount of flintwork, including a broken plano-convex knife and a transverse arrowhead. A possible site of interest is at Havant. Excavation of a Roman villa at *Spes Bona*, Langstone (see Gilkes 1998) also recovered at a depth of *c* 1.5m (5ft) Neolithic flint including scrapers, fabricators, 'late' arrowheads, and bones including cattle long bones and boars' tusks. Where boars' tusks are found in Neolithic contexts this is usually in pits containing 'structured' deposits, but there is no mention here of pottery nor of context (Warren 1926–30). Further afield, 40 sherds of Grooved Ware were recovered, along with some waste and burnt flint, during topsoil stripping at Paradise Lane, Fareham (SU 5945 0715; Hughes 1977).

Polished axes have been recovered as stray finds from Church Field, Hayling (SU 710 020; Gardiner 1988, cat no 235; Portsmouth Museum) with at least one other, poorly provenanced, from Hayling Island (*op cit* cat no 237; Portsmouth Museum). Further afield on the coastal plain, polished and unpolished axes and fragments are quite numerous around Titchfield and Fareham to the west and Chichester to the east. Many more, of course, are known from the Downs.

The focus of Neolithic activity in southern Hampshire is on the Chalk downlands and two Neolithic long barrows occur on the Portsdown Ridge to the north-west of Langstone Harbour. Bevis's Grave (SU 6923 0642) was originally one of the longest in Hampshire (88m) though it is now largely destroyed and its original shape unknown. It is oriented west-east along the axis of the ridge (RCHME 1979). The Portsdown Barrow (SU 6665 0641) was a short rectangular example, probably originally *c* 30m long, oriented west-east, now destroyed (RCHME 1979). There is, in addition, an oblique reference to the excavation of a Neolithic long mound on Hayling Island 'midway between the National Schools and Tournerbury' which uncovered remains of a windmill formerly standing on the mound (Keeble-Shaw 1958, 108; Williams-Freeman 1919) – however, it is now clear that this is the Bronze Age burnt mound mentioned above.

Bronze Age

Bronze Age flintwork and pottery are again recorded from the islands. On Long Island an urn containing a cremation was recovered from the mudflats in 1982 (LI.54) with the remnants of an urn 'and contents', together with fragments of several others, including one with fingernail decoration, on North Binness (NB.59; but note a possible confusion in the SMR records here which quotes same accession number for both entries). Fragments of pottery and 'other finds' are also reported from Baker's Island (BI.58).

To the south of Farlington Marshes 25 pieces of Deverel-Rimbury pottery, representing at least three pots, were recovered from a pit exposed in the intertidal zone whilst, to the south-west of the marshes, a barbed and tanged arrowhead was recovered with other finds of probable Bronze Age date in 1969 (FM.55). Hooper reported finds of late Bronze Age pottery here also (FM.56). In the north-west corner of the harbour numerous pottery fragments and flints collected by Draper suggest the presence of an urnfield (FM.51, FM.52). Overall, there is a strong possibility of the presence of one or more flat urnfield cemeteries on the north-western fringe of the harbour. A further cremation burial in a Deverel-Rimbury urn was recorded at Langstone (SU 7151 05000; Soffe 1980; see Chapter 3) together with late Iron Age and Romano-British artefacts, and a pit containing briquetage and wheel-made pottery.

On Hayling Island, Bronze Age flint artefacts are reported from one of the shingle banks (HI.38) and pottery from south of the old oyster beds with the possible remains of a hearth (HI.41), though Iron Age pottery was also present. On the northern shore of the harbour at Brockhampton, a number of finds of Bronze Age pottery are suggested from areas which appear to be raised shingle beaches (Ha.61).

A hoard of four decorated copper alloy rings and a palstave was found near St James' Hospital, Portsea, in 1945 (PI.50; Rowlands 1976, cat no 68). A hoard of 29 palstaves, two armrings, and a quoit headed pin was found in cutting a mains trench at Gable Head, South Hayling, in 1960 (Rowlands 1976, cat no 60). A group of six middle Bronze Age palstaves from the southern beach at Hayling (Hayling Beach) is housed in the British Museum (Lawson 1999, 95). Another middle Bronze Age hoard, of 20 palstaves and also from Hayling (Hayling Island II, near Fleet) was recovered in 1995 (Lawson 1999, 98). In 1993 a late Bronze Age bronze 'founder's' hoard containing 134 objects was discovered by a farmer in a field on Hayling Island, near Newtown (SU 7175 0195). It included at least eleven palstaves plus fragments, fragments of several spearheads, possible dirk fragments and other broken implements, and a large number of bronze lumps and casting jets (Lawson 1999, 101–2). Fragments of at least one pot were also recovered (D Allen pers comm; A J Lawson pers comm). Bronze slag is reported from North Binness Island from 'site near the sea wall' (NB.127) but no description or quantification is provided. An unpublished late Bronze Age founder's hoard not recorded by Lawson (*op cit*) is noted in the SMR as a find of the cutting edges of 'two Bronze Age socketed axes and fragments of waste bronze' and were from the spoil created by the yacht basin on north Hayling Island, near Duckard Point (HI.43) and retained by M Rule.

The coastal plain has produced very little evidence of Bronze Age settlement or burial sites though finds of late Bronze Age pottery and flintwork from positions close to the shoreline in West Sussex (eg Chichester Harbour, Cartwright 1982), and the discovery of a Bronze Age site in Havant (Crosby 1993) and Bronze Age pits containing large quantities of pottery at Bosham (Gardiner and Hamilton 1997) probably indicate the nearest known settlement sites. A middle Bronze Age barrow at Westhampnett (Fitzpatrick and Allen in prep) suggests funerary activity on the coastal plain. The nearest known Bronze Age settlement on the adjacent Chalk is that at Chalton (Cunliffe 1970; 1993, 132–4), an unenclosed site comprising two circular buildings terraced into the hillside. These were associated with a range of domestic equipment and Deverel-Rimbury pottery.

Iron Age

Iron Age finds are recorded on the islands and in the north-western part of the harbour, as well as on the western shore of Hayling Island. However, it should be noted that much of the pottery originally identified as being of Iron Age date is actually more likely to be later Bronze Age (see Chapter 4). Quantities of pottery, fired clay, and briquetage are noted, together with occasional hearths and areas of burning. Pottery is recorded from the foreshore of Long Island (LI.47) and North Binness (NB.73), the latter being of late Iron Age date. Briquetage from North Binness (NB.126) and south of Farlington (FM.119; FM.123), and in the north-west corner of the harbour (FM.33, FM.57) could be of Iron Age or later date.

Most evidence of apparent Iron Age activity comes from the western shore of Hayling Island south of the old oyster beds. Here Bradley recorded a number of principally salt production sites in areas which have since been covered over. Finds include evidence of hearths and burning associated with pottery and briquetage (HI.66; HI.75; HI.76; HI.82). A large quantity of Iron Age pottery with associated patches of burnt clay and calcined flints was observed to cover an area of approximately 3 × 2m in section on the shoreline in 1969 (HI.70). A series of hearths with associated pottery was recorded during topsoil stripping in 1967 and these are said to be Iron Age though it is recorded in the SMR that the finds have not been examined by an archaeologist (HI.71). Pottery was also recovered during reclamation works at Storehouse Lake, Brockhampton in 1971 (Ha.74). Salt production sites of Iron Age date are also known from Portsmouth and Chichester Harbours (Bradley 1992). Pottery and briquetage from Langstone have already been mentioned (Soffe 1980).

Two Iron Age sites on Hayling Island are of some importance, the late Iron Age temple in the northern part and Tournerbury univallate camp in the southern part. The former consisted of a circular structure of c 11m diameter facing east into a trapezoidal courtyard. A pit in the centre contained pottery, animal bone, Celtic coins, and brooches of the 1st century BC. The courtyard produced quantities of metal finds including jewellery, horse harness and chariot fittings, currency bars, and c 170 coins including many continental issues, again mostly of the latter half of the 1st century BC and early-1st century AD (King and Soffe 1994; 1998). Limited excavations through the rampart of Tournerbury indicated two-phased construction (Bradley and Fulford 1975) but nothing is known of the interior of the fort.

Otherwise, Iron Age finds are rather few and far between around Langstone. Occasional finds of pottery are reported from Portsea and Hayling and coins of both the Atrebates and the Durotriges also occur (eg Ha.89b). Langstone apparently falls on the boundary between the two distributions of tribal coinage (Sellwood 1984). To the north-west, a small Iron Age settlement site of the 5th–3rd centuries BC was excavated near Fort Wallington, Fareham, in 1972 (Hughes 1974), but the main distribution of known Iron Age sites on the coastal plain is to the west, around Chichester, itself the site of a late Iron Age *oppidum*, and on Selsey. Excavations in advance of construction of the A27 Westhampnett Bypass, just east of Chichester, produced evidence of the

largest known late Iron Age cremation cemetery in the country as well as other features and finds (Fitzpatrick 1997; Fitzpatrick and Allen in prep).

Romano-British

Romano-British finds occur, again, on the islands. Part of a storage jar of Rowlands Castle Ware was recovered from South Binness Island in 1978 (SB.83) and was marked with the batch number XIII. Baker's Island produced Roman pottery from at least three places, mostly coarsewares of 1st century AD date, and some briquetage (BI.87). North Binness also produced pottery from more than one location on the southern foreshore, including fragments of storage jars, samian, and 2nd century AD material (NB.27; NB.88b; NB.88c), and an area of brick and tile fragments (NB.88a).

Further finds of pottery, mostly of the 1st or 2nd century AD, are noted from in and around Farlington Marshes (FM.84; FM.85; FM.86) and from the western shore of Hayling Island (HI.38; HI.75; HI.82) where they are again associated with areas of burning, briquetage, and spreads of brick and tile, including what appeared to be wasters, indicating the presence of brick or tile kilns (HI.79). Saltworking on the harbour margins again seems to have been an important activity, as it continued to be in Portsmouth and Chichester Harbours at this time (Bradley 1992). It is quite likely that existing saltworkings would have continued in use, possibly even into the Middle Ages (see below), but the fact that most evidence comes from the intertidal zones, and is therefore in a highly mobile environment, makes any detailed discussion of the evidence or its dating very difficult. Part of an early Roman flagon was recovered from the shoreline at Brockhampton Mill Lake in the north-east of the harbour (Ha.90).

A few Roman coins are reported from several places on Hayling Island, including a group of four from the foreshore to the south-west of the road bridge to Hayling (HI.2). At least two of these were 4th century bronze issues of the House of Constantine (AD 307–37).

The Iron Age temple (HI.81) on Hayling was replaced by a larger, stone-built, structure in AD 60–70. The circular structure was rebuilt, its walls lined inside and out with painted plaster, and a porch added, whilst the courtyard enclosure was enlarged and replaced by a galleried *temenos* having a double enclosure wall and internal colonnade. A fairly elaborate entranceway was also added (King and Soffe 1994; 1998). Full details of the site have yet to be published.

On the mainland, three Roman villas are known near Havant. One was partly excavated in the 1920s. At least one room of a corridor style house was excavated, having an apsidal end and hypocaust. A frigidarium with a floor of large ceramic tiles was also examined, with an open gutter lined with roof tiles leading away from it to the north (Warren 1926–

30; Hughes 1976, 70–2; Scott 1993, gazetteer). A rather larger villa is recorded at *Spes Bona*, Langstone Avenue, Langstone (Gilkes 1998) which included a bathhouse, and further afield, an aisled farmhouse was excavated at Crookham Farm on Portsdown above Langstone Harbour, and produced bonding tiles, *tegulae*, box flue tiles, and *pilae*, indicating the presence of a tilery (Soffe *et al* 1989).

Two Roman roads are known. A major road from *Noviomagus* (Chichester) to *Clausentum* (Bitterne, Southampton) runs east–west across the head of harbour on roughly the route now followed by the A27/M27, whilst a lesser road runs from Hayling Island to Rowlands Castle. Recent excavations at Oak Park School, Havant, failed to find the latter road which was thought to run across the site, though limited evidence for Romano-British occupation was recovered, in the form of ditches and pottery (Crosby 1993).

A hoard of ten *Antoniniani* are recorded from Portsdown (Hampshire County Council 1982, 3). Finds from Portsea are apparently scarce but a hoard of 927 silver 4th century coins is recorded (*ibid*, 3) and various small-scale rescue excavations to the north of Portsmouth have revealed Romano-British features, suggesting the presence of small domestic sites and cemeteries (RCHME 1992).

Langstone lies in the rural hinterland between these major Roman settlements, around both of which further evidence of Romano-British occupation is known. The Roman Palace at Fishbourne (Cunliffe 1971) lies just to the west of Chichester and the later Roman, so-called 'Saxon Shore' fort of Portchester (Cunliffe 1975) is at the head of Portsmouth Harbour to the west. The presence of small, rural, domestic farmsteads along the road which runs across the top of the harbour is to be expected but there is no indication of any major Roman sites apart from the temple. Inland, on the Chalk, several areas of presumably agricultural settlement are known, for instance around Chalton (Cunliffe 1977; 1993, 248–51).

Saxon and medieval

No finds of Saxon objects are recorded in the SMR from the harbour or its immediate hinterland though pre-Conquest settlement around the harbour and on Hayling is recorded in *Domesday* (VCH 1908, 128–50). Numerous documents exist pertaining to land ownership and tenure in the medieval period, and imply that a priory existed in the southern part of Hayling and that this priory, during the reign of William I, was attached to the Abbey of Jumièges near Caen, Normandy, which held about half the island in demesne and the overlordship of the rest by the gift of the king. VCH further reports that at least part of the Priory and a considerable area of land was lost to the sea in the 14th century and may now lie buried in the mudflats (*op cit*; Soffe 1995). This has led to much speculation about the location of this lost

ecclesiastical foundation. Recent research by Reger (1994 and forthcoming) has shown that the information provided in VCH is actually a misinterpretation by Longcroft (1857) who said that a Priory or Priory church existed and indicated that it was of considerable importance, though its where-abouts were unknown. By a misinterpretation of the taxation records, Longcroft 'proved' that the old parish church at Hayling had been 'lost', where in fact the taxation records refer to loss of 'land'. He also mixed up details of the 'extents of the Alien Priories' which were surveyed in 1324, claiming that land belonging to the Priory had been lost earlier in the reign of Edward II. This incorrect ascription was misread by Cox in the VCH (*ibid*) to claim that the Priory itself had been lost.

Reger convincingly argues that the loss was in fact loss of land rather than of a building, and that the loss was actually of its agricultural produce over a period of years because of seasonal flooding by salt water, rather than permanent physical loss. It is more than likely that no Priory ever existed on Hayling, but that Jumièges supplied a *Prior*, who may have resided in the manor house (Reger 1994; forthcoming). Hayling Priory as it existed was non-conventional; its Prior was appointed directly by Jumièges and had probably only been so appointed since the early-13th century. Reger (1994; forthcoming) indicates that the prior probably resided in the old manor house, though Soffe (1995) disagrees and suggests that there were simple buildings near the parish church.

Earliest mentions of Farlington are as a Royal manor leased by the king to various tenants, including one William de Curci in 1187 (VCH 1908, 148), whilst Warblington Manor is known to have been in the possession of Earl Godwin before the Conquest and in 935 King Athelstan granted seven *manse* at Havant to his theyn Witgar (*op cit*, 129).

Medieval material recorded in the SMR and directly related to the harbour largely consists of structures associated with saltworking. Saltworking on Hayling Island is attested in *Domesday* (VCH 1908, 128) and again from the 11th century (*ibid*, 129). Salterns recorded at Wade Court Farm, between Langstone and Warblington (HI.96) are probably of medieval date and finds have also been made here of the rim of a medieval cooking pot and fragments of a green-glazed, 12th–14th century jug in the same area (HI.94). On Portsea, salterns situated on the north side of the creek at Great Salterns are probably those also mentioned in *Domesday* (PI.100).

Some of the oyster beds at Hayling are also likely to be of medieval date, or have medieval antecedents. Oyster culture is recorded from at least the 14th century (VCH 1912, 468) and some former salterns sites were reused as oyster beds (*see below*). Oyster farming continued in the post-medieval period – extensive dredging is reported in 1856 (*op cit*, 468) – until it was closed down in the 1920s following an outbreak of food poisoning (Moore 1984; see Fontana and Fontana, Chapter 2 for further details of the saltworking and oyster industries in Langstone Harbour).

Fishing is also recorded as an important feature of Langstone in the medieval and post-medieval periods, though the harbour fisheries were considered to be in decline by 1813 (VCH 1912, 468). Mullet, bass, turbot, cod, and whiting are all mentioned as catches. Smuggling has also been an activity in the harbour, and probably still is. In 1829 and 1835 it is recorded that parts of elaborate wooden rafts kept submerged and used by smugglers to carry cargo across the mudflats, were found in the harbour.

Post-medieval: finds and industrial and defensive features

There are numerous archaeological features of the post-medieval period around the harbour including industrial sites and the many defensive structures. Those of direct relevance to the harbour include: a very worn 19th century trade token from Long Island with a representation of the Market Cross at Chichester on the reverse (ident J A Davies); a number of the old oyster beds along the western shore of Hayling Island, some now buried under reclamation; and 18th–19th century saltworkings on Portsea at Great Salterns, now largely built over. The swing bridge of 1867 (HI.99), made of wood on massive iron columns, which carried the railway from Langstone to Hayling Island, is a notable feature of the north-eastern corner of the harbour, whilst the sea lock at Eastney Lake is an important feature in the south-west corner. This lock was part of the ill-fated Portsmouth to Arundel canal project which opened in 1822 but failed to attract much trade. The lock quickly began to leak and was closed in 1827 (Moore 1984). Other major industrial monuments in the area, including water pumping stations and brickworks, are summarised by Moore (*op cit*). Remains of the Langstone train service built in the latter half of the 19th century can still be seen in a number of structures across the south side of Sinah Lake.

The remains of a Mulberry Unit construction site is still visible on Hayling Island in the beach on the east side of the main channel (Hughes 1990; this vol). Several pillboxes also survive (SU70SW 83; SU60SE 66; SU60SE 65) together with the remains of a decoy lighting system (eg BI.103).

In the north of the harbour, at Warblington Bay, a causeway (the Wadeway) leading south from Langstone High Street across the corner of the harbour towards Hayling is known to have been in existence by 1552 (Ha.102). Spreads of 17th and 18th century broken glass bottles are noted from the south-east corner of the harbour (D Fontana, pers comm), but there is no indication at present as to where these may have originated.

The harbour foreshore, particularly along the length of the west coast of Hayling Island and in the north-eastern area, contains many wooden stakes and posts. Some of these seem to form small, rectangular or circular enclosures or sinuous lines, sometimes connected by hurdling. In other areas, apparently haphazard clusters of posts occur in no recognisable pattern. These structures, which are typical of harbours and estuaries around the coast of Britain, relate mostly to mooring and fishing activities. Their detailed recording formed part of the Langstone Harbour Survey (Chapter 2).

Wrecks

There are several wrecked vessels within Langstone Harbour. Just north of the entrance is a Phoenix Unit, a concrete caisson built as part of the Mulberry Harbour designed for the D-Day landings (50 47.92N 01 01.40W). The sections were to be towed across the channel to Arromanches and St Laurent on the Normandy coast. Here the Phoenix units were joined end to end to form breakwaters. The section left in the harbour is one of the smaller Type C units, it has broken its back but is otherwise almost intact. Another World War II marine casualty is a small landing craft sitting on the edge of the intertidal mudflats in Sinah Lake (50 48.45N 01 00.20W). It can be seen protruding through the water at most states of the tide.

The additional three known wrecks are all below low water and only accessible by diving. The oldest is the *Withern* (LH.112). She was a bucket dredger lost in 1926, four cables (4/10ths of a nautical mile) north of Ferry House (50 48.08N 01 01.72W). Today she lies in a north–south orientation, with her bow a few metres south of an isolated danger marker buoy. Half a kilometre to the north-east lies the shattered remnants of the paddle tug *Irishman* (LH.111). She was heading up the channel with a small grab dredger under tow on May 8th 1941 when she detonated a magnetic mine (50 48.28N 01 01.31W). She sank with the loss of all hands and she dragged her tow with her. She now lies badly broken adjacent to an isolated danger marker buoy near Sword Point. The *Percy* (LH.113) was the grab dredger being towed by the *Irishman*. She remains relatively intact, sitting upright on the seabed over half a kilometre to the south (50 47.95N 01 01.48W).

Other submarine locations that are known but not recorded by survey included the site of Prison ships, once moored in the main channel during the Napoleonic Wars, sites where fishermen had snagged their nets at locations along the edge of the main channel, and incongruous deposits of large flat stones seen in both Sinah Lake and Milton Lake.

Undated finds and features

A number of areas which have produced prehistoric material have also yielded notable quantities of burnt flint. Such concentrations, though strictly speaking undatable by themselves, are generally considered to be indicative of prehistoric activity and in some areas, especially close to water, they may be of such density and size to be termed 'burnt mounds'. The function of these is unknown. The Langstone concentrations noted during previous work seem to be generally small and some are probably the remains of hearths, possibly of various dates. General domestic activity such as cooking fires, saltworking, and metalworking and cremation pyres are all activities which could have produced these spreads of burnt flint and, in some cases, there is no clear evidence that they are genuinely prehistoric. Some of the saltworking sites known to be of medieval date have also produced quantities of burnt flint.

Also in the SMR is reference to a mound protected with earthworks on North Binness Island (NB.125). Neither Draper, Hooper, nor Bradley record this feature and Bradley has no recollection of having seen it (pers comm). This island also reveals on aerial photographs the presence of long, narrow, linear marks running approximately north–south across it but which are not clearly identifiable on the ground. They seem most likely to be associated with post-medieval draining of the saltmarshes but have not yet been adequately investigated.

There are also areas where large boulders and heavy stones form lines and what appear to be small, but insubstantial, 'enclosures'. These are mainly now above LWM and therefore not permanently immersed. They may be associated with saltworking but have not been closely investigated. Other wooden and stone or brick structures also occur, some of which are probably of World War II origin.

2 Results of the Langstone Harbour Archaeological Survey *by Michael J Allen, Julie Gardiner, and Neil J Adam*

The nested survey and archaeological fieldwork strategy employed (see Chapter 1) produced a series of data which is the consequence of the individual tasks. The walkover survey provides data which range from the point specific to general harbour-wide distributions; it is not a complete nor definitive record of all the remains in, or from, the harbour. The survey included general descriptions of the nature of the present-day environment as well as the occurrence of eelgrass and provides evidence of diffuse artefact scatters and of specific findspots. At a more specific level the gridded artefact collections and excavations provide detailed information from single locations. Although it is tempting to report these data strictly by fieldwork task, as this is probably the simplest way to deal with a mass of archaeological data, it is more applicable to present the information by moving from the general to the specific regardless of recovery method. Recovery methods and the varying accessibility of some areas impose some constraints of confidence on interpretation of archaeological significance which must be taken into account. This report concentrates on the prehistoric to Roman periods where artefacts are plentiful and archaeological features relatively common. Apart from the summary historical background (Gardiner, Chapter 1), the important medieval and post-medieval periods are dealt with in a more cursory manner. The detailed historical aspects of the harbour are subject of on-going research (V J L Fontana in prep)

The aim, therefore, is to present the results of the fieldwork first at the general, harbour-wide level (this chapter) and then by focusing on areas where more specific data has been acquired (Chapter 3). The data are used to characterise those locations and periods of activity and provide the basis for interpreting the role and development of human societies within the study area. They also enable examination of how, during each archaeological period, those societies lived and utilised local resources which are known to have changed significantly over the past 10,000 years (Chapter 7). The detailed surveys provide information which is location and event specific and are described more conventionally.

All finds and environmental data are presented in the conventional manner by category (Chapter 4 and 5) Combining the evidence of fieldwork, finds, and palaeoenvironmental analyses allows us to interpret the development both of the physical 'harbour' and of the communities who lived and utilised this area together with the adjacent chalkland and maritime resources (Chapter 7).

Areas covered by fieldwork
by Neil J Adam, Michael J Allen, and Julie Gardiner

The walkover survey covered the majority of the accessible saltmarsh and intertidal foreshores; its main objective was for database enhancement and standardisation of both recording and collection (Fig 8). More limited underwater augering and swimover surveys (Figs 8 and 10) extended searches into the submarine zone which occupies the largest area but which is also the least extensively covered by overall survey methods. However, as we will see later, more extensive underwater survey would have been unlikely to have recorded significant archaeological evidence missed by the less extensive, but locally more intensive, underwater archaeological work.

Extent of mapping

Aerial photography and photogrammetry covered the entire study area and included the full harbour fringes and hinterland. The physical survey, through the digitisation of aerial photographs and GPS survey on land was therefore more extensive than archaeological fieldwork which only encompassed all land and intertidal foreshores, as exposed by low neap tides, and small test areas of the marine environment.

Extent of archaeological fieldwork

In terms of the survey fieldwork, the study area comprised the whole of Langstone Harbour below high-water and a limited area of shingle beach and permanently dry land beyond (ie the littoral zone which comprises the part adjacent to the shore and includes mudflats and shingle seaward of the 'cliffs' and sea defences). In practice, the limits of the harbour are quite clearly defined by seawalls, roads, pasture, fences, and other property boundaries. No fieldwork was undertaken on the dry-land side of these margins, though the desktop study covered a considerably wider area (see Archaeological background, Chapter 1).

Walkover survey

Langstone Harbour covers an area of some 23 km^2 and, for the purposes of field recording, the entire harbour was divided into arbitrary blocks (Fig 8) for

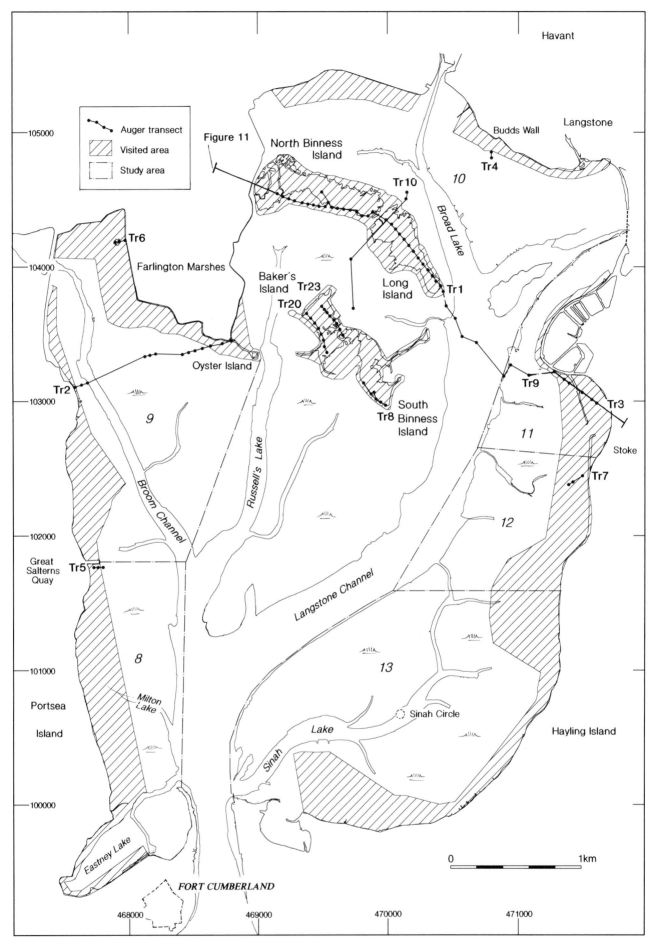

Havant

Langstone

Budds Wall

Tr4

10

Figure 11

North Binness
Island

Tr10

Broad Lake

Long
Island

Tr1

105000

Auger transect
Visited area
Study area

Tr6

104000

Farlington Marshes

Baker's
Island   Tr23
Tr20

Oyster Island

Tr2

103000

9

Russell's Lake

South
Binness
Island

Tr8

Tr9

Tr3

Stoke

11

Tr7

12

102000

Great
Salterns
Quay   Tr5

Broom Channel

Langstone Channel

101000

8

Milton
Lake

13

Sinah Circle

Portsea

Island

Sinah

Lake

Hayling Island

100000

Eastney Lake

0   1km

FORT CUMBERLAND

468000   469000   470000   471000

Figure 8   Archaeological Walkover Survey areas, auger transects and the areas visited. Drawn by S E James

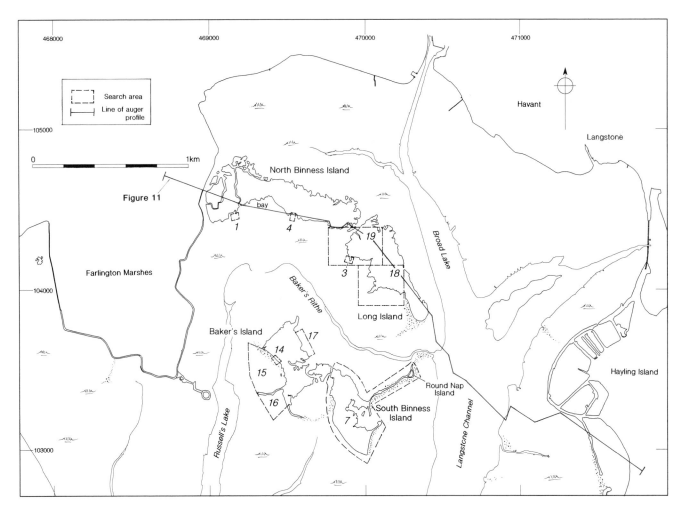

Figure 9   Main archaeological study areas on and around the four island in the north of the harbour. Drawn by S E James

the systematic walkover survey. Those around the harbour edges were divided at convenient, recognisable, topographic points at the shoreline and extended into the harbour essentially as far as the edges of the permanent channels. These were designated Areas 8–13 (Fig 8). The four main islands were sub-divided into a series of smaller areas designated Areas 1, 3, 4, 7, and 14–26 (Fig 9; Appendix 1). The central part of the harbour, with its main channels and intervening mudflats, was essentially inaccessible as well as being of extremely low archaeological potential (see below) and was not given a search area number, but a number of specific locations were sampled and investigated by the HWTMA team. The area numbers are retained in archive but are generally not used in this report, except for some of the more detailed study areas on the islands where it is more convenient to use them than longer descriptive labels. They are labelled on Figures 9, 26, and 29–31.

The intention was to carry out the walkover survey over as much of the harbour as physically possible. In practice, some areas proved more difficult to access than others, generally because of the depth and softness of the mud (see Langstone Harbour setting, Chapter 1) and, thus, the proportion of each 'area'

which could be searched varied. The landward zones of three of the four main islands and Oyster Island were systematically searched (see Plate 12, Chapter 1, above) and walked in their entirety, only South Binness Island was more cursorily investigated. As the saltmarsh vegetation cover obscured much of the ground surface above the HWMT no artefact scatters were recordable but upstanding structures and ground features such as ditches were recorded. The intertidal zones of all the islands were searched thoroughly as far out into the harbour as it was possible to walk, with limited swimover surveys used to augment and increase the coverage (see Fig 10, below). The landward side of the harbour edges, above high-water was not rigorously searched as these areas were generally either developed, or under permanent grassland, and will have been more readily covered in the past by standard archaeological fieldwork and observations which are included within the desktop study (Fig 7).

The intertidal mudflats and shingles were investigated to limited and varying extents. On average the intertidal areas were systematically searched for about 200m from the HWMT (see Plate 1, Chapter 1, above), though the range was from perhaps as little as 50m below the northern seawalls to as

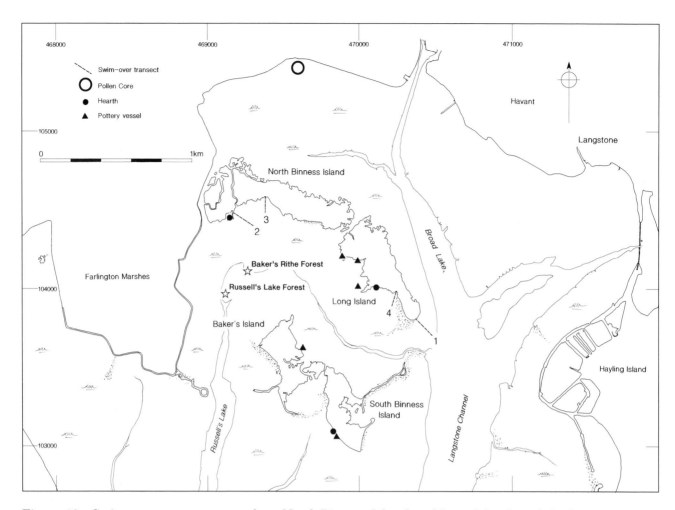

Figure 10   Swimover survey transects from North Binness Island and Long Island, and the location of major finds around the islands. Drawn by S E James

much as *c* 600m along parts of the Hayling Island side. At the lowest tides it was possible, in places, to cross on foot between the islands leaving only a fairly narrow channel permanently inaccessible. On the north-eastern fringes of the harbour accessibility was reduced by the outfall of the Budds Wall sewage works, although other more detailed fieldwork was subsequently undertaken here (Wessex Archaeology 1999). On the north-western edge of the harbour, where the Broom Channel emerges, very soft and dangerous clays existed, enabling considerably less archaeological examination of the mudflats. The auger survey was successful here, but only two of the fourteen auger points could be surveyed by the Portsmouth team because of these conditions. In contrast, the western margins (the east coast of Portsea) and eastern margins (west coast of Hayling Island) of the harbour offered extensive tracts which allowed regular and systematic searches up to 600m from the shingle shore. During the summer tides, for instance, it was possible to walk between Round Nap on South Binness Island and the southern tip of Long Island and rapidly search the soft muds in between.

The fieldwalking teams consisted of between two and four experienced archaeologists, working for only 2–3 weeks in each season. The team was often accompanied by Arthur Mack, who provided not only an extremely detailed knowledge of the local microtopography and current state of the intertidal muds, but also brought over 40 years of experience of working and collecting artefacts in this region. When trained his keen eyesight and recognition skills soon made him a proficient and invaluable member of the survey team.

Underwater survey

Physical constraints, limited resources, and restricted times of access meant that only limited swimover survey was possible. A series of spot searches was conducted in eight separate locations around the central channel and in Sinah Lake (Fig 14), while the swimover survey was restricted to four transects off the south and east coasts of Long Island and North Binness Island (Fig 10; see below). More detailed submarine survey and recording was undertaken at one site, the so-called Sinah circle, just as more detailed study was undertaken at specific locations in the intertidal zone.

In summary, most of the intertidal and shingle foreshores were searched to at least 200m beyond High-water mark of Mean Tides (HWMT). This was achieved by combinations of walkover and swimover survey and by the planning and mapping of wooden structures (see below). Although thorough, systematic artefact recording and collection was not undertaken throughout the harbour, the recording was sufficiently detailed for all major scatters, features, and structures to be identified. One must remember, however, that the shingle and muds are mobile over long periods, and areas not accessible for recording during the 1993–5 seasons of fieldwork may become exposed, or be eroded, in coming years, just as some areas producing artefacts in the 1960s are currently not available for study (see below). The islands, having been isolated in the preliminary field assessment as having the highest potential for artefact recovery, were systematically searched and we are confident that, in spite of the saltmarsh vegetation which prevailed, all significant archaeological distributions and sites were identified where exposed. It is obvious that the searches were most effective on the coastal edges of the islands and harbour where the sediments were exposed in section in the cliffs and in plan on the foreshores. Within the harbour, the least well-explored zone was that underwater. However, underwater auger transects were able to further define the stratigraphy and expand archaeological interpretation. Detailed surveys of submarine sites were restricted to a few specific locations and shipwrecks.

The development of the harbour sedimentation: the results of test-pits and auger survey
by Michael J Allen with Neil J Adam

The aims of the auger survey were to establish the basic sediment stratigraphy of the harbour and to identify and delimit the extent of layers of archaeological and palaeoenvironmental importance in order to assist in the interpretation of harbour development. One of the fundamental premises was that although Langstone is a harbour today, its long-term coastal history remained unknown and it cannot necessarily be assumed to have always been a harbour. It undoubtedly included a period 10,000 years ago when the area was an expanse of dry-land, albeit dissected by rivers.

The auger survey attempted to:

- provide a database which could be manipulated to enable the mapping of the augered silts to the underlying drift geology of the harbour in relation to archaeological features and deposits

and

- provide a reliable terrain model to set the archaeological results in some context.

Each auger transect provided a profile of the Holocene sediments which could be related to the modern topography. Together, the suite of transects

Plate 14   Methods: augering in the mudflats off North Binness Island (Elaine A Wakefield)

would provide data for determining sediment parcels and the three-dimensional graphic reconstruction or modelling of sediment distribution. The three-dimensional sediment maps should, in turn, enable both the sedimentological development of the harbour to be outlined, and some predictive modelling of where additional archaeological data might potentially exist. To our own auger data could be added information from the larger and deeper bore holes reported by Mottershead (1976, figs 6 and 7), and the *Chirp* data reported by Dix in Chapter 1 (Location, geology, and topography).

It was hoped that the larger auger survey would establish the basic sediment sequence and also aid in isolating the location and extent of layers of archaeological importance. A further aim was to explore the archaeologically relevant horizons. The relationship of artefacts to sediment units would be established by first examining sediments which could be directly related to localised areas of exposed archaeological remains. Subsequently, their extent could be mapped by limited augering in areas where artefact scatters were not exposed (eg within parts of the intertidal zone and saltmarshes). In both intertidal and saltmarsh areas limited test-pit excavation was

Table 2 Summary location of auger transects and the numbers of boreholes made.
The proportion of augerholes surveyed *vs* recorded provides some index of the difficulty of
the physical environment in which the augering was conducted

Transect No	location	No of boreholes	No surveyed and OD heights	% recorded
1993 season				
T1	Farlington Marshes to Long Island	48	43	89
T2	Farlington Marshes to Kendall's Wharf	14	2	14
T3	Hayling Island towards Long Island	12	7	58
T4	Budd's Wall to Langstone Channel	7	2	28
T5	Great Salterns Quay to Russell's Lake	5	3	60
T6	Farlington Marshes to Broom Channel	5	4	80
T7	Knotts Marsh to Upper Rithe	5	3	60
T8	South Binness Foreshore	5	5	100
T9	Long Island to Upper Rithe	8	6 + 1 incorrect OD	87
T10	The Grounds to Binness Rithe	4	4	100
1994 season				
T20	Across centre of Baker's Island	8	8	100
T21	Across Oyster Island	3	3	100
1995 season				
T23	Along north-east coast of Baker's Island	8	8	100
T24	TP 2007 to scatter 2053	3	1	33
TOTAL		135	100	74

also conducted to help amplify the nature and extent of archaeological horizons. This exercise enabled questions to be addressed as to the sedimentary context of the archaeological debris: for instance, were artefacts exposed on hard clays in the intertidal areas lying within a sediment which was contemporaneous or had those sediments been eroded, with the artefacts now residing on an arbitrary, erosion-produced surface?

Augering is a precision recording and sampling technique. At Langstone all augering (whether on land, in the intertidal zone or underwater) was undertaken by hand using a 30mm diameter gouge auger with a 1m long sample chamber (Plate 14). This enabled the recovery of sediments to depths of up to 3.5m or until gravels or chalky (presumably Devensian meltwater) deposits were reached. The only reasons for aborting at depths less than *c* 3.5m were either difficult surface conditions or the tenacity of the deposits and friction created by the auger in clays at depth. The basic sediment record was gathered in the field and then detailed and summarised (see Chapter 1). The augering provided a detailed picture of local variations in sediment as well as revealing the main sediment facies. This data, however, was summarised and sediments ascribed to broad sediment parcels (*sensu* Needham 1992), which are recorded as units. Auger locations were

surveyed in three-dimensions using GPS, however, physical working difficulties also affected the Portsmouth GPS team, with the result that some 26% of the auger sites (35 boreholes) either could not be reached by the GPS team or the survey canes were lost to the sea before they were recorded (Table 2 and see Chapter 8). Although detailed auger records exist for the 34 sites, they could not be used because neither their precise location nor, more importantly, their Ordnance Datum levels were known, even though their relative position to other auger points could be approximated.

Most auger holes were bottomed on either impenetrable shingle or degraded chalk. The underwater augering, however, only penetrated a maximum of about 1m of sediment. Sediments at depth (usually over 1m) containing many chalk fragments and predominantly chalky or calcareous silts were assumed in the field to be derived from chalk meltwater deposits originating from periglacial processes on the chalk scarp of Portsdown *c* 1km to the north. Although these deposits represent erosion of chalk derived material, in retrospect they need not necessarily have been wholly derived during the Devensian (or other) cold epoch. This is particularly significant when examining the deeper, undifferentiated deposits described by Mottershead (Wimpey 1962; Mottershead 1976) which, because of

Plate 15 Recording the stratigraphy exposed in the cliff section on North Binness. The saline alluvial gley soil (Avery 1990) shows distinct horizonation and bands of archaeological material, see Figure 27 (Elaine A Wakefield)

their greater depth (10m+; –10 to –11m OD), provide sediment sequences covering much longer periods of time. Mottershead considered this entire sequence to be Flandrian which, if correct, calls into question our own field interpretation of late glacial deposits at only 2–3.8m depth (*c* 0 to –1.5m OD).

Sediment mapping

Two major cross-harbour auger profiles comprised a number of transects and were augmented by a programme of numerous shorter, local auger transects (Fig 8). A total of 14 transects was surveyed, comprising 135 hand auger points. The main transects (Tr1 – Tr9 – Tr3 and Tr2 – Tr10 – Tr4) forming the two cross-harbour sediment profiles account for over 90 of the auger holes (70%), extended from the dry-land margins, across the islands to the intertidal zones and submarine bottom. These two major terrestrial transects across the northern part of the harbour were augered at 50m intervals in the accessible intertidal and terrestrial zones and at 100m intervals in the submarine areas. These were augmented by a series of smaller transects (Fig 8) comprising some 40 auger holes which were largely sited on the harbour edges (Tr5, Tr6, Tr7, Tr8, Tr20, Tr21, and Tr23).

Archaeological context

The smaller auger transects sought to augment the major transects which were sited in the intertidal areas of the harbour. They also sought to relate artefact scatters to localised sediment sequences (eg transect 23, Baker's Island). This information could then be extrapolated to sediment units on a larger, if not harbour-wide, scale. This local data was integrated with the results of small-scale test-pit excavations through the saltmarshes and the inspection and recording of the sediments in the 'cliff' face (Plate 15). More specific augering, such as three points augered between artefact scatters on Baker's Island (Tr24), were positioned in areas of archaeological finds on the higher, more landward, side of the intertidal mudflats (especially in the area of the former Little Binness) and further points were augered through the bases of test-pits on both North Binness and Baker's Islands, extending the excavated sequences.

The sedimentological framework

The general drift geology is outlined by Dix and Scaife in Chapter 1. Previously recorded major cores from the harbour (Wimpey 1962; Mottershead 1976) indicate blue-grey undifferentiated marine silts over peats at –11.9m and –10.75m OD. These peats probably represent deeply incised former channels of the Broom and Langstone Channels and their surfaces probably date to about 7000 BP (ie *c* 5850 cal BC, pollen zone VIIa). Unfortunately, the Wimpey boreholes do not provide a detailed profile of the sediments as they are too coarsely spaced. Geotechnical pits on the western edges of Langstone Harbour at the Portsmouth Sailing Club, Kendall's Wharf (SU676 036), provide some information on the landward side of the harbour, which was not augered by the project. The excavation of three geotechnical pits for determination of the mechanical properties of the sediments, undertaken for the County Architects Department (Hampshire County Council 1992; R Banham, HCC pers comm), revealed 2–3m of firm to stiff brown-yellow silty sandy clay with occasional fine to medium gravel flint. Beneath this to depths of about 3.6m was a dense brown orange yellow gravel with a sandy silty clayey matrix (?Reading Beds).

Transect results

The auger transects on 'land' were undertaken at between +2.50m OD and –0.08m OD with the majority in the intertidal areas being below +1m OD. In contrast, those recorded by submarine augering were undertaken at between –0.76m and –4.97m OD in transect 9 and consistently at +0.01m OD in transect 10.

The longest transect (Tr1, Tr9, and Tr3) crossed Farlington Marshes, North Binness Island, and Long Island. The results were complicated by a number of factors. Sediments recorded in augering were significantly different in colour, but not texture, from those seen in the exposed cliff section. It became apparent that many of the deposits which were grey to brown in colour, would change markedly in colour when exposed to air and allowed to weather and oxidise. This was tested by augering close to the exposed 'cliff' section. Thus, although the auger information provides a vital basis for understanding and interpreting the sediment history, the resolution of data relating specifically to archaeological horizons is not as simple nor as clear as that seen in the cliff sections. This has made the initial and cursory interpretation of the auger survey data particularly problematic, but the resolution of information we are attempting to gain is, nevertheless, significantly higher than any other geotechnical or borehole records undertaken in the area. These have recorded silts and sands, but not differentiated any variations or units within the basic facies (see Mottershead 1976, fig 7).

The following is a brief resumé of the sediment sequences for each transect taken from the auger log data. This provides the basis for understanding the occurrence of the *in situ* archaeological finds, it also provides the basis for the interpretation of the Holocene sediment history for the entire harbour in Chapters 6 and 7.

Transect 1: Farlington Marshes to Long Island

On Farlington Marshes the topsoil (+1.02 to +1.93m OD) lay over varying depths of silty clay and stiff clay down to a depth of 1m + and which increased in depth towards the centre of the field and thinned out again towards the seawall. On North Binness and Long Islands (+1.5 to +2.0m OD), below a silty clay topsoil containing much organic material, the sequence was fairly consistent. A layer of silty clay up to 0.3m thick sealed a yellowy-brown stiff clay with organic inclusions within which was contained a large amount of archaeological material, including pottery, worked and burnt flint, animal bone, and charcoal. On Long Island a layer of grey clay occurred above this yellowy-brown clay on the higher parts of the island. Below the yellow clay was another yellow-brown or

reddish-brown clay beneath which was the degraded chalk. An apparent bank across the western end of Long Island proved to be shingle. At the south-eastern end of the island the reddish clay lay directly under the topsoil with no archaeological horizon apparent.

The area of the mudflats between the two islands did not reveal the clay with organics, which seems to have been eroded, but features cut into the lower clay survived.

Transect 2: Farlington Marshes to the Kendall's Wharf (Portsmouth Sailing Club)

Augering from the Farlington end of the transect across the intertidal zone (+0.4 to –0.08m OD) revealed a consistent sequence of sand over up to 0.75m of reddish clay over degraded chalk. In some places pockets of grey clay were encountered while, in others, the sand directly overlay degraded chalk.

Augering out from the Sailing Club on the other side of the channel was restricted by the softness of the mud. Here c 0.5m of grey silty clay was encountered overlying the chalk with some pockets of sandy clay. An auger point close to the seawall revealed yellowish-brown clay with much gravel and a hole in the cricket pitch showed 2m of makeup over gravel.

Transect 3: Hayling Island towards Long Island

In the intertidal foreshore off Hayling Island (–0.06 to –0.31m OD) in most cases augering stopped at a depth of c 1m on reaching impenetrable shingle. Sediments consisted of grey clay with pockets of gravel and silty clay up to 1m deep, in some places overlying degraded chalk rather than shingle. Further out, pockets of reddish-brown clay over chalk were encountered.

Transect 4: Budds Wall to Langstone Channel

Close to the shore a light brown sandy clay overlay shingle (–0.83 to –1.17m OD); further out from the shore this gave way to grey sandy clay overlying degraded chalk at about 1m depth. In one auger hole a brown/grey clay with organic inclusions was recorded at c 1.20m.

Transect 5: Great Salterns Quay towards Russell's Lake

The muds at Great Salterns (c –0.25m OD) proved to be very soft and dangerous and only a short transect was augered. The sediments consisted mostly of grey silty clay over shingle but further out, yellowish-brown and then reddish-brown clays underlay the grey clay with flint inclusions, becoming impenetrable with depth.

Transect 6: Farlington Marshes to Broom Channel

A short transect was made across mudflats at the north-west corner of Farlington to a small islet (+1.37 to +2.07m OD) known previously to have produced archaeological remains. At the shoreline gravel and shingle mixed with brick and other debris indicated infill. On the island itself yellowish-brown clay only 0.2–0.3m deep gave way directly to degraded chalk. Around the firm ground of the island a peaty loam overlay grey clay, then degraded chalk.

Transect 7: Knott's Marsh, Hayling Island to Upper Rithe (Cockle Rithe)

At the shoreward end of the transect shallow deposits of reddish-brown clay overlay shingle. Further out sand overlay up to 1m of stiff grey clay which was too difficult to auger through. Further out still, the sequence was sand over yellowish clay over reddish-brown stiff clay with flint and some pockets of grey clay. At the south-western end of the transect the reddish clay disappeared to be replaced by grey sandy clay over shingle.

Transect 8: South Binness foreshore

A 250m transect was undertaken along the upper southern foreshore of South Binness at an altitude of +1.2m to +1.6m OD. Each hole revealed rather different results but essentially a series of grey and yellowish-brown silty clays was encountered giving way to degraded chalk in the north and shingle in the south. Pockets of grey silty clay and reddish-brown clay occurred. Archaeological material on the foreshore appeared to be eroding out of the yellowish-brown clay, including an almost complete pot, devoid of rim or base, standing upright in the clay. A single auger hole taken some 25m inland revealed the presence of the yellowish-brown clay beneath a peaty topsoil and grey silty clay.

Transect 9: Long Island to Upper Rithe

Augering undertaken underwater by HWTMA completed the main west–east transect across the harbour. The augering started at the harbour floor at between –0.76m OD and –4.97m OD within the Langstone Channel. These uniformly recorded light grey clays to 1m – the full depth of the auger chamber (ie to between –3.45m OD and –5.77m OD).

Transect 10: The Grounds (North Binness Island) to Binness Rithe

A second submarine augering transect of four boreholes between North Binness and Baker's Islands provided data for the south-west to north-east transect. Although conducted by submarine techniques at high water, the harbour floor at this point was at about 0m OD. The auger penetrated to a maximum of 1m and revealed grey (green) silts and clays with some sand.

Transect 20: Across Baker's Island

A short transect of 8 auger points across Baker's Island (c +2m OD) revealed the yellowish- to greyish-brown stiff clays overlying intermittent areas of grey clay at 1.6 to 2.7m depth. The compacted silts with chalk inclusions were encountered in most holes at about 2.5m depth.

Transect 21: Across Oyster Island

Three reference points were augered on Oyster Island (c +2m OD). The same general sequences were recorded with the greyish-brown clays over pale brown clays to depths of 3.9m. The degraded chalk was recorded at depth of in excess of 3.9m and not encountered in all holes. This was not due to the excessive depth OD of the chalky deposits, but to the height of the island, which is at least partly artificial, requiring more sediment to be penetrated before the base deposits were reached.

Transect 23: North-east coast of Baker's Island

The main transect of eight holes through Baker's Island showed organic and peaty surface horizons over grey and greyish-brown silty clays over white compacted calcareous and chalky clays.

Transect 24: Baker's Island (between test-pits 2007 and artefact scatter 2053)

This transect was undertaken specifically to examine the sediments in relation to artefact scatters and the sediment exposed in the test-pits. A short line of three auger holes approximately 20m apart were excavated to define the edge of artefacts scatters 2051–6 and test whether archaeological material survived below the soft muds which appeared to have accumulated along this particular part of the island. It was located in a line some 20m inland from, and parallel to, the north-eastern coast of Baker's Island.

In broad terms the sequence consisted of a peaty topsoil over a mixed peat and clay subsoil, sealing a grey clay overlying a firm clay, which itself lay over a chalk rubble and clay mix. The main sub-division within this sequence consisted of holes which found a firm light yellowish-brown clay below the soft grey clay and those which found a very firm yellowish-brown clay in the same part of the stratigraphic sequence. This yellowish-brown clay appeared to be identical to the material exposed by erosion on the north-eastern coastline, on which flint scatters 2051–6 were found. One fragment of possibly worked flint was noted in the softer light yellowish-brown stratum which suggests that this layer also has archaeological potential. However, augering found no evidence of any significant scatters of material.

No artefacts were recovered from any of these layers and as a result it was assumed that the artefact spread did not penetrate this far inland. It was initially assumed that the hard yellowish-brown clay on which the coastal artefact scatters were found underlay all other deposits making up Baker's Island, but it appears that the coastal spreads of flint are limited to the present shoreline and, in particular, the areas of firm yellowish-brown clay. The material visible in the cliff section must therefore be considered to be the last remains of the primary flint deposits from which the scatters are derived, with significant implications for the future survival and recovery of archaeological data on this island. The augering showed that the firm yellow-brown clay does not underlie the island, rather it occurs in isolated islands or knolls, some of which have been exposed by coastal erosion, while further patches may remain under Baker's Island itself.

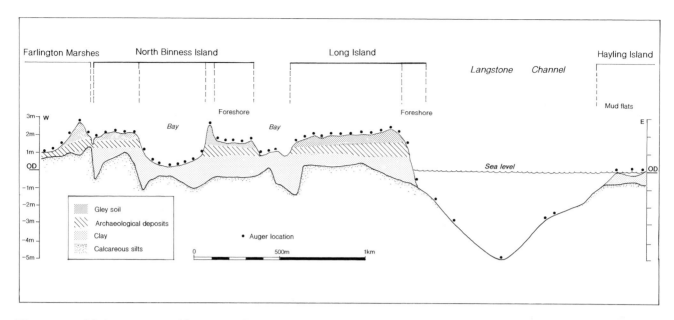

Figure 11   Main auger profile across the harbour from Farlington Marshes to Hayling Island, showing the archaeological layers in relation to the islands. Drawn by S E James

The sediment sequence

Many deposits were easily recognised from both their characteristics and stratigraphic position across the survey. Other deposits were identified which, although they displayed some variability, were considered to form a single sedimentary unit based on sediment characteristics and stratigraphic location. Variations may have been due to the local water conditions; it was evident that some units were more gleyed than others. This can effect colour and visual characteristics but not texture, structure, nor stratigraphic relationship. We were, therefore, able to distinguish a series of major horizons across much of the survey.

Uniformly across the entire survey beneath Farlington Marshes, the islands, and underwater across Langstone Channel is a greyish, slightly calcareous, silty clay containing very small rounded chalk pieces which, in places, is possibly seen as directly overlying the chalk or chalk mud. This deposit underlies all the deposits from which archaeological artefacts have been recovered including the Mesolithic flints, and thus has been taken as the 'archaeological base' for this survey. Other Holocene deposits within the harbour are known to be significantly deeper than this (see Mottershead 1976, fig 3). The upper surface of this basal horizon, where not eroded, generally lies at about –0.5 to –0.75m OD but with undulations, possibly created by former minor channelling, giving peaks at 0.5m and troughs at –1.6m OD. Across the Langstone Channel the underwater augering encountered its eroded surface immediately below the recent soft muds at heights as low as –4.97m OD (Fig 11). The chalky content of this widely distributed deposit may be related to an episode of solifluction during a late glacial cold phase. On the basis of this assumption, and the fact that no archaeological artefacts were associated with the deposits, this has been taken to be the archaeological base – ie 'natural' – to the survey.

Above the grey calcareous silty clay was a hard 'yellow clay' which was archaeologically sterile. This was distinguished by its stronger yellowish colour (mainly light yellowish brown, 10YR 6/6 to brownish yellow, 10YR 5/3) with uniform fine texture and lack of chalk inclusions, which resembled the Reading Beds in some places. Where eroded, exposed, and weathered, this unit forms a hard surface and was recognised as the 2Cg2 horizon of the saline alluvial gley soils across the islands (see North Binness Island below); when very wet (but exposed) it becomes grey in colour. Nowhere was this unit seen to contain any archaeological artefacts; where it was exposed as a planar erosion surface on the southern foreshores of the islands in particular, artefacts were seen to lie on, but not in, it and some archaeological features were certainly cut into it. The contact between this horizon and that above, although clearly recorded in a number of places, was more difficult to record consistently than that with the grey calcareous deposits below. In general the overlying deposit was a subsoil and this has been described in pedological terms where it is exposed in the 'cliffs' of the islands.

The most significant deposits were these subsoil horizons (Cg and 2Cg1) of the alluvial gley soils which contained the majority of the archaeological artefacts, and from or through which many of the archaeological features were cut. These deposits are characterised by their generally yellowish-brown (10YR 4/6 – 5/6 – 6/8) to greyish-brown (10YR 5/2) colours, with predominately silty clay and locally sandy silty clay matrix. They occur uniformly at between about +0.75m and +1.75m OD. The deposits are vertically variable; although largely stonefree, horizons or lenses of stones occur, some of which contain burnt flints. These deposits occurred predominately under saltmarshes on the islands, but were also traced through Farlington Marshes (Fig 11).

Fringing the littoral zone on the harbour's edge were intertidal soft muds and shingle which were assumed to be relatively recent temporary deposits. The muds were consistently unconsolidated silts and silty clays, commonly with a small, fine sand content. They were always easily distinguishable from the firm yellow clays where a sharp erosion surface could be detected in the auger. Even where the moisture content had softened the upper portions of this 'yellow clay', the colour and texture boundary was always sharp. Texturally these two were easily separated suggesting that the present unconsolidated intertidal silts were not wholly derived from the 'yellow clays'.

Localised palaeochannels were identified during hand augering, the most pronounced being a narrow peat-filled channel on the eastern edge of Farlington Marshes. Another was recorded in the northern part of the harbour from which a peat core was extracted in 1979 and analysed for pollen (Scaife, Chapter 5).

Archaeological significance

The survey has demonstrated that all the flint- and artefact-bearing deposits lie over the 'yellow clay' unit and that many artefacts have been eroded and fallen onto the exposed and eroded surface of this unit. All the sediments augered within the marine element of the harbour itself are significantly below this OD. Artefact-bearing deposits lie stratigraphically and physically above the calcareous grey silts and the 'yellow clay'. Essentially, these only survive on higher ground which today is represented by the remnant islands and the Farlington Marshes. As these islands are continuing to erode, the higher ground containing the archaeological finds is clearly a diminishing resource (see below).

In terms of the artefactual record, whether the chalky deposits really relate to periglacial processes or are early postglacial in origin, is irrelevant. These deposits can realistically be seen to be the 'archaeological base', even if they belong to postglacial periods covering the earlier Mesolithic (9th millennium BC) for which there is very little archaeological evidence either within the harbour, or within the vicinity of Langstone on the coastal plain and southern extremities of the chalk downland (see Chapter 1). Indeed this suggestion of the sediment timescale would fit well with Bellamy's comments on the Holocene sequences, particularly along the southern coast where he reports that 'As sea level approaches the present level, river valleys along the coastline are infilled with thick sequences of fine-grained sedi-

ments in a continuum of temperate fluvial and estuarine environments, eg the valley of the River Ouse, East Sussex (Jones 1971)' (1995, 60).

All deposits of archaeological or palaeoenvironmental significance (except palaeochannels) are now restricted to the islands which are remnants of former land masses dating back to at least the later Mesolithic (7th millennium BC onward), and probably earlier. Channels incised through the harbour are not recorded, or represented in our auger survey. Boreholes by Wimpey (1962) record peats in only two out of at least 13 locations. It is no coincidence that the only two occurrences of peat at –10.75 and –11.9m OD are adjacent to, but some 5–6m below, the present course of the Broom and Langstone channels. We can be relatively confident that these peats represent the land surfaces on the edges of, or peat forming within, stream courses in the former deeply-incised valleys.

The relationship of the archaeological finds to the sequences

The combination of the augering, test-pits, and recording of artefacts in the 'cliff' sections of the islands show that artefacts of at least Neolithic to Bronze Age date occur *in situ* in discrete horizons in the low cliffs. The surface of Farlington Marshes (c +1.00 to +2.00m OD), North Binness Island (c +1.85 to +2.15m OD), Long Island (+1.75 to +2.00m OD), South Binness Island (+1.15 to +1.6m OD) and Baker's Island (+1.4 to +1.6m OD) is relatively constant. In each case the upper foreshores are up to about 1.5m OD but the exposed hard 'yellow clay' of the bays of the Islands are at +0.1 to +0.5m OD. All of the islands, therefore, contain the archaeologically significant horizon (occurring at between +0.75 and +1.75m OD); their foreshores, predominantly the south facing foreshores, all expose the hard 'yellow clay' at heights of below +1.5m OD, ie below the occurrence of the archaeologically significant horizon. Thus the augering suggests that the artefacts on this surface have eroded from contexts which have now been removed. This hypothesis is examined from a number of other perspectives – the archaeological record, the location, nature, and integrity of the archaeological artefact distributions, and the environmental information.

The horizon on which the artefact scatters occur in the intertidal zone is the present day planar erosion surface and is arbitrary in relation to their former location within the now eroded sediment sequences (Fig 12). Artefacts may also have moved laterally, as well as having dropped vertically on to the present-day surface with significant consequences for their interpretation; this probability is examined in the analysis of artefact distributions by Gardiner later in this chapter. The archaeologically relevant sediment units were, therefore, largely restricted to the four main islands which are the remnants of a much larger archaeological resource.

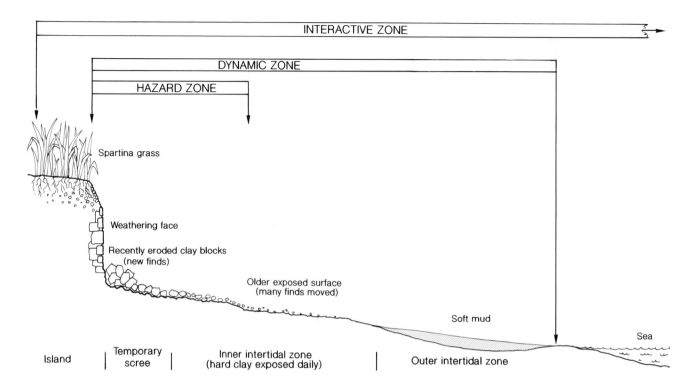

Figure 12   Defining the coastal zone: the interaction of the human environment with the physical environment across the foreshore and intertidal zone. Drawn by S E James, after DoE 1993, fig 1.1

Walkover and swimover surveys

The walkover and swimover surveys were the first element in the nested fieldwork strategy intended to enhance the SMR, provide further information on artefact scatters in the area, and to identify areas of specific interest and potential for further work. As described above, the preliminary survey covered as much of the harbour as could be physically walked. Thereafter, investigations were confined to those parts of the harbour where the potential for interpretable archaeological distributions were at their highest, including areas where archaeological finds had been reported in the past.

The areas covered by the walkover survey have been outlined above. In practice most artefacts were recorded in the higher intertidal zones. Further out, in softer muds, few significant archaeological finds were made, indeed, many areas of mudflat were consistently largely devoid of any surface stones. Where finds were made (eg Sinah Lake) these were invariably of medieval or post-medieval date. This lack of both visible artefacts and natural stone, which was confirmed by the swimover surveys, was sufficiently consistent for a very large part of the current harbour to be considered to be of very low potential for the recovery of archaeological data and no further work beyond the preliminary search was undertaken. In contrast, the walkover survey conducted on the islands and closer to the main harbour shoreline was able to identify areas of both high and low potential. From these it was possible not only to determine

those parts of the harbour where the greatest quantities and variety of artefacts were available for study, but also to comment on the effects on artefact distributions of the current tidal and sedimentary regimes acting within the harbour area.

Walkover survey
by Neil J Adam

The following summarises the general nature of the harbour-edge intertidal zones which were not the subject of further detailed examination (see Appendix 1). The finds and structures recorded in these areas are incorporated into the more detailed discussions which follow and the 'Areas' themselves are not discussed again individually or by name hereafter.

1   Portsea Island east coast: Fort Cumberland to Great Salterns Pier (Fig 8, Area 8)

The eastern coast of Portsea Island forms the western edge of Langstone Harbour and this area covers the south-western corner of the harbour from Fort Cumberland, across the inlet at Eastney and along the western shore as far as the Great Salterns pier. Above the High-water mark of Mean Tides (HWMT) the entire length of the Portsea Island coast has been extensively developed, mostly in the past 150 years. The greater part of the intertidal zone is covered with a very soft silt around 1.0 to

1.5m in depth, while the foreshore comprises loose shingle mixed with modern building rubble, general waste, scrap metal, and the hulks of several abandoned modern wooden boats. Large areas of former harbour have been reclaimed, initially for saltworking, with the earliest reclamations probably begun in the medieval period (see Fontana and Fontana, below). With the demise of saltworking much of this reclaimed land has become rough pasture. A substantial seawall has been constructed along the entire length of the coast, including a sheet piling and concrete quay at Great Salterns. Residential and limited industrial and recreational development, together with road construction, fringe the harbour beyond. The intertidal zone along the Portsea coast consists of firm shingle beach with patches of sand, varying between 50 and 200m in width. This beach gives way to extremely soft, accreting mud. In some places this mud has become substantial enough to support wild sea grasses which have, in turn, trapped further mud to create a number of small islets some 200–300m off the coast, particularly to the north of Great Salterns pier.

The main geographical feature of this section of coast is the Eastney Lake at the southern end of the harbour. This is in-filled with soft accreting muds with a shingle beach at the HWMT. This area, sheltered behind the coastal bar, forms a small subsidiary harbour supporting yachting facilities and is generally full of small boats. The Eastney Ferry runs between a pontoon at the extreme tip of the coastal bar to Hayling Island.

Three archaeological features were noted; all probably of post-medieval date. A small sub-circular promontory of shingle and gravel which encloses a small pool of stagnant water is situated on the southern beach in the south-west corner of the inlet at Eastney (Eastney Lake), the outer edge of which is partially enclosed by a horse-shoe of timber stakes (timber structure t4, Figs 13 and 19). No datable material was recovered and the recent development of the shore has led to large amounts of modern rubble being dumped across the site (the *Glory Hole*). This feature may be the remains of a 17th century haven or harbour structure, and although there is no firm evidence to support this theory, it is recorded on de la Fabvollière's map of *c* AD 1600.

Two parallel lines of roundwood timber posts *c* 150m long were noted just to the north of the Eastney Inlet (timber structure t5, Figs 13 and 19). These were thought to be the remains of a 19th century jetty or landing stage which has been replaced by a concrete ramp to the south. The remains of two mooring points were noted on the southern side. About 100m south of this landing stage was a roughly rectangular array of square-sectioned posts, the northern elements of which were revetted with timber planking (t5, Fig 19). A metal girder was also present within the array. These are the remains of the lock entrance to the long defunct Portsmouth to Arundel canal.

2 Western harbour: Broom Channel, Farlington Marshes, and the north-western corner (Fig 8, Area 9)

The foreshore of Portsea Island from Great Salterns Pier to the head of the Broom Channel consists of loose shingle peppered by bait-digging holes and modern jetsam. The intertidal zone consists of soft unconsolidated silt up to 1m deep, with local pockets, especially around the head of the Broom Channel, as deep as 3m. In this area along the north-eastern coast of Portsea expanses of soft unconsolidated muds are dominant. At the head of Broom Channel and along the western margins of Farlington Marshes are a mixture of accreting and eroding small banks and ephemeral islets. These comprise patches of unconsolidated silts on which localised saltmarsh struggles to become established, and areas of the former mainland which have become detached from Farlington. The two largest of these islets with a well-developed saline alluvial gley profile (unripened gley soil) were found to contain strata of burnt and worked flint and prehistoric pottery in their eroding margins. These were formerly part of Farlington Marshes, from which they are separated by channels filled with dark soft muds which can only be crossed on foot with difficulty.

Oyster Island is the most prominent of these small islands, situated at the southern tip of Farlington Marshes, and contains a series of timber and brick structures and from which isolated Mesolithic finds were recovered, it is dominated by post-medieval material. This site is discussed separately below.

Farlington Marshes were enclosed by a concrete seawall in the 1970s, effectively cutting them off from the erosive and depositional processes of the harbour itself. Prior to this the marshes were a rich source of archaeological finds (see below). The muddy islets give way to a firm shingle beach which survives for 200m along the south-western coast. The intertidal zone around the edge of the Farlington seawall consists of a mixture of firm shingle and sand areas with large patches of dark-grey and very soft mud. The western side of the coast is characterised by deep and very soft muds, particularly in the channel separating Farlington from North Binness Island.

3 Northern coast (Fig 8, Area 10)

The north shore itself is lined with a low modern concrete seawall infilled with modern rubble, some of which has spilled out onto the shingle and mudflats. The mainland coast between Farlington Marshes and Hayling Island is again characterised by a shingle and sand beach some 100m in width, giving way to extensive dark-grey soft muds from which no archaeological finds were recovered. A number of small recently established islets can be observed between 200 and 300m off the coast, some of which have erosion faces, particularly on their southern

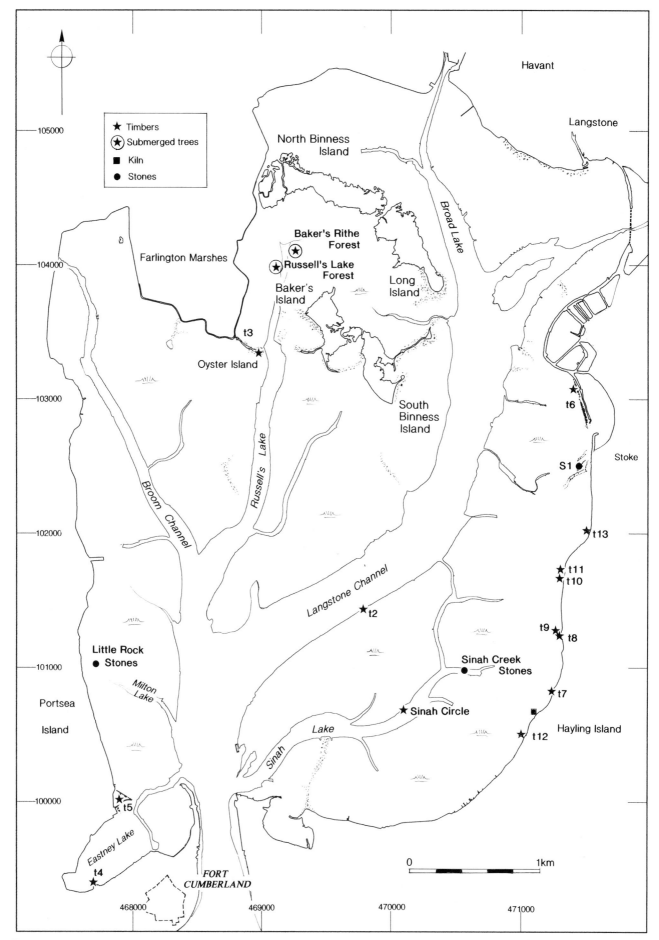

Figure 13 Timber and other structures around the edge of the harbour. Data Portsmouth University, drawn by S E James

sides, exposing 'cliffs' of mud and silt up to 0.75m high. Halfway along this section of coast the beach gives way to a soft mud-filled channel where a freshwater channel, in which sea trout still run today, empties into into Broad Lake from Budds Wall. Large quantities of modern debris have been dumped along its length and no archaeological features or deposits were noted along the northern coast apart from the Wadeway, a causeway which leads south from Langstone High Street towards Hayling Island (see, for instance, Draper 1990, 106–7, and accompanying photograph). This causeway is known from documentary sources to have been in existence from at least 1552 (VCH 1908), and green glazed pottery (?16th century) was recorded in the vicinity but not recovered (N J Adam pers comm).

4   Hayling Island (west coast) (Fig 8, Areas 11 and 12)

The west coast of Hayling Island forms the eastern edge of Langstone Harbour, beginning with the modern road bridge which joins it to the mainland, along with the timber supports for a former rail bridge which runs in parallel with, and to the west of, the road bridge. The northern end of this stretch of coast (Area 11) is dominated by a series of saltwater lagoons used as oyster beds (see Fig 13). The recent oyster beds comprise a series of seven pans of varying sizes made of dikes or building rubble. These occupy the site of salterns which were in use from the Middle Ages through to the mid-19th century (see Fontana and Fontana, below). Directly to the south of these lagoons is a shingle and sand beach partially enclosed by a shingle bar. Lines of roundwood and squared stakes (timber structure t6) were found on either side of the 500m long and 40m wide shingle bar. The lines of stakes included two parallel lines on the western side of the bar stretching for about 200m. Several small circular timber remains of 19th century oyster beds were found on both sides of this bar while, on the headland to the south, a series of five pairs of parallel lines made up of rectangular chalk blocks and flints was also identified (S1) radiating from the headland at Stoke up to 300m into the intertidal zone. The lines were about 2m apart and *c* 20m long, some of which were joined at their seaward ends by single rows of chalk and flint blocks set at right-angles. Their precise function is unclear, although they may also have been associated, in the past, with oyster farming.

To the south of the headland (Area 12), down to the mouth of the harbour, the Hayling Island coast consists of shingle and sand beach between 100 and 150m wide, giving way to soft accreting muds in the intertidal zone up to 400m wide. A number of mud islets can be seen some 400m off the coast, at the low-water mark, close to the edge of the Langstone Channel.

The remains of what appeared to be a post-medieval brick-built kiln (HI.107) were found just above the HWMT (1m OD) where the shingle beach meets the current land mass some 1.5km north of the harbour entrance (Fig 13). A single sherd of Romano-British pottery was also recovered from the the high-water strand line 125m south of the kiln.

Where the shingle beach gives way to muds, a series of timber jetties and what appear to be fish traps, were noted at intervals along the entirety of the coast (t8 to t13, Fig 13). All of these were presumed to be either late post-medieval or modern in date and are described in more detail by Fontana (below). A single line of more substantial timber posts is located at the southern end of the coast, close to the Kench inlet, near the harbour mouth. These are aligned south-east to north-west along the top of a natural gravel bank which runs from the inlet towards Sinah Lake within the harbour itself. These posts are believed to represent the remains of a late Victorian railway bridge which was never completed. Dominic Fontana (pers comm) reports the former presence of substantial quantities of post-medieval bottle glass in the south-east corner of the harbour.

Swimover survey
by Garry Momber and Sarah Draper-Ali

The swimover involved detailed swim searches along four transects (Fig 10), listed below from west to east:

Transect 2: 150m, running south, from ditch 1711 perpendicular to south-west end of North Binness Island; elevation 2.50 to 1.50m

Transect 3: 100m, running south from known pottery scatter on south side North Binness Island; elevation 1.09m to 0.60m

Transect 4: 100m running south perpendicular from artefacts on south side Long Island; elevation 1.92 to 0.15m

Transect 1: 100m, running south-east, from defined flint scatter, perpendicular to east end of Long Island; elevation 2.04 to –0.33m

The swimover surveys off the south of North Binness Island and Long Island recorded very few archaeological artefacts and identified no archaeological deposits or features. The main reason for this singular lack of results was the dense coverage of green algae (eg *Enteromorpha* spp and *Ulva*, see Tubbs 1980) on the harbour floor which hid any potential material from the swimmers. (For a more detailed discussion of this technique's successes and failures see the section on review of methodology below, Chapter 8).

Subtidal Transect 2: from ditch 1711 North Binness Island

At the shoreward end many flints and pebbles over firm grey clay were noticed over the first 30m near the shore. Most items of potential archaeological interest were evident nearer the shore, and this is where the artefacts were recovered from swimover (and walkover). Stone-free sediments occurred in a band, but a covering of silt and weed was evident as the transect moved below chart datum (60m along transect) and made the observation of any material, had it been present, very difficult.

TRANSECT PROFILE 2: 150m

record collected
20m   pot sherd, flint-gritted (Bronze Age)
24m   pot sherd crumb, flint-gritted (Bronze Age)

Subtidal Transect 3: from pottery scatter North Binness Island

Scatters of flints, stones, and pebbles were more abundant near the shore above the low-water mark (where observation was difficult due to the shallow depth and tides). Firm grey clay was evident in occasional exposures beneath the soft silt on the lower foreshore. Heavy sediment deposition and a blanket of *Enteromorpha* weed obscured the seabed on the second leg (50–100m) of the transect.

TRANSECT PROFILE 3: 100m

record collected
13m   burnt flint
30m   pot sherd, flint-gritted (Bronze Age)

Subtidal Transect 4: from artefact scatter Long Island

Sandy gravels and a lot of flints were noted for the first 14m. The firm grey clay was evident near the shore and beneath the soft silt. In deeper water the blanket of *Enteromorpha* green algae lay over a fine black silt. The visibility was reduced to zero if the algae was moved and the silts disturbed. Scatters of flint pebbles and stones were more abundant near the shore above the low-water mark, and absent beyond this, however soft sediment deposition and green algae grew thicker further along the transect.

TRANSECT PROFILE 4: 200m

record collected
11m   black pot sherd, flint-gritted (Bronze Age)
30m   burnt flint

Subtidal Transect 1: from flint scatter Long Island

Grey clay with flint pebbles and fragments were present over the first 50m of the transect. Softer sediments, more sediment deposition was more evident and flints and stones were much less frequent, becoming absent in the second 50m.

TRANSECT PROFILE 1: 100m

record collected
9m   flint flake
13m   pebble
34m   burnt flint

Most of the finds were evident nearer the shore and no artefacts were recovered more than 35m from the exposed foreshores recorded by terrestrial survey.

Underwater spot surveys
by Garry Momber

To complement the archaeological work on land, the swimline surveys, the wreck surveys, and the site-specific archaeological work below water, a series of eight underwater surveys (Fig 14, nos 1–8) was conducted by the HWTMA. Sites were chosen in a variety of environments within the harbour to investigate known or suspected anomalies. It was hoped that inspection of these areas would give an insight into the nature of the seabed and any artefacts found therein. The results of these, where significant, are presented by site location, but are detailed in the archive (see also Review of methods, Chapter 8).

A seabed search was carried out along a channel at the eastern end of Sinah Lake. The focus of the search was a group of stones, possibly foreign to the region, which are reported below (Sinah Creek stone scatter, Bingeman and Momber, below).

Langstone Channel

A circular search was conducted in the Langstone Channel to the north-east of the *Irishman* wreck in an area where fisherman's nets had been known to snag (Fig 14, no 1; 50 48.50N 01 00.50W). The depth of the dive was an average of 5m below OD. The sea floor at this location consisted of silty sand with low-profile sand bars running up the length of the channel. The seabed was heavily colonised by filter feeding polychaeta.

Another circular search was located further south in the Langstone Channel in an area of known net fasteners (Fig 14, no 2; 50 48.12N 01 01.40W). The seabed was sandier than that encountered north-east of the *Irishman* and had sparser populations of polychaeta. A large outcrop of sedimentary rock was recorded on the east side of the channel. Layering of the rock was evident, giving plenty of opportunity for nets to snag. A number of isolated timbers were noted although they were all relatively modern.

South-east of South Binness Island

A series of circular searches was undertaken to the south-east of South Binness Island in an area

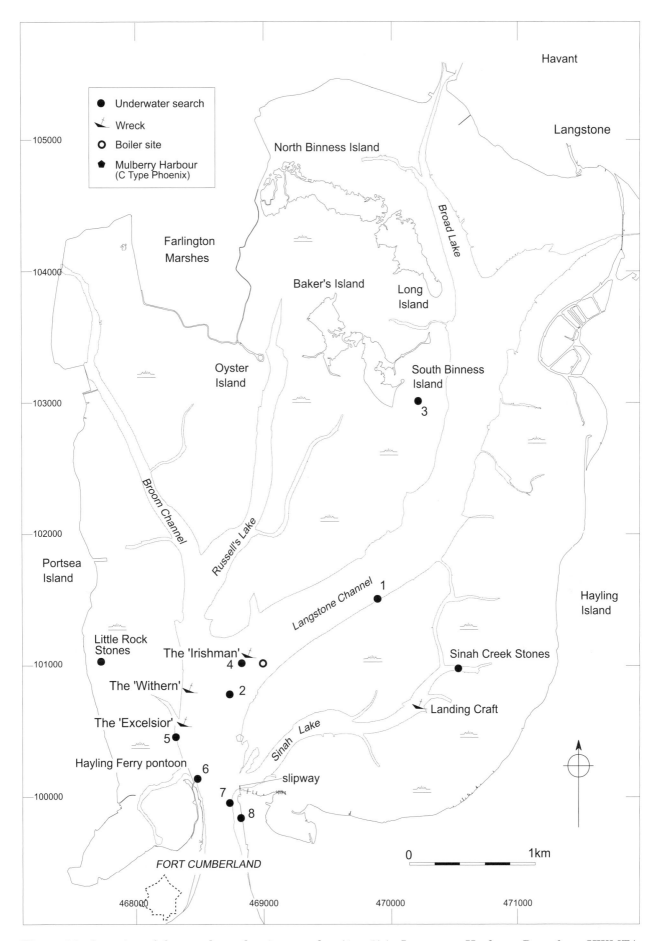

Figure 14 Location of the wrecks and swim searches (1 to 8) in Langstone Harbour. Data from HWMTA and Portsmouth University, drawn by S E James

directly offshore from finds of flint tools eroding on the foreshore (Fig 14, no 3; 50 49.30N 01 00.20W). A large number of scattered clusters of flints and shells lay on a silty seabed through which intermittent patches of underlying clay were exposed. The flints were sitting in and on the clay and a number were recovered for examination aboard the vessel but no worked items were present.

West of the Irishman

Searches 80m west of the *Irishman* obstruction buoy identified a large bank of rock which appeared to be layered sandstone (Fig 14, no 4; 50 48.28N 01 01.35W). This was in an area of known net fastners. It was similar to the rock recorded in Langstone Channel (50 48.12N 01 01.40W). A timber with a treenail was found, its position was 13m along the swimline at a bearing of 300° back along the line. There was an isolated timber with no evidence of an associated structure nearby.

Hayling Ferry pontoon

Wreckage was reported and recovered during trawling (50 47.90N 01 01.80W) in the channel north of the Hayling Ferry pontoon. A search focused along the edge of the west bank in the main channel 300m north of the Ferry pontoon (Fig 14, no 5). The seabed was silty sand colonised by seagrass (*Zostera*). At approximately 3m below chart datum wooden wreckage was found. One large plank with treenails measured 3m × 0.3m. Nearby, other timbers lay protruding from the sand although they did not appear to be part of a cohesive structure. Preliminary investigation suggested the timbers were relatively modern.

Investigations below Ferry Pontoon (Fig 14, no 6; 50 47.80N 01 01.70W) were conducted in an area believed to be below the site of prisoner hulks from the Napoleonic Wars. This was located directly to the east and north of the Hayling Island Ferry where it had been reported that artefacts remained scattered on the sea bed. A series of north–south swimline searches covering 20m at 3m spacing were conducted just off the jetty and to the north. The seabed consisted of a silty sand with gentle undulations essentially inhabited by peacock worm (*Sabella pavonina*). A number of scattered artefacts were noted including animal bones 2.5m east of buoy 06 and a scatter of pottery and pieces of clay pipe stems (none of which were removed from the seabed) 15m to the north of the buoy.

A second series of searches was conducted on the east of the channel, to the south of the public slipway (Fig 14, nos 7 and 8; 50 47.65N 01 01.50W). The seabed here was sandy, interspersed with boulders on the edge of the bank. No artefacts were identified.

Chirp sub-bottom profile survey of the harbour
by Justin K Dix

Over the last 30 years a variety of marine seismic reflection techniques have been used to investigate a range of submerged archaeological sites (eg Frey 1971; Chauhan and Almeida 1988; Rao 1988; Redknap 1990). The principal aim of these early investigations has focused on site prospection. However, as the concept of placing archaeological artefacts in their geomorphological context has developed, the importance of regional geological surveys to marine archaeological investigations has significantly increased. To date, the success of such investigations has been limited by the researchers' access to appropriate state-of-the-art technology. The majority of the early acoustic systems were incapable of: producing an acoustic pulse with sufficient resolution to be able to identify artefact material whilst maintaining the penetration capability necessary for geological interpretation; providing data in a format necessary for post-acquisition image enhancement; operating in the shallow water depths found over many archaeological sites.

Over the last decade, the development of *Chirp* seismic reflection devices has provided a potential tool ideal for archaeological operations. *Chirp* is a high-resolution, digital, frequency-modulated (FM) sub-bottom profiling system that is capable of obtaining cross-sectional profiles of the sea-bed with a vertical resolution of decimetres (15–30cm: Quinn 1998) and a maximum penetration depth of 30 to 40m in unconsolidated sediments. These systems can operate in shallow water depths ($\geq$2.5m) and can acquire data in an industry standard format (SEG-Y) which enables its straightforward transfer to off-line processing packages (Quinn *et al* 1998). The *Chirp* source differs from conventional, single frequency, sub-bottom profilers by having a repeatable, swept-frequency, pulse (in the range of 1 to 12kHz). This results in the data having a significantly improved signal-to-noise ratio (ie greater clarity), whilst the wide range of frequencies within the single pulse limits the classic trade-off between penetration and resolution. It should be noted that for the reconstruction of palaeolandscapes that are buried beneath coarse grained stratigraphies (coarse sands and gravels) it might be preferable to use lower, single frequency, sources (eg boomers).

Irrespective of which seismic device is deployed, the resulting images represent reflections from boundaries of high acoustic impedance contrast (acoustic impedance being the product of the density of a medium and the speed of sound through a medium). Consequently, any effective geoarchaeological interpretation of the seismic images requires appropriate calibration. Ideally, this would be achieved by the acquisition of core material, or in the case of artefact identification, excavation by divers. In the absence of such operations, reference can be made to any extant datasets such

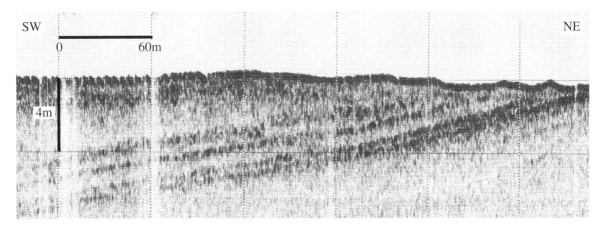

Figure 15a Chirp *section of the Upper Cretaceous to Middle Eocene sequences of Langstone Harbour (Justin Dix)*

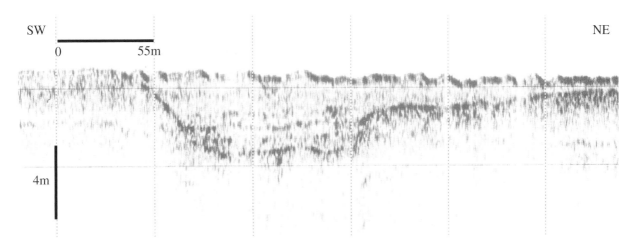

Figure 15b Chirp *section of incised channel running obliquely to the modern day Langstone Channel (Justin Dix)*

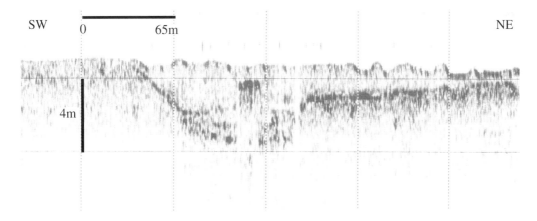

Figure 15c Chirp *profile of the unidentified anomaly in Langstone Channel, see Chapter 3 (Justin Dix)*

as Admiralty Chart data; commercially acquired geological and geophysical information; and adjacent terrestrial information. In the case of the Langstone survey no *in situ* core material was recovered, so all interpretations presented here are based on extant data.

Langstone and Broom Channels

The submerged river valleys of the Solent system, including Langstone Harbour, represent ideal conditions for the deployment of the *Chirp* system. A three-day *Chirp* survey was undertaken in April

1996 covering ground within both the harbour and the adjacent Solent coastline. In the harbour, the survey covered the main Langstone and Broom Channels with a total of 40 line kilometres of *Chirp* data being acquired. The stratigraphy derived from this work can be simply subdivided into an incised bedrock basement overlain by a thin (<2m) superficial cover of unconsolidated silts and sands. Internal reflectors within the bedrock sequence identify a series of gentle (<2.5°) southerly dipping units (Fig 15a), which is concordant with the structural context of the area derived from the terrestrial geology (see Chapter 1). A more detailed analysis of the stratigraphical style of these reflectors provides a good correlation with the regional geology with units from the Upper Cretaceous to the Mid-Eocene being identified.

Over the majority of the harbour area, the Tertiary bedrock surface has been incised to create a series of channels that are concordant with the current bathymetry. The maximum depth recorded during the survey was c –16.5m OD, at the entrance to the harbour, however, this probably represents over deepening by tidal currents which reach a maximum of $1.7ms^{-1}$ during Mean High Water Springs. The lack of superficial cover contrasts markedly with the adjacent bedrock channels within the East Solent, which are frequently covered by more than 15m of unconsolidated sediment (Dix unpublished data). The exceptions to this are a series of small (c 100m width), incised channel profiles identified in the Langstone Channel (Fig 15b). Here the average altitude of the bedrock surface is between –5.5m OD with a maximum depth of incision of –8.75m OD being recorded. The orientation of the survey lines parallel with the current channel prevented a complete reconstruction of the system, but these oblique cuts suggest that a meandering channel system, at an angle to the north-east–south-west oriented Langstone Channel, existed prior to the marine transgression.

The seismic characteristics of the unit overlying bedrock in the Broom and Langstone Channels suggest that they are fine grained homogeneous sediments (silts), an interpretation corroborated by both Admiralty Chart data and subsequent diver inspection. The exceptions to this are a series of strong discontinuous reflectors in the base of the small, incised channels. Comparison with the seismic stratigraphy derived for the East Solent (Dyer 1975; Dix unpublished data) suggests that they are gravel horizons representing higher energy, probably fluvial, conditions. In the central channel towards the mouth of Langstone Harbour the seismic characteristics of this upper unit changes with the unit thinning (<1m), having an overall stronger acoustic return and with the development of mobile bedforms. Again, calibration with extant data suggests that the bedrock in this area is covered by sands and gravels. As no core material was directly retrieved from the submerged sections of harbour it has not been possible to directly date the units described here.

However, comparison with the known record of basin evolution from terrestrial data, one can ascribe the bedrock incisions to be related to the polyphase development of the Solent River system. The subsequent fill stratigraphy probably represents deposition following the Flandrian transgression. High energy environments dominated the mouth and central channel areas, resulting in the deposition and subsequent movement of a thin veneer of sand and gravel. Further into the harbour the energy conditions reduced, resulting in the deposition of finer grained material, albeit the rate of accumulation is significantly lower than anticipated.

Chirp *anomaly*

A final point of interest was the identification of an anomalous target within the Langstone Channel at NGR 470470 102510 (Fig 15c). This strong acoustic reflector occurred at a depth of c 0.8–1.75m beneath the sea bed and directly above a buried palaeochannel. A high-resolution survey (5m line spacing) was conducted over the site in order to limit the extent of the anomaly. The dimensions of the target are c 25m by c 10m (± 1m) and its acoustic characteristics are comparable with wooden targets identified in the East Solent (Quinn *et al* 1997). A small excavation of this site has failed to identify any artefact material, but it is suggested that further investigations should be considered. This discovery was investigated by excavation (see Adams, Excavation of the *Chirp* anomaly, Chapter 3, below).

Artefact collections, distributions, and analysis
by Julie Gardiner with Neil J Adam

Artefacts were recovered during both the rapid walkover survey and from the more detailed gridded artefact collection units and test-pits. Further finds were made on an unsystematic basis before and during the period of the survey by Arthur Mack and Dominic Fontana and are included in the discussions which follow (though note that a few pieces collected after much of the artefact analysis and writing of the relevant text had been completed have not been included since they constitute essentially redundant information). The total numbers of artefacts by area within the harbour is given in Table 3; the full database by Survey Collection Area is held in archive.

Post-depositional artefact movement
by Julie Gardiner

There have been many finds of artefacts on the shores of Langstone Harbour, in fact in many cases artefacts are prolific. Bradley and Hooper (1973) pointed out that concentrations of artefacts on the intertidal foreshores in particular could be derived

Table 3 Summary of all artefacts from the Project (excluding pots 360 and 380)

	Flint (no)				Pottery (no/wt)						Other finds			
	Cores & waste	Scrapers	Other tools	Total flint	Bronze Age/ ?BA	Iron Age	Roman	Saxon	Post-medieval	Total pottery	Burnt flint (wt)	Animal bone (no)	CBM (no)	Other (no)
North Binness S shore West	451	9	8	468	87/5938	1/14	51/1824	–	–	139/7776	8017	27	11	5
North Binness S shore East	175	7	3	185	5/27	–	22/350	–	–	27/377	13628	1	147	31
Long Island SW shore	1133	63	18	1214	297/5080	1/14	5/52	–	4/40	307/5186	20252	2	1	1
South Binness	125	16	9	150	130/2256	–	52/470	–	–	182/2726	472*	6	10	5
Baker's Island west	439	28	5	472	34/412	–	102/1670	2/4	–	138/2086	24099	191	4	3
Baker's Island East	1246	144	38	1428	15/228	1/33	27/749	–	2/144	45/1154	3817	1	4	14
NE corner of harbour	115	2	1	118	10/158	–	2/15	–	–	12/173	1828	1	–	1
Oyster Island	55	2	2	59	–	–	6/93	–	3/181	9/274	2508	–	–	3
Eastney E shore	–	–	–	–	–	–	–	–	1/23	1/23	–	–	–	–
Hayling Island W shore	19	6	–	25	–	–	1/35	–	1/405	2/440	–	–	–	–
Total	3758	277	84	4119	578/14,099	3/61	268/5258	2/4	11/793	862/20215	74621*	228	177	63

* plus contents of pot, too heavy to carry home

from *in situ* material eroded from the cliffs as a receding shoreline passed through the site. The precise location and height (OD) may, therefore, be in question, and Bradley and Hooper (*op cit*) requested the need for more precise information on the stratigraphic position of these artefacts.

The distribution of artefacts is affected by the distribution of the various types of sediment within the harbour. Since most of the sediments are mobile and are subject to a variety of erosive forces, the most obvious of which are the daily and seasonal tides, the distributions observed during the survey cannot provide a *definitive* picture of true patterns of human activity in the harbour area at any period in the past or present. While a principal aim of the project was to attempt to undertake regression analysis and *inter alia* terrain modelling of the archaeological data through time, it was acknowledged from the outset that no such analysis could be undertaken without thorough interrogation of the dataset in relation to the taphonomic processes which have acted on it since at least the early postglacial.

Whether *in situ* artefacts of different periods contained within the sediments of the harbour occur in correct stratigraphic relationship with one another or not, virtually the entire dataset available for study had lost any stratigraphic context before observation and occurred as a palimpsest of material lying on the unprotected surface of the harbour foreshore. The vast majority of the archaeological material came from the intertidal zones around the main islands in the northern part of the harbour. Some areas of the harbour shoreline itself also produced artefacts but in only a few, isolated concentrations.

The islands of the harbour are composed of clays and muds of saline alluvial gleyed soils essentially held in relative stability by the growth of *Spartina* grass and other marshland flora. The surfaces of these saltmarsh islands are, as we have seen, generally not available for artefact collection. Topographically the islands present low but discontinuous cliff faces, rarely rising to more than +1.5m OD, on their southern, seaward, sides with a mixture of shingle banks, gravel spreads, and deep mudflats around the remainder of their coastlines. They are further dissected by many small creeks and rivulets containing soft mud. Each island presents an individual pattern of topographic features dependent on its position in relation to the main channels and tidal currents, and the position and extent of the loose sediments change through time in response to shifts in those channels and currents.

The islands are eroding and, with them, the artefacts they contain (see Chapters 4 and 6). The archaeological material is largely contained within, and is clearly visible, in the 'cliff' sections (see above and see Plate 10, Chapter 1, above). Deposition of the artefacts onto the foreshore seems to occur in one of two principal ways: they either drop out of the cliff section as it is eroded by wave action, particularly on a spring tide or storm surge, or more gentle erosion of the overlying sediments following vegetation

dieback leaves low but upstanding areas of artefact-rich deposits which are gradually eroded away. Clearly the foreshore is not a uniform surface; in addition to low 'headlands' of clay the presence and relative positions of muds, gravels, creeks and spreads of seaweed and eel grass provide a varied surface 'texture' on which the artefacts may be deposited and from which they may be subsequently removed. Microtopographic variation in this generally mobile environment is therefore likely to have significant effect on the movement and observable distribution of artefacts at any one point in time.

Larger scale and longer term trends in sediment transport within and around the harbour as a whole affect not only the distributions of archaeological material but also, and more importantly for our purposes, their visibility on the surface. Long-term cycles of mud accretion, gravel accumulation, and erosion are not necessarily observable on a day-to-day basis but it is known that, for instance, areas of the west coast of Hayling Island were prolific in artefacts during the 1960s but are now buried beneath accreting muds which mask any further archaeological material not already lost to erosion. It has not been possible to monitor such large scale movements over the relatively short period of the survey and indeed, over the three years in which fieldwork was undertaken, such movements are less likely to have had an impact on the available database than have other factors. Undoubtedly the most significant of the post-depositional processes to have acted, and to continue to act, upon the archaeological data is erosion, and erosion at a very local scale.

The islands of the harbour were once part of the dry-land coast and maps dating to *c* 1600 (Portsmouth Record Office 44A/1), 1716 (Lempriere map; Portsmouth Record Office G/MN/421), and a map of 1773 (quoted in Bryant 1967) provide some indication of relatively recent progressive erosion on the Farlington side. Farlington Marshes themselves are now protected by a seawall. The causes of erosion over the 10,000 years or so since the end of the last ice age will have varied and the rates of erosion fluctuated in response to many changing factors. The 'natural' factors involved, such as sea-level change, are described in Chapters 5 and 8 where the physical development of the harbour through time is discussed. As described above (Chapter 1), unlike its neighbours of Portsmouth and, to a lesser extent, Chichester Harbour, Langstone has never been subject to much development, but the human use of the harbour itself, and of the Solent and adjacent coastlines, are almost certain to have affected the maritime regime within it, particularly during the last 150 years or so. Some parts of the coast, in the north of Hayling Island for instance, have been 'made-up', there is some development of the mouth of the harbour, seawalls have been constructed and dredging occurs. Given the relatively shallow nature of the harbour (see Fig 60, Chapter 7, below), even fairly localised changes to the coast and depth of water have the potential to alter the flow and velocity of the tides and main channels which may, in turn, cause changes in the rate and extent of both erosion and accretion in different parts of the harbour.

Spartina was only an accidental introduction to southern England at the turn of the century (Haynes and Coulsen 1982) and recent dieback of this community is having detrimental effects. Certainly there has been a marked acceleration in erosion of the main islands in recent years. This has partly resulted from the progressive loss of *Spartina* grass, that which basically holds the islands together (Haynes and Coulson 1982). *Spartina* dieback is a phenomenon that is not unique to Langstone but is occurring in other saltmarshes of southern England and is the subject of current research (eg May 1969; Allen and Pye 1992; Goodman and Williams 1961). Whether it was erosion that led, in the first place, to the dieback, or the dieback that led to increased erosion is not clear (Nyman *et al* 1994): either way it is a vicious circle and, from the archaeological point of view, the principal effect of *Spartina* dieback is that the saltmarsh margins become unstable and increasingly susceptible to wave erosion so that the archaeological resource contained within the saltmarshes, which is fragile and irreplaceable, is rapidly being lost. A separate, but related project in Langstone Harbour since the start of the present survey has been the monitoring and measurement of *Spartina* dieback. As this monitoring has only been in progress for a short period, and monitoring of erosion cycles needs to be conducted over periods in excess of 25 years (Collier and Fontana undated), it is not yet possible to adequately predict rates of erosion in the past. Resolution of this problem is not aided by the difficulties encountered by previous workers in the harbour in accurately locating findspots on available maps – that is, they did not know precisely where they were so we cannot measure subsequent changes in the size and shape of the islands on the basis of their finds recording.

Integrity of the archaeological deposits
by Julie Gardiner and Michael J Allen

Given the potential mobility of the archaeological material within Langstone Harbour, the question which had to be asked before any detailed analysis could begin was to what extent there may have survived any internal integrity to the assemblages, both temporally and, more importantly, spatially. The loss of material from the islands onto an essentially planar surface immediately destroys their stratigraphic context. What needed to be determined was whether, at any point in time (see discussion of auger results above), the material lying on that surface retains any spatial coherence in the sense that it may be 'held' in its new position for a time before being moved. If artefacts are being moved very quickly around the foreshore area then any discussion of their distributions can only be on a very general level

and the overall assemblage can be expected to have no more, and probably even less, meaningful structure than a typical ploughzone assemblage. In that respect, many of the problems and pitfalls encountered in interpreting ploughzone assemblages are also applicable to those from intertidal situations and it is therefore important that analysis be undertaken at a level which is appropriate to the nature of the recoverable data.

Taphonomy and considerations of site formation

Although gravely seabed sediments (where archaeological artefacts could be considered to be analogous to gravel) are largely considered immobile during Holocene wave and tidal current regimes (Hamblin and Harrison 1989), at the sea margins such as intertidal and immediate subtidal off-coast zones, gravel mobility is known to be potentially high, even in the quietest tidal environments (Will and Clark 1996).

A small experiment was conducted to determine whether there was much movement of artefacts during the period of survey in August 1995. This limited observation involved the daily monitoring over two weeks after tidal ingression of a 2×2m square (square 2000) selected more or less at random on Baker's Island. The area containing stones and archaeological artefacts was marked out with four sturdy metal pins and daily photographed and planned. These records showed no significant movement of the coarse artefacts component; none of the flints or stones had perceptibly been moved within the square, but over the observation period fragments of seaweed and green algae (eg *Fucus vesiculosus* and *Enteromorpha*) and shell (inc *Hydrobia* spp and *Crepidula fornicata*) were seen to pass over and through it. In the extreme short term (ie during 1 week of seasonally low tides) artefacts and gravels did not move extensively. Observations were, however, conducted over both a very short time span and during August at a time when other elements (eg weather and tidal range) were at their least aggressive and, thus, less conducive to direct physical movement of material. The weather was mild and the timing chosen because of the low tides, thus their erosive power was probably at its lowest. It does, however, confirm that the season at which the fieldwork was conducted was most opportune in that conditions could be expected to be optimal for observing a high proportion of the assemblages which we believe to have a relatively high degree of integrity, in the short-term at least – for fuller explanation see Integrity of the archaeological deposits, below and Chapter 6.

Movement of large, flat stones and other material, such as potsherds, can be accomplished by 'rafting'. Seaweeds (eg bladder wrack, *Fucus vesiculosus*) attach themselves to such objects which are lifted and floated by the tide. This phenomenon was clearly observed during the survey, notably with regard to two huge conjoining pottery sherds, one of which (weighing over a kilogram) had been rafted by its attached frond of bladder wrack about 100m from its partner (see below), such kinetic movements can occur even on very low energy tides (see location of rafted sherd on Fig 26 below). The movement of even larger items is also noted by the loss of two sarsen stones weighing *c* 5kg from the lower intertidal zone was noted in a period of three months (see Chapter 6). Arthur Mack also reported skid marks about 15m (50ft) long in the soft silty peat surface at Russell's Lake where a flint boulder covered in seaweed and weighing about 5kg (8–10lbs) was dragged seaward across the surface of the isolated peat shelf at low tides. A large number of waterlogged wooden tree trunks and branches up to several metres long were also lost to the sea during the reporting of this survey project (see Chapter 6).

Other significant movements will occur when the surface upon and within which material lies is, itself, moved. Erosion of the low cliffs, which predominately occurs during the winter months (Arthur Mack pers comm; pers obs), causes artefacts to drop onto the foreshore along with loose soil and mud. Tidal swash not only removes the loosened sediment context, but in so doing can also transport artefacts over short distances. Artefacts resting on firm substrates high up on the intertidal zone and near the cliff margins are less likely to move in calm conditions as relatively high energy is needed to lift them and waves will be at their lowest velocity. On loose and mobile muds further out, artefacts will both sink into and be moved with, the muds. Even within the two week periods of fieldwork, areas of mud were seen to be highly mobile with local intertidal topography being resculpted by each tidal cycle. Again, these observations were undertaken when such movement must have been at its lowest.

There is a wealth of geological and hydrological literature concerning tidal currents and the movement of particulate material (eg Lou and Ridd 1997; Orford *et al* 1995; Celik and Rodi 1988), indeed the hydrological and current patterns are well documented for Langstone itself (eg Webber 1980; Dyer 1980; Henderson and Webber 1977). Much of this geological literature, however, deals only with the movement and mobility of natural clasts (stones). Other papers written from a geological perspective tend to deal with erosional and depositional processes at a somewhat larger scale and over longer periods than are required within the archaeological framework, whereas sedimentation studies (eg Dyer 1980) tend to deal with primarily fine particulate material (clays, silts, and sands rather than clasts), and over short, immediate, time durations of only years or decades. Further, many of the hydrological studies cannot be seen to apply directly to archaeological artefacts, which have been observed to behave differently to many natural clasts (Schick 1986).

Significantly, however, archaeologists have specifically considered the problem of the movement of

archaeological clasts in experimental terms (Schick 1986), and from artefacts distributions and occurrence (Shackley 1978). Flints from the Solent shores have been used (Schofield 1989) to discern the effects fluvial action may have on the structure and integrity of artefact distributions. At Rainbow Bar, Hill Head, at the tidal outlet of the Meon (SU 5280 0240), Lower Palaeolithic and Mesolithic flint artefacts were recovered from intertidal locations by Chris Draper (1951) and more recently by John Schofield (1989). An extensive lithic scatter, covering some 2 acres (*c* 0.8ha; Draper 1951) and representing at least two distinct periods of activity, was present on the intertidal muds and gravels. Schofield considered fluvial displacement and site formation, and used his empirical data in direct comparison with experimental data on the level of artefact displacement by fluvial disturbance described by Schick (1986), and the more detailed data given by Shackley (1978). All three agree that artefact movement is a significant factor in flint assemblages recovered from fluviatile environments. Schick essentially indicates that at *all* levels of fluvial disturbance, larger artefacts will display better rates of recovery and, conversely, flakes and debitage recovery will diminish with artefact size (*op cit*, 81): the smaller pieces will have been moved.

We must, therefore, consider some of the sorting effects and total or selective displacement which might have affected the artefact distributions observed in Langstone Harbour. Work by Hjulstrom (1939), Menard (1950), and Lane and Carlson (1954) demonstrates that particles of the size of flint and pottery artefacts can be moved at low velocities; Shackley (1978) and Fahnestock and Haushild (1962) demonstrate that the behaviour of archaeological material will depend on a combination of factors including:

- flow characteristics (velocity, depth, and duration), of which tidal deluge displays one of the greatest variances of all of these factors and is especially significant in the context of Langstone Harbour
- bed conditions (particle size and bed form), which is relatively uniform within Langstone Harbour
- the physical characteristics of the archaeological material (shape, size, and density), which is highly variable among the Langstone collections

Some of the sorting effects described by these authors suggest that flint artefacts less than 150mm in maximum dimension may exhibit continuous or near-continuous movement in a flow of velocities of only 0.75m/sec (Schick 1986, 49; ie well below standard wave velocities in Langstone Harbour), once the material has been 'released' from the sediment bed. Perhaps surprisingly, larger artefacts (eg cores) may be similarly transported or show even greater movement, despite greater weight (Schick 1986, 49), because they are large enough to physically extend into the turbulent boundary layer where higher flow velocities compensate for their greater mass.

Cores will tend to slide or roll and at water velocities of 0.75m/sec core transport is almost continuous. Although gradual increase in flow velocity can effectively separate smaller from larger elements, a sudden powerful surge (ie wave) effects nearly *all* the assemblage components simultaneously, and cores, flakes, and pottery may move nearly as rapidly and as far despite the considerable variation in size and mass. A rapid decrease in flow velocity enables most entrained elements to lose momentum and be almost simultaneously deposited, resulting in relocation and displacement of the assemblage with little selective bias, but with potential internal spatial reordering. Thus wave action with rapid surging increase in water velocity and a similarly rapid decrease in velocity has the potential to relocate whole assemblages by continual, repeated, small-scale movements with a cumulatively significant effect.

In considering this effect in Langstone we must also add the nature of the bed form and substrate, and here we assume a muddy low-lying substrate, which would always be the product of erosion of the saltmarsh profiles that survive from the islands to Farlington Marshes. This is significant because movement of objects and artefacts has been demonstrated to be impeded in mobile sandy substrates but significantly improved over substrates of very fine grained silts and clays (Schick 1986, 53).

When submerged, the upper sediments on the foreshore are lifted *en masse* into suspension. This is clearly apparent on many tides and presented problems for the divers during the swimover surveys. When underwater, the unconsolidated sediment masses in suspension have elastic mobility (ie move as single fluid mass) and may move incorporated artefacts within them. Items with greater mass may end up in contact with the firmer substrate which will impede artefact mobility. In the unconsolidated sediments artefacts will settle to the base and all subsequent sediment movement may occur over displaced artefacts. These will not then move unless:

- there is total rapid sediment movement (eg on a storm surge)
- gradual removal of the sediment leaves the artefacts open to redisplacement
- high velocity directed water movement (channels) occurs moving both sediment and artefacts (artefacts within the sediment mass), in the case of Langstone possibly out of the harbour entirely and into the Solent

All three processes can be observed to be at work in Langstone Harbour by the geomorphic landforms they produce and by changes in the observable distributions of artefacts and sediments at different places in the harbour over time (see below). A model of potential artefact displacement is presented in Chapter 6.

There is great potential for both sediment and artefact movement in Langstone despite the low relief and environmentally 'quiet' nature of the harbour. Indeed Schofield concludes, from his examination of the Rainbow Bar material, that lithic collections in a fluviatile situation may bear little relation to the original assemblage in terms both of density and distribution, and intrasite spatial patterning. There is, therefore, the possibility not only that a high proportion of large artefacts (eg cores and axes) may be significantly displaced from their associated assemblages, or have been moved to an apparent association with unrelated artefacts, but also that foreshore assemblages in areas where more than one period of activity is represented are likely to have become mixed. At Langstone, as discussed below, both the coarse and finer components are present but assemblages produced at different times have clearly become mixed.

In summary the most likely erosive events which need to be considered are:

- movement after erosion of cliffs (ie 'cliff fall' and tidal swash removing the sediments)
- rafting of larger artefacts from the firm intertidal muds
- movement of material in the softer intertidal muds
- movement of material within the major channels to the harbour mouth and beyond

Integrity of the Langstone assemblage

There are three potential areas of the harbour itself where *in situ* material may be observable: in the cliff sections, by excavation into the saltmarshes, and by the excavation of any archaeological features encountered on the foreshore. Examination of the cliff sections at various places on North Binness and Long Islands revealed a discontinuous band of artefacts, burnt flint, fired clay, ceramic building material (CBM), and flecks of charcoal contained within one or more pedogenic horizons (see Fig 27 and Plate 30, Chapter 4, below). In some areas this material seemed to be confined to prehistoric flintwork and burnt flint, in others to Roman pottery and burnt flint, sometimes with fired clay fragments and/or CBM, in others to a mixture of material of different dates.

A small number of test-pits was excavated on North Binness and Baker's Islands to examine the stratigraphy of the islands in plan. It was only possible to dig eight test-pits within this important, ecologically designated area in the time made available and without causing too much damage to the saltmarshes, and the choice of position was determined largely by the nearby location of known or potential archaeological features or deposits. From the test-pit evidence it was possible to obtain a better understanding the deposits making up the islands (see above) but, unfortunately, only a few artefacts were recovered and none of the test-pits produced a clear stratigraphic sequence of archaeological material. Disappointing as this proved it was not altogether surprising given the tiny percentage of the area that could be examined in this manner.

A number of archaeological features were apparent on the foreshore and small scale excavations were undertaken of several of these (see below). Again, although artefacts were recorded, the evidence was generally inconclusive as to the date of origin of the features; a radiocarbon date from hearth 1702 on North Binness Island gave a date of 1410–1060 cal BC (OxA-7366, 2995 ± 55 BP) consistent with the several more or less complete pottery vessels which were encountered buried in the soft mud of the foreshore. In each case the upper part of the vessel had been lost so it was not possible to determine the level from which any pit had been dug to contain them. All these pots, however, proved to be later Bronze Age in date.

In order to assess the possible degree of integrity of the foreshore assemblage a series of density plots was produced for various categories of artefact recovered from the 2 × 2m gridded collection areas (see Plate 30, Chapter 4, below), two of which were located on the southern shore of North Binness and one in the northern part of the south-western shore of Long Island (Survey Areas 1, 4, and 3 respectively). The categories plotted were: for flint – burnt flint, blades and blade cores/trimmings, flakes/miscellaneous debitage and flake cores/trimmings, scrapers, and other tools; for pottery – Bronze Age/early Iron Age/indeterminate and Roman sherds. Flint artefacts were plotted by number, pottery by number of sherds and weight, and burnt flint by weight. Ceramic building material was also plotted but this could only be done by number of fragments recorded as most CBM was discarded in the field. A selection of the plots is reproduced here (Figs 16, 17, and 18).

Initial examination of the distribution plots reveals interesting differences between the three areas. In Area 1 (Fig 16), on the southern foreshore towards the west end of North Binness Island, there is a wide scatter of material throughout the 500 grid squares. Most categories occur in relatively low densities throughout and where concentrations of any one material do occur there is no obvious correspondence with concentrations in any other material category. There is a general, but not particularly marked, trend for more material to occur in the southern, seaward part of this collection area.

Area 4 (Fig 17), towards the east end of North Binness Island, which comprised 375 grid squares, shows a very different distribution. The total amount of flint and pottery recovered from Area 4 was around 35% of that from Area 1 but there was nearly twice as much burnt flint. Most of the material was recovered from the northernmost third of the gridded area, with just a very few pieces apparently randomly distributed through the remainder. The north-west corner is blank on all the distribution plots and there is a broad correlation between the highest densities of burnt flint, waste flint flakes, and Roman pottery. Area 4 also produced a

substantial quantity of CBM, mostly of post-medieval date, which was concentrated in an area of c 10 × 10m at the western edge of the collection grid.

Area 3, on Long Island (Fig 18), produced the most distinctive patterning. In this area, which produced much more worked and burnt flint than Area 1 but only two-thirds as much pottery from 500 grid squares, there are two distinct zones where materials of all types are concentrated. At the north-eastern edge of the gridded area there is a dense concentration of burnt flint, waste flakes, blades, and flint cores, and a scatter of pre-Roman pottery. A much denser concentration of pottery extends in a roughly diagonal band from the north-west to approximately the centre of the gridded area; the greatest amount of pottery (number of sherds and weight) occurring at this central point. This diagonal distribution is reflected in the other categories of material to a greater or lesser extent, with the highest numbers of flint waste categories coinciding with that of the pottery. Burnt flint also follows a similar pattern but with a number of foci along the diagonal and one to the south of it.

Taking these distributions at face value we might suggest that there were definite zones of archaeological activity in Areas 3 and 4 and only a low-density 'background' scatter of material in Area 1. To test this suggestion, three further factors were introduced: the location of any archaeological features, the microtopography and surface 'texture' of the collection areas, and the distribution of weed cover which may have masked artefacts during collection.

Archaeological features in Area 1 comprised a ditch (1711) and one irregular pit which may be the remains of a hearth (1702) and a narrower ditch (1704) running parallel to 1711. The more ephemeral remains of a third ditch (113) lie just to the west of the gridded area at an approximate right angle to 1711. The positions of these features in relation to the grid for Area 1 are shown on Figure 16. A concentration of pottery is actually focused on hearth 1702 but most of this was recovered before the grid was established and was partly the reason for the collection grid being placed here and the position of both this feature and 1711 cannot be determined from the distribution plots taken from the total collection squares alone. Although over 400g of flint-gritted pottery were recovered from 1704, there is again no indication of its presence within Area 1 on the basis of the distribution of the gridded surface finds.

No features were recorded in Area 4. Area 3 was positioned to examine in detail the area around one of the buried pots on Long Island which was discovered and excavated in 1993 (vessel 350), and two further pots eroding out of the foreshore were recovered in 1997 (vessels 360 and 380) on the foreshore to the south (see Fig 29, below). All the pots were presumably originally placed in small pits but no trace of any cut features could be seen. Vessel 360 was inverted. The position of pot 350 (Figs 18 and 29) is slightly offset from the main distributions of

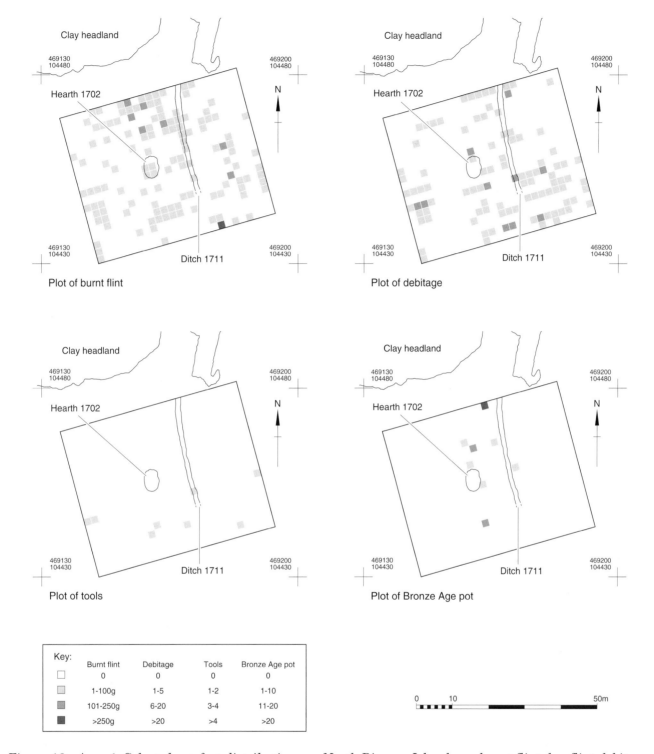

Figure 16 Area 1. Selected artefact distributions on North Binness Island: a = burnt flint, b = flint debitage, c = flint tools, d = BA/flint-gritted pottery. The positions of the archaeological features are marked together with the position of the cliff face. Drawn by Rob Goller

artefacts, lying on the edge of the diagonal band of material (see below).

During fieldwork, plans of the collection areas were drawn directly onto gridded paper which showed the position of any topographical features and patches of seaweed and eel grass together with changes in the nature of the foreshore surface across the areas. The corners of the collection areas and points referring to specific features were surveyed to provide accurate horizontal and vertical coordinates.

As can be seen from comparison between Figures 16, 17, and 18, the microtopography and surface 'texture' have significant bearing on the distributions which were observed.

Area 1 comprised open but relatively firm mudflats lying at around +0.5m OD with an essentially smooth surface and no significant vegetation cover. Artefacts in this area are more or less randomly distributed. Some 23% of the pieces of flint debitage recovered are under 25mm maximum dimension and

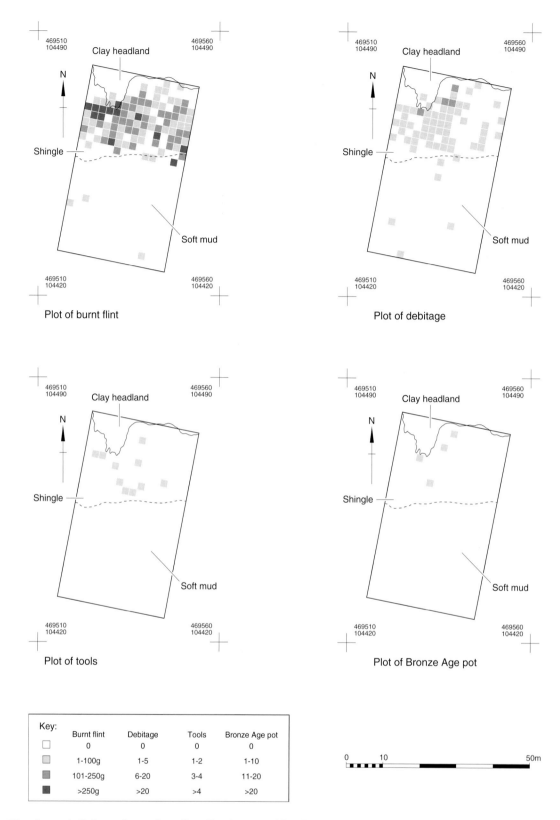

Figure 17 Area 4. Selected artefact distributions on North Binness Island: a = burnt flint, b = flint debitage, c = flint tools, d = BA/flint-gritted pottery. The position of the cliff face and shingle beach are indicated. Drawn by Rob Goller

do not occur in any concentrations – which suggests that there is no obvious sorting of flintwork by size (see above). Concentrations of large and heavy sherds of flint-gritted pottery and several large fragments of well-preserved animal bones first alerted the field team to the presence of features 1711 and

1702 during the initial fieldwork season in 1993, but these features, which are clearly visible at low tide, did not provide the same focus for material when revisited in 1994. A very large sherd of pottery, weighing over 1kg (see Fig 48 and Plate 33, Chapter 4, below), from directly above 1702, conjoins with a

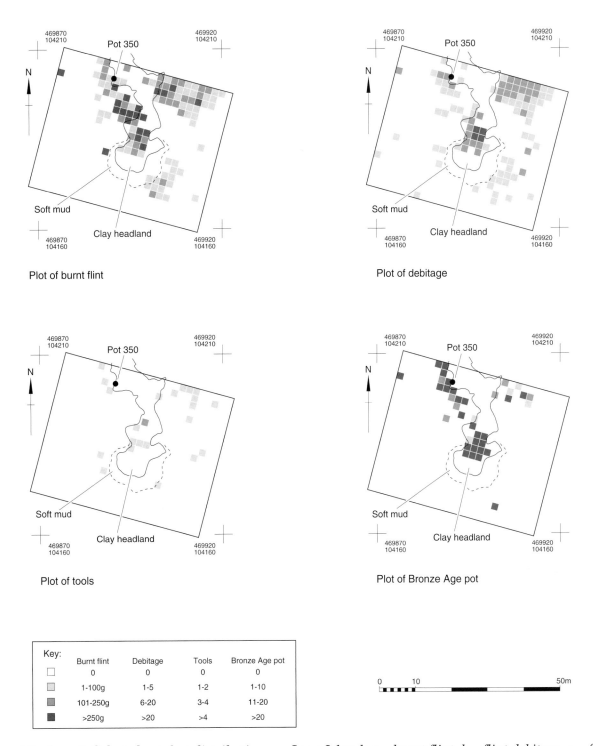

Figure 18   Area 3. Selected artefact distributions on Long Island: a = burnt flint, b = flint debitage, c = flint tools, d = BA/flint-gritted pottery. The position of the cliff face and the eroding clay headland are indicated. Drawn by Rob Goller

clean, sharp break, with an equally massive piece also recovered from the foreshore in 1993. These two and a number of other pieces recorded with them are all part of one vessel but were separated by a distance of some 100m. The average sherd weight excluding components of this vessel is just 8g and it may be that pottery is more subject to sorting than the flintwork. A number of sherds, particularly the larger pieces (Plate 33, Chapter 4, below) had proved attractive to seaweed (esp bladder wrack) which firmly anchored itself to the pottery. This, coupled

with the essentially tabular nature of broken sherds, makes them susceptible to movement because smaller sherds can be lifted by even fairly gentle wave action whilst larger sherds are 'rafted' as the seaweed floats and carries them – see above. These observations indicate that artefacts accumulating on the foreshore in Area 1 are being moved rapidly by the tides and that the velocity of water moving around this part of North Binness is fairly high.

Area 4 encompasses part of the cliff which occupies the extreme northern edge of the area and, in particular, its north-western corner where *Spartina* grass grows to the edge of the cliff. The cliff gently falls away from a height of +2.45m OD in the north-east corner of Area 4 to +1.99m at its north-west corner. Below the cliff is a strip of coarse flint gravel which occupies most of the northern third of the collection area (Figs 17 and 26). South of this is firm, open mudflat with no significant weed cover and with a patch of fine gravel in the south-eastern corner lying at +0.86m OD. The distribution plots show clearly that the bulk of the material in Area 4 was recorded on the coarse gravel 'beach' beneath the cliff line, with a notable concentration below the headland in the north-western corner, from which a few artefacts had become displaced onto the mudflats beyond. The distributions in Area 4 suggest a slower rate of artefact transport away from the eroding cliff line, material apparently being 'held' on the gravel beach for a while before being washed away. This observation should not be unexpected because, in this situation, artefacts form only a small percentage of the mobile coarse material whereas, on the mudflats, they constitute a much larger proportion so that a greater percentage of the total available artefacts will be moved at any one time. Although the material is not *in situ*, it seems likely that the observable quantity of artefacts and composition of the assemblage in Area 4 retains some of its original integrity, at least in the short term.

In Area 3 the diagonal zone of high artefact density reflects the occurrence here of an eroding 'headland' of firm clay extending out from the cliff itself which lies just to the north of the collection area, surrounded by areas of mudflat. At the southern end of the 'headland' was an area of soft 'silt' representing material being eroded out of it. The 'headland' has a maximum height of *c* +0.75m OD with the mudflats lying at +0.24 to +0.43m OD. Some of the blank areas for artefact recovery result from the presence of dense patches of seaweed and green algae. Pot 350 lay at the western edge of the headland, on the northern side of where a shallow 'bay' is being more rapidly eroded; the densest concentration of burnt flint, and highest densities of waste flakes and Bronze Age pottery, lie within, and on the edge of, this 'bay'. Overall Area 3 produced a considerably larger assemblage than Areas 1 and 4 and it appears that, as in Area 4, artefacts are being 'held' on the foreshore for some time before becoming dispersed. In this case, however, it is the presence of firm, tenacious clay which is largely responsible for the observable distributions but, although the archaeological data are recovered from the clay itself, the artefacts cannot be considered to be *in situ* as they are exposed to wave action. Of the three areas examined in detail, Area 3 seems likely to have produced the most coherent assemblage.

The results of this spatial analysis show that a variety of factors are currently involved in the composition and distribution of artefacts around the foreshore and that the dynamics of artefact movement vary from place to place and are likely to be very localised and complicated. In general, open mudflat locations are likely to see the rapid and widespread dispersal of material while areas of coarser texture, such as shingle beaches, will hold the material for a time before higher tides or storms remove some or all of it. Where artefacts occur on eroding clay headlands they are not only closest to their original stratigraphic position but also seem to be held more firmly, though the clay itself may erode quite rapidly. These results are interesting in view of the work undertaken by other researchers into the movement of artefacts in fluviatile environments discussed above. How long artefacts may remain 'in position' on the foreshore in any one location, however, is currently impossible to predict. Very little of the flintwork shows much evidence of water-rolling in the form of rounded edges, or edge damage which occurs very easily when struck flakes collide with other stones or each other. Not surprisingly, by contrast, most of the pottery and other ceramic material is abraded.

The broad conclusion which may be drawn from this is that, while very little of the observable archaeological data remains *in situ*, and all of it is subject to a variety of dynamic forces, the material lying on the foreshore surface may be taken as providing a 'snapshot' of the harbour assemblage at a particular moment in time. Over a period of a few weeks at least the overall assemblage retains sufficient integrity for significant information to be obtained regarding its composition, date, and, to some extent, its function. The present survey has observed essentially *different* assemblages during each phase of fieldwork, and assemblages which are different to those observed by earlier fieldworkers. Similarly any future fieldwork will observe different assemblages again to those recovered during the present survey. However, by careful and appropriate analysis combined with the accuracy of measurement and mapping provided by the GIS database, and by comparison with the results of previous work in the area we can begin to build-up a picture of the development and human use of Langstone Harbour through time.

Distribution of archaeological material

As already stated, the vast majority (*c* 97%) of archaeological finds recovered during the survey come from the intertidal zones of the islands in the northern part of the harbour. A single sherd of orange-glazed post-medieval pottery was found on the foreshore at Eastney and very small quantities of flint and Roman and later pottery were recovered from various points along the western shore of Hayling Island. Although some areas of shingle occur above the low-water mark on these coasts both are mainly covered by thick accreting muds which, in places, proved too soft and dangerous to work in.

No archaeological finds were made along the northern coast or on Farlington Marshes although it was formerly productive in artefacts (Bradley and Hooper 1973). In addition to the timber structures described below, a small quantity of artefacts and burnt flint was recovered from the immediate foreshore of Oyster Island with further small concentrations occurring on patches of firmer clay between Oyster and Baker's Islands.

Considerably more productive in artefacts was the area lying to the south-east of Farlington, where the harbour forms a bay draining the now canalised Ports Creek into the Broom Channel. The small clayey islets here are known to have produced material in the past, but no artefacts were recovered during the survey. In the far north-west corner, however, an old headland supporting what appeared to be a fairly well-developed unripened gley soil horizon produced over 100 flint artefacts, quantities of burnt flint, and pottery of both Bronze Age/early Iron Age and Romano-British date.

North Binness and Long Islands produced most artefacts from the wide arc of their southern and south-western sides respectively. To the west of North Binness, between it and the Farlington seawall, is a fast-flowing channel while the south-eastern tip of Long Island extends closely towards the main Langstone Channel. In neither area do artefacts survive. The northern sides of both islands support deep, soft muds and are subject to strong tidal flows which move up and down the Langstone Channel and Broad Lake and 'behind' them. No artefacts were recovered from these mudflats.

Between these two islands and the southern two, Baker's Island and South Binness, is an area of mudflat drained to both west and east by tributary channels of Russell's Lake and the Langstone Channel. The immediate foreshore of the northern islands varies from fairly firm mudflats with patches of seaweed to shingle beaches lying beneath the low cliffs. Deep mud fills the narrow channel between North Binness and Long Island. The shingle beaches are prolific in archaeological material and a number of features were recorded in addition to the large quantities of 'loose' finds. The distributions are not even along the shoreline. Two main concentrations were found along the southern coastline of North Binness, one at its western end and the other in the eastern half. Each was around 50m in diameter and produced quantities of worked and burnt flint, pottery, animal bone and fragments of fired clay. Similar material was recovered from the south-west facing shore of Long Island, with one particular concentration, c 35m in diameter.

The coast of Baker's Island was found to be surrounded by a halo of prehistoric material, extending out from its foreshore and into the intertidal mudflats and shingle bars which enclose it. Similar types of material were found to those on North Binness and Long Islands. Small but intense concentrations of worked and burnt flint were found along the north-eastern coast of Baker's Island where they were particularly noted to correspond with remnant 'headlands' of firm clay. The spreads of

material continued along the south-western coast of South Binness Island, situated just to the south-east of Baker's Island. On South Binness the scatters continued up from the intertidal zone onto the raised shingle beach which surrounds that island but few finds were made on the shingle spit which extends towards Long Island. Baker's Island also supports a number of wartime structures and various undated, but probably post-medieval, banks.

Methods of analysis
by Julie Gardiner

It had been hoped that data collection would indicate clear spatial variation in the distribution of artefacts of different periods so that individual assemblages could be examined in considerable detail. It quickly became apparent, however, that such was not the case and that while some concentrations of artefacts indicated activity at specific times, rarely if ever could those activities be seen to be spatially discrete from material representing those of other periods. In essence, the archaeological database had to be regarded as a single, mixed assemblage and dealt with on much the same basis as if it had been a ploughzone assemblage. While the identification of spatial and temporal variations in this assemblage were obviously central to the interpretation of the use of the harbour, interrogation of the data had to be conducted at a rather lower level than originally intended, and the interpretation of the results is necessarily presented on a more general level than might otherwise have been possible.

In addition to the overall problems caused by the mixing of assemblages, further difficulties are engendered by the methods of collection. Not all the material was collected on the same basis: in addition to the total collection conducted over the three gridded areas there were a number of individual 2 × 2m total collection squares and large areas of the foreshore which were subject to rapid walkover survey and from where only a 'representative' sample of artefacts was recovered. Ceramic building material, fired clay, glass, and foreign stone were not systematically collected, partly because of the quantities of modern material involved and partly because of the sheer difficulty of carrying the material across the mudflats. Such a varied strategy inevitably introduces biases into the database, as does the inclusion of significant, but unsystematically collected artefacts recovered by individuals other than the archaeological fieldwork team during the course of the survey.

The basic methods of field collection and recording of artefacts are described above (Chapter 1). An initial scan of all the recovered artefacts was conducted at the end of each season of fieldwork so that a broad assessment of the data could be achieved and strategies for further fieldwork formulated. This scan was undertaken by the author with subsequent checking by the various specialists involved.

Analysis of the various material classes was carried out independently but for the purposes of interpretation and discussion the chronological and spatial distributions of the material were further examined using a structured, but simple, nested method of analysis. All the artefacts in each major material category were assigned to one of several groups of data based on the method of collection employed, these being, in decreasing order of reliability:

- artefacts from the total collection Areas 1, 3, and 4; excavated features and test-pits
- artefacts from individual 2 × 2m total collection squares
- artefacts from rapid walkover surveys in areas subsequently subject to more detailed analysis
- artefacts recovered in the rapid walkover surveys
- artefacts recovered by unsystematic collection

In this way it was not only possible to distinguish easily from among the 417 'contexts' producing pre-modern finds (excluding those producing only burnt flint) recovered by different methods, but also to compare and contrast evidence from different parts of the harbour collected at the same level of detail. The first of these groups provides the most reliable information since collection was objective once the position of the grids or excavation areas had been established. Confidence in the composition of the material recovered from other collection units decreases as the subjectivity of the location and collection strategy increases. By working from the most reliable to the least reliable data for each of the main areas producing artefacts the level of confidence in interpreting the patterns that may be revealed is substantially increased, while interpretation is concomitantly tempered by an appreciation of the flaws in the dataset. This approach is hardly ground-breaking in its originality but provided a simple and effective way of sorting a mass of essentially two-dimensional data while allowing the analyst to appreciate and take into consideration the inherent imbalances in the dataset imposed both by the nature of the terrain and the methods of collection.

The composition of the assemblages recovered from the three gridded collection areas provided the base on which to overlay the less reliable data collected by other methods from North Binness and Long Islands. The strategy employed on Baker's Island meant that only a series of individual 2 × 2m total collection squares could be investigated within the time available and these were positioned in relation to specific areas of known archaeological potential and without direct reference to one another. The Baker's Island data is, therefore, less reliable than that for the northern islands but the actual collection within the squares was conducted on the same basis as for those in the gridded areas. Over the top of this information can be added that from the walkover surveys and unsystematic collection. On South Binness only three total collection units were

employed and, indeed, the island could only be visited for a day in 1993 and another in 1995. The data for this island is therefore the least reliable.

Of the categories of artefact recovered the flint assemblage was subjected to the most detailed analysis. It forms by far the largest of the assemblages recovered and appears, over short periods at least, to have been the least subject to post-depositional movements. Although detailed spatial analysis was not possible, the quantity of flint artefacts was more than sufficient for an assessment to be made of its basic technological characteristics and internal chronology, and for some general comments on the distributions of various elements within it. The obvious chronological mixing and unstratified nature of the material suggested that detailed metrical and technological analysis would not prove particularly informative and they were not, therefore, undertaken. Details of the methods employed are given in the flint report, below.

The pottery assemblage from the survey is comparatively small and, again, mixed in date, as well as being in generally poor condition. With the exception of a few partially intact vessels of prehistoric date, the material mostly consists of small quantities of abraded sherds in a limited range of fabrics, a proportion of which is of ambiguous date. Again, it was not felt that detailed fabric analysis would be very helpful in interpreting the assemblage. Summary fabric descriptions of the urns and of a few other notable sherds are given.

All recovered finds (some material having been noted in the field but not recovered, see above) were washed, counted, and weighed; burnt flint was subsequently discarded. Human cremated bone and environmental samples were processed according to standard Wessex Archaeology procedures as outlined in the relevant sections below, where the particular methods of analysis employed are also described. Finds categories other than flint, pottery, and human bone were briefly examined and are described below. All material is held in archive for future research.

Survey of wooden structures around the harbour shoreline
by Dominic Fontana

A number of reasonably sizeable timber structures distributed around the shoreline of the harbour (Fig 19; Plates 16 and 17) were identified during the rapid walkover survey (above). Some of these structures are certainly fairly modern, particularly those associated with the remains of the Portsmouth and Arundel Canal situated around Milton Lock. These timbers are probably the remnants of a jetty and the barge guide posts on the seaward side of Milton Sea Lock. The canal was opened in 1822 and closed just five years later in 1827. This rapid closure was as a result of the leakage of seawater from the canal pond into the domestic water supplies of the adjacent settlements

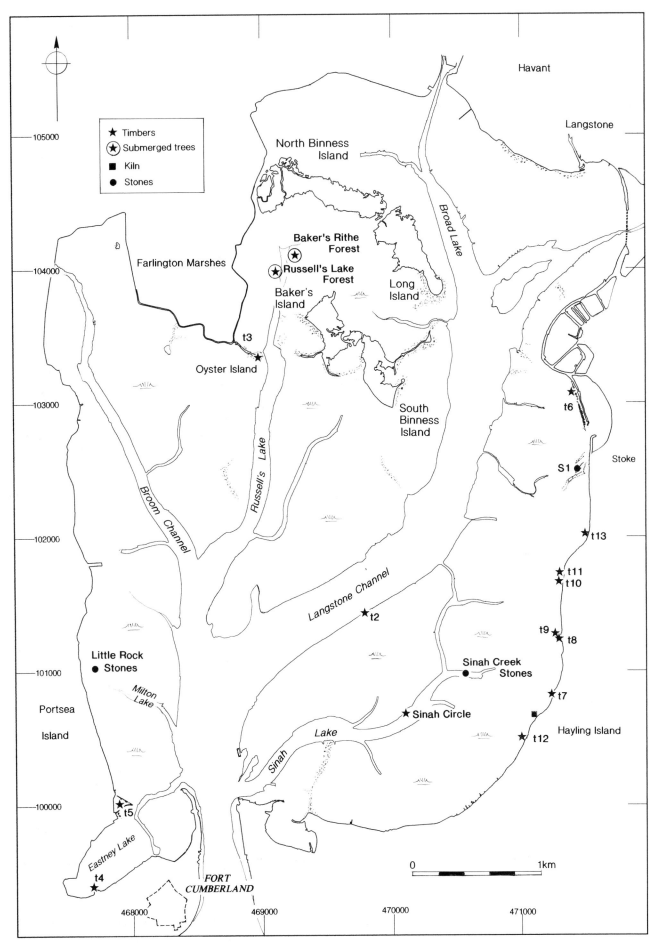

Figure 19   Timber and other structures around the edge of the harbour. Data from Portsmouth University, drawn by S E James. Note timber structures are not to scale

Plate 16   Timber structure t13 on the west coast of Hayling Island, see Figures 19 and 20 (Dominic Fontana)

(Vine 1965). In other parts of the Harbour there are also timber structures that are probably associated with the 19th century oyster farming industry. These are located in the north-east of the Harbour along the Hayling Island coastline and at the southern tip of Farlington Marsh at New Milton Fishery, known locally as Oyster Island (see Chapter 3).

Among the other timber structures are a whole series of jetty remains which included a series of six lines of timber stakes distributed along the western coast of Hayling Island that extend from the coast out into the Harbour. These are both covered with water and exposed by each tidal cycle. Others included S-shaped lines of stakes, which are interpreted as fish traps, located along the length of the Hayling Island coast, with the series beginning some 450m to the south of the chalk block lines. A few other timber structures were present around Eastney Lake. In addition to those found in Langstone Harbour other timber structures have been observed in both Portsmouth and Chichester Harbours.

The rapid walkover survey only identified their presence and recorded any artefacts in the vicinity which might relate to the features. For this project the constituent timbers of each of these structures have been simply surveyed as point locations (see Figs 20 and 32). More detailed survey (but not description) was undertaken. They are mentioned here merely noting their existence, and provide a subject for further study at a later date. They were surveyed using a total-station electronic theodolite into the control network which was established using high-precision Global Positioning System survey (see Fontana, Chapter 1). This ensured that each timber in all features was recorded in three-dimensional coordinates and fitted to the Ordnance Survey national grid and Ordnance Datum (Newlyn) height datum (OD). Thus, the survey records accurate positions of the individual constituent timbers that were visible at the time of survey (1993). The form of these surveyed features are summarised below (all OD heights are to the base of the timbers).

Timber structures

Because of the form of the timber structures, visibility, and the good condition of the timbers below the

Plate 17   Part of the complex timber structure on Oyster Island (t3), the timbers in the foreground are in the north west quadrant on the top of the island. This view from the top of Oyster Island is looking south west over the oyster shell midden (dark patch in the mud flats) (Elaine A Wakefield)

mud surface, it has been assumed that they are of quite recent origin (but see Bell *et al* 2000). However, it is important to appreciate that the fine particle mud provides highly anoxic conditions which preserve organic materials well. As such, a simple visual assessment of the condition of the timbers may give little guide to their age. The form of the jetty features, however, suggests that most are probably post-medieval, and some contain metal bolts, fastenings and bands. The fish traps are more difficult to date. Lines of stakes along the water's margin are a common form of net and basket fastenings and parallels are known in many estuary and harbour locations (see Geraint Jenkins 1974) such as the Severn (eg Godbold and Turner 1992; Nayling 1997), Westward Ho!, Devon, (Balaam *et al* 1987) and the Kent and Essex coastlines (Wilkinson and Murphy 1995). In the Severn there are photographs and historical and archaeological records of these in use from medieval to recent times (Godbold and Turner 1992; Nayling 1997; Salisbury 1991), and in Westward Ho! similar lines of stakes are radiocarbon dated to the Roman period. The cursory nature of the historical survey for this project was not able to

provide details of jetty structures nor of fish traps. The detailed chart of 1783 for the area by Lieut Murdoch Mackenzie, which elsewhere records the presence of fish traps, does not chart beyond the mouth of the harbour entrance. None of the maps examined in the brief historic survey (Fontana and Fontana, below) dating from 1575, 1607, 1665, and 1716 (eg Christopher Saxton's map of Hampshire, John Norden's map of Hampshire, and the larger scale maps of Fabvollière and Lempriere) showed any fish traps. That is not to say that they did not exist, only that we did not find any.

Timber Structure t2

This structure (LH.129) was first noted by Arthur Mack in 1993. It is situated well out on the intertidal mudflats towards the middle of the harbour just to the south of the main Langstone Channel. It sits on top of an intertidal mudbank which is exposed at low tide. The structure is formed of six visible timbers (there may well be more extant beneath the soft mud) which are rough-hewn sections of timber and sharpened to a point. Their heights ranged from −0.294m to −0.188m OD. The condition of the sub-surface timber is good with clear indications of metal working. The function and date of this structure is unclear – though it is possible that it is the remains of some form of fish trap. At present it is only accessible by boat with a short walk across very soft and treacherous mud.

South-western harbour fringes: Fort Cumberland to Great Salterns Pier (Area 8)

Timber Structure t4

This structure of 64 timbers whose base level heights ranged from +0.627m to +1.141m OD. This structure (Pl.98) is located on the southern side of Eastney Lake and forms an inverted horseshoe shape (Fig 20) which encloses a shingle bank. It is comprised of roundwood stakes and stands about 0.3m high. The original structure was considerably larger extending southwards beneath what is now the Lumsden Road housing estate. Interestingly, the full extent is shown on the 1898 Ordnance Survey map of the area as the tip of a small enclosed area named *The Glory Hole* (see Historical survey, below). The depth of the enclosed area is not great, probably no deeper than 0.5m (−0.5 to −1m OD) which would limit its use as a haven. It may be the site from which clay was dug to make bricks for the building of Fort Cumberland in 1788, buts its origin may well be earlier. There is a small and rather indistinct linear feature shown in J A Burt's copy (1890) of la Fabvollière's map of around AD 1600 at this point. This might this suggest that this structure forms the remains of a medieval or Tudor haven.

Timber Structure t5

The 196 timbers in this area, whose ground level heights ranged from +0.098m to +1.949m OD, are arranged in three groups (Pl.104). The southern group consists of guide posts for the entry to the sea lock entrance to the Portsea section of the Portsmouth and Arundel Canal (Fig 20). These are quite substantial posts, some of which reach to over 2.4m in height. These were probably new in 1822 when the canal opened. The canal closed five years later in 1827 (Vine 1965) and so they are unlikely to have been replacements for the original equipment. The middle group of posts form two parallel lines with two areas projecting south in the middle of the run. It is possible that these are the remnants of a landing jetty. The age of this structure is unknown. However, there is the possibility that it is associated with the Prison Hulks which were moored in Langstone Harbour in the early-19th century (Smith 1994). The third grouping is to the north and is situated alongside the sea wall. It is probably the landward end of another jetty which extends eastward.

North-west coast of Hayling Island (Area 11)

Timber Structure t6

The heights of this structure (HI.105) of 307 timbers heights ranged from −0.654 to +0.812m OD. It is most likely part of Harry Lobb's Oyster farm of the late 1860s (Lobb 1867). The South of England Oyster Fishery was established in Langstone to develop a 'scientific' oyster farm. These timbers probably form part of the oyster pens (Fig 20). There are two large brick built 'drains' associated with these timbers (see Non-timber structures, below).

West coast of Hayling Island (Area 12) and Sinah Common (Area 13)

Amongst the most intriguing of the harbour's various timber structures are six lines of timbers that run out into the harbour from the west coast of Hayling Island (timber structures t7, t8, t10, t11, t12, t13) in Areas 12 and 13. The date of construction of these structures is unknown, as is their function. They are located in a very sheltered part of the harbour. At high tide the water remains shallow, not exceeding 2m depth, this constrains the maximum wave sizes that may occur under stormy conditions. The minimum distance across the mudflats from the relatively deep water of the Langstone Channel to the timber structures is *c* 800m, and in places reaching distances as much as 1.5km (Fig 19).

Timber Structure t13

This array of 385 timbers (HI.134), whose heights ranged from +0.228 to +1.468m OD, resembles other lines of timber stakes along the coast of Hayling Island although it is a sinuous curve and bifurcates in the middle of its run (Fig 20; Plate 16). The stakes at the coastal end of the line are slender but reasonably substantial at around 150mm to 250mm diameter. The timbers at the seaward end of the structure are mostly smaller, in the 100mm to 150mm size range. Most of the timbers are roundwood standing about 100 to 150mm above the surface of the mud. It may be another form of fish trap. Its date is unknown.

Timber Feature t11

A line of 32 posts (HI.137) projecting westwards for 32.9m from Hayling Island shore about 57m north of timber feature t10. This is unusually close in comparison to the other timber lines (t7, t8, t12, and t13) which are sited along the Hayling Island shore. The ground level around the lowest timber was 0.19m and highest, at the shoreward end, at 0.84m OD, giving a range of just over one vertical metre. These other timber structures are spaced along the shore at

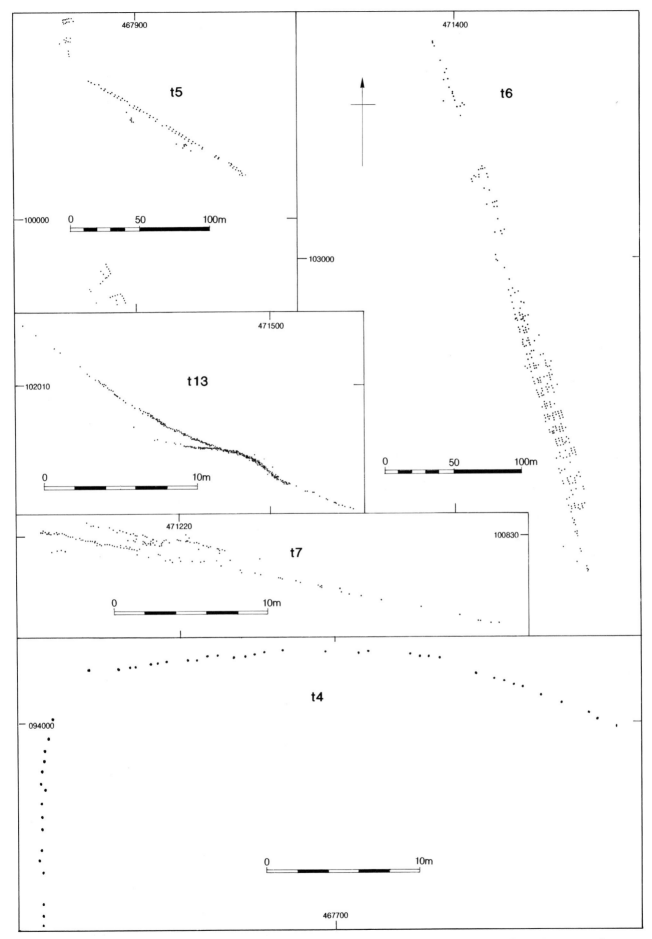

Figure 20 Plans of selected timber structures around the harbour edge. After data from Portsmouth University, drawn by S E James

intervals of approximately 400m or, interestingly, 440 yards or one quarter of a mile. This even spacing along the shore might suggest that this spacing is important to their function, whatever that may be. The closeness of t11 to t10 may also indicate that these two lines may be functionally part of the same structure.

Timber Feature t10

This is a line of 233 timber post (heights range from –0.266 to +1.668m OD) which project westward from the Hayling Island coast (HI.132). They are placed more thinly towards the coast and bunched together towards the seaward end.

Timber Feature t8

t8 (HI.131) is a complex array of array of 132 stakes (heights +0.105 to +1.445m OD). There seem to be some ovoid sub-structures in the middle of the run. This is probably a fish trap of unknown date.

Timber Feature t9

A simple line (HI.136) of only 15 timbers (+0.171 to 0.433m OD) just to the north of this structure t8. It is so close that it could be considered a part of t8. The shoreward end of the structure is at 0.43m OD.

Timber Feature t7

Adjacent to t8 is another complex arrangement of 159 stakes (HI.130) placed into the mud projecting out from the west coast of Hayling Island (Fig 20) whose heights ranged from –0.006 to +1.065m OD. There are some sub-structures, or divisions, in the middle of the run of timbers. It is undated, and is also probably a fish trap.

Timber Feature t12

The structure comprising 78 timbers (heights ranging from +0.233 to +1.099m OD), is situated adjacent to a small stream outfall and it faces southwest (HI.133). The structure consists of two lines of roundwood stakes driven into the mud which cross each other in the middle of their run to form a shallow and slightly curved X shape. Below the surface the timbers remain in good condition retaining the bark on the outside. The tops of the stakes stand generally less than 100–150mm above the surface of the mud. As yet it is unclear what is the function of the structure although it may be the remains of a fish trap. Its location suggests that this is likely as the structure is covered and uncovered by most tides.

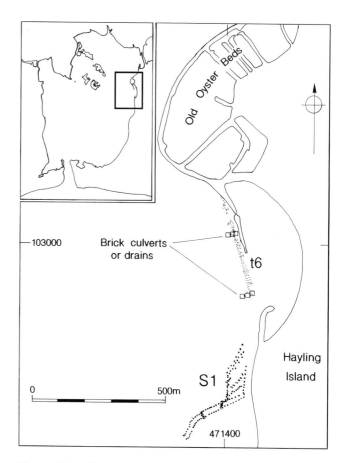

Figure 21   Stone structures and brick culverts off the coast of Hayling Island. After data from Portsmouth University, drawn by S E James

Non-timber structures around the harbour perimeter foreshore
by Neil J Adam

Several non-timber structures were recorded in the intertidal zones around the perimeter of the harbour. Some of these are probably associated with various timber structures which were recorded in detail by Portsmouth University (Fontana, above; Fig 20).

A line of worked chalk blocks was found running along the coast *c* 150m south of the old Hayling Island Oyster Beds in the same area as timber structure t6, together with which it probably originally formed part of an oyster farm (Fig 21). Two large drains or culverts built of a double skin of bricks run across the foreshore towards the low-water mark in the same area.

Further lines of chalk and flint blocks were found to the south, radiating out from the Stoke headland in a pattern similar to the spokes of a wheel. Although intrinsically undatable these are likely, again, to be the remains of oyster pens. The Ordnance Survey 1:2500 scale map SU 70 SW plots the lines made by these blocks and labels them as 'Old Oyster Beds'.

A complex of lines of stones (HI.106) was surveyed (S1) on the surface intertidal muds (1m OD) at Stoke close to Knott's Marsh (centred on SU 7045 0245), and the location of each stone recorded in detail by the total station survey for incorporation into the GIS. These form oyster pens and they are marked on the OS map as such. The stone lines clearly form trapezoidal pens leading out into the mudflats but set at an angle to the coast, running south-west to north-east – presumably aligned with the main tidal flow (Fig 19). A sinuous double line of stones leads off to the south-west towards the head of a channel known as Cockle Rithe and is crossed in two places by what appear to be double rows of stones, possibly intended to pond water as the tide receded. On the outside of the pens are the remains of what appear to be wooden hurdles which were probably used to retain oyster spats while allowing for the through-flow of water. A number of roofing tiles were found scattered towards the seaward end of the structure below the surface of the mud. These were formerly used in oyster beds, stacked into small towers, as a means of collecting and nurturing oyster spat (Yonge 1960). It is possible that these too are associated with the activities of Harry Lobb (see Historical survey, below), although they could be earlier.

The remains of a post-medieval brick-built structure set back against a low cliff were identified at about High Water mark of Mean Tides (HWMT) on the Hayling Island coast (SU 4712 1007). It was horseshoe-shaped in plan and measured 3m east–west and 2.2m north–south. The front of the structure did not survive above the level of the shingle beach but the back wall stood to c 1m. It was built entirely of brick faced with a white, probably, lime, wash blackened in places by scorching. Scorched bricks and brick fragments littered the general area. This structure is likely to have been a brick kiln; brickmaking is certainly known in the vicinity from the 19th century (Moore 1984).

A brief historical survey
by Val Fontana and Dominic Fontana

This section is a brief survey of some the documentary sources that provide evidence for some activities that have gone on, both in and around Langstone Harbour, during the past millennium. It complements the archaeological desk-based study that preceded fieldwork (Chapter 1). This survey is not a full documentary research, but a summary concentrating on a few pertinent themes that are, to a greater or lesser extent, reflected in the archaeological record of the harbour. A more detailed history of Langstone Harbour is given in Tweed's book 'A history of Langstone Harbour and its environs . . .' (Tweed 2000). Sources used are the Hampshire Sites and Monuments Record (SMR), Victoria County History for Hampshire (VCH 1908; 1912), Portsmouth Papers, and printed records of Portsmouth Corporation. Other sources briefly examined were those in the Public Record Office, Portsmouth and Hampshire Record Offices, Portsmouth Library (Local Studies Section), and local newspapers. The location of the main sites referred to are shown on Figures 2 and 3.

The main themes discussed in this section fall under the following headings:

1   Reclamation of land from the sea (and inundation by it)
2   Salt extraction from the sea
3   Oyster cultivation and fishing
4   Military activities

Significant land reclamation has occurred around the margins of the harbour since the 17th century. Salt extraction from sea water has been an industry of the south coast of England since at least Roman times, including in Langstone Harbour. Over the past 200 years, oyster cultivation has had an important and changing role. This began as a simple gathering of naturally-occurring oysters and developed into an organised, commercial effort in the 19th century, before returning to its earlier harvesting status in the mid-20th century. Military activity too has left a significant mark on the development of Langstone. Indeed, it was as late as 1959 that the military relinquished its control over the harbour.

Other activities in and around the harbour encompass such traditional activities as fishing, flour milling, and general transportation of goods and people. Smuggling in the 18th and 19th centuries to avoid government duty on the import of goods was undoubtedly prevalent, Langstone village being a noted haunt of smugglers, and included the usual items of lace, brandy, and tobacco. In addition there was smuggling of people, particularly of Roman Catholic priests after the Reformation and before the *Catholic Relief Act of 1778* (VCH 1908, 174; Caron 1974). In addition there was the housing, in hulks, of convicts awaiting transportation to the American colonies and Australia. Finally there were the many unrealised, and often over-ambitious, projects that had been planned and, in some cases, started in Langstone Harbour during the 20th century. These included the plans for turning Langstone into a commercial harbour to rival Southampton. More recently, there were proposals to develop Farlington Marsh into a international flying boat base, which would have involved closing the harbour entrance to create a vast lake on which the flying boats would take off and land. The latter project was abandoned because of the Munich Crisis in 1937 (Sparks 1938), and subsequently overtaken by developments in aviation technology that made large land-based aircraft practicable (HRO 15M74/DDC182).

Land reclamation and inundations

Langstone Harbour has continued to change its general shoreline in historic as well as prehistoric times. The main areas of reclamation are on the western side of the harbour, from Farlington, in the north, down the eastern shore of Portsea Island. The west coast of Hayling Island has changed little over recent centuries, except for reclamation in the north-west. A comparison of Daniel Favereau de la Fabvollière's map (c 1660; BL Add MS 16371a) with today's shoreline would suggest that the east shore of Portsea Island has changed considerably. It should be noted, however, that Fabvollière copied his map, without any major topographical changes, from an original surveyed by Edward Mansell in 1626 (Hodson 1978). In the 1660s numerous indentations were indicated on the map which may have over succeeding years subsequently disappeared, leaving an almost straight north–south shoreline. By the 1960s, the two branches of Eastney Lake were filled, leaving an inlet half the size of the original. This is now the only inlet left. The reduction of Eastney Lake was rather more piecemeal than that of the other inlets and was connected partly with the development of the ill-fated Portsmouth and Arundel Canal in 1822 (Vine 1986, 81–83), and the rebuilding of Fort Cumberland in the late-18th century (Magrath 1992).

In 1788, when Fort Cumberland was being rebuilt (Magrath 1992, 5), it was decided to make bricks nearby using clay available on the southern shore of Eastney Lake. This reduced the need to transport bricks from the Bay House works at Gosport to Eastney, an expensive and perhaps hazardous operation. The result of the brickmaking was the creation of a large hole which was filled in the 1920s. In about 1910, Ferry Road was constructed across the mud so that people travelling to the Hayling Island Ferry did not have to pass close to the Fort and rifle ranges. The mudflats between Ferry Road and Fort Cumberland Road were filled-in the early 1960s with rubble from the Dockyard. Subsequently, the whole of this area became known locally as 'The Glory Hole' (V J L Fontana pers obs; oral history).

Household rubbish was tipped into the southern part of Milton Lake (Velder) at the turn of the century (Gates 1928, 216). In 1962 a chalk bund was put across Milton Lake, closing it off from the sea, so that tipping could take place in the remaining area. This was completely filled by 1970 and now forms Milton Common which sports two freshwater lakes that developed from the numerous freshwater springs arising in this part of Portsea Island (V J L Fontana pers obs; oral history).

The large indentation, formerly known as Gatecombe Haven, was cut off from the sea in about 1660 and a large portion of it developed as The Great Salterns Salt Works (CTB&P 1660–7, 38; CSPD 1664–5, 72–3). This area was incorporated within the Borough boundaries in 1895 by Act of Parliament (Gates 1928, 184); and much of the low-lying land that had been the salterns was acquired and infilled with household rubbish (Gates op cit, 216). This caused the owners of Great Salterns House to sue for £10,000 compensation and, in turn, led to the Corporation building two refuse

'destructors' near Baffins Pond to deal with the rubbish. By 1926 the tipping was nearly completed and most of Great Salterns was opened as a Corporation golf course. In 1931 the destructors were dismantled and the Corporation reverted to 'controlled' direct tipping (Gates undated 1, 104–5; undated 2, 120–1).

In 1877, when Hilsea Lines were rebuilt in response to the threat of invasion by the French (Saunders 1997), the north-east corner of Portsea Island was reclaimed from saltmarsh and turned into a rifle range, firing out over the harbour. By the mid-1930s the rifle range had disappeared and in 1941 the final and northern portion of the Eastern Road was opened and crossed Portcreek at this point (Blanchard undated). Portcreek itself was also altered in the mid 1860s; from being somewhat sinuous it was straightened out and dams with floodgates built at either end, so that it would remain flooded at all tides, thus forming an extra moat to the Hilsea Lines. The French threat had disappeared by 1897 and by then the dams had been breached to allow free passage of water and boats. The remains may still be seen at the Langstone end of Portcreek next to the western side of the Eastern Road Bridge (Patterson 1967).

Major reclamation occurred in 1771 along the northern shore of the harbour. Part of the largest island, then known as Binner's Island, was incorporated into the mainland by dividing it and building sea walls across the island to the mainland. This became Farlington Marsh and was used as pasture land, thus releasing more fertile land at the foot of Portsdown Hill for arable use (Bryant 1967). William Cobbett wrote in his *Rural Rides* (Cobbett 1830) that, in the 1820s, from Bedhampton to Fareham, at the foot of Portsdown Hill, 'The land is excellent. The situation good for manure. The spot the earliest in the whole kingdom. Here, if the corn be backward, then the harvest must be backward'. That part of 'Binner's Island' not incorporated into the Marsh is now North Binness Island (PCRO map 1716, DC/PM2/12). Reclamation also occurred during the early 1970s at Broad Marsh on the northern shore of the harbour, where the Bedhampton and Brockhampton streams emerge and in the north-western part of Hayling Island where former salterns and oyster beds have been infilled since the late 1960s (V J L Fontana pers obs).

To what extent inundations by the sea have contributed to changes in the harbour shoreline (as opposed to erosion of the islands) during the historic period is more difficult to assess. Repeated major inundations of Hayling Island are reported during the medieval period. In 1324–5 Hayling Priory (see Chapter 1) lost £42 worth of property to the sea and the hamlet of East Stoke (on the Chichester Harbour side of Hayling Island) was lost. In 1340 a 'great part' of the island was flooded (to be followed by the loss of half the population to the Black Death in 1346) and further inundations are recorded in the 17th century (VCH 1908, 129).

The salt industry

In common with some of the other harbours of the Solent coast, Langstone is an ideal area for salt production (eg Bradley 1975). It is sheltered and there is plenty of low-lying marsh that may be enclosed to make salt pans. The technology involved in salt production has barely changed over at least 2000 years. In the later-prehistoric and Roman periods salt water collected in simply enclosed brine pits at high tide was transferred to crude pottery vessels (briquetage) for drying and transportation (see Morris 1994 for a recent discussion). Throughout the historic periods, and continuing today at, for instance, Lymington, the basic process has involved the pumping of brine by windmills into large lead or iron pans to be boiled (Lloyd 1967). As the brine becomes more concentrated the salt crystallises and is removed with rakes and shovels. The residual liquid is then drained off. This drained liquor, known as 'Bittern', was traditionally used to produce Epsom and Glauber Salts. The crude, generally brown, salt that was left was known as 'Bay Salt'. This was either sold or further purified by dissolving in freshwater and re crystallising to produce a high quality white salt. The presence of freshwater and the ease of delivering fuel by sea (charcoal or, from the 17th century, coal, mainly from Newcastle) are further factors that favoured the development of the salt extraction industry in Langstone Harbour (Rochester undated).

Evidence for salt production in Langstone can be traced from at least the Iron Age, through medieval times (see Chapter 1), till the latter half of the 18th century, when it went into decline, disappearing altogether by the second quarter of the 19th century (Counsels Brief 1844, PCRO G/MN 78). La Fabvollière's map shows nine salt works; two of these, Paulsgrove and Wymering, are labelled 'Old Saltworks', which may imply that they had been in existence for a considerable time but were probably no longer productive. One of these, Wymering, is mentioned in Domesday as having a salt pan along with several others (Hinde 1985): Havant (2) valued at 15d; Hayling Island (1), 80d; Bedhampton (2), 45d; Copnor (1), 8d; Cosham (1), 14d which suggests a thriving late-11th century industry.

Bradley (1975; 1993, and see Chapter 1) provides considerable evidence for an early salt industry in Langstone Harbour dating from at least the Iron Age and possibly earlier (see Chapter 2). Finds of briquetage, in particular on the west coast of Hayling Island, were numerous in the 1960s though many of the relevant areas are not currently accessible for collection of material. Actual evidence for Roman salt production in Langstone Harbour is sparse though it can be reasonably inferred (Bradley 1993). However, Skelton (1826) records that St Augustine of Hippo, in his book *The City of God* (c AD 410), mentions that the salt made around the shores of Hayling was 'superior to every other made on the British Coast', though it has not been possible to verify the accuracy of the quotation. If correct, this indicates that salt production in the harbour in Roman times was more than just a small, local affair. In geographical terms, the position of Langstone, essentially at the crossing of a main east–west and a lesser north–south Roman road, would make it ideally situated to provide salt to the likes of *Noviomagus* (Chichester), and various smaller settlements such as that at Rowland's Castle and local villas.

During the 13th/14th centuries, the salt production industry in England went into decline because good quality salt was being imported from Europe, in particular Brittany, while salt workers were being tempted away to industries such as woollen production (McKisack 1959). However, the industry around Langstone survived, probably because of the developing port of Portsmouth and the need to supply both the army and ships with salted meats, etc. There are a number of cases where the Crown requires 'that the Bailiffs of Portsmouth prepare 50 does, casks and salt and export same to king in Gascony' (Cal Lib Roll 1253; 1254, vol 4, 140, 160).

In the 17th century salt production became more industrialised. In 1598 Robert Bold acquired Portsea Manor, which included the right to rent from the Crown the 40 acre salt works at Copnor, where he remained Saltmaster until 1626 (Counsels Brief 1844, PCRO G/MN 78). These salterns are also marked on la Fabvollière's map (c 1660), on the spur of land between Velder (Milton) Lake to the south and Gatcombe Haven to the north, with Baffins Pond to the west providing a source of freshwater. After 1626 the works were granted by the king to Sir Edward Sydenham for a rent of 6/8d pa (Counsels Brief 1884, PCRO G/MN 78; CSPD 1664-5). Not long after, in 1660, Dr William Quatermain, physician in ordinary to the King, and Richard Alchorne petitioned Charles II to grant them Gatcombe Haven so that they could enclose it and develop a salt works there. This they did and by 1664 The Great Salterns Salt Works was established (Counsels Brief 1844, PCRO G/MN 78). The brine pits covered the area to the east and south of the lake. Low-lying pasture land was developed to its west.

The other main salterns around Langstone Harbour in the later–17th century were at Cosham and North Hayling. Unfortunately for the Langstone industry, in 1670, about the time that Great Salterns was being developed, rock salt was discovered during the excavation for coal near Northwich in Cheshire (Rochester undated) and, during the subsequent 100 years, this developed into the main source of salt in Britain. There is a possibility that Cheshire rock salt was imported to Great Salterns during its declining years where it was dissolved in sea water to make more concentrated brine. This was certainly the case at Lymington (Cross 1965; Lloyd 1967, 90).

Though the potential for a prosperous salt industry was present in Langstone Harbour, it never really developed to the extent that it might have done. The Audit Office list of salt duties paid to the Excise in the early-18th century indicated that

Portsea was not very productive. In 1705 the Portsea collecting area (extending from Hamble to about Pagham), in which Great Salterns Salt Works was the largest, collected £4647, whereas Chester collected £95,770! (CTB&P 1706–7, vol 21, cccxiv) The suggestion that salt manufactured in the Portsea area was mainly used by the Admiralty for salting meats may not be entirely true. A report (PRO 1796, T64/233) to the Commissioners about the Portsea Salt Duty collection area in 1796 says that: 'In the present year to April 1796 the greatest part of the salt made at this collection will be shipped for exportation . . . '. The discovery of rock salt in Cheshire probably made it cheaper for the Admiralty to obtain their salt from there.

At the beginning of the 19th century the Great Salterns Salt Works were closed and, in 1830, the estate, including some of the saltmaking equipment, was sold by the Crown as a private estate to Mr Francis Sharp for £11,000. The saltworks at Hayling lasted a little longer, but by the mid-19th century they too had ceased to be productive (*Hampshire Telegraph* 12 April 1830).

Oyster fisheries and fishing

It goes without saying that general commercial fishing around the Langstone Harbour area has gone on from time immemorial. Although recorded as important in the medieval and early post-medieval periods (VCH 1912, 468), it has never developed into a major industry and was certainly noted to be in decline by 1913 (*ibid*). In general it has remained very much a local affair supplying local markets, in particular Portsmouth, with such fish as mackerel, mullet, bass, sole, plaice, eels, and prawns. Turbot, cod, and whiting are also mentioned as catches in the medieval period (*ibid*). The largest proportion of fishermen involved in Langstone Harbour came from Emsworth to the north of Chichester Harbour.

Although not documented here, the Roman fondness for oysters and the natural occurrence of the round flat oyster (*Ostrea edulis*) in the shallow waters of the south coast (Yonge 1960) means that oyster fishing is likely to have been an activity in the harbour since at least Roman times.

Oyster fishing in Langstone Harbour fell into three categories:

1) Gathering mature oysters from the wild for direct selling
2) Gathering immature oysters from the wild, or buying from a breeder, for laying on private beds so that they may grow in ideal conditions to a suitable size and regular appearance for sale
3) Laying mature oysters in controlled conditions so that they may breed and form free swimming larvae that settle as spat on special collecting devices from which the fisherman could collect young oysters and lay elsewhere to fatten for market

Since the end of the last century species other than *Ostrea edulis* have been imported for commercial exploitation and laying, in particular the Portuguese oyster (*Crassostrea angulata*), which only occasionally breeds in these waters, but is able to cope with adverse conditions such as thicker sediment and longer periods of exposure. No shells of *Crassostrea* have been found in Langstone Harbour (Bennett and Fontana 1955) nor have records been found of it having been introduced (the species usually on sale in the supermarkets today are *Crassostrea virginica* or *C. gigas*). The following discussion, therefore, concerns *Ostrea edulis* only.

Ostrea edulis is reproductively described as a protoandric hermaphrodite (Yonge 1960); starting as male producing sperm it alternates through its life with periods as male followed by periods as female producing ova. Fertilisation occurs inside the shell and after a few days development the ciliated larva is released into the sea to be distributed by the forces of nature. After a few days drifting the larva becomes spat which settles and cements itself to a suitable hard surface and continues to feed and grow. Three to four year old oysters are of ideal size for eating.

There have been considerable natural oyster beds off Shoreham, Selsey, the Isle of Wight (Cole 1956; Winder 1992), and in Langstone Harbour itself. Up until the end of the 18th century these supplied a sufficient quantity of oysters for local requirements and some surplus for transportation to the Kent and Essex beds for relaying. As demand grew and more boats from outside the area arrived to dredge for oysters, the depletion of the beds reached a point where they were no longer capable of self-maintenance. Regulations were introduced (Cole 1956, 8) with a closed season between May to August, and a minimum size of oyster that could be fished of 2½ inches (64mm), but these regulations were neither observed nor enforced. In 1796 (PCRO 1798, CCR, 5–17, 47–49, and 77) a meeting of the Portsmouth and Portsea Fishery requested that a reward should offered for the reporting of anyone dredging for oysters at improper seasons. So serious was the denudation of the beds that, by the 1830s local fishermen, mainly from Emsworth, were being deprived of their income and having to go 'on the parish'. The *Hampshire Telegraph* (20 August 1833) reported the ' . . . need to regulate oyster fishing. Otherwise the whole brood in Solent will be lost. Langstone Harbour fishermen may be thrown out of work by unwarrantable conduct of 40 to 50 vessels from Medway with heavy dredges who pull undersize oysters'. These undersized oysters were taken away and laid in beds along the Thames to grow to a marketable size. However, it was not until the *Sea Fisheries Act* of 1868 that some regulation was imposed.

As a response to the depletion of the natural oyster beds, members of a local family, the Russells, obtained leave in 1821 to build a house on a small island off Ware Point in Carsticks Channel, known

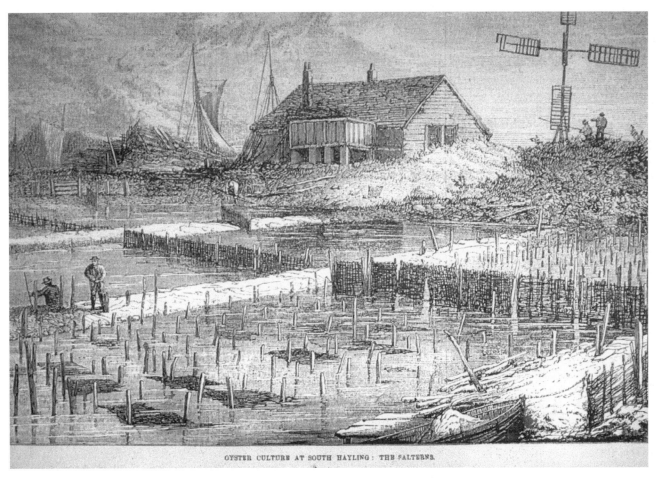

OYSTER CULTURE AT SOUTH HAYLING : THE SALTERNS.

Figure 22   The South of England Oyster Company's breeding ponds and Hayling Island; note the windmill for pumping water. From the Illustrated Times *15 August 1868*

today as Oyster Island in Russell's Lake (see Figs 20 and 32). They prepared beds by laying down sand, old shell and gravel in the mud along the edge of the channel just below low-water mark. Young oysters purchased from the Emsworth fishermen were put down for fattening to marketable size. The Russell's, having established their beds, were then continually at odds with the Emsworth oyster dredgers. In 1839 local fishermen, finding their old sources depleted, tried to dredge over the Russell's laying beds and found themselves prosecuted for fishing on what they considered to be common ground. This led to a fracas, law suits, and prosecutions (*Hampshire Telegraph*, 2 November 1840) which were not resolved until the 1868 *Sea Fisheries Act* which made it possible for grounds below low-water mark to be held under a several or regulating order. By 1895 these beds were well established and had become the over-wintering beds of the Whistable Oyster Company (PCRO DVIF/7/5).

Various attempts were made in the 19th century to create breeding beds for oysters where spats could be restricted to specific places from which it would be easy to collect, and then lay for fattening. A French mason named Rivedoux suggested a method as early as 1834 for use on the Ile de Ré off the Biscay coast near La Rochelle (Lobb 1867, 7–16) but his idea was not pursued until 1858. His idea was to confine breeding oysters in specially constructed 'parcs' (ponds), so that the released spat would not be swept away. Within these 'parcs' suitable surfaces, such as hazel hurdles or roof ridge tiles, were placed for the spat to attach itself. When the spat had grown to about the size of a new penny (20mm diameter) they were detached and placed for 3 to 4 years in fattening beds to grow for market.

In 1865 Harry Lobb, an entrepreneurial British businessman, went to France to study the system, returning to set up the South of England Oyster Company with the intention of developing breeding oyster beds based on the French system in north-west and south-east Hayling Island. The beds on the western side of Hayling Island were to occupy those that had been partly developed earlier for oyster laying by a Mr Crouch. In his report Lobb writes (1867):

> There are from fifteen to twenty boats for oyster dredging leaving Langstone Harbour, and dredging in the neighbourhood of Ryde, Cowes, Calshot etc, and bring the oysters into Langstone Harbour, where they are sold by the tub for laying down. Mr Crouch has been accustomed to purchase these oysters and laying them down for fattening.

Mr Crouch's beds were those at the north-west corner of Hayling Island, between the west coast of the Island and the embankment for the railway which was being built over the mudflats to carry a line connecting Havant with South Hayling at the Kench (Mitchell and Smith 1984). This embankment was never completed although the remains of it may still be seen.

The beds on the eastern side of Hayling Island were developed from the old saltworkings. Deeds relating to the transfer of oyster beds here came to light in 1995 (Mr V Pierce-Jones pers comm). One set, concerning the sale in 1880 of the beds and oyster rights to a certain Geofrey Lewis Austin from the South of England Oyster Company Ltd contained a very interesting map showing a breeding pond or 'Fusaro'. This map ties in with the lithograph from the *Illustrated Times* of 15 August 1868 (Fig 22). This pond was located on the north shore of Cockle Rithe, Hayling Island (it has now become the Boating Lake at Coronation Holiday Village). 'Fusaro' refers to Lake Fusaro, near Naples, just south of Cumae, Italy, where the method was also used (Yonge 1960).

Lobb and his manager, Hart, at first had some success with this method and so wrote a series of optimistic reports of the work (Lobb 1867). However, in contrast to the situation in France, a good spat fall in Langstone Harbour was erratic and therefore unreliable. The sea around Hayling was too close to the threshold of conditions required for successful oyster breeding. A general decline set in which was exacerbated by sewage pollution. There were further difficulties presented by the arrival of new competitors such as *Crepidula fornicata* (slipper limpet), *Elminius modestus* (barnacle), and *Urosalpinx cinerea* (american tingle), and the importation of hardy foreign stocks of oyster, such as *Crassostrea* sp. The foreign stock introduced diseases, such as the flagellate protozoan *Hexamita* which, in 1920–1, decimated the oyster population on the south coast. The Langstone oyster farming industry came to a final end in the 1920s when it was closed down following an outbreak of food poisoning (Moore 1984). One or two attempts have since been made to revive it, none has yet succeeded.

Military and related activities

Military and related activities in Langstone Harbour are presented later in this volume with the review of the Mulberry Harbour remains (Hughes and Momber, Chapter 3).

The Hayling Island railway

One of the most important factors dominating the later history of Langstone Harbour, especially from the latter half of the 18th century, has been the military requirements. For example, there is a detailed report (PRO 1854, RAIL 1149/31) dated 16 March 1854, setting out the Admiralty's requirements regarding the structure of a proposed railway bridge

between Langstone and North Hayling. In other places this would have been solely the province of the Board of Trade and not a concern of the military. This report took into account some memorials received from local firms and individuals, including one from the Portsmouth and Arundel Canal Company, who had paid £3580 towards the expense of opening the road bridge, as well as expenses of £20,000 towards making a cut in the creek to deepen the navigable channel. Proposals for a solid embankment across the creek were, not surprisingly, not acceptable to them. The Admiralty themselves felt that the creek should remain open to navigation. They stipulated that 'The railway across the creek be constructed for a length of not less than 560ft (170.7m), on open pile work, with an opening span of not less than 40ft (12.2m). In addition there was to be a clear headway of not less than 7ft (2.1m).

This railway was intended to run over the mudflats some 1000 yards off the western shore of Hayling, ending at a station just south of the Kench, where a port was to be developed. The line was never finished as it proved impossible for the engineers to make the embankment stable. Harry Lobb, the oyster entrepreneur, thought that the mudflats between the Hayling shore and this railway embankment could be developed as oyster beds. In his report of September 1865, Lobb (1867, 34) describes the area as being bounded on the west side by ' . . . the railway embankment, stretching out about half a mile, and terminating in the piles forming a bridge over Sinah Lake.' He goes on, 'There is one to two miles of embankment to be made, completing the western boundary, when 900 acres of mudland will be enclosed, with the exception of Sinah Lake, which runs under the previously mentioned bridge.'

It can be concluded from this is that the outer edge of the oyster beds on the north-west corner was built on part of the original embankment. The distance from the southern edge of these beds to Sinah Lake is about 2 miles. In addition there is the remains of a shingle embankment south of Sinah Lake running to the end of the Kench. However, despite these plans, the railway was eventually built to run on land and not across the mudflats, following the western shore of Hayling Island, terminating near West Town. The first train ran in July 1867; the line finally closed in 1963 (Magrath 1992).

18th and 19th century defences

It was not until 1959 that the Queen's harbour Master in Portsmouth relinquished control of Langstone Harbour when a civilian harbour Board was set up a year later. Military control of the harbour had been maintained since the mid-19th century because of the concerns that the garrison of Portsmouth and its dockyard could be attacked from the land side. As a consequence there was felt to be a need to control shipping that entered Langstone Harbour. In the early-18th century,

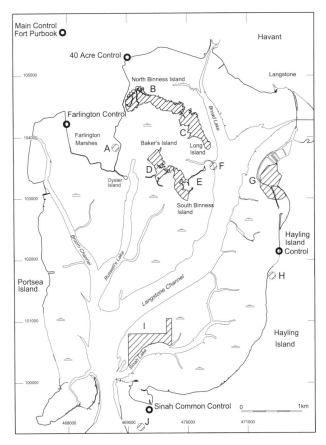

Figure 23   Location of WWII decoy sites in the harbour (after Jenkins 1986, drawn by S E James): A Farlington starfish; B North Binness Is 'Q' lighting; C Long Is 'Q' lighting; D Baker's Is 'Q' lighting & fires; E South Binness Is 'Q' lighting & fires; Round Nap Is 'Q' fires; G Old Oyster Beds 'Q' & leaky lights; Hayling Island 'Q' fires; I Sinah Sands 'Q' & leaky lights; J Sinah Common starfish

Talbot Edwards, an engineer (Magrath 1992) noted that an enemy force could cut off Portsmouth from the mainland, by entering into Langstone Harbour and capturing Ports Bridge. By 1715 a small bastion armed with canon had been established on Eastney Point. But the threat from the French, during the War of the Austrian Succession, led to the realisation that a more substantial defensive establishment was required at the entrance of the harbour. In 1746 the construction of Fort Cumberland was commenced; it was rebuilt in 1785.

In 1857, England thought itself again to be under threat of invasion by the French. The defences needed updating as a result of the advent of the rifled canon, which had a greater range and was much more accurate than the old muzzle loading guns. Amongst the records of Lord Panmure, the Secretary of State for War, is a letter from Prince Albert, dated 12 August 1857 (Douglas 1908), which states that the Queen has pointed out that there is a need 'for a work in the rear' (of Portsmouth), connecting Hilsea Lines with Fort Cumberland. In the event nothing

was done, but Lumps and Eastney Forts were strengthened, whilst along the top of Portsdown a series of brick-built forts was constructed along with the three Spithead forts (Saunders 1997).

Prison hulks

In 1785, Fort Cumberland was almost completely rebuilt using mainly convict labour who resided in the hulks moored inside Langstone Harbour. Under the *Transportation Act* of 1718, convicted felons were sent to the British colonies in America. However, in 1776, during the American War of Independence, the use of ships hulks as floating prisons was established by the British government as a temporary measure until an alternative place for transportation could be established. This was eventually to be Australia. This prison system lasted for 67 years (Smith 1994). There were three such hulks moored in Langstone Harbour: *La Fortunée* 1785–1802; the *Ceres* 1785–91; and the *Portland* 1802–16. These hulks were unhealthy places to keep prisoners, in spite of being frequently washed with vinegar in an attempt at disinfecting them. *La Fortunée* was subject to very severe criticism by the inspectors in a report of 1802 (Smith 1994). They pointed out that, in 1797 when the largest number of convicts were on board, only nine died, whereas in 1801 some 120 died.

> The present compliment of *La Fortunée* is about 300, near fifty of whom are invalids, or cripples on deck, besides eleven confined to their beds, and as many more in the hospital ward. The complaint that has been most prevalent begins with a low fever, and ends with diarrhoea or dysentery. (Smith 1994).

By 1852 all of the hulks had been destroyed and the convicts transferred to new prisons ashore, for instance at Portsea. The hulk of *La Fortunée* was destroyed by the convicts in 1802. Suitable ships timbers were sold, whilst others remained in the mud. Parts of a pump, probably from *La Fortunée*, were found quite recently (A Mack, pers comm).

The 20th century

Langstone was a centre for both construction and diversion during the two World Wars. There was one of the locations for the construction of the Mulberry Harbours (see Hughes and Momber, Chapter 3, below), the disposal of old ammunition explosive on Farlington Marshes and the use of the islands in the harbour as the sites for air raid decoys (Fig 23) with the intention of diverting the enemy planes away from Portsmouth Dockyard (see *Battle over Portsmouth*, Jenkins 1986). There is still a great deal of research to be done on the question of the military influence on the harbour, especially during the two World Wars of the 20th century.

3 The site investigations
by Michael J Allen and Julie Gardiner

The artefact distributions described above have been considered on a harbour-wide and chronological basis only, isolating specific areas or locations of concentrations of recovered and recorded finds. Several 'structural features' are discussed below as 'sites'. These include sites of palaeoecological significance, such as the find of submerged ancient trees, and locations of surveyed stone scatters (natural or otherwise). More strictly archaeological 'sites' were the wood stake structures (Sinah circle and on Oyster Island), timber structures along the harbour's edge, archaeological features and specific *in situ* find spots of pottery vessels formerly cut well into the ground, but now eroding out of the wave cut foreshores. Because of the combination of the density of artefact scatters, the presence of archaeological features and the occurrence of *in situ* vessels, each of the four main islands is also dealt with as an archaeological 'site'

Submerged ancient 'forests'
by Alan Clapham and Michael J Allen

The presence of preserved trees is considered here as they were associated with datable organic old land surfaces which are considered important in understanding the physical and vegetational development of Langstone. They are considered as 'sites' in spite of a lack of direct evidence of human activity or even of the occurrence of any artefacts except rare occur-

rences of burnt flint. Because of their importance in understanding and describing the basic nature of these sites, the full environmental reports relating to the trees in Langstone are presented in Chapter 5.

Two small areas 175m apart of poorly preserved and isolated submerged trunks and branches were identified in Langstone Harbour by Arthur Mack and were surveyed and sampled by the project team (M J Allen, D Fontana, J Gardiner, A Mack) and Alan Clapham in 1997. The location of each can be seen in Figures 10 and 19. The first, in Baker's Rithe (centred on SU 6926 1041) to the north of Baker's Island, had been first noted by Arthur Mack nearly 25 years previously, at which time there were at least eight tree stumps covering a small area of about 6 × 6m and at c –1m OD. Arthur did not see any trees at this spot again until 1995, when only one stump and a series of associated roots and a section of trunk remained (see Plate 36, chapter 5 below). He brought this to the project's attention but the site could not be recorded and sampled until August 1997 (Plate 18), at which time only the stump remained with some roots and a few vestigial remnants of fallen branches (Fig 24).

On the same survey trip a few relict stumps and fallen trunks were noted on the northern edge of Russell's Lake on peat at –0.5m OD. These had not previously been noticed by Arthur Mack, though he had passed this spot very many times by boat. This suggests erosion of soft mobile mud of up to c 0.25m depth, exposing timbers lying on the hard clay

Plate 18   The submerged 'forest' at Baker's Rithe with Baker's Island itself in the distance. Several of the tree stumps and the long, horizontal branch BC can be seen (see Fig 24). This photograph was taken on an extremely low tide in September 1997, allowing only about 45 minutes for recording and sampling. Most of the wood was removed in the storms of Christmas 1999 (Julie Gardiner)

shelf beneath. In both areas peat deposits were exposed at low tide and were sampled for wood identification, waterlogged plant remains, pollen, and snails.

Each stump and trunk was mapped using the GPS system and composite figures based on field plans and GPS data produced (Figs 24 and 25).

Baker's Rithe submerged trees (LH.68)

At Baker's Rithe an area of only 3.5 × 2m of preserved timbers survived on a peat ledge at about –1m OD in September 1997. The peat itself was between 0.15 and 0.26m deep and, where the deeper profiles survived, comprised of a thin 'surface' layer (maximum 0.06m) of dark brown to very dark brown fibrous peat over a brown fibrous peat with wood and woody root fragments. Preservation of the timbers was better and more locally concentrated than those at the edge of Russell's Lake, nevertheless the loss of both timbers and the peats over 25 years, and even between 1995 and 1997, is demonstrated. The area was archaeologically planned with datum points surveyed by the GPS.

The surviving trees only consisted of one *in situ*

oak stump (BB) (Plate 36, Chapter 5 below) 0.22m in diameter, a large fallen oak trunk or branch (BA) nearly 0.5m in diameter, and oak and yew branches (BC and BD respectively), with a few loose wood fragments (BE). Roots of another tree were recorded around oak stump BB but proved not to belong to this tree; they were yew and were probably a part of the fallen slender 0.08m to 0.2m diameter yew branch BC (Fig 24). The oak stump BB dated to 2310–1950 cal BC (R-24993/2, 3735 ± 60 BP). An isolated alder (*Alnus glutinosa*) tree trunk (trunk CA) was recorded 32m to the north-west next to a 4m wide peat-filled channel.

Following very low tides and erosion of the surface at Baker's Rithe in December 1999, Arthur Mack observed the exposure of more fossil trees covering an area of nearly 10m^2 (30ft^2). It was covered with branches and included another tree stump. Scouring of the surface had exposed and revealed the roots of stump BB and a another fallen trunk, clearly showing where it had broken in antiquity. This discovery was made as this monograph was being submitted for publication and no further survey work is reported here. The significance of this in terms of erosion and monitoring are outlined in Chapters 6 and 8 respectively.

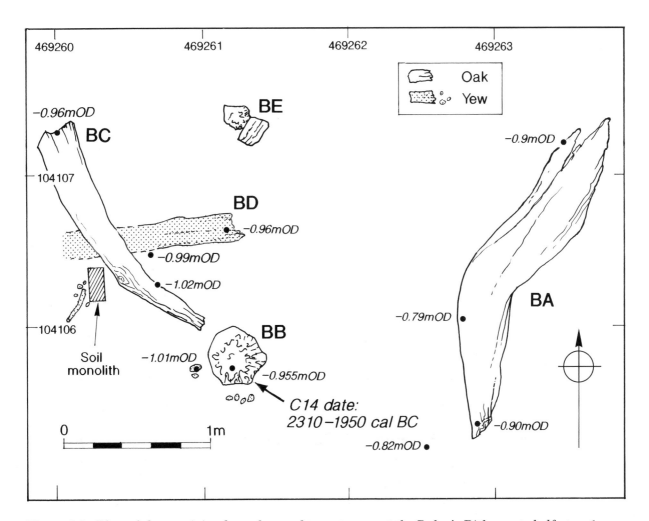

Figure 24 Plan of the surviving branches and tree stumps at the Baker's Rithe peat shelf at c –1m OD as recorded in September 1997 (from a roughly measured field sketch, drawn by S E James)

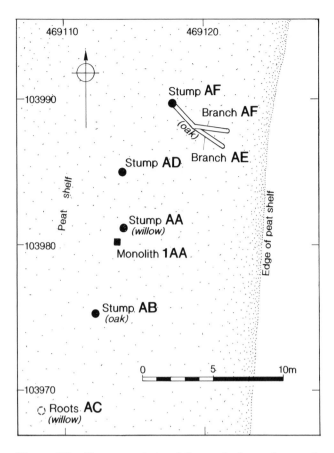

Figure 25   Survey points of the main branches and trunks on the peat shelf at c –0.5m OD north of Russell's Lake; based on GPS survey in September 1997. Data from Portsmouth University, drawn by S E James

Russell's Lake submerged trees (LH.65)

The find of three dispersed *in situ* oak and willow trunks, one group of roots (willow), and two branches (oak) on the northern edge of Russell's Lake, indicates the recent erosion of the soft clay facies above the timbers as they had never been previously seen by Arthur Mack. The relict area of preserved wood again lay on a 0.2m deep peat shelf at about –0.5m OD and were dispersed over an area of about 25 × 12m near the edge of the peat shelf. This peat shelf, although only 175m from that at Baker's Rithe, was nearly 0.5m higher, and the peats (see Fig 55, below) were very different – this does not necessarily imply, however, that they are of different date. The peat here was dark brown woody peat which was more variable in thickness than that at Baker's Rithe. It was generally about 0.2m deep, but away from the trees was up to 0.48m deep, and where the peat shelf ended at edge of Russell's Lake was only 0.12m thick. A thin humic mud slurry existed over its exposed surface, and was dissected by a number of narrow (0.3m) rivulets which cut through the peat onto the gravel and sands or clays below. The main peat stratigraphy was a homogeneous dark fibrous peat with wood fragments throughout, and with isolated lenses of sand and shells occurring both at its base and within it. Because of the wide spacing of the tree finds no archaeological planning was undertaken in this subtidal area. The locations of all samples were also recorded by GPS, together with spot locations on each stump, trunk, or root ring, and locations of samples of undisturbed sediment taken for pollen and plant macrofossil analyses. Unfortunately, due to technical problems in the field with the GPS system, none of the data from Russell's Lake can be regarded as reliable. Point locations of their relative position can be seen in Figure 25.

The branches/fallen trunk (AF and AE) were relatively slender (c 0.2m diameter), but the main trunk/branch (AF) was over 4m long and branch AE was in excess of 2.5m long. They were straight with the remnants of only a few other branches growing from them. Oak branch AE was radiocarbon dated to 3350–2910 cal BC (R-24993/1, 4431 ± 70 BP).

Trees from the sites
by Alan Clapham

A total of thirteen stumps and trunks was sampled for microscopic identification. The conditions of the sites, which were covered in marine mud and only accessible for less than an hour, and the position of the stumps and trunks, which were barely visible above the surface of the marine mud, meant that it was not possible at either site to record the exact length and diameter of each tree stump and trunk as outlined by Clapham *et al* (1997). Although the direction of fall of each stump was recorded they show no preferential orientation.

The preserved and recorded trees and identifications

Baker's Rithe

	species		
Trunk BA	*Quercus* sp	oak	
Stump BB	*Quercus* sp	oak	2310–1950 cal BC
next to BB	*Taxus baccata*	yew	
Roots at BB (burnt flint in peat)	*Taxus baccata*	yew	
Branch BC	*Quercus* sp	oak	
Branch at BC	*Taxus baccata*	yew	
Branch BD	*Taxus baccata*	yew	
Loose wood BE	*Quercus* sp	oak	
Stump CA	*Alnus glutinosa*	alder	

North of Russell's Lake

	species		
Stump AA	Salicaceae	willow	
Stump AB	*Quercus* sp	oak	
Stump AEA	*Quercus* sp	oak	
Roots AC	Salicaceae	willow	
Stump AD	not sampled		
Branch AE (part of AF)	*Quercus* sp	oak	3350–2910 cal BC
Branch AF (part of AE)	*Quercus* sp	oak	

All oak samples examined have very close rings suggesting that they survived under ecological and physiological stress (see Clapham, Chapter 5, Waterlogged plant remains for further discussion).

North Binness Island
by Neil J Adam and Michael J Allen

North Binness Island is at the northern end of Langstone Harbour, with Farlington Marshes to the west, Broad Lake to the north, Long Island to the east, and Baker's and South Binness Islands to the south, separated by a channel. Its maximum extent is some 900m east to west and 250m north to south (Fig 26). The island is flat and low-lying, being no more than +2.5m OD, and is covered with a thick matting of saltwater grasses. The only other obvious vegetation is a small coppice of trees towards the eastern end of the island. The northern coast is characterised by soft accreting muds cut by the outflows of the many rivulets which dissect the entire island. The southern coast mainly consists of firm shingle mixed with sand and very firm yellowish-brown clay. Along this southern coast the island forms a slight cliff, varying between 0.5 and 1m in height, within which archaeological materials can be clearly seen in the exposed section.

Part of the cliff section, in collection Area 1, was cleaned and recorded in some detail. An unripened gley soil (Jarvis *et al* 1984), typically formed under saltmarsh vegetation in marine alluvium, was apparent – these lithomorphic soils are now termed saline alluvial gley soils (Avery 1990). Seven distinct archaeological layers or contexts were identified (Fig 27, Plate 19), however, these should not be confused with pedogenic horizons since some of the archaeo-

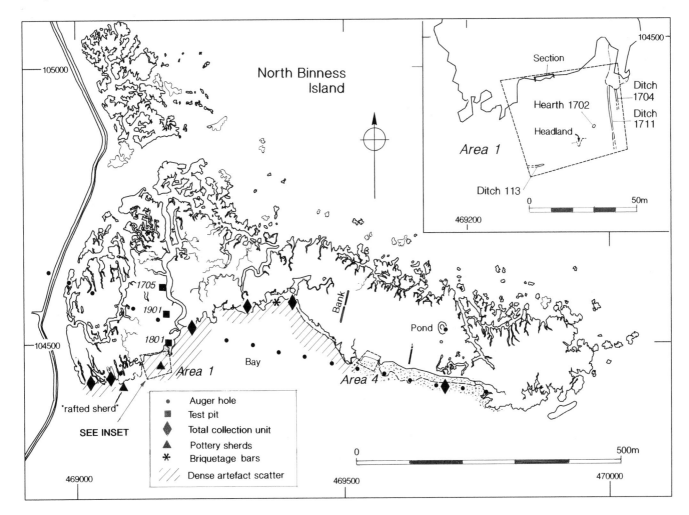

Figure 26 North Binness Island showing the study areas and major find spots (outline based on data from Portsmouth University, with additions). Insert shows the ditches and hearth in Area 1. Drawn by S E James

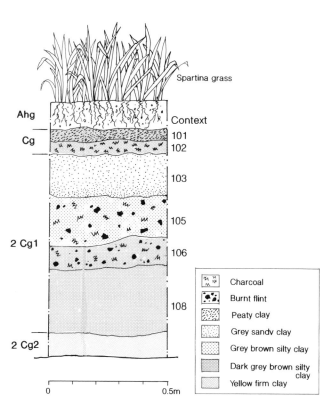

Figure 27   Representative soil profile exposed in
the 'cliff' section showing the archaeological
stratigraphy. Drawn by S E James

Plate 19   Recording the stratigraphy exposed in the
cliff section on North Binness. The saline alluvial
gley soil (Avery 1990) shows distinct horizonation
and bands of archaeological material, see Figure 27
(Neil J Adam)

logical layers are lenses of burnt flint or charcoal
within a pedogenic horizon (the difficulties of describing the sediments are outlined above).

The thin (0.1m), dark brown peaty topsoil with
saltmarsh vegetation is the Ahg horizon over a dark
greyish-brown peaty/humose silty clay (layer 101)
and a 0.06m thin layer of greyish-brown silty clay
with occasional lenses of charcoal flecks (layer 102)
comprising the Cg horizon. Two layers with archaeological material are both part of the 2Cg1 horizon
and are separated from the charcoal above by an archaeologically sterile and stone-free deposit of grey
sandy clay (layer 103). The archaeologically significant layers were a greyish-brown silty clay (layer
105) and a dark greyish-brown silty clay 0.2m thick
(layer 106) both of which contained burnt flint, charcoal, and some fired clay. A lower dark grey silty clay
layer (layer 108) which was not recorded to have contained any archaeological artefacts although some
charcoal was recovered, was up to 0.35m thick and
was distinguished from that above by its stonefree
nature and moderate blocky structure. It lay over the

firm mid yellowish-brown clay 2Cg2 horizon. This
forms the main foreshore and, when very wet,
becomes grey in colour.

A layer some 0.15m thick of burnt flint and fired
clay was observed in the profile exposed in the cliff
section (Fig 27) facing the ditches (see below) within
Area 1, including a concentration which may indicate a hearth. Similar intermittent lenses were
recorded along much of the 'bay' on this south coast
between Areas 1 and 4. Another layer of material,
possibly a part of the same horizon, about 0.05m
thick was noted in the 0.4m high cliff exposure
400m further east of the first concentration in Area
1. The basic sequence and presence of archaeological deposits could be followed along the cliff face.
The density and composition of archaeological finds
varied but not sufficiently for specific 'sites' to be
identified. Pottery from this area included coarse
flint-gritted sherds of probably Bronze Age date and
some Romano-British coarsewares, of special note
was at least one piece of kiln bar on the foreshore
(NB.91).

A line of three test-pits, aligned approximately
south to north, were dug across the island from the
northern edge of Area 1 (Fig 26) in an attempt to
recover further finds and to relate the archaeological
features recorded on the foreshore with uneroded
stratigraphy within the island. Each test-pit was 1.5
× 1.5m, they were located between 20 and 25m apart,
and were excavated and reinstated by hand under

the terms of Notice and Consent documents prepared by the RSPB and approved by English Nature (ref no 27).

The southern and northern test-pits produced identical saline alluvial gley soil profiles comprising a dark grey humose/peaty Ahg horizon over grey clay 2Cg1 subsoil over the firm yellowish-brown natural clay (2Cg2). This profile mirrored both the stratigraphy exposed on the coast and that seen on all of the islands. The central test-pit, about 50m north of the cliff section, did not reveal this typical profile. Beneath the saline alluvial gley soil was a mixed deposit of grey and yellowish clays indicating disturbed ground up to at least 0.56m, but was not bottomed before the test-pit became flooded with sea water. As the total area excavated was very small, relatively few artefacts were recovered from any of the test-pits, except for a lens 0.2m thick within the disturbed layer of the central test-pit which contained charcoal (not sampled), burnt flint, flint flakes, and pottery sherds. Included among the pottery were fragments of a 4th-century Roman vessel, along with body sherds of Romano-British greyware and fragments of flint-gritted, probably Bronze Age, pottery. These finds are significant in that they indicate the preservation of surviving archaeological horizons and deposits within the island. The small size of the test-pit did not allow either the bottoming of the profile, nor the establishment of the shape of the feature, if that is what this excavation had indeed encountered.

This sequence (test-pits and cliff-edge) appears to show at least one and possibly two 'phases' of human activity on North Binness Island. The burnt flint and charcoal deposits (contexts 105 and 106 especially, but also 108) are clear evidence for human activity, although no structural features were noted in the section. The charcoal deposits from layers 101 and 102 may suggest some degree of reoccupation (speculatively Romano-British), and the absence of burnt flint may suggest that this later phase was less intensive and more spasmodic than the first, or of a different nature (see Chapter 4). The peaty topsoil was free of archaeological material, reflecting the fact that North Binness has effectively not been occupied or intensively used in the recent past (and certainly not within living or recorded memory). Unfortunately, the absence of any physical stratigraphic link between this sequence and the intertidal features (see below) means that the latter cannot be directly related to either of these two horizons, although it seems likely that the features probably relate to the earlier phase.

A small 'knoll' of topsoil and subsoil measuring roughly 2 × 2m was found c 5m to the south-west and seaward of the hearth 1702, and some 40m south of the current shoreline. This was interpreted as the remains of a headland dating from an earlier phase of coast which had since been eroded by tidal action, leaving the knoll stranded in the intertidal zone. This demonstrated that all the archaeological features found on the foreshore reported below (the hearth and the ditches) were once a part of land, the remnant of which is the current North Binness Island. The features recorded by the survey are those places where these original 'dry-land' features disturbed the underlying clay below the island's soil horizon. Now that the soils have eroded, only these disturbances in the clay survive.

Features on the intertidal foreshore (+0.5m OD): NB63a

A group of four archaeological features – three ditches and a possible hearth – was clearly visible on the intertidal muds to the south of North Binness Island, c 300m from its western end (Figs 26 and 28), with a particular concentration of artefacts noted in the cliff face nearby. These were identified in the initial walkover survey in 1993 and the area designated Area 1 for more detailed survey, gridded artefact collection, and excavation in subsequent seasons. A small 'headland' on the cliff section from which two of the ditches appeared to emerge had collapsed before excavation took place and it was impossible to discern their stratigraphic relationships. Test-pitting (see above) failed to record them 'inland'. It is doubtful that either feature would have been identified if tidal action had not exposed them in the intertidal zone. Although no direct stratigraphic relationship could be demonstrated between any of these features, their occurrence together in a small area seems unlikely to be coincidental given the paucity of other archaeological cut-features recorded in the survey. The features were assigned three-figure context numbers in 1993, the excavated cuts of two of the ditches were later given four-figure numbers used throughout the survey for detailed recording.

Three of the four features were narrow ditches, filled at their exposed surface with dark brown humic silts. Two (1704 and 1711) were aligned north–south, virtually parallel and about 5m apart. Sherds of Bronze Age pottery, some Romano-British pottery, burnt flint, and fragments of animal bone were recovered from the then current surface of both ditches. They occurred in close proximity to a shallow pit or hearth (1702) from the surface of which was recovered a quantity of burnt flint, animal bone, a bone point, and 18 sherds of pottery. These included a very large and unusual flint-gritted sherd which conjoined with an equally huge piece recovered about 100m away to the west. On the uncleaned intertidal surface, ditch 1704 measured approximately 0.5m wide and petered out down the foreshore after only c 7m, while ditch 1711 was 0.75m wide and was recorded for some 28m before disappearing in the lower intertidal shore. Ditch 1704 was narrower and less well defined than ditch 1711, and unlike ditch 1711 it did not contain a distinct reddish-brown infill, nor a scatter of archaeological artefacts on its surface. The third ditch (113) was 0.5m wide and about 35m offshore. It was aligned east–west, ran parallel to the

Plate 20   Ditch 1711 on the foreshore of North Binness Island as first discovered, looking south out into the harbour. Note the spread of artefacts and animal bone on the surface (Elaine A Wakefield)

coast for a recorded distance of *c* 5m, and produced flint-gritted Bronze Age pottery from its surface (see Table 15, below).

Ditch 1711 (also recorded as 111 in archive)
see Plate 20

The ditch was recognised in the intertidal clays as a distinct reddish-brown infill scattered with animal bone and few pottery sherds. The ditch was exposed for over 28m and a 3m section of ditch 1711 was fully excavated (Plate 21). This section was established *c* 2m from the headland from which the feature emerged and its surface was at 1.03m OD at the north of this section, but only 0.41m OD at the south. Excavation revealed a narrow, flat bottomed ditch 1.2m wide at the surviving surface, 0.15–0.25m at the bottom, and 0.75m deep. The eastern edge was slightly shallower in slope than the western. It contained five distinct layers (1712 and 1714–7, Fig 28) of mainly grey and yellowish- or reddish-brown sandy clays with varying inclusions of subangular

flint and chalk. The main fill (1715) was a light–mid grey, anaerobic, slightly silty clay, 0.47m thick, containing subangular flint pebbles, a quantity of burnt flint and three struck flakes. The upper fills contained animal bone fragments (cow) and charcoal flecks. Two subcircular 'features' which intruded on the eastern edge of the ditch may be evidence of side collapse.

The north-facing section of the ditch was monolith sampled for pollen adjacent to a column of eight contiguous small bulk samples for snails (Fig 28).

Hearth 1702 (also recorded as 112 in archive) see Plate 22, Figure 28

A discrete feature (1702) about 10m to the west of ditch 1711 was identified in 1993. The large number of finds from the surface of this feature suggested that it was a pit or hearth and it was excavated in 1994. It was ovoid, *c* 1m long and 0.75m wide, and was situated on the wave cut foreshore at 0.69m OD. It proved to be only 0.05m deep with steep sides and a

Plate 21 Ditch 1711 on the foreshore of North Binness Island after excavation (Neil J Adam)

Plate 22 Hearth 1702 on the foreshore of North Binness Island, as first seen. Note the spread of pottery, animal bone, worked and burnt flint on the surface (Elaine A Wakefield)

flat base and was filled with dark brown silty loam. However, this shallow depth contained large sherds of at least two flint-gritted vessels, including fragments of the large pot found in 1993, fragments of animal bone (mainly cow), some worked and over 2 kg of burnt flint. This appears to be the severely eroded base of a hearth. Charcoal from this features gave a date of 1410–1060 cal BC (OxA-7366, 2995 ± 55 BP), see Chapter 5.

Features on the island

Two further features were noted within the island's interior. A linear upstanding 'earthwork' some 100m long and aligned north–south was identified from aerial photographs *c* 30m west of the trees and was visited by the field team. No clear function or date could be established, but it was probably a field boundary of some description and is thought to be of post-Roman date and possibly related to the major reclamation and creation of Farlington Marshes in 1771 (see Chapter 2, Historical survey). A shallow, oval pond 50m east of the trees was augered and was shown to be filled with soft dark-grey mud. It appears on air photographs of 19 April 1929.

Artefact scatters

Artefact scatters occurred along the southern foreshore (NB.14, NB.35), particularly in the western part of the island. Two areas were examined by means of individual 2 × 2m total collection units (see detailed archaeological investigations, Chapter 1, above for details) and the principal concentration of prehistoric material was that in which Area 1 was placed. The total collection area (50 × 40m) was established over the features described above and 500 individual collection squares were examined. Large amounts of both struck and burnt flint were recovered together with Bronze Age pottery. Artefacts were not recovered from every square; some of those lower down the foreshore being obscured with seaweed etc (see Gardiner above and Fig 16). Less dense scatters of burnt flint, worked flint and pottery sherds occurred about 150–200m to the west of Area 1, and all along the southern coast for about 80m as far as Area 4. The density of scatters varies; the denser scatters occurring around the low cliffs and eroding headlands. One such scatter, about 100m to the east of Area 1 on a small eroding headland in

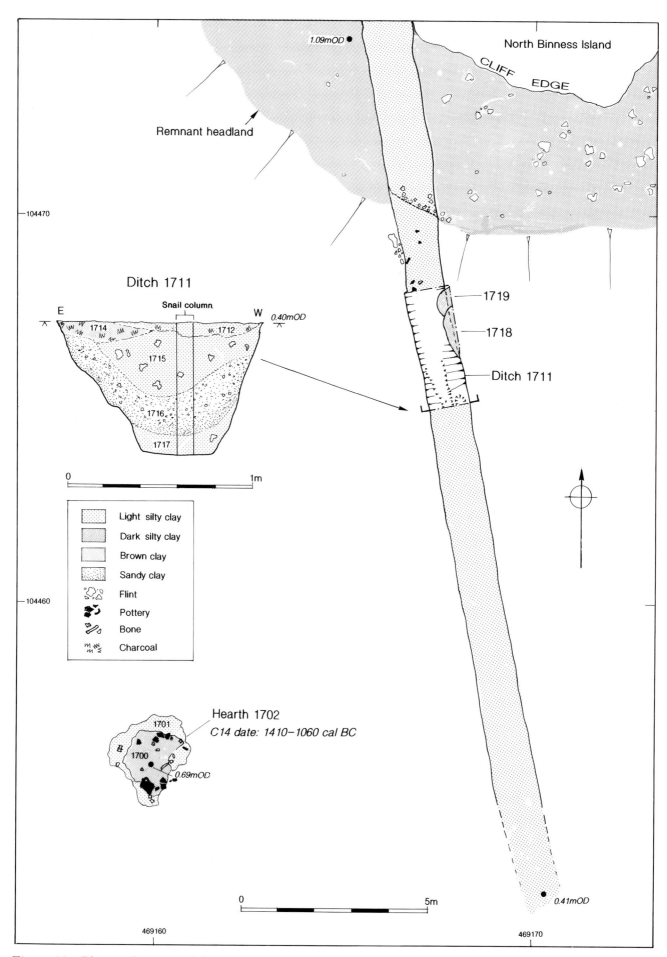

Figure 28 *Plan and section of ditch 1711 and plan of hearth 1702 on North Binness Island, Area 1. Drawn by S E James*

which was a large (*c* 1.8 × 4.3m) oval patch of grey clay, produced worked and burnt flint as well as fragmentary animal bone. This was probably not a discrete archaeological feature, but a relict patch and remains of an eroded headland.

One rich area, approximately in the centre of the southern coastline, was designated Area 4 and an area of 30 × 50m subject to a gridded total collection. In Area 4 large quantities of post-medieval ceramic building material, including bricks, peg tiles, and modern glass may suggest the former presence of a small building. The majority of this material lay within 15–20m of the low mud cliffs where burnt flint, worked flint, and pottery were all noted within the clay subsoil (see Gardiner, above, and Fig 17).

Subsequent to the fieldwork conducted within this project, Arthur Mack reported the recovery of fired kiln bars and Romano-British pottery (possibly including samian), from the cliff in North Binness bay, between Areas 1 and 4 (NB.91). The kiln bars, which were poorly fired, vegetable tempered, and probably made of local clay, may have been in a shallow feature. Briquetage kiln bars indicating saltworking were recovered previously from this approximate location by Prof Barry Cunliffe (pers comm).

Long Island

Long Island is situated to the south-east of North Binness Island with a gap of less than 20m between them. It is aligned north-west to south-east and measures *c* 750m by 250m north to south at its widest point (Fig 29). It is identical in topography, pedology, and plant cover to North Binness Island, but with no trees. The north-eastern and south-western coasts mirror the characteristics of the northern and southern coasts of North Binness, while a number of rivulets dissect the island. A bar of shingle, now covered with saltwater grasses, runs along the north-eastern coast.

The southern coast of Long Island is a low cliff similar to the that of North Binness with localised layers of burnt flint and pottery in a 2Cg2 horizon of unripened or saline alluvial gley soil. On the western shore in the southern part of the island, one headland (in Area 18) showed prime evidence of erosion and the Ahg and Cg had been truncated leaving the 2Cg1 horizon containing artefacts exposed in plan to natural agencies of tide and weather. Seaward of the headland, all the top sediment has eroded away leaving hard clay and chalk out to the channel between Long Island and the north side of South Binness Island.

Features on the intertidal foreshore

Four archaeological features were identified on Long Island during the survey, all of which were on the south-western coast of the island (Fig 29). These included three individual middle–late Bronze Age vessels buried in what is now the foreshore of Long Island, and a circular feature filled with fragments of burnt flint and presumed to be a hearth.

In 1993, during the rapid walkover survey, an apparently complete middle–late Bronze Age pot (350) was spotted only 0.5m from the cliff, its 'rim' level with the surrounding shingle at +0.69m OD just off the most north-easterly headland of the island close to the present 'cliffline' (Area 19). The area around the pot was cleaned and it became evident that the 'top' of the pot had been removed by wave action (it was not possible at this stage to determine which way up it was) (Plate 23). The pot, which in the field appeared to be of prehistoric date and was expected to contain cremated human bone, had presumably been set into a small pit but no trace of a cut could be seen. It was stuck fast in the tenacious clay (Plate 24). Its contents, principally large fragments of burnt flint, were removed and a sample retained for palaeoenvironmental analysis but the pot itself could only be removed by breaking it into pieces and bagging it in sequence so that several conjoining sherds were kept together in each bag for later reassembly. It proved to have been standing upright and to be of later Bronze Age date, flint-gritted with a finger-impressed cordon. No bone was present. Quantities of worked flint were recorded in this part of the foreshore (LI.15) and the area immediately around the position of pot 350 was chosen for further detailed survey and designated Area 3 (details of the specific distributions across this area are presented above – Gardiner, Artefact collections distribution and analysis).

In 1997 Arthur Mack spotted two further pots (360 and 380) as 'rings' of pottery exposed on the foreshore off Long Island and in imminent danger of being lost. One was less than 80m from vessel 350 in a similar location, on an eroded headland high up on the foreshore and less than 10m from the island cliff. A large pottery ring *c* 0.35m diameter (vessel 380) was recorded and carefully excavated. Despite being high up on the foreshore (+1.15m OD), upon excavation the vessel was found to survive to no more than 30mm high, the remainder having already been lost to the sea. The remains of the vessel were lifted intact but flotation of the contained soil proved it to be devoid of burnt flint, charcoal, and any bone.

The third vessel (vessel 360) was some 225m south-south-east of pot 350 and was well out on the foreshore (+0.43m OD), about 60m from the island (Fig 29). This vessel was removed as a single intact block. It was extremely soft and fragile and was removed and allowed to partly dry out in order to harden the pottery before detailed recording and careful excavation of its interior. Like vessels 350 and 380, no cut could be discerned for the feature in which the vessel was placed. The vessel was a flat-bottomed, straight sided jar 280mm in diameter and survived to a height of 180mm. Although, when found, it appeared to be upright, it was subsequently shown to have been inverted and no elements of its base survived. Careful excavation in three 50mm

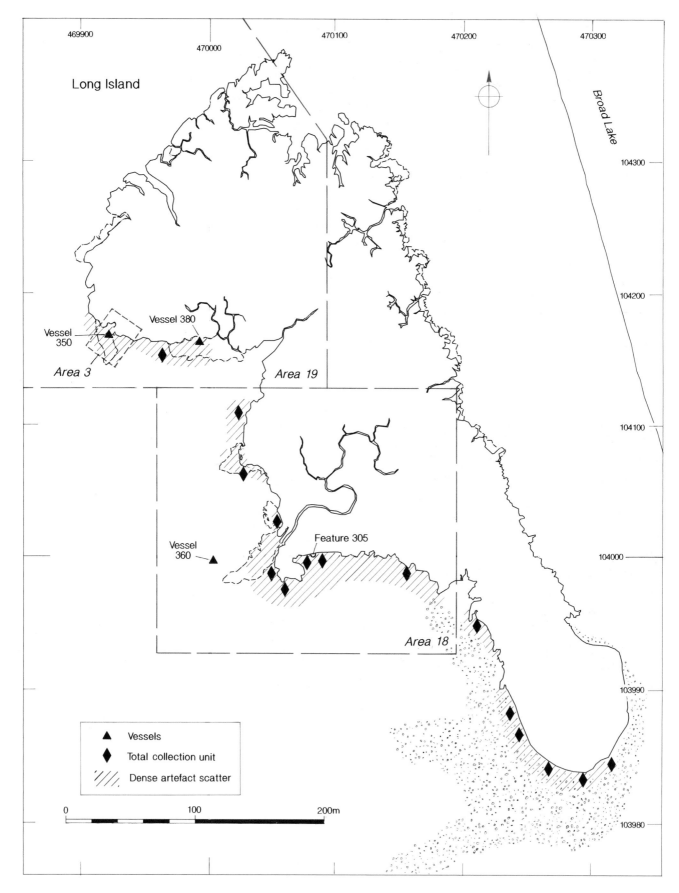

Figure 29   Plan of Long Island, showing the study areas and major find spots (outline based on data from Portsmouth University, with additions, drawn by S E James)

Plate 23   Pot 350 as found, showing as a ring of pottery in the shingle on Long Island (Elaine A Wakefield)

Plate 24   Excavation of pot 350 on Long Island. The overlying shingle has been removed to expose the surface of the yellow clay beneath. Note that there is no indication of a cut feature (Elaine A Wakefield)

spits and floating of the soil showed it to be completed devoid of any stones (except on the present-day surface) and charcoal. Cremated human bone was present; the majority of this was recovered in the third (ie lower) spit in a tight cluster (100 × 50mm) against one edge, suggesting that either it was in a leather or textile bag on the base of the vessel or that the lightweight cremated bone in the 'upper' part of the vessel had floated away (J McKinley pers comm).

Further round the coastline and approximately 300m south-east of vessel 350, on the south-facing coast of the wide bay forming the lower half of Long Island, a subcircular feature (305) was encountered in an area producing dense scatters of worked and burnt flint (Plate 25). The feature was *c* 2m in

diameter and showed as an area of mid-grey silty clay against the surrounding bluish-grey clay with approximately 80% of its surface composed of burnt flint fragments. It is considered to have been a hearth.

Artefact scatters

The north-east coast (Area 18) was similar to the north coast of North Binness Island comprising an irregular shoreline with frequent water channels running seawards through thick accumulations of soft silt and mud. No archaeological artefacts or

Plate 25 Excavation of small, dense scatters of worked and burnt flint, hearth 305 on Long Island, possibly of Bronze Age date (Elaine A Wakefield)

features could be seen although they may exist buried beneath the soft unconsolidated silts.

The south-western shore, in contrast, was prolific in artefact scatters all the way down to its south-western tip (LI.28). A general scatter of worked and burnt flint extended along nearly 400m of the shore-line, being densest on the eroding headland around 200m east-south-east of Area 3. In an attempt to identify areas of greatest concentration, or most significant assemblages along the shoreline, a series of individual 2 × 2m total collection units was established at roughly 50m intervals along the shoreline (collection units 379–399, Figs 18 and 29). The flint assemblages were largely recovered from the eroding soil profile and comprised relatively large quantities of flint (nearly 700 pieces) from the 21 small collection units. The assemblages included Mesolithic flakes and diagnostic late Neolithic–early Bronze Age tools including a laurel leaf and arrowheads, and a number of scrapers. Large quantities of burnt flint were recovered, but very few sherds of pottery.

One of the most significant artefact scatters (LI.15) identified in this manner was again sampled as a large (50 × 40m) single collection area (Area 3) which straddled the eroding headland where vessel 350 was located. It comprised 500 individual 2 × 2m total collection squares in an area (Figs 29 and 18) – the details of the specific distributions are given above (Gardiner, Artefact collections, distribution and analysis). Apart from the vessel, no further features were observed, but concentrations of both worked and burnt flint were present, mostly around the base of the low cliffs of the headland where material was being actively eroded out of the yellow clay subsoil. Many of the squares and grids searched contained no artefacts because of the maritime grass cover across the headland and patches of dense seaweed and algae in the intertidal zone. The flint assemblage is a mixture of late Mesolithic plus late Neolithic–earlier Bronze Age and heavier material probably of late Bronze Age date (see Gardiner, above).

Surface material included later Bronze Age flint-gritted wares with a few Romano-British coarse- and fineware sherds. A large quantity (97 sherds) of Bronze Age pottery (371g – excluding the vessels) was recovered and only 5g of Romano-British pottery. Much of the prehistoric pottery was of a similar fabric to vessel 350 which was recovered from this collection area. Nearly 17kg of burnt flint was also recovered.

Despite two seasons of field survey and examination of aerial photographs, no features were identified on Long Island itself, nor were any artefacts recovered from either its vegetated surface or the muddy rivulets.

Baker's Island

Baker's Island lies to the south of North Binness and Long Islands, from which it is not directly accessible on foot, and some 450m off the eastern coast of Farlington Marshes. It lies just to the north-west of South Binness Island, from which it is separated by a 50m wide channel filled with accreting mud which can be crossed with care at low tide. The island is aligned north-west to south-east, measuring 400m in length and 300m in width (Fig 30). Its northern, southern, and eastern foreshores are heavily dissected and covered with soft accreting muds, within which are many small patches of firmer clays, while the western coast consists of a firm shingle and sand beach some 50m wide giving way to an intertidal zone of very firm yellowish-brown clay with patches of sand. The southern peninsular is dominated by two shingle bars, between which lie firm yellowish-

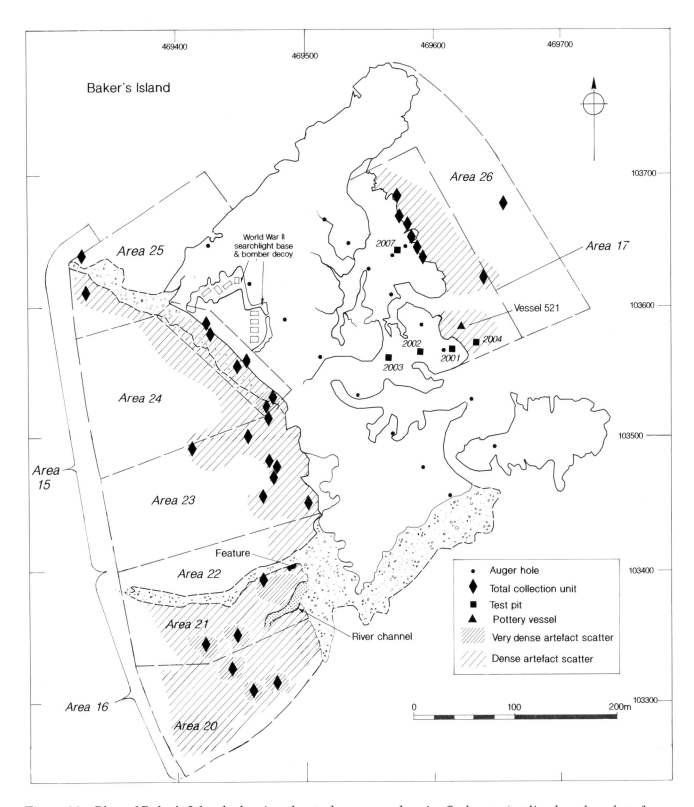

Figure 30   Plan of Baker's Island, showing the study areas and major find spots (outline based on data from Portsmouth University, with additions, drawn by S E James)

brown clays and intertidal muds. The island interior has been cut by a number of rivulet channels of varying sizes, while the land itself rises towards the south-western and north-eastern edges with a low, but locally conspicuous, promontory at the north-western point (+2m or more OD). The rivulet channels vary from 0.20 to 1.5m in width and from 0.20 to

at least 1.2m in depth. There are no cliffs as there are on the northern islands; much lower bluffs do however exist, marking the limit of the high water. Like the other islands, its interior is covered with the usual carpet of saltwater grasses, succulent plants, and sea heather which form a spongy skin over the saturated peaty clay topsoil. The soil profile was typical of the other islands; a humic soil over silty clay with a stiff yellowish clay which formed the fore-shore, and which was locally covered with expanses of gravel.

An auger transect consisting of eight auger holes was conducted north-east to south-west along the shoreline (Tr 23) and revealed a peaty topsoil (Ahg) over a mixed peaty and clay subsoil (Cg) sealing a grey clay (2 Cg1) over a firm yellowish brown clay (2 Cg2)sometimes containing a fine chalk rubble. In places the 2 Cg1 horizon also contained a lighter yel-lowish brown clay akin to the subdivision of this horizon on North Binness (Fig 27). This is a slight variation on the soil profile already described for North Binness and Long Islands

Features and possible features on the intertidal foreshore

No major prehistoric features such as the ditches on North Binness Island were found. Nevertheless, a series of more ephemeral and largely eroded features and evidence of post-medieval activity were re-corded.

A small cluster of features was recorded on the southern peninsular of the island between the elbow of two shingle bars. These included a large amor-phous feature (c 8 × 1m) on the surface of which was a concentration of burnt flint at the southern elbow of the two shingle bars about 10m from the shore (Fig 30, Area 16). It was partly obscured by the northern shingle bar. Apart from burnt flint, no other arte-facts were recovered from the surface of its fill, and although unexcavated, it is considered than it might relate to a spread of Bronze Age pottery only 10m to the south-east.

A ridge of slightly raised dark clay, probably eroding more slowly than the surrounding foreshore deposits and about 5m wide, ran from close to the shoreline into the mudflats for some 60m (Fig 30, Area 16). It was noted to the south of a prominent shingle bar, with an S-shaped plan running in a me-andering south-west to north-east course with a marked turn. Two total collection units were estab-lished along its length (2028, 2029) and its surface produced worked and burnt flint, Bronze Age pottery, and fragmentary animal bone. A concentra-tion of burnt flint and potsherds with some animal bone occurred at around its mid point. Cleaning of the surface showed the 'feature' to be of irregular width (0.5–4.0m) and shape, it was 4m wide where it met the coast and narrowed gradually, but irregu-larly, to a pointed terminal about 50m out in the mudflats. From its irregular shape and alignment it was concluded that this was probably an infilled former rivulet or 'leak' which used to run across Baker's Island when it extended further seawards. Two 0.1m diameter timber roundwood stakes were recorded just beyond its south-western end but their location may be fortuitous and unconnected with the feature.

Off the north-eastern coast the badly degraded remains of the lower part of a pottery vessel (pot 521) were discovered in 1994, adjacent to the cliffline in an area where patches of firm yellowish-brown clay survived and worked and burnt flint was abundant. As only a very short time was available for work on Baker's Island in this season, and the pot was leather-hard and very fragile, it was removed in a block and allowed to dry out. Unfortunately the pot itself disintegrated but the contents included a small fragment of human bone, charcoal, and burnt flint fragments. As with the pot on Long Island it was assumed that this vessel had been placed in a small pit and so, in 1995, an area 5 × 5m around the findspot was carefully cleaned in the hope of finding any further features and of examining the context and stratigraphy in which the pot had been placed or cut. Unfortunately, during the intervening winter, erosion of this area had occurred and the headland had retreated between 2 and 3m so that any deposits associated with the potbase had been removed from the area around the find spot.

A line of small circular features (possibly post-holes), each about 0.3m diameter, was seen in the western coast (in the eastern part of Area 15). Re-examination of these features in 1997 showed that one still contained a rotted squared wood post, one with a metal bolt, and therefore can be considered to be modern. These may relate to a former landing structure, but more probably to the wartime features on the island itself (see below).

Almost in the centre of the western shoreline a dark red/black patch was noted on the shingle beach c 1.0 × 0.75m in size which was covered with burnt flint fragments (2040) reminiscent of a hearth. No obvious cut feature was revealed by excavation and several other such dark patches were noted on the foreshore of Baker's Island. These may be no more than differentially surviving patches of clay but close inspection of several revealed the presence of burnt flint and they may represent the vestigial remains of hearths.

Structures on the island

Evidence for human activity in the north-western corner of the island was clearly visible. This con-sisted of two main areas, the first of which was a series of five brick-built shelters (BI.103), each around 1.5m in width and 5m long. The walls of these structures included a regular pattern of gaps in the brickwork. Each building was covered with a flat re-inforced concrete roof around 0.30m thick. The origin and function of these buildings is not known for certain, although they are believed to have been used as night bomber decoys during World War II, to lure air attacks away from Portsmouth. The effectiveness of these decoys is reinforced by the presence of the large bomb crater on North Binness Island.

The partially upstanding remains of a flint-walled building were also found on the north-western point of the island. Two 1m long fragments of the north-western and south-eastern walls survive to a height of around 1.6m, while the foundation courses of the rest of the building can still be seen clearly at ground level. From these observations it was possible to estimate the original size of the building at around 8 × 3m. The building's origins are unknown although it is marked on a 19th-century map of the island and labelled as 'old walls'.

The building appears to be situated at the south-western end of an elongated enclosure delimited by a 1.2m high bank and ditch earthwork. This area measures *c* 55 × 15m and itself contains a series of smaller banks and ditches forming three further rectilinear enclosures. These smaller enclosures appear to become progressively larger towards the north-eastern end of the main enclosure with that at the south-western end measuring 10 × 8m, the central one 20 × 10m, and that at the north-eastern end 22 × 12m. Some sherds of Romano-British pottery, two sherds of possibly Saxon pottery and some fragments of burnt flint were noted within the make-up of the outer bank during investigations of a gap in its north-eastern corner. This pot and flint was assumed to be redeposited material which was disturbed by the construction of the bank and was not thought to date the earthwork itself. The enclosures were interpreted in the field as either being oyster beds or salterns. With no firm dating evidence available both the enclosures and the flint-walled building were assumed to be post-medieval in origin.

Artefact scatters

Baker's Island is prolific in flint artefacts and pottery except on the northern shore, which faces onto Russell's Lake, and in the softer mudflat area in the heavily eroded 'bay' on the eastern side. A general survey along the western coast (Area 15 and 16; BI.17) and the eastern coast (Area 17; BI.16) enabled the characterisation of these scatters which were investigated in more detail in the following season.

Baker's Island was found to be rich in prehistoric material along its western coast. The majority of this exists in the form of large spreads of material over the intertidal zone, while only a small proportion, far smaller than on North Binness and Long Island, was noted sealed within the island cliffs. Along this western shore (Area 15; BI.17) typical mudflats lead onto sand and a low 'cliff' on the islands edge. A walkover search was conducted over up to 150m of the intertidal foreshore into the harbour. Several major scatters of worked flint were noted which consisted of a mixture of Mesolithic and late Neolithic–early Bronze Age flintwork. The Mesolithic material is probably late Mesolithic (?6th millennium BC) and includes blade cores. The late Neolithic–early Bronze Age material includes a possible miniature axe. Some Bronze Age pottery was recovered and a few sherds of Romano-British wares, mostly coarseware.

The southern peninsular of the island was formed by two shingle bars between which the intertidal muds contained a general spread of worked and burnt flint (Area 16; BI.17) ending abruptly about 200m from the shore. A small assemblage of Mesolithic and late Neolithic–early Bronze Age flints was recovered and a few large sherds of coarse-flint tempered, Bronze Age pottery. Several discrete flint scatters were investigated in detail along this western shore. One concentration of worked and burnt flint on the edge of the nearby shingle bar was investigated in more detail by cleaning a 7.5 × 7.5m area and then excavating a 2 × 2m square (TP 2006) to examine the relationship between the artefact scatter and sediments in this area and any possible feature it might represent. In addition to a number of worked flints and almost 2kg of burnt flint, a quantity of flint-gritted pottery, and over 170 small (largely unidentifiable) fragments of animal bone were recorded.

The northern shoreline was largely soft intertidal muds and no archaeological material could be seen, or accessed, along this margin so a detailed walkover survey was not conducted along this stretch of the island. Only around the gravel spit on the western end of this coastline (Area 17 = 25; BI.16) were small clusters of flint recovered. In contrast, on the eastern side the coastline is similar to the western-side coast, with some eroding cliffs and recently isolated headlands forming small 'islands' a few metres off the coast. The intertidal mudflat, however, differs from the western coast; immediately beyond the cliffs and eroding headland soft and deep mud exist deposited just off the coastline. Unlike comparable areas of North Binness and Long Island (northern coasts), some archaeological material was recovered from the several small eroding headlands. These included a general scatter of worked flints along a 100m stretch with spreads almost 20m into the intertidal zone. Small patches of firmer yellowish-brown clay existed as small 'islands' in the soft intertidal mud about 40m from the coastline; these contained large concentrations of burnt flint, worked flints, including waste flakes, and some Bronze Age pottery.

Most of the flint assemblages from this area consisted of waste flakes although some scrapers, cores, boring tools, and a fragment of a leaf shaped arrowhead were found. The Mesolithic flintwork included two serrated blades. A series of targeted collection squares examined several of these scatters in more detail (Fig 30).

The extent of archaeological deposits and artefact scatters: test-pit excavation and augering (Tr24)

It was apparent that the artefact scatters were eroding from the cliffs and that they thus continue into the interior of the island where they were blanketed within the soil profile and masked by the present vegetation. A test-pit (TP 2007) was excavated (1.5 × 1.5m) about 20m from the coastline in the interior and about 20m from scatter 2053 in an attempt to examine the extent of this scatter. The test-pit exposed the typical saline gleyed soil despite excavation to comparable levels to those exposed on the foreshore, no archaeological artefacts were recovered. It can be concluded that this particular scatter did not extend this far inland (20m), but may also indicate that these scatters are spatially discrete and are not a large and ubiquitously spread across the island. Their apparent distributions along the foreshore are therefore largely a real reflection of the former scatters, rather than being wholly a product of differential erosion. A line of three auger holes parallel to the eastern coast (Tr24) confirmed the evidence observed in the cliff face, but did not succeed in defining the edge of the artefact scatters.

A transect of four test-pits (TP 2001 to 2004) was excavated at 20m intervals approximately northeast to south-west across the saltmarsh on the northeastern edge of the island and extending into the intertidal zone from the areas adjacent to the find of the pot base 521, Area 17 (Fig 30). The transect attempted to trace inland the archaeological horizons associated with the pot base on the foreshore. The test-pit on the intertidal zone revealed patches of the deposits which could be equated to those from which pot base 521 was recovered (Fig 30). The conditions (extremely soft and sticky deposits) did not enable the recognition of comparable deposits in the two closest test-pits on the island. The furthest test-pit, nearly 80m from the findspot, revealed the typical saline gleyed alluvial soil profile, however the presence of interleaving layers of yellowish-brown clay above the natural base may indicate the extent of the archaeological deposit. No artefacts were recovered except a single burnt flint fragment from the topsoil, and this represented the total artefact recovery from this exercise.

South Binness Island

South Binness is the southernmost of the four main islands in the northern part of the harbour, lying to the south of Long Island and west of Baker's Island. It is a long, narrow, irregular island, approximately 600m north–south. A 400m long narrow shingle bar to the east gives the island a maximum width of 240m east to west. This bar, called the Wadeway (SB.128), and not be confused with the Wadeway from Langstone village to Hayling Island, although covered by the high tide, provides a 'causeway' at low tide to a small promontory known as Round Nap Island, only the top of which (+2m OD) lies above HWMT. This is separated from the south-eastern tip of Long Island by some 250m of mudflats and channel though it is possible, with care, to cross between the islands on a low tide. An embayment to the south of the Wadeway ends in a low headland known as Deadman's Head (+1.5m OD). The southern shores of South Binness (SB.18) consist of firm shingle beaches up to 50m wide with patches of

eroding clay on the landward side, with mudflats on the northern sides (Fig 31). As on Baker's Island there are no coastal cliffs though the land rises gently to about +2m OD at the south-western shoreline with the shingle beach sloping relatively steeply. Many small creeks drain into the northern embayment.

Exposures in the sides of rivulets on the southern part of the island confirmed by a single auger profile revealed the familiar saline alluvial gley soil profile. An exploratory auger transect was conducted along the south-western foreshore (Tr8), revealing the 'natural' stiff yellowish-brown clay to vary between grey and yellowish-brown silts with pockets of reddish-brown clay. These overlay degraded chalk in the north and shingle in the south.

Features on the intertidal foreshore

South Binness was not as closely surveyed as the other islands as access is both more difficult and more restricted (only two days were available during the entire fieldwork for its investigation). During a rapid walkover survey in 1993 another pottery vessel was discovered *in situ* on the south-western shoreline at the 'top' of the shingle beach (Fig 31). It was an almost complete flint-gritted vessel of later Bronze Age date (vessel 774/1; SB.18d), devoid of rim or base, set upright in the clay. On removal it was clear that, although it contained a few burnt flint fragments, as with the vessel 350 from Long Island, no bone was present, although this may have been lost to erosion. The contents were sampled for palaeoenvironmental data.

Approximately 30m to the south-west of pot 774/1 a band of reddish clay 0.7–1m wide extended for 2–3m out from the shoreline. The seaward end of this appeared burnt and contained a small quantity of Roman pottery sherds, flecks of charcoal, burnt flint, and what appeared to be holes containing darker clay and possibly the carbonised remains of wooden stakes. There was no obvious form or date to this 'structure', however, and it is possible that the 'stakes' are decayed roots. This was interpreted in the field as a possible hearth.

A second hearth was a clearer circular feature (2058) measuring 0.5m in diameter towards the southern end of the west coast. Like similar features on Baker's Island it was filled with a dark grey silt with abundant inclusions of burnt flint.

Artefact scatters

General collection units along the western foreshore consisted of five 50m wide strips (SB.18). Other units were areas of the foreshore rather than collection squares. Quantities of worked flint were observed on the south-eastern foreshore, but fewer elsewhere. Artefacts were, in particular, noticed in a 260m length of this shoreline just above the shingle and no

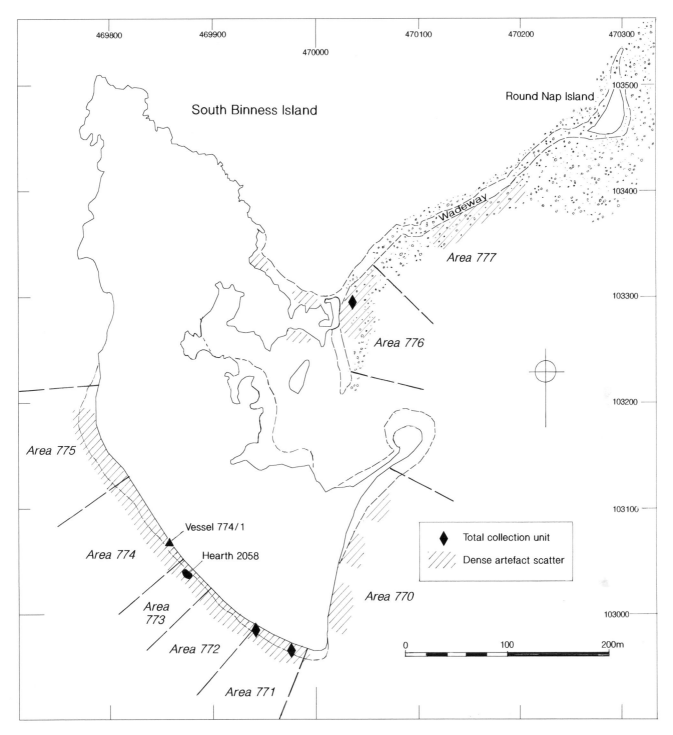

Figure 31   Plan of South Binness Island, showing the study areas and major find spots (outline based on data from Portsmouth University, with additions, drawn by S E James)

material was noted in the mudflats beyond, which began 25–30m offshore. A concentration of flintwork, Bronze Age pottery, and a few sherds of Romano-British pottery occurred in the southern 40m stretch where hearth 2058 was recorded. The flintwork included diagnostically Mesolithic material, including a tranchet adze, as well as late Neolithic–early Bronze Age and late Bronze Age material. Along this coastline fired clay was recovered and a fragment of a fired-clay object, possibly a loomweight.

A second concentration (2059) was on the land-ward end of the Wadeway running for c 30m and produced one unfinished, but well made, plano-convex knife, several large scrapers, and some Bronze Age pottery. An area to the south of this, marked on an OS map in the 1930s as having produced artefacts, produced none during this survey.

Artefacts were present over much of the shingle beaches on the south-east and south-west shores of South Binness and in various small concentrations along the Wadeway and around its junction with the main part of the island.

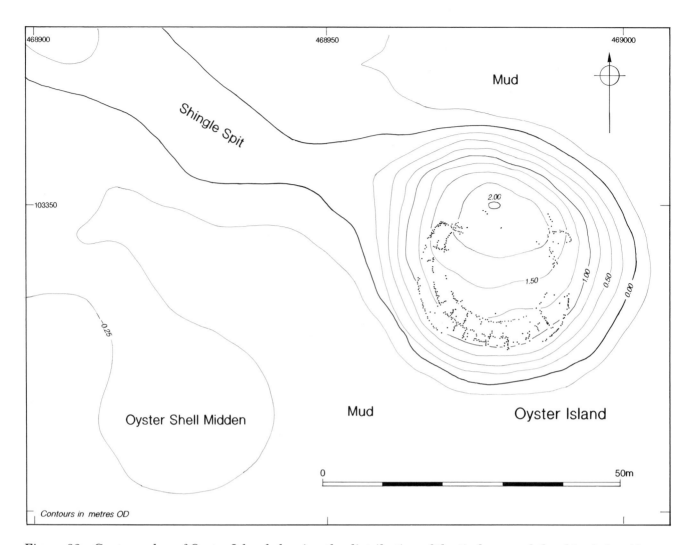

Figure 32   Contour plan of Oyster Island showing the distribution of the timbers, and the shingle bar (data from Portsmouth University, drawn by S E James)

Oyster Island
by Neil J Adam and Dominic Fontana

The small, roughly circular mound situated off the southern tip of Farlington Marshes (Figs 19, and 32) is known locally as Oyster Island and comprises a small raised shingle-covered mound, 120m in diameter, joined to Farlington Marshes at low tide by a 250m long shingle bar. The island itself is a mound of clay with a 0.3m thick layer of loose shingle. A thin, unripened humic gley soil exists on the top of the mound. Most of the shingle and gravel is greater than 0.03m in size and shows considerable wear from tidal action. It is reported that the island was built up to accommodate the building on it and is therefore, in part, artificial (Bryant 1967, 8).

A submerged 'causeway' exists linking Oyster Island (OI.135) and the mainland and Farlington Marshes, and a second shingle bar extends from the causeway westward linking it to Baker's Island. The 'causeway' rarely dries out but is usually walkable at low tide. Both the shingle bars, from Farlington Marshes to Oyster Island and from Baker's Island to the causeway run east–west, and therefore at right

angles to the present tidal flow. At present this flow can be quite strong on a falling tide and it is unlikely that these bars are natural in origin, probably having been artificially built-up to enable easier access on foot. Indeed, the bar linking Farlington Marshes and Oyster Island exhibits a significant 'dog-leg' where the ebb tidal flow has caused the bar to migrate southwards, again supporting the contention that it is unlikely to be a naturally deposited shingle bar. These shingle bars may have been laid down by the Russell family during the early years of the 19th century as a part of their oyster farming operations (see Fontana and Fontana, Historical survey, Chapter 2, above).

All of Oyster Island, apart from the north shore, is ringed by a double row of timber posts (t3); some squared and others roundwood stakes (OI.108). These are thought to represent the remains of Oyster pens which are likely to date to the mid-19th century, although no datable material was recovered directly associated with the structure.

The walkover survey of the island (an area of 35 × 25m; *c* 900m²) recovered few finds, but burnt and worked flint, plus flint-tempered pottery, was recovered from the surface of the mudflats around it, together with some Romano-British coarseware sherds. The flintwork is mostly large and poorly struck but includes two rough blade cores; it is of later Bronze Age affinity. Finds recorded from nonsystematic survey (by Arthur Mack and Dominic Fontana) included a small collection of cores, a Mesolithic tranchet adze and debitage, possibly including Mesolithic material, with other modern debris including post-medieval pottery and a number of copper alloy fragments and slag, some possibly being bomb fragments and shrapnel. A few fragments of animal bone were recovered from the surface and included both cow and horse.

Two auger holes, bored on the highest point of the mound, confirmed the hypothesis that the main islands in Langstone Harbour contain thin soils (unripened gley soils) over heavier marine silts clays and gravels. Two features of archaeological interest were noted in addition to the timber posts; both are probably of post-medieval origin.

- A ditch averaging 1.5m wide was identified running for about 35m across the island and aligned with both northern extremes of the post circle. It was covered in part by a thin layer of loose shingle and large flint nodules and its full length and width could not be determined. A single auger sounding indicated that it was only 0.25m deep and filled with a dark-grey, slightly sandy clay with inclusions of undiagnostic waterlogged wood. No datable material was recovered from the fill although post-medieval brick and tile were noted on its surface. It seems likely that it associated with the timber posts.
- The remains of an early-20th century support building and a WWI searchlight position.

Despite isolated Mesolithic finds from Oyster Island (recovered A Mack; ident J Gardiner) the general paucity of ancient archaeological artefacts and the high percentage of modern material scattered across the island lead to the inescapable conclusion that the timber ring and ditch are very probably 18th or 19th century in origin.

Timber structure (t3)

The timbers of Oyster Island were surveyed in detail. A total of 744 timbers survive of which 568 were surveyed (t3, Fig 32) and their heights ranged from +0.50m OD to +2.08m OD indicating considerable variability (OI.108). Most of the posts survive to a height of 0.5m. There are three distinct timber structures; two on the mainland end of the shingle bar that may have provided some coastal protection for the small brick and flint built house which once stood there (marked on the 1947 Admiralty Chart as 'red roof conspic.'). The other, more substantial structure surrounds the southern side of the island and forms three concentric semicircles about 22.5m diameter with 'cells' created by further posts placed radially (Fig 32). Most of these timbers were reused ships timbers. They were about 150mm (6in) square, many with treenails, and seem to be half carlings – beams supporting the deck (Mack pers comm). The southern area is surrounded by blocks of dressed stone, possibly placed for reinforcement purposes. In the south-west of the island (c 25m) is a substantial midden of discarded oyster (Ostrea edulis L.) shells.

This is a substantial structure consisting of three semicircles with internal cells created by the radially placed lines of posts and several 'strategically' placed blocks of dressed masonry. It bears similarities with another concentric structure found in Caernarfon Bay, Wales and described by Momber (1990; 1991). This structure is of medieval date and, at c 300–350m diameter, is larger than that of Oyster Island. It is identified as a fishtrap and is circular in plan with an enclosure at its seaward end to trap fish (see Hutchinson 1994, 136–7). These traps are apparently self-baiting with marine worms colonising the silts which accumulate, attracting small fish which in turn attract larger species (Hutchinson 1994, 137). The masonry blocks in the Caernarfon Bay structure strengthened it and Hutchinson (op cit) suggests that it would have had nets fastened over the entrance.

Although strong parallels can be seen in the Caernarfon Bay structure, the strong historical connection with oysters in Langstone Harbour, the site name, form, and the occurrence of an oyster midden cannot be disregarded. This structure certainly served as an oyster bed in its latter (post-medieval) life, but whether this was a modification and reuse of a structure that was originally constructed as a fishtrap has to remain speculative.

World War I brick structure and searchlight base

On top of the island are the foundations of two brick-built structures (OI.109). The first of these is a rectangular building with a concrete base in front surrounded by brick and mortar rubble. The foundations are aligned on a south-west to north-east axis and are situated in the very centre of the island, measuring about 30 × 5m. The remains of a tiled floor are still visible, with a concrete base in front of the structure. The foundations of the second structure formed a circular platform about 4.4m in diameter (Plate 26) with reinforced concrete supports in the centre. Following erosion in December 1999, this 'platform' was standing proud as a circular column of bricks nearly 0.9m (3ft) high (Mack pers comm, compare with Plate 26). Near it was a square column of bricks, possibly a building foundation or support. These structures are the remains of an observation post and searchlight control station respectively, built to monitor traffic in Langstone Harbour during World War I. At the time of survey (1993–4) both structures only survived as single line of foundation bricks, but building rubble littered the whole island with glass from the searchlight itself.

Plate 26   The World War I searchlight base on Oyster Island, photographed in 1994. Heavy storm surges at Christmas 1999 left the base standing over a metre proud of the mudflats and revealed more brick walls not visible on this photograph (Elaine A Wakefield)

Creek Field, Hayling Island (1955)
by A M ApSimon

Creek Field, properly '10-acre Creek' (otherwise, 'Crake', 'Crate', or 'Big Creek'), lies in North Hayling on alluvium underlain by Chalk, in the north-west corner of Hayling Island (Fig 2). It is bounded to the west by a sinuous old sea-bank. To the north are saltings and to the south-west it abuts 'Little Creek' field, also enclosed by the sea-bank. Both fields lie between 4 and 3m OD and are permanent pasture. The alluvium here over the Chalk is post-Bronze Age.

The site (SU 7185 0352) was discovered in 1955 by Mr Noel Pycroft (who provided most of the detail of this account) and his father, during hand-digging of brickearth for brickmaking in Pycroft's brickworks (White 1971, 90; Pycroft 1998). The first indication was the finding of a large Bronze Age pottery jar (HI.36). The jar, which was substantially complete (except that its upper part had collapsed into the lower part), was upright, tilted at about 45°. The upper part was only about 0.23m (9in) below the surface, the base about 0.5m (20in) deep, allegedly resting on traces of a small hearth. Mr John Budden (of Chalton Manor Farm) did not observe any hearth during the excavation, nor any associated material. The jar was removed complete to Cumberland House Museum, Southsea; nothing was found within it. It is now in Portsmouth City Museum (acc no 47/55).

Subsequent investigation on site by Mr Arthur Corney, then of Portsmouth City Museum, showed that the jar had been deposited outside and a short distance to the west of the doorway of a circular house, perhaps 4.2–4.5m (14–15ft) in diameter. The doorway was marked by two postholes, the wall of the house by a ring of pieces of 'blue daub', suggesting a wattle structure. The interior is described as

having a floor of chalk lumps about 0.1–0.15m (4–6in) thick. The lower parts of three further pots, standing upright, their bases about 125mm (5in) in diameter, were found about 6m (20ft) north of the house; another to the west of it. A saddle quern was found in the field boundary ditch 80m north of the site.

The circumstances of the deposition of the Creek Field Bronze Age jar, and its connection with the house, are obscure. It is however believed that the house still exists beneath back-fill, and it is hoped to provide answers to these and other questions by further investigation.

The 'brickearth' at the site was about 0.75m (2ft 6in) thick, beneath ploughsoil 0.12–0.15m (5–6in) thick. Elsewhere it varied in thickness, up to 10ft (3m) being proved in localised 'pits', probably solution features, one of which was found about 25m west of the hut site, apparently with pottery 'at all depths'. At the western side of the field, where the brickearth was about 1.2m thick, Mr Corney demonstrated the presence of two old land surfaces in it, the lower attributed to the 3rd century AD, the upper to around AD 1100. The brickearth was underlain by chalky clay 'marl', with flints, to about 0.3m thick, overlying broken chalk. In all, an area of about 90m square in the south-west corner of the field was dug out for brickearth. In the course of this, Romano-British or Iron Age saltmaking structures, investigated by Richard Bradley, on behalf of M Rule, in 1964 (Pycroft 1998, 64) were found at the west side of the field and a further 6–10 hearths, probably associated with saltmaking, were found scattered across the area.

Little Creek Field produced another hut-circle about 5–6m (15–20ft) across, marked by a ring of burnt wooden posts going down into the marl, with a hearth in the middle full of burnt bone. Finds from it

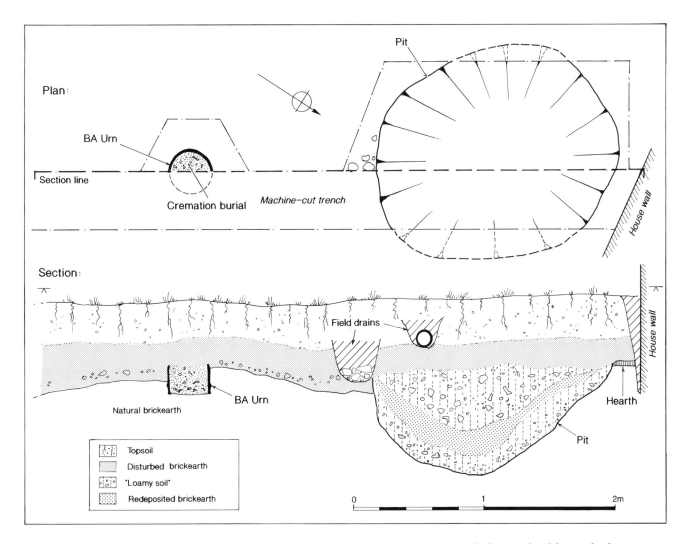

Figure 33   Plan and section of pits and hearth recovered in the service trench during building of a house (Mulberry) north of Mill Lane, in Langstone village in 1979. Drawn by S E James, based on field drawing by G Soffe

included burnt flint, wood charcoal and decomposed wood, and pieces of pottery, thrown away, but believed to be middle Bronze Age. A large dump ('about half-a-ton') of Romano-British pottery was also found in the field in 1946, as well as a polished discoidal flint knife of late Neolithic type from a probable solution feature, and about 35 hearths, believed to be associated with middle to late Iron Age saltmaking. When the cess-pit was dug for Pycroft's house, *Buena Vista*, immediately south of Creek Field, traces were found of three graves, oriented west–east and containing decayed extended inhumation burials with flints placed over the head positions.

Pits near Langstone Village (1979)
by Grahame Soffe

The find reported here is situated in Langstone itself, 50m north of Mill Lane (Ha 44; SU 7151 0500). The area forms the south-west extremity of the low-lying, narrow, brickearth peninsula of Langstone

village, 200m north of the present high-water mark. On either side of this peninsula are alluvial valleys containing shallow deposits of riverine silt over flinty gravel. Adjacent to the site, however, the lowest reaches of the western valley contain estuarine alluvium indicating that the area known as South Moor (or Mere) was formerly subject to tidal flooding. It is now protected by an old sea bank, Budds Wall. The site lies on the edge of this estuary, on poorly drained brickearth of the Park Gate series (Hodgson 1967).

Features were discovered by Mr Noel Pycroft in 1979 in a machine-cut trench when building a house, *Mulberry*, on land formerly an orchard. The service trench, running south from the house, bisected a middle Bronze Age cinerary urn, an oval pit, and a fragment of hearth dating to the mid-1st century AD (Fig 33). The features were recorded by the writer under 'rescue' conditions but, prior to this, the rim and parts of the urn remaining *in situ* were photographed and removed by Mr Nicholas Hall of Havant Museum. Other fragments of the urn and what could be found of the cremated bones it had contained were

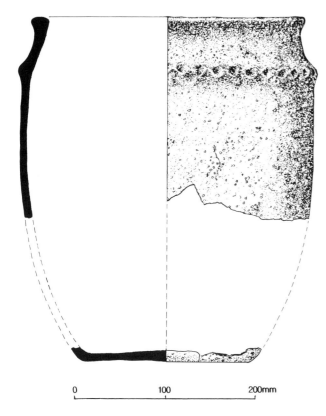

| 0 | 100 | 200mm |

Figure 34   Middle Bronze Age barrel urn from Langstone village. Drawn by Valerie King

recovered by the writer from both the trench and its spoil heap. The urn was reconstructed (Fig 34) and the discovery briefly reported (Soffe 1980; 1981), but the note in Hughes (1982, 36), suggesting that *two* barrel urns may have been found, is incorrect, as is the grid reference cited for the site location. The urn, cremation, and material from the pit are lodged with Hampshire County Museums Service (Acc No A1981 80H)

The middle Bronze Age urn and cremation burial

The barrel urn (Fig 34) was found inverted and set into natural brickearth. The pit into which it had originally been placed was not clearly defined, probably because it had been rapidly refilled with brickearth without inclusions of extraneous material. Part of the rim and upper part of the vessel including the cordon survived *in situ* but the lower body had been lost in an overlying layer of disturbed brickearth. Sherds representing about 55% of the base had collapsed into the interior over the cremated bones, with one base sherd being recovered from the spoil heap. Although, around the urn there was a slight rise in the surface of the natural brickearth, there was no evidence for an overlying barrow and the burial probably belongs to a flat cemetery (see Chapter 7).

The urn itself is of typical barrel shape, 370mm in height (reconstructed) with a rim diameter of

300mm and a base diameter of 185mm. A single horizontal cordon with finger-tip impressed decoration is applied to the outer wall of the vessel 50mm below the bead rim. The cordon diameter is 330mm. The wall thickness varies from 7 to 10mm. The vessel is hand-made and the surfaces well smoothed. The fabric has reddish-brown oxidised surfaces with slight traces of reduced blackening, but the core is heavily reduced. The fabric is fairly friable, suggesting a clamp firing temperature of *c* 650°. The clay is calcareous with a ferruginous content and 50% crushed flint, some calcined with a grit size of 0.5–1.5mm predominating and a scatter of iron ore inclusions, all homogeneously distributed. Two grains of iron-stained sedimentary quartzite were observed in the thin section.

The cinerary urn is an example of one of the simplest forms of decorated vessels belonging to the local manifestation of the 'Deverel-Rimbury' tradition of the middle Bronze Age. Apart from the three vessels reported in this volume (see Chapter 4), one of its closest local parallels is the cinerary urn from Portsdown (Nicholls 1987), which is almost identical in size and form with a similar fabric.

Only just under 8g of cremated bone was recovered, representing a tiny proportion of the original burial. The fragments ranged in size up to just over 10mm. Some of these fragments were identifiable, confirming the remains as human. One skull fragment and one long bone fragment, probably from a tibia, were noted but the remaining pieces were unidentified. As this was clearly such a small part of the original deposit it was not possible to suggest the age or sex of the individual (assuming that the bones were part of only one individual).

The late Iron Age/early Roman pit and hearth

An oval pit 1.82m by 1.54m and 0.80m deep, had been dug into the brickearth (Fig 33). The lowest filling (layer 1) was a dark loamy soil containing numerous burnt flints, animal bones, pottery and small fragments of abraded fired clay, possibly the remains of burnt daub, briquetage, and tile. This layer had been sealed with a layer of clean brickearth (layer 2). Layer 3, the upper filling, was very similar to layer 1, containing numerous burnt flints, some pottery, but no bone. On its north side the pit abutted an area where the surface of the undisturbed brickearth was burnt to a depth of *c* 30mm, probably a hearth more-or-less contemporary with the pit. Its extent could not be recorded because it was truncated by the foundation trench of the modern house. Two teeth, maxillary molars of cattle, were bedded into the feature.

Pottery

The pottery from layer 1 could be divided into two fabric types (A and B), the first also occurred in layer 3 together with a third fabric (C).

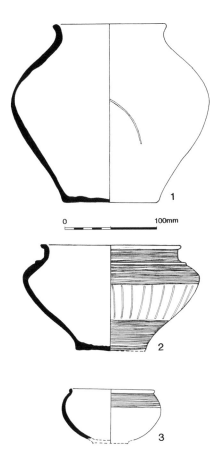

0   100mm

Figure 35   Late Iron Age Atrebatic vessels from the pit in Langstone village. Drawn by G Soffe

Fabric A: Reddish-brown to grey sandy ware, fired grey to black on the outer surfaces.

Figure 35, no 1. Jar with everted rim and traces of a single impressed and burnished curved line. Probably handmade.

Figure 35, no 2. Cordoned bowl, high shouldered, upright neck, black burnished and decorated with horizontally burnished bands above the shoulder and above the base and vertical burnished lines in a band below the shoulder. Probably wheelthrown.

Not illustrated. Cordoned bowl with high shoulder, upright neck and out-turned bead rim, similar to above. Probably wheelthrown.

Figure 35, no 3. Small bead-rimmed bowl. Possibly wheelthrown.

Not illustrated. Fragments of bead rim.

Fabric B: Rowlands Castle ware. Hard light-grey sandy ware with occasional calcined flint and ironstone grits.

Not illustrated. Two body sherds of a large handmade storage jar from layer 3.

Fabric C: Black, slightly vesicular ware with flint grit and grog tempering.

Not illustrated. One body sherd.

The occurrence of high-quality cordoned bowls and other forms of Southern Atrebatic type belonging to the 'Aylesford-Swarling' tradition, makes this small group of some significance. They are similar to vessels from the Westhampnett cremation cemetery, near Chichester (Fitzpatrick 1997, graves 20637, 20650) datable to the mid- to late-1st century BC and this is the date range usually assigned to the form. However, their relationship here at Langstone with early-Rowlands Castle ware (Hodder 1974), suggests their continued use into the mid-1st century AD when the industrial production represented by Rowlands Castle and other local Romano-British sources is thought to be have started (although M Lyne has recently suggested a pre-Conquest origin for the industry in Fitzpatrick 1997, 123). This is reflected in the broad date range for Southern Atrebatic pottery, up to AD 43, given by Cunliffe (1991, 584), who illustrates similar bowls from Chalton, 11 km north of Langstone. At the Langstone villa (at *Spes Bona*) itself, Lyne illustrates different late Iron Age forms occurring in the mid- to late-1st century AD as the 'Atrebatic Overlap' encountered very thinly at Chichester and Fishbourne (Gilkes 1998, 58–9).

Other fired clay material

The abraded fragments of fired clay were difficult to identify. Some had fabrics similar to Roman tiles and bricks of the 1st and 2nd centuries AD and have therefore been tentatively identified as such. The rest of the material could be broadly divided into two fabrics. The first was very friable, poorly mixed clay with considerable banding, suggestive of daub. The matrix contained a medium scatter of rounded quartz grains, 0.03–0.05mm, and rare threads of finely divided whiter mica. Considerable rounded iron ore particles were also present. The second fabric was finer than the first, and better mixed and fired at a higher temperature. In thin section the matrix was seen to contain a high tenor of fine angular quartz silt, no grains measuring more than 0.06mm. The ferruginous clay contained no other inclusions. The second fabric may have been related to some aspect of salt boiling, as it would be adequate for refractory activities involving high temperatures, containing as it does, a high proportion of free silica to matrix. Neither fabric, however, belongs to briquetage vessels involved in the evaporation of brine, as these, when positively identified, are invariably porous, containing considerable voids resulting from the burning-out of organic matter. Very large stony temper is also sometimes added to raw clays to achieve porosity. In the absence of an intensive local clay sampling programme, it was not possible to attribute any of these fabrics to any local clay or brickearth source.

Animal bones

The small collection of animal bones recovered from layer 1 consisted entirely of the food refuse from domestic animals. They comprised:

Cattle: Proximal radius, split sagittally. Maxillary molar

Sheep/goat: Humerus shaft. Mandibular 3rd molar

Pig: Juvenile distal tibia with unfused epiphysis

Horse: Proximal metatarsal from gracile animal. Possibly a pony or small horse; too large for *Equus asinus*

This collection would be in keeping with a date in the mid- to late-1st century AD for the pit but the number of bones is too low to make any more reliable interpretation.

Discussion

Although it is possible that the contents of this pit, particularly the burnt flints, may suggest local brine-boiling activity, it is not possible to be certain that any of the fired clay represents briquetage vessels. The presence of pottery and animal bones indicates that the pit was primarily used for the disposal of domestic refuse and a general scatter of sherds of the entire area around it and the hearth adjacent to it suggest occupation in the vicinity. The presence of Rowlands Castle type pottery and fragments of tile or brick shows that the settlement may be just post-Conquest in date but early enough for local late Iron Age southern Atrebatic forms of pottery to be in continued use. The proximity of probably extensive mid- to late-1st century Roman buildings at Langstone immediately to the northeast of this site (eg villa at *Spes Bona*, Gilkes 1998), and the presence of the late Iron Age and early Roman temple complex just to the south on Hayling Island (King and Soffe in prep) must have a bearing here and the pottery from the pit group can be easily compared with the sequences and assemblages recovered from these excavations.

Sinah circle structure
by Jon Adams, Kit Watson, and Michael J Allen

A circuit of timbers was identified on the edge of Sinah Lake in the south-east corner of the present harbour among one of the largest expanses of mudflats (LH.93). The site is at about –2.7m to –3m ± 0.5m OD, on the northern edge of Sinah Lake and is rarely exposed, and then only by exceptionally low tides when it is just accessible on foot. It is normally, however, underwater and has only once (in 1993) been seen exposed by such low tides by Arthur Mack in over 40 years.

Discovery
by John M Bingeman and Arthur T Mack

The discovery of this enigmatic timber 'circle' was made by Arthur Mack during exceptionally low tides in March 1993 and a rapid investigation was made by him and John Bingeman. An initial survey was made by sketching the nature of the site (Fig 36). This survey revealed 27 (later revised to 28 on the recovery of an additional stake in 1994) upright

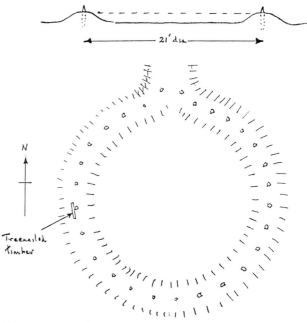

Figure 36   Sketch plan of the Sinah Circle by John Bingeman (from Bingeman 1995)

timbers in an approximate circle of about 6m in diameter, and was recorded as being surrounded by a low mud bank with a 'porch' or 'funnel' due north (Fig 36). The timbers of the circuit included roundwood posts and split timber 'planks', some of which had been loosened as a result of snagging during oyster dredging. Remains of 'wattling' were also recovered loosely associated with the timbers, and surrounding the stake circuit was an apparent low, but distinct mound. Two of the timbers (Bingeman 1995, 4) were removed for further examination prior to survey of any form and passed to Dr Tomalin for comment of which only stake OO is reported here). A further timber (AD) was later removed in March 1994 by HWTMA. All of these stakes were timbers which had been split and then trimmed with metal adzes and had been associated with some small 'wattles'. Its resemblance in plan to a Bronze Age roundhouse and the recovery of Neolithic and Bronze Age structures on the opposite side of the Solent at Wotton, Isle of Wight, fuelled suggestions that this might be a Bronze Age terrestrial structure which had become submerged. This was considered particularly pertinent in view of the Bronze Age timber from near Wadeway, north Hayling Island (Williams and Soffe 1987).

A further, more detailed sketch record of most of the individual timbers was made in conjunction with HWTMA in July 1993, detailing their existing heights above the seabed sediments and shape (Fig 36). This survey, three months after the first discovery, showed that the timbers were consistently 5–

6mm longer than when surveyed previously, confirming that the seabed in this part of the harbour continues to be scoured. At the request of HWTMA, the Langstone Harbour Board approved a Preservation Order to prohibit fishermen from trawling through the site. The prohibited area was defined by four marker buoys.

Archaeological survey

After the discovery had been brought to the attention of Sarah Draper-Ali and Garry Momber (HWTMA) and the local NAS scheme, its survey and investigation was formally incorporated into the Project with a detailed schedule of works designed by the archaeological team to ensure the maintenance of the seamless concept. John Bingeman and Arthur Mack were also of the opinion that the site was eroding fairly rapidly, and the presence of small loose fragments of twig around the base of the larger upright timbers tended to support this view. One erosive process could be seen in action. The site was well populated by swimming crabs whose favoured position was tucked up under the timbers. They could be observed scraping away sediment to embed themselves against the timber and this activity is certainly contributing to the progressive removal of sediment. As the sediment levels round the timbers are lowered more of their hitherto protected surface becomes exposed to attack by microbiological organisms. Although the rate at which the site was eroding was unknown, the priority was to record the structure as quickly as possible.

An underwater survey was conducted jointly by Jon Adams (then NAS), HWTMA, and Kit Watson (Wessex Archaeology) and the surveys entered into the project GIS by Portsmouth University. The aims were to archaeologically map and plan the site, excavate portions of it to determine the nature of its construction and conditions under which it was built (ie dry or wet), sample the wood for detailed examination, identification, and dating, and to consider the circle within the context of other timber structures in the harbour. The development of an accurate, measured plan was required before other options could be considered.

A systematic archaeological swimover survey recorded the visible archaeological material around a 10×10m search area centred on the readily observable elements of the structure. The entire 100m² area was systematically searched in 1m lanes running east–west and the structure systematically cleaned of weed and searched for both features and artefacts in a rolling programme of clean, search, record, and survey. No large stones, embedded pebbles, or stable deposits were removed as the intention was to be as non-destructive as possible. Particular care was taken to avoid any damage by finning (ie damage by the swimmers flippers or fins), small scale excavation, or abrasion from ropes which might compromise the stability of the site before it

was sufficiently well recorded. Details of the shape and orientation of each timber were recorded to augment the timber records made previously by Bingeman. A three-dimensional survey of all features and bathyometry of the seabed topography within the survey area were undertaken, together with a complete two-dimensional survey using offsets to record any other archaeological features.

The three-dimensional data were processed to provide both conventional plans (Fig 36), comparable to land-based surveys, and three-dimensional images (see Adam *et al* 1995, fig 3) of the structure, topography, and associated sediment patterns. All surveys were related to both the Langstone GIS and the OS grid, which enable this data to be compared with historic changes within the harbour and to sea-level change.

In addition, a further three-dimensional web of datum points was established by Jon Adams for a photomosaic of the timbers using the computer program (*Web for Windows*) in which the metrical measured survey was 'rectified' by computer analysis (see Chapter 1). An attempt was made to produce a photomosaic in which each photograph would have recorded at least two known locations (tagged timbers), but visibility was too poor for its completion.

Nature of the structure: results of the survey

The structure appeared be on a slightly raised area and about 6m in diameter. There were discontinuities in the sequence of timbers that otherwise seemed to be fairly regularly spaced. The timbers were in a rough circle and depth measurements confirmed that the south-east side was slightly higher than the surrounding seabed, though elsewhere it appeared to be almost the same. The timbers appeared to be of two basic types. The larger appeared to be split oak stakes, the smaller posts being single poles. In between some of the uprights there were some timbers lying horizontally on the seabed, although from survey alone it was not certain whether they were associated. There were also what appeared to be fragments of withy-like twigs, such as might come from a hurdle. Some were lying loose on the surface and none was observed in any coherent wattle or hurdle-like pattern although they did seem to be associated with the timber uprights. Many were still embedded in the sediment and were roughly aligned post to post. There were also several flint nodules around the site, though again, whether these were related to the structure was not clear.

The structure consisted of 24 of the original 27 roundwood timbers and split timbers (Plate 27) planned in 1993. They formed a roughly ovoid shape about 7m in diameter with a distinct gap to the north-east in which stake AE was located; there were no central structures, features, or posts. It is not certain whether the gap was real or represented the erosion and/or removal of stakes from this point; at least three of the stakes reported in earlier work had

Plate 27   Timbers of the Sinah Circle structure. Note the poor visibility typical of Langstone Harbour (Jon Adams)

been removed and other loose stakes may have been lost. Some stakes, presumed to have come from the structure, have also been recovered. Many of the uprights were found to be leaning, but the direction of lean was not consistent. Bingeman observed that one stake had changed its lean from east to west between 1993 and 1994, almost certainly due to an oyster trawl during the winter. The fact that not all the timbers are upright may be the result of impact from fishing or dredging gear, though the possibility that not all elements were originally set vertically cannot be discounted.

Many of the split upright timbers stood exposed between 0.068m and 0.365m above the seabed sediments (Plate 27), and the roundwood elements were 0.063m to 0.215m tall. The exposed portions displayed moderate degrading – the spit uprights were worn to ragged points and many of the roundwood elements were worn to the wood core. Relatively undegraded wood surfaces existed at the base of the uprights in areas where the sediment had only recently been eroded to expose the timbers.

Within the circle was a scatter of large (0.2m) chalk pebbles, not noticed elsewhere on the local seabed in the survey area (Fig 37). Many were noted around the timber uprights, but not enough were present to be confident that they were an intentional part of the structure, or that they had become trapped naturally by the timber circuit. It seems more likely that their introduction into the circuit was intentional. No other features were recorded.

The sediment within the stake circuit was a shallow light grey/brown sandy silty clay with many shells (*Ostrea edulis*, *Littorina* spp, *Mytilus edulis*, *Cardium edule*, and *Crepidula fornicata*) containing both flint and chalk pebbles. Where the seabed had been eroded by tidal scouring a grey-blue 'marine' silt was exposed over about half of the survey area, inside and out of the stake circuit.

Coarse pebbles and stones occurred in particular at the junction of these two layers and represented the residue of the upper eroded surface. Where wooden elements such as the plank AP and areas of wattling were covered, they were buried by the grey-brown sediment, but it could not be determined if this was entirely a later deposit, or one largely contemporary with the structure that had been eroded and redeposited. The stones in Figure 37, were shown by excavation to be largely confined to the surface and were not a part of the seabed sediment matrix. These stones were probably chalk, and those stones in the pebbly silt were flint cobbles.

Excavation

In view of the continuing doubts as to the circle's function and date, and the ongoing erosion, it was felt that there was a strong case for an excavation to try and furnish the required information. A principle aim would be the acquisition of a timber sample, either for dendrochronology or ^{14}C. Rather than simply extract the timber like a tooth, a small trench would be dug to reveal the structure below seabed level and the contexts. To that end an excavation was carried out in the spring of 1995 by a team from the University of Southampton and the HWTMA.

A sector of the circle between stakes BE and AN was chosen on the south-western perimeter of the circle; it included two of the large split stakes as well as the other smaller poles (Figs 37 and 38). An initial area 1.8 × 0.65m was investigated and after removal of the loose, mobile upper sediments, further details of the structure were immediately revealed. Running around the stakes was a ditch-like feature in which all the various timbers were set. It was cut, worn, or gouged into the natural seabed clay (Fig 38a). A sondage was excavated through this feature,

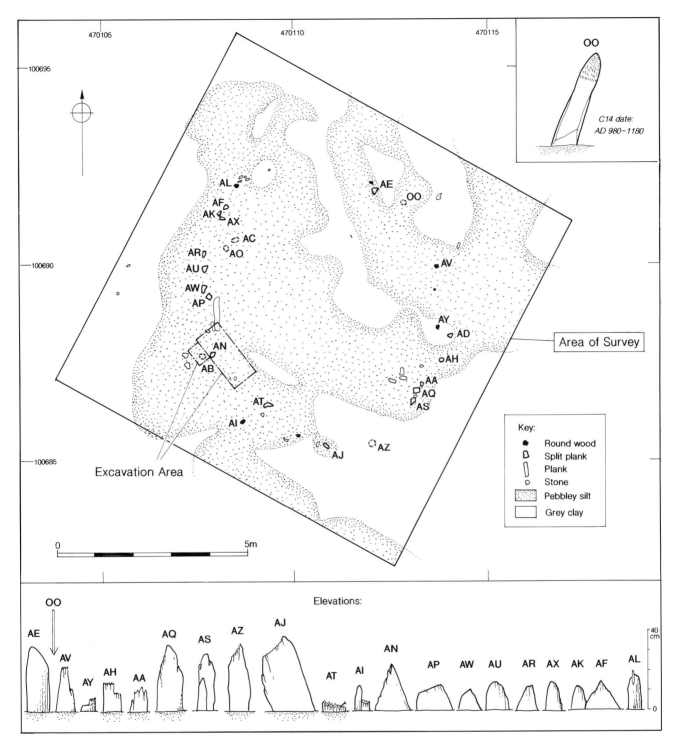

Figure 37   Survey of the Sinah Circle (Wessex Archaeology and HWMTA) with sketches of selected wooden posts based on originals by John Bingeman. Drawn by S E James

working in towards the timber 'AN' to be extracted for examination and dating (Fig 38b). The fill of this 'ditch' was a soft silty clay with many shell fragments and small twigs (Fig 39).

Embedded in the surface, though not within the fill, were occasional flint nodules. One was large enough to avoid being 'rafted' away by attached weed. Several oyster shells were found adhering to the lower part of timber 'AN'. Another significant component of this fill was a substantial quantity of *Crepidula fornicata* (slipper limpet). This was a

species accidentally introduced from America in the late-19th century (Barrett and Yonge 1958).

The timbers were clearly of various, but nevertheless distinct types (Fig 40). These were:

1   large cleft oak piles ('stakes')
2   intermediate sized poles *c* 75–90mm in diameter
3   smaller vertical stakes *c* 40mm in diameter
4   twigs that still had bark on them and apparently laid in some way, more or less along or through the various uprights

116

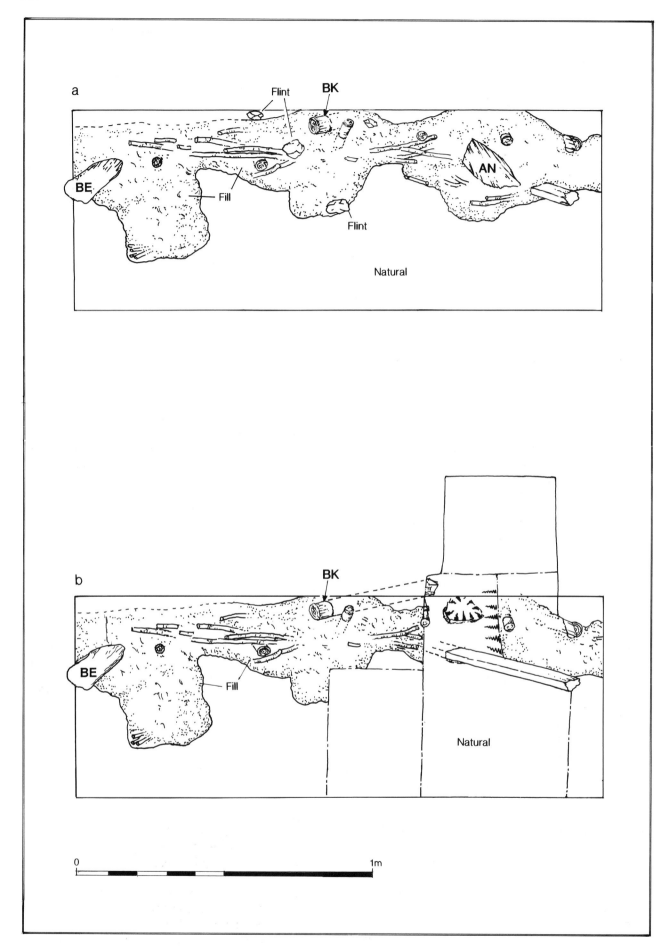

Figure 38   Plan of excavation area in the Sinah Circle a) before excavation, and b) after excavation, showing the exposed wooden elements, for orientation and labelling of timbers see Figure 37 (Jon Adams)

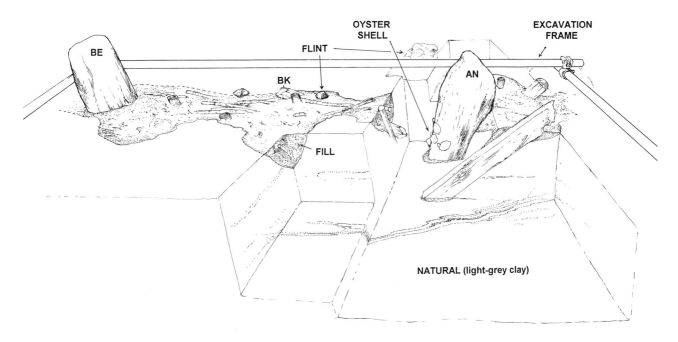

Figure 39   Isometric drawing of excavation of the Sinah Circle (Jon Adams)

The latter were around 10–20mm in diameter. This suggested some sort of hurdle-like structure in which the twigs would be 'rods' and the verticals would be 'sails'. However, it was by no means certain that these 'rods' were laced or woven in any way. Nor do the 'sails' seem to be in alignment. It is possible that if hurdles were successively replaced in this sort of environment one might expect the sort of confused remains we now find. On the other hand this may have been a coarser arrangement (Fig 41) and further excavation might demonstrate which is nearer the mark. The timber (AN) was duly extracted and removed.

Detailed examination of the base of the timbers indicated that they were not dropped into postholes, and this was confirmed by excavation and removal of post AN; it was evident that timber AN had been hammered or pile driven into soft silts as no posthole was found. The area surrounding each post was, however, often highly disturbed, probably by selective burrowing by marine organisms.

Three of the stakes (AN, AD, and OO) were examined and identified by Rowena Gale as oak (*Quercus* sp, see wood report, below). The structural condition of the stakes enabled her to suggest that they were well preserved and particularly striking: the wood, although dark, worm-eaten and decayed on the surface, was firm and pale with no discoloration only 2–3mm below, indicating that the wood was probably not of any great age (details of the wood are given below). Some of the roundwood elements had clearly been cut using a sharp, flat metal blade.

Small roundwood elements and fragments of hurdles were recorded lying horizontally on, and partially embedded in, the seabed; these were slight, insubstantial elements. Other elements of 'wattle', reported from previous dives, have not been identified and seem to have been lost from the site. All the samples of the stakes and hurdles that were examined were oak roundwood. Also on the seafloor was a plank with a squared hole cut in one end laying on, but partially covered by, the uppermost sediment. Another plank (AP) over 365mm long, 110mm wide, and 30mm thick, recorded by Mack and Bingeman, had four treenail holes, and one broken off treenail

Over 20 slipper limpets were recovered from samples taken during excavation of the seabed deposits within the circuit and from the stake molds. Slipper limpets (*Crepidula fornicata*) are a significant find because they are not recorded on the south coast of England before about 1880 (Barrett and Yonge 1958) when they were accidentally introduced with oyster spats from North America (McMillan 1968). They are now enormously prolific and a pest on oyster beds, especially round the south-east and south coasts as they compete with oyster for food and smother the oyster beds. They are not known in Langstone Harbour prior to the 1860s (Tubbs 1980).

Twenty four of the timbers, one stave, and a recumbant plank were described (see below), and shows that 14 were split wood, squared timbers, or triangular posts which were probably reused old wood, four were planks and six were roundwood stakes (Table 4).

The stakes

The main stakes of the circuit were divided into two types – roundwood and split timbers. The roundwood stakes were uniformly about 68mm to 95mm in diameter, and although bark still adhered to two (AO and AN), the other inspected had clearly been cleaned of the bark. The splitwood stakes were simply cleaved and were either radially split resulting in crudely triangular cross sectioned uprights (AF, AK, and AR), or tangentially split producing planks (AN).

118

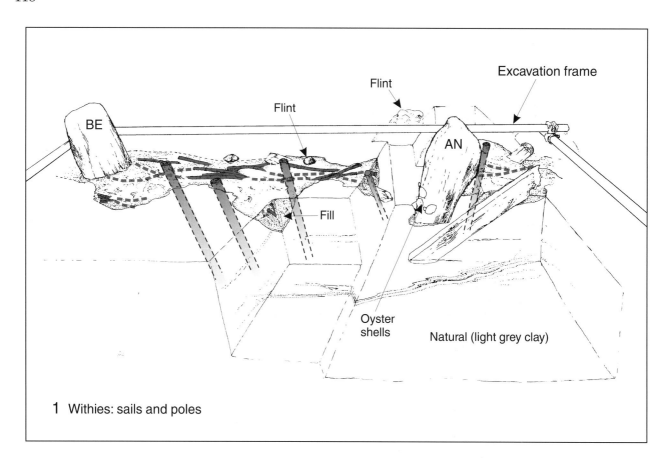

1 Withies: sails and poles

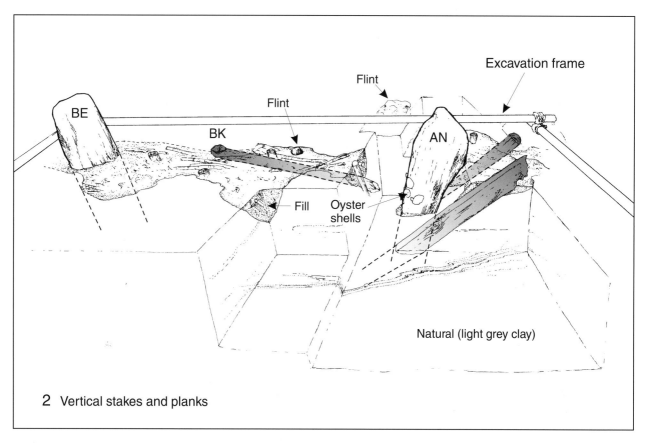

2 Vertical stakes and planks

Figure 40   Interpretation of structural elements of the Sinah Circle 1) withys, sails, and poles, and 2) vertical stakes and planks (Jon Adams)

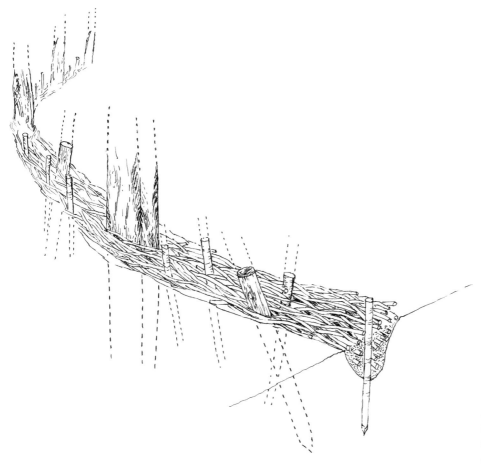

Figure 41   Reconstruction of the wattle and stake circuit of the Sinah Circle (Jon Adams)

The wood surface of the stakes was porous where it had been attacked by marine organisms, but this decay was only surface deep (2–3mm). Disturbance to the mud around the stakes was probably the result of selective burrowing by marine organisms, ie the effect of benthic zone fauna discussed by Ferrari and Adams (1990). Exposed structures can provide attractive new habitats for a range of benthic species which have the potential to cause mechanical damage to the structure by widening cervices selected for habitation (Collins and Mollinson 1984, quoted in Ferrari and Adams *op cit*). In particular, species such as squat lobsters (*Galathea squamiferae*) and European lobsters (*Homarus gammarus*) burrow against timbers (Howard and Bennet 1979) to depths of 0.2m exposing previously sealed and protected wood to other deleterious, wood-boring organisms. Furthermore, the timbers may be loosened and subsequently prone to loss. Thus decay is related in part to burrowing organisms creating local instability (Ferrari and Adams 1990) and accelerating decay at this point. Marine wood borers, including the shipworm mollusc (*Teredo navalis*) and its allies *Pholadacea* and the indigenous gribbles (*Limnoria lignorum*, *L. quadripunctata*, *L. tripunctata*, and *Chelara terebran*) are all recorded from the Solent and, in particular, Southampton Water (eg Coughlan 1976; Holmes and Coughlan 1973) and have acted upon the Sinah structure.

Many of the split timbers have degraded to ragged points and roundwood stakes have been attacked by gribble to the core wood at the top. In both cases, relatively undegraded wood was exposed in bands at the base of the uprights.

The three uprights (AD, AN, and OO) removed were identified before submission for dendrochonology.

The wattle rods and sails

Wattle and sails were present and were found as a mixed mass of wood between the uprights. Where these have been identified they were all oak. The rods were about either 8mm or 16mm in diameter, with small sails (upright staves around which the rods were woven) up to 40mm across, but only fragmentary lengths of these were recovered for inspection. On neither the rods, nor sails, nor on the seabed around them, was there any evidence of daub, imported clay, mud, or other materials that might represent walling material.

No artefacts were recovered in association with the structure which could provide direct evidence of date or function, though the presence of oyster shell and slipper limpets may be significant in this respect. On the mudflats of Sinah Lake, few artefacts have been recovered, but the majority of those finds date to the post-medieval period.

Table 4   List of stakes from the Sinah circle structure and their dimensions

Stake	Type/description	Species	Width (mm)	Breadth (mm)	Height above seabed (mm)	Lean (if recorded)
AE	Split wood plank	–	110	70	320	26°
OO	Roundwood; not planned in situ	oak	120	120	total length 490	
AV	Roundwood	–	93	93	215	
AY	Roundwood	–	68	45	63	
AD	Roundwood	oak	84	82	total length 330	
AH	Roundwood	–	90	90	143	40°
AA	Splitwood, squared timber	–	85	60	115	
AQ	Split timber	–	133	145	320	53°
AS	Split timber, double 'post'	–	75	65	280	38°
AZ	Squared timber	–	120	95	315	
AJ	Split timber plank	–	220	135	365	
AT	Split timber, splintered	–	120	135	68	
AI	2 x squared roundwood timbers	–	30 35	30 35	160	
AB	– not described					
AN	Split timber plank – 4 slipper limpets at point, one crushed	oak	170	85	225 (but total length 890mm)	
AP	Recumbent splitwood plank	–	195	90	130	
AW	Split timber; faceted triangular	–	105	57	100	
AU	Split timber (double post)	–	135	85	135	
AR	Split timber, triangular post	–	90	70	110	
AO	Splitwood plank	–	50	nr	length 760	
AC	Roundwood stake	–	40	38	length 140	
AX	Split timber	–	105	120	143	
AK	Split timber, triangular post	–	105	80	120	
AF	Split timber, triangular post	–	173	90	144	
AL	Roundwood squared stake	–	95	75	180	
AM	Stave; reclining	–	30	30	length 170	

Timber identifications from the structure
by Rowena Gale

The wood from three stakes (AD, AN, and OO) recovered from the Sinah circle structure by Bingeman and others during preliminary investigations were examined and identified. A further wooden stake (AN) and fragments of hurdles (objects 4 and 5) recovered from underwater survey by Jon Adams during the 1995 season were also examined and identified to species.

Materials and methods

Thin sections of the transverse, tangential longitudinal, and radial longitudinal planes were taken using a double-sided razor blade and mounted in 70%

glycerol on microscope slides. The anatomical structure was examined using a Nikon Labophot binocular light-transmitting microscope at magnifications of up to ×400. The anatomical structure and diagnostic features were compared and matched to authenticated reference material.

Stakes

All roundwood stake samples (objects AD, AN, and OO) were from oak (*Quercus*) roundwood. The samples were waterlogged and well preserved. Stake AD was of particular note in that the wood, although dark, worm-eaten, and decayed on the surface, was firm and pale with no discoloration only 2–3mm below. The structural condition of the stakes from

Sinah circle suggested that these items were not of any great age.

Rods and sails (hurdling)

The samples of rods included a large number of short fragments, which were divided into two groups according to diameter and subsampled, two sails were also examined.

Sails: two sail fragments:

Quercus sp, oak. These were of similar diameters (approx 40mm) and each included about 4 growth rings. They were wedge shaped (measuring approx 10mm tangentially) and were spit before use.

Rod fragments:

Quercus sp, oak.
  Larger diameter rods
    17mm, 3 growth rings (2nd ring very wide)
    15mm, 9 growth rings
    15mm, 7 growth rings
  Narrow diameter rods
    10mm, 4 growth rings
    7mm, 5 growth rings
    7mm, 5 growth rings
    7mm, 2 growth rings

The method of construction of the hurdle is unknown. The rods were used whole and appear to have been selected for uniformity of diameter rather than age (see details of larger rods), dividing into two main diameter sizes, of which the narrower fragments probably represent the tapering ends of the rods rather than a separate element of the structure.

Dating

Three timbers (AD, AN, and OO) were submitted for dendrochonological analysis, but were unfortunately unable to produce a date (see Groves, Chapter 5). A roundwood oak stake (OO) which, unlike many of the planks and split timbers including the carefully excavated timber AN, was not obviously a reused timber, was submitted for radiocarbon dating. The determination of 980 ± 50 BP (GU-7275) indicates a date of cal AD 960–1180 .

Interpretation

In a wider context, the walkover survey of the Sinah area (Area 12), which extended well into the intertidal muds, recovered very little archaeological material. However, it produced more post-medieval pottery sherds than most other areas surveyed. No prehistoric flintwork or pottery was recovered from the locality.

A circle of posts is, by itself, neither functionally diagnostic nor intrinsically datable and it is not known how many of the timbers were reused. There are, however, a number of strong supporting clues as to the date and function of this enigmatic structure. What the evidence as a whole suggests is an aquatic structure of stakes and withy, either roughly laced through the uprights and pinned with small 'sail-like' poles to the seabed, or secured to the stakes as hurdles. The Sinah circle contains a number of different types of upright which indicate different patterns of use and reuse of wood, and which may also suggest either different functions (eg split timber and uprights performing a load-bearing function, roundwood acting as infill) or different phases of construction. The timbers themselves are not large enough to be considered as having performed a significant load-bearing function which militates against this being a substantial building such as a roundhouse. Those stakes which have been examined are oak roundwood which have been sharpened to a point by an iron blade (possibly an axe), though otherwise unmodified.

From the nature of the context it did not seem that the construction was assembled during a period of lower sea-level. The structure was built in very soft silts, in water, on a clay or clay-and-'cobble' seabed and the timbers seem to have been driven into the seabed at low water. The presence of associated wooden poles, wattles, and flat planking suggests that the layer of silt within the circle accumulated either during the life time of the structure or subsequently, during the collapse, or disturbance of the structure.

The structure may have provided containment for flint or a similar substrate that is no longer present. The cobbles within the structure may be a part of the original construction. We can reconstruct the remains as a circle of largely unworked, though crudely pointed, sharpened, timber posts selected from local driftwood and available timbers and woods within the area. These timbers were (Fig 40) hammered into the harbour muds at some point within the contemporaneous intertidal zone presumably on the edge of a deeper channel. Oak wattling (Fig 41) provided an enclosed 'basket' 7m in diameter which would have allowed for the through flow of water while retaining anything placed inside the structure. The floor was probably laid with cobbles and stones.

Are there any parallels for similar structures? Although when the site was originally recorded a small but pronounced and well-defined bank was sketched around the posts of the circle with a possible 'porch' or 'entrance'; see Bingeman's sketch (Fig 36), this feature was only recorded as a low rather flattened bank by subsequent formal surveys by the HWTMA, Wessex Archaeology, Jon Adams, and Portsmouth University but computer enhancement of the digitised contour surveys records it clearly (see Adam *et al* 1995, fig 3). This bank comprised sediment around the waterlogged timber elements (rods, sails and, planks) between the upright posts. Little evidence of the 'porch' or 'funnel' was recorded despite computer enhanced images of the contour and archaeological survey, although a vague gap in the seabed sediment is broadly coincident with this feature (compare Fig 36 with Fig 37 and Adam *et al* 1995, fig 3).

The implication, clearly, is of a marine function. This factor, when taken in collaboration with the rest of the evidence from the harbour, described below; the presence of metal toolmarks; and the radiocarbon date all point towards a historic rather than prehistoric date. In its intertidal position this structure is certainly unusual but a close parallel can be found in the unlikely setting of Lake Fusaro, near Naples, in Italy where very similar structures were used as oyster pens (Fig 42; Yonge 1960, fig 59; Fontana and Fontana, above). Here, in the 19th century AD, oyster larvae and spats were raised and fattened in 'Oyster Pyramids' piles of cobbles and stones which raised the spats from the muddy bottom, and which were ringed by stakes. The spats settled on and anchored themselves to the stones and both stones and spats were protected by the stake ring and wattling. Together the structure provides an ideal housing pen for rearing of oyster spats. A number of marine shell were found within the structure the majority of which were oysters, but also cockle, periwinkle, slipper limpet, and mussel were present (see Allen and Wyles, Chapter 5)

While it would be more satisfying, and certainly less contentious, to be able to cite a rather more local parallel we can be fairly confident that the Lake Fusaro connection is more than mere coincidence. In 1874–5, Harry Lobb, the director and owner of an large oyster farming business in Langstone Harbour (*South of England Oyster Company*), expressed his concern that the natural oyster beds of the United Kingdom were becoming almost exhausted and that private beds were '*an actual necessity*' (Lobb 1867). He is reported to have established direct contacts with oyster farmers in Italy, and of all places with Lake Fusaro, and in the 1860s at least two *parcs* were prepared (Philpots 1890, 344) along with various experimental oyster spat beds. It is also recorded that small individual 'ponds' were constructed so that the oysters could be transferred to growing parcs near to the Langstone

Figure 42   Lago Fusaro Oyster parc (from Yonge 1960 after Coste 1861, drawn by S E James)

Channel where they could enter upon the final stage of fattening (*op cit* 1890, 429), perhaps the Sinah structure was one of these. There is no precise record of where these experiments were conducted but the remarkable similarity between the remains of the Sinah structure and the Lake Fusaro examples strongly suggest that here are the remains of one of his, presumably unsuccessful, experiments. One other enigmatic structure is, however recorded in the SMR along the west coast of Hayling Island in the area of the old oyster beds (HI.118). It is described as a circle of postholes, possible a hut circle 18.3m (60ft) in diameter with the postholes 6.1m (20ft) apart. Pointed carbonised ends of the posts 130mm (5 ins) in diameter were reported to surround the central area of flints. Perhaps this too is another oyster parc? Unfortunately it was not examined during this project.

The 9th century AD radiocarbon date, is however, difficult to reconcile with this. While it is known that the timber used to make oyster pyramids or similar structures could be reused wood and anything that was conveniently to hand (see Oyster Island for instance), the time span between the early-medieval date and the Lobbs' oyster parc of the 1860s is a little hard to bridge. The single radiocarbon date cannot, as hoped, be correlated with any dendrochronological dates and the result is open to the usual difficulties posed by single dates, even without the possible reuse of structural material. Bearing in mind this proviso, are we perhaps

Table 5   Finds around Sinah Sands mudflats

Context	Flint			Pottery	Total
	Cores	Debitage	Scrapers	Post-Med	
1993	–	–	–	1	1
?peat	3	3	1	–	–
1994	–	13	5	2	20
Total	3	16	6	3	28

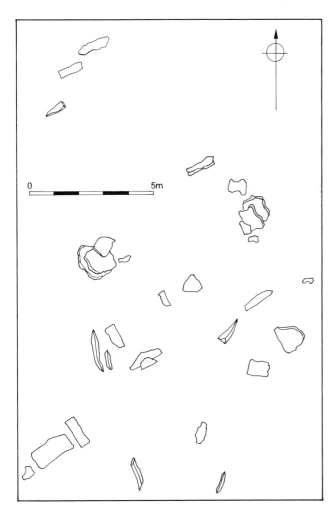

Figure 43   Plan of Sinah Creek stone scatter (after Garry Momber, drawn by S E James)

dealing with an earlier fishing structure that has a fortuitous resemblance to later oyster farming structures? The only datable artefacts recovered from the vicinity in the walkover survey were post-medieval sherds (Table 5).

Other underwater sites
by Garry Momber

Investigations adjacent to the Hayling Island ferry pontoon were conducted on the site believed to be below the prisoner hulks from the Napoleonic Wars. Nothing of interest was found. Wooden wreckage on the edges of channels in Langstone Harbour was recorded by contour searches, particularly along the edge of the main channel 300m north of the Hayling ferry pontoon.

Sinah Creek stone scatter
by John M Bingeman and Garry Momber

An incongruous deposit of stone slabs in a tributary at the eastern end of Sinah Lake (50 48.22N 0 59.95W) was investigated. The group of stones, superficially similar to Mixon rock (a series of distinctive yellow and grey beds of limestone with Alveolina limestone beds), were in Sinah Creek about 500m further up-creek from the timber stake circle (SU 701 007; Fig 45). The group comprised a series of about 30 large flat stones (up to 1.6 long by 0.75m wide) scattered over an area of area of about 18m × 12m (Fig 43). They were surveyed by HWTMA. These are large enough to be structural (ie a jetty), but no structural form was noted, and it is thought that they might perhaps be the remains of a cargo of building stone or even ballast. The stones were interestingly regular; many appeared to be of similar size of just over 1m wide and just under 0.1m thick. Some also had regular, roughly right-angled corners, although there was no evidence that they were worked. Fifteen of the stones were lying flush with the sea floor while sixteen were at a slight angle of up to 30° from the seabed. Two stones were almost vertical and rise to a height of 0.8m. A sample of stone was given to Professor Peacock whose comments are given below.

The stone
by D P S Peacock

A sample from an area of large stones on the seabed off Sinah Point was submitted for petrological opinion. The rock is a fine grained, buff, glauconitic sandstone of flaggy and friable habit. It is quite different to the fossiliferous oolite from the Mixon reef and suggests that the stone derived from that locality can be dismissed.

The material was not examined *in situ*, but consideration should be given to the likelihood of this being a natural pavement caused by the erosion and disintegration of a thin lens of sandstone within the London Clay or Bracklesham Beds (depending upon the precise location of the find). The rock is insufficiently indurated to be of much use as a building stone although it might have been used in rubble building, as there is a dearth of material in this area. It could have been ballast, loaded elsewhere and dumped at Sinah, but there is no reason to suggest that it is anything other than a local Tertiary sandstone lens.

Little Rock Leak stones
by Arthur T Mack

On the south-western foreshore, a leak known locally as Little Rock Leak runs east–west for 400m (50 48.03N 01 00.18W). The name most likely comes from the fact that along its length it is lined with large flat stones, some vertical and others lying flat. It seems likely that these may be a local Tertiary sandstone lens as suggested by Professor Peacock for similar stones at Sinah Creek.

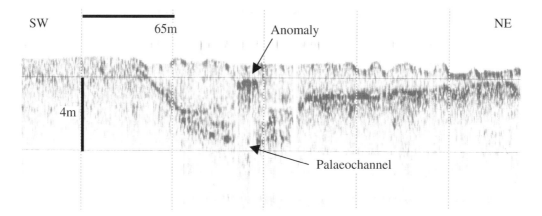

SW ⟶ 65m ⟶ NE

Anomaly

4m

Palaeochannel

Figure 44 Chirp *profile of an unidentified anomaly buried to a depth of approximately 1.7m in Langstone Channel (Justin Dix)*

Excavation of the *Chirp* anomaly
by Jon Adams

Following the detection of a buried anomaly that was both a very hard acoustic reflector and relatively discrete spatially (Dix, Chapter 2), it was decided to excavate the feature in order to identify it. It must be admitted that the 'ship-shape' of the feature added a certain frisson of excitement, although this was tempered by the depth at which it was calculated to lie below the harbour floor (1.75m). On the basis of the material found on the adjacent islands, it seemed unlikely that cultural material, let alone a large seagoing craft, could have come to lie this deep. A probe survey was attempted but due the depth of sediment the results were inconclusive.

An excavation was mounted (by the University of Southampton and HWTMA) to investigate the anomaly. The feature was revisited using DGPS and *Chirp*. The mean centre was judged on the basis of several passes and marked with a buoy. An area 2.5 × 2.5m was gridded to define the excavation area. Over four days the sediment was progressively reduced down to the level at which *Chirp* had detected the reflector (Fig 44). A trench almost 2m square and about 1.7m deep was excavated (Fig 46). At exactly 1.75m a coherent, compacted layer of flint nodules was revealed (Fig 46). Many had marine growth adhering, including oyster, demonstrating that they had once formed the bed of a waterway, perhaps one of the many palaeochannels picked up by *Chirp* in the same survey (Dix this volume).

This was a highly effective correlation of *Chirp* data with excavation and points the way to further investigations of this type, where high-resolution profiling can help determine the site of excavation, so maximising cost-effectiveness and bottom time.

Wrecks
by Garry Momber

A number of wreck sites are known in Langstone Harbour (Fig 45) but very few details are recorded.

The HWTMA aimed to address this discrepancy by locating some of the sites and conducting surveys with the aid of the local knowledge of Arthur Mack and John Bingeman. Information collected during dives has enabled the recording of a number of wrecks by documenting their current condition and dimensions. The divers were able to validate the SMR information and provide information of the length, breadth, elevation and, orientation of each wreck.

The Withern

The *Withern* (LH.112) was a bucket dredger which was lost four cables (4/10ths of a nautical mile) north of Ferry House (50 48.10N 01 01.73W) in 1926 (Fig 45). The wreck lies on one side with a north-south aspect. The northern end of the shipwreck terminated approximately 2m to the east of the isolated marker buoy. The Sonardyne Homer Pro acoustic measuring system was used to record the longer distances. A hand held unit interrogates transponders which are fixed on datum points. The position of the hand held unit can then be calculated (see Chapter 1). A network of three transponders was set up around the *Withern*, one to the west, amidships, and the other two at the north and south extremities of the wreck. The distance between these two transponders was recorded as 34.9m which equates to the overall length of the wreckage. The Langstone elevation at the highest point of the wreck reached 4.5m above the seabed on the west side and 3m above the seabed directly to the east. This was located at 25m from the northern point of the wreck where width of the structure measured almost 8m. Initial observations infer the bows lie to the north as the structure tapers into the seabed in this direction and the majority of the wreck lies to the south. The remaining structure is becoming heavily degraded, it is lying on its starboard side which has become crushed beneath its own weight.

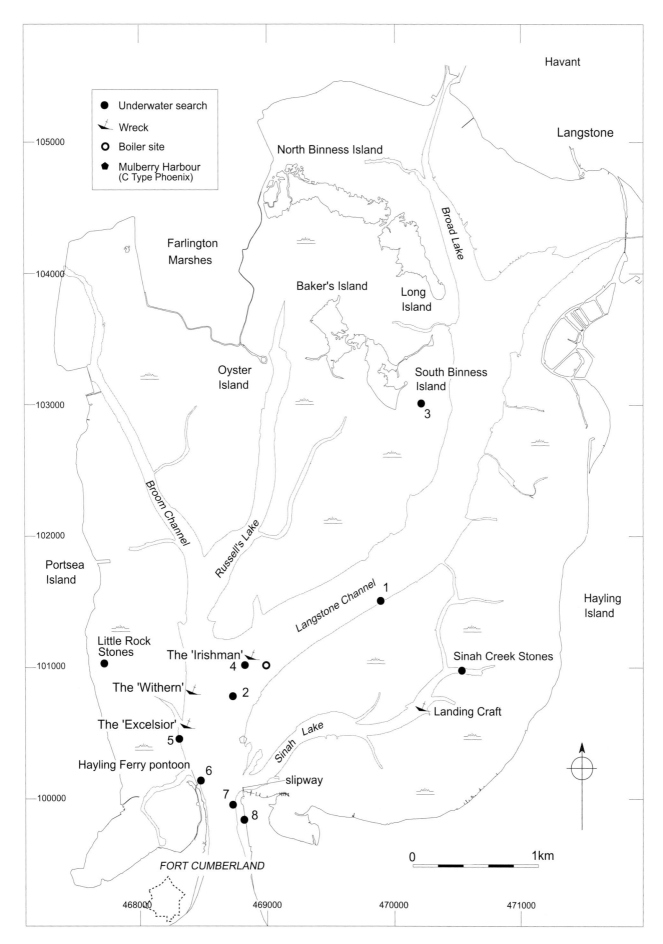

Figure 45   Location of the swim searches and wrecks in Langstone Harbour. Data from Portsmouth University, drawn by S E James

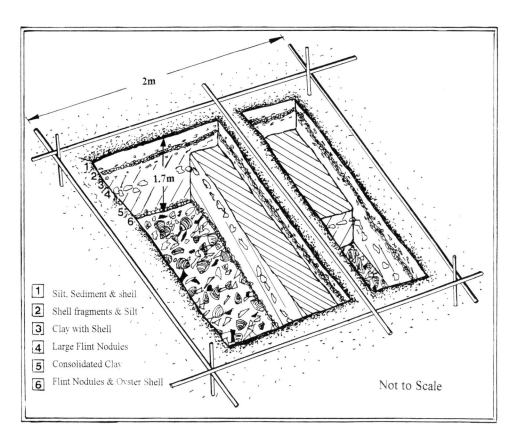

Figure 46 Plan of excavation of the 'Chirp Anomaly' (after G Momber, see HWMTA 1997, 7, drawn by Garry Momber)

1 Silt, Sediment & shell
2 Shell fragments & Silt
3 Clay with Shell
4 Large Flint Nodules
5 Consolidated Clay
6 Flint Nodules & Oyster Shell

Not to Scale

Facing west are the remains of the port side consisting of broken and eroded metal plates. Despite the corrosion, a boarding ladder still remains *in situ* 27m from the bow. A large number of artefacts could be seen scattered around the wreckage which include both metal and ceramic objects although time did not permit detailed assessment.

The Irishman

The paddle tug *Irishman* detonated a magnetic mine on May 8th 1941. She sank with the loss of all hands (50 48.28N 01 01.33W). She now lies badly broken adjacent to an isolated danger marker buoy near Sword Point (LH.111, Fig 45). A single dive was undertaken on the site and survey measurements taken. An estimate of the extent of remaining debris was produced although only limited survey was possible in respect of the confused and scattered nature of the site.

The wreck site lay to the north of the marker buoy and breaks the surface at low water. It predominately consists of substantial amounts of bent and twisted metal around a structure spread over an area of at least 30m, with elements of the wreckage rising over 2m from the seabed. Discernible elements also included a bucket from the paddle wheel and hull frames. The upper parts of the structure were predominately covered with kelp (*Laminaria digitata*) which became sparser with depth.

The complexity of the site restricted comprehensive survey, but an estimate of remaining debris was

produced, although only limited survey was possible. More time was necessary than was available to understand the wreck fully, and the Navy have now cleared the site with explosives.

Boiler site

An anomaly 100m to the west of the Irishman was investigated (isolated object marker buoy 50 48.28N 01 01.22W). The object had been the cause of net fasteners (ie snagged fishing nets) and recorded as an anomaly on echo sounders when traversed by boat. The object was a boiler, possibly from the *Irishman*. It measured 2.35m wide, 3.54m long, standing 1.77m from the sea floor. The boiler was sketched (Fig 47) and its position plotted. It is now believed to have been cleared by the navy.

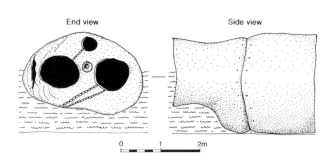

End view   Side view

0   1   2m

Figure 47 Plan of boiler of the paddle tug Irishman *(after Momber, drawn by S E James)*

The Excelsior

The *Excelsior* (LH.138) is a well-preserved 80ft self propelled barge sitting upright on the seabed north of Langstone Pontoon (50 48.00N 01 01.75W). The wreck is not recorded on the Hampshire SMR and the date of loss is currently undetermined. She was powered (still retaining her propeller *in situ*), with her hull structure and large areas of the main deck remaining intact.

The shipwreck lay with her bows to the north along a north–south aspect. The length of the ship measured 22m with an elevation from the seabed of 2.5m at its highest point. The width between the port and bow quarters measured 3.4m while the width amidships was calculated at 3.5m. The ship had a rounded stern, 1m deep by 3.4m wide. The cargo hatch begins 5.5m from the bow and was 9.5m long. There was no evidence of cargo in the hold although a thorough investigation was not undertaken. Aft of the cargo hatch, the upper parts of the wheel-house cover had gone, leaving a structure 0.5m high, this being the same height as the cargo hatch and the guard-rail. The remains of the wheel-house measured 4m in length.

The Mulberry Harbour remains
by Michael Hughes and Garry Momber

The harbour also contains relics from World War II. These remains have not yet been subject to survey but are of historical value and should be acknowledged.

Directly north of the Hayling Island ferry pontoon, a large concrete structure sits proud of the water at all states of the tide (50 47.91N 01 01.40W). The structure is a large caisson built as part of the outer breakwater for the Mulberry Harbour at Arromanches in Normandy. It is a *C Type Phoenix Unit*. These were constructed all along the south coast, submerged so as to be concealed from German reconnaissance, then refloated and towed across the channel as part of the D-Day landings. This unit is one of the many that did not make it across the channel; it now rests with its back broken, oriented approximately 345° along its length.

Mulberry Harbour construction site

The pre-fabricated harbours, which were used in the D-Day *Overlord* and *Neptune* operations to provide shelter and landing facilities for vessels, troops, and machinery during the invasion of German-occupied France, were code-named *Mulberry,* and comprised, like that just described, a number of component parts (Futter 1981; 1982) with different functions.

These included deep water shipping breakwaters, codenamed *Bombardon*, floating pierhead units and roadways codenamed *Whale*, temporary inshore breakwaters consisting of scuttled ships codenamed *Gooseberry*, and permanent inshore breakwaters consisting of concrete caissons codenamed *Phoenix*.

There was a number of sites around the Hampshire coast where these different components were constructed – in Portsmouth Dockyard, on the beaches at Stokes Bay, Gosport, and Stone Point, at Lepe (Hughes 1992), as well as in the Beaulieu River. A number of the concrete caissons were built at the Langstone Harbour site (Hodge 1946). These, together with another 140, were towed across the Channel in the days following D-Day and strategically sunk off the Normandy coast at Arromanches (where the remains of some of the caissons can still be seen on the beach and offshore) and Omaha Beach.

The caissons reinforced the temporary Gooseberry blockship breakwaters which were installed during the initial Allied landings, as the latter could be brought across the Channel under their own power more quickly than the Phoenix units, which had to be towed by tugs (Wilson and Sully 1947). The Phoenix breakwaters were reinforced in the autumn of 1944 by the addition of supplementary strengthened caissons when it became apparent that they were to continue in use longer than the 90 days originally planned (Wood 1947).

On the foreshore, to the south of the Ferry Inn on the south-west corner of Hayling Island, are the remains of a Mulberry Harbour construction and launching site. They consist of a row of concrete slips which are still visible in the shingle on the Hayling Island side of the Langstone Harbour entrance Channel (50 47.60N 01 01.42W). The slips form parallel lines in the intertidal zone together with parts of the construction and assembly areas and winch-house foundations used to launch the caissons sideways into the sea at high tide. The type B2 caissons that were built at Hayling measured 62m long, 13.4m wide, and 10.7m high. They were divided into twenty-two compartments arranged in rows of eleven separated by dividing concrete walls 300mm thick at intervals of 5m. These compartments were to provide stability during sinking. Gangways 1.8m wide were constructed around the sides and end of the caissons 6m below the top to carry scaffolding during construction, bollards for towing, and holes for pumping out water during refloating operations (Hodge 1946).

The caissons were made of concrete slabs and assembled by a largely unskilled labour force. The type B2 did not carry anti-aircraft guns and only the sections at either end were roofed over with horizontal concrete slabs. Altogether 24 B2 caissons were built including the seven at Hayling Island.

In the absence of a dry-dock or facilities for building the caissons while floating, the assembled units were launched into the sea sideways. This operation was carried out when the units had been assembled to a height of 6m and weighed 2000 tons. They were then completed whilst afloat, towed away and 'parked' on the seabed at Selsey or Dungeness until needed, when they were refloated ready for towing to

Normandy. The work at the Hayling Island site was carried out with the technical assistance from Messrs Holloway Bros (London) Ltd, who had developed the basic techniques used in the construction and sideways launching of heavy craft during work on a prototype alternating pier head at Conway, in North Wales.

Landing craft

In Sinah Lake, within 100m of the stake circle, the bows of a landing craft rise from the mudflats (50 48.03N 01 00.18W). The site is marked with an isolated object marker buoy and is exposed in all but the highest tides.

4   The finds assemblages

Nearly all of the artefacts recorded during the Langstone Harbour Archaeological Survey Project are surface finds and unstratified material; ie they have not been recovered from sealed and excavated contexts. Most finds were made during the systematic walkover surveys and from total artefact collection units, or by Arthur Mack. The few exceptions to this were where excavations were conducted of the features such as hearth 1702 and the section of ditch 1711 on North Binness and the excavation of whole pots from clays on the foreshores. Very few artefacts were recovered from test-pit excavations and the only objects removed from exposed cliff sections were where detailed recording of the sediments was undertaken.

Worked flint
by Julie Gardiner

A total of 4119 flint artefacts was recovered during the survey, 95% of them from the intertidal zones of the four main islands. A number of additional pieces, notified subsequently by Arthur Mack, have been examined, but have not been included in the totals here. The material ranges in date from Mesolithic to Bronze Age and the initial examination did not indicate the obvious presence of any discrete groups of artefacts belonging to any one period. For the purposes of analysis, therefore, all the flintwork was considered as one mixed assemblage. Examination of various aspects of the composition and distribution showed that some spatial variation is discernible and that it is possible to indicate areas where the flintwork represents material of predominantly one period or another.

Raw material

Flint is available in abundance in the area of Langstone Harbour today, occurring as vast quantities of gravel nodules washed up on the shoreline and forming gravel banks and beaches. In prehistory, however, while flint may have been easily accessible, its immediate source would have been significantly different. The harbour has developed in a region where the dipping Tertiary deposits of the Hampshire Basin are overlain by Quaternary sands and gravel, see Chapter 1, and probably represent a mixture of glacial, fluvioglacial, and river terrace material. The gravel washing around in the harbour today is almost certainly derived from these sources but it is probable that throughout much of the prehistoric period it would have been available on or close

to the dry-land surface or as river gravels: ie it would have formed a terrestrial and riverine resource rather than a maritime one. Also, to the north of Langstone, the Bracklesham Beds are abundant in flint nodules which could have been washed down by the former rivers running into what is now the harbour, as could surface-derived material from the Chalk downs.

Although initially described as deriving from 'a flint source within the chalk' (Bradley and Hooper 1973, 17), the raw material used to produce the Langstone flint assemblage is indistinguishable from the material currently present in the harbour. It consists of water worn nodules and rounded pebbles of varying size but generally weighing under c 300g, with the majority under c 100g. The colour of the flint varies widely from pale grey and buff, through various shades of grey and brown, to black, and from translucent through to completely opaque. Cortex colour also ranges from white and buff, often with an unpleasant greenish stain, through pale brown, dark brown, and black. For the most part cortex is thin and smooth from water rolling. A few pieces, generally of relatively large size, appear to be Chalk flint with a thick, white, less worn cortex. The vast majority of pieces are in fresh condition with sharp edges and little cortication and remarkably little edge damage (see above); only a minority give the appearance of having rolled around in the sea for very long.

The quality of the raw material varies considerably. Whilst some pieces clearly shattered early in the attempt to work them, others produced thin, fine blades of high quality or were capable of being pressure flaked (see Plate 31, below). Internal flaws account for many of the abandoned cores and a number of frost shattered fragments were used as make-do cores and implements. Many pieces bear 'pot-lid' scars resulting from frost action. Where the raw material is black and completely opaque, frost shattering may have resulted in a small number of naturally fractured pieces being identified as possibly struck, but the incidence of this is less than 1% of the total. Overall, the flint is most reminiscent of the raw material employed at Hengistbury Head, Dorset, which was based on the use of Pleistocene gravel and Bracklesham Bed nodules (Gardiner 1987a).

Cores and debitage

Cores and debitage comprise 91.5% (n = 3758) of the total worked flint recovered (Table 3, Chapter 2). Of this total 250 cores, core fragments, and core trimmings (6.1% of total assemblage) are present, of

Table 6   Cores, classification of complete cores

No platforms	Blade cores				Flake cores				Total
	1	2	3+	Total blade cores	1	2	3+	Total flake cores	
No	22	16	7	45	18	12	31	61	106
% bl/fl cores	48.9	35.6	15.6		29.5	19.7	50.8		
% total	20.8	15.1	6.6		17.0	11.3	29.2		

Table 7   Weights of complete flint cores

1–25g	26–50g	51–75g	76–100g	101–125g	126–150g	151–200g	201g+	Total
6	31	33	11	6	8	9	2	106
5.7%	29.2%	31.1%	10.4%	5.7%	7.5%	8.5%	1.9%	

which 100 (40% of core debris) represent the production of predominantly blades and 150 (60%) the production of predominantly flakes. A breakdown of core types is provided in Table 6 and of core weights in Table 7. Single, two-, and multi-platform blade and flake cores are present (Clark *et al* 1960), of which almost half the blade cores are single-platform, and just over half of the flake cores are multiplatform. One core is just possibly a discoidal arrowhead core. A few 'cores' are little more than tested pieces fashioned on large, heavy flakes or frost shattered pieces and these usually display only a few removals. The smallest of the cores weighs just 19g and the largest (excluding a 446g nodule with one or two flake removals of dubious prehistoric origin from Hayling Island) 289g. Over 75% of the cores weigh under 100g (Table 7).

Many of the cores seem to have been abandoned because of internal flaws and frost damage, though some were abandoned when they could have been worked down further. The crude nature of some pieces clearly results from a poor standard of workmanship rather than the quality of the individual nodule. An interesting feature of the core assemblage is the very high incidence of core trimmings (n = 130; 52% of total core assemblage). Without exception these are all core edge trimming flakes – no core tablets were recovered. Of these trimming flakes, 53 (40.8%) appear to be from predominantly blade cores and the remainder from predominantly flake or indeterminate cores. In general the blade cores display a higher standard of workmanship and control than do the flake cores, even allowing for the variable quality of the raw material, suggesting a chronological separation.

No detailed metrical analysis of the debitage was undertaken because of the obviously mixed nature of the flint assemblage. Debitage was divided visually into blades (breadth:length ratio of < 2:5), flakes, and miscellaneous debitage, the latter of which accounts for many of the angular, shatter fragments which

have resulted from the breaking up of cores, frost shattering of struck pieces, and the poorly controlled use of hard hammers.

Of the 3508 pieces of non-core debitage, only 608 (17.3%) are blades or blade fragments (see Plate 31, below). This is an unexpectedly low total for the number of blade cores. Negative blade scars on the cores and trimmings seem to correspond reasonably well with the range of blade sizes present. There is little to suggest from the blade assemblage that there has been any *obvious* sorting of this material, either post-depositionally or during recovery, which might have resulted in the removal of smaller, lighter pieces which might be considered to be most easily lost to erosion (see Chapter 2) or missed during collection: in fact, if anything, it is the larger blades that could be under-represented. Examination of the debitage from the total collection grids showed that *c* 15% of non-core pieces, both blades and flakes, are under 25mm in maximum dimension, which accords well with, for instance, excavation assemblages from sites along the route of the Dorchester Bypass, Dorset (Bellamy 1997, table 25), and at Hengistbury Head (Gardiner 1987a). Artefact recovery was also consistently undertaken by the same individuals who were experienced in fieldwalking for flint artefacts. However, the possible loss of a small-blade element must be borne in mind and it is notable that no microburins or other evidence of microlith manufacture were recovered (see below).

Waste flakes come in a wide range of shapes, sizes, and thicknesses and more closely reflect the variability of the raw material than do the blades which, to some extent, have been more carefully produced from better prepared cores. A high proportion of the flakes, and some of the blades, were produced using hard hammers on broad platforms, resulting in many pronounced bulbs of percussion, often with incipient cones, and obvious mis-hits, and *c* 12% of flakes exhibit hinge or step fractures. The incidence

Table 8 Flake classes, total collection squares only

Area	Total flakes/blades	Primary	Secondary	Tertiary
North Binness Island; 1 + 175–8	369	44/11.9%	72/19.5%	253/68.6%
North Binness Island; 4 + 473–4	136	21/15.4%	21/15.4%	946/9.1%
Long Island; 3 + 388–90	624	35/5.6%	351/56.3%	238/38.1%
Long Island; 18	294	25/8.5%	87/29.6%	182/61.9%
Long Island south	30	5/16.7%	12/40.0%	13/43.3%
Baker's Island; 20–22	66	15/22.7%	30/45.5%	21/31.8%
Baker's Island; 23–5	300	46/15.3%	121/40.3%	133/44.3%
Baker's Island; 26	622	56/9.0%	173/27.8%	393/63.2%
Total	2441	247/10.1%	867/35.5%	1327/54.4%

of these breaks can be partly accounted for by the variable quality of the raw material but the overall impression is that much of the flake debitage is the result of a lower standard of workmanship than is the blade debitage which, again, has chronological implications.

All non-core debitage from the total collection units was examined for the extent of surviving cortex and divided into primary (>75% cortex), secondary (25–75%), and tertiary (<25%) categories (Table 8). Overall only c 10% primary flakes were recorded, with c 36% secondary and 54% tertiary, although there is considerable variation across the harbour. This is an unexpectedly low percentage of primary flakes and high incidence of tertiary pieces, especially given that the incidence of cores is unremarkable. The apparent over-representation of tertiary pieces may be partly explained by the very high incidence of core trimmings which strongly suggests that 'good' cores were being rejuvenated and worked out despite the presence of an abundant source of raw material. A similar pattern was observed by the author among a series of late Neolithic–early Bronze Age surface flint assemblages in northern Hampshire, though here the use of readily-available and generally much larger nodules resulted in the rejuvenation of cores by the use of core tablets rather than edge-trimming flakes (Gardiner 1988, 420). At Hengistbury Head, a similarly low proportion of primary flakes (c 13%), high incidence of tertiary flakes (c 62%), and occurrence of cores/fragments (5.8% of assemblage) was recorded from Site 6 (Gardiner 1987a). Here, however, the raw material was of consistently better quality than in Langstone Harbour and only seventeen (8.7% of core debris) core trimmings/rejuvenation flakes were recorded. At Hengistbury the cores demonstrated a wasteful use of the raw material and, unlike at Langstone, selection of particular types of flint for the manufacture of implements was apparent and many pieces were manufactured on primary and secondary flakes.

Implements

A total of 361 flint implements was recovered, accounting for 8.8% of the total flint assemblage. This relatively high proportion of implements by comparison with many 'terrestrial' assemblages, is partly the result of the unsystematic recovery of pieces by non-archaeological fieldwork team members and by the more subjective recovery of 'representative' samples of flintwork from the rapid walkover surveys.

Two hundred and seventy-seven of the identifiable tools (77%) are scrapers. The scrapers are manufactured mainly on broad flakes and irregular, miscellaneous pieces of debitage, and range from the very rough and ready to the quite finely pressure flaked. The assemblage includes 26 (9.5%) long end scrapers and five (1.8%) hollow scrapers, and although 25 (9.1%) examples are small and weigh 12g or less, only eight (2.9%) of these may be classified as 'thumbnail' scrapers. The area and angle of edge retouch varies considerably but is generally an unremarkable 30–60% and 40–60° with a few very steep examples and a few very shallow. One steep end scraper is made on a huge flake, weighing some 256g, but fewer than ten of the remainder weigh over 60g. The average scraper weight is 26.5g. It is impossible, therefore, to separate the scrapers chronologically.

The non-scraper tool assemblage (n = 84) by area of the harbour is shown in Table 9. The flake-tool assemblage consists of a restricted range of forms, of which piercing and fabricating tools are the most common. The flake knife from North Binness is neatly retouched on both long edges of a broad blade and the plano-convex knives (Plate 28), though not of very high quality, are pressure flaked. Otherwise the flake tools are fairly roughly made, generally on thick and irregular flakes. Two blades from Baker's Island have fine serrations along one long edge.

Thirty pieces exhibit what appear to be small areas of genuine edge retouch, including one with

Table 9 The tool assemblage excluding scrapers

Location	Core tools						Arrowheads					Flake tools									Total
	A	B	C	D	E	F	G	H	I	J	K	L	M	N	O	P	Q	R	S	T	
North Binness S shore West	1	–	–	–	–	–	–	–	–	1	–	1	–	–	1	–	–	–	1	3	8
North Binness S shore East	–	–	–	–	–	–	–	–	–	–	–	–	1	–	–	1	–	–	–	1	3
Long Island SW shore	–	–	–	–	1	–	2	1	1	3	–	1	1	1	–	1	–	–	1	5	18
South Binness	1	–	–	–	–	–	1	1	–	–	–	–	–	1	–	1	1	–	2	1	9
Bakers Island West	1	–	–	1	–	1	–	–	–	–	–	1	–	–	–	–	–	–	–	1	5
Bakers Island East	4	1	1	2	1*	–	2	–	–	–	1	2	1	1	–	–	–	2	3	17	38
NE corner of harbour	–	–	–	–	–	–	–	–	–	–	–	–	–	–	–	–	–	–	–	1	1
Oyster Island	1	–	–	–	–	–	–	–	–	–	–	–	–	–	–	–	–	–	–	1	2
	8	1	1	3	2	1	5	2	1	4	1	5	3	3	1	3	3	2	7	30	84

A = tranchet adze/sharpening flake; B = pick; C = tranchet tool; D = hammer; E = axe fragment * = polished; F = ?miniature axe; G = leaf arrowhead; H = laurel leaf; I = oblique arrowhead; J = transverse arrowhead; K = barbed and tanged; L = piercer; M = denticulate; N = fabricator/slug; O = tanged piece; P = plano-convex knife; Q = flake knife; R = serrated flake/blade; S = bifacially retouched; T= edge retouched

*Plate 28   Selection of
flint tools (top row)
Plano-convex knife,
oblique arrowhead,
unfinished laurel leaf,
plano-convex knife,
broken borer (bottom row)
broken bifacially
retouched implement,
possible miniature axe,
transverse arrowhead,
broken pick (Elaine A
Wakefield)*

*Plate 29   Tranchet adze
and four adze sharpening
flakes from the survey
(Elaine A Wakefield)*

apparent edge gloss such as would result from the cutting of plant materials. Other possibly irregularly retouched pieces occur, but have not been so classified as they could equally have incurred post-depositional edge damage. Six other pieces, all broken, have either two retouched edges, one of which has invasive retouch, or are fragments of bifacially worked flakes, none of which is of identifiable form.

Sixteen core tools and fragments were recovered. A possible flaked axe in a burnt and damaged condition comes from Long Island and a rather neater, but possibly reworked, piece from Baker's Island is probably a miniature axe. A broken polished axe was also recovered from Baker's Island. The tranchet tool from Baker's Island has a very steep 'blade'

giving it a 'pushplane' appearance and there are three hammers and a small, crude pick, also from Baker's Island. A few of the cores have small areas of battering suggesting that they were used as hammers, but only three hammerstones were recovered. Apart from the polished axe, all of these pieces are manufactured from larger nodules of locally available flint. Two tranchet adzes, and four of the five sharpening flakes (Plate 29), by contrast, are all manufactured from a fine-grained mottled grey flint with some toffee-coloured banding which has the appearance of chalk-derived flint and does not seem to occur elsewhere in the assemblage except in the form of one finely made oblique arrowhead. The fifth sharpening flake clearly comes from a large adze. It is in a toffee-coloured flint which may be derived from the Bracklesham Beds but the original implement was clearly made from a nodule which would have been unusually large for the local material. A third tranchet adze, from South Binness, was unfortunately lost but was again manufactured from a large nodule of what appeared to be chalk flint, though not the same material as the other adzes, as was the polished axe.

The arrowheads include examples of all the principal types of the Neolithic and early Bronze Age (Plate 28). The leaf arrowheads all exhibit neat pressure flaking but the possible example from Baker's Island seems to have broken in manufacture, as did the laurel leaves from South Binness and Long Islands, on the latter of which it can be seen that several efforts were made to thin this internally flawed piece before it snapped. A broken, bifacially worked fragment from Baker's Island could also have been intended to be a laurel leaf. In addition to the oblique arrowhead mentioned above, two rather more rough and ready transverse arrowheads were also recovered; all three are from Long Island. A small, neat, barbed and tanged example was found by Arthur Mack on Baker's Island. With the exception of the oblique example mentioned above, all the arrowheads could be made on locally available flint.

Chronology, dating, and distribution of the flint assemblage

There are, unfortunately, relatively few individually diagnostic pieces amongst the flint assemblage. Certainly most of the blade cores and trimmings and some of the blades are of Mesolithic date and the general size and proportions of the blades and blade scars and presence of tranchet adzes and sharpening flakes points towards the presence in the harbour area of a later Mesolithic (c 7000–5000 BC) assemblage. Similarly, the many broad and squat flakes, crude flake cores, accidental flake fractures, use of hard hammer technique, and a tool assemblage restricted mainly to piercing, scraping, and fabricating tools amongst the rest of the material indicates a substantial mature Bronze Age element (c 1600–800 BC). In between, however, is a range of scrapers, indeterminate flakes and cores, and some flake tools and arrowheads of typically late Neolithic–early Bronze Age type (c 2600–1600 BC) which accords well with finds made by earlier fieldworkers in the harbour.

As with most ploughzone assemblages, distinguishing between these various elements can only be done on a broad and semi-quantitative basis since probably more than 90% of the flint artefacts cannot be assigned individually to any tight timescale within the possibly 6000 years during which the various components of the overall assemblage were in regular use in southern England. By employing the fairly basic methods of structured analysis described in Chapter 2, the composition of the flint assemblage in various parts of the harbour could be examined for chronological and spatial variation.

Although the initial finds scan did not indicate the presence of discretely located groups of flintwork belonging to any one period, the impression of the fieldwork team actually in the field was that parts of Baker's Island produced more obviously Mesolithic material than flintwork of other periods, or from other parts of the harbour. The finds scan suggested that there might well be a more pronounced Mesolithic element amongst the material recovered from this island than elsewhere but it had also to be considered that the positioning of the individual collection units, which were targeted to sample obvious flint scatters, might, even subconsciously, have been influenced by the observation of blades. The finds scan noted a general background presence of blades in most of the collection areas, and of blade cores and trimmings, the latter of which are not necessarily distinguishable from other forms of debitage in the field and which, as a result, might be considered to provide more positive, less subjective, evidence of Mesolithic activity.

In order to determine whether it was possible to identify more closely any chronological patterning in the flintwork the composition and relative proportions of the various elements of debitage, independent of any identifiable or datable tools, were examined more closely for all areas of the harbour where total collection units had been employed. In the first instance, all cores and other debitage from those areas which had been subject to total artefact collection – either by grid or individual squares – were tabulated and a series of ratios calculated. These ratios were:

- ratio of blades to flakes
- ratio of blade cores and trimmings to blades
- ratio of flake cores and trimmings to flakes
- ratio of blade cores to flake cores
- ratio of all cores to all other debitage

The areas concerned were the three collection grids, the central area of the south-western coast of Long Island to the south of Area 3 (designated Collection Area 18 in the field; Fig 18), the southern part of that coast, and the various collection zones in different parts of Baker's Island. To the collection grid data were then added those from the nearby individual collection units in the western part of the south coast of North Binness (to the Area 1 data), the eastern part of that coast (to Area 4), and collection squares located just south of, but on the same part of the foreshore, as Area 3 (to Area 3). Broad patterns began to emerge and, where general consistency was observed across the range of calculations for adjacent collection areas, the results for those areas were combined and compared to both the original calculations and those for other areas. Since there is an inevitable degree of subjectivity involved here in assessing the significance of the variation in the ratios calculated, especially where collection areas were somewhat arbitrarily

Plate 30 Typical flint artefacts from Langstone Harbour, here collected from a single Total Collection Unit on Baker's Island (Elaine A Wakefield)

defined rather than being topographically distinct, various combinations were tried for adjacent areas, for instance, Collection Areas 20–3, 21–2, 23–4, etc (see Fig 30 for location of Collection Areas) until a 'best fit' was achieved for the set of ratios calculated. Details are tabulated in archive and the final set of calculations is presented in Table 10.

The three total collection areas in North Binness West, East, and Long Island North, provide the most objective view of the flint assemblage because, although initially selected because of the presence of specific features or concentrations of artefacts, each covers a contiguous area of 1600, 1500, and 2000m² respectively. When the small areas comprising the extra collection squares have been added in, the density of flints per square metre is very low (0.23, 0.11, 0.33) but, as described above, the distributions within these areas are not regular and seem to relate largely to microtopographical features of each (see Chapter 2). There are also notable differences in the composition of the assemblages. The western part of North Binness produced more than double the amount of flintwork than the eastern part but with barely a quarter of the number of cores/fragments. Overall, there is a very low ratio of cores to other waste. The eastern part of the shoreline, by contrast, has a very high ratio of cores to other waste, a higher proportion of blades and blade cores to flakes and flake cores, and a higher incidence of primary flakes. Nine and ten implements respectively were recovered, comprising 2.3% and 5.6% of the flintwork in these two areas. The range of tools in the eastern area (four types, of which two-thirds are scrapers) is more restricted than in the western (seven types).

Long Island North, which produced the largest assemblage of flintwork of the three, falls between the other two in terms of the ratio of cores to other waste. Although this area has a similar ratio of blades to

flakes to the western part of North Binness, overall the characteristics of this group of material are closer to those of the eastern part of North Binness than the western area. The proportion of blade cores compared to flake cores is higher than for either of the North Binness areas. This area produced the largest number of blade cores and trimmings of any area surveyed and, with the exception of the eastern side of Baker's Island, the largest number of blades. It produced 29 implements from total collection units, of which all but three are scrapers. This greater emphasis on blades is also apparent in the middle part of the foreshore on Long Island. Although a much smaller number of collection areas was employed here, the ratios of blade cores to blades, and of blades to flakes is similar to the northern zone but there are very few flake cores, especially in proportion to the number of both blade cores and flakes recovered. Only eight implements were recovered, of which two were Neolithic arrowheads. Collection units further south on Long Island present generally similar results to the northern part, except that there are, again, fewer flake cores and trimmings and no implements.

In the field, as stated above, the assemblage from the eastern part of Baker's Island suggested a greater presence of Mesolithic material than elsewhere. This area produced the largest number of blades from any of the collection areas and, indeed, almost the greatest quantity of flint. The various ratios calculated for this area distinguish it from the rest of Baker's Island and certainly indicate a greater emphasis on the presence of both blades and blade cores, producing the highest ratio of blades to flakes of any of the collection areas. However, it must be remembered that the collection units on Baker's Island were not contiguous and only 86m² were subject to total collection (Plate 30). The density of

Table 10 Analysis of debitage (total collection squares only)

Area	Total debitage	Blades	Flakes	Ratio bl:fl	Blade cores & trimmings	Ratio blade cores:bl	Flake cores & trimmings	Ratio fl cores:fl	Ratio bl cores: fl cores	Ratio all cores: all waste	No/% implements
North Binness S shore west	375	41	328	1:8	1	1:41	5	1:65.6	1:5	1:61.5	9/2.3%
North Binness S shore east	169	10	126	1:12.6	9	1:1.1	24	1:5.3	1:2.6	1:3.9	10/5.6%
Long Island SW shore north	671	72	552	1:7.7	20	1:3.6	27	1:20.4	1:1.4	1:13.3	29/4.1%
Long Island SW shore centre	308	39	255	1:6.5	11	1:3.5	3	1:85	3.7:1	1:21	8/2.5%
Long Island SW shore south	35	4	26	1:6.5	2	1:2	3	1:8.7	1:1.5	1:7	0/0
Bakers Island South-west	71	8	58	1:7.25	0	0:8	5	1:11.6	0:5	1:14.2	9/11.3%
Bakers Island North-west	317	31	269	1:8.7	6	1:5.2	11	1:24.5	1:1.8	1:17.6	19/5.7%
Bakers Island East	653	118	504	1:4.3	12	1:9.1	19	1:26.5	1:1.6	1:21.1	39/5.6%
South Binness	40	6	28	1:4.7	2	1:3	4	1:7	1:2	1:5.7	3/7.0%
Total	2639	329	2147	1:6.5	63	1:5.2	101	1:20.6	1:1.6	1:14.7	125/4.5

bl = blades; fl = flakes

flints recovered from Baker's Island East, however, is by far the highest of the whole harbour (23.3 per m^2). The field team noted that material seemed to concentrate in small dense clusters where patches of eroding clay survived (see above) among the mudflats. In so small an area as currently comprises Baker's Island (no more than 650 × 500m) it is unlikely that these individual clusters represent discrete 'sites', though there is potential for the survival of evidence for areas where different activities were undertaken. In this respect it may be interesting that the western and north-western parts of the island produced a much higher proportion of primary flakes than the east (Table 8). Baker's Island also produced the greatest number and variety of implements (67) from any of the areas employing collection units, 39 of them from the eastern part of the island. These include retouched blades, adze sharpening flakes, and a pick, supporting the suggestion of an identifiable Mesolithic element.

The assemblage from the three collection squares on South Binness is too small by itself for sensible comment to be made.

To what extent these spatial variations in the relative proportions of different categories of flint artefacts are significant is difficult to assess. However, several points emerge from the total collection unit data:

- There is, overall, an unusually high percentage of core trimming flakes, and low percentage of primary flakes.
- Gridded collection in the western part of Baker's Island produced an assemblage of debitage which is distinctly different to that of the eastern part and Long Island and a wider range of tool types.
- The debitage from Long Island includes a comparatively large number of blades and blade-core debris and is more similar overall to material from the eastern part of North Binness than the western part.
- There is a much clearer Mesolithic element present among the flintwork from Baker's Island than from elsewhere, including diagnostic artefacts. There appears to be a much higher density of flint present on the foreshore on this island than elsewhere and some indication of differences in the composition of the assemblages from different parts of the island.

To the total collection square data can now be added the remainder of the assemblage from the less systematically collected contexts, in particular the remaining implements.

Additional flintwork recovered from Baker's Island West includes a further three cores, two of them flake and one a blade core, and eight scrapers. 'New' tool types are the polished axe and the barbed and tanged arrowhead of Neolithic–early Bronze Age date. Only a handful of additional waste pieces were recovered from North Binness East. For Long Island the additional information from the south-western shore needs to be combined as precise provenances are not available for some of the material. A further twelve cores and fragments (ten flakes, two blades) were recovered and over 80 additional pieces of debitage, of which 47 (67%) were blades. Eighty-one implements, of which 31 (38%) are scrapers, can also be added to the total. The range of implements from Long Island is greater than for either area of North Binness, with twelve categories represented. Interestingly, especially in view of the strong blade element among the debitage, these categories include two additional types of arrowhead and a plano-convex knife. When combined with the arrowheads and axe fragment found in the gridded collection the diagnostic artefacts point towards a late Neolithic–early Bronze Age presence here, in which case it may also be relevant that thirteen (52%) scrapers weighing under 12g, including three thumbnail scrapers, are from Long Island.

A considerable quantity of additional flintwork was recovered from Baker's Island during rapid walkover survey and unsystematic collection. From the south-western and north-western parts of the island were collected a small amount of debitage together with four scrapers and a miniature axe. Baker's Island East was again the most prolific area with nearly 600 additional pieces of debitage, including 39 cores/fragments (19 blade and 20 flake), 182 blades (35% of the additional total non-core debitage), and 143 implements. Of these, 114 are scrapers, two are tranchet adzes, and seven 'new' tool types were recovered. The barbed and tanged arrowhead, tranchet tool, and 'slug' are most likely to be late Neolithic–early Bronze Age and the polished axe Neolithic or early Bronze Age. The tranchet adzes are Mesolithic in date but the remainder are not chronologically diagnostic.

South Binness Island received less attention during the survey than the other islands, largely because of problems of accessibility, both physically and because of restrictions imposed by the needs of the itinerant bird population. Only three collection units were employed and the remainder of the collection was undertaken by rapid walkover survey of the shingle beaches, banks, and firm mudflats. Only 150 struck flints were recovered, mostly from the shingle beach of the southern shore, where a tranchet adze, a fabricator, one plano-convex, and one flake knife were also found as well as eight scrapers. The northern shingle bar of South Binness, known as the Wadeway and Round Nap, was apparently once quite prolific in flintwork but only a small amount of material was recovered in the survey, including a further eight scrapers, a leaf arrowhead, a laurel leaf, and two broken, bifacially retouched flakes.

The addition of the remainder of the assemblage recovered in the survey, therefore, generally reinforces, rather than contradicts the broad trends identified in the analysis of the debitage. The only obviously difference is in the addition of a series of chronologically diagnostic implements on Long

Island which suggest a significant late Neolithic–early Bronze Age element which was not apparent from the waste material.

Previous collections

In 1981, as part of her doctoral research (Gardiner 1988), the present author briefly examined flintwork from Langstone Harbour held by Portsmouth Museum. This material included almost 1500 artefacts collected by Chris Draper and, especially, by Richard Bradley and Barri Hooper. In 1996 it was proposed to re-examine this material, however, in the intervening period, archive material held in the museum stores had been rehoused and only a small proportion of the flintwork could be reidentified among the boxes. This was particularly unfortunate as most of the debitage seemed to be missing and could not, therefore, be compared with the survey data, no specific analysis having been undertaken in 1981. More recently collected material was examined. In the description which follows, information from both museum visits has therefore been combined. The composition of the museum collections are summarised in Tables 11 and 12.

Bradley and Hooper and Draper concentrated their efforts on the margins of Farlington Marshes and the foreshores of North Binness and Long Island, the other two main islands being generally inaccessible for most of the time. Artefacts came mainly from the foreshore and from cliff sections where the presence of hearths was also noted (Bradley and Hooper 1973, 19). Although there are records of Draper finding a variety of artefacts on both South Binness and Baker's Islands, some of them relating to Portsmouth Museum records (eg Wymer 1977, 117–8), no flintwork from these islands could be found in the 1996 museum visit and nor was any observed by either the present author or by Suzanne Palmer when examining Draper's personal collection, in 1981 and for the *Mesolithic Gazetteer* (*ibid*) respectively.

Overall, a similar range of artefacts was present in the museum collections to those found during the survey. However, there are some notable additions. Bradley and Hooper recovered four fragments of polished axe, one of which (Bradley and Hooper 1973, fig 3, no 39) is an almost complete, part-polished example of a Gardiner type 4a (Gardiner 1988, 80–3) axe which the author considers to be of Bronze Age rather than Neolithic date (note that because of its fairly steep blade Bradley published this as an adze). Several other core tools are reported and a slightly different range of flake tools, though in terms of probable function these are all related types (Gardiner 1987b). Most notable among the flake tools is the addition of four microliths and three serrated blades. A crude tanged arrowhead (Bradley and Hooper 1973, fig 3, no 28) completes the repertoire of Neolithic–early Bronze Age arrowheads present in the harbour. It is interesting to note that the majority of

core tools recovered by Bradley and Hooper from the northern islands are of typical late Neolithic–early Bronze Age types while the majority of core tools recovered during the survey (twelve out of fourteen) came from the southern islands and two-thirds of those are of Mesolithic date.

Note is also made (Table 13) of other material recorded as coming from the harbour, but not personally observed (see Chapter 1 and Allen *et al* 1993). From this list, it is again noticeable that diagnostically Neolithic–early Bronze Age implements are recorded from the northern islands, and Farlington, with additional, probably Mesolithic items predominantly from Baker's and Long Islands.

Discussion

Interpretation of the flint assemblage from Langstone Harbour must be tempered by the knowledge that virtually none of the material is *in situ* and all is subject to erosive forces which have and will move artefacts around the harbour. The use of total collection grids and squares provided an essential control and allowed some assessment of the integrity of the data. This suggested that, although ultimately all the archaeological finds are mobile, distributions in the cliffs and on shingle and clay headlands will retain some coherence and provide a snapshot picture of the data at any moment in time that bears some relationship with the original distribution of that material. However, this is by no means an exact correlation and care had to be taken that analysis was conducted at an appropriate level of detail. Observed differences in the composition of the survey data from place to place are the result of only a semi-quantitative analysis employing a simple, nested strategy of interrogation within which absolute numbers are essentially unimportant and, indeed, potentially misleading. Strict chronological separation of the vast majority of the assemblage was impossible and the methods of analysis used were therefore aimed at identifying broad trends in the data through both space and time.

Table 14 provides a summary comparison of the proportions of the major tool categories recovered by Bradley and Hooper and by the survey. Those authors noted the preponderance of scrapers and limited number and variety of other tools present in the harbour, with an emphasis on piercing and fabricating tools. These observations are certainly borne out by the survey data (Table 9), though the interpretation of them requires some reconsideration in the light of recent research into post-Neolithic flint industries.

Bradley and Hooper (1973) published most of their flint assemblage as being of Neolithic date, and indeed many of the diagnostic implements they recovered are of typical late Neolithic–early Bronze Age form. They also acknowledged the presence of a Mesolithic element which Jacobi, in his seminal paper on the Mesolithic of Hampshire (1981), con-

Table 11 Summary of collections held in Portsmouth Museum

A Examined 1996 (exc Bradley & Hooper)

Area	Bl cores/ trimmings	Blades	Fl cores/ trimmings	Flakes & misc deb	Scrapers	Other tools	Total
N Binness 1920s, 1970–82	–	17	5	106	33	8	169
Long Island 1959–81	1	33	9	138	7 + 1 scraper/ borer	6	195
Long Island E end 1973	–	4	3	117	3	1	128
Farlington Marshes 1978–87	4	9	4	29	17	7	70
Total	5	63	21	390	61	22	562

B Examined 1981: Bradley & Hooper and Draper collections
(figures in brackets indicate additional examples in published report (Bradley & Hooper 1973) but not identified in Museum)

Area	Bl cores/ trimmings	Blades	Fl cores/ trimmings	flakes & misc deb	Scrapers	Other tools	Total
North Binness (Bradley & Hooper)							
NB 1	–	–	–	–	35	7 (+4)	42 (+4)
NB2	–	–	–	–	(2)	–	(2)
NB3	–	–	–	–	12	6	18
NB6	–	–	–	–	14	2	16
North Binness (in same box but not listed in publication)	–	–	some	c 200 bl/fl	–	9	9 (c 200)
Long Island (Bradley & Hooper)							
L2	–	–	–	–	35	4	39
L3	–	–	–	–	136	24 (+12)	160 (+12)
L4	–	–	–	–	6	1	7
L5	–	–	–	–	29	6	35
L6	–	–	–	–	53	7 (+8)	60 (+8)
L7	–	–	–	–	24	2 (+7)	26 (+7)
L8	–	–	–	–	31	4 (+3)	35 (+3)
L9	–	–	–	–	5	2	7
L11	–	–	–	–	24	2 (+5)	26 (+5)
L12	–	–	–	–	3	1	4
Long Island	–	–	–	c 200 bl/fl	–	–	(c 200)
Farlington Marshes	–	–	–	–	–	–	–
Bradley & Hooper	–	–	–	–	97	7	104
Draper	–	–	11	305 bl/fl	19	65	400
Total	–	–	11+	305 (c 400)	523 (2)	149 (39)	988 (c 441) = 1429+

NB = Norton Binness; L = Long Island; bl = blade; fl = flake

Table 12 Implements in Portsmouth Museum other than scrapers

Area	Core tools					Arrowheads				Flake tools									Total
	A	B	C	D	E	F	G	H	I	J	K	L	M	N	O	P	Q	R	
NB1	1	–	–	–	–	–	–	1	–	–	–	1	–	–	4	–	–	(4)	7 (+4)
NB3	1	1	–	–	–	–	–	–	–	–	1	–	–	–	3	–	–	–	6
NB6	–	–	–	–	–	–	–	–	–	1	1	–	–	–	–	–	–	–	2
North Binness (in same box but not listed in publication)	–	–	–	–	–	–	1	–	–	1	2	–	–	–	–	–	–	5	9
L2	1	–	–	–	–	–	–	–	–	–	–	–	–	–	–	–	–	3	4
L3	–	–	–	–	–	2	–	–	–	–	5	–	(4)	1	10	–	–	6 (+8)	24 (+12)
L4	–	–	–	–	–	–	–	–	–	–	–	1	–	–	–	–	–	–	1
L5	–	–	–	1	–	–	–	–	–	2	2**	–	–	–	1	–	–	–	6
L6	1	1*	–	–	1	–	–	1	–	–	–	–	–	–	3	–	–	(8)	7 (+8)
L7	–	–	–	–	–	–	–	–	–	–	–	–	–	–	2 (+1)	–	–	(6)	2 (+7)
L8	–	–	–	–	–	–	–	–	–	–	1	–	–	–	3	–	–	(3)	4 (+3)
L9	–	–	–	–	–	–	–	–	–	–	1	–	–	1	–	–	–	–	2
L11	–	–	–	–	–	–	–	–	–	–	–	–	–	–	2	–	–	(5)	2 (+5)
L12	–	–	–	–	–	–	–	–	–	–	1	–	–	–	–	–	–	–	1
Farlington Marshes	–	–	–	–	–	–	–	–	–	–	–	–	–	–	–	–	–	–	–
Bradley & Hooper	–	–	–	–	1	–	–	–	1	1	–	1	–	–	2	1	–	–	7
Draper	–	–	1	–	–	–	–	–	–	–	1	–	–	–	–	2	3	58	65
N Binness 1920s, 1970–82	–	–	–	–	–	–	–	–	–	1	1	–	–	–	–	–	–	6	8
Long Island 1959–81	–	–	2	–	–	–	–	–	–	2	–	–	–	–	1	–	1	–	6
Long Island E end 1973	–	–	–	–	–	–	1	–	–	–	–	–	–	–	–	–	–	–	1
Farlington Marshes 1978–87	–	–	–	–	–	–	–	–	–	4	–	–	1	–	–	–	–	2	7
	4	2	3	1	2	2	2	2	1	12	16	3	1(4)	2	31 (1)	3	4	80 (34)	171 (39) = 210

Areas are those defined in Bradley and Hooper 1973

A= polished axe frag/flake; B = flaked axe frag; C = pick; D= heavy duty; E = core tool; F = laurel leaf; G = oblique arrowhead; H = triangular arrowhead; I = tanged arrowhead; J = piercer; K = fabricator/rod; L = spurred; M = notched; N = plano-convex knife; O = flake knife; P = serrated bl/fl; Q = microlith; R = ret/ut

* = listed as PC knife in publication; ** 1 listed as adze in publication

Table 13   Summary of chronologically diagnostic flint implements recorded prior to the present survey

	N Binness	Long Island	S Binness	Baker's	Farlington	NW corner of harbour	W coast Hayling
Palaeolithic		4 flints					
Mesolithic		cores	cores	core	core		Meso site, no details
		flakes		flakes			
		blades	blades	blades	ut blade		
		scrapers		scrapers			
			pick	pick			
				tranchet adze			
				axe			
					saw		
Neolithic–early Bronze Age					cores		
			flakes		flakes	flakes	
	scrapers	scrapers	scrapers		scrapers	scrapers	
		arrowheads			leaf; barbed & tanged arrowheads		
		plano-convex knives					
	polished axe frags			polished axe frag	polished axe flake		knife
	adze						
					borers/awls		
Bronze Age						flakes	
					scraper	scrapers	scrapers
						borer/awl	

Table 14   Summary comparison of major tool assemblage elements (no/%)

Source	Location	Scrapers	Core tools	Arrowheads	Flake tools	total
Bradley & Hooper	Farlington Marshes	97/93.3%	1/1%	1/1%	5/4.8%	104
Bradley & Hooper	N Binness & Long Island	523/71.3%	12/1.6%	7/1%	151/16.1%	693
Survey	N Binness & Long Island	105/78.4%	2/1.5%	8/5.9%	19/14.2%	134
Survey	Entire assemblage	277/76.7%	16/4.4%	13/3.6%	55/15.2%	361
Total		1002/77.6%	31/2.4%	29/2.2%	230/17.8%	1292

sidered to be late Mesolithic (post-6500 BC). That late Mesolithic element is confirmed by the survey data but a large part of the remaining assemblage should no longer be assumed to be Neolithic. Research into post-Neolithic flint industries during the 1980s–1990s has shown that the later Bronze Age is characterised by the occurrence of an essentially crude flint industry based on the expedient production, use, and discard of a restricted range of simple flake tools, dominated by scrapers but most frequently also including fabricators, piercers, knives, and somewhat non-specific items generally categorised as spurred, tanged, and denticulate pieces. Bronze Age assemblages frequently include a high proportion of simple edge retouched pieces associated with a generally poor standard of work-

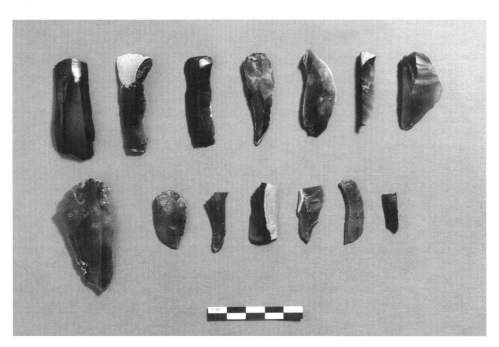

Plate 31 Selection of flint blades (Elaine A Wakefield)

manship, lack of core and blank preparation, and the production of broad, squat, thick flakes showing many accidental breakages (see for instance Ford *et al* 1984; Fasham and Ross 1978; etc). The bulk of the Langstone assemblage is typified by just these characteristics and tool types. However, the transition from a late Neolithic–early Bronze Age industry to a later Bronze Age one, within a mixed assemblage such as we have from Langstone, is impossible to isolate – nevertheless the survey data points strongly towards a greater mature Bronze Age element than a Neolithic one, amongst the debitage at least.

Combining all the available information on the flintwork from Langstone Harbour we can offer a few salient comments on the date and distribution of the material. The principal surviving Mesolithic component seems to be on Baker's Island, as recognised in the field, and on Long Island which, interestingly, was not obvious to the field team. South Binness may also support Mesolithic artefacts but our information from this island is comparatively slight. Baker's Island produced the greatest number of flints during the survey and most of the diagnostically Mesolithic tools. These include tranchet adzes and sharpening flakes, picks, and serrated blades, to which can be added the products of previous work in the form of further tranchet adzes, picks, and serrated and retouched blades. Undoubtedly some of the scrapers and possibly some of the fabricators may also be Mesolithic. Farlington Marshes also produced Mesolithic material in the 1960s and 1970s including quantities of debitage, three microliths, a pick, and both serrated and retouched blades. The lack of a true microlithic element is notable, given that there are plenty of pieces in the assemblage of an appropriate size and shape.

The composition of the Mesolithic assemblage is interesting. The presence of tranchets, their sharpening flakes, and of picks suggests some heavy work. They may have been used for the cutting down of trees, as is frequently assumed for such artefacts, or they may be considered as more general purpose tools performing a variety of functions. Either way, the tranchet adzes at least were not made here but were brought, by people, to what is now Langstone Harbour. The assemblage does not include the range of manufacturing and processing tools typical of many late Mesolithic 'sites' (see Jacobi 1981 for example) – there are no burins, microburins, gravers, or awls, for instance (or indeed microliths if some of these are considered to be parts of composite tools rather than purely projectile points). Overall, the suggestion is of a limited range of activities. It has been noted, above, that there is a low percentage of primary flakes overall in the harbour. Baker's Island East, in particular, has produced very few primary (or secondary) flakes and has a comparatively low ratio of blade cores to blades and flake cores to flakes (Plate 31). One possibility, therefore, is that the area was being visited repeatedly, and perhaps for very short periods, in order specifically to exploit its flint resources, with some knapping taking place locally but most material, including probably cores, being taken away. The range of flake tools and very few microliths or associated debitage (coupled perhaps with the presence of hearths – see below), suggests little more than basic maintenance activity for small parties of individuals who may only have been resident for a few days at a time. It is equally possible, of course, that flint was only one resource being exploited, but there is certainly no evidence for a 'base-camp' type assemblage (eg Binford 1980; Jacobi 1981) suggesting any long-term residency.

Neolithic activity is also difficult to pinpoint since although, relatively speaking, quite a large number of diagnostic implements have been recovered, it is impossible to separate out much of the post-Mesolithic assemblage any further. There is no clear evidence of an earlier Neolithic presence, though it would be unlikely to be obvious in such a mixed assemblage anyway; the presence of an occasional leaf-shaped arrowhead is not particularly significant in chronological terms (given the 1500+ years during which this form was current), and probably represents no more than casual hunting losses. A single polished axe is of interest but, again, not of great significance as these implements were in use over at least two millennia.

In recent years, flint specialists have realised that the transition from late Neolithic to early Bronze Age is not reflected in the flint industry to the same extent as it is in the ceramic evidence, and it has become customary to regard flint assemblages of the mid-3rd to mid-2nd millennium BC as part of a continuum (a technological assemblage often simply referred to as LNEBA). Tools diagnostic of this technological continuum recovered during this survey are few, they consist of a tranchet tool, plano-convex knives, fabricators, a 'slug', a fragment of a flaked axe, and a possible miniature axe. Essentially undiagnostic but undoubtedly of mixed date are, again, scrapers, piercers, flake knives, and some of the less specific flake tools. Arrowheads include all the principal types of the Neolithic and early Bronze Age, with just one or two examples of each. Bradley and Hooper noted that the incidence of arrowheads was quite low (c 1% of implements), certainly by comparison with many excavated assemblages. However, examination of a large number of mixed surface-collected flint assemblages from central southern England by the present writer (Gardiner 1988, table 9.3) suggests that the combined total of arrowheads from the harbour is unremarkable for a tool assemblage of this size (c 3.6%). Only one of the arrowheads is of clearly imported flint; all the others could have been made and used on the spot and there is one possible core for producing transverse arrowheads among the survey material (though this is a very poor example if correctly identified and most of the local flint would not be suited to this method of core preparation). The presence of plano-convex knives and barbed and/or tanged arrowheads might suggest a specifically early Bronze Age element but it was noted both by Bradley and Hooper (op cit, 23) and above that thumbnail scrapers of the type frequently associated with such implements and with Beaker pottery are notably few.

Bradley and Hooper recorded similar types of implements to the survey but with the addition of a few core tools. As with the Mesolithic material, the range of activities indicated by these tools is limited. It seems likely that flint remained an exploited resource and though it is difficult to comment on the complete industry present in the harbour at this time because of the problem of separating out the debitage, there does not seem to be any evidence for settlement as such. Even allowing for the redating of much of the assemblage, Bradley and Hooper's assertion that it is essentially non-domestic in character, possibly representing seasonal, short-term grazing and associated activities, seems very reasonable. In terms of distribution, there is no obvious concentration of material among the survey data though there is a suggestion, reinforcing that from the earlier finds, that the main focus was on the foreshore in the wide bay of the eastern end of North Binness and Long Island, in which case it is quite possible that any such focus has been largely lost to erosion or buried by accretion.

Much of the Langstone flint assemblage is here assigned a mature Bronze Age date of c 1600–700 BC. As already stated, the technological characteristics of the debitage, the preponderance of scrapers, piercers, and simple edge-retouched pieces all point to a notable Bronze Age presence. The polished axe, recorded as an adze by Bradley and Hooper, and the tanged arrowhead (op cit, figs 3, nos 39 and 28 respectively) probably belong to the late-2nd millennium rather than any earlier. Because Bronze Age flint assemblages are characterised by a similarly narrow range of simple tool forms, which were probably made very quickly, used, and discarded, it is probable that these implements were used for a variety of scraping, boring, and cutting functions where metal tools were either less efficient or simply too expensive. By this stage, the use of flint was in decline as metal tools and weapons came into general use, but it is very likely to have continued in expedient use, perhaps most frequently away from settlement sites.

It should not be expected that the human use of the Langstone area from the middle Bronze Age onwards will be as clearly reflected in the flint assemblage as in other categories of material but, taken by itself, the flintwork is again not suggestive of long term residency. The debitage suggests that activity may have been predominantly focused on what is now North Binness and Long Island and the very low ratio of cores to flakes in some parts of the foreshore suggests that much of the core assemblage is missing. A possible scenario is that the harbour area was being used again essentially for seasonal grazing, with the butchering of animals and preparation of hides taking place alongside. The presence of a few fragments of possible saddle quern and a spindle whorl suggest that such visits were of more than a few days duration (if they are not more recent introductions – see below).

It is also possible that flint was being removed from the area, perhaps to more permanent settlements further inland on what is now the coastal plain. One such settlement site was recently investigated at Grange Road, Gosport (Hall and Ford 1994) where pits and postholes were associated with post-Deverel-Rimbury pottery, loomweights, a small flint assemblage, and carbonised grain. However, when taken in combination with other categories of artefact recovered in the survey, other possibilities emerge (see below and Chapter 7).

144

Plate 32   Unusual sandstone axe/chisel from Long Island (Elaine A Wakefield)

Stone axe or chisel
by Julie Gardiner

A ground and polished stone axe or chisel was found in 1995 by Arthur Mack near the east end of Long Island. The object (Plate 32) is made from an irregularly shaped, tabular piece of what appears to be a fine grained, orange-brown sandstone. It is worked on all sides with surfaces ground and irregularly polished to produce a rather lopsided, chisel-like blade. The dimensions of the object are as follows: max length = 139mm, max thickness = 18mm, width of blade = 45mm, width of butt = 32mm. The raw material is clearly not local to Langstone Harbour and its form is unusual. Little more can be said other than that, while it is possible that this is an ethnographic piece (a few exotic imports such as an Egyptian faience scarab beetle have been found in the harbour area), this object is probably a 'one-off' item made from an appropriately shaped piece of rock, most likely in the later Neolithic or early Bronze Age when such opportunistic use of suitable raw materials is not unfamiliar (eg Gardiner 1988, figs 3.12 and 3.13).

Pottery
by Rachael Seager Smith, A M ApSimon, Lorraine Mepham, and Julie Gardiner

A total of 960 sherds of pottery derived from the Langstone Harbour area was examined, including seven Bronze Age vessels (Table 15 and Table 17, below). This includes all the sherds recovered during the survey, and the surface material gathered by Arthur Mack and Dominic Fontana. In addition are sherds previously found in this area held within the collection of Portsmouth Museum (see below). At least some of the sherds published by Bradley and Hooper (1973, 24–7) were also examined. The assemblage was rapidly scanned to establish the nature, date range, and condition of the assemblage but no detailed analysis was undertaken. The results of the scan are summarised by chronological period.

Overall, the assemblage encompassed sherds dating from the middle Bronze Age to the post-medieval periods. No sherds of medieval date were recognised, and most of the pottery was too featureless for a close date to be suggested. Few featured sherds were present and, in general, the condition of the assemblage was poor. Coastal erosion and tidal movement has frequently resulted in severe surface abrasion. In addition, coarse, flint-tempered fabrics dominate the assemblage. Such fabrics are invariably difficult to date, and in the absence of chronologically diagnostic vessel forms, surface treatments and decorations, or reliable contextual associations with intrinsically datable artefacts of other material types, it is impossible to assign many of these sherds within the period between the middle Bronze Age and around the later-4th century AD with any degree of certainty. For the purposes of this report, except where a predominance of sherds definitely datable to another period occur in close association, the coarse, flint-tempered sherds have been assigned a Bronze Age date. This is likely to overestimate the percentage of Bronze Age pottery recovered from this particular assemblage compared with that of other periods, but it at least allowed a consistent approach to the problem of quantifying these fabrics, which were very common during the later Bronze Age, although by no means confined to it. Details of the far smaller number, and the distribution of definite Bronze Age sherds are summarised below.

Table 15   Number of pottery sherds by period and area recovered during fieldwork

Table 15a   Pottery from the survey

Area/location	Bronze Age	probable BA	Iron Age	Romano-British	Saxon	Post-med
North Binness						
General	–	3	1	28	–	–
Area 1 (inc ditch 113)	23 + 1*	5	–	8	–	–
Ditch 1711	1*	–	–	–	–	–
Hearth 1702	5 + 21*	–	–	–	–	–
Ditch 1704	12 + 16*	–	–	–	–	–
Area 4	–	5	–	22	–	–
Test-pits	–	–	–	15	–	–
Total	40 + 39*	13	1	73	0	0
Long Island						
General	–	2	1	5	–	2
Pot 350	154	–	–	–	–	–
Pot 360	70	–	–	–	–	–
Pot 380	29	–	–	–	–	–
Area 3	–	141	–	–	–	2
Total	253	143	1	5	0	4
South Binness						
Area 7	–	18	–	52	–	–
Pot 774	112	–	–	–	–	–
Total	112	18	0	52	0	0
Baker's Island						
General	2	9	1	24	–	2
Area 14	–	2	–	6	–	–
Area 15 (inc 22–25)	9	4	–	76	–	–
Area 16 (inc 20 + 21)	7	12	–	20	2	–
Area 17 (inc 26)	–	–	–	3	–	–
Test-pits	4	–	–	–	–	–
Total	22	27	1	129	2	2
All other areas						
	–	10	–	9	–	5
TOTAL	466	210	3	268	2	11

Table 15b   Pottery in Portsmouth Museum

Museum coll						
Farlington	7	41	3	68	–	–
North Binness	143	23	–	169	–	1
N Binness/Long Island	45	–	–	–	–	–
Long Is, vessel 1981/367	168	–	–	–	–	–
Baker's Island	7	–	–	–	–	–
Total	370	80	3	258	–	1
OVERALL TOTAL	836	290	6	526	2	12

* = large globular (handled) vessel

Bronze Age

Table 15a indicates a total of 676 Bronze Age or possible Bronze Age sherds, of which only 466 or 69% are reliably of Bronze Age date, the remainder being sherds of coarse flint-tempered fabrics. However, of these 466 sherds, 404 are from just four vessels and if these are counted individually, then the percentage of datable sherds falls to just 12% of the total. On the other hand, given the probable function of the vessels identified, it is quite possible that *all* the Bronze Age pottery relates to very specific activities (see below).

Sherds of middle Bronze Age date were found, together with sherds of later date extending into the Roman period, on the surface above, and excavated from the hearth on the western side of the south shore of North Binness (1702) (Fig 48). These included two sherds in a fine, well-sorted flint-tempered fabric probably from a globular urn and a variety of small rim fragments which may have belonged to vessels of the Deverel-Rimbury tradition. However, most of the flint-tempered pottery from this area of North Binness was of late Bronze Age or earliest Iron Age date, also of coarse flint-tempered fabrics. Rim sherds from jars with flat, internally thickened rims, one with an applied cordon decorated with finger-nail impressions, were recognised. Body sherds from other vessels with similar decoration, and bases with expanded base angles were also present.

Among a group of sherds found on the south-west shore of North Binness above and close to the hearth (which gave a radiocarbon result of 2995 ± 55 BP; 1410–1060 cal BC) and ditches were two very large and well-preserved sherds from a thick-walled vessel of unusual globular form, with one surviving handle and an applied cordon (Fig 49). It is hand-made with a moderately sorted coarsely flint-tempered fabric (grits up to 5mm across, 10–20% frequency). The exterior surface especially has been carefully finished, probably wiped with a cloth or slightly gritty hands using roughly horizontal strokes; towards the base of the vessel there are traces of a thin clay surface slurry. The sherds are predominantly oxidised and although the pinkish-red colouring of the vessel is unusual, the firing is comparatively uniform. Other plain, thick-walled, flint-gritted body and base sherds from these contexts are also attributable to this vessel. Wall thickness ranges from 9mm to 17mm. Nothing survives of the vessel rim. The vessel is discussed further below.

Two middle Bronze Age lug-handled jars and their wider implications
by A M ApSimon

Jar from North Binness Island

The very large, undecorated jar, from hearth 1702 and its immediate surroundings is represented by 39 sherds, perhaps 18% of the pot. The vessel has a slightly concave in-turned neck, with a well defined

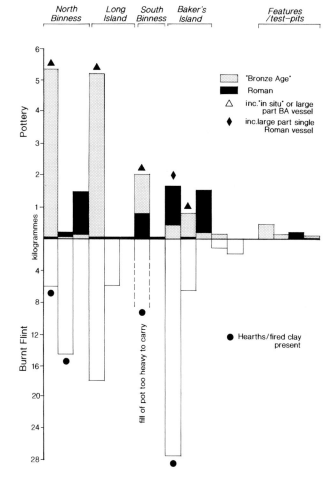

Figure 48   The relative proportions of burnt flint and 'Bronze Age' and Roman pottery from the four islands. Drawn by S E James

junction between the neck and the broadly convex-sided body (Fig 49, Plate 33). The upper end of the moulded handle springs from a horizontal girth cordon applied to the base of the neck. The base sherds indicate a simple flat base about 12–16mm thick and at least 200mm in diameter. Voids in the lower sherds and some internal shrinkage cracks suggest poor mixing of clay, but no shrinkage cracks are visible outside. Other sherds from the same context, generally from smaller pots than this, but similarly flint-tempered include: a rounded rim sherd with concave neck ending in a rounded shoulder with fingernail or similar impressions, in finer, dark reduced fabric with fine flint temper to 1.5mm, 9mm thick; and some moderately to more heavily flint-tempered reduced wares, including simple base-wall junctions and a sub-rounded rim 15mm thick.

The lug-handle, with its 30–35mm diameter aperture, seems better suited to taking a thick cord than serving as a hand grip. Its shape and relatively small size suggests that there were originally at least two and more probably four such handles. These might have been arranged in two diametrically opposed pairs, as on the nearby jar from Creek Field, Hayling Island, but the length of cordon preserved is insufficient to decide between this and the possibility of

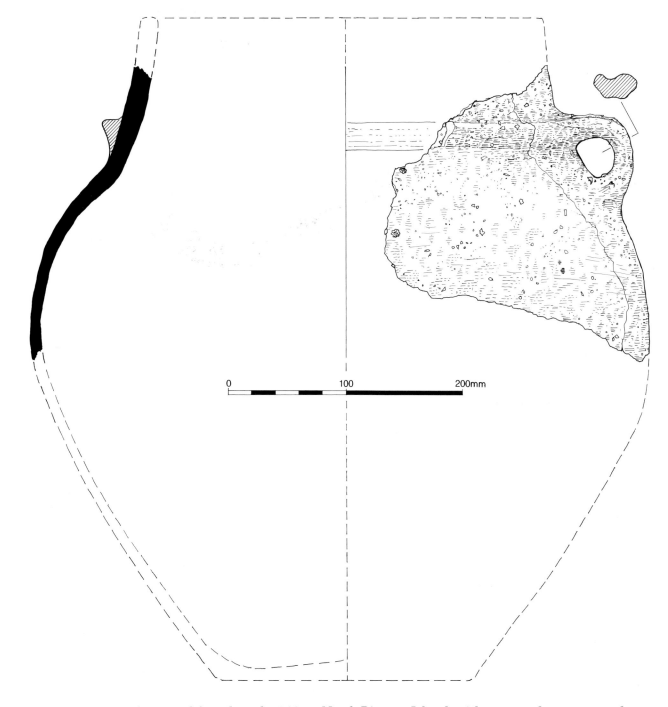

Figure 49   Bronze Age vessel from hearth 1702 on North Binness Island, with suggested reconstructed profile. Drawn by S E James

four lugs placed equidistantly around the circumference. Note that this latter location is incorrectly referred to as Crate Field in the SMR and by Rudkin (1980, no 73).

The reconstructed profile suggests a maximum body diameter of about 520mm. Conservative estimates might suggest a height of *c* 550mm, a rim diameter of *c* 340mm and a basal diameter of *c* 220mm (Fig 49), making this unusual vessel one of the largest known Bronze Age pots from Britain, perhaps only exceeded by the jars from Creek Field, Hayling Island and Portscatho, Cornwall (see below). The jar's bipartite form with slightly concave neck and convex body can be compared to

'Globular Urns' of the Deverel-Rimbury series, as for example a globular urn of Ellison's type 1A from phase D of the cemetery at Kimpton, Hampshire (Dacre and Ellison 1981, fig 14, D14), attributed to the early middle Bronze Age. It might be regarded as just a gigantic globular urn, except that the combination of well defined junction between body and neck, and evenly convex body, is unusual on globular urns in the central Wessex area. These are generally no more than half the size and 1/8 the volume of this jar, forming the fine-ware component of the series. However, type 1A globular urns up to 0.4m high and 0.43m in diameter occurred at Thorny Down, Winterbourne Gunner, Wiltshire

Plate 33 Pottery from hearth 1702, North Binness Island. The huge conjoining sherds together weight over 1.5 kg and belong to a huge, very unusual globular vessel (see text). The hearth produced a radiocarbon date of 1410–1060 cal BC (Elaine A Wakefield)

(Stone 1941); and similarly a jar, *c* 0.42–0.44m tall, was present at Compton Way, Oliver's Battery, Hampshire (Hawkes 1969, fig 3; King 1989). This latter jar, intermediate in size between the two extremes, has a slightly concave inward sloping neck bearing lightly tooled decoration resembling that on type 1A globular urns of the Central Wessex group. This is separated from the rounded body by a horizontal girth cordon from which spring the lower ends of 4 moderate sized lug handles with 12mm horizontal piercings, which Sonia Hawkes (1969, 16–17) saw as suggesting 'remote Cornish ancestry'.

Jar from Creek Field, North Hayling

Despite being prominently on display in Portsmouth City Museum where it was seen and became familiar to many archaeologists, the pot (PCM acc no 47/55) discovered in Creek Field, Hayling Island appears to have escaped publication or mention (excepting Rudkin 1980). Although its fabric and the features to which attention has been drawn suggest that it can be assigned to the middle Bronze Age with a fair degree of probability, it nevertheless remains true that this pot is difficult to parallel.

The jar, as restored, is 578mm (22.8 in) high, rim thickness generally 13–14mm, minimum 12mm, external rim diameter 279mm, base diameter 260–8mm, maximum diameter (from drawing) 536mm, measurement ridge to ridge of cordons 48–50mm. Two of the lug-handles are complete, one 7/8 complete, one broken and restored. The oval openings in the lugs are about 35 by 15mm. The pot is quite hard fired, the inside darker in colour but not reduced, there are no shrinkage cracks. The exterior surface is not burnished or especially smooth but has been wiped, leaving the temper slightly protruding. The calculated volume is 76.8 litres.

The drawing (Fig 50b) is old but accurate, with only minor divergences from measurements taken on the pot. Features to note are the evenly curved globular body; the sharp junction between sides and the base, which is no thicker than the wall; the pair of ridged cordons which are placed high on the body and appear to be worked up rather than applied; the shallow inward sloping neck and simple upright rim, and the two opposed pairs of lug-handles bridging the space between the cordons. There is no evidence of how the handles are fastened, probably they are applied rather than tenoned through the walls. No ring or coil joins are apparent and the pot is without decoration. Dr D F Williams' examination shows that the pot is finely tempered with crushed flint. This pot is now believed to have been associated with a roundhouse – see Creek Field, Chapter 3 – (Bradley pers comm; ApSimon and Williams in prep).

The fabric is moderately hard and rough, red to reddish brown in colour (Munsell 2.5YR 5/6 to 4/4), with a few patchy grey areas on the outer surface. The surface of the fabric is dominated by many small patches of white flint, giving it a distinctive visual appearance. The small, sharply arched, handles have a slightly coarser texture than the rest of the jar, possibly to give extra strength when used to lift the large vessel.

Dr Williams comments that there seems to be no reason to suspect anything other than a source for the pot on Hayling Island itself. Many of the middle–late Bronze Age coarsewares of the region, as exemplified in the assemblage from the present survey, are similarly tempered with crushed flint, often calcined. However the average size of the flint present in the Hayling Island vessel seems to be of a smaller size grade than generally appears to be the case for such large vessels (see for example, Bell 1977; Hamilton 1984; J Nicholls 1987).

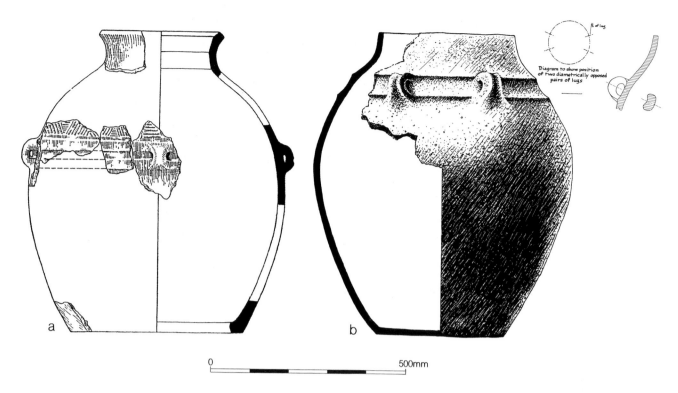

Figure 50   a) Trevisker series jar from barrow at Portscatho, Gerrans, Cornwall (from Hencken 1932, fig 34C), and b) Bronze Age jar from Creek Field, Hayling (drawn by Arthur Corney, Portsmouth City Museums)

Cornish analogues and maritime implications

Lug-handles similar to the North Binness example occur on pots of the early–middle Bronze Age Trevisker series in south-west England, sometimes with their upper ends attached to applied cordons, as here. Although the effective limit of that series is in south Dorset there are outliers in the Isle of Wight and isolated finds much further east at Hardelot, Pas-de-Calais (Mariette 1961) and now Monkton, Kent (Bennett and Williams 1997). The gabbroic fabric of the pots from Hardelot Plage, Pas-de-Calais (ApSimon and Greenfield 1972; Parker Pearson 1990; 1997) indicated that they were in all probability made in the Lizard peninsula, 500km from where they were found, and must necessarily have been transported by sea. Evidence of sea-bottom finds of bronzes almost certainly derived from Bronze Age shipwrecks (Muckelroy 1980; 1981; Needham and Dean 1987) points to the reality of such early and middle Bronze Age voyages, both coasting and cross-Channel (Tomalin 1988; Parker Pearson 1990; Bradley 1990). It would be no surprise therefore to discover pots attributable to or influenced by the Trevisker series in the hinterland of Langstone Harbour, while cross-channel voyages could with equal probability bring pots from a wide stretch of continental coast.

The North Binness jar, however, has no other features which would justify its attribution to the Trevisker series and the lug handles could simply be a functional development for handling such a large vessel. It may be noted that there do not appear to be any comparable pots among post-Deverel-Rimbury plainware styles (Barrett 1980) or later pottery in southern England. The very large 'globose' handled jar found with the late Wilburton phase hoard from Isleham, Cambridgeshire (Coombs pers comm) does not, as reconstructed, show any significant similarity to the jars described here. Looking beyond the Channel, there is nothing comparable in Urnfield or Iron Age pottery from the Lower Rhine and Low Countries or in the pottery of the 'Bronze final' in the Paris Basin and the north of France.

For the Creek Field jar, as for the North Binness Island pot, the possibility of contact with the Trevisker series requires discussion, since lug-handles springing from paired moulded girth ridges, or cordons, certainly occur in it. There the underlying form is that of ridged form 2B Food Urns (Tomalin 1988; 1996), on which the paired girth ridges provided an opportunity for the aesthetically satisfying integration of the added handles with the formal design of the pot. Two such examples are Urn 1 from Crig-a-Mennis, Perranzabuloe (Christie 1960, fig 4 and pl xv) and Chysauster, pot P4 (Tomalin 1996, fig 15). None of these however has a closed form anything like the Creek Field jar. The only Trevisker series vessel comparable in shape to the Creek Field pot is the massive barrel or 'amphora' shaped handled jar from a barrow at Portscatho, Gerrans, Cornwall (Borlase 1872, 205–6, figs 1, 2; Hencken 1932, 121–3, fig 34C [here Fig 50a]; ApSimon 1961, 14), whose remarkable character and exceptional size were noted by Hencken. On this jar, the space between the cordons is bridged by small arched lug-handles – two survive, though the paired flat-faced applied girth cordons are not immediately assimilable with the girth ridges of form 2B Food Urns and are not set high on the pot but on the belly at the point of greatest girth. A second large Trevisker series jar, from the Bronze Age settlement at Kynance Gate, Mullion (Creeth 1958; Thomas 1960), has two large pierced lug-handles springing from similarly placed cordons, but though convex sided and with an upright neck and constricted mouth, is less 'globular' than the first. The 'closed' form of these two jars is, however, without antecedent in Cornwall, indicating that the ultimate origins of the Creek Field jar must lie elsewhere.

Dr David Tomalin (1988) has recognised the formal identity between lug handles from Trevisker and those on the large 4- or 5-handled jar from the primary 'Wessex' burial under barrow G5, Winterbourne Stoke, Wilts (Annable and Simpson 1964, 105, no 265; Tomalin 1988, fig 4). He identified that jar, with its haematite-burnished fabric and constricted mouth, as an import from either Jersey or the north coast of Brittany. He suggested that the introduction of this and other *vases à anses* and copying thereof, was contemporary with the arrival of bronze smiths responsible for making Armorico-British C series bronze daggers (Gerloff 1975), with landfalls at Portland and Wight evidenced by further *vases à anses* finds from there. This would then be the moment at which jars with constricted mouths entered the pottery repertoire in southern England, before the distinctive features of the Trevisker series developed. Tomalin considered that separate movements to Cornwall were indicated by the close links between gold lunulae from Harlyn Bay and Kerivoa and St Potan (Côtes-d'Armor), and a possible *vase à anse* copy at Trethellan Farm (Woodward and Cane 1991, fig 44 no 21). He noted handle sherds, from field-walking, at Saint-Nicolas-du-Pélem (Côtes-d'Armor; Le Prevost and Giot 1972; Giot *et al* 1979, 181), suggesting that lug-handles comparable in size to Cornish examples might be present in little known domestic assemblages in Armorica, of which only the 'table ware' found its way into burials.

Extremely large jars do indeed occur on the far shore of the Channel, as for example from a ring ditch at la Chapelle-de-l'Iff, Languenan, Côtes-d'Armor (Briard 1984, 163–6, fig 100). Radiocarbon dates of 1420–1010 cal BC (2990 ± 70 BP, GIF-5564) and 1440–1050 cal BC (3030 ± 70 BP, GIF-5565) from the ditch fill suggest that the jar could be contemporary with the North Binness Island jar. Though quite different in form, it had similarly thin sides, with the same simple junction between the sides and the equally thin flat base, as is found on Armorican *vases à anses*, on Trevisker series jars, on the Creek Field jar, and possibly on sherds among the North Binness find. It seems permissible to suggest that a commonality of underlying traditions is involved.

A large lug-handled jar, attributed to the Kelheim group of the Straubing culture, from the Regensburg (Hochweg) hoard on the upper Danube in Bavaria (Eckes 1938), is a pointer to the probable source. This jar (Eckes, Taf 3, Abb 1), 3/5 the size of the North Binness jar, is similarly proportioned, with a globular body separated from a short upright neck by a horizontal cordon, to which are attached the upper ends of two large upstanding moulded lug-handles. In this case the cordon is notched and also carries two horizontal tongue lugs, features found in southern England in the 'Inception Series' of Biconical Urns (Tomalin 1983; 1988), which Gerloff (1975) argued had their origins in the same general region of southern Germany. The bronzes in the Regensburg hoard date it to the transition from the final, Langquaid phase (Reinecke A2, Christlein 4) of the early Bronze Age, to the initial, Lochham phase (Reinecke B) of the middle Bronze Age (Paszthory and Mayer 1998, 10). Dendrochronology suggests dates for this transition in the 17th to 16th centuries BC (Becker *et al* 1989), a century or so older than the earlier end of the date range for the North Binness jar, though the type may have had a long life.

Given the rarity of comparably large jars with lug-handles in the early and middle Bronze Age of the coastal zone of central southern England between Christchurch and Chichester, it is a natural assumption that these two pots, both flint-tempered and thus probably locally made, represent the maximal size storage jar component of an as yet poorly known local middle Bronze Age Deverel-Rimbury tradition, in which normal sized globular urns may have been the 'table-ware' component. Such a tradition would be representative of a regional 'notional polity', as discussed by Tomalin (1988). They are, though, not closely similar and so not necessarily closely contemporary; if the reddish fabric of the Creek Field jar is a reminiscence of early Bronze Age haematite burnishing, then that jar might be early within the middle Bronze Age. Significantly, closest to the Creek Field pot, in shape of rim and concave neck, are two early Bronze Age jars, that from Winterbourne Stoke G5a already noted and the lost plain jar, c 0.45m tall, from Winterbourne St Martin, Dorset (Sydenham 1844, 330, pl 17, 3), found with glass (?), faience, and bone beads, and a cowrie shell.

In this context, and given the suggested origins for the North Binness jar, it is surely significant that stylistic elements analogous to those of Globular Urns – shapes, lug handles, decorative modes – are widely present in early Bronze Age pottery across southern Germany (Gersbach 1974; Koninger and Schlichtherle 1990), even including forms like 'Jersey Bowls', but with handles (Gersbach Abb 10, 6, 8). These elements, together with applied strip cordons reminiscent of South Lodge Barrel Urns, are traceable back to Hundt's (1951) late Neolithic Cham culture. The probable mechanism for long distance transmission of these stylistic elements is the network of exchanges which brought Arreton style metalwork to southern England, together with the *Fremde-Frauen* (foreign women; Jockenhövel 1991), given in marriage to cement alliances, for whose presence in the early and the middle Bronze

Age, exotic bronze pins and ornaments are evidence. Such women brought status with them and came to positions of status, in which they could take the lead in fabricating vessels in prestigiously exotic styles. I believe that Calkin (1964, 44–5) was correct in looking to entry points on the south coast for the introduction of these new styles and it may be that the coastal region round Langstone Harbour played a greater role in the process of total transformation of the ceramic repertoire at the early to middle Bronze Age transition than has hitherto been recognised. It is conceivable that wide-ranging early Bronze Age prospection for new sources of tin was a catalyst in these processes of change.

Though neither can be regarded as 'fine-ware' and both were finally deposited in low-lying situations apparently away from any substantial settlement focus, their style, their thinness and their detailing make them, like the Portscatho jar, masterpieces of the potters' art – probably valued and carefully preserved. They may even have been used for special activities such as brewing and serving drink, or as containers of salt or brine. The paired arrangement of the lugs on the Creek Field pot is extremely unusual. A similar arrangement occurs on certain Central-European late Bronze Age bronze cauldrons which are provided with two crossing 'bucket handles'. Perhaps, with use of a stout cord, the arrangement could help control the jar when tipping it.

Buried Vessels

The upper part of a late Bronze Age vessel came from well out in the intertidal zone of the southern foreshore of Long Island (Pot 360; Fig 51). The fabric is coarsely tempered with poorly sorted, crushed calcined flint <0.6mm in size, but the exterior surface has been relatively well finished and smoothed. The vessel has a long upright neck above a slight shoulder, and the rim, which has an unusual lid seating around the inside edge, is slightly flared.

The base of another vessel probably of late Bronze Age date was found on Long Island (Pot 380). This also is in a coarse, flint-tempered fabric, but is in very poor, friable condition, and the base itself is extremely fragmentary. The form of the vessel is unknown.

An almost complete late Bronze Age–early Iron Age vessel was found on the south-west shore of Long Island (Pot 350; Fig 51). The fabric is tempered with coarse, poorly-sorted crushed flint 0.5–7mm across. Impressions of organic materials were noted on the underside of the base only, suggesting that it had been placed on a bed of straw, chaff or grass during manufacture or while still leather hard. The vessel has an expanded base angle and the exterior surface is finished with vertical finger-smearing beneath an applied horizontal cordon decorated with finger impressions. The upper part of the vessel was poorly represented, but three rim sherds, of plain, rounded, slightly inturned form were noted. Body and base

sherds probably from at least two similar, although slightly thicker-walled, vessels were found on South Binness Island (Pot 774/1), but very severe surface abrasion prevented the reconstruction of these. All three of these vessels appear to have been placed upright in pits in the ground. At least one other similar vessel was recorded from the eastern part of Baker's Island (Pot 521). The surviving base and lower part were lifted *en bloc* as the fabric was very fragile. It was allowed to dry out slowly but, unfortunately, completely disintegrated.

Other buried later-Bronze Age vessels recovered previously include the cremation burials in vessel acc 1981/367, Long Island (see below) and one from Langstone (Soffe 1980; see above) along with five others from the north and north-west coast of Hayling Island (Williams and Soffe 1987).

Iron Age

Three rim sherds from known Iron Age forms were recognised. One sherd, a flared rim from a fineware bowl, was made from a very fine sandy fabric with rare fine flint. Both the other Iron Age sherds occurred in moderate to coarse flint-tempered wares, illustrating the difficulty of dating these fabrics in the absence of chronologically distinctive material. All three sherds were surface finds.

The fineware sherd is of early–middle Iron Age date, and was found on the southern tip of Long Island. The two other sherds probably belong to the late Iron Age (c 100 BC–AD 43). These comprise an internally thickened rim from a jar found on the eastern side of Baker's Island and a sherd from a high-shouldered bead rim jar, found on the south-west shore of North Binness.

Romano-British

A total of 268 sherds were recognised. Sherds belonging to this period were found in most areas of Langstone Harbour but were especially common on the west side of Baker's Island.

The assemblage was dominated by sherds of sandy grey coarseware. Recognisable forms included all the commonest types of the four centuries of 'Roman' Britain – necked jars with upright and everted rims, bead rim jars, large storage jars with a variety of profiles, 'dog-dishes', dropped flanged bowls and dishes, as well as flasks, flagons, and lids, but overall featured sherds were again few in number (Table 16). The nearest and most likely major source for these sandy greywares were the Alice Holt/Farnham kilns (Lyne and Jefferies 1979; c 40km distant), but products from the New Forest (Fulford 1975a; c 50km distant) and a variety of smaller, more local centres such as those at Shedfield (Holmes 1989; c 15km distant) and Rowlands Castle (8km distant) may also be present.

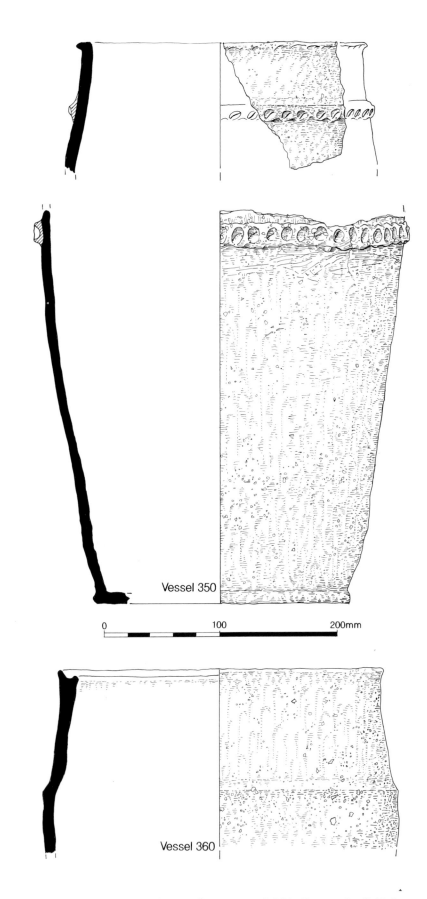

Vessel 350

0   100   200mm

Vessel 360

Figure 51   Pottery from Long Island: sherd; vessel 350; vessel 360. Drawn by S E James

Table 16 Langstone Roman and Post-medieval pottery forms (number of examples)

| Location | Romano-British coarse wares | | | | | | | Romano-British established wares | | | | Post-medieval | | | | |
| | Jars | | | | Bowls/dishes | | | Samian | | Oxford red-slip | New Forest | White ware | Jack-field ware | Cream stone-ware | Orange-glazed | Glazed earthen-ware |
	upright	everted rim	bead rim	un-certain	drop-flanged	dog-dish	G-B copy	Dr 18	Dr 33	C49	Bowl	flagon	teapot			
N Binness																
Area 1	1	1	–	–	1	–	–	1	–	1	–	–	–	–	–	–
Area 4	–	1	–	2	–	–	–	–	–	–	–	–	–	–	–	–
south – A Mack	–	–	–	14	–	–	–	–	1	–	–	–	–	–	–	–
Long Island																
Area 3	–	–	–	–	–	–	–	–	–	–	–	–	–	–	–	–
Area 19	–	–	–	–	–	–	–	–	–	–	–	–	–	1	1	–
Baker's Island																
Area 16, 20–3	–	–	–	1	–	–	–	–	–	–	–	–	–	–	–	–
Area 14, 15, 24–5	3	2	–	2	–	1	–	–	–	–	–	–	–	–	–	–
gen A Mack	–	5	1	–	–	–	1	–	–	–	–	–	–	–	–	–
South Binness																
Area 7	–	3	1	–	–	–	–	–	–	–	–	–	–	–	–	–
south A Mack	–	–	–	–	–	–	–	–	–	–	–	–	–	–	–	–
north A Mack	–	–	–	–	–	–	–	–	–	–	1	–	–	–	–	–
Harbour edge																
NW corner – Area 5	–	2	–	–	–	–	–	–	–	–	–	–	–	–	–	–
Eastney – Area 8	–	–	–	–	–	–	–	–	–	–	–	–	–	–	1	–
Hayling Island shore – Areas 2, 13	–	–	–	–	–	–	–	–	–	–	1	–	1	–	–	–
A Mack finds																
Sinah Lake	–	–	–	–	–	–	–	–	–	–	–	1	–	–	–	–
Oyster Island	–	–	–	1	–	–	–	–	–	–	–	–	–	–	–	3

Table 17 Langstone Harbour Pottery Vessels

Pottery vessel	Island	Area	Date	Size (∅ × surviving ht if buried)	Sherds	Wt (g)	Form and decoration	Fabric	Drawn
	North Binness 69160/04201.76 0.67m OD	Area 1, hearth 1702	MBA 2995±55BP 1410–1060 BC	∅ c 370mm (r)	38	c 4800	urn, globular finished/wiped with a cloth, strap handle and cordon, see ApSimon's comments	moderately-sorted coarse flint tempered fabric	Fig 49
Pot 350	Long Island 69889.37/04201.27 0.69m OD	Area 3	LBA	∅ 310mm (r) × 330mm	154	4510	straight sided vessel, finger impressed cordon, flat rim, expanded base, finished with vertical finger smearing, plain rounded rim	coarse poorly-sorted crushed flint, impressions of straw, chaff	Fig 51
Pot 360	Long Island 70183.25/03983.37 0.43m OD	Area 18	LBA	∅ 280mm (b) × 180mm	70	1936	upper part of large jar, slightly flared, lid-seated rim, slight shoulder	coarse, poorly sorted, crushed calcined flint	Fig 51
Pot 380	Long Island 69911.52/04205.37 1.15m OD	Area 18	LBA	∅ 20mm (b) × 30mm	29	316	base only; vessel form unknown	coarse, poorly sorted, crushed calcined flint	–
PCM acc no 1981/367	Long Island 7020 0410		LBA jar/urn	∅ 250mm × 120mm	168	2315	flat base, vertical sides containing cremation	coarse, poorly sorted, crushed calcined flint	Plate 35
Pot 774/1	South Binness 69873.02/03052.76 1.40m OD	Area 774	LBA	∅ c 280mm	112	2013	straight-sided vessel	coarse poorly-sorted crushed flint, impressions of straw, chaff	–
Pot 521	Baker's Island 69563.91/03722.26 1.09m OD	Area 17	prehistoric	–	–	–	disintegrated on lifting	fine gritted	–

(r) = rim; (b) = base

A few flint-tempered sherds were also identified as being of Roman date; the flint grits being slightly less frequent, smaller, and better sorted than those in the fabrics assigned a prehistoric date. These probably belong to the 1st–2nd centuries AD, a similar range of fabrics being known from a variety of sites further east, in Hampshire (Stuart and Birkbeck 1936; Hawkes 1985, 69–76; 1987, 27–33 and 1989, 94–6; Neal 1980, 135–9; Wessex Archaeology 1989; Seager Smith and Woodward in press). Grog-tempered wares, similar to those known across Hampshire and south-east Wiltshire from the late-3rd century AD onwards (Fulford 1975b, 286–91), were also represented by a handful of plain body sherds from large jar forms.

Sherds of samian were the only imported wares to be recognised in the assemblage, no other imported finewares, mortaria, or amphorae being present. Fragments from a Dr 18 platter and a Dr 33 cup were the only recognisable forms, all the other sherds were small, very abraded featureless bodies. Late Roman (late-3rd–4th century AD) finewares of British origin were also present. Sherds of red slipped, colour-coated, and parchment wares from the New Forest, including one parchment ware mortarium sherd and several sherds from colour-coated indented beakers, were identified. One sherd from a red colour-coated bead rim bowl made in the Oxford region (Young 1977, type C49) was recovered from the south-west shore of North Binness (test-pit 1901).

Saxon

Two Saxon sherds were found on the south-west side of Baker's Island although 20 sherds of Roman pottery were also found in the same area. Both the Saxon sherds were featureless bodies in an organic-tempered fabric. The use of organic materials as temper is generally considered to be a characteristic feature of early–middle Saxon date (c 5th–8th centuries AD).

Post-Roman

No medieval and only ten sherds of post-medieval pottery weighing 800g were recovered during the survey. The rim and part of the body of a black Staffordshire Jackfield Ware vessel, probably a teapot, could be the remains of an unfortunate late-18th or early-19th century picnic on the shingle beach at Hayling Island! The pedestal base of a 16th–17th century whiteware chafing dish comes from Sinah Lake in the south-east of the harbour. The fabric seems too coarse for a French import, and the vessel may instead be locally made, perhaps in the Poole Harbour area, although the only known whiteware production centre of this date known here, at East Holme, Purbeck, has as yet yielded no chafing dishes (Terry 1987). The remaining sherds comprise one body sherd in 19th–20th century cream stoneware and seven sherds of assorted orange and green-glazed earthenwares, five of which are of indeterminate source and 16th–20th century date. The green-glazed sherd is probably a Verwood type and one other sherd is in a micaceous fabric which might have a south-western origin. None of the vessels represented would be out of place in a south-coastal location.

Previous finds: Portsmouth Museum collections
by Julie Gardiner and Rachael Seager Smith

A total of 712 sherds, including sherds from three individual vessels, found in the Langstone Harbour area are held within the collection of Portsmouth Museum (Table 15b). Most of this material derives from fieldwork summarised by Bradley and Hooper (1973). Bradley and Hooper note that a few of their sherds from the shoreline of Langstone Harbour '... show characteristics possibly diagnostic of a later Bronze Age date. Their fabric is coarse and unevenly fired with large flint filler and they show raised and applied cordons and lugs.' (*ibid*, 24), however, the largest section of their pottery report concentrates on material from a site at Paulsgrove, on the edge of Portsmouth Harbour. In 1973, a middle Iron Age date was deemed most appropriate for this material (*ibid*, 27) although subsequent refinements in the ceramic chronology of the 1st millennium BC (Barrett 1980) mean that, today, this material would be assigned to the late Bronze Age/early Iron Age. Similarly, the remainder of pottery from Langstone Harbour has been considered to be of Iron Age date (Bradley 1975 and pers comm to JPG; SMR records of same). In fact, all the material examined in the museum is of similar date range and character to that recovered during the more recent fieldwork in the area, and is mainly of late Bronze Age/early Iron Age or Romano-British date.

Four hundred and fifty sherds including those from three individual vessels were assigned a Bronze Age date. The majority were again of coarse, flint-gritted fabrics. The three vessels and 202 of the sherds can be reliably dated to the Bronze Age on the basis of vessel form or decoration. Six sherds, all of flint-gritted fabrics and probably of middle Bronze Age date were identified amongst the material from North Binness. These comprised a rim probably from a bucket urn, four body sherds with horizontal cordons and one body sherd with intersecting horizontal and vertical cordons decorated with finger impressions, possibly from a globular or barrel urn.

The three individual vessels identified were of late Bronze Age/earliest Iron Age date. One, the lower part of a large jar (acc no 1981/367), contained a cremation burial (McKinley, below), and was found on Long Island (see Plate 35; Chapter 5, below). Numerous thin-walled, flint-tempered body sherds, some decorated with a horizontal cordon, from a single vessel were found on the north part of Hayling Island (acc no 1955/47/1). The third vessel, represented by seven coarse flint-tempered base sherds, with an expanded base angle and vertical smoothing on its exterior surface (acc no E/91/2), was found on Farlington Marshes. Other material characteristic of this period includes plain, slightly inturned jar rims, internally bevelled jar rims, upright or slightly inturned rims decorated with finger-nail or tip impressions, sherds from weak-shouldered jar forms, and sherds decorated with plain or finger impressed cordons. Expanded base angles and vertical finger smearing on the exterior surface of sherds were also common features among the collection. Findspots concentrate on North Binness and Long Islands.

Bradley and Hooper's collection from North Binness also includes a rod-handle fragment, oval in cross-section and made from a moderately well-sorted, fine flint-tempered fabric. For the reasons described in the introduction, this sherd has been included in the Bronze Age category although its actual date is unknown. Of the 25 sherds recorded under the same museum accession code (1971/208/3), two are probably middle Bronze Age, eleven are probably of late Bronze Age/earliest Iron Age date while the presence of two Romano-British sandy greywares suggests that at least some of the flint-tempered sherds may be of similar date.

Two middle Iron Age sherds, both rims from saucepan pots, were recognised. Both were plain, one was made from a sandy fabric, the other was flint-gritted. These were recorded as being from Langstone Harbour or Farlington Marshes (acc no 1978/706) and currently represent the only material of this date from the area. However, a late Iron Age/early Romano-British sherd from a bead rim jar also found on Farlington Marshes (acc no 1978/186/53) was noted in the museum collection.

In total 258 sherds of Romano-British date were identified, predominantly derived from North Binness and Farlington. The same range of fabrics and vessel forms present among the material from the survey were recognised in the museum collection, the sandy greywares again dominating the assemblage. However, one particular vessel form – large cable-rimmed or 'bee-hive' jars – was noted in the museum but not from the survey. Although not exclusively produced by the Alice Holt industry, these vessels are among its most characteristic products, appearing c AD 180, and continuing with few changes for the next 250 years (Lyne and Jefferies 1979, 51). Similar vessels were also made in the New Forest (Fulford 1975a, type 40). It has been suggested that these vessels were ceramic bee-hives, but no definitive proof of this has ever been recovered and a variety of dry storage functions are perhaps more likely.

Finewares were again poorly represented. The collection from North Binness included three small samian body sherds, two New Forest colour-coated ware sherds, one from an indented beaker (Fulford 1975a, type 27), and two parchment ware sherds, one from a mortarium. Another New Forest colour-coated ware base sherd had been found at Farlington.

Other recorded pottery finds

Information gleaned from SMR and publication records is summarised in Chapter 1, above. Most notable among the previously recorded, but not recently examined, pottery finds are the following. Bradley and Hooper (1973) record a single sherd of Neolithic pottery from their fieldwork. It is a flint-gritted, damaged rim sherd with impressed decoration, possibly Peterborough ware, from Emsworth. There are records of Deverel-Rimbury urn fragments from the north-west corner of the harbour and to the south of Farlington Marshes with sherds of other later Bronze Age urns on North Binness. Williams and Soffe (1987) record a total of five late Bronze Age urned cremation burials from the north-west of Hayling Island and one from Langstone village.

Various concentrations of Roman pottery are recorded from North Binness, including storage jars with finger impressions recovered with 'Iron Age C' pottery on the southern shore, and some samian. The rim and shoulder of a small Rowlands Castle storage jar with a batch mark XIII was recovered from South Binness and a variety of 1st-century AD coarseware sherds came from at least three locations on Baker's Island in 1958.

No Saxon pottery is recorded in the SMR and no medieval material from the islands, though sherds are reported from Brockhampton Sewage Works and 12th–14th century cooking pots and a green glazed jug from Wade Court Farm, both of which are close to the present harbour.

Discussion

The small number of identified middle Bronze Age sherds probably all belong within the Deverel-Rimbury tradition but the assemblage is too small and fragmentary to bear close comparison with other assemblages from the area or to indicate specific activities leading to its deposition. With the exception of the two probable globular urn sherds (both of a fine, well-sorted flint-tempered fabric), all the other middle Bronze Age sherds are thick-walled with large, poorly sorted and unevenly distributed flint inclusions. These fabrics are comparable with those recovered elsewhere in central Wessex (Seager Smith and Woodward in press), although individual vessels were locally made. The two middle Bronze Age globular vessels may indicate some form of specialised activity of which we cannot be certain. Both were probably buried in some form or another, rather than broken in antiquity and discarded on to an open surface.

The late Bronze Age/early Iron Age assemblage exhibited most of the characteristic features defined by Barrett (1980) – simple, rounded, inturned or internally bevelled rims, externally expanded base angles, and vertical finger-smearing. Decoration was not common on the sherds examined (only thirteen of the Bronze Age sherds from the museum collection, for instance) and was confined to fingernail or -tip impressions on the top of rims and plain or finger-impressed cordons. Much of the assemblage probably belongs to Barrett's 'post-Deverel-Rimbury' tradition dated to the earlier part of the late Bronze Age, although the presence of one sherd from a fineware bowl, considered to be of early Iron Age date, implies that at least some of the coarsewares belong to this later period. No analysis of vessel form or size, customarily used to suggest the functions of ceramic vessels (Barrett 1980; Ellison 1981), was undertaken because the assemblage was considered to be too fragmentary.

One of the individually deposited vessels (museum acc no 1981/367) was used to contain cremated human remains. An urn of a flint-gritted fabric and probably of late Bronze Age date was previously found inverted over cremated human remains on the line of the M27 motorway across Portsdown (J Nicholls 1987, fig 2). The SMR records also suggest the presence of a Bronze Age urnfield in the north-west part of Langstone Harbour, but no further details are available. It is possible that a number of the vessels (eg vessels 350, 360, 380, 1981/367, and possibly 774/1 and 521) represent outliers of this cemetery. Vessels 1981/367 and 360 contained cremated human remains, and a few fragments of cremated human bone were present in 380 and 521.

Another vessel, found during the survey (vessel 350; Fig 51) contained large quantities of burnt flint, but no bone. The other vessels were more fragmentary, and although apparently deposited in an upright position, little more is known about their associations. Similar deposits of isolated vessels occur elsewhere, although the exact nature of the reasons and beliefs behind them or the frequency with which they were made are unknown. One such vessel, represented by the base of a flint-gritted jar containing burnt flint and charcoal, was found on Portsdown (J Nicholls 1987). This vessel is likely to be of late Bronze Age date and no other features were recorded in its vicinity.

At Twyford Down, Hampshire, eight late Bronze Age/early Iron Age pots were found at approximately even intervals along one or two alignments, possibly implying the existence of a topographical feature subsequently destroyed by ploughing (Seager Smith and Woodward in press). The vessels were not associated with human cremated bone although one (ibid, fig 25, 23) contained substantial quantities of burnt flint. Recent research (ie Bradley et al 1994; Drewett 1982; Ford 1982) has indicated that a complex process of land division was taking place over much of southern England during the late Bronze Age and special deposits marking and 'legitimising' such boundaries have been noted on Salisbury Plain (Bradley et al 1994). While it is possible that the Langstone vessels indicated a similar process of land division, too few vessels were recovered for alignments or other patterns to be observed and the possibility of deposition for other reasons cannot be excluded. Given the recorded presence of burial urns in several parts of the harbour, a function associated with human burial seems likely (see also Burnt flint, and Human bone, below).

The Romano-British pottery spans all four centuries of Roman rule (c AD 43–410), although the paucity of diagnostic sherds means that most of the collection cannot be dated with any precision. No clearly-defined, datable groups were recovered by the survey. The assemblage contains the usual range of fabrics and forms found in collections from small-scale, rural farming communities in southern England and all elements of it can be paralleled among the larger collections from the vicinity (Fulford 1975b; Cunliffe 1971; Down 1979). The assemblage is overwhelmingly dominated by sherds of sandy grey coarsewares derived from the major sources of ceramic supply to this area. Interestingly, Black Burnished ware from the Wareham-Poole Harbour region of Dorset is absent. This widely traded ware was present at both Bitterne Manor, Southampton (Cotton and Gathercole 1958, fig 22, no 3) and Fishbourne by c AD 120 (Cunliffe 1971, fig 74, nos 2 and 3) and continued to play an important role in assemblages from the Hampshire/Sussex coast into the 4th century AD (Fulford 1975b, fig 162). Continental imports were restricted to a handful of samian sherds, ubiquitously found in small quantities on even the lowest status of Romano-British sites. None of the other imported finewares, amphorae, or mortaria common in Roman assemblages from this area were found. Late Roman finewares from British sources were also scarce, represented by a few sherds from the Oxfordshire and New Forest industries.

The coarseware vessel forms present indicate their use for everyday food preparation, serving, and storage purposes while the very small quantities of samian, New Forest, and Oxfordshire wares represent finer tablewares. There is no evidence from either the quantity or the quality of the pottery recovered to suggest large-scale or high-status settlement and although the harbour is ideally located as a centre for both coastal and cross-channel trade, the scarcity of ceramic imports indicates that this potential was not exploited during the Roman period. Despite often severe surface abrasion, the sherds recovered are larger than expected for material derived from the manuring of arable fields with domestic refuse although the lack of subsequent ploughing in this area would, of course, have a beneficial influence on their survival. It is possible that the sherds derive from small-scale settlement activity, possibly largely based on an agricultural or pastoral economy although no definite traces of settlement were identified by the survey. Equally they may relate to more specific activities such as saltworking which was practised in the harbour area from at least Roman times, probably earlier (Bradley 1975; 1992; see Chapter 1 and below). The distribution of sherds suggests that Baker's Island, North Binness, and Farlington served as foci for this activity.

The very small quantities of Iron Age and Saxon pottery recovered clearly indicated that the area of the harbour currently comprising the islands, at

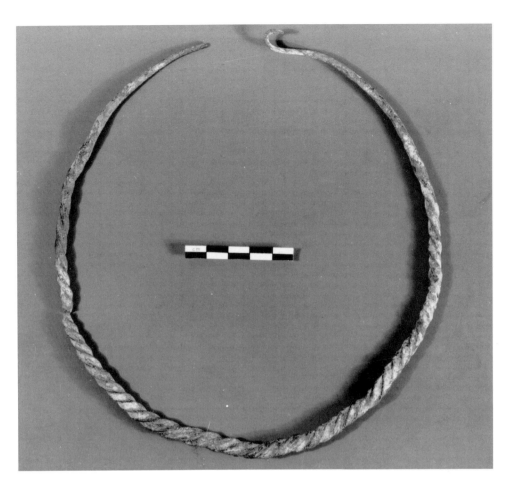

Plate 34 Spiral twisted torc from Russell's Lake (Elaine A Wakefield)

least, was not an important centre of activity at these times. No Saxon finds are recorded in the SMR despite *Domesday* references to pre-Conquest settlement around the harbour (VCH 1908, 128–50) and the known presence of a priory on Hayling Island by the reign of William I (site unconfirmed).

Copper-alloy torc
by Andrew J Lawson

A copper-alloy torc was found in Russell's Lake, north of Oyster Island by a local fisherman about 20 years ago (A Mack pers comm) and was donated to Portsmouth City Museum. The object is a spiral-twisted torc, presumed to be of bronze, 180mm in diameter and 560mm in circumference. It was formed from a square-sectioned rod (7mm wide) and has plain-tapered and hooked terminals (Plate 34). One terminal is missing and the torc is now in two pieces. It has no record of conservation work but is in sound condition with a dark-green patina and in places a powdery blue-green surface.

The British spiral-twisted torc series, whether in bronze or gold, is generally thought to be based on ornaments common in northern Europe (Butler 1963, 137–44; Eogan 1967, 130). Rowlands (1976, 88) cites 23 find-spots for torcs in southern Britain, their distribution (*ibid*, map 22) being mainly in two groups, one in East Anglia and the larger in Somerset, Dorset, and south Wiltshire: new finds have extended this distribution pattern eastward but it

remains generally valid. Prior to the reporting of the Langstone torc, only three finds had been made in Hampshire, namely in the hoards from Plaitford, Woolmer Forest, and South Wonston (Lawson 1999, table 1). Further examples occur in a collection thought to be from the Isle of Wight and others in the hoards from West Ashling, Lavant, and Hollingbury, West Sussex (J Kenny pers comm).

Torcs are not usually found in isolation but associated with other ornaments, as is apparent from the list above. It is possible, therefore, that the Langstone example was only one object recovered from a once larger deposit. Bronze torcs are usually placed in the Taunton metalworking tradition, dated between *c* 1450–1250 cal BC, although the gold series may have been longer lasting (Needham 1996, period 5), and have been used to propose commercial or cultural links between (the Montelius III tradition of) northern Europe, northern France, and Britain in the middle Bronze Age (Rowlands 1976, 89).

Other finds from the survey
by Lorraine Mepham

Small quantities of other categories of archaeological material were recovered or recorded during the survey. These comprise ceramic building material (CBM), fired clay, slag/clinker, stone, glass, worked bone, and metalwork. Much of the CBM, or fired clay, and glass recorded in the field was not collected for reasons stated in Chapter 2. Representative samples

Table 18   Other finds recovered during survey fieldwork

	Area	Slag	CBM	Fired clay	Cua	Fe	Glass	Stone	Quern	Other
N Binness	1	–	8	–	–	1 lump corroded	–	–	–	–
Long Island	3	–	1	–	1	–	–	–	–	–
N Binness	4	–	146	–	–	3	12 inc 1 bottle	1	–	2 x mortar
N Binness	19	–	2	–	–	–	–	–	–	–
N Binness	F1702	–	–	–	1	–	–	–	–	–
Walkover	5	–	–	–	–	–	–	1	–	–
Walkover	7	2	–	–	–	–	–	–	–	1 spindle whorl
Walkover	15	–	–	–	1	–	–	–	–	–
context	105	–	1	–	–	–	–	–	–	–
context	108	–	1	–	–	–	–	–	–	–
context	403	–	–	13	–	–	–	–	–	–
Oyster Is		1	–	–	3	–	–	–	–	–
Baker's Is	(1993)	–	–	–	–	–	–	–	–	1 Pb fish wt
	E Bay	–	–	–	–	–	–	–	–	1 hone/polisher
	(1994)	1	1	–	–	–	–	1	4	–
	21/22	–	3	–	–	–	–	–	–	–
	24	1	1	–	–	–	–	1	–	–
	25	–	–	–	1 shrapnel	–	–	–	–	–
	26	–	3+1 tile	–	–	–	–	–	–	–
Baker's Is	general	–	–	1	–	1 shapnel	–	1	2 saddle	1 coin 1 antler kife handle -modern
PORTSMOUTH MUSEUM										
N Binness	1982		–	–	2 shrapnel	–	–	–	–	–
N Binness	1981		–	–	–	–	–	–	–	cremation burial
Long Is	1971		–	–	–	–	–	–	–	lots briquetage
Farlington M			2	1	–	–	–	–	2 rotary	–
Langstone			–	–	–	–	–	–	–	iron spearhead
TOTAL		5	170	24	10	5	12	5	8	–

of CBM/fired clay were recovered where these materials occurred in any quantity. Where only a few pieces were recorded from the total collection units these were generally retained. A summary of the 'other finds' is presented in Table 18.

Ceramic building material consists largely of well-worn fragments of roof tile, with some smaller, undiagnostic fragments. The thickness of the identifiable roof tile indicates a late-medieval or, more likely, a post-medieval date range for this material, and it is probable that the remaining fragments are

also of this date. Material noted in the field but not recovered included further roof tiles and machine-made bricks representing the remains of several small buildings of known post-medieval to modern date. The fired clay consists almost entirely of small amorphous ceramic fragments lacking surfaces or any other diagnostic features. These fragments, all in soft, friable, oxidised fabrics, are of unknown date or origin, although some might be very abraded fragments of CBM. One piece was identified as part of a cylindrical spindle-whorl; this is in a coarse, flint-tempered fabric quite distinct from the other fired clay fragments, and is likely to be of later-prehistoric date, probably late Bronze Age.

The slag/clinker probably derives from metalworking, although the precise activity represented is unknown. This material is undatable.

Obviously non-local stone, and identifiable objects, were collected. Two pieces of igneous rock, probably granite, may represent building material. Four fragments of ?greensand appear to derive from querns, one identifiable as a saddle quern, the remaining three may be rotary fragments. All four came from Baker's Island, as did two other possible quern fragments, and one possible whetstone.

A worked bone, or possibly antler, handle was recovered from Baker's Island. This is of uncertain but probably post-medieval date. In addition, a small fragment of unidentifiable worked bone was recovered from the surface above hearth 1702 on North Binness. This piece measures 6mm wide by 2mm thick, with a subrectangular section, broken at one end with a surviving length of 44mm. The complete end tapers to a rounded point. The whole piece appears polished, perhaps through use; this may be the tip of a pin or needle.

The metalwork includes both iron and copper-alloy objects. The iron objects are very corroded, but probably represent nails. Amongst the copper alloy, one small perforated disc is probably a fishing weight, of uncertain date; another fragment has part of a screw thread and is almost certainly of modern date. Other fragments are unidentifiable. Most of these pieces represent shrapnel and bomb fragments of World War II.

The presence of a variety of materials and objects of many possible dates within a harbour environment is hardly surprising. Of note, however, is a possible prehistoric ceramic spindle-whorl fragment from South Binness and the possible quern fragments from Baker's Island. Baker's Island supports a number of modern, including wartime, structures for which a variety of building materials have been introduced. It is possible, therefore, that these pieces are introduced but two further saddle quern fragments are recorded, one in 1958 and the other by Chris Draper in 1969.

It is possible that some of the CBM may be earlier than the post-medieval date offered by the only identifiable pieces as there are records, by Bradley and Hooper (1973; also Bradley 1975) and in the SMR, of fragments of Roman brick and tile on North Binness and on the west coast of Hayling Island where the inclusion of wasters suggests the presence of kilns. A further SMR record states that large Iron Age pottery sherds were found over an area of 'over 10ft' (3m) associated with patches of burnt clay and calcined flint, suggested to be a 'potter's hearth' to the south of the old oyster beds on Hayling Island. The greatest quantity of CBM recorded in the survey was from the eastern part of North Binness (total collection grid Area 4) where it was clearly post-medieval in date. However, a small concentration on the south shore of South Binness appeared to be associated with the remains of a wooden structure, represented by possible stakeholes and fragments of wood and charcoal, and 30 sherds of Roman pottery.

Briquetage
by Julie Gardiner

No briquetage was recorded during the survey. This is surprising in view of the quantity of this material recovered by previous workers in the harbour area. Bradley and Hooper (1973; also Bradley 1975; 1992) recorded significant concentrations of briquetage, associated with Iron Age and Roman pottery, 'pot boilers' (burnt flint), and possible hearths, at various places on the northern part of the west coast of Hayling Island. These areas are, unfortunately, now either reclaimed or covered by thick muds so that they were not available for study during the survey.

Briquetage including a 'fired clay strut' is recorded from Baker's Island, associated with 1st century AD pottery with further finds, including struts and pieces 'from evaporating parts' on North Binness, south of Farlington Marshes, and in the north-west corner of the harbour. In the latter case both 'Iron Age' and 1st–2nd century AD pottery are also recorded. Barry Cunliffe (pers comm) remembers finding briquetage kiln bars on North Binness, and Arthur Mack also found a kiln bar on the North Binness foreshore after the project fieldwork had been completed.

In Bradley's (1975) view, saltworking in Langstone Harbour is evident from at least the Iron Age, possibly earlier in view of the redating of some of the pottery recovered by him and Barri Hooper (see above). The use of Portsmouth, Langstone, and Chichester Harbours for saltworking during the Roman period is well-attested (eg Bradley 1992) and in the medieval and post-medieval periods Langstone was well-known for its salt production (see Fontana and Fontana, Chapter 2). Early saltworking is likely to have been a short-term summer activity. As Bradley points out (1975, 21), even the 'large scale post medieval industry in Hampshire was limited to four months of a dry summer while comparable evidence from Brittany suggests the period from May to August.' Such seasonal activity would fit well with the pottery and flint evidence from the Langstone survey, even in the absence of any currently surviving briquetage in the area.

The lack of briquetage from the survey is probably a direct result of erosion of the islands and inaccessibility of the Hayling coastline resulting from reclamation and mud accretion. The fact that it was present in some quantity on the island coasts until at least 1970, but seems to be rare today, may provide important evidence for former coastline positions and regression.

Table 19   Total burnt flint recovered from the survey, by weight

	Wt (g)
North Binness S shore west (surface)	5864
North Binness, Area 1, hearth F1702	1388
North Binness, Area 1, ditch F1704	194
North Binness, Area 1, ditch F1711	571
Total	8017
North Binness S shore East	13628
Long Island SW shore north (surface) inc 350	17160
Long Island SW shore, centre	1958
Long Island, Area 3, pot F305	large quantity not recovered
Long Island SW shore south	1134
Baker's Island SW	3787
Baker's Island NW surface	18557
Baker's Island Test pits	1755
Total	20312
Baker's Island E	3817
S Binness (inc contents of pot too heavy to carry home)	472+
NW corner of harbour (Area 9)	1828
Oyster Island	2508
Total	74621

Burnt flint
by Julie Gardiner

Very large quantities of burnt flint (74.6kg; Tables 3 and 19) were recovered during the survey, from virtually all areas examined, and much more was noted in the field. This material occurred as both scatters and dense concentrations on the foreshore, as concentrations visible in the cliff sections, and, in a few cases, associated with and inside more-or-less complete pottery vessels found buried in the mud (Fig 51). Excavated features and test-pits also produced burnt flint. In some instances the sheer weight of burnt flint made it impractical to recover. That which was retrieved was washed, weighed, and then discarded.

None of the main areas examined in survey were devoid of burnt flint and the largest collections made were on Baker's Island, particularly in the northwestern part, the eastern part of North Binness, and the northern part of Long Island. Burnt flint is intrinsically undatable though concentrations are frequently found in archaeological excavation and fieldwalking (see Buckley 1990, for example, for

recent discussions). In prehistoric contexts mounds of burnt flint are quite common and they frequently occur close to water, but their function and date is open to question. Where dating evidence is available they seem to be Bronze Age or later and have most often been interpreted as cooking places – though the general lack of cooking or other domestic debris associated with them seems a little at odds with this interpretation. In Langstone Harbour any 'mounds' are likely to have been long since destroyed by erosion and the long history of human activity in the area precludes much discussion of their chronological significance.

Some of the concentrations of burnt flint are datable to the later Bronze Age as the material fills and surrounds pots of this age which were found buried in the mud (Figs 49 and 51). Fragments of human bone was found in one of the pots recovered in the survey, scraps in two others, and a substantial amount along with charcoal in one found previously (see below). The other vessels contained no human bone but, if they can all be considered to have been associated with human burial, then it is possible that these concentrations represent the remains of pyre sites from which the lighter elements such as ash, charcoal, and cremated bone have been removed by wave action (J McKinley, below).

In cliff section, some concentrations appear to have been discrete hearths though the chronological relationship with any pottery or other artefacts is equivocal; there is no particular reason why the remainder of this material should be as early as Bronze Age in date. The total collection grid in the eastern part of North Binness (Area 4), for instance, produced over 13.5kg of burnt flint compared with only five sherds of pre-Roman pottery (Fig 48, above). However, large quantities of post-medieval ceramic building material, including bricks and peg tiles, and quantities of modern bottle glass suggest the former presence of a small building close by and it is possible that the burnt flint relates to the presence of a hearth or open fire associated with it.

Some small, dense concentrations of flint which appeared to be hearths were excavated (see below), for instance on Long Island (feature 305) and Baker's Island, but apart from the flint itself no evidence for associated material such as fired clay or animal bone debris was found and only in a few instances was there any evidence for fire. Other concentrations of burnt flint in this area were noted to occur with Roman rather than Bronze Age pottery. On Oyster Island no associated features and very few finds of pre-modern date accompanied the scatters of burnt flint noted here in the survey.

A further possibility is that some of the burnt flint at least relates to former saltworking activities in the harbour, represented by previous finds of briquetage, as described above.

Wooden harpoon
by Michael J Allen

A wooden 'harpoon' was dredged from the grey silty clays of Sweare Deep by local fisherman and bought by the current owner Eric Mcleod. It was found at about SU 730 045 on the edge of the Sweare Deep channel (Bingeman and Mack pers comm), which connects Chichester and Langstone Harbours north of Hayling Island. On recovery it was thought to have been stuck in the mud as if thrown or shot (Bingeman and Mack pers comm). The object was conserved by the Portsmouth City Conservation Offices along with material from the Mary Rose. The wood had been air dried and treated with PEG CEPG 4000 when examined and sampled for radiocarbon dating (Allen 1997a; Allen and Pettitt 1997). No formal identification was made on the PEG 4000 impregnated artefact, but conservation at the Portsmouth City Conservation office recorded it has being probably yew (*Taxus baccata*), which is often used for this type of implement.

The object is 538mm long and about 8mm in diameter tapering to a weathered point. The well finished cylindrical shaft varies between 7.5 and 9mm in diameter and gently tapers to a worn blunted point at the butt end (Fig 52). Heavy weathering and pitting is more evident along this taper, suggesting that it

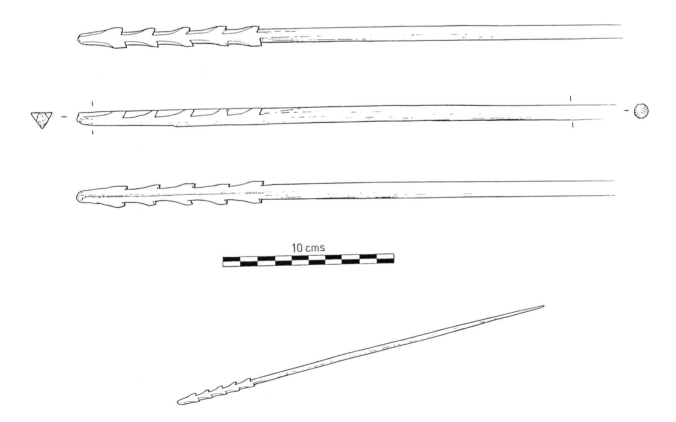

Figure 52 Medieval wooden harpoon from Sweare Deep. Drawn by Norman Lacey

may, in part, be a product of, or have become accentuated by, post-depositional weathering and erosion. If it was stuck into the muds then the butt end would have become more water worn. The remaining length of shaft is smooth and well finished. No tooling marks can be distinguished, largely because the shaft has been well finished. The head of the harpoon is unusual, it is triangular in cross section; an almost perfect equilateral triangle with each face 13.5mm long. Into the upper flat face a series of five paired 'barbs' have been cut. The pairs of barbs are 20mm long and splaying at about 15°, making them 12mm wide and only projecting about a couple of millimetres beyond the diameter of the shaft. The 'nose' of the harpoon is worn, weathered, battered and blunted and therefore it is impossible to discern if this had been tooled into a fine point.

Initially, immediate parallels were sought amongst bone harpoons and fishing spears of the Magdalenian to Mesolithic periods, though known artefacts of this date are all uniserial rather than biserial. A prehistoric date for this fish spear is ruled out by the 13th–14th century AD AMS radiocarbon date (710 ± 40 BP, OxA-6459; see below). The object is certainly designed for spearing or harpooning, and its recovery from Sweare Deep, on the edge of both Langstone and Chichester harbours is entirely consistent with this. Its preservation is due to its loss at sea and the fact that it was embedded in fine clays. Medieval parallels for this object in wood (Earwood 1993) or bone (MacGregor 1985) are, however, scarce. Nothing resembling it is noted by Earwood (1993) among wooden domestic objects in Britain from the Neolithic to early-medieval periods. These are mainly confined to bucket, bowls, staves, and spindles etc or elements of fishweirs (eg Salisbury 1991) or boats (Goodburn 1991). Nothing as far as the author can locate has been recovered from, for instance, waterlogged and estuarine deposits in London, Poole, Bristol, or Viking deposits in York, despite the known fishing contacts in these locations.

Fish spears or harpoons are known from glacial deposits, largely made from bone or antler, such as the recent find of an antler harpoon from Gransmoor, Yorkshire, found embedded in a piece of wood (Sheldrick et al 1997) of 12th-millennium BC date. Beyond these records the archaeological literature is surprisingly impoverished. Despite Steane and Foremen's discussion of spearing, harpooning, and shooting of fish in the medieval period (1991), they cite no parallels of even similar artefacts, with the exception of late-glacial items (eg Smith and Bonsall 1991) and for example the Hoxnian yew spear from Clacton-on-sea (see Wymer 1999, colour plate 15). The fact it may resemble late-glacial objects is not unsurprising for such a utilitarian object with no functional reason for change in design.

On balance it seems likely that this is probably local, as opposed to an ethnographic medieval import. It probably formed part of a medieval fishing kit, possibly for sea fishing as well as in the harbour. It is unlikely that it could be used for large sea fish as

the harpoon shaft is far too slender, but it would be ideal for flat fish, especially in shallow waters with a relatively low tidal reach, such as Langstone Harbour. In retrospect the lack of parallels is not surprising. Although many medieval urban waterside waterlogged deposits have been excavated, eg London, Bristol, and York where waterfronts and domestic buildings have been excavated, these are not contexts from which one might expect to recover organic fishing tackle. This find was purely fortuitous and provides an useful addition to the wealth of other wooden artefacts, and in particular those related to medieval fishing.

Human bone
by Jacqueline I McKinley

Unburnt human bone

During the walkover survey of the west coast of Hayling Island a single, unburnt, human bone was recovered from the surface of the intertidal foreshore. The bone was an almost complete right tibia, but lacking its proximal end. Although water worn, the fragment from an unsexed adult of about 18–45 yrs, was in good condition. The Platycnemic index (degree of meso-lateral flattening of the tibia) of 80.4 is within the Eurycnemic range. A small squatting facet was observed.

The isolated find could be of any period and dating the find is difficult; it could be prehistoric but it could equally well represent a drowning in the harbour from the medieval period to the 20th century.

Cremated human bone

Cremated bone from four late Bronze Age urned burials was received for examination including vessels 1981/367 (Long Island), base of vessel 521 (Baker's Island), and vessels 360 and 380 from Long Island. One further vessel from Long Island (350) contained no cremated bone.

One of the urned burials (acc no 1981/367) had been excavated from Long Island in 1981 and stored in Portsmouth Museum; the vessel was damaged and fragmentary but largely complete (Plate 35). The residues from the fill had been retained and were scanned. The burial from Baker's Island (pot 521) was excavated during the survey; only the base survived and the vessel was badly damaged and very friable and disintegrated on drying out. The burials from the foreshore of Long Island were excavated and recovered in 1997; vessel 360 was almost complete and inverted, whilst only the lower 20mm of vessel 380 survived.

All four burials were recovered from foreshores and had been subject to regular coverage by water at high tide. Relatively little is known about potentially associated features in the vicinity of the burials; the urns were inserted into small pits cut from the level

Plate 35 Later Bronze Age cremation urn (1981/367) and contents recovered from Long Island in 1981. The remains are those of an adult female (Elaine A Wakefield)

of, or through, the archaeologically rich clay layer visible in cliff sections which survives locally on the foreshore as residual 'headlands' (see above). Pot 521 from Baker's Island was recovered from such a 'headland'.

Methods

The fill of vessel 360 was excavated in four, 50mm spits, the sub-contexts being retained throughout. Analysis followed the writer's standard procedure for the examination of cremated bone (McKinley 1989; 1994a). Age was assessed from the stage of tooth development and eruption (Beek, van 1983); the stage of ossification and epiphyseal bone fusion (Gray 1977; McMinn and Hutchings 1985; Webb and Suchey 1985); tooth wear patterns (Brothwell 1972); and the general degree of cranial suture fusion and degenerative changes to the bone, including Brooks (1955). Sex was assessed from the sexually dimorphic traits of the skeleton (Bass 1987; Gejvall 1981). Full details are in archive.

Results

The situation of the cremation burials from Long Island, on the present foreshore where they have been subject to tidal flooding, has resulted in substantial infiltration of the fills by small sea shells (*Hydrobia* spp) and, to a lesser degree, seaweed. It is probable that some of the original contents of vessel 380 were lost as a result of truncation, and some may have been washed-out by the action of the sea, particularly the lighter, spongy bone. Some of the contents of the better preserved vessel 360 may also have been lost to the sea, particularly fragments of charcoal

which would float. Although the loss of some small bones/fragments from the latter cannot be conclusively excluded, given the position of the bone concentration within the fill 100–150mm below the rim (see below), any substantial loss is unlikely. The presence of a few fragments of burnt flint and flecks of charcoal in the small-fraction residues from burial 360 indicates the original inclusion of some redeposited pyre debris.

The bone from all the cremation burials was in good condition and did not appear water-worn or abraded, both compact and trabecular bone being well represented in the three relatively undisturbed burials. There is no indication of deliberate fragmentation of bone prior to burial in any of the burials (McKinley 1994b).

A minimum of four individuals are represented amongst the cremated bone (Table 20). Two fragments of adult bone were recovered amongst the infant bone from the burial in vessel 380. Whilst it is possible that the deposit represented a dual burial of an adult and an infant, had that been so one would have expected the adult bone to have survived in preference to that of the infant, being larger and heavier, and to have recovered more bone from the base of the vessel. The adult bones in this instance are more likely to represent intrusive remains; since there were no neighbouring burials, the contamination probably resulted from the reuse of an inefficiently cleared pyre site (McKinley 1994a, 6–7 and 83).

In the burial from vessel 360, *ante mortem* tooth loss was noted in 2/12 socket positions, with dental abscesses in 3/12 including the right maxillary incisors. There was a possible well-healed fracture in one clavicle shaft. The pitting and osteophytes (new bone) recorded may be indicative of the early stages of joint disease.

Table 20 Summary of human bone from cremation burials

Burial in pot no	Bone wt	Age	Sex	Pathology
360	404.6g	adult *c* 30–45 yr	??female	- *ante mortem* tooth loss; abscess; fracture – left clavicle; pitting – left temporo-mandibular; osteophytes – atlas
1981/367	1079g	adult *c* 19–25 yr	??female	
380	31.2g	infant *c* 2 yr + 2 frags adult bone		
521	2.4g	> infant		

Pyre technology and ritual

The cremated bone was predominantly the buff-white colour indicative of full oxidation (Holden *et al* 1995a and b). A small proportion of fragments from all skeletal areas from burials in vessels 360 and 380 showed varying hues of blue and grey, and a few fragments of skull vault and one tarsal bone from vessel 1981/367 were slightly blue-grey.

In the burial from vessel 360, there may be some significance in that, where elements from both sides were recovered, the left side (scapula, patella) was less well oxidised than the right, but the observations most probably reflect a general deficiency in the quantity of fuel used or time available for cremation. A substantial quantity of bone (*c* 100g) from the burial in vessel 360 remained amongst the unsorted small fraction residues (> 2mm), where it was mixed with large quantities of marine snails (*Hydrobia* sp) and snails. The quantity of bone recovered represents, at maximum, 40% of the expected weight of bone from an adult cremation, but more probably *c* 25%. The majority (72%) of the bone was recovered from spit 3, only 9% being found in spit 4, the lowest spit at the mouth of the vessel. There was no bone in the upper 50mm of the fill.

It is probable that bone was lost from vessel 521 as a result of the tidal erosion which had removed most of the pot itself, leaving too little to allow comment on its possible original state.

The total weight of bone presented for vessel 1981/367 is slightly less than was in fact present. The 5mm and 2mm fractions were not fully sorted in post-excavation, the residues only being scanned for identifiable skeletal elements, consequently there was slightly more cremated bone in the 5mm fraction than was weighed and much more in the 2mm fraction. The quantity of bone recovered demonstrates that much, though certainly not all, of the bone was collected from the pyre for burial, probably in excess of 67% (McKinley 1993). Such weights of cremated bone from Bronze Age burials are most frequently found in association with primary 'barrow' graves, though not exclusively so (McKinley 1997a). The writer believes it likely that the quantity of bone collected from the pyre for burial may, at least in the Bronze Age, have been seen as a expression of 'status'. The lack of background information associated with burial 1981/367 precludes further comment on its probable nature, though it seems likely that it formed part of a larger urnfield represented by reported finds of other urns in the northern part of the harbour.

The largest bone fragment recorded was 80mm (burial 1981/367), and the majority of the bone from the two, relatively undisturbed, adult burials was recovered from the 10mm sieve fraction.

The majority (39%) of the bone from the burial in vessel 380 was between 5–10mm, with a maximum fragment size of 29mm; the young age of the individual and truncation of the burial leading to substantial reduction in bone fragment size. There is no indication of any deliberate fragmentation of bone prior to burial (McKinley 1994b). Elements from each skeletal area were recovered within each burial and there is no evidence to suggest any deliberate selection of specific bones for deposition.

The position of the bone within vessel 360, where it was largely confined to one side and concentrated in the central spit 3 rather than in the basal spit 4, suggests the bone may originally have been placed within a bag prior to deposition within the urn. There is also the possibility that some form of organic material was originally included in the burial, helping to confine the bone within one area of the upright vessel.

Several small fragments of cremated animal bone were recovered with the human bone from vessel 1981/367, a not uncommon occurrence in burials of this period. The animal or parts of the animal would have been cremated with the deceased as pyre goods.

Relatively large quantities of charred wood (136.7g) were recovered within burial 1981/367, including several large fragments (max 0.20 × 0.20 × 0.15m) probably representative of the pyre structure (as opposed to stem-sized brushwood in-fill). Unfortunately, the stratigraphic relationship between the bone and the charred wood is not known. The latter undoubtedly comprises pyre debris either accidentally or deliberately included in the burial and the large size of the fragments may be significant to their inclusion. Small amounts of probable pyre debris, comprising burnt flint and charcoal, were also recovered in the fill of and in the area around Vessel 521.

The inclusion of small quantities of pyre debris in Bronze Age cremation burials or graves has been noted in other burials of this period. Its presence suggests the likely close proximity of the pyre site to the place of burial, which may account for at least some of the large quantities of burnt flint recovered during the survey and in previous work in the area (see above).

Discussion

A small, but increasing number of Bronze Age cremation burials have now been recovered from adjacent islands in Langstone Harbour (see Chapter 7 and Williams and Soffe 1987). Mostly urned burials, some, like those recorded here, have the appearance of 'secondary' burials, perhaps part of a larger assemblage, whilst others have the characteristics of 'primary' burials (vessel 1981/367) containing a substantial quantity of bone (McKinley 1997a). All contain some redeposited pyre debris,

indicative of the close proximity of the pyre site to the place of burial.

Animal bone
by Pippa Smith and Michael J Allen

Animal bones from the Langstone Harbour survey were recovered during the three field seasons (1993, 1994, and 1995). Bone was recovered from walkover and detailed surveys, excavations, and test-pitting with, in addition, fewer than 50 bones picked up at various times by Arthur Mack and Dominic Fontana (Table 21).

Only bone from features (ie from excavation or recovered from the surface of features in walkover survey) can potentially be dated. Those from the excavation of saltmarsh soil profiles and from general collection of the foreshores and total area collection provide a background of material for which a reliable date cannot be ascribed. The relatively low rate of recovery of bone was partly intentional as the

Table 21   Animal bone, recovered from excavation and fieldwork

	Cow	Horse	Large mam	Deer/ s cow	Sheep/ goat	Small mam	Unident	Large bird	TOTAL
FEATURES									
North Binness Area 1									
Hearth 1702	4	–	7	–	–	3 [2 bnt]	1	–	15
Ditch 1711	3	–	–	–	–	–	–	–	3
Ditch 1704	–	–	1	–	–	–	4 [1 bnt]	–	5
TOTAL	7	–	8	–	–	3	5	–	23
SURFACE FINDS									
North Binness Area 1									
Surface	1	–	–	–	–	–	–	–	1
Long Island									
3314	–	–	–	–	1	–	–	–	1
94\0003	–	–	–	–	1	–	–	–	1
South Binness									
Surface (Area 7)	–	1	–	–	–	–	–	–	1
Round Nap	–	–	–	–	2	1	–	–	3
Baker's Island									
TP 2006	–	–	–	–	1	–	*	–	1 + *
Area 16	–	3	1	–	–	–	–	–	4
Area 20/21	–	2	–	1	–	–	–	–	3
Area 26	–	–	–	–	–	–	1	–	1
Surface	–	1	–	–	–	–	–	1	2
Oyster Island									
surface	3	2	1	–	–	–	–	–	6
TOTAL	4	9	2	1	5	1	1 + *	1	24 + *

* = small unidentifiable fragments

fieldwork strategy was to collect only bones that were potentially significant or directly associated with features. Some bone, however, was recovered during total area collection survey. Few bones are complete enough to measure and the data set is too small for metrical analysis to be meaningful.

Almost half of the assemblage was recovered from excavated features or their surfaces in Area 1 on North Binness. These features are considered to be later Bronze Age in date and produced predominantly cattle bones. The largest assemblage was recovered from hearth 1702 and included a cattle horn-core, patella, metacarpal, and pelvis fragment with vertebrae, a rib, and skull fragments of a large mammal, possibly also cow. Three fragments of small mammal, possibly sheep/goat were recovered, two of which were burnt.

A right cattle radius and metatarsal were recovered from the surface of ditch 1711 with a pelvis fragment from its upper layer. The smaller ditch, 1704, produced large mammal and an unidentifiable fragment from its surface.

Material recovered from the walkover surveys, total collection units, or other collections are predominantly fragments of larger mammals (cattle and horse) or larger bone fragments of smaller animals or birds. Only two bones were recovered from Long Island, both sheep/goat maxillary teeth. Only four fragments (three teeth) were recovered from South Binness, three of which are probably sheep/goat, with one horse molar. Only Baker's Island was significantly different in that the majority of bone was horse and included tibia, femur and radius fragments as well as teeth from a number of different areas. No cattle/deer and only one sheep/goat fragment was recovered. A long bone of a large bird (possibly a brent goose) was also recovered; not altogether surprising for one of the most important bird reserves on the south coast of England.

Comment on the assemblage

Few bones are complete enough to measure and the data set is too small to get anything out of metrical work. A closer look with a comparative collection may enable differentiation between some of the cattle/deer identifications (Table 21).

5 Absolute dating evidence and palaeoenvironmental data

ABSOLUTE DATING EVIDENCE

Radiocarbon evidence
by Paul Pettitt and Michael J Allen

Five radiocarbon dates were obtained from the wood and charcoals from the project.

1 Wooden harpoon
2 Charcoals from hearth 1702 on North Binness
3 Wooden Stake (OO) from the Sinah circle structure
4 Yew roots (near BB) from the submerged woods at Baker's Rithe
5 Oak branch (AEA) from the submerged woods at Russell's Lake

1 Wooden harpoon

The only obvious parallels for this wooden object appeared to be Lateglacial bone implements; though no example could be found that matched it closely. As it was recovered by dredging there was no archaeological context, nor any other associated artefacts. A small sample AMS radiocarbon date was provided by the Oxford University Radiocarbon Accelerator Unit.

Radiocarbon evidence
by Paul Pettitt

A 300 mg sample was drilled from the midshaft of the harpoon. The object had been preserved using PEG (see above). It received the standard Oxford mild chemical purification treatment for wood, with the objective of isolating the datable cellulose from contaminating agents such as dust, lignins, and humic acids. As PEG 4000 is soluble in methanol, the process was initiated with a methanol rinse, which successfully removed the preservative. Thereafter, the sample was given a hydrochloric acid wash, a rinse and a subsequent caustic wash in sodium chloride, another rinse, and a further acid wash and rinse. Following the pretreatment, the purified cellulose was combusted in an oxygenating environment. The resulting carbon, in the form of CO_2, was measured by the Oxford accelerator mass spectrometer (AMS). The $\delta^{13}C$ of the sample was –26.6 per mil, as expected for a sample of wood, and the resulting age, in radiocarbon years BP is as follows:

OxA-6459   710 ± 40 BP

When calibrated, using the OxCal program developed in-house, it can be seen that, at the 95% level of confidence, the harpoon dates to the 13th–14th centuries AD, with the weight of probability in the 13th century. This is illustrated in Figure 53.

2 The hearth (Feature 1702)

The sherds of a large handled globular pottery vessel were found in the top of hearth 1702. During excavation and sampling several smaller sherds of the same vessel were recovered from within the hearth. Although some of these sherds are very large, the form, function, and date of the vessel remain enigmatic and ensuing debate among a number of recognised pottery specialists provided a date range of early Bronze Age to early Roman (see Chapter 4)! An absolute date was therefore considered imperative both in terms of national ceramic typology and for the chronology of the use and environment that existed on North Binness. As the vessel is securely related to this feature a selection of identified twiggy charcoals (greater than 9.5mm) was submitted for radiocarbon dating in order to date both the hearth and the unusual pottery vessel. The charcoal was collected by careful sampling in the field and laboratory flotation and all charcoals larger than 2mm were extracted and separated for radiocarbon dating. These were identified by R Gale as Pomoideae, *Fraxinus* sp, *Alnus* sp, *Prunus* sp, and *Salix* sp.

A radiocarbon determination of 2995 ± 55 BP (OxA-7366) calibrates to 1410–1060 cal BC, indicating that both the hearth and the large globular vessel are middle–late Bronze Age. The significance of this date in relation to the pottery vessel is discussed elsewhere.

3 The Sinah circle

The Sinah circle provides an interesting structure today located deep in the intertidal zone. Its age is important in understanding both the nature of the structure, and the environment in which it was constructed. The structure contained both worn split planks and roundwood stakes. An oak roundwood stake was selected for radiocarbon dating as this was considered more likely to directly relate to the construction of the structure; the split planks might be more likely to be reused structural wood and/or represent driftwood. One roundwood oak stake (OO)

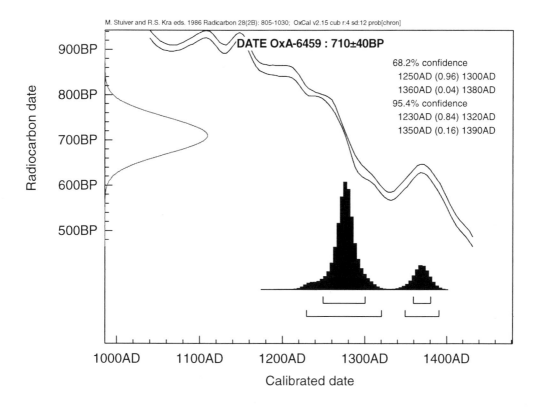

M. Stuiver and R.S. Kra eds. 1986 Radiocarbon 28(2B): 805-1030; OxCal v2.15 cub r:4 sd:12 prob[chron]

Figure 53   Radiocarbon distribution from the Medieval wooden harpoon

Radiocarbon results

Site/find	Material	Lab no	Result BP	δ^{13}C ‰	Calibration
Harpoon	wooden harpoon	OxA-6459	710 ± 40	–26.6	cal AD 1230–1390
Sinah circle	oak stake OO	GU-7275	980 ± 50	–24.5	cal AD 980–1180
Hearth 1702	charcoal	OxA-7366	2995 ± 55	–24.2	1410–1060 cal BC
Baker's Rithe	oak stump (BB)	R-24993/2	3735 ± 60	–22.16	2310–1950 cal BC
Russell's Lake	oak branch (AEA)	R-24993/1	4431 ± 70	–27.83	3350–2910 cal BC

recovered from the Sinah circle structure was submitted for radiocarbon dating. This and two other stakes had previously been submitted for dendrochronology but no results were possible on these items (see below).

The determination of 980 ± 50 BP (GU-7275) indicates a date of cal AD 960–1180 encompassing the later-Saxon and earlier-medieval period. This is a surprise in view of the general lack of artefactual evidence from the harbour representing this period. The structure at this time must have been constructed within the harbour, rather than in a terrestrial situation, and this is discussed in detail in Chapter 3. Whether the radiocarbon result dates the construction of the Sinah circle, however, is another matter and is discussed in Chapter 3.

4   The submerged 'forests'

Small samples of sapwood were removed from one of the main trunks or branches from each of the sites investigated to provide some indication of their age. No datable artefacts were recovered from the area, in fact each area was largely devoid of any finds excepting isolated pieces of burnt flint.

The two radiocarbon determinations indicate that both areas of submerged wood are of Neolithic date. That at Russell's Lake belongs to the later Neolithic, while that at Baker's Rithe, nearly half a metre lower, was nearly a millenium later, but still generally late Neolithic in date.

Dendrochronology
by Cathy Groves

Three oak timbers from the Sinah stake circle were submitted for dendrochronological dating. All three timbers were prepared, and but only one contained in excess of 50 rings and no match could be found for the measured pattern.

Dendrochronology sample details

Stake	Total number of rings	Sapwood rings	Average ring width (mm)	Comments
OO	c 40	c 20	c 1.2	*Rejected*: pith present, bark present, ?felled summer
AN	65	–	2.0	measured
AD	c 20	c 5	c 2.0	*Rejected*: pith present, bark present, felled summer

The general principles and techniques of dendrochronology and its application to timber assemblages are discussed elsewhere (eg Baillie 1982; Hillam 1998). Basically for a structure to be considered suitable for dendrochronological dating some of its major structural timbers need to contain a minimum of 50 growth rings. Ring patterns with less than 50 rings are generally unsuitable for dating purposes as the sequence may not be unique (eg Hillam *et al* 1987). It is also usual to sample at least 6–10 timbers per phase whenever possible as this increases the likelihood of producing a site master curve, which incorporates the data from a number of matching ring patterns, and hence improves the chances of obtaining a date (eg Hillam *et al* 1987). Multiple sampling also reduces interpretative difficulties that may arise from the reuse of structural timbers.

Three samples of oak wood were made available from the Langstone Harbour structure. Details of the samples are given in the table.

Stakes OO and AD did not contain sufficient rings to be considered suitable for full analysis, thus these were rejected before measurement. Stake AN was analysed using standard dendrochronological techniques (Hillam 1998). The ring sequence derived from stake AN was compared to numerous reference chronologies and in particular to those spanning the last 500 years, as it had been suggested that the structure may be associated with 19th century oyster beds. However, as no consistent results were obtained the search was widened to include both the historic and prehistoric periods. Unfortunately no conclusive results were produced thus the timber remains undated by dendrochronological techniques. It is concluded that the trees were subject to a lot of ecological stress during growing (see discussion by Clapham, below on the Neolithic trees from Baker's Rithe and Russell's Lake), and this is why their ring patterns do not fit in with any dated reference chronologies, nor even those from Wootton Quarr, Isle of Wight (Hillam in Tomalin *et al* forthcoming). Although absolute dating has not been possible, some general information on the environment in which they grew can be suggested. It is likely that the distressed growth patterns occurred because local growing conditions were unfavourable, and this stress may be due to the proximity of the trees, from which these stakes were obtained, to saline water and saline water ingression.

THE PALAEOENVIRONMENTAL EVIDENCE,
edited by Michael J Allen

Introduction: landscape and land-use development

The opportunities for excavation during the survey were very limited and, consequently, so were the opportunities for obtaining samples for palaeoenvironmental reconstruction. Where excavations were conducted bulk samples were taken for charred and waterlogged plant remains (hearth 1702, ditch 1711, and pots 350, 360, and 380 from Long Island, and 774/1 from South Binness) and, in appropriate cases, subsamples were removed for the recovery of snails. Sampling for snails and pollen was undertaken from the exposed ditch section, otherwise the most significant palaeoenvironmental evidence was obtained from additional fieldwork undertaken specifically for the recovery of suitable plant macrofossil samples and pollen cores.

Most significant of these was a deep peat and alluvial sequence discovered by Dr Keith Fowler, of Portsmouth University in 1978, and cored by Scaife and Fowler in 1993 in the north of the harbour, east of Farlington Marshes, in the *Spartina* grass north of Chalkdock Lake at SU 4696 1054. A long pollen core was analysed by Scaife and specific coring programmes in 1995 and 1997 were undertaken to obtain fresh and datable material.

The second programme of specifically palaeoenvironmental investigation was that of survey and sampling of the Baker's Rithe 'forest' and Russell's Lake trees in August 1997, during which trees were recorded and sampled, associated peats bulk sampled for radiocarbon dating and recovery of plant macrofossils, and undisturbed monolith samples taken for pollen analysis. Close sampling for snails was also undertaken from suitable, more obviously calcareous, contexts. Identifications of wood from the Sinah circle structure and of cremated human bone from the later-Bronze Age vessels have been reported above.

Preservation varied; snails only occurred in pockets such as within the 'complete' pottery vessels and lenses of material stratified within the peats, but were almost absent from most of the stratified archaeological deposits. Pollen was present in the deep peat and alluvial stratigraphies, but again absent from the sampled archaeological contexts.

The aim of the limited palaeoenvironmental programme was to ascertain the basic nature of the landscape during prehistory to provide some indication of the local environment during times when human activity occurred. Key among these aims was that of ascertaining the marine and fluvial influence which might have provided one of the major attractions for prehistoric populations.

Pollen analysis at Farlington Marshes: a vegetation history of Langstone Harbour
by Rob Scaife

The 'submerged' intertidal peat deposit identified in 1978 in Farlington Marshes, north of Chalkdock Lake on the northern periphery of Langstone Harbour (SU 4696 1054 – between SU 4694 1053 and SU 4697 1054 – K Fowler pers comm 7/4/94) is the only such submerged peat thus far identified in Langstone Harbour (Fig 10) with the exception of those small shelves recorded at Baker's Rithe and Russell's Lake which are associated with waterlogged subfossil trees (Fig 10 or 19). This is unusual given the widespread occurrence of such 'submerged' peat and sediment along the Solent margins elsewhere in Hampshire, Dorset, and the Isle of Wight. This site has previously been used in undergraduate studies (eg Ullet 1993) and was originally cored by the writer and Dr K Fowler in 1979. The present project has afforded the opportunity to carry out a more detailed pollen analysis on that original core which could provide data on the palaeovegetation and environment of the local region. Unfortunately no material survived suitable for radiocarbon dating the sequence.

Extent of the submerged peat

Previous work by Fowler (pers comm) had consistently recorded submerged peat stratigraphies to *c* 3m depth between SU 4694 1053 and SU 4697 1054. A programme of exploratory coring in 1997 by the writer, Dr M Allen, Dr D Mauquoy, and S Wyles, sank in excess of 26 boreholes using a 20mm diameter gouge auger across the area. Although within the vicinity of the previous peat find, none of the cores peppered across the area encountered peat despite coring to depths in excess of 3m. It can be concluded from this that the peat originally identified by Fowler does not represent a submerged peat shelf, but is much more restricted in its extent and is probably a peat-filled channel and, as such, is not necessarily sea-level related. The implications of this are discussed further in Chapter 7.

Method

Cores for pollen analysis were obtained using a 0.5m chamber Russian peat corer. Standard techniques were used for the extraction of the contained subfossil pollen and spores (Moore *et al* 1992). Pollen was identified and counted using an Olympus biological research microscope fitted with Leitz optic at ×400 and ×1000 magnification. Pollen counts of between 250 grains in poorer mineral sediments and 900 in alder rich peat were made for each of the 17 levels examined. The average pollen sum was 400 grains. Data have been presented in standard pollen diagram form, calculated and plotted using Tilia and Tilia Graph, with the pollen calculated as a percentage of the sum (total dry-land pollen, hereafter tdlp), and spores and marsh groups as a percentage of the sum and the requisite group. This work was carried out in the Department of Geography, University of Southampton. The plant taxonomy follows that of Stace (1991) and for pollen that of Moore *et al* (1992) but with modifications according to the Stace, *Flora Europaea* (Bennett *et al* 1994; Stace 1991).

Stratigraphy

A total of 2.5m of sediments and peats was recovered from this site with the undulating incised saltmarsh surface being at *c* +3.25m OD. The stratigraphy was characterised as follows:

Depth in metres

0–0.3	Grey silt (sediment) containing *Spartina* rootlets
0.3–0.6	As above but fewer rootlets
0.6–1.44	Grey (marine) silts and clays; homogeneous with little plant debris
1.44–1.47	Transition (lighter sediments)
1.47–1.50	Lower transition (darker/humic)
1.50–1.65	Brown detrital peat mottled by lighter clay
1.65–2.02	Brown, highly humic detrital/monocot peat. No organics
2.02–2.10	Peat with clay fraction
2.10–2.40	Wood in humified detrital peat. Wood at 2.13–4m; 2.17–2.41m; 2.23m
2.40–2.90	Pale grey silts with occasional organic lenses

Pollen characterisation and zonation

Four principal local pollen assemblage zones (lpaz) can be recognised (Fig 54) from the base of the pollen profile at 2.9m to the top of the peat sequence at 1.5m. These zones are characterised and delimited as follows:

lpaz LANG:1, 2.90–2.60m. Poaceae-Cyperaceae: This zone is characterised by the lowest values of arboreal pollen in the profile and conversely the highest percentage totals of herbs. The latter are dominated by Poaceae and Cyperaceae. Trees and shrubs comprise *Betula* (to 9%), *Quercus* and *Corylus avellana* (expanding to 14% and 15% respectively). Other tree/shrub taxa include small numbers of *Betula*, *Ulmus*, *Tilia* (at the top of the zone), *cf Fagus*, and *Salix*. Aquatic/marginal aquatic *Myriophyllum spicatum*, *Typha/Sparganium*, and algal *Pediastrum* are noted. Spores of *Equisetum* (8%), *Pteridium aquilinum* (15%), and monolete *Dryopteris* type spores (8%).

lpaz LANG:2, 2.60–2.36m. *Pinus-Corylus avellana* type- Cyperaceae-*Dryopteris* type. Herb percentages decline throughout this zone with tree and shrub pollen expanding (to 50% and 40% respectively). *Pinus* is dominant (36%) with *Corylus avellana* type (expanding to 40%). *Betula* (10%), *Quercus* (reduced to 5%), and *Salix* (2%) remain. Non-arboreal pollen (especially Poaceae and Cyperaceae) decline markedly to the top of this zone. Some sporadic occurrences of marsh and aquatic taxa are noted (*Myriophyllum spicatum*, *Callitriche*, *Menyanthes trifoliata*, and *Typha latifolia*). Spores of *Dryopteris* type are important and percentages expand sharply in this zone to a peak of 48%. *Polypodium vulgare* is present from the base of this zone. Conversely, *Pteridium aquilinum* declines.

lpaz LANG:3, 2.36–1.64m. *Quercus-Tilia-Alnus-Corylus avellana* type. This pollen zone spans the greater part of the peat sequence. The broad characteristic of dominant tree pollen comprising *Quercus*, *Ulmus*, *Tilia*, *Corylus avellana*, and *Alnus* nevertheless show some variations in relative importance. Whilst separation into individual pollen assemblage zones was not felt justified, these changes are described as pollen assemblage sub-zones (pasz).

pasz LANG:3-A, 2.36–2.20m. *Ulmus* (5%), *Quercus* (27%), *Tilia* (15%), and *Corylus avellana* type (36%) expand. A single *Fraxinus* record is noted. Conversely *Pinus*, *Betula*, and herbs decline.

pasz LANG:3-B, 2.20–2.04m. Delimited by a 'peak' of *Pinus* (13%) associated with a higher inorganic content of the peat. *Corylus avellana* type attains its highest percentage values (50%). *Alnus* and *Tilia* are reduced.

pasz LANG:3-C, 2.04–1.64m. *Tilia* (25%) and *Alnus* (70%) expand to their highest values while *Quercus*, *Ulmus*, and *Corylus* remain important. *Pinus*, *Betula*, *Salix*, Poaceae, and Cyperaceae die out from the base of this sub-zone.

lpaz LANG:4, 1.64–1.48m. This upper zone corresponds with the lithostratigraphic transition from peat to the overlying marine sediments. Palynologically, this is characterised by a sharp reduction in *Tilia* while some *Ulmus*, *Quercus*, and *Corylus avellana* type remain. There is a sharp expansion of herb pollen numbers and diversity (41%). *Chenopodium* type (17%) and Poaceae (16%) are

dominant. Asteraceae and Plantaginaceae types are of note. *Pteridium aquilinum* (30%) attains its highest percentage.

Inferred vegetation history

The study of intertidal peat deposits and associated submerged forests has a long history in this region of the south coast. Clarke, in 1838, recorded a variety of wood taxa recovered in Poole Harbour, Dorset. Narthorst (1873) subsequently discussed early floras (Arctic) from South Coast localities. Clement Reid was, however, pioneer in his study of submerged forests, recording subfossil plant material from Southampton Water at Stone (1893), Parkstone, Poole, Dorset (1895), and from Corfe, Dorset (1896). These studies were a prelude to his classic texts *The Origin of the British Flora* (1899) and *Submerged Forests* (1913). Little further study was accomplished until that of Godwin and Godwin's (1940) publication on deep peat deposits excavated during dock building in Southampton and from Weevil Lake, Portsmouth Harbour (Godwin 1945).

Similarly, early and deep peat has been recognised by Mottershead (1976). Whilst these works allude to the question of relative sea-level (eustatic) changes, more recent advances in radiocarbon dating and biostratigraphical analyses (pollen and diatoms analysis) have allowed a better understanding of Holocene sea-level changes and coastal palaeoenvironments which have been related in many cases to submerged archaeology. In the Hampshire Basin, Solent region, basic radiocarbon-dated vegetation chronologies exist for Poole Harbour (Haskins 1978; Long *et al* 1999), the Isle of Wight (Scaife 1980; 1982; 1987), and the more generalised work of Waton (1982a; 1982b). These act as useful bench marks for study of vegetation in marginal environments such as the coastal fringes. Sea-level index curves have now been established for the Holocene of the South Coast including the Solent (eg Long 1992; Long and Innes 1993; Long and Tooley 1995; Long *et al* 1999; and Long and Scaife 1996). These data provide useful palaeovegetation data related to relative sea-level change.

The sequence of peats obtained from Langstone clearly relates to a period prior to marine inundation. Whilst it is possible that the peat and sediments were deposited in environments changing in relation to eustatic change, it is also possible that these fen carr peats relate solely to local topographical situations – that is, a palaeovalley with high watertable suited to development of a valley fen community. At present, no radiocarbon dates are available from the sequence and, thus, recourse is made to correlation with known sequences noted above.

In the pollen profile (Fig 54), the pollen assemblage zones/sub-zones in part reflect the varied stratigraphy present. Lower mineral sediments clearly show different woodland characteristics being dominated initially by localised *Betula*, *Quercus*, *Ulmus*, *Alnus*, and *Corylus avellana* type. However, all of these taxa have

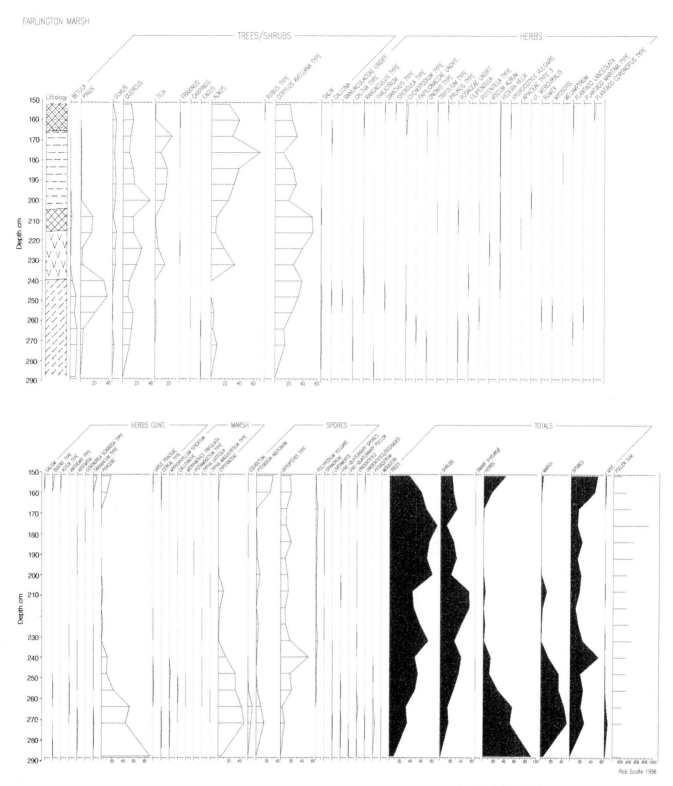

Figure 54   Pollen diagram from north of Chalkdock Lake, Farlington Marsh (Rob Scaife)

relatively high pollen production and anemophilous dispersion which may indicate local over-representation of these taxa. Open, grass and sedge dominated herb communities appear more important. Although this clearly reflects deposition in a freshwater fen with dominance of sedges and other marginal aquatic plants, an open-aspect vegetation with scattered trees is evidenced. These communities/pollen assemblages appear to be of

early-Holocene age (Flandrian Chronozone I; Pre-Boreal). The presence of some thermophiles (eg *Quercus* and *Alnus*) possibly negates a late-Devensian age, which shows an almost completely treeless environment at a number of regional sites (Scaife 1980; 1982). Characteristically, after this transitional phase, *Pinus* and *Corylus avellana* become dominant in lpaz LANG:2 and accord with the vegetation of the Boreal (Flandrian

Chronozone Ib and Ic) for the region. These two basal zones thus appear to represent the early post-Devensian vegetation changes at a time when sea-levels were some 18–20m lower than at present, allowing migration and colonisation by pioneer tree types into the region. Without radiocarbon dating, the age of zone LANG:1 and LANG:2 remains, however, conjectural. This is especially the case since although the basal dominance of herbs and importance of pine and hazel is noted, there are present unexpected records of *Fagus* and early occurrence of *Alnus* and *Tilia*. Reworking of local interglacial sediments may be responsible for these records.

Pollen assemblage zone LANG:3, sub-zone A shows the clear demise of *Pinus* but rapid expansion of *Tilia* and *Alnus*. If no hiatus is present, by comparison with radiocarbon-dated similar events at Gatcombe Withy Bed and Borth Wood Farm, Isle of Wight, this may relate to the middle Holocene (Flandrian Chronozone II; Atlantic period). At both of these sites organic peats overly sediments and have provided radiocarbon dates of *c* 7000 BP (Scaife 1980; 1987). This is in broad accord with the start of the middle-Holocene Atlantic period of increased temperatures and humidity (Godwin 1975). However, although there is a small but progressive transition from mineral sediments to peat, the possibility of a hiatus must be considered as it is possible that rising sea-levels may have influenced this peat development (see below). Radiocarbon dating may, in the future, clarify this. Pollen spectra show the 'on-site' dominance of alder carr woodland also evidenced by wood macrofossils. The terrestrial/dryland environment supported dominant lime/linden woodland. The percentages of this entomophilous and largely underrepresented taxon also clearly indicate growth very local to the site. Typical deciduous woodland elements (oak, elm, and hazel) are also evident. These may have been growing in association with *Tilia* or as separate woodland communities on soils of differing characteristics (*cf* the monoclimax/polyclimax arguments relating to mixed oak forest).

In pollen assemblage sub-zone 3-B, there is a reoccurrence of *Pinus*. This event was similarly present in the diagram of Ullett (1993). Whilst this may be considered as a localised recolonisation of *Pinus* in the local region, this 'peak' occurs with increasing amounts of silt in the peat. Thus, it appears more likely that reworking of older sediments is responsible (ie lpaz LANG:2). Some increase in herbs is also noted, although poorer representation of these than pine would be expected because of less robust pollen structure and morphology. The alternative of *Pinus* maintaining a position in the local environment cannot, however, be discounted. Previous workers have provided tentative evidence for continuation of localised stands of pine perhaps growing on poorer soils in the Hampshire Basin (Haskins 1978; Scaife 1980, 1991; Cameron and Scaife 1988). In sub-zone 3-C, there is a return to pollen spectra which are typical of the middle Holocene and early Flandrian Chronozone III (Neolithic prior to widespread defor-

estation). Here, there is the clear domination of *Tilia* whose underrepresentation in pollen diagrams is well known (Andersen 1973) due to entomophily and production of smaller numbers of pollen grains than many other tree taxa. The values recorded here clearly indicate the local dominance of *Tilia* woodland throughout the time-span represented in lpaz LANG:3. Such domination of lime woodland in southern and eastern England during the middle and later Holocene has been reviewed by a number of researchers (Moore 1977; Scaife 1980; Greig 1982) and its spatial distribution by Birks *et al* (1975) and Birks (1989). Such woodland would have been growing in close proximity to the sample site but on the soils of the better drained interfluves. The floral changes evident in pollen zone LANG:4 correspond with the change to sediment lithology associated with marine transgression. Palynologically this is indicated by the expansion of percentages of herb taxa including possible halophytes (Chenopodiaceae and large pollen grains of Poaceae which may include *Spartina* and *Elymus*).

Dating

Radiocarbon dating is awaited but, until obtained, comparison with existing regional data has been attempted. With pollen zone LANG:1 and LANG:2 dating will not be possible because of insufficient organic material in the sediments and their high alkalinity. However, it appears that these zones correspond with the early Holocene, Flandrian Chronozone I; that is the pre-Boreal and Boreal. As noted, it is unclear whether a hiatus is present between LANG:2 and LANG:3. At this boundary, the expansion of *Tilia* and *Alnus* is highly diagnostic of the beginning of the middle Holocene, Flandrian Chronozone II (Atlantic). If a hiatus is present, then certainly the peats of zone LANG:3 postdate the Boreal/Atlantic transition of *c* 7000 BP (5900 cal BC). The temporal span of the peat is, however, enigmatic. The widely recognised phenomena of the 'elm decline' and lime decline are not apparent in this pollen profile. The former is dated variously at 5500–5000 BP (4250–3750 cal BC); the latter is less synchronous but with a broad span of dates relating to middle–late Bronze Age woodland clearance. Their absence could be attributed to:

i) The site being marginal low-lying land where these events might not be clearly represented.
ii) The peat deposit (LANG:3) being wholly middle-Holocene in age; that is from *c* 7000–5000 BP (5900–3750 cal BC).

The latter is considered most likely. Wootton Quarr, Isle of Wight has produced similar foreshore peats with radiocarbon dates of *c* 5500–4500 BP (4250–3250 cal BC) for their upper contacts with the overlying marine silts.

Plate 36 Fragment of tree stump BB from Baker's Rithe, photographed in 1995 (John M Bingeman)

Pollen from other locations in Langstone Harbour

Samples were prepared for pollen from several other locations in Langstone Harbour. These included monoliths 1AA and 4BC taken from the stratigraphy associated with the submerged trees at Russell's Lake and Baker's Rithe respectively. In addition, subsamples from the middle–late Bronze Age hearth 305 and late Bronze Age pot 350 on Long Island, and the late Bronze Age pot 774/1 on South Binness Island and ditch 1711 on North Binness Island were examined. Pollen was not well preserved in suitable quantities in any of these samples to enable further investigation.

However, it can be noted that samples from Russell's Lake, which were prepared twice in an attempt to recover useful pollen spectra, did contain degraded *Tilia* and *Quercus* pollen. It is possible that these peats may have developed under a dry carr woodland in which microbiological activity was high, causing destruction of the pollen. This view accords with the evidence postulated from the plant macrofossils (Clapham, below).

Identification of tree stumps and trunks at Baker's Rithe and Russell's Lake
by Alan Clapham

The identifications of the trunks (Plate 36) and stumps at both sites are given in Table 22. The preservation of the tree remains was sufficient to allow the identification of all stumps and trunks sampled. Five identifications are from the trees sampled at Russell's Lake and eight are from Baker's Rithe. At Russell's Lake, the dominant species was oak (*Quercus* sp) with three tree remains being of this species, the other two were of willow/poplar (Salicaceae). At Baker's Rithe, the dominant species was yew (*Taxus baccata*) with three other trees being identified as oak and one of alder (*Alnus glutinosa*).

Oak was, therefore, the most common find, with six of the tree stumps and trunks so identified. Yew was the second most common (four of the tree stumps and trunks), two of the tree remains were identified as willow/poplar and only one as alder.

The species identified at Langstone are commonly found in submerged forest deposits (Clapham 1999) especially oak, willow/poplar, and alder. The presence of yew in both submerged forest and buried forest deposits is becoming more common as rescue excavations, especially in the south-east, are increasing. Other sites in the past have contained this species but it appears that the finds of yew are restricted to the south and south-east. Godwin (1975) records yew being found in the lower deposits of the fenlands where they have been found *in situ* at the edge of river banks, with deformed roots which show restricted growth on the riverside of the stump. It has been debated and much discussed as to whether yew has changed its ecology, as in the present day yew is usually restricted to highly calcareous, dry soils, when in natural communities. The increasing number of identifications of yew in submerged and buried forest deposits suggests that there has been some restriction in the ecological range of this species. In the light of the increasing numbers of identifications of yew, a review of the ecology of this species is needed in the near future. The identification, in past studies of submerged forests, of pine (*Pinus sylvestris*) also needs to be reconsidered as it may have been misidentified yew (Clapham 1999).

In summary, the two deposits of tree remains in Langstone Harbour revealed four species of tree – oak, alder, willow/poplar, and yew. Russell's Lake contained both oak and willow/poplar and Baker's

Table 22 The identifications of the preserved trees at Baker's Rithe and Russell's Lake

	Species	OD	Date
Baker's Rithe			
Trunk Stump BA	*Quercus* sp	−0.90/−0.90/−0.79	
Stump BB	*Quercus* sp	−0.96	
Next to BB	*Taxus baccata*	?−1.01	
Roots at BB (bnt flint in peat)	*Taxus baccata*	?−1.01	2310–1950 cal BC
Branch BC	*Quercus* sp	−0.96/−1.00/−1.02	
Branch at BC	*Taxus baccata*		
Branch BD	*Taxus baccata*	−0.95	
Loose wood BE	*Quercus* sp	Not recorded	
Stump CA	*Alnus glutinosa*	−1.00	
North of Russell's Lake			
Peat at sample 001		−0.54	
Peat at sample 002		−0.53	
Stump AA	Salicaceae	−0.65 – peat surface at −0.58	
Stump AB	*Quercus* sp	−0.57	
Roots AC	Salicaceae	−0.47	
Stump AD	not sampled	−0.58	
Branch AE (part of AF)	*Quercus* sp	−0.81/−0.73	3350–2910 cal BC
Branch AF (part of AE)	*Quercus* sp	−0.81/−0.74	

Rithe oak, yew, and alder. This distribution of species may well be an artificial one, as the original extent of the submerged forest is unknown and may reflect local differences in ecology. The analysis of the plant macroremains preserved within the deposits associated with the tree remains (below) helps to throw light on this situation. All samples identified as oak showed very narrow growth rings, with the early and late wood being very close together. This suggests that the oak trees were under substantial stress during their lifetime, but were able to survive. This stress may have been due to the high watertable which must have been present in the area. Oak trees are able to survive waterlogged conditions, even immersion in saltwater, for considerable periods as long as there is some period of a lower watertable (Heyworth 1978; Clapham 1999).

Waterlogged plant remains (Baker's Rithe and Russell's Lake)
by Alan Clapham

Two monoliths were taken from the deposits surrounding the tree remains in Langstone Harbour, one from Russell's Lake (monolith 1AA) and one from Baker's Rithe (monolith 4BC). The description of each monolith is given below and, in both, there appeared to be very little variation throughout the section apart from in monolith from Baker's Rithe

(4BC) where the top 30mm appeared to be darker brown in colour.

Method

Standard techniques for processing of waterlogged plant remains were employed by sieving the sample through a series of granulometric sieves of 2mm, 1mm, 0.5mm, and 0.3mm. All samples were sorted in distilled water using a low-power (×10–40) stereomicroscope. All critical identifications were made using the modern seed reference collection housed in the Pitt-Rivers Laboratory, Department of Archaeology, University of Cambridge. A uniform sample size was adopted of 0.1m³ (0.2m³ for Russell's Lake). All botanical nomenclature follows that of Stace (1997).

The waterlogged plant remains from Baker's Rithe (monolith 4BC)

Depth 190mm

0–30mm	Dark-brown fibrous peat than that below. Sample at 0–30mm
3–190mm	Brown fibrous peat with wood and woody root fragments present
	Samples taken at 3–83mm, 83–136mm, and 136–190mm

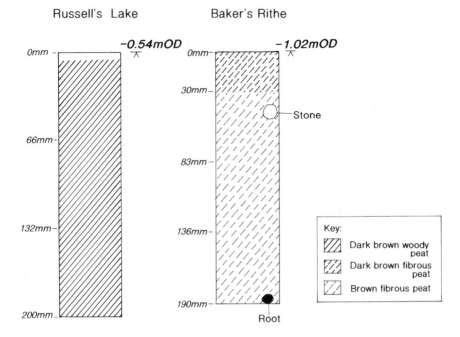

Figure 55 *Peat profiles from the submerged 'forests' (based on originals by Clapham)*

A total of four samples each of 0.1m³ was analysed for plant macrofossils from this monolith. Again the samples were not rich in plant remains and the results are presented in Table 23 and Figure 55.

0–30mm

This sample contained many buds, budscales, and leaf fragments, the latter were, unfortunately, too fragmented to identify. The most common species was *Oenanthe aquatica*, along with *Rubus fruticosus*. Other species recovered as single finds include *Ranunculus* subgenus *Batrachium*, *Betula* sp, *Alnus glutinosa* female cone, *Chenopodium* sp, and *Solanum dulcamara*.

The habitats represented include woodland, with the finds of *Betula* sp and *Alnus glutinosa* female cones, but the majority of the remains are found in damp conditions (as is alder), for instance *Oenanthe aquatica* and *Solanum dulcamara* which have also been found to be associated with other submerged forest deposits (Clapham 1999). The identification of *Ranunculus* subgenus *Batrachium* suggests an aquatic component to the sample although some species of this subgenus are found and are able to survive on damp terrestrial ground. As these were associated with yew and oak it is possible that the sample represents some kind of carr woodland consisting of oak, yew, birch, and alder, with a ground flora of species usually found in damp habitats.

Other remains recovered from this sample include frequent fragments of moss, worm cocoons, *Cenococcum geophilum* sclerotia, and charcoal fragments. Cladoceran (water flea) eggs were common, suggesting that there was standing water present, as could be expected in carr habitats.

30–83mm

This sample contained a large number of budscales and a larger number of plant taxa, of which *Ranunculus* subgenus *Batrachium* was dominant. Other species included *Urtica dioica*, *Viola riviniana*, *Rubus fruticosus*, *Solanum dulcamara*, *Cirsium palustre*, *Lemna* sp, and *Carex* sp. In the majority of cases these were only single finds. Woody species included a fragment of yew and a fragment of a hawthorn type fruitstone. Fragments of mosses were rarely encountered in this sample. Cladoceran eggs were abundant and worm cocoons were also recovered.

This sample also suggests the presence of fen/carr woodland, which is supported by the finds of large numbers of buds and budscales. The identification of yew wood and the hawthorn fruitstone fragment is also evidence for this interpretation. The presence of worm cocoons suggests a temporary lowering of the watertable as does the presence of the seed of *Lemna* sp. This aquatic species only produces fruit and seeds either in very hot summers or in drought conditions which may have been induced by the lowering of the watertable during summer. It can be envisaged that the woodland consisted of damp loving species such as *Viola riviniana*, *Solanum dulcamara*, *Cirsium palustre*, and sedges, interspersed with areas of standing or slow moving water containing *Ranunculus* subgenus *Batrachium*, *Lemna* sp, and Cladocerans (water fleas).

83–136mm

No buds or budscales were recovered from this sample and the number of taxa identified was reduced compared to the previous two samples. The dominant plant taxa was nutlets of *Carex* spp, along with achenes of *Ranunculus* subgenus *Batrachium*. The only other plant species encountered was *Urtica dioica*. Fragments of mosses were also rare but the sclerotia of *Cenococcum geophilum* were recorded in great numbers.

This sample appears to represent a more open environment and perhaps one that was considerably wetter than the previous two. However, the presence of the fungal sclerotia and the worm cocoons again suggests that there was a temporary reduction in the watertable. No woody or tree species appeared to be represented within the sample.

136–190mm

Very few plant remains were recovered from this sample and very few were whole seeds. The most common was *Ranunculus* subgenus *Batrachium*. Other plant taxa include *Viola riviniana*, *Rubus fruticosus*, *Lemna* sp, and *Carex* sp. The sclerotia of *Cenococcum geophilum* were not recorded in such great numbers as in previously described samples.

Once again, a fen habitat with standing or slow moving water is represented. A temporary lowering of the watertable is suggested by the presence of the fungal sclerotia. The presence of a *Lemna* seed also suggests a temporary drying out, as mentioned above.

Discussion

In general, it appears that the samples from this monolith, if taken from the bottom upwards, probably represent the development from a fen habitat to one of fen/carr woodland. In the lowermost two samples no representatives of woody or tree species are identified, the only species that can be considered to be perennial is *Rubus fruticosus*. A temporary drying out phase is indicated throughout the profile by the presence of the sclerotia of *Cenococcum geophilum* and worm cocoons, but in two samples, at 136–190mm and 30–83mm, this is supported by the presence of *Lemna* sp seeds which only produces fruit and seeds in very hot or drought conditions. The temporary lowering of the watertable during the summer months may induce it to produce fruit.

Although the number of taxa recovered from each of the samples is small (this is most likely a function of the small sample sizes involved) the following conclusions can be made. It can be suggested that the plant remains extracted from the peat deposits surrounding the stumps and trunks represent fen conditions which at first are open but gradually become wooded. The tree species involved include oak, yew, willow/poplar, birch, and alder, with an understorey of hawthorn. The ground flora is dominated by species which prefer damp conditions or high watertables such as *Oenanthe aquatica*, *Viola riviniana*, *Solanum dulcamara*, *Urtica dioica*, and *Cirsium palustre* but can also tolerate drier conditions. Other species prefer open standing or slow moving water such as *Ranunculus* subgenus *Batrachium* and *Lemna* sp. Water fleas (Cladocerans) would also thrive in these water conditions. These pools of water occasionally dry up as the watertable is lowered, most likely in the summer. This is supported by the presence of sclerotia of *Cenococcum geophilum* and worm cocoons. The presence of seeds of *Lemna* sp also helps to substantiate this interpretation.

The effect of waterlogged conditions can also be seen in the tree species. In oak the annual growth rings are all narrow suggesting that the trees are under ecological and physiological stress, narrow rings are usually associated with drought but a surplus of water can produce the same effect and is known as 'physiological drought'. All of the remains identified as oak at Langstone have similar narrow rings showing that, although they were under stress, they were able to survive.

The waterlogged plant remains from Russell's Lake (monolith 1AA)

Depth 200mm

0–200m   Dark fibrous peat with wood fragments present throughout. Three contiguous samples taken: 0–66mm, 66–132mm, and 132–200mm.

Because of the uniformity of the monolith only the top sample, 0–66mm, was analysed. The sample contained many monocotyledonous stems and roots as well as burnt flint fragments. The results of the analysis can be found in Table 23. There was very little in the way of waterlogged plant remains. A single seed of *Chenopodium* sp, two fragments of *Suaeda maritima* and *Rubus fruticosus*, and one nutlet of *Schoenoplectus lacustris* were recovered. A single leaf of *Sphagnum* sp, was also identified. Other extracted remains included two charcoal fragments, and five worm cocoons. The sclerotia of the soil fungus *Cenococcum geophilum* were common.

There is little that can be deduced about the deposits surrounding the tree remains at this site. The identification of *Rubus fruticosus* suggests the possibility of a forest floor, but the presence of *Schoenoplectus lacustris* suggests that it was very wet, perhaps close to a stream or area of standing water. The remains of *Suaeda maritima* shows that a maritime influence was not too far away, although the possibility of modern intrusion cannot be ruled out. The presence of the worm coccoons and the sclerotia of *Cenococcum geophilum* suggests that

Table 23   Table showing the waterlogged plant remains and macrofauna identified from Russell's Lake and Baker's Rithe

Site		Baker's Rithe, Monolith 4BC				Russell's Lake, 1AA
Sample		1	2	3	4	1
Depth (cm)		0–3	3–8.3	8.3–13.6	13.6–19.0	0–6.6
Volume (cm^3)		100	100	100	100	200
Species	**common name**					
Taxus baccata wood	yew	–	f	–	–	–
Ranunculus subgenus *Batrachium*	water crowfoot	1	3+21(½)+15f	1+10f	5f	–
Urtica dioica	nettle	–	1	1+2f	–	–
Betula sp	birch	1	–	–	–	–
Alnus glutinosa female cones	alder	1	–	–	–	–
Chenopodium sp	goosefoot	1f	–	–	–	1
Suaeda maritima	annual sea-blite	–	–	–	–	2f
Viola riviniana	common dog-violet	–	1	–	1f	–
Rubus fruticosus	bramble	3	3	–	2f	2f
Crataegus sp	hawthorn	–	1f	–	–	–
Oenanthe aquatica	fine-leaved water-dropwort	3+2f	–	–	–	–
Solanum dulcamara	woody nightshade	1	1	–	–	–
Cirsium palustre	marsh thistle	–	1	–	–	–
Lemna sp	duckweed	–	1	–	1	–
Schoenoplectus lacustris	common club-rush	–	–	–	–	1
Carex sp lentic	sedge	–	1f	–	–	–
Carex sp trigonus	sedge	–	–	27+13f	2	–
Sphagnum sp leaves	sphagnum moss	–	–	–	–	1
Musci		frequent	rare	rare	–	–
Buds		24	11	–	–	–
Budscales		4	–	–	–	–
Charcoal fragments		2	3	1	–	2
Cenococcum geophilum		103	rare	100s	rare	common
Cladoceran eggs		common	common	–	–	–
Insect remains		rare	frequent	rare	rare	
Worm coccoons		3	4	2		5

Key: f = fragments, (½) = half achenes

there may have been periods of a lower watertable which would permit the survival of the trees.

Discussion and conclusion

The variation of tree species between the two areas could be due to sampling similar ecologies, but ones which were growing nearly a millennia apart (3350–2910 cal BC and 2310–1950 cal BC), albeit both in the later Neolithic. Nevertheless, species found at the two sites occur in very similar habitats and rely on high watertables. The presence of *Suaeda maritima* at Russell's Lake suggests a maritime influence, possibly a saltwater river or inlet. The variation between the two is compounded by the smallness of the areas sampled. If larger areas were available for sampling a more even distribution of species might be discovered.

The interpretation of the waterlogged samples alongside the tree remains at each site is based on the two sets of evidence being broadly contemporaneous. The only way to prove the contemporaneity of the trees and these samples is by radiocarbon dating both the woody remains and the surrounding peat deposits. Other evidence suggests that the two datasets are contemporary, such as the findings of large number of buds and budscales in the uppermost samples as well as the identification of an alder female cone and that of yew wood fragments from within the samples, (although these could be of a later date). The presence of the *Betula* sp seed from the uppermost sample from Baker's Leat, without any wood being identified, could have been due to either the seed belonging to the allochthonous element of the sample being deposited from further afield either by wind or water, or the fact that there was no birch wood preserved within the areas of sampling.

The presence of burnt flint in the Russell's Lake sample could suggest the presence of human activity, apart from this there is no other evidence of anthropogenic activity in any of the samples, although a small number of charcoal fragments were found in most samples, but these may be natural, see Table 23.

Snails
by *Michael J Allen*

Land snails were examined from several archaeological features, the most satisfactory in taphonomic terms were the old land surfaces of the late Neolithic trees (peat shelves and Russell's Lake and Baker's Rithe) and ditch 1711 excavated on the southern foreshore of North Binness Island. Samples from the Bronze Age hearth on North Binness and Bronze Age pot fills on Long and Baker's Islands were less satisfactory as the origin of the assemblages is not as well understood. The aims were to attempt to establish the general environment in which these features and objects were placed; in particular it was important to establish the presence or absence of the maritime and intertidal environment which characterises the area today.

Peat at Baker's Rithe

A small spot sample was taken from the brown fibrous peat at Baker's Rithe adjacent to monolith 4 BC from which the waterlogged plant remains were examined (Clapham, above). The samples were taken from well within the deposit, and the mixed surface was avoided. This sample, therefore, equates with Clapham's samples between 30 and 190m. The sample was very difficult to

disaggregate in water so it was freeze–thawed several times as this had proven effective in aiding dissagretation on similar deposits at Westward Ho! (Bell 1987). The assemblage from this single sample was in marked contrast to all other assemblages examined from Langstone (Table 24). It was dominated by marsh and slum species, with few dry-ground fauna. Five specimens were burnt and a small (2g) piece of burnt flint was recovered, but no charcoal. Further, *Hydrobia* were almost absent and no indications of brackish-water or marine contexts were present, in fact the only aquatic species was *Lymnaea truncatula*, a distinctly freshwater species.

The shells were not well preserved and considerable time was expended matching with reference material to ensure identification to species where possible. A number of species are restricted to marshes and wetlands (*Vertigo moulinsiana*, *V. antivertigo*, and *Zonitoides nitidus*). *Vertigo antivertigo* is typical of marshes and sedge fens but avoids places were water-levels fluctuate marked (Kerney 1999) and can be common in grassy floodplain and tussocky vegetation containing dead biomass (Robinson 1988). Although only one shell of *V. moulinsiana* was recognised, it is restricted to wetlands and usually to lowland rivers and lakes; more importantly this species is stenotopic (an 'indicator species') and usually lives on the stems of *Carex* sp or *Glyceria maxima* in fen environments (Butot and Neuteboom 1958; Bishop 1974; both quoted by Evans *et al* 1992, 68). It occupies niches close to the ground but in the autumn will ascend taller vegetation such as *Phragmities* and *Alnus* (Phillips 1908). The stenotopic nature of *V. moulinsiana* is of particular interest because *Zonitoides nitidus*, which also occurs in this assemblage, as well as being characteristic of wetlands, is particularly common in emergent vegetation on the edge of rivers where it lives on decaying *Phragmites* or *Carex* litter in muddy ground.

The dry-ground fauna present is a restricted one, and shade loving and rupestral species (*Clausilia bidentata*) are present, few dry open country species were recorded (Table 24). One of the most notable species was *Zonitoides excavatus* which is a calcifuge, avoiding base-rich (calcareous) soils and is absent in the chalkland soils around Langstone Harbour both in modern and subfossil assemblages (Kerney 1999 and pers obs). In contrast to the dry open grassland habitats indicated by the Bronze Age assemblages described below, the overall impression here is of local wet riverside marshland (fen) with some drier ground and trees such as ?*Alnus* (carr) in the vicinity. This evidence corresponds well with the environments of the later Neolithic wood indicated by the waterlogged plant materials (Clapham, above). It is tempting to consider that the burnt flint and burnt shells were a result of human activity, and that any associated wood charcoal had floated away, but this does not help us provide any better idea of the date of this peat formation.

Table 24 Langstone Harbour: mollusc data from ditch 1171, hearth 1702 and pots 350, 521 and peat at Baker's Rithe

Feature				ditch	1711				hearth 1702	pot 521	pot 350	pot 360				Baker's Rithe
Sample	191	192	193	194	195	196	197	198	190	521	350	360.1	360.2	360.3	360.4	peat
Context	1717	1716	1716	1716	1715	1715	1715	1712	1702	521	304	3470	2847	3176	4962	3–19
Depth (cm)	60–70	50–60	40–50	35–40	30–35	20–30	10–20	0–10	spot	spot	spot					
Wt (g)	1500	1500	1500	1200	1300	1500	1500	1500	1 ltre	1 ltre	1 ltre	3470	2847	3176	4962	
Terrestrial Mollusca																
Carychium tridentatum (Risso)	–	–	–	–	–	–	–	–	–	–	–	–	–	–	1	–
Oxyloma/Succinea spp	–	–	–	–	–	–	–	–	–	–	–	–	–	2	–	1b
Cochlicopa lubrica (Müller)	–	1	–	–	–	–	–	–	–	–	–	–	+	2	1	–
Cochlicopa spp	+	–	–	+	–	–	+	–	1	–	–	–	–	2	1	+
Vertigo antivertigo (Draparnaud)	–	–	–	–	–	–	–	–	–	–	–	–	–	–	–	2
Vertigo cf moulinsiana (Dupuy)	–	–	–	–	–	–	–	–	–	–	–	–	–	–	–	1
Vertigo pygmaea (Draparnaud)	2	1	–	3	–	1	–	–	1	–	–	–	–	1	4	–
Vertigo spp	–	–	–	–	+	–	+	–	+	–	–	–	1	–	–	3b
Pupilla muscorum (Linnaeus)	+	+	+	1	1	–	–	–	–	–	–	–	–	1	3	1
Vallonia costata (Müller)	1	2	4	3	–	–	–	–	–	–	–	–	–	2	2	–
Vallonia excentrica Sterki	2	3	2	1	–	4	+	–	3b	–	–	–	–	–	3	–
Vallonia spp	–	–	–	–	–	–	–	+	–	–	–	–	2	–	–	2
Punctum pygmaeum (Draparnaud)	+	–	–	+	–	–	–	–	–	–	–	–	+	1	1	1
Aegopinella nitidula (Draparnaud)	+	1	+	–	–	–	–	–	+	–	–	–	–	–	–	–
Zonitoides excavatus (Alder)	–	–	–	–	–	–	–	–	–	–	–	–	–	–	–	2b
Zonitoides cf nitidus (Müller)	–	–	–	–	–	–	–	–	–	–	–	–	–	–	–	1
Clausilia bidentata (Ström)	–	–	–	–	–	–	–	–	–	–	–	–	–	–	–	2
Trichia hispida (Linnaeus)	3	2	4	2	1	2	–	–	4b	–	–	–	–	1	2	–
Cepaea spp	–	+	–	+	–	–	+	–	–	–	–	–	–	–	–	+
Fresh-water Mollusca																
Lymnaea cf truncatula (Müller)	–	–	–	–	–	–	–	–	–	–	–	–	–	–	–	2
Brackish-water & Marine Mollusca																
Hydrobia ulvae (Montagu)	2	1	1	4	1	4	4	6	–	–	–	8	12	7	4	8
Hydrobia ventrosa (Pennant)	–	–	–	4	3	6	8	9	28	61	37	397	221	156	180	2
Taxa*	4	6	3	5	2	3	+	+	4	0	0	0	2	7	7	9
TOTAL*	8	10	10	10	2	7	+	+	9	0	0	0	3	12	17	18

*excluding *Hydrobia* spp, b = some were recorded burnt

Peat shelf at Russell's Lake

A small sample of the base of fibrous peat was examined from the peat shelf at Russell's Lake where it seems to lie on a chalky substrate. Only *Hydrobia* were recovered from this and these were observed to be abundant on the chalky substrate exposed in a small rivulet. As nearly half of the specimens were obviously live when sampled this assemblage is not tabulated.

Ditch 1711, North Binness Island

A column of eight contiguous samples was taken through the sediment sequence exposed in the excavated, cleaned southern section of ditch 1711, adjacent to the soil monolith (Fig 28). The monolith of undisturbed sediment was subsampled and analysed for pollen (see above) and the column of disturbed sediment samples was processed for snails, following standard methods outlined by Evans (1972). Because of the weakly calcareous nature of the deposits and the lack of any obvious inclusions, where possible, samples of 1500g were processed. The apparently stone-free fills proved, on processing, to be so – no residue was encountered on the 0.5mm, 1mm, or 2mm mesh sieves. The largest residue recorded was in the 5.6mm fraction and was only 24g (ie 1.6% of total wt) from lower in the ditch fill. All the mollusc and other remains were recovered from the flot (0.5mm).

Snails were sparse, and shells very thin and fragile, except for the few *Hydrobia* spp present. The low numbers of shells do not allow detailed interpretation of change in the local environment during the period of the infill of this ditch and the main aim of analysis was to establish the general, rather than specific, nature of the environment. There are, however, sufficient specimens to enable the establishment of:

a) the basic environment in which the ditch was cut and

b) the general nature of the environment in which the ditch survived.

The ditch is now situated in a strongly marine environment. In particular we wished to determine the presence and nature of any marine, estuarine, or fluvial elements, as opposed to terrestrial components, in order to establish whether the ditch was dug in open dry grassland, held freshwater, or was always present in a marine, intertidal environment.

The depauperate assemblages are presented in Table 24, from which two definite components can be defined and are discussed separately below.

Non-marine snail assemblages

The terrestrial assemblages comprised of few poorly preserved specimens with thin shells. The species most common were *Vallonia excentrica*, *V. costata*, and *Trichia hispida*, with some *Vertigo pygmaea* occurring. All are species typical of very dry open terrestrial habitats. No species of running or standing water, or even damp conditions, were identified. Detailed examination of the *Vallonia* sp was conducted to ensure that none was *V. pulchella*; a species which occurs in the wettest habitats of the *Vallonia* species (Evans 1972, 161) and lives particularly ' . . . at the roots of grass in moist fields and meadows' (Ellis 1969, 162), on rich, moist grassy floodplains (Robinson 1988), and often with other more mesic species, as seen, for instance, at Balksbury, Hampshire (Allen 1995). None of the *Vallonia* species could be identified as *V. pulchella*. Similarly all the *Vertigo* species were carefully examined, as members of the Vertiginidae subfamily are physically similar to each other, and this subfamily contains species that are commonly found in fens, marshes, alder carr, and *Phragmites* (*V. antivertigo*, *V. moulinsiana*, *V. lilljeborgi*, and *V. genesii*), or damp poor marshy grassland (*V. substriata*). However, these are individually easily distinguished by their distinctive apertural and teeth arrangements (Evans 1972, 55–9; Kerney and Cameron 1978, 70–6; Cameron and Redfern 1976). Where only apical fragments have survived the shell microsculpture of *V. pygmaea* is distinctive. Needless to say only *Vertigo pygmaea* was present; a species particularly characteristic of dry grassy places, also found in sand dunes and only very rarely in marshes (Cameron and Morgan Huws 1978, 72; Evans 1972, 143–5). It is essentially a species of very open country, and is most common in dry short-turfed grassland, where it thrives.

The heliophile *Helicella itala*, probably the most xerophile in the British fauna, was not recorded, but the assemblage is undoubtedly one of very open dry grassland – some indication of local shade provided by either the ditch micro-habitats or by longer grassy vegetation is possibly indicated by the presence of *Aegopinella nitidula* and *Punctum pygmaeum*, the only members of the shade-loving group defined by Evans (1972; 1984) present in the assemblages. More robust shells of *Pomatias elegans*, *Discus rotundatus*, or Clausiliidea were not present, even as non-apical fragments. There is no evidence of damp conditions or running or standing water in the ditch. The absence of *Helix aspersa*, a snail introduced in the Roman period, cannot however, be taken to indicate a pre-Roman date.

Brackish-water and marine shells

In complete contrast to the terrestrial assemblages was the presence of a number of weathered, but thick-shelled, small brackish-water snails of *Hydrobia ulvae* and few specimens of *H. ventrosa*. One of the former was notably swollen with a bent spire, probably due to infestation by a parasitic nematode worm (McMillan 1968). All specimens were stained a light orange-brown. *H. ulvae* is a species common in estuaries and saltmarshes (Macan 1977); it inhabits these environments on most parts of the British coast, and is present in abundance in Langstone today where it chiefly feeds on *Ulva*, and other green algae (eg *Enteromorpha* sp), and is resistant to both drought and changes in salinity. *H. ventrosa* inhabits quite brackish creeks and lagoons, usually living among algae on the mud in brackish water. It is locally common and present in Langstone today, particularly in the northern sheltered areas to the east of Farlington Marshes. Both these species occupy an environment which is in complete contrast to that suggested by the terrestrial assemblage. The composition and fragile nature of the terrestrial assemblage indicate that this is contemporary with the ditch sediments. The more robust *Hydrobia* which litter the foreshore today are likely to be intrusive. The species is not known to burrow, and although no obvious macropores were noticed in the sampled sections, nevertheless when *H. ulvae* does occur, it often does so in great abundance, as in Langstone today.

These species, in contrast to the non-marine assemblage, are probably allochtonous and therefore do not indicate the presence of marine environments in the immediate vicinity. They are more likely to have been washed in at high sea-levels, probably on winter or early-spring high tides giving rise to flooding events which carried the shells into the established drier hinterland. Nevertheless, this might suggest the presence of marine influence either from tidal rivers or within direct shore-flooding distance of the ditch. However, the distance that ditch 1711 was from the sea cannot be established as *Hydrobia* spp have been recorded more than 15km inland, washed up on river floodplains in high spring tides, where the nearest living population was *c* 12km downstream (Landport floods, Lewes; Allen pers obs).

From the snail assemblages we can conclude that the ditch was cut into and survived in an open, dry, established low-lying grassland, possibly pasture. It was, however, subject to occasional inundation by the flooding of tidal rivers or estuaries, or from coastal flooding.

Bronze Age hearth 1702, North Binness Island

Snails were extracted from a 1 litre sample which was processed by laboratory flotation for charred and waterlogged plant remains. Snails were extracted from the flot (0.25mm) and the residues. The shallow feature produced a mixed assemblage almost identical to that from the nearby ditch. *Vallonia costata*, *Trichia hispida*, *Vertigo pygmaea*, and *Cochlicopa* spp were all present in low numbers and as fragile shells. Again, a very dry, open environment is indicated. Three of the seven terrestrial specimens were strongly burnt, indicating that they were contemporary with the hearth (*Vallonia excentrica* and *Trichia hispida*). As in the ditch, a number of

Hydrobia spp was present, but here only *H. ventrosa* was identified from 28 orange-stained specimens. None of the large number of *Hydrobia* showed any evidence of burning possibly indicating that they were not really contemporary with the hearth.

Pot 350, Long Island

After removal of a large quantity of burnt flint fragments, the remaining contents of pot 350, from Long Island, were bagged and returned to Wessex Archaeology for processing for charred and waterlogged plants, and the snails extracted from the flots and residues. Large numbers of stained *Hydrobia ventrosa* only were found.

Pot 360, Long Island

The vessel was emptied in four spits and the entire contents were floated for the recovery of human bone and the snails retrieved. The upper sample was dominated by *Hydrobia* sp; many stained orange with, presumably, iron and a number still retaining their periostricum and two were live when sampled. The numbers of *Hydrobia* per kilogram decrease with depth down the vessel, from which we can conclude that most are probably recent.

The small, but significant, open-country assemblage indicates very dry, open conditions (*Pupilla*, *Vallonia*, and *Vertigo*). Some longer grass or shade may be inferred by the presence of *Carychium tridentatum* and *Aegopinella nitidula*, but no evidence of damp or marsh environments is indicated. In conclusion, the different preservation of the robust *Hydrobia* shells leads us to believe that these are all intrusive and originate from post-Bronze Age environments.

Pot 521, Baker's Island

The pot shadow on Baker's Island was sampled as a single sample. It was processed, despite the pot itself not surviving. Only *Hydrobia* were present in this sample.

Marine shells and shellfish
by Michael J Allen and Sarah F Wyles

The harbour typically provides a habitat for many marine shellfish species living in the littoral and on the seabed. These include oysters (*Ostrea edulis*), edible hard-shell clams (*Mercenaria mercenaria*), slipper limpets (*Crepidula fornicata*), limpets (*Patella vulgata*), and periwinkles (*Littorina* spp). Few marine shells were collected during the walkover survey, therefore, only those from archaeological or excavated features were retained. A few shells were recovered from excavation or were noted but not collected in the walkover survey while those collected during the submarine augering provide a general indication of the species present in the surface muds today.

During the descriptions of sediments from submarine augering in transect 9 (Long Island to Upper Rithe) samples of sediment were removed for sediment clarification (see Chapter 1), and for the recovery of any inclusions. Several small shells were recovered from the chamber of the 10mm diameter gouge auger to depths of 0.84m. Four of the seven auger points recovered 22 shells and several fragments; the species present were periwinkle, cockle (*Cardium edule*) prickly cockle (*Cardium echinatum*), carpet shell (*Veneruperis* sp), *Scrobicularia plana*, *Gibbula* sp, Rissoidea, and *Hydrobia* spp (details in archive).

During the survey and excavation of the Sinah circle structure, several shells were recovered in excavation. These were representative of those within the area but do not represent total collection. The 15 shells include oyster (5), cockle (4), periwinkle (4), slipper limpet (1), and mussel (*Mytilus edulis*) (1). With the exception of the slipper limpet, which is a well-known pest on commercial oysters, all the other species are edible.

Immediately to the south of Oyster Island, a substantial midden of oyster shell debris was recorded and estimates indicate that this small midden (*c* 0.5m × *c* 1.2m) included several hundred broken valves, including many juveniles. Only a grab sample was available of this collection, however, but included 27 oyster valves (8 of which were juvenile), 17 oyster spats, and 3 edible hard-shell clams. The collection recovered seemed to include either modern or recent specimens (especially the edible hard-shell clams) as well as possibly older elements. Further investigation was not possible to determine the nature of this collection, and two further visits in September and November 1997 could not relocate the site.

Perhaps the most significant point that arises is the contrast between the species recovered 'randomly' from the seabed by augering with those carefully recovered from the Sinah structure. Admittedly the two collection methods are not comparable and the auger will only capture the smaller shells, nevertheless, no shells, or even microscopic fragments, were recovered of any of the edible or commercial shellfish recovered from Sinah circle structure, which it is suggested produced commercial shellfish, or species known to be directly associated with them.

Charred plant remains
by Alan Clapham, Joy Ede, and Michael J Allen

Four bulk samples of 1–10 litres size were obtained from features in Langstone Harbour. These were processed to determine the presence of charred plant remains and charcoals. Although all samples were wet, none was waterlogged. The samples were processed by standard flotation methods, the flot initially retained on a 0.25mm mesh (to check for waterlogging) but then retained on a 0.5mm mesh and the residues fractionated into 5.6mm, 2mm, and 1mm fractions and dried. The coarse fractions (<5.6mm) were sorted, weighed, and discarded. The flots were scanned under a ×10–30 stereo-binocular microscope and presence of charred remains quantified by Sarah F Wyles (Table 25). Apart from charcoal, which was present in all samples (Table 26) and is reported by Gale below, only the sample from the hearth 1702, on North Binness Island, produced charred plant remains.

Table 25   Assessment of the charred plant remains

Feature type/no	Context	Sample	Flot size ml	Grain	Chaff	Weed Seeds		Charcoal >5.6mm	Other	Residue Charcoal >5.6mm
						unburnt	burnt			
North Binness (hearth)										
Feature 1702	1702	190	15	B	–	–	–	A	*Hydrobia*	8
Long Island (pit fill)										
Feature 305	306	938	100	–	–	–	–	A	mollusc	–
Pot 350	304	391	50	–	–	–	–	B	mollusc	–
Baker's Island (pot fill – no pot)										
Pot fill	521	521	30 (75)	–	–	–	–	A	mollusc	20
South Binness Island										
Pot 774/1	774	790	25 (75)	–	–	–	C	A	–	–

Key: A = ≥10 items, B = 9 – 5 items, C = < 5 items, (h) = hazelnuts, smb = small mammal bones
Note: flot is total, but flot in brackets = % of rooty material.

Table 26 Charcoal identifications

Feature	Sample	Pomoideae	*Fraxinus* sp	*Alnus* sp	*Prunus* sp	*Salix* spp	*Corylus* sp	*Ulmus* sp
hearth 1702	190	5	3	1	1	1	–	–
?hearth 305	938	–	–	–	2	–	8	1
pot 521	521	–	–	–	21	–	–	–
	totals	5	3	1	24	1	8	1

Two cereal grains were present but the preservation of both was too poor for them to be identified to genus or species (JE). This may, in part, be the result of direct heat during charring. However, repeated wetting and drying in saltwater conditions on the current foreshore cannot have helped preservation.

The fills of pots 350 (Long Island) and 774 (South Binness Island) were analysed (AJC). In both cases the samples were dominated by large numbers of charcoal fragments. A single fragment of *Chenopodium* sp was identified from pot 774. From pot 350 monocotyledonous roots and stems were also found. The only other remains found associated with the charcoal fragments within the pots were numerous fragments of burnt flint. This suggests that the charcoal (and pieces of burnt flint) may represent the remnants of the fire on which the pots were sitting.

Charcoals
by Rowena Gale

Three samples of charcoal were submitted for examination, these were from hearth 1702 on North Binness Island (sample 190), which was submitted for radiocarbon dating; from the fill of a possible hearth on Long Island (305; sample 938); and material from the fill of pot shadow 521 from Baker's Island.

All samples included fragments of charcoal measuring up to 10mm in radial cross-section, though many from the hearth 1702 were considerably smaller. The fragments were prepared for examination by fracturing to expose the transverse, tangential and radial planes and supported in sand. The anatomical struc-

ture was examined using a Nikon Labophot incident-light microscope at magnifications of up to ×400, and matched to reference material.

The sample from the hearth 1702 was most diverse, with the samples from the pot 521 and possible hearth 305 producing few taxa. The taxa recovered were as follows and are summarised in Table 26.

Pomoideae	This group comprises several members which are anatomically similar: hawthorn (*Crataegus*), apple (*Malus*), pear (*Pyrus*), whitebeam (*Sorbia aria*), rowan (*S. aucuparia*), and wild service (*S. torminalis*)
Fraxinus sp	ash
Alnus sp	alder
Prunus spp	blackthorn, cherry, or bird cherry
Salix sp	willow
Corylus sp	hazel
Ulmus sp	elm

The fragments from the hearth 1702 were too small to assess the likely age of the wood. If the charcoal derived from fuel residues and was gathered as firewood (as opposed to the burning of woodworking waste or disused structures), it would, for convenience, almost certainly have been gathered locally. None of the species identified is likely to have tolerated the saltmarsh or mudflat environments flanking the periphery of the harbour today, although alder and willow would probably have flourished in less saline areas of wetland. Taxa such as hawthorn (and other members of the Pomoideae), *Prunus*, and ash prefer drier, non-saline conditions.

6 Erosion of our history: evidence for net sediment loss and artefact displacement and redistribution

by Michael J Allen

Before reviewing the taphonomy and origin of the mapped artefact distributions and dense scatters, we need to consider these in relation to the erosion processes operating within the harbour. This is best reviewed by examining the general evidence for erosion in the harbour over the past few centuries in order to lay down a historical base, and then to examine the distribution and occurrence of the products and landforms of erosion: gravel, muds, wave-cut intertidal platforms, and cliffs.

We have discussed artefact displacement in a theoretical construct above (Chapter 2, Integrity of the archaeological deposits), but now employ the results of the survey and analysis of the artefact distributions in combination with our records and knowledge of tidal and erosion processes in the harbour, to re-examine the evidence on a number of temporal and spatial scales. We can then attempt to discern which elements of those mapped distributions may relate to the processes of erosion and redistribution and which of, or how, these distributions relate to patterns of past human activity.

Resolution, time-scale, and stasis

At the immediate local scale we can see changes within the harbour on a daily basis and certainly on a yearly basis, but how do these relate to the long-term history of Langstone Harbour? At the historic scale we can see relative stability in that few major overall changes in the harbour morphology can be seen in the mapped evidence back to about AD 1600, and most are a direct result of reclamation (see Chapter 2, Historical survey). Traditionally there was a land connection between the mainland and the Isle of Wight which was recorded by *Diodorus Siculus* as late as 90 BC (Stagg 1980). From a much longer archaeological perspective we can see that, in the Mesolithic for instance, the Isle of Wight was not an island as the coast was in excess of 40km to the south of its present position (Fig 56) – so Langstone, then, was far from coastal in any sense of the definition.

It is important to understand the physical development of the harbour because this landscape is the stage upon which past communities performed their daily activities. Its setting and scenery define the nature of those acts. Processes of erosion, sedimentation, and soil formation that have created the harbour we see today also have a role in modelling the occurrence and nature of the artefact distributions recorded in this survey and previously (eg Bradley and Hooper 1973; Draper 1958; 1963).

The subject of erosion, displacement, and redistribution has to be viewed at different scales of resolution in both time and space. Statements about the relative rates of events or occurrence of erosion may only be relevant to specific scales of time or space. For instance, historical map evidence covering the entire 23 km² of the harbour over a period of only a few centuries, indicates little significant change in the harbour and island morphology and thus may, superficially, be taken to indicate no major erosion. Viewed over a longer time-period, the indications given and cited in previous chapters that the small islands are actually relics of much larger land masses provide a different perspective. Certainly the presence in prehistory of the islands as we see them today would make some of the interpretation of archaeological activity presented here (see Chapter 7) difficult. Further, any statement that infers that erosion has not, and is not, occurring belies the observed evidence of all who know and have worked in the area. The artefact scatters themselves are a product of erosion, whether of coastal recession and cliffing (lateral erosion), lowering of intertidal wave-cut platforms exposing material, or redistribution, removal, and rafting. The presence of the large-scale artefact scatters and the palaeoenvironmental evidence (pollen, snails, and submerged trees), in combination with the analysis of dated horizons and sea-level data, provide a picture of much wider landscape change over several millennia.

Moreover, there is evidence to suggest that there are both long periods of stasis and stability and periods in which changing relative sea-level and local currents significantly change the dynamics of the tidal system leading to episodes of accelerated erosion or deposition. It is because of this cyclical variability that measurement over the short-term may not be directly relevant to the longer time-period (see below). The following discussion aims to clarify the nature and scales of erosion in both a historical and archaeological perspective and, ultimately, in terms of the taphonomy of the artefact scatters recorded.

General tides and coastal change (natural environment)

Evidence of general sediment load movement in the Solent and Langstone Harbour

Recent sedimentological and hydrological studies aid in establishing the presence, if not the specific occurrence, of erosion within the Solent basin. Probably most significant among these is the NERC report, which although nearly twenty years old, provides an excellent summary of the Solent (NERC 1980), to which can now be added some more specific local studies.

Both Langstone and Chichester Harbours have higher average tidal ranges (c 3m) than Portsmouth and the western Solent (Webber 1980, 28, fig 4). Sediments within Langstone Harbour mainly comprise fine silts and organic matter, accumulation having been locally assisted by the rapid growth of *Spartina* marshes since the late-19th century. However, angular flint gravels occur over the surface of some mudflats and similar material outcrops along channel and creek beds and as beaches at about high-water. Radioactive tracer surveys in Langstone Harbour have shown that, even on neap tides, a proportion of sediment load is discharged into the open sea through the harbour mouth, indicating considerable tidal excursion and a degree of turbulent exchange (Webber 1980, 34). In the Solent as whole there has been 'considerable net loss of the area of intertidal sediment since at least the eighteenth century' (Tubbs 1980, 2), and this change is most apparent on the shores of the main body of the Solent where there has been a progressive narrowing of the intertidal zone. Although the change has been less dramatic in the harbours, low-water channel widths have clearly increased (Tubbs *op cit*).

Because of the non-linear relationship between sediment transport rates and near-bed current velocities, the *direction* of net sediment transport may differ significantly from, or even oppose, the direction of near-bed residual current velocity (Gao and Collins 1997). The time-scale over which net sediment transport rate is meaningful is controlled by the time-scale in which changes in seabed morphology take place. Changes in the net transport rates may occur because of the combination of wave action and the time-asymmetry of tidal currents in the eastern Solent. Within Langstone it is likely that net transport is directed towards the upper reaches of the harbour under calm conditions; it would be directed towards the sea during stormy periods.

Mapping by Portsmouth University (Collier and Fontana undated) showed a marked residue flow from Chichester Harbour to Langstone Harbour around the Sweare Deep on the northern side of Hayling Island (see Webber 1980, 24). The rate of sediment accumulation in the saltmarsh and mudflats can be examined by the vertical distributions of a series of radionuclides (^{210}Pb, ^{137}Cs, ^{238}Pu, $^{239,\ 240}$Pu, ^{241}Am, and ^{60}Co). Despite expected local variability across southern England, sediment accumulation rates for saltmarshes are relatively consistent (Cundy and Croudace 1996; Long *et al* 1999). This suggests that a regional effect, such as a rise in mean sea-level, is the main driving factor behind sediment accumulation, and dominates local effects such as sediment compaction and site location on an individual marsh. These studies give an average vertical accretion rate of between 4.2 and 4.7mm per year – mmyr^{-1} – (depending upon the nuclide used) which approximates to the relative sea-level rise in the Solent region. The rate may be slightly high due to the comparatively recent development of the marshes (post–1870). This rate of 4–5mmyr^{-1} average accretion rate is similar to the 4.5–5.5mmyr^{-1} rate derived from independent tide-gauge data at Portsmouth (Woodworth 1987) and indicates an apparent increase in the rate of mean sea-level rise prior to this century, from 1–1.5mmyr^{-1} over a millennial time-scale (Long and Tooley 1995) to 4–5.5mmyr^{-1} over the last century.

A similar acceleration in the rate of sea-level rise has been observed in the Severn Estuary (Allen and Rae 1988; J R L Allen 1991), which was tentatively attributed to changes in the local tidal regime, but a eustatic (global) cause for such acceleration is unlikely with current global sea-level rise estimated at 1–2mmyr^{-1} (Gornitz 1995). The estuaries of the Solent have some of the most complex tidal regimes in the UK and distortion of the tidal curve (and hence mean sea-level) may have occurred following both natural and anthropogenically driven changes in water depth and coastal morphology. However, this acceleration has occurred over a large part of the Hampshire coastline suggesting either a regional change in the tidal regime or an acceleration in crustal subsidence.

Although there is evidence of recycling of sediments within Langstone, and to a certain extent from Chichester to Langstone, there is an overall net loss of sediment. Sediment loss is exacerbated by *Spartina* dieback, and after mobilisation and movement within the harbour. Net loss is through the harbour mouth where a large delta of gravel, sand, and mud exists.

Evidence for coastal stability: the historical evidence

First, the speed of erosion within the harbour needs to be carefully considered in terms of scale, longevity, locality, and nature. For instance, examination of historic maps (see Fontana and Fontana, Chapter 2) indicates that, since the 1600s, the general configuration of the harbour and of land masses clearly identifiable as the four islands, has undergone comparatively little obvious change. In the earlier prehistoric periods, however, this was far from the case and the area in the Mesolithic is unrecognisable in its present day configuration; the sea was some 40km to the south (Fig 56), and the area was undoubtedly an inland, albeit low-lying, landscape.

Historical maps are not necessarily locally spatially accurate, as Fontana has outlined in Chapter 1. However, they are useful in providing a historical context to the overall development of the harbour morphology, if not to specific shorelines. We can examine the gross changes in the mapped area even if we cannot deal with the historical maps at the

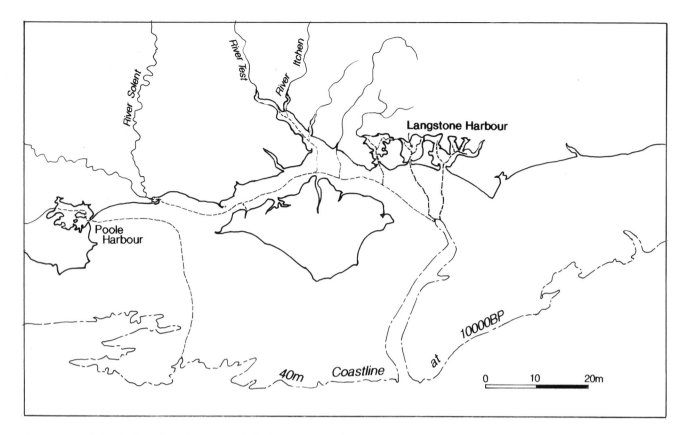

Figure 56   Mesolithic shoreline; simplified palaeogeographic reconstruction of the shoreline prior to the opening of the Holocene at 12,–10,000 BP. Note: this reconstruction use estimates of bathymetry taken from Dyer 1975, and does not take into account the more complex palaeochannels recently reported from the west of the Isle of Wight by Velegrakis et al *(1999) nor any possible changes in tidal range (after Long and Scaife 1996)*

same scale of resolution as those created by Portsmouth University for this project.

A cursory examination of maps dating from *c* 1665 (Fig 57), taking account of inaccuracies, nevertheless provides some indication of gross changes, and the rate of that change over the mapped period (three centuries). We must, however, be mindful that islands which are of greatest interest to us because of their rich archaeological results have probably received only the most summary and cursory historical mapping. In contrast to our study, these areas were not of great significance to the cartographers because they were not important or valuable land nor was great accuracy in mapping needed for their navigation. In addition, as we found, they are difficult to gain access to and negotiate, and thus to map as accurately as other areas. These factors indicate that the accuracy of the surveying of the islands is likely to be worse than elsewhere in the harbour. That said, changes in their general size and shape will have been recorded.

Major changes are shown in the harbour along the eastern coast of Portsea Island which are largely a result of reclamation (see Chapter 2). Despite the relatively poor mapping of the islands some significant changes can be seen. The most dramatic was entirely man-made and was the incorporation of elements of 'Binners' Island into the mainland creating

Farlington Marshes in 1771 (compare Fig 57b with Fig 57c) leaving North Binness as an separate island. Apart from this we can see significant changes in the shape of Long Island from a more blocky shape to its present linear form (Fig 57). Whether this indicates erosion at its northern and southern shores as we suspect, or deposition along its eastern and western margins is not immediately clear. Archaeological fieldwork, however, tends to suggest that the island is comprised of older stable, rather than new (250 years) deposits from which we may conclude that some erosion has occurred. Similarly, a fifth island is mapped; this is presumably the small knoll known as Round Nap Island, indicating that it too, was a larger land mass from at least *c* 1665 to 1810 (Fig 57).

More significant than the changes outlined both above and in the historic survey (Chapter 2), is the evidence of stasis, of relatively little change in the harbour morphology, and of stable coastlines on a harbour-wide scale over the past three centuries. In particular the Hayling Island coastline is mapped as a consistent coastline from *c* 1665 to 1995 with surprisingly little change in its form and shape, with the exception of development and, in particular, of the construction of the oyster beds (Fig 57). Similarly, much of the northern coast remains essentially unaltered; the major changes being around

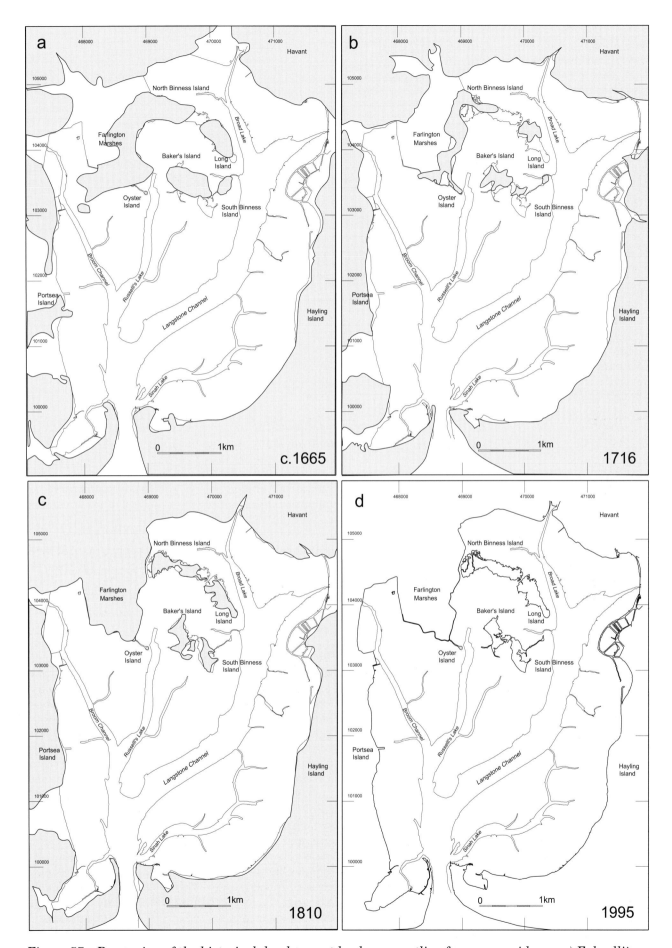

Figure 57   Regression of the historical development harbour coastline from map evidence, a) Fabvollière c 1665, b) Lempriere 1716 c) Ordnance Survey 1810 d) Portsmouth University 1995. Drawn by S E James

river inlets which have subsequently been tamed and embanked.

Overall therefore, in recent historic times there seems to have been general stability and lack of gross morphological change within the harbour, excepting that resulting from human intervention. Needless to say, some of these reclamations, in particular the creation of Farlington Marshes, may have significantly altered tidal and current regimes within the harbour and thus changed sediment movements and redistribution and altered littoral cell budgets (*cf* Bray *et al* 1995).

Evidence for coastal erosion

When the Flandrian transgression breached the Isle of Wight–Purbeck Ridge it created the Solent as we know it and cut off the Isle of Wight from the mainland. This breach resulted in rapid erosion, over the last 'few' thousand years, of the plateau-gravel covered Tertiary clays. It released large quantities of clays, sands, and gravels into the environment of the Solent River system and the English Channel. The fact that erosion is continuing indicates that the equilibrium configuration has not yet been reached.

In this volume we consider that many of the artefact scatters and distributions are a result of cliff retreat, ie erosion within the harbour. Although the configuration of the harbour and, in general, the islands within, does not seem to have changed significantly (on cartographic grounds) in the past 200 years (Fig 57), this does not necessarily indicate that cliff erosion has not occurred, nor that this erosion has not released artefacts onto the foreshore. We can see that the harbour is a highly dynamic ecological and sedimentological system; but also that, within the past century, there is evidence of increased sedimentation, *Spartina* dieback, and erosion, indicating changing equilibriums in these harbour systems. At the very large scale, ie millennial, it is evident that erosion must have occurred as the harbour has been created from a much larger, former landmass.

Evidence of erosion on the local scale and over very short time-periods (up to five years) are provided by our own records and observations during fieldwork (1993–5), by major finds subsequent to that fieldwork phase (1997), and by detailed records of erosion measurements by the RSPB (RSPB unpublished data). Some assessment of erosion over the whole harbour, again at the short time-scale of mainly 25 years, but up to 65 years, was attempted for the RSPB by detailed examination of aerial photographs by Portsmouth University (Collier and Fontana undated). Historical mapping also indicates erosion of specific areas, rather than coastlines, and finally less useful are some anecdotal and unquantified observations made by the archaeological field team. The various forms of evidence are examined below.

Map evidence

Map evidence for Langstone (Fabvollière 1665; Lempriere 1716; 1773; military survey 1797–1810 and the more recent Ordnance Surveys) shows that, although coastal retreat seems minimal (Fig 57), Tubbs (1980, 1) suggests that the area of saltmarsh has declined steadily through erosion. The 48ha of saltmarshes that remain represent only relics of formerly extensive tracts which, at their greatest extent, probably occupied a large portion of the upper northern part of the harbour. In the Solent in general there has been abundant cartographic evidence to suggest considerable loss of intertidal sediments and general recession of the mixed saltmarshes, particularly since the 18th century. Tubbs (1980) specifically points out that, in Langstone Harbour in particular, maps of 1600, 1716, 1773, and the military survey of 1797–1810 on which the first Ordnance Survey was based, and the more recent Ordnance Surveys of the 19th and 20th centuries, show that the area of saltmarsh has declined steadily, presumably through erosion; a process clearly discernible today (Tubbs *op cit*). There is a narrowing of the intertidal zone generally, probably accompanied by a lowering of the profile of the remaining muds and possibly by a change from a generally convex to a generally concave cross-section. The lowering of the intertidal profile accentuates cliffing at the margins of mixed saltmarsh and *Spartina* marsh alike and thus increase their vulnerability to wave attack. Indeed, it can be demonstrated that, since the 1950s, sediment throughout the Solent has been lowered by up to 1m, as many current sea wall defences now have their footings exposed.

Observations

Observation and recording of a number of small islets to the south-west of Farlington Marshes suggests again that they are eroding vestiges of a former larger landmass rather than accreting sediments of inundation. Elsewhere in the same general location, recycling of sediment has also led to the accumulation of muddy silts at the head of Broom Channel in the north-west corner of the harbour and the creation of small islets up to 10m in diameter upon which saltwater grasses have begun to establish themselves. There is no indication from the stratigraphy and structure of these deposits that they are of any great antiquity; they display little consolidation and pedogenically have few developed features. Similar sediment banks are seen on the northern side of Sinah Lake, and small islets are forming about 200m offshore. These too have begun to be colonised by grasses and other saltwater marshes. However, between 1995 and 1997 the southern extremity of these islets was removed down to a hard stiff clay, emphasising the recycling

Plate 37 A good example of cliff erosion on Long Island. Note how lumps of clay have dropped on to the foreshore and are gradually reduced in size and as they are increasingly exposed to the waves. Arthur Mack is pointing out eroding cliff features (Garry Momber)

and redistribution of sediments within the harbour system. Superficially all the islets look similar, but on closer examination, some are *Spartina* covered with developed stratigraphy and even stony horizons (they are land relicts), and others are unconsolidated temporary silt reservoirs.

In addition to this, the submerged trees on the peat shelf in the northern edge of Russell's Lake were first noted by Arthur Mack and the survey team in August 1997 (Chapter 2). The soft mobile muds above them had been removed, exposing them for the first time in over 30 years. Just over two years later (December 1999–January 2000) most of the timbers had been lost to the sea. In their isolated location there is no question of human removal or interference, apart from our own survey sampling. We have reported the limited extent of the Baker's Rithe waterlogged trees (Chapter 3), the remains of which had been depleted since their first discovery nearly 30 years previously. Although the area of peats were extensive, the area of exposed wood at the time of survey (August 1997) was only 3.5 × 2m (see Fig 24). Less than three years later, the low tides of December 1999 exposed an area of almost 10m² of branches and fallen trunks (Mack pers comm), demonstrating the dynamic and changing nature of the intertidal environments, the significance of which for survey are outlined in Chapter 8.

The impact and erosive force of the waves can be seen by the loss of shingle and sediments on the harbour-most side of Oyster Island during the very low tides and storms that occurred in the period December 1999–January 2000 (Mack pers comm). The removal of over 0.6m of shingle and clay deposits left nearly 0.9m of the brick foundation exposed on the harbour-facing side of the searchlight base (see Oyster Island, Chapter 3). In addition the movement, by nearly 0.5m and rotation by c 30°, of a large

concrete slab, about 4.4m in diameter, over its brick-built support (see Plate 26), testifies to the erosive power and force of the sea to mobilise even very large, dense, and certainly not floatable, items. This makes the movement of any individual artefacts, or even removal of whole artefacts scatters, pale into insignificance.

Individual erosion points

We have seen that sediment accretion occurs within the harbour (above) and that there is significant evidence that the rate of accretion has increased this century. Small scale erosion events have also been studied within the space of the fieldwork of this project. The cliffline on the north-east coast of Baker's Island receded by 0.6m over the winter of 1993–4, leaving the site of vessel 521 at least 0.45m from the cliffline (see Fig 30) where before it had been virtually adjacent. Cliffing occurred on the southern coast of Long Island and resulted in the loss of most of vessel 380 before its discovery and recovery in November 1997. The horizontal retreat observed in September and November 1997 was of cliff fall and mass movement (Plate 37); observations which are paralleled by records made by J R L Allen (1989). Lowering of the wave-cut platform between 1995 and 1997 in the same general area revealed and removed the uppermost portion of vessel 360, situated on the outer, or lower, foreshore (see Fig 29). A fresh clay scree was present along the cliffs of Long Island in autumn 1997 containing pottery and other artefacts. Over a period of two months this clay scree was observed to be reduced from an average height of 0.35m to less than 0.15m and the width of detritus debris against the cliff narrowed from about 0.9m to 0.45m. During this later stage, the clay talus seemed to contain more stones and artefacts, presumably as a result of the loss of fines (ie silts and clays).

Turning to the main harbour foreshore, the differing recovery patterns between those reported by the archaeological field team here (1993–5) and those of Bradley and Hooper in the late 1960s (1973) may be at least partly accounted for by limited erosion. Previous fieldwork found briquetage to be common along the Hayling Island coast; much was eroding from wave-cut exposures and this friable material was easily recovered along stretches of the foreshore (Bradley pers comm). Small scale test-pit excavations by a youthful Richard Bradley indicated the presence of identifiable archaeological horizons (Bradley 1992). The field survey, nearly 30 years later, failed to recover briquetage, or to identify briquetage, or other finds, in wave-cut exposures, despite careful scrutiny and knowledge of the former recovery in specific locations. Admittedly, some previous exposures are now covered by walls or other developments but, in others, the artefacts were simply not there. The lack of recovery cannot be attributed to field reconnaissance or methods, and reasons must be sought elsewhere. The most probable is that discrete and possibly isolated areas of archaeological artefacts no longer exist; the coastline has either eroded beyond the site, with the artefacts destroyed and redistributed (briquetage is particularly fragile and will not survive long in a consistently wetting and drying environment), or the erosion which, in the late 1960s, released the artefacts recovered by Bradley and Hooper (1973) has now abated, or arrested. This stasis will provide stable erosion faces, and release of artefacts on to the foreshore will be dramatically reduced. The scale of erosion and exposure required to facilitate the recovery of relatively large quantities of artefacts from a dense artefact scatter need not be large. This evidence does not necessarily contradict the mapped evidence of high stability and relatively little alteration and erosion of the Hayling coastline overall or, in some cases, covered by recently accreting muds.

RSPB erosion records

More controlled erosion studies have been carried out by the RSPB, concerned about the loss of the precious island resource for roosting and migrating birds. These erosion monitoring studies were purposely placed along the southern coastlines of North Binness and Long Islands (Fig 58) where erosion has been most evident and perceived to be a threat to the longevity of the islands themselves.

A total of six specific measurement studies were examined on North Binness and three on Long Island. Five erosion studies were conducted on the south-western shore of North Binness (RSPB area a1, a2, a3(a), a3(b), b) around our survey Area 1, and a sixth (RSPB area c) beyond the Binness 'bay' and to the east of our survey Area 4. On Long Island three studies were conducted; two on the north-western end of the island to the west and east of the find spot of vessels 350 (RSPB areas a1 and a2), and a third along the south-western coast on which feature 305 was found (RSPB area b).

Each study consisted of lines of 2–7 wooden stakes erected broadly parallel to the cliffs. These provided base-lines from which erosion was monitored by taking measurements at 0.25m intervals along the baselines to the top of the cliff, giving 684 erosion measurement points. By recording this on an annual basis between 1988 and 1996 annual and cumulative rates of cliff retreat were monitored. These data provide a record of 4215 measurements from which 3693 measurements of erosion loss could be calculated. Although, at present, the available data (RSPB unpubl) spans a maximum of only seven years (where archaeologically we are dealing with centuries or millennia), it shows coastal retreat at every survey point (see below).

The overall results of this small-scale study on the erosion-prone southern shores of North Binness and Long Islands shows that some locations along the coastlines (predominately higher up the foreshore and on the inner parts of any small promontory) demonstrated relative stability over the seven year observation period. In some areas retreat of only a few centimetres was recorded (eg protected indurated coastline of areas a2 and a3(a) on North Binness Island). In contrast, on more exposed smooth coastlines, especially those on Long Island and some areas of North Binness (RSPB area b), retreat of up to 1.23m was recorded in a year, and up to 2.07m over a five-year period. These recession rates are not atypical – similar rates of shoreline retreat have been recorded in a number of similar coastlines in southern and south-western England. In many such shorelines retreat at *average* rates up to 1m yr^{-1} is common (Allen 1989). Retreat may be due to a number of factors (Allen and Rae 1987) and may include channel migration (Marshall 1962), changes in sediment supply and regional tidal conditions (Allen 1987), or eustatic changes (Gornitz 1995).

Coastal retreat in the measured areas, however, averaged up to 0.34m yr^{-1} and in one location to only 0.02m yr^{-1} (over 5 years). Rates of erosion were particular high on the southern promontories of Long Island, and it is perhaps no coincidence these areas of consistently high erosion were also the findspots of pottery vessels 360 and 380, and hearth 305. Rates of erosion drop significantly on inland areas of headlands such as area b on North Binness where rates of erosion drop from 34mm yr^{-1} to 9mm yr^{-1} over a stretch of 47m and on Long Island (area b) from 37mm yr^{-1} to 3mm yr^{-1} over a coastline length of 46m. In this latter stretch, the highest rate of erosion equates to the find of hearth 305 and one of the dense artefact scatters.

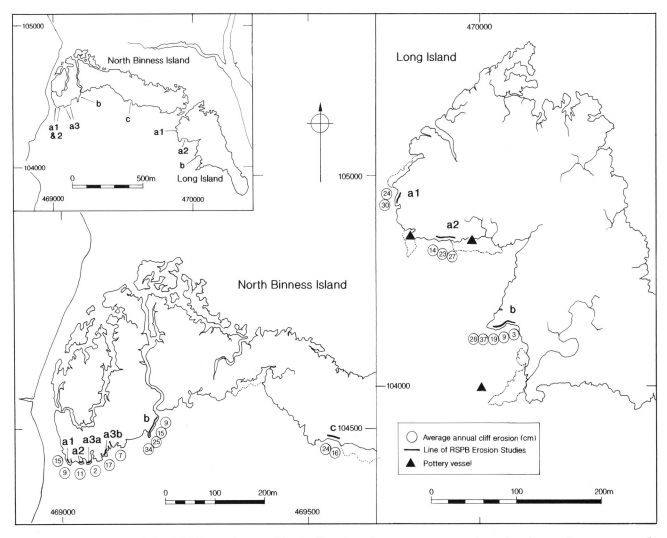

Figure 58   Location of the RSPB erosion studies indicating the average annual erosion in centimetres at each survey point over a study period of 5¼ years (between 1988 and 1994), based on data from the RSPB, Langstone. Drawn by S E James

An erosion model: the taphonomy and formation processes that expose and rearrange the recorded assemblages, Figure 59

Geomorphic features of erosion in Langstone Harbour

The low-lying mixed saltmarsh cliffs and muddy alluvial coastline in Langstone are typical of many muddy coasts of Britain. Records by J R L Allen in the Severn estuary, in particular, have produced a wealth of information about the current processes of erosion and the mechanism for, and products of, erosion and land formation in these environments. The Langstone Harbour environment is analogous to many of the estuarine areas studied by Allen (eg J R L Allen 1987; 1989; 1990a; 1990b; 1991 etc) and, thus, the identification of comparably simple erosion features (J R L Allen 1993) provides evidence of process and mechanisms for land change.

Allen provides models of three chief high-tide shoreline morphologies (J R L Allen 1993, fig 2); smooth transition from mudflat to saltmarsh, bold marsh cliff, and marsh ramp with wave scoured spurs and furrows. Our survey has certainly revealed the presence of the two more dynamic features: cliffing on bold, but low, marsh cliffs, and wave-scoured spurs and furrows. On the southern margins of the islands, in particular Long Island and North Binness, bold low clifflines (to *c* 1m) occur, and mapping demonstrates embayments, a typical product of erosion, but also cliffing and cliff-edge fall (Plate 38 – compare with Allen 1993, fig 2b and fig 3) as a result of wave erosion and mass movement. Cliffing also occurs to a lesser extent on some of the Portsea coastline, but this is largely Tertiary clay and the shoreline is higher relative to sea-level and the intertidal foreshore covered with gravel. These factors reduce the impact of waves and thus cliffing and mass movements are not as pronounced as on the islands.

The artefacts on the foreshore are not *in situ*; the distributions are jumbled and do not directly relate to their original distribution on a point by point

194

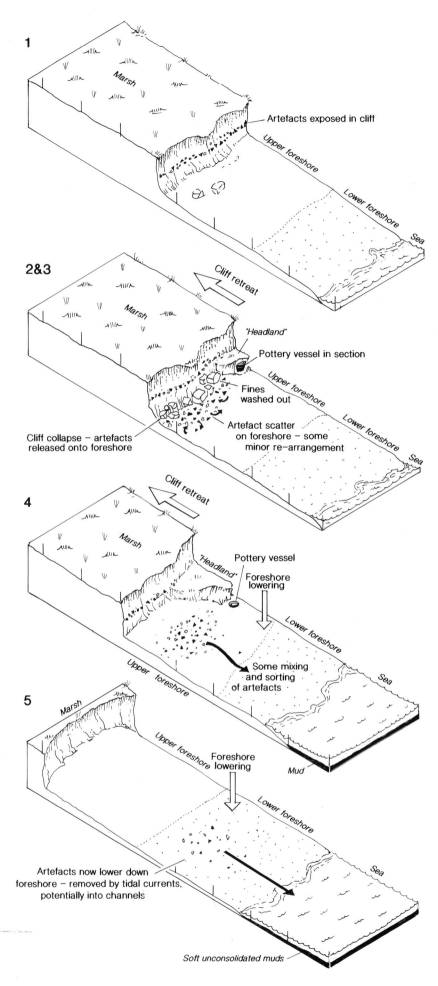

Figure 59   Model of stages of recession erosion showing movement, redistribution across the intertidal zone and ultimately loss into the marine environment. Drawn by S E James

*Plate 38   Eroding clay
headland on Long Island
(Elaine A Wakefield)*

scale. At a more general level, although no clear patterning can be discerned within the scatters, the
distribution and characteristics of the scatters themselves provide relatively detailed information of the
more general activities which created them, especially in comparison with known assemblages in
southern England (Gardiner 1988).

Mottershead (1976, 16) conveniently points out
that one of Bradley and Hooper's (1973) most salient
points in addressing the artefact scatters on the
intertidal foreshores was that one has to be careful in
relating them to post-Mesolithic rise in sea-level
(*sensu* Rankine 1962), and that the scatters may
have been derived by erosion of *in situ* materials
from the cliffs as a receding shoreline passed through
the site. In view of the research conducted within
this project we can now firmly address this point, and
offer some models for the creation of some of the distributions encountered, and in so doing understand
the significance and integrity of the scatters (see
Gardiner, Chapter 2).

The artefact scatters recorded are, by the nature of
the survey project, nearly wholly recovered from
exposed surfaces. A few have been recorded from
exposed 'cliff' sections and the excavation of a ditch
and hearth where they are in secure stratified horizons, but these are the minority of the very large
artefact assemblage from the survey.

The largest category of artefact recovered is prehistoric flintwork (over 4000 items), followed by
pottery. Careful account has had to be taken in analysis of the essentially mobile nature of the sediments
and the artefacts they contain. A simple, nested
method of analysis was employed to test the integrity
of the assemblages and examine the spatial and temporal distribution of the artefacts. In many respects,
the material resembles a ploughzone assemblage.
Details of how it was analysed are presented in
Chapter 2. Most of the artefacts recovered come from

the intertidal mudflats on the south sides of the four
main islands. Many previous finds of prehistoric
date are also recorded from Farlington Marshes and
remnant islands to the south, from the north-west
corner of the harbour, and from the west shore of
Hayling Island.

The stages of erosion

The following erosion model has been developed from
the evidence of the nature of the *in situ* artefacts
from records of the exposures in the shallow cliffs,
the results of the walkover and swimover surveys,
analysis of artefact distributions and scatters, and
our own observations of current erosion and cliffing
on the islands. The model was developed, re-exam-
ined, and modified following three post-fieldwork
visits. It is based on the original occurrence of stratified archaeological material in sealed deposits (Figs
11 and 27) and proposes the likely movement and redistribution of this material (Fig 59).

Stage 1   An artefact scatter becomes exposed in
cliff section by coastal recession

Artefacts exposed in the cliff section are susceptible
to weathering out of this largely stone-free matrix.
Items such as burnt and worked flints and pottery
weather from the section and fall onto the intertidal
wave-cut platform or into the cliff scree or talus. The
relatively few items are then subject to possible
movement and redistribution in tidal swash.
However, the tide is at its lowest energy at this point.
Nevertheless fragments of pottery on Long Island up
to 48 × 34mm were seen to be moved in gentle conditions as each tide broke against the cliff (September
1997).

Plate 39 Exposed and eroding clay surface on Long Island (Garry Momber)

Stage 2 Coastal recession and cliffing of exposures with *in situ* artefacts

Cliffing, as a result of coastal recession, results in mass movements and the accumulation of a 'scree' of clay 'blocks', normally no more than $0.3 \times 0.3 \times 0.2m$, and probably essentially the soil peds (Plate 37). Such debris is temporary. It is subject to weathering, breaking down the blocks to smaller blocks, and to physical wave impact and degradation by even gentle wave action. These processes tend to sort and remove the fines (silts and clays) leaving a gravel (artefact) scree on the upper intertidal margins. Artefacts are, therefore, dropped onto the wave-cut intertidal platform. They essentially maintain their spatial integrity, though slightly modified, but lose vertical integrity and are stratigraphically and con-textually no longer related. With the loss of 'context', most of the microflora and fauna (pollen, diatoms, foraminifera etc) are also lost, together with any pedological and soil micromorphological informa-tion. Numerous, formerly stratified, artefact groups may now reside on a single planar surface. Intrin-sically associated palaeoenvironmental data such as terrestrial shells and some bone will float away along with charcoal (pers obs) and other lighter, less dense items. Small low 'headlands' of the basal soil profile are sometimes left as a result of this cliff retreat (Plates 38 and 39); here artefacts are noticeably more common (see Figs 16 to 18). Little removal of the coarser component occurs at this stage (Fig 59).

Stage 3 Minor rearrangement of the scatter on the upper intertidal foreshore

Depending upon the height of the foreshore in rela-tion to OD, tidal regime, aspect, and location within the harbour, the scree and artefact scatter on the upper intertidal foreshore may be subject to minor rearrangement. The gravel scree is particularly subject to movement in the winter and autumn months when even large flints can be moved by tidal action and were observed to do so during the survey (September–November 1997). In these conditions we anticipate that some sorting of smaller, less dense, and more tabular objects may occur, introducing the first sorting bias in the artefact assemblage. The artefact scatter may reside in the upper intertidal foreshore location for considerable periods of time and, in general terms, will maintain some internal integrity (Fig 59).

Stage 4 Further coastal recession and migration of the upper intertidal foreshore

As coastal recession progresses in saltmarshes (see for example J R L Allen 1987; 1993), the upper intertidal foreshore will migrate shoreward past the artefact scatter. The exposed foreshore lower down the intertidal zone is subject not only to greater wave energy, but also to lowering of the wave-cut platform. The artefact scatters in these zones (mid intertidal foreshore) are subject to more rigorous wave action and swash and more regular submersion, and larger items are more likely to be anchors for seaweed and thus prone to rafting (see Chapter 3, Figure 26, where one sherd weighing over 1kg was rafted nearly 100m from its partner in recent times). Over the short-term there may be a tendency for gravel and artefacts to form a shingle bank along the foot of the cliffs or along the high-water line.

Stage 5 Migration of the mid intertidal foreshore

Continuing coastal recession (perhaps less than 100m from stage 1, depending of the aspect, location, and OD height) will place the artefact scatter on the lower intertidal zone where it is only uncovered at low, or very low, tides. Although there may be a tendency in the short-term to concentrate artefacts and gravel in a strandline along the high-water line or at the base of the cliffs, the long-term effect is to remove these from the foreshore and redistribute them seawards. The intertidal foreshore may have been lowered by in excess of 1.2m (see for instance the heights of the foreshore at the find spots of vessel 350, 360, and 380, where heights vary by 0.72m over a distance of only 60m; see Table 17), and here may be prone to movement of submerged material. The lower intertidal zone is characterised by either soft grey mud, or a hard, stone-free, yellowish clay wave-cut surface. Any artefact scatters are therefore likely to be buried or removed once in this location. Northern shores of the islands are permanently soft intertidal mud, in contrast the southern shores which fluctuate and alternate between soft mud and hard clay surfaces. Alternation between the two occurs along the foreshore but its distribution, especially on the lower foreshore, fluctuates by time over both the weekly and seasonal time-scale.

Despite the generally quiet habitat of the harbour environs, tidal velocities in the low intertidal foreshore are capable of moving large items. We have already noted the rafting of very large pottery sherds on the foreshore of North Binness Island (Chapter 2), but other more substantial objects were also moved and lost during the survey. Two sarsen blocks each weighing in excess of 5kg were placed on, but actually sank in, the soft unconsolidated mud of the lower intertidal zone off Long Island (September 1997). On deposition they were nearly submerged in the soft mud. Revisiting the same location only two months later showed that this soft mud which, two months earlier, was at least 0.2m deep, had been removed to a yellowish-brown hard clay surface with only patches of soft clay, about 0.05m deep. One of the two sarsen boulders had moved more than 50m seawards and was out of reach of both tape and surveyor. The second was not within a 100m radius of its original location; it could not be found, and was assumed to have been moved into the channel separating Long Island from Baker's Island. It is unlikely that it would have been collected by casual visitors, fishermen, or ornithologists. This demonstrated removal from muddied foreshores, or possibly loss under deeper muds lower down the foreshore beyond the intertidal range and within the channels. Even more significant evidence was reported by Arthur Mack in January 2000, following the exceptionally low tides and bad storms of the preceding month. A large flint boulder about 5kg in weight and covered in seaweed had been dragged by the tides seawards about 15m across the peat shelf of Russell's Lake, scouring a deep 'skid mark'. The main branches and trunk of the submerged forest north of Russell's Lake had all but been lost together with most of the tree stumps (see Fig 25). The heavy branch/trunk (AF) had been totally removed; in its waterlogged condition it could not have floated away. Remnants of the smaller branch, which was over 2m long, only survived because its shorter branches penetrated the peat and mud anchoring it in place.

Taphonomy and origin of the mapped artefact distributions

From the above we can consider some of the major overall effects of erosion upon artefact displacement, redistribution and removal, in general non-site specific, terms. Gardiner's analysis of the artefact distributions themselves (Chapter 2) concurs with both the theoretical constructs (Allen and Gardiner, Chapter 2) and the evidence above of erosion processes. Where artefact scatters occur on the high foreshore they have largely just lost their stratigraphic context and the finer resolution of their internal distribution. Following cliff mass movement and the release of artefacts, dropping up to 0.7m from the stratified cliff contexts onto the foreshore, the artefacts are subjected to wave action with disturbance limited movements of flints and pottery; other smaller and less dense artefacts and ecofacts (cf M J Allen 1991) are, however, lost. This general pattern is demonstrated by the artefact plots in Areas 4 and 3 (Figs 17 and 18) which show basic internal integrity, but some loss of detailed patterning, if it ever existed.

Artefacts on the surface of the foreshore lower down the dynamic zone (Fig 12 and 59) tend to be either larger, denser, or embedded within the firm context of an archaeological feature. The fact that the middle foreshore is largely devoid of all coarse clasts supports the view that both finds and stones have been removed from these zones and are lost to the survey. Underwater survey confirmed that these components do not reside in the low-water tidal stretches around the foreshores, and the only places where concentrations of gravel occur in the harbour are in the main channel beds and under the soft unconsolidated muds. By far the largest concentration is in the huge delta of gravel and sands outside the mouth of the harbour. This is material swept from the channels and out into the Solent on the retreating tide.

Thus, artefacts remain resident and undisturbed *in situ* for millennia. Upon cliffing and mass movement they are released onto the hazard zone (Figs 12 and 59) where they have moderate residence time at the foot of the cliffs. Residence can initially be temporarily on a low headland (Fig 59) and then among a clay-block scree or talus before deposition on the wave-cut upper foreshore floor, often with other detritus of similar size density. Features within the island and land deposits may be truncated by cliffing and coastal retreat, exposing *in situ* contexts and features cut into the foreshore clays. Once the cliffs retreat well beyond the site and some lowering of the foreshore occurs, artefact residence time is severely reduced. The distribution of artefacts plotted on the surface of ditch 1711 demonstrates this (Fig 28). Most finds are removed relatively rapidly from the mid foreshore and transported across the lower foreshore into the channels. Once deposited in the channels we have no indication of their residence time, however, the very large delta of detritus and coarse clasts at the mouth of the harbour indicates that the present sand tidal system is very dynamic.

Loss by truncation in such locations is demonstrated by the finds of pottery vessels 350, 360, and 380 on Long Island as pottery 'rings' (see Plate 23, Chapter 3 above). Vessel 350 was found within 0.5m of the cliff edge (+0.69m OD). It was 310mm in diameter and 330mm of the vessel survives from which we can postulate a former total vessel size of about 410mm; ie a loss of about 90mm, plus the upper portion of the feature fill. In this case about 80% of the vessel survives, in contrasts to vessel 360 found *c* 60m from the shoreline and well out on the intertidal foreshore at +0.43m OD (see Fig 29). This was inverted and of similar size to vessel 360, but only 180mm of the vessel survived. If the vessel was of the same proportions, then 230mm has been lost and less than 45% survives. We cannot, however, model the loss or truncation merely by location relative to the current cliffs or position on the intertidal foreshore. The depth to which each vessel was buried is unknown and may have varied; pot 380 was within a few metres of the shoreline, high up on the intertidal foreshore, at +1.15m OD but less than 30mm of this vessel survives, indicating a loss of over 90% of this vessel.

Inference on coastal erosion to the occurrence of artefact scatters

We can use the information discussed above to understand the general occurrence of the artefact scatters. Nearly all artefact scatters are skirts or halos of material on the upper foreshore and, on the islands, these are predominately on foreshores facing either southwards (seawards) or a major channel. These halos are, in general, only a few metres wide, beyond which the mid foreshore is stone-free. Artefacts that survive within this stone-free zone are either those in features exposed on the wave-cut foreshore, large artefacts not as readily moved by wave action, or those rafted along the shore. This close-shore artefact distribution is, therefore, entirely a product of erosion and does not reflect past activity, but the occurrence and varying densities within it do reflect concentrations of specific activities.

At the more specific level of interpreting function and activity within the artefacts scatters, the effect of larger particle size movement and erosion can be examined by the detailed analysis of the content of the assemblages and by comparing these with known, previously studied prehistoric artefact assemblages in Sussex, Hampshire, and Dorset (*cf* Gardiner 1988). This can be used to gauge any obvious bias within the assemblages which we might attribute to processes of natural erosion and displacement, rather than displaying different functions between the assemblages. Assemblage composition and distribution can be compared with known and expected distributions and assemblages and any differences questioned in terms of cultural activity, disposal practices, taphonomy, and possible rearrangement by erosion.

7   The physical development of a harbour: 9000 years of human activity

by Michael J Allen and Julie Gardiner

The survey and research described above provide us with a number of pieces of a 'jigsaw'. We can try to put these pieces together and emerge with a story of the development, in physical and social terms, of the area we know today as Langstone Harbour. This will be discussed as far as possible using the present evidence, however, we know that there are large elements which we can only touch upon and which can be improved and refined with further research. Some of that research is outlined and proposed in Chapter 8.

Sea-level history and the physical development of the harbour landscape
by Michael J Allen

The importance of sea-level change cannot be over estimated, especially in a low-lying, near-marine landscape such as Langstone Harbour (Plate 40). This is all the more significant when attempting to view change and development of human communities over the past nine millennia, during which significant changes have occurred that have a direct impact upon the physical and ecological nature of the defined study area. At the outset we can see that Langstone differs in its physiography and morphology from both Portsmouth and Southampton harbours. The latter have major, deep, and maintained channels in which peat occurs (Fig 60) and have been recorded by antiquarian investigations (Portsmouth: James 1947; Godwin 1945; Southampton: Everard 1954a; Godwin and Godwin 1940; Hodson and West 1972; Hooley 1905; Shore 1905; Shore and Elwes 1889; see Archaeological and palaeo-environmental background, Chapter 1). Langstone, by comparison, is a broad shallow basin (Fig 60), more akin to Chichester Harbour (see Langstone Harbour setting, Chapter 1).

Recent evidence from Southampton Water shows that the history of the Holocene evolution of this estuary has been dominated by sea-level rise and

Plate 40   Typical view across the mudflats of Langstone Harbour at or around low tide (Elaine A Wakefield)

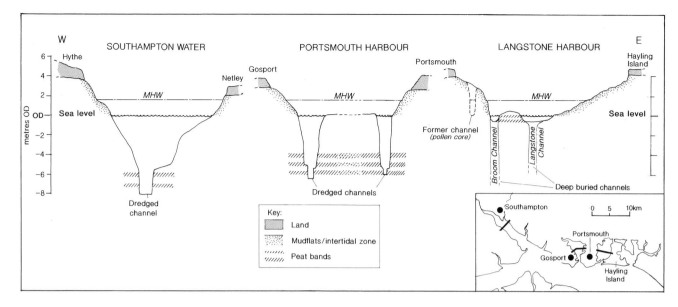

Figure 60 Cross profile comparing, Southampton, Portsmouth and Langstone Harbours, showing the deeply incised channels and buried levels in Portsmouth and Southampton, and the shallow eroded nature of Langstone. Drawn by S E James

coastal inundation (Long and Scaife 1996). The outer reaches of Southampton Water were first inundated and drowned at about 7000 BC, with extensive mid-estuary drowning of the extensive alder-dominated woodland at about 5000 BC (c –5m OD). Mean sea-level was at c –6m OD at about 3500 BC and rose at a broadly linear rate of 1.1mm per annum. After c 3000 BC rate of sea-level rise began to fall slightly, and most sea-level rise was due to local crustal subsidence. The high, more marginal dry-land peats at about –2 to –1.5m OD (eg Bury Farm) were submerged by about 1000 BC, after which saltmarsh sedimentation persisted. At the start of the project evidence of this type of inundation was seen as the model for the creation of Langstone Harbour. However, when the radiocarbon determinations of the data from Langstone are plotted on to a local sea-level curve generated with data from Southampton Water (Long and Scaife 1986, fig 18) and central southern England (Devoy 1982; 1987b; Tooley 1990), we can see that all the Langstone dated events and surfaces fall well above the curve (Fig 61). Unless significant local massive warping is invoked, this conclusively indicates that the peats and levels within Langstone were not coastal. They are estuarine and higher up the river profile than coastal sites. Thus, although inundation of these sites is indirectly generated by sea-level rise, they are not coastal peats, nor can this information be used to generate local sea-level curves.

In the earlier Mesolithic (9000–7000 BC) we can see that the coastline was some 40km to the south of the present harbour (Fig 56) and that very large, deeply incised palaeochannels existed draining into the former Solent River and Channel. Within this system peat has been mapped infilling channels but also 'onlaps on to a shallow basin' (Bellamy 1995, 54) at between –20 and –22.7m OD. Pollen spectra from the upper portion of the sequence at Chalkdock Lake suggest a broad date of 7000–6000 BC. From Bellamy's map we can attempt to reconstruct an idea of the general nature of the physiography in the earlier Mesolithic. This provides a base and start for the regression analysis and development of the harbour as we see it today.

Infilled channels are represented in Langstone Harbour by the localised occurrences of peat at c –13m OD beneath the Langstone and Broom channels (Mottershead 1976) indicating their former incised, ravine-like nature. The larger drainage channels have been mapped as the Solent River and extended courses of the Adur and Arun (Bellamy 1995, fig 1). The formation of peats at –13m OD in the deeply incised, narrow, buried channels beneath the Langstone and Broom Channels relates to the 'Solent Transgression' and flooding about 8000–6800 BP (R J Nicholls 1987) c 7000–6000 cal BC. The landscape comprised two parts; the dry-land basin below the chalk providing large plains in which local still-water pools may have occurred, and the rivers in deep ravines with flat valley floors with constrained floodplains supporting rich damp vegetation and facilitating the formation of floodplain and possibly channel peat. Access to these rivers would certainly have been easier nearer the Downs and the coast, but the exact configuration of the ravine sides in the Langstone location is undetermined and open to speculation. The underlying geologies are London Clays and Reading Beds with Bracklesham Group (gravel and sands) to the south (see Fig 4) which will not form steep cliff edges. We can speculate that long relatively gentle, but pronounced, slopes existed into the 'ravines'. Only in the north, where the valleys cut through chalk, may steeper slopes of perhaps 30° occur with localised river cliffs.

Gradual, but essentially constant, sea-level rise in

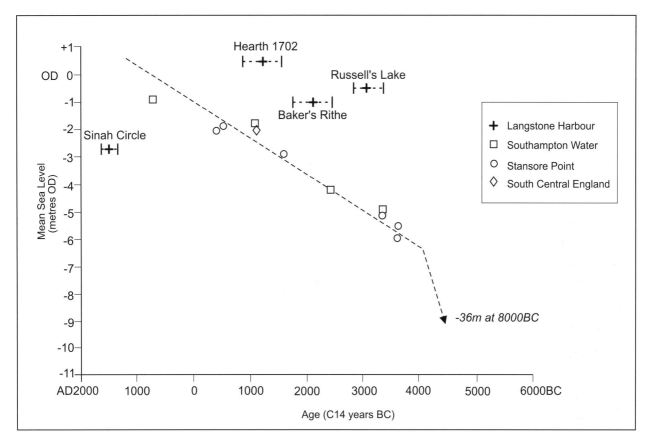

Figure 61   Mean sea-level changes (after Long and Scaife 1996, fig 17) with data from Southampton Water (Long and Scaife 1996) and Stansore Point (Long and Tooley 1995), and central southern England (Devoy 1982; 1987b, and Tooley 1990), and Langstone Harbour (this volume). Age errors of c ± 100 years and altitude errors of ± 0.5m should be assumed for each index point. Drawn by S E James

the 9th–4th millennia BC resulted in alluviation of the valleys and infilling of these formerly pronounced topographic features. Continual accretion of fine-grained over-bank and channel alluvium, as seen in some of the major river valleys in Sussex (Burrin and Scaife 1984; Scaife and Burrin 1983; 1985), would have raised the valley floor, reducing the topographic contrast between the plain and incised valley. Much, but not all, of the valleys were infilled. Largely inorganic sedimentation (Mottershead 1976), driven by rising sea-level, resulted in these topographically significant features being completely infilled by the later Bronze Age, thus dramatically altering the perspective of this landscape into a single plain, fringed with slightly higher ground, through which rivers meandered in a shallow valley. Drainage velocity would have decreased with the rising sea-level and localised pools of standing water may have formed in this poorly drained landscape.

Given that the later Neolithic peats in Langstone Harbour (submerged 'forests' at –1 and –0.5m OD) are at a much higher OD even than the widespread Bronze Age and Iron Age coastal peats (–3m OD) from sites such as Stansill Point, Southampton Water, and Wootton Quarr (Long and Tooley 1995; Long and Scaife 1996; Scaife pers comm), it appears that the Langstone deposits are indirectly sea-level

controlled by decrease in river velocities and ponding within the inland river basin as an indirect result of relative sea-level rise (Fig 62), rather than directly controlled by relative sea-level changes (Scaife pers comm). In other words, the driving force behind both the locally wet habitat and its subsequent burial is not controlled by sea-level; it is purely the result of local environmental factors of the evolving low-lying river system. Although freshwater pools existed, there is tentative evidence of brackish conditions by the later Neolithic, this is largely because of the tidal nature of the former Broom and Langstone channels (see below). The deep ravines that existed in the Mesolithic were significantly alluviated by the later Neolithic, surviving as broad, but defined, low valleys in the later Neolithic and Bronze Age.

Seasonal or extreme flooding events may have created some inland brackish lagoons and provided the first opportunity for the growth of occasional more maritime flora (*Suaeda maritima*) within the study area.

Minor fluctuations in sea-level and of the morphology of the coastal plain and its river channels and levees could relatively rapidly change this predominately low-lying freshwater landscape with seasonal brackish lagoons to one with frequently flooded river floodplains and eroding channel edges. By the middle–late Iron Age the river valleys were fully

Plate 41   Aerial view of Langstone Harbour at low tide from the south with Portsdown in the distance. Note the exposed mudflats in the harbour giving a better impression of the extent of land in the past. (Reproduced with permission of the Langstone Harbour Board)

alluviated and the streams and rivers flowing in only very shallow valleys. Much of the area was within the tidal reaches, and the action of waves, and seasonally higher water levels, would allow flooding of large areas of the adjacent land. Tidal action and flooding allow 'over topping' of the valleys and provide the first major impetus for lateral and more widespread erosion and artefact displacement in the area.

Soon inland saltmarsh and deeper standing water could have existed, perhaps forming over a period of a millennium in later prehistory. By the late Iron Age and Romano-British period, Langstone existed as a shallow muddy harbour, fringed with saltmarsh and stronger brine pools (see Plate 41 for an indication of this environment); in many respects it reflects that which developed in Chichester Harbour (Cunliffe 1971), with shallow gravel-floored navigable channels and silt infilled surrounds. Chichester Harbour was only made navigable to larger ships in Roman times by large-scale modifications of the

harbour edges and construction of an artificial terrace and quay wall. This created, or modified, a huge lagoon-like inlet at Fishbourne. It is not known how water was retained in its upper reaches but Cunliffe suggests that some kind of mole built out across the harbour end probably kept the water back at low tide while the constant flow from freshwater streams maintained the level. He also postulates that lock gates were provided in the mole to allow ships to sail up the 10m (30ft) wide channel dredged alongside the terrace edge to Fishbourne. This provided water only just 1m deep, but sufficient for quite large Roman vessels to berth (Cunliffe 1971). No such constructs or intensive activity can be seen in Langstone, but the physical environment was probably not dissimilar. By the Saxon period we can see that the Sinah circle structure, located at −2.7 to −3m OD, was well below sea-level (Fig 61; below), confirming it as a marine, rather than terrestrial, structure. The depth of water here, confirms the presence of a true inlet and harbour.

The occupation of the developing harbour landscape
by Michael J Allen and Julie Gardiner

This narrative aims to highlight the main and, in our view, most important episodes of activity in the human history of Langstone Harbour. In the earliest Mesolithic (9th–8th millennium BC) the presence of the peat at the base of the two main channels indicates deeply incised valleys as much as 14m deep and probably up to 200m wide in places, but elsewhere as narrow as 20–25m. These deep 'ravines' dissected a lowland plain some distance from the coast. However, our first evidence of significant human activity is in the later Mesolithic perhaps three millennia later.

The general lack of spreads of bone in comparison with other intertidal surveys, such as the Hullbridge Basin (Wilkinson and Murphy 1995), and an allied absence of pottery scatters rather than isolated features and individual vessels, is not just a case of survival (see North Binness Island excavated features), but points to a general lack of settlement in the studied landscape throughout prehistory. The evidence may confirm a series of localised and specific activities, rather than more generalised settlement activities such as have been detected in intertidal studies elsewhere (eg the Welsh Severn, Bell *et al* 2000, and the Hullbridge Basin, Wilkinson and Murphy 1995).

Upper Palaeolithic (before 10,000 BC) and earlier Mesolithic 10,000–6000 cal BC)

Despite the abundance of evidence for Lower Palaeolithic occupation of the gravels on the northern side of the former Solent River, Langstone Harbour itself has only produced a single handaxe, from intertidal muds on the west side of Hayling Island. The Palaeolithic evidence from southern England has recently been reviewed in detail (Wymer 1999) and need not be discussed further here. Four, possibly five, individual finds of Upper Palaeolithic date are recorded, three of which were actually seen by one of the present authors (JPG) and were all in a very rolled condition. Apart from indicating the presence of people in the area at some stage during the Upper Palaeolithic, they provide no clues as to what activity occurred here, nor is there any evidence for natural local environmental conditions (vegetation, and the impact of man on these environments). Evidence for these conditions is unlikely (Allen 1996, 60), but evidence of the broader palaeogeographic framework (sedimentological regimes etc), has been largely elucidated by the Quaternary research summarised earlier.

Earlier Mesolithic activity along the coastal and hinterland stretches of southern England is sparse, and activity of this period within the study area has, to date, eluded recovery. Analogy, however, with recent discoveries around the Isle of Wight provides some important indicators. A submerged cliffline has been recorded at Boulder off the north-east coast of the Isle of Wight. A peat level lying at the base of the submerged cliff at –10m OD has produced *in situ* Mesolithic flints and microliths (Dix and Momber pers comm). An oak bole resting on this peat ledge gave a date of 8390–8060 cal BC (Tomalin pers comm). Further dates and examination of this area is being carried out by HWTMA and Southampton University. With such sparse evidence, we can only point to low scale and specialised exploitation and use of resources not found within the Langstone area at this time. Submerged clifflines with peat, preserved trees and associated flintwork off the Isle of Wight, however, indicate the possibilities of similar environments off the south coast of Hampshire.

Late Mesolithic (6000–4500 cal BC)

The evidence in Langstone for the Mesolithic is restricted to the 6th–5th millennium BC, ie the late Mesolithic (Atlantic). The landscape was quite alien to that which we know now. Not only was it well inland, but two deep ravines, perhaps 50 to 150m wide in places, provided major routeways from the coast to the Downs while the bowl now forming Langstone Harbour was in excess of 14m above the ravine floors. Base camps, hunting camps and other temporary Mesolithic sites may have been concentrated in these routeways, but their discovery was beyond the scope of this survey project being buried by *c* 10m of inorganic silts beneath the current harbour. Through these pronounced valleys freshwater streams flowed over flint gravel-strewn beds and rich vegetation grew and died along the braided and meandering river margins forming peats. The valleys and their sides were not deep- nor steep-enough to preclude access to the streams and gravels, though in the northern extent of the Langstone area access was much easier. The streams flowed on through the lowland basin to the sea some 30km or so away. The upper reaches of one of these smaller peat-filled channels in fen-carr in Chalkdock Lake provide an indication of the local vegetation (pollen zone LANG:3). In the valley, open grass and sedge with freshwater fen with alder carr existed. On the low-lying basin, some 14m above the stream floor, dry-land supported lindens (lime), possibly with some oak, elm, and hazel: these mixed oak forest elements were certainly present in the hinterland. This high local biodiversity and range of habitats and resources made this a landscape rich in many elements that would have been attractive to the Mesolithic population. The upper dryer plain may have provided fine hunting grounds for mobile and even transient herds, in particular of deer and cattle. The opportunity to exploit the widespread exposures of Pleistocene river gravel led to a landscape that was never highly, nor intensively occupied, but repeated visitation led to one which is redolent in Mesolithic artefacts (Fig 62).

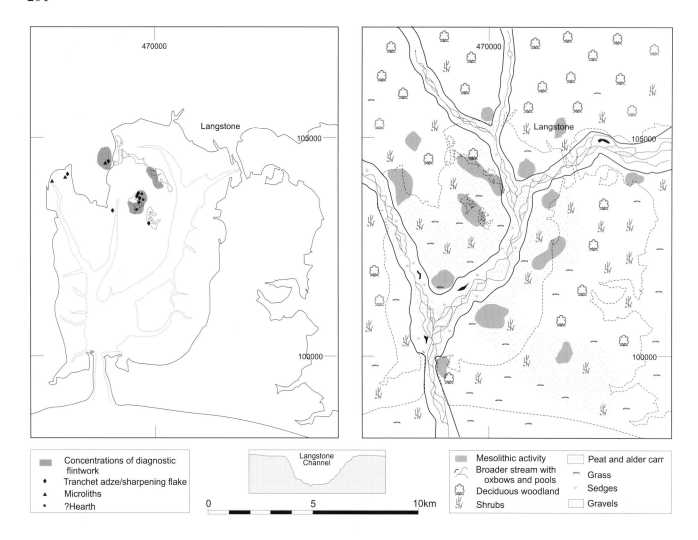

Figure 62   a) (left) Distribution of known Mesolithic activity in the harbour, and b) (right) reconstruction of the Mesolithic landscape. Drawn by S E James

The composition of the late Mesolithic flint assemblage is interesting; it is extremely limited and largely confined to waste material and a restricted range of tools including tranchet adzes and sharpening flakes, picks, scrapers, and serrated and retouched flakes. The assemblage does not include the range of manufacturing and processing tools typical of many late Mesolithic 'sites' (eg Jacobi 1981). Overall, the suggestion is of a limited range of activities.

The raw material used is local though it would have been available as a 'dry-land' (river gravel), as opposed to a marine, resource. The tranchet adzes/flakes, however, are all of imported material – presumably brought in as complete artefacts. Overall it looks as though the area was being visited repeatedly for short periods, in order specifically to exploit its flint resources, with flint cores, tool blanks, and probably unworked nodules being transported out of the immediate area for use elsewhere. The composition of the assemblage suggests little more than basic maintenance activity for small parties of individuals who may only have been resident for a few days at a time. Other, less archaeologically recoverable resources were almost certainly being exploited, but there is no evidence for a 'base-camp' type assemblage (cf Binford 1980; Jacobi 1981) suggesting any long-term residency. Nor have any typical 'hunting stand' type assemblages been identified, though that does not mean that they may not have existed in areas now eroded away (lower down the stream valleys where access may have been easier), or perhaps buried in the alluviated valleys (Allen and Gardiner forthcoming a).

We can envisage this rich and diverse area being an ideal hunting ground, principally for the flint but possibly for prey too; the prey being likely to be herds of large mammals which were exploiting the open lowland vegetation and freshwater provided by the rivers. Migrating herds attracted to drink in the valleys provided Mesolithic communities with opportunity to ambush their prey. Upon making their weapons and tools, and effecting a kill, butchery and dismemberment could have occurred at the kill-site

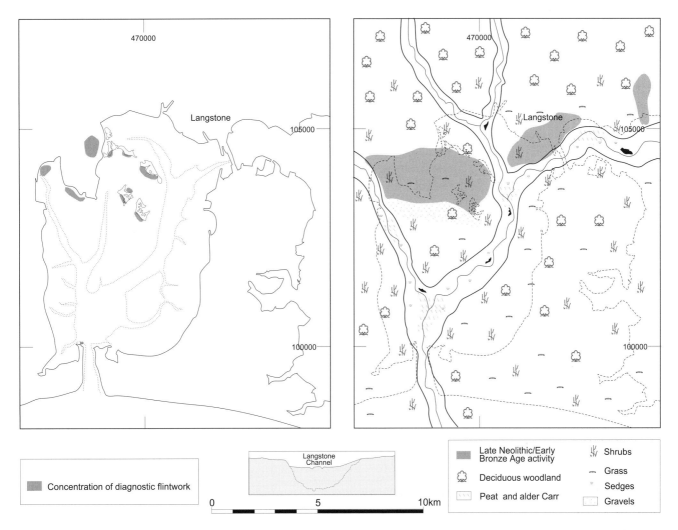

Figure 63   a) (left) Distribution of known late Neolithic / early Bronze Age activity in the harbour, and b) (right) reconstruction of the late Neolithic / early Bronze Age landscape. Drawn by S E James

allowing the removal of the most useful elements of the dismembered carcass to a base or home-camp. The Mesolithic 'occupation', if we can call it that at this time, is likely to have been further inland on the chalk fringes, or the chalk itself.

Late Neolithic–early Bronze Age (2600–1750 cal BC)

Our next concentrated episode of activities lies within the late Neolithic–early Bronze Age, which we can date to about 2600–1750 cal BC. The pollen spectra from Chalkdock Lake do not, unfortunately, extend into this period of habitation, nor have we any other sealed sources of palaeoenvironmental evidence. The dated submerged peat floor at Baker's Rithe (2310–1950 cal BC) indicates the development of fen into fen/alder carr woodland with oak, yew, and hawthorn locally. Using the waterlogged seed and sub-regional evidence we have a relatively good body of data with which to outline the environment and nature of the late Neolithic and early Bronze Age landscape.

Site/find	Material	Lab no	Result BP	Calibration
Baker's Rithe	oak stump (BB)	R-24993/2	3735 ± 60	2310–1950 cal BC
Russell's Lake	oak branch (AEA)	R-24993/1	4431 ± 70	3350–2910 cal BC

Low-lying, largely freshwater rivers probably existed in the former deeply incised river valleys with freshwater pools and alder carr (alnetum) (Allen and Gardiner forthcoming b). Infilling and alluviation with inorganic fine-grained sediments during the later Mesolithic to earlier Neolithic period presented much shallower, gentle, though still significant, valley profiles (Fig 63). Although the streams may have been tidal, and the area was a part of the coastal plain, there is no evidence to indicate a strongly maritime nor definitely coastal (ie shoreline) environment. Direct evidence of trees with notably close rings indicates a stressed environment, possibly caused by this increased local salinity. Extensive peat blankets formed in the wet floodplains in the river valleys. Open grassland and alder carr existed in the valleys and adjacent to the rivers but, in all probability, open woodland dominated by lime existed in the main on the drier and higher adjacent land. The fringing chalkland would have supported denser mixed oak, hazel, and lime woodland.

There is no clear evidence for activity in the earlier part of the Neolithic. Earlier publications (eg Bradley and Hooper 1973) recorded much of the material from Langstone as being of Neolithic date but, although implements attributed to the late Neolithic–early Bronze Age have been recovered, much of the assemblage can now be seen to be later in date. At face value, a relatively large number of tool types were recovered (Table 9), but it is significant that these all belong to very few functionally-related groups and the assemblage is dominated by scrapers (75%+). In view of the nature of the locally available raw material it is likely that most large core tools and at least one of the arrowheads were brought into the area as artefacts; the remainder being made on the spot for immediate use and discard. Here, we agree with the assessment by Bradley and Hooper (1973) that this is an essentially non-domestic assemblage, possibly representing seasonal, short-term grazing and associated activities. No contemporaneous pottery is recorded.

The lack of large scatters of pottery and of animal bones like those excavated at the Stumbles, Hullbridge (Wilkinson and Murphy 1995) is notable in Langstone. In contrast to the Stumbles, for instance, we can envisage the Langstone area being used for short-term visits for occasional hunting and the continued exploitation of flint resources. We can also postulate grazing (largely cattle). Thus Langstone had the capability of contributing to an important part of the Neolithic economy and life style. The area itself was not settled or occupied, it was peripheral but not marginal to the occupied areas (Fig 63). It was exploited through choice, not necessity and provided specific and important resources for local Neolithic communities. Long-term, settled occupation was largely concentrated on the adjacent chalklands where abundant evidence survives in the form of long and oval barrows and causewayed enclosures (Trundle), and where there is also evidence of widespread use of the Downs shown by the flint scatters (Gardiner 1988; 1996). Recent excavations (Westhampnett) on the coastal plain, previously thought to be largely devoid of monuments and settlement evidence in the late Neolithic and early Bronze Age with the exception of ubiquitous distributions of artefacts, have found the presence of more typical domestic or funerary activities in this period. This indicates clearances within the woodland and more permanent activities and settlement forms. Although these do not seem to exist in the Langstone area, probably because of its subtly different local environment and altitude, such activity may exist on the higher ground running though Langstone village itself and at Gosport (see below).

Middle Bronze Age–late Bronze Age (1600–700 cal BC)

Recently, contrary to previous belief, evidence for settlement and burial activity of middle and late Bronze Age date has been found on the coastal plain of Hampshire and West Sussex. There is extensive evidence of settlement and for farming systems with enclosures, fields, hut platforms, and designated burial grounds on the chalk. The discovery, therefore, of roundhouses on the coastal plain at Creek Field, Hayling Island (HI.36) and Gosport (Hall and Ford 1994), of field systems and barrows at Westhampnett, West Sussex, and specialist activities at Bosham (Gardiner and Hamilton 1997) indicates that extensive areas of the southern landscape were being utilised as parts of a much larger farming economy. Societies were not isolated single extended family units farming locally, but broader communities exploiting and utilising a much wider and more diverse economic region. It is within this wider social context that we can place the evidence from Langstone Harbour. Two radiocarbon determinations from the area confirm activity locally at this time.

Site/find	Material	Lab no	Result BP	Calibration
Stake (Williams and Soffe 1997)	wood, oak	HAR-8375	2850 ± 100	1320–820 cal BC
Hearth 1702 (this vol)	charcoal	OxA-7366	2995 ± 55	1410–1060 cal BC

By the middle Bronze Age the Langstone area saw slow-running streams meandering through a gently undulating, low-lying grassland fringed with localised saltmarsh. We can assume that the development of larger freshwater pools, mires, and alder carr occurred along the stream courses, with poor meadow on the interfluves interspersed with stands of oak, alder, yew, and willow. Concomitant with this was the development of saltmarsh and a stronger maritime environment created by the tidal rivers. The islands in the northern part were a continuous landmass, as was probably most of the harbour, only dissected by the rivers and associated tributary streams (Fig 64). Extensive, but not thick, peat formed along the stream courses, and had already choked some of the smaller courses in the northern part of this basin, which were virtually redundant as waterways. The streams were tidal – all exiting the area and heading towards the coast as a single channel through what is now the harbour mouth – and there is possibly some evidence of the first development of local saltmarshes. Increasing salinity in the rivers and the development of local saltmarsh provide a more maritime feel to the coastal plain here, but the area was still not on the coastline, though it was within easy access of it (Fig 64).

Much of the Langstone flint assemblage is here assigned a mature Bronze Age date of c 1600–700 BC. Because the Bronze Age flint assemblages are characterised by a narrow range of simple tool forms, which were probably made very quickly, used, and discarded, it is probable that these implements were

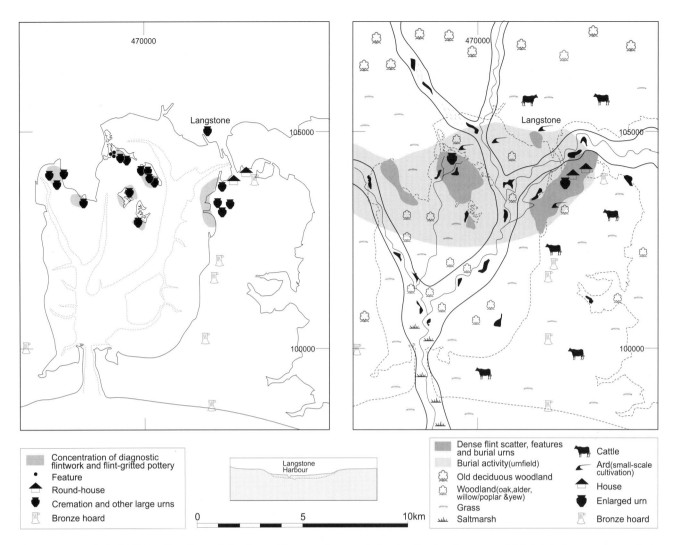

Figure 64 a) (left) Distribution of the later Bronze Age activity in the harbour, and b) (right) reconstruction of the later Bronze Age landscape and activities. Drawn by S E James

used for a variety of scraping, boring, and cutting functions – where metal tools were either less efficient or simply too expensive – and are very likely to have continued in expedient use (see also Young and Humphrey 1999). The flintwork is again *not* suggestive of long-term residency. A possible scenario is that the harbour area was again being used essentially for seasonal grazing, with the butchering of animals and preparation of hides taking place alongside, and probably removal of the carcass as very little bone was recovered. It is also possible that flint was being removed from the area, perhaps to more long-term settlements on permanently dry land on what is now the coastal plain, for instance, at Creek Field, Hayling Island (ApSimon this volume), Knapp Farm, Bosham (Gardiner and Hamilton 1997), and Grange Road, Gosport (Hall and Ford 1994). The study area, by its topographical definition, only examined the lower-lying land; more permanent settlement may have been located on the slightly higher ground indicated by the sites listed above (Fig 64).

The pottery assemblage from Langstone includes a large proportion of medium–coarse flint-tempered pottery, much of which is of later Bronze Age (post-Deverel-Rimbury) date. Some sherds of probable Deverel-Rimbury globular urn were identified. The assemblage includes parts of five crude urns, and the remains of at least one other, found buried in the foreshore muds, having presumably originally been inserted into small pits. Four of these vessels contained human remains (Table 20), and produced between 2.4g and 405g of cremated bone. Others were apparently filled with burnt flint (eg vessel 350), which itself was recovered in large quantities during the survey, though it is possible that some lightweight cremated bone has been lost to the sea. Previous finds in the harbour area include the remains of several other urns; some associated with cremated bone, particularly in the north-west corner of the harbour, suggesting the presence of an urnfield. The surviving remains of a pot found in 1981 contained the cremated remains (1079g) of a young ?female adult and a quantity of pyre debris. It is possible that some of the burnt flint concentrations represent the remains of pyre sites.

The remains of an unusual enlarged, globular, handled vessel, the surviving part of which weighed

Table 27 List of recorded later Bronze Age vessels, largely cinerary vessels many reported with cremated bone

No	Vessel	NGR SU	Location	Date found	Description	No	Reference /note	SMR	Project No
1		67900430	Farlington Marshes, east side	1979	25 pieces of 'Deverel-Rimbury' from three pots in a pit [C Draper]	3	unpubl	SU60SE 26A	FM.53
2		69350465	North Binness Island	1953	Bronze Age urn fragment with fingernail decoration 'Deverel-Rimbury vessel' with contents (and sherds of 2–3 other vessels eroding from southern shore) [C Draper]	1	Rudkin 1980, no 74	SU60SE 53	NB.59
3		70200410	Long Island	1981	Urn with cremated bone (PCM acc no 1981.367) 2–3 other urns [C Draper]	3	Hughes 1982, *Arch in Hants* 1981, 36	SU70SW 54	LI.45
4	350	69890420	Long Island, north-west	1993	straight-sided vessel, finger impressed cordon, flat rim, expanded base, finished with vertical finger smearing	1	This volume	–	LI.15d
5	360	70180398	Long Island, off west coast	1997	slightly flared jar	1	This volume	–	LI.28d
6	380	69910420	Long Island, north-west	1997	a flat bottom jar 320mm in diameter, base only survived	1	This volume	–	LI.15e
7	521	69560372	Baker's Island, north	1994	unknown	1	This volume	–	BI.16d
8	744/1	69850305	South Binness Island, south	1993	flint-gritted straight-sided vessel, LBA, devoid of base or rim	1	This volume	–	SB.18d
9	–	71510500	Langstone village, Mill Lane	1979	One MBA barrel urn with a cremation burial [G Soffe] HCM Service acc no A1981 80H	1	Soffe 1980; this volume	SU70SW 53A	Ha.44
10	–	72610427	north of Hayling Island, Duckard Point	1968	Inverted Bronze Age urn containing cremated bone [M Rule] note Founder's hoard near by Rudkin 1980, no 75	1	unpubl	SU70SW 21	HI.40
11	–	71880359	Creek Field, Hayling Island	1955	Large jar with two pierced lugs on shoulder. [Pycroft/Budden] PCM acc no 47/55	1	Rudkin 1980, no 73 This volume	SU70SW 1	HI.36
12	–	71850354	Hayling Island, north- west coast of	1969	Three inverted cinerary urns found while digging brickearth, [Pyecroft]	3	unpubl	SU70SW 20	HI.39
13	–	72209920	Elm Close, Hayling Island	Before 1980	fragmentary bucket urn	1	Rudkin 1980, no 71	–	HI.64

nearly 2kg, was found on the foreshore of North Binness, within a hearth. The date of this vessel is secured by a radiocarbon date of 1410–1060 cal BC, its fabric contains medium–coarse flint fragments but has a smoothed outer surface and a strap handle which ApSimon considers is probably related to the Deverel-Rimbury series. One parallel has been found on Hayling Island which ApSimon considers to be of middle Bronze Age date and 'French with a Cornish accent' (pers comm).

The apparent lack of evidence for settlement and permanent residence (in terms of the expected range of typical domestic features and structures) tends to enhance the suggestion of limited specialised activities within the area now defined by Langstone Harbour itself. The presence of several bronze ornaments and of at least four metal hoards also points in this direction (see below).

In terms of a settlement context for the activity represented in Langstone Harbour, we can suggest that the area provided a supplement to the farming economies of the main settlement areas, and was, again, peripheral to those settled areas, even if settlement at this time extended onto the slightly higher land in coastal plain (eg Creek Field on Hayling Island, Gosport and Bosham). Although the area was not 'marginal', the use of the land and its resources became increasingly more so, in terms of food and economic resources, to later-Bronze Age communities. It did not provide a key resource base in the mature Bronze Age farming economy as it had done to the preceding economies of more mobile, hunting and foraging lifestyles of the Mesolithic and Neolithic. Few fragments of bone were found in Bronze Age features suggesting small scale consumption or 'picnicing'. Further, the necessity to obtain good flint in this period was also less.

The rich soils of the chalk downland (Allen 1992; 1994; 1997b) provided intensive farming opportunities but, later in the Bronze Age, as populations grew and, more importantly, as degradation of some of the chalkland soil occurred through these tillage practices (cf Allen 1992; 1997b; forthcoming), so some pressure to utilise areas off the prime downland was evident, but the choice of local cereal cultivation in the Langstone area was one of economics and convenience. Detailed arguments for this are presented elsewhere, but it has been suggested (ibid) that the increasing need to bury the dead in large monuments (round barrows) or in areas designated for burial (flat cemeteries) seems at odds with the potential pressure of farming land. Undoubtedly many Bronze Age barrows are sited on ridges and hilltops where they can be seen and displayed, but it is no coincidence that these are also areas which had suffered the most severe soil erosion and degradation; ie burial and funerary rites were not placed on prime agricultural land, but at its fringes. Perhaps we can use the same argument to understand the use of the northern part of the study area as a large burial ground and as the location for metal hoards.

Burial

This study alone has recovered five mature Bronze Age vessels neatly buried; three on Long Island, and one each on Baker's and South Binness Islands (Table 27). Although, on recovery, not all contained cremated human bone, they may have done so originally and they strongly indicate funerary rather than domestic practices. In addition, previous finds have included a vessel with a relatively large quantity of cremated human bone from Long Island (acc 1981/367) and a number of other vessels are reported from the north-west corner of the harbour (Bradley and Hooper 1973). A further five cremation vessels are known from north and north-west Hayling Island (Williams and Soffe 1987; Soffe forthcoming – quoted in 1987), and one from Langstone village (Soffe 1980; Williams and Soffe 1987). Much, if not all, of the northern part of what is now the harbour seems to have been used as an open flat cemetery (Fig 65). Its southern extent is unrecordable as this has been lost to the harbour. The cemetery would have been overlooked by the living on the Havant–Gosport ridge and higher ground within Hayling Island, but would not have excluded the use of the land for occasional, probably seasonal, pasture (Fig 67). The move to the lowland of the study areas might also reflect the designation of land for burial away from the chalk and set apart from the previous systems (barrows) which is not a part of the later Bronze Age communities' 'ancestral land'.

Some further suggestions can be made regarding the use of the area as a cemetery. The urns themselves are, typically of this period, large and heavy (320×420mm and c 6kg). If nothing else this simple fact may be a clear indication that the northern harbour area was dry land at the time since carrying several kilograms of pottery vessel and bone over any distance across mud and through saltmarsh would be a daunting task (field team pers obs!). Settlement within this area has been recorded on Hayling Island within 500m of the current shoreline, but on slightly higher land. Several reasons can be offered to suggest that the whole funerary ritual may have taken place within the harbour area, as opposed to the higher fringes. The large spreads of burnt flint may well represent the remains of actual pyre sites. The clay which is, today, eroding from the cliffs would have been accessible and suitable for potting and the pots themselves are heavily flint-gritted. At least one pottery vessel (350) was clearly finger-finished and appeared to have been placed on a bed of straw, chaff, or grass during manufacture (see Chapter 4). In short, the funerary urns need not have been carried any distance, but were made 'on-site' using a by-product of the cremation process itself as one of the potting ingredients, for immediate deposition with the deceased. It is possible that most of the recovered later Bronze Age pottery relates specifically to funerary use of the area. A single cremation requires a pyre with about one tonne of good burning

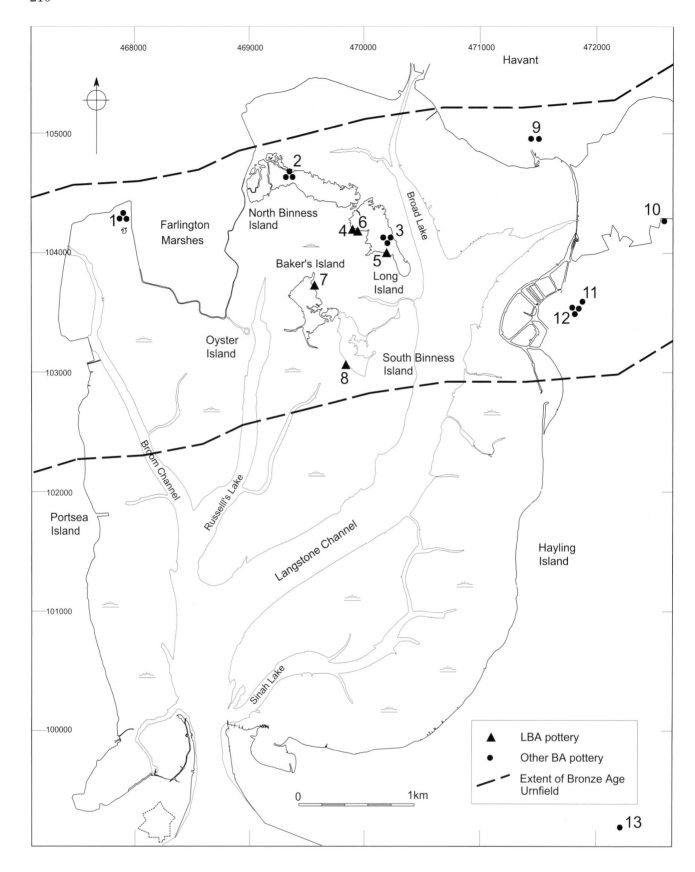

Figure 65 Location of buried later Bronze Age pottery vessels and postulated extent of the Bronze Age unfield cemetery. Drawn by S E James

(oak) wood (McKinley 1997b) and, by inference, some of the wood too must have been local and growing in the area. Not all of it could have been brought in.

Metalwork

Four Bronze Age metal hoards are reported from the Langstone hinterland, as well as a hoard of four solid rings and a looped palstave, and a single twisted spiral torc (Chapter 4) from within the harbour itself. The contents of most of these hoards have recently been described in detail by Lawson (1999) who draws attention to the predominance of palstaves in Hampshire middle Bronze Age hoards generally, and of the presence of ornaments (rings, a quoit headed pin, the torc). There is a distinct pattern in the distribution of palstave hoards of this period, the majority of Hampshire examples occurring on the coastal plain (*ibid*, fig 11.5). The Hayling Island I hoard is, in contrast, unusual in that not only does it also contain a number of late Bronze Age forms but its 'character is completely different' (Lawson 1999, 103). The palstave hoards contain essentially complete, 'working', examples of a very common tool type while the Hayling Island I hoard, in common with many definitively late Bronze Age hoards, includes a variety of tools and weapons and broken and molten items, including spearheads and probably a sickle. It was found with at least 30 sherds of heavy, flint-gritted pottery from a globular shaped urn with a rim diameter of *c* 120mm. Of fifteen late Bronze Age hoards in Hampshire, seven are dominated by weapons, and, of these, only the Hayling example occurs on the coastal plain (*ibid*, fig 11.8).

Richard Bradley (1990, chapter 3), drawing on work by Taylor (1982) and R Thomas, among others, has considered the role and significance of metal hoards. He reminds us of the connection between metal objects and 'watery places' but particularly draws our attention to the coincidence that the deposition of personal wealth (ie weapons and ornaments) in rivers (note the find of the torc) occurs at the same time that the custom of conspicuous burial in upstanding monuments is largely replaced by the development of flat urnfields. The two rites are hardly synonymous but there may be indications that the deposition of weapons and 'ritual' hoards is associated with the burial of individuals and the concomitant removal of their personal property from circulation. In the late Bronze Age, when the hoarding of broken tools and, especially, weapons becomes relatively common, it has generally been assumed that such deposits are utilitarian, representing the eminently sensible hoarding of recyclable metal. But, as Bradley points out, the nature of these hoards may be deceptive and there is a noticeable tendency for mixed hoards containing both weaponry and tools (as in the case of Hayling Island I) to occur in coastal or riverside locations where they more or less enclose the deposition of specifically watery deposits. Coastal hoards also frequently include imported metalwork from the Continent and an increasing emphasis on the value of exotic metal, even if in the form of ingots or broken artefacts, seems evident. Ingots are present in the Hayling Island I hoard.

The later Bronze Age sees widespread changes in many aspects of settlement, economy, and material culture and Bradley considers that the changes of emphasis apparent in the deposition of both individual watery deposits of metal weapons and of hoards are symptomatic of such changes '. . . if the provision of funerary offerings was detached from traditional locations and traditional burial rites, there would be scope for new developments. This is particularly true if the practice of making such gifts was assimilated into an equally long-lived tradition of votive offerings in watery locations – a tradition which had hitherto run in parallel to the provision of grave goods' (Bradley 1990, 136).

It may be in this sort of context that we can view the major assemblages of the later Bronze Age from Langstone Harbour. The area was a low-lying river basin which came to be used as a flat urnfield. The presence of metal hoards, most significantly of the Hayling Island I hoard, may not be indicative of settlement but of just the relationship outlined by Bradley. While it is certainly true that late Bronze Age settlements may survive as little more than pits and pots, the flint assemblage from Langstone does not suggest long-term sedentary activity, and the significant Bronze Age finds are specifically of large urns, probable pyre sites, fragments of human bone and metal hoards. Together these reinforce the picture that Langstone was peripheral to the main settlement area but held a special significance for funerary and associated rituals.

Specialised activities

The large, cordoned, and handled vessels (North Binness Island and Creek Field, Hayling Island) were not funerary urns, unlike the other large vessels. They represent unusual, almost unparalleled forms, but that from North Binness was ascribed to the later Bronze Age on the basis of fabric and general characteristics (see ApSimon, Chapter 4) even before confirmation by the radiocarbon determination. The function of such unusual vessels is unknown. ApSimon draws on parallels in Cornwall for vessel form, and suggests that such rare types may 'even have been used for special activities such as brewing and serving drink, or as containers of salt or brine' – an interpretation which is not at odds with other evidence from the survey area.

Although ApSimon (Chapter 4) dismisses another large vessel of later Bronze Age date from Isleham, on the south-east edge of Cambridgeshire (Coombs pers comm 1997), found associated with a Wilburton phase hoard, on the basis of ceramic form and style, this, and the two vessels reported here all have one

212

thing in common: their location. All three were found in areas known to be low-lying fen in the Bronze Age. ApSimon also provides a coherent argument for strong maritime associations with these and the other parallels he cites from Cornwall and Hardelot, Pas-de-Calais. It is plausible that they all relate to specific activities or functions peculiar to these landscapes, but as yet, this remains unknown. Saltworking may be one such activity, though at this stage this must remain conjectural.

Jetties and causeways

It was hoped that this research might recover evidence of Bronze Age, or at least prehistoric, waterlogged wooden structures such as have been found before (Williams and Soffe 1987, see Fig 66), but none was recovered, nor identified. In other intertidal surveys wooden structures, whose preservation had tended to suggest a post-medieval date, were proven by radiocarbon determinations to be of prehistoric origin. Although this is possible for some of the fishtraps around the harbour (Fontana, Chapter

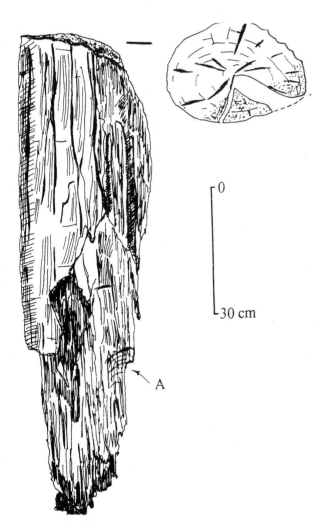

Figure 66 Wooden stake from North Hayling drawn by G Soffe (from Williams & Soffe 1987) with permission of the Hampshire Field Club

2), the nature, bracing elements, and jointing of others tend to confirm post-medieval, or possibly medieval, harbour jetties and associated structures – hardly surprising in a busy harbour. The record of close alignments of oak timber stakes (Williams and Soffe 1987) associated with 'an area of wattle' (HI.49), one timber of which dated to 1320–820 cal BC, at Northney on the north coast of Hayling Island is better understood in the light of recent excavations at Testwood Lake, Totton, north of Southampton (Fitzpatrick *et al* 1996a; 1996b). Here, wooden timber structures were originally considered to be jetties, but recent evidence (1999) indicates that they were causeways. Close set, sharpened, oak and alder timbers in the Blackwater valley, Essex (Wilkinson and Murphy 1995), provide evidence of major middle and late Bronze Age causeways (or jetties) across small channels. The evidence from Northney may well be a parallel, indicating the desire to reach Hayling Island, or the Langstone Harbour area, by the construction of a wooden causeway, over which probably both man and animals could pass. It reinforces the importance of the Langstone area and that in the late Bronze Age it remained an integral part of a much larger social and economic system, but was not the location of settlement or intensive activity.

Location of activities across the wider landscape

Just as Locock has defined the occurrence of a range of activities in specific topographic zones on the Avon Levels during the later Bronze Age (Locock forthcoming, fig 4), we can see a similar range and location of activities in the Langstone area (Fig 67). As with the Avon Levels (Locock forthcoming) we can define distinct topographic zones and apply the rudiments of Locock's model to the Langstone area.

Chalk Down and Chalk scarpfoot

Barrows lie on top of the Chalk Down and associated with them are field systems of the mature Bronze Age. Most, however, lie on the landward side with their aspect to the north, rather than the scarp slope towards the Langstone arena. The scarp itself, as well as the Downs, we can safely assume provided a good source of wood for burning and building on the lower land of the Langstone area.

Low-lying, but 'dry' land

The land fringing Langstone 'harbour' and lying at about 2–3m OD supported settlement, eg Gosport (Hall and Ford 1994) and Creek Field (this vol), and it is in this area, on Hayling Island in particular, that several metal hoards have been recovered (Lawson 1999), see above.

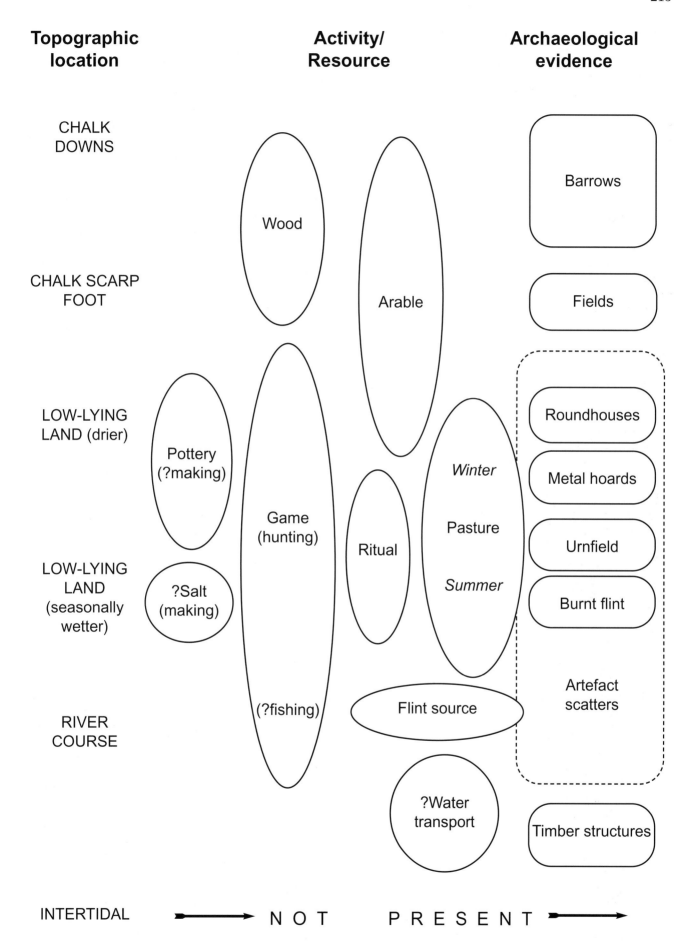

Topographic location

CHALK DOWNS

CHALK SCARP FOOT

LOW-LYING LAND (drier)

LOW-LYING LAND (seasonally wetter)

RIVER COURSE

INTERTIDAL

Activity/ Resource

Wood

Arable

Pottery (?making)

Game (hunting)

?Salt (making)

Ritual

Winter Pasture *Summer*

Flint source

(?fishing)

?Water transport

NOT PRESENT

Archaeological evidence

Barrows

Fields

Roundhouses

Metal hoards

Urnfield

Burnt flint

Artefact scatters

Timber structures

Figure 67   Model of the use of the various topographic zones in the later Bronze Age

Low-lying, seasonal wet / saltmarsh

Evidence indicates the use of this zone for craft activities, seasonal pasture, and possibly saltmaking. The origin of saltmaking in this area is undefined. There is evidence of localised saltwater conditions and brackish pools, and of the presence of large and unusual pottery vessels, but we have no secure evidence that saltworking occurred at this time, though we know it was well established in the later Iron Age.

River courses

The rivers provided access to flints and gravel – raw material for tools – as well as access to the sea by boat. Jetties, wharfs, or causeways were constructed into, or on the edge of, the larger rivers such as at the north end of Hayling Island (Williams and Soffe 1987).

Intertidal zone

The intertidal zone, in contrast to the Avon Levels and the Stumbles (Essex), did not exist as such within the majority of the Langstone study area. The exploitation, and indeed the location, of this zone in the later Bronze Age is not yet defined.

Iron Age and Romano-British

From the evidence of rising sea-levels and the parallels we can draw with Chichester Harbour and Fishbourne (see above), we can postulate that the area became distinctly wetter and more maritime in nature during the Iron Age and Romano-British periods. Although we cannot be precise about the nature of the 'harbour' at this time, a small rise in relative sea-level would make a significant impact upon the basin; the flooding of the rivers in their now very shallow, or almost non-existent, valleys would be locally extensive. The middle–late Bronze Age flat cemetery extending from the north-west corner of the harbour, through the islands to Hayling Island and Langstone, suggests a generally open, cleared tract of land rather than a dense complete woodland cover, although some woodland presumably existed to provide the fuel for the cremation pyres. The widening of the rivers by only slight changes in relative sea-level would flood relatively large areas of this low-lying basin, and saltwater ingression would have enabled expansion of the saltmarsh communities to the detriment to those of dry land. This provided the first major impetus for lateral erosion in the study area. Saltmarsh and brackish lagoons of a coastal inlet and proto-harbour existed in the early Iron Age, rapidly expanding, as relative sea-level rose, to a much larger harbour with fringing dry land. This compares well with the development and natural enlargement of Chichester Harbour around

Fishbourne over the same period, and presumably the inner reaches of Portsmouth Harbour too (Fig 68). A period of changing local landscape does not necessarily hinder, nor arrest, the range of activities comprising prehistoric behavioural patterns. In the Welsh Severn Levels, for instance, Bell *et al* (2000) found that it was precisely during periods of change that many of the activities and settlement for which they found evidence occurred.

Iron Age–early Roman

Saltworking

Although we have indicated that much of the 'Iron Age' pottery recorded by Bradley and Hooper (1973) can more appropriately be considered to be later Bronze Age in date, this may not apply to most of the material associated with briquetage. The associated quantities of briquetage, hearths, and Iron Age pottery can safely be considered to provide evidence of Iron Age saltworking (Bradley and Hooper 1973; Bradley 1975). Much of this seems to be later Iron Age and associated with saucepan-style pots, as at Creek Field, and also at Paulsgrove in Portsmouth Harbour (Bradley and Hooper 1973).

Iron Age evidence is limited in the study area and most is associated with saltworking, as Bradley has previously indicated (1975; 1992). The recent survey recovered a solitary fragment of briquetage from the islands, primarily suggesting that the evidence has been eroded away, and the relevant areas of Hayling are now either buried in mud or under concrete. Although our fieldwork failed to recover much evidence of this activity, we have been able to draw upon the unpublished evidence of late Iron Age saltworking pans on Hayling Island excavated by M Rule (see Bradley 1992; and HI.72). With this and the site at Paulsgrove as exceptions, none of the briquetage was in sealed stratified contexts; it was found on the intertidal surfaces associated with pottery scatters and finds. Saltworking, or the recovery of briquetage, 'kiln furniture', and burnt flints, is evident in a number of locations in Langstone, as it is in Chichester and Portsmouth Harbours. These occur especially along the west coast of Hayling Island adjacent to Creek Field (HI.38, HI.69, and HI.77), in North Binness Island Bay (NB.91, NB.126, probably largely of Romano-British date), and in the north-west corner of the harbour along the western margins of Farlington Marshes (FM.31, FM.33, FM.57, FM.119, FM.120, and FM.123). The most significant is the salt production site complete with 'boiling pits' and flues in Creek Field, Hayling Island (HI.72).

There remain some ambiguities over the date of origin of this industry. Although finds at Creek Field and some along the margins of Hayling Island are undoubtedly Iron Age, some of the pottery associated with distributions of briquetage may be later Bronze Age, although this has not been confirmed. We no

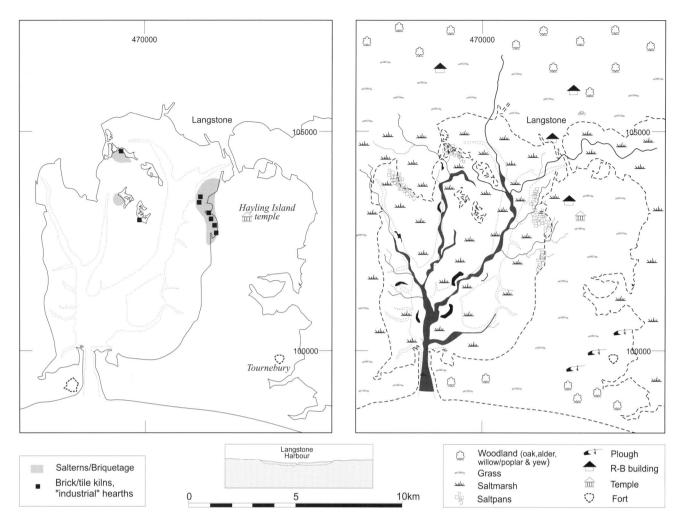

Figure 68   a) (left) Distribution of the late Iron Age and Romano-British activity in the harbour and b) (right) reconstruction of the late Iron Age / Romano-British landscape and activities. Drawn by S E James

longer have the direct association of pottery and briquetage (Bradley and Hooper 1973) because much of the material could not be relocated in Portsmouth Museum at the time of the survey. Since some, but not all, of the pottery reported by Bradley and Hooper (*op cit*) can now be redated to the late Bronze Age this opens the possibility that some of the briquetage may also be of this date, and one of the postulated functions of the large globular Bronze Age pots might also connect them with salt and brine. This would be exciting, but unusual as saltworking evidence this early is still very rare in the British Isles. Only two Bronze Age saltworking sites are known; one at Brean Down, Somerset (*c* 1700–1600 cal BC) where the evidence was associated with roundhouses in the sandcliff (Bell 1990) and the other in the Hullbridge Basin (River Crouch, Essex) dated to 1460–1000 cal BC (HAR-5733, 3020 ± 90 BP; Wilkinson and Murphy 1986, 187; 1995). Furthermore, the environmental evidence from Langstone does not indicate the strongly coastal locations seen at both Brean and Hullbridge Basin, in fact, although brackish conditions existed, the size of open water is likely to have been small. Given that the survey found virtually no Iron Age pottery (Table 15) and no briquetage, we cannot be sure how much

of the briquetage is Iron Age, or even Roman, but we must assume it is more likely to belong to this later date. Although we can speculate on these earlier origins and parallel them with other late Bronze Age sites in southern England, the local evidence is not yet convincing. Undoubtedly this is an area for further research but, without firm dates for the briquetage recorded by Bradley and Hooper (1973), we must await that research before embarking upon any further speculation.

Occupation and settlement

There is, in fact, very little evidence for other activity in the harbour area during the later part of the Iron Age, apart from the temple site and a less well-known univallate fort (Tournerbury Camp) on Hayling Island. How much the temple reflects the importance of the saltworking industries in both Langstone and Chichester Harbours remains questionable, but there might be some meaningful relationship between the presence of a temple and its associated economy, and the salt industry (Fig 68).

Notably, Iron Age wetlands elsewhere in the country which supported saltmarshes have been able to reveal evidence of short-term and temporary occupation with wooden buildings and the use of the area as seasonal pasture (Goldcliff; Bell *et al* 2000). No evidence of this has yet been recovered from Langstone, but neither have many of the wooden structures around the harbour been recorded in detail or dated in this survey. We are, therefore, unsure of the role of the Langstone area, or even the harbour, in the Iron Age: the fort and temple have already been mentioned, but in the wider landscape there are major hillforts, settlements, and cemeteries at the Trundle, Chichester, and Westhampnett. In social terms, Langstone appears to have been relatively unimportant and this may not have been purely a 'natural' or accidental development. Although lying firmly within the territory of the Atrebates in the later Iron Age, Langstone has been shown to lie on the boundary of two major Iron Age coin distributions (Sellwood 1984). It is also within the area that is most likely to have come under Roman influence at a comparatively early stage and which may well have seen considerable political and social upheaval in the last centuries BC. This is not the place to review the relationships between the native tribes, the Roman Empire and the Belgae (see, for instance, Cunliffe 1991, chapter 6), but it is undoubtedly true that the coastal regions to the east of Langstone were heavily influenced (and ultimately invaded) by Rome while at least one major trading emporium on the western part of the Solent coast developed at Hengistbury Head, providing a focus for cross-channel trade.

Of the Solent 'harbours' it was Chichester that ultimately became of greatest importance – presumably for political reasons as much as anything – eclipsing Hengistbury and eventually boasting not only *oppidum* status but also the early Roman palace at Fishbourne. Langstone, without the deliberate modifications made at Chichester, may have been little more than a rather smelly, muddy marshland during the late Iron Age–early Roman period. It seems, literally, to have been a quiet backwater, peripheral to the areas of socio-political control and extensive agricultural and market systems, and marginal in terms of its environment and economic resources.

Romano-British

The relatively small quantity of Roman pottery recovered during the survey spans all four centuries of Roman rule though with a slight emphasis on the earlier part of that period. Although in comparison with the Bronze Age pottery (Table 15), 526 sherds of Romano-British pottery seems a high total, we must bear in mind a number of aspects. Pottery in the Roman period was a much more common and widespread commodity than in prehistory; Romano-British pottery is kiln-fired at relatively high temperatures and generally has fine inclusions (sand etc) rather than having been fired in bonfire clamps at low temperatures and tempered with coarse flint grits. The result is that the durability of the pottery is significantly different. The Bronze Age pottery is much more friable and considerably less robust, as was demonstrated by the leather-hard condition and final disintegration of vessel 521 from Baker's Island. In short, the fact that nearly 50% of the pottery sherds are Romano-British cannot be used as a relative comparison of importance or of intensity of use during this period.

The assemblage contains the usual range of fabrics and forms found in collections from small-scale, rural farming communities in southern England and all elements of it can be paralleled among the larger collections from the vicinity (eg Fulford 1975b; Cunliffe 1971). It is overwhelmingly dominated by sherds of sandy grey coarsewares derived from the major sources of ceramic supply to this area. Interestingly, Black Burnished ware is absent. Continental imports are restricted to a handful of samian sherds. Late Roman finewares from British sources were also scarce, represented by a few sherds from the Oxfordshire and New Forest industries.

The coarsewares indicate their use for everyday food preparation, serving, and storage purposes, while the very small quantities of samian, New Forest, and Oxfordshire wares represent finer tablewares. There is no evidence from either the quantity or the quality of the pottery to suggest large-scale or high-status settlement and although the harbour would, by this time, have been ideally located as a centre for both coastal and cross-channel trade, the scarcity of ceramic imports indicates that this potential was not exploited during the Roman period. It is possible that the sherds derive from small-scale settlement activity, possibly largely based on an agricultural or pastoral economy, although no definite traces of settlement were identified by the survey. Equally they may relate to more specific activities such as saltworking, brick or tile manufacture, and oyster farming, for which there is certainly evidence, though currently not more closely datable.

The evidence for the later Romano-British period, therefore, probably indicates contained 'native' activity (not settlement) with isolated exploitation representing low-level local industries. Unlike Chichester, no major Roman roads converge on the area; there are no palaces or Saxon Shore Forts; and only a couple of modest villas in the neighbourhood. One major Roman road passes to the north of Langstone Harbour linking *Noviomagus* (Chichester) to Portchester and *Clausentum* (Bitterne, Southampton); it rather by-passes Langstone Harbour. A smaller road does link Rowlands Castle, a local pottery production centre, to Hayling Island, and we can suggest that pottery and salt were exchanged along this route.

Some of the briquetage scatters reported previously (Bradley and Hooper 1973; Bradley 1975) are associated with Romano-British fabrics; again located in the principle areas of Iron Age saltworking on the fringes of Farlington Marshes (FM.84, FM.86

and FM.87), west coast of Hayling Island (HI.75, and HI.76), and North Binness bay (NB.88, NB.91). Thus, the saltworking industry continued well into the Roman period, and Langstone was noted for its salt in these times. Records as early as *c* AD 410 mention the superior quality of the salt from around the shores of Hayling Island (see Fontana and Fontana, Chapter 2). Saltmaking may have been more than just a small local affair, but need not necessarily indicate importance, high status, nor even major settlement and associated occupation with this low-intensity, seasonal industry. Lack of evidence of major Roman settlement or building activity supports this view. There is, however, evidence of settlement, or villas, on the higher land at Langstone village, and on the west coast of Hayling Island. Further structures are suspected in Havant itself (Hughes 1976, 70–2), which may have been a small Roman town. Despite the influence and effect of Romanisation in the surrounding areas, with the palace at Fishbourne in the early period and emerging importance of Portchester in the later, Langstone Harbour and its margins seem largely to have remained unchanged in socio-economic terms from the later Iron Age. It remained a relatively quiet backwater, peripheral to these other important centres, but playing its part in servicing them and their communities in its own small way.

Although we can speculate that amongst local industries was oyster fishing, there is no archaeological nor historical evidence to support this. We know that oysters existed, but were not necessarily fished or farmed, in Chichester Harbour (note the oyster shell on the Roman helmet dredged from Chichester Harbour). Elsewhere in Britain, low-lying coastal fringes were subject to major reclamation. Along the Severn Estuary in both South Wales (Allen and Fulford 1986) and Gloucestershire (Allen and Fulford 1990) and Avon (Rippon 1997) in England, land was enclosed, embanked, and reclaimed for agriculture and pasture (Rippon 1996). At none of the south-coast harbours (Portsmouth, Langstone, nor Chichester) is this paralleled nor is there any similar evidence. This is discussed further below.

The use of the Langstone area was for low-level exploitation of salt, possibly of oysters, and of additional seasonal grazing of the marsh and meadow. In terms of economy, activity, and social status it was far from the busy centres of Chichester, villas such as those at Chilgrove and Upmarden (Down 1979), or even other rural centres such as Westhampnett.

Saxon

There is little archaeological evidence from this survey, or previous archaeological investigations, of Saxon activity in the area. The main source of evidence is the confused historical records of an ecclesiastical establishment on Hayling Island (see Archaeological background, Chapter 1) and the

surviving Sinah circle oyster parc (cal AD 980–1180 – assuming that the timber is not reused from an earlier structure). With such sparse evidence we can elaborate little except to say that these two sites may not be unconnected; it may not be coincidental that an oystery survives, perhaps one that served ecclesiastical patrons: see for instance Winder's discussion (1991) in relation to oyster middens in Poole Harbour and their monastic connection.

This lack of activity is perhaps surprising in view of the earlier evidence of activity and of the rich harbour and harbour-edge resources available in the Saxon period. Intertidal salt and flood marshes elsewhere around the British Isles show major phases of reclamation by enclosure and embankment from the 10th century onwards. Large areas of reclamation can be seen in Norfolk, the Welsh and English Severn Estuary, and the Thames Estuary. Indeed, by the 10th century most coastal margins show embankment and drainage and, by the medieval period, reclamation was evident and the improvement of embanked and reclaimed land can be seen to be significant, reflected in higher land values and taxation records (Rippon 1999).

Medieval and post-medieval activity

We have dealt primarily with the prehistoric development and use of the area. By the medieval period Langstone was certainly a harbour in which fishing, oyster farming, and saltworking were important industries (VCH 1908; 1912). A number of fishtraps (*cf* Bannerman and Jones 1999) and oyster parcs were recorded around the harbour. A find of a wooden barbed harpoon from the channel linking Langstone with Chichester Harbour has been dated by AMS radiocarbon dating to the 13th–14th centuries AD. Although this artefact seems to be unparalleled in the British record, it is a harpoon-type implement ideally suited to the catching of flatfish in shallow water.

Site/find	Material	Lab no	Result BP	Calibration
Sinah circle, this vol	oak stake OO	GU-7275	980 ± 50	cal AD 980–1180
Harpoon (Allen and Pettitt 1997)	wooden harpoon	OxA-6459	710 ± 40	cal AD 1230–1390

By the 12th–13th centuries mixed agriculture was practised in widespread reclaimed saltmarsh landscapes around Britain. They were especially used for arable cultivation; they were not marginal landscapes but rich farming land. Pressure to use this land and the expense of embankment and reclamation was compensated by the fertility, use, and higher value of the land (Rippon 1999).

At Langstone, and indeed Chichester and Portsmouth, we see no such embankment and reclamation despite the known important Saxon and medieval population and the presence of potential markets. We must conclude that the reason lies not in a difference in the size and significance of the populations, but in the nature of this saltmarsh at Langstone during the 5th–15th centuries. It seems evident that only thin strips of coastal saltmarshes existed, rather than the large expanses such as are seen especially in the Severn Estuary. This limited extent of saltmarsh made the large investment in time and fiscal resources unjustified at Langstone.

Post-medieval wooden structures

A number of wooden structures have been recorded and mapped in the harbour and along its edge. A number are long alignments of stakes and posts almost certainly relating to fishing (*cf* Salisbury 1991) and other marine activities. One circular structure (the Sinah circle) was found comprising about 24 oak posts in a circle of about 11m diameter. Analysis of the wood suggested a medieval or post-medieval date, but they provided a Saxon radiocarbon determination from a roundwood post carefully selected as being less obviously reused driftwood, and excavation of the posts showed that they had been driven into soft sediments (rather than dropped into an excavated posthole). This pointed to a structure constructed in the intertidal zone, and may relate to other structures used for oyster fishing and breeding. Indeed oyster fishers are known in the harbour in the 19th century, though the only direct parallel for this structure is known in Lago Fusaro, Italy. Significantly, there are documentary records of direct contact between oyster fishers here and those in Lago Fusaro (Yonge 1960).

Discussion and conclusions: preconceptions and marginality

We recognise that in all of our collections and reconstructions there are local biases in recovery and redistribution of artefacts within the harbour. These are discussed in detail in Chapters 2 and 6. Intertidal areas as a whole also suffer from skewed destruction through continued phases of regression and transgression (Louwe Kooijmans 1993). In Langstone, however, the development of the 'harbour' does not seem to have suffered this cyclical type of regime, as the creation of the harbour, and thus the intertidal zone, occurs relatively late in the history of its development. It has largely suffered continual regression, or lateral erosion.

Although most of the artefact scatters reside on the upper wave-exposed surfaces devoid of contemporaneous deposits, this maritime, wave-cut local environment is anathema to the artefact scatters. The long held belief that Langstone was a drowned landscape, like many harbours of the south coast (Dyer 1975), has been disproved. Apart from the narrow, deeply incised buried former courses of the Broom

and Langstone channels which may contain narrow strips of earlier Mesolithic (9000–7000 BC), Atlantic, and Sub-boreal land surfaces, the main area of Langstone Harbour is largely eroded and eroding. The assumption and hope that there might be extensive areas of submerged prehistoric land surfaces seems to be unfounded.

Physically these intertidal and fringing 'harbour' areas are considered, today, to be 'marginal'; indeed they represent the zone where present-day land and sea meet. Their low-lying situations, propensity to flooding and groundwater seepage, and soft geology, make them marginal areas for the construction of modern domestic houses; they are not suitable for residential settlement at the start of the 3rd millennium AD without considerable modification. Archaeologically and conceptually they are also often considered to be marginal in the sense that the areas were not of great importance to prehistoric or historic communities; they were superfluous regions which did not provide significant contributions to the economy and lifestyle. Although, today, many of these areas are indeed marginal for settlement, we must be wary of the preconception since, in fact, in many areas, as has been discussed above, quite the reverse may be true (see Louwe Kooijmans 1993).

The area need not be in constant, nor intensive, use to make it important, if not key, to economy and lifestyle. The uses of the harbour area extend to prehistoric societies who lived outside the locality, and whose necessities and needs were provided for by the area now defined as Langstone Harbour. One of the significant aspects of the Langstone area is its lack of general domestic debris such as pottery and bone. Much of the prehistoric pottery represents placed, funerary items. Bone was generally sparse. This contrasts with other intertidal survey areas such as Goldcliff (Bell *et al* 2000) and Hullbridge (Wilkinson and Murphy 1995). Large quantities of domestic refuse and even prehistoric structures were found in the former, and large assemblages of Neolithic pottery, requiring little, or no, excavation were exposed on surfaces in the latter. The preservation and large quantities of artefacts seem to be features of many intertidal zones; Langstone is no exception, but here those artefacts (largely flint scatters) represent predominantly resource procurement rather than use.

The environmental evidence has indicated that a marine flavour to the area did not really develop until later prehistory, and thus many of the activities prior to this were involved with the exploitation of dry-land fauna and flora of low-lying terrestrial habitats. The area provided a hunting ground for herds of animals, raw materials (flints), and later, grazing or herding for domesticates and even, possibly, local small-scale cultivation.

The area was first exploited for its terrestrial resources, then its marine resources (salt, fish, oysters), and now for marine recreation; ie it is the water itself that now provides the resource-base in human terms. In this respect then, we can see the role of the area shifting its position through time in the requirements of the population – it *has* become progressively more marginal in economic terms throughout prehistory and early-historic times. In historic times it played an important role in the fishing industry but now is largely exploited for recreation – thus we can see renewed importance to the local communities in the post-medieval and modern times. Ironically it is this tranquil marine environment that is largely responsible for destroying the evidence of its past use.

Why is there no permanent or seasonal prehistoric settlement in this area?

Many other intertidal zones are characterised by settlement, whether permanent or seasonal, and the exploitation of locally diverse resources. In many cases human activity is seen to occur, not during periods of landscape stability, but during periods of change engendered by changing relative sea-level. We might expect, therefore, evidence of structures and of domestic or specialised seasonal dwellings especially during the later Bronze Age to later Iron Age when the major changes in the physiography of the area occurred. Certainly the low-lying dry land was exploited for funerary purposes in the mid to later Bronze Age and the new and changing marine resources for saltworking in the mid to later Iron Age. No evidence of seasonal dwellings associated with pasture or agriculture, nor any artefact assemblages of this nature have been recovered during this, or previous, surveys. More permanent settlement evidence may have been lost to the harbour itself, which represents about 76% of the study area, but most seems to be on the slightly higher ground of Hayling and Portsea Islands. This provides land more suitable for long-term settlement, within easy daily access of the lower land of the Langstone basin. It is this local configuration that has probably ensured that the basin was devoid of the structures and settlement seen at Wootton-Quarr, Isle of Wight (Tomalin *et al* forthcoming), Goldcliff (Bell *et al* 2000) and Hullbridge (Wilkinson and Murphy 1995). All other sites are located on more simple planar surfaces which have suffered inundation, exposure, and erosion. Langstone has a locally simple, but more complex topography than these sites.

Conclusions

The following statements can be made and conclusions may be drawn:

- For much of the prehistoric period the area was low-lying coastal plain bisected by probably two rivers (the Langstone and Broom Channels) but with low-lying freshwater pools and mires.
- Langstone was not a marine inlet of any size until the Iron Age (after *c* 800 BC).

- Langstone is an eroded not a drowned landscape. The islands are relics of the former mainland, but lower pools did exist, represented by the submerged alder carr woodland.
- No evidence for permanent or long-term domestic settlement has been found within the current harbour area during any period. It seems to have been used at various times for the exploitation of specific, possibly seasonal, resources including flint, salt, oysters, and grazing.
- The area was not 'marginal' for most of the prehistoric period. Although we consider the area to be marginal today, it can only be considered as such in terms of construction of settlement and domestic buildings. In prehistoric terms it contained a wide and diverse range of resources which were specifically exploited and complemented prehistoric occupation nearby. Langstone provided an ideal ecotonal location and was exploited as such through its changing physical and ecological history.
- Human activity throughout the prehistoric–Romano-British periods was sporadic and specific.

The main activities for each episode of activity can be summarised as follows:

- Mesolithic (*c* 6000–4500 BC): exploitation of flint sources. Flints were exploited locally from gravels eroding in the river banks – other activity is not visible, this area was just one part of a larger Mesolithic arena.
- Late Neolithic–early Bronze Age (*c* 2500–1600 BC): seasonal activity, probably mainly grazing and some hunting. An important resource area to complement the hunting, farming, and foraging Neolithic life style, evidence for which ranges across the coastal plain and on the Downs locally.
- Middle–late Bronze Age (*c* 1400–850 BC): grazing, funerary activity, ?saltworking and ?metalworking, metal hoarding. An important resource area, probably at least one urnfield, grazing, saltworking industries to accompany evidence for settlement as represented on Hayling Island, at Gosport, and on Portsdown and the Downs beyond.
- Romano-British (AD 43–510): Saltworking, ?oyster farming, ?brick/tile manufacture. The quantity of Roman pottery is low compared to any Roman site, it is nearly all local, low-status domestic wares.
- The islands are currently eroding, removing the archaeological evidence and its context. Erosion of the islands is evident from the auger survey and from limited present erosion studies. Many of the findspots and features recorded in earlier work are now beyond the intertidal zone. Most of our recent information however only represent two or three decades, whereas, archaeologically, we are talking of between 200 and 1000 decades of erosion – we have therefore observed it over just 0.002–1.5% of the time it has occurred, which is hardly representative.

Examining the large body of data this project has collected and the 53 new SMR records ('sites', distinct scatters, features etc) it has produced (Appendix 2), only serves to emphasise all the significant elements of the project. The fact that so much was recovered indicates erosion and renewal of the archaeological artefacts on intertidal areas. Changes in the overall distributions and chronology reflected, reinforces the variability of the distribution.

Palaeolithic	0
Mesolithic	5
Neolithic	3
Neolithic/Bronze Age	5
Bronze Age	15
Bronze Age/Iron Age	2
Iron Age	0
Iron Age/Romano-British	0
Romano-British	3
Saxon	1
medieval	2
post-medieval	7
undated	10

List of the new 'sites' discovered by this project, by period.

The distribution of these sites by period also emphasises the periods of activity resulting from debris (artefact) loss and past activity. And this is reflected too, in the weight and comprehension of our understanding of each period, and in the discussion presented above.

8 Langstone Harbour multidisciplinary project: a retrospective

Archaeological work in the terrestrial and intertidal zones
by Michael J Allen and Neil J Adam

Site and structure survey: the walkover survey

The general walkover survey of the harbour was extremely successful in detecting previously unknown archaeological sites. The location and mapping of the material scatters was probably one of the most important contributions to the archaeological aspect of the Langstone Harbour Survey, in that it not only mapped the areas of high archaeological potential but also discovered a sedimentological relationship between the firm clays and archaeological deposits. The walkover survey also found the features off North Binness Island, the only evidence so far for pre-medieval 'settlement' on any of the islands. In the course of the survey the team also noted a number of important aspects relating to the processes of erosion and deposition around the harbour.

Against these results it can also be said that the survey was severely limited in a number of ways. For practical reasons it was limited to the foreshore and the intertidal zone. Although an attempt was made to extend the search area with a swimover survey, this was not very effective (see below). In addition, large areas of the intertidal zone at many points around the islands and the coast itself were too dangerous to traverse because of the depths of soft muds and survey could not be extended across these areas (see Fig 8). As a consequence, less than a third of the intertidal zone exposed at low water was visited during the two seasons of walkover survey. The tides severely limited the length of time available for investigation each day and would often require working either very early in the morning or late in the evening.

The walkover survey was conducted by teams of no more than three archaeologists and may have been more effective with a slightly larger team. However, numbers were limited in Langstone because of the environmentally sensitive nature of the area, most of which is an RSPB bird sanctuary. The walkover survey proved good at finding surface scatters and exposed features but, just as terrestrial fieldwalking is very effective on ploughed fields but of limited use in pasture, so comparable survey was not effective on land covered by vegetation.

Test-pitting and excavation

Test-pit excavations were conducted in an attempt to relate the stratigraphy of the islands to the artefacts found scattered on their intertidal foreshores. The number of test-pits was limited because of the sensitive nature of the environment and saltmarsh through which excavation was conducted.

Physical excavation was problematic. The saturated nature of the clay-rich soils of the saltmarsh meant that excavation was a slow and messy business, and the test-pits themselves quickly became flooded, even in the summer, before a full sequence of deposits could be uncovered and recorded. Despite the wealth of artefacts both on the foreshore and within the cliff sections, only one test-pit (of nine excavated) recovered any archaeological material. In retrospect almost as much information would have been gained from a series of auger holes which would have been more expedient and less intrusive.

Features on the foreshore that were investigated by excavation were only exposed for a few daylight hours, leaving limited time in which to work, and the nature and size of the excavation had to be limited. During excavation of features, as with the test-pitting, the saturated nature of the deposits and proximity to sea-level meant that the physical mechanics of digging and spoil management were problematic. Continual flooding of features at high tide required pumping and re-cleaning of excavated deposits and sections at the beginning of each day.

Artefact collection strategies (and analysis strategies)

Artefact collection strategies, both during the walkover survey (see above) and in controlled total artefact collection (Table 1), were highly effective and efficient. The walkover survey enabled selection of suitable areas for more rigorous collection policies. All artefact collection was, however, limited to the firmer, upper intertidal zones. Areas around the north of the islands were prone to sediment influx and the soft mud here could not be searched.

Augering

The use of a simple gouge auger was highly successful on land, within the intertidal zone and underwater. The only area inaccessible to augering was the soft intertidal muds that were inaccessible at low tide, and at high tide were too shallow to enable diving. The augering was very rapid and effective; in excess of 100 augerholes of up to 3.5m depth were recorded by a two-man team in fewer than five days.

Mapping in the harbour

The use of GPS equipment which enabled the use of single 'radar probes' at relatively long distances from fixed stations was probably the only effective way of recording such rapidly collected and disparate arrays of data in such wide ranging, and often treacherous, conditions. The only failure of the survey was purely a logistical, rather than mechanical, one. As teams from different organisations undertook the archaeological survey and the mapping it was not always possible or cost-effective for them to be in the field together. All points to be surveyed and recorded were marked with labelled canes, but in some cases these were lost to the sea or by the weather before they could be recorded. As a consequence, for instance, 25% of the 135 auger points were not recorded (see Table 2). This was also true of some of the archaeological features and excavations which were recorded thoroughly by tape, but not inputted into the project GIS.

Conclusions: project time-scales and efficacy

The fieldwork required for a project in this type of terrain cannot be conducted wholly during short-duration intensive fieldwork campaigns as on terrestrial sites. The unpredictable and constantly changing nature of the local environment precludes this. Most fieldwork tasks are subject to uncertainty of individual tides as well as the weather making conditions that are less easy to combat in intertidal environments than wholly terrestrial landscapes. Tasks in locations at low water are severely restricted by the tides and, even during the limited time-period available, effort usually has to be expended cleaning up after the tidal ingression and re-establishing some basic points.

General survey, in particular, is most appropriately conducted by small teams carrying out small scale searches over long periods of time; the complete antithesis to terrestrial excavation which may best be conducted by large teams working intensively over short periods. Thus, intertidal projects are not easily conducted within the time-scales, nor fieldwork frameworks, designed primarily for projects on dry land. Further, the constantly changing and eroding nature of these landscapes means that no survey can be definitive. Unlike in conventional fieldwalking surveys, where material may be moved up and down the soil profile and laterally across field surfaces but, nevertheless, remains present in the ploughsoil, intertidal surveys record a sample of the material that is exposed and available *only* during the time of survey. A return visit, even a few days later, may record a completely different assemblage. As such, it is necessary to repeat the exercise at suitable intervals to re-evaluate the evidence (see recommendations for further research, below) as this project has done for some of the evidence reported previously by Bradley and Hooper (1973). Biases in

the assemblages recorded by these two surveys are largely due to the erosion, removal, or inaccessibility of some areas and artefacts, rather than to differences in the recovery methods. In fact, the difference in recovery between the two surveys is important in emphasising this bias, and in Langstone is most markedly seen in the wealth of briquetage recovered in the 1960s compared with the dearth of such material recovered during the present survey.

Working underwater: an evaluation of the underwater methodologies
by Garry Momber

The underwater work throughout the Langstone Harbour Project was conducted as an extension of the terrestrial studies. The seamless approach was adopted where certain survey methods used on land were continued below the water. In addition, a variety of other techniques were used to determine their effectiveness in the harbour environment.

Archaeology underwater

It is easy to overlook and underestimate the constraints faced by archaeologists working underwater. When archaeological tasks are performed on land the emphasis is on the methodology deployed and skill of the practitioner to complete them accurately. Underwater, the environment is totally alien. Before archaeological skills can be utilised, mastery of the weightless submarine world must be accomplished.

On land the project manager is seldom concerned with the ability of his field workers to deal with their working environment. Below the water, without total control, the material being studied may easily be disturbed or destroyed. These problems are compounded where the water is turgid and subject to tidal movement as in Langstone Harbour. Even where currents are light, deposition can cause problems as the seabed can be covered in a soft film of sediments which, if disturbed, cause visual blackouts. Consequently, survey underwater needs to be flexible, it involves considerable preparation and is a much more time consuming exercise than on land.

The constraints imposed by diving and working in the Langstone Harbour environment result from the following problems:

- Limited visibility and clarity
- Image deformation due to optical distortions of water
- Distorted perception resulting from exposure to pressure in the underwater environment
- Difficulty in navigating because of limited visibility and currents
- Adverse weather conditions disturbing visibility or preventing diving
- Water movement affecting controlled searching

- Disturbance of suspended or seafloor sediments by divers
- Marine floral growth obscuring seabed or plankton obscuring visibility

Swimover survey

Swimover surveys were restricted to the south shores of North Binness and Long Islands. The survey was hampered by a substantial covering of marine growth obscuring the seabed. The weed itself was covered by a deposit of silt so, when this was disturbed, vision was totally obscured. Silty seabeds make searching for small objects, such as flints, very difficult. The presence of silts suggests that the artefacts may be buried and, unless there is a current able to disperse disturbed sediment, attempting to shift and investigate below is futile. Nevertheless, where the bed was less obscured, the method was successful, even though little was found and thus the results were initially disappointing.

For a swimover survey to be more effective in this environment, a water suction dredge could be used to help clear the seabed of the overburden and suspended sediments, allowing the diver a clearer view of the seafloor.

Swimline/corridor surveys and circular and contour searches

All more controlled searches suffer the same problems of visibility described above. These surveys were very effective when searching for larger objects (rather than archaeological artefacts such as flints and pottery sherds) especially in areas where the seabed contained coarse-grained material. They proved to be quick and efficient once the baselines had been established.

Circular searches were of limited value in low-visibility water as many concentric circles needed to be performed to gain good coverage and a single search with a 30m radius required a swim of almost 200m. Tidal problems were also encountered and further difficulties with baselines snagging on undulations in the seabed – a problem that was not readily apparent in low visibility. In retrospect, this method was not suitable for large controlled survey in Langstone Harbour. It was, however, a good method for identification of the seabed topography and seabed material.

Contour searches proved effective on inclines. The main limitation was the inability to locate the position of small objects accurately which were more effectively located during swimline and corridor searches.

The swimline and corridor surveys took a little longer to set up, but once they were in place survey was quick and efficient. Problems included the growth of weed (described above) and disturbance of the seabed.

Site surveys: Direct Survey Measurement (DSM)

Archaeological sites were recorded using DSM where accurate sets of relative positions could be calculated. A network of measurements was taken between points on the objects to be surveyed and the data was input into the 'Web For Windows' software. This form of survey proved to be quick and efficient, but as it only gives the spatial relationship between points, further detailed recording is necessary to record the surveyed objects.

Wreck surveys

Evaluation of the Homer system

The Sonardyne Homer is an underwater acoustic measuring system consisting of transponders, beacons, and a hand held unit. The hand-held unit interrogates beacons with an acoustic signal. The return time for the signals to pass between the hand unit and the transponder is measured and the distances through water are calculated.

The comparative accuracy of the Homer unit proved to be within 0.01m. The main problem with the equipment is in maintaining a stable fixed position for the hand-held transmitting unit as readings are taken from each of the beacons. This can be very difficult under the influence of swell and current or without a solid holdfast. Nevertheless, Homer provided an effective method for general survey, especially over longer distances providing a very valuable time saving tool. Tape measures were quicker and more accurate over short distances.

Tape measured surveys

Surveys of the *Irishman*, the *Withern*, and the *Excelsior* were conducted with a tape measure. At longer distances the tape measure bowed with the currents, resulting in differences in readings of over 6%. For instance, the distance between the transponders on the *Withern* was recorded as 34.9m using the Homer Unit, but 37.2m using a tape measure.

Augering

Augering was undertaken using narrow gouge augers. It would have been less successful if the substrate was harder or deeper as the only force available underwater is the inertia the diver is able to generate by moving up and down. Augering proved very successful and accurate in the silty clay of the Langstone Harbour bed, the less successful element was not the augering itself, but the acquisition of accurate locations of the seabed auger point using the GPS.

Conclusions
by Michael J Allen

There can be no doubt that the underwater aspect of this project completed our seamless approach. The results of the underwater augering, in particular, provided the basis for our understanding of the physical development of the harbour, and the use of the harbour in later years was highlighted by the work on the Sinah circle. Most of the underwater activities were highly successful. Underwater work in Langstone throughout was hampered by poor visibility and much of the bottom surface was obscured by vegetation growth at the time of the survey. One major practical factor stands out from this survey work. Underwater activities require considerably higher investment in person-time than any comparable land-based task and usually take many times longer. They require a much more planned and considered approach, even before entering the water, than most dry-land based tasks. Further, all tasks such as searching, excavation, and recording take much longer underwater; divers are restricted by the length of each individual dive, and by the physical differences with working in air. A comprehensive survey and search of large areas of the sea bottom is not feasible underwater as it might be on dry land, due to the considerable investment of time that would be needed for satisfactory completion. Accordingly some modifications or adaptations of methodology are required to accommodate this, usually by designing a suitable sample-search strategy.

The seamless approach was a success, providing excellent parity with the results from land-based fieldwork. Parity in the time expended to collect those results, however, can never be achieved and any future research design needs to take account of this and design and modify all fieldwork programmes accordingly.

Multidisciplinary multi-team project: a retrospective
by Michael J Allen and Dominic Fontana

Coordination and concept

Survey review (GPS)

In order that all archaeological points such as auger holes, survey grids, and recorded cliff-section points could be surveyed either by GPS survey or Total Station survey, the archaeological field team placed tagged canes at all significant points. This was intended to enable the archaeological field team and the survey team to work with reasonable autonomy. It was expected that this would improve the efficiency of the teams in the field: for instance, in case weather or other conditions precluded completion of the Total Station survey while archaeological fieldwork was in progress the points could be identified and recorded at a later date. Where excavation or test-pitting was being undertaken, this had the added advantage that the archaeological work could be concluded without having to wait for the survey team, thus maximising the very limited available fieldwork time. Underwater survey points were recorded in a similar manner, although the fixing of points had to be done during diving with the survey team in full attendance.

Unfortunately, in some cases a time interval of only several days between the archaeological activity and the survey resulted in the loss of canes before recording (up to 25% in the case of the auger survey). In a few cases the survey team failed to find the relevant survey pins within the period of the fieldwork project. This can be ascribed to the difficulty of working the terrain, the inexperience of the survey team of working with archaeological data, and in some cases, the failure of the archaeological fieldwork team to be more precise about the points required for survey. In a number of cases (excavation of the ditch and on North Binness for instance) missed pins on the foreshore were resurveyed five years later by more traditional means during the post-excavation phase in 1998–9, and pins or canes removed.

Accuracy of surveying and considered requirements: the GIS base

The questions of to what precision and accuracy the archaeological data should be surveyed are rather difficult to answer in simple terms because there are many variables to be considered in the decision process. In theory, one should always strive for the highest possible accuracy that is achievable at all times. However, this is not a very practical aim in the light of the difficulties of working in the intertidal zone where a rather more pragmatic view must prevail. Therefore, *what* and *where* must be addressed in relation to the *size* and *scale* of the find or search area and at the same time the informational (capital) value of the data that is to be collected.

The survey team considered it most important that the surveying of find spots be as precisely recorded as was reasonably possible and that the full information value of the finds at that point be retained and incorporated into the GIS, despite the fact that, in many cases, the position from which they were recovered may bear little relationship to their location prior to erosion from their 'archaeological' context. In other words, that *what* is found *where* should be fully recorded regardless, and ascribed to a point in three-dimensional space.

This level of find recording for the GIS only happened to a limited degree. As discussed above, the difficulties of the working environment and the archaeological field team's great familiarity with their existing working, recording, and reporting practice made the transition to the slightly different approach requested by the survey team's surveying and GIS data recording needs, less than straightforward.

The method of autonomous working had both positive and, in retrospect, negative aspects. The ability to work as autonomous teams had major beneficial implications on costs. In particular it enabled the archaeological fieldwork, survey, and excavation to be started or completed full-time according to a predetermined and agreed programme of work, while members of the survey team were not available due to other work commitments. It provided greater flexibility in the field, which was required in these difficult working conditions with limited access time (tides) and the necessity for daily decision making to operate effectively. Contra to this was the problem created in liaison and communication, normally an unconsidered part of teams working in the field together. The survey team was regularly informed of all the archaeological discoveries and the communicated details of the fieldwork were logged on a regular basis, however, the fieldwork was often disparate and sporadic and it was often difficult to explain the exact location, nature, and number of all the activities conducted.

The fundamental need for close liaison between the archaeological field team and the survey team was undoubtedly underestimated at the planning stage. Despite the availability of a mobile telephone (bearing in mind, that this was in 1993 when the mobile telephone was still something of a rarity and it was primarily provided for safety) the archaeological field team could not always communicate their finds immediately to the survey team. Communication was partly hindered by personnel logistics; the two teams were not always in the area or contactable at the same time due to unconventional working times, limited access to some areas, and the impracticality of having the survey team on hand at all times.

The survey team was regularly informed of archaeological discoveries but occasionally failed to find the the relevant positions of the finds due to the difficulty of explaining exact location. In retrospect this led to significant difficulties for the survey team, who were inexperienced in recognising significant archaeological locations ie the section points and datum lines marked in the field by labelled bamboo canes and iron grid pegs. On several occasions the canes marking points were missing or were missed because they were visited for survey 5 or 10 days after archaeological fieldwork. Perhaps some were removed by itinerant wildfowlers but most were lost to the tide despite, in some cases, being firmly planted over 0.5m in the sediments. The difficulty of relocating some spots was highlighted at one point in the north of the harbour, east of Farlington Marshes, and in the long *Spartina* grass north of Chalkdock Lake. The cane, despite the provision of verbal description, map reference, and map locations could not be found by the survey team, but was visited and its location reaffirmed by members of the archaeological team on no less than four occasions, the last being more than four years after its original placing. The recording, therefore, of precise three-dimen-

sional coordinates of archaeological data was perhaps rather less complete than was anticipated and might have been hoped.

That such difficulties occurred is most interesting from the point of view of planning future work of this kind. Significantly, the problems arose from differing cultures prevalent in the archaeology and geography teams and the fact that the funding and conditions did not enable them to physically work together. The archaeological team's aim was to collect a sample of the data to facilitate the interpretation of the physical environment and the understanding of human action in the past. Their data collection and recording was standard and typical of archaeological sites, including those in the intertidal zones such as Goldcliff, Gwent and Blackwater, Essex. The needs of the GIS development, however, were rather different, in that it attempted to amass as complete a dataset as possible of individually and precisely recorded data to create a system which integrated data through the function of location. In other words, the GIS sought only to record data of what occurred at each place and where that place was (in three dimensions) while the archaeological data collection was required to provide a representative sample of information in each area and of each type. Consequently, much of the information was not as usable as the survey team had hoped because they had not realised that, as in any archaeological project (be it excavation or surface collection), most of the artefacts (eg flints) were not individually datable, nor was the precise three-dimensional location of artefacts on wave-cut erosion surfaces at the time of recovery necessarily absolutely spatially relevant to their former *in situ* position and, therefore, to the archaeological integrity.

Clearly such differences of approach placed very different pressures upon each team. The archaeological team knew that its field time was limited and, although they needed to accrue sufficient evidence quickly, they knew that the fieldwork was only ever meant to survey and sample and that this would provide, as with most archaeological investigations, sufficient information to enable analysis and archaeological interpretation. Despite the selective collection policy (see Methodological approach, Chapter 1) there were over 4100 obviously worked flints, in excess of 990 sherds of pottery (c 23kg), some 504 other objects, and a sample of burnt flint (74.62kg) probably representing about 4000 individual pieces; there were 26 survey areas, 1375 collection units, 55 total collection units, 7 excavated features, 5 detailed cliff section records, and 14 detailed survey and section points. The survey team, however, needed to gather three-dimensional positions such that the locations of sites could be combined with the archaeological information of date and function. The two distinct aims of data collection are not immediately directly compatible. A GIS requires that the information is kept at a unaggregated (point specific) level and that each is well located and unambiguously numbered, which results in a wealth of unrefined data, while archaeological understanding and interpretation requires selective classification and aggregation.

An archaeological survey including the location and pinpointing of the approximately 10,000 selectively retrieved artefacts, in addition to all points required for all the features, contexts, and survey areas of the project alone (probably in excess of 35,000), would have taken the field team an estimated 2000 days. At this level of recording the fieldwork undertaken and reported here would have taken in excess of sixteen seasons, or years, just to complete at the same level of work, let alone embark upon the analytical and reporting phases.

Archaeological data processing

Archaeological recording inevitably involves the aggregation of data in order to reveal patterns which are meaningful in terms of the interpretation of past human cognitive actions, rather than just the visual display of the spatial location of the data points resulting from those actions. Essentially, all archaeological work is subjective and interpretational at every level and stage, whereas GIS relies on the initial aquisition of objective data. The problem, as clearly revealed by this survey and in the foregoing discussion, is striking a balance between practical fieldworking considerations and preservation of as much as possible of the informational value that the recorded dataset holds. While the two can never be fully reconciled it is important to remember that future researchers may require to interrogate the data recovered by the survey in ways which may not yet be invisaged. Both the 'conventional' paper and graphic archive compiled by the archaeological team, and the digital data compiled by the survey team form equivalent and vital parts of the survey archive.

GIS development and applicability

At first sight, the necessity of the GIS to this project may be considered questionable. Certainly, as the project was actually conducted, the GIS offered little beyond a set of digital base maps which were used in the construction of the illustrative maps for this report. Nevertheless, that a GIS was built and developed had considerable, but possibly hidden, benefit to the project. The construction of the GIS required precise surveying of as many of the points of archaeological significance as possible. Since much of the project's data was referenced to a national coordinate system the future usefulness of the data that was collected during the course of this project was greatly enhanced. It will be possible for future researchers to use this geographically coordinated data as a visualisation tool. It will enable them to understand something of the distribution of archaeological material as it was experienced by this

particular project. Data which was collected during earlier studies is of great value to archaeological investigations but researchers often experience significant difficulties when attempting to utilise such data. These records were analysed, the artefacts examined, and the data from this assimilated into the information available to the archaeological team so that it could be used to support their interpretation of the site and its past.

However, as Gardiner notes, 'A major difficulty with all of the finds from the islands is the lack of accurate maps available to the collectors.' (Chapter 1, Archaeological background), and she further records that 'Bradley and Hooper at least tended to assign all finds from one island to a generalised, approximate, grid reference'. This suggests that the location of any particular find spot derived from these earlier studies is difficult to determine with any degree of precision or reliability. Whilst this does not preclude the data collected by these studies from being useful for this current work, it makes the data less valuable than it might have been if accurate locations had been provided.

As has been noted in this report, there is a strong relationship between the erosion of the coastline of the islands in the harbour and the appearance of archaeological material on the foreshore (Chapter 6, An erosion model). It has also been noted that areas where the earlier workers found particular types of material have not yielded similar finds during this study's fieldwork. This may indicate that there has been some change to the erosion habit of those places where artefactual material was found in the past (Chapter 2, Distribution of archaeological material). Clearly, it would be advantageous to know exactly where individual finds were found in both the earlier and current studies, enabling a fuller examination of the evidence for erosion might be made. This requires precise recorded positions for individual finds or artefact scatters. Moreover, it follows from this, that researchers in the future might also gain advantage from being able to recreate the distributions that were found in the course of this fieldwork programme of this study and thereby integrate this data with their own collected at some point in the future.

The real value of the GIS created for this project was not realised. Apart from the mapping, the postexcavation analysis was carried out by simply using time-honoured archaeological recording methods and data handling methods. The data collected by this study for the GIS, however, potentially has a future beyond the confines of this report. Much of the data that has been collected is actively and effectively available to future researchers. The data must be maintained such that it retains as much of its 'research capital' (Fontana *et al* 1999) as is reasonably possible. The development of this project's GIS has ensured that the data, which has been collected and processed for the GIS, is already in an appropriate form for Web dissemination. The data may therefore, be quickly placed on the Web and made available to a much wider research audience than may be achieved via a traditional paper publication.

Although the GIS was not immediately useful to the archaeological team in the preparation of this interpretative report, it has provided a vehicle for the collection, manipulation, and dissemination of the project's data by means of the Web. The GIS will thereby enable future researchers to gain easy access to a geographically referenced data set.

The use of the data for regression analysis, modelling the physical development and shape of the harbour over 9000 years, and for three-dimensional modelling of the sediment recovered from the auger survey was not employed through machine-based analysis. Although the auger data represents a large dataset, the distribution of the sampled points was not appropriate for the construction of a sequence of DEMs by means of computer surfacing packages. The auger points were predominantly located at 50m intervals along transects which crossed the harbour from Farlington Marsh in the north to the coast of Hayling Island in the east. This introduced a strong geographical linearity to the data distribution. Shorter auger transects in other areas of the harbour were between 0.75km and 2.3km away from the main auger transect, thereby leaving large gaps between themselves and the other sampled points. The resultant linear distribution of sample points imposed problems for the construction of a digitally created surface.

Many different software systems were available to the project all of which could produce a surface from the collected data. All such systems rely upon surface interpolation algorithms to 'fill in' the gaps between the measured points (in this case the auger points). If the distances between such points are large and, possibly more importantly uneven, then the interpolated result will 'drift' away from what might be the 'true' value. This is the case with the auger data distribution as it was collected. In order to achieve a high quality computer generated surface the distribution of sampled points needed to be more evenly spread across the harbour.

The areas available for augering were largely limited to the islands and this prevented the collection of more data points to improve the measured distribution pattern. The inability to create three-dimensional subsurface terrain models negated the realisation of many of the dynamic project aims (see Origins and aims of the project, Chapter 1). In order to obtain an approximate model of the levels of sediment across the harbour Wessex Archaeology used QuickSurf to manipulate and visualise the auger data (archive). The cross-section (Fig 11) has provided an adequate basis for interpretation.

The application of all the elements held in the GIS was not directly relevant to the interpretation of the archaeology. The GIS elements are, therefore, redundant in the interpretations presented here. At the time AutoCAD and QuickSurf were available to the archaeological team. Neither of these packages are GIS applications and they did not possess any GIS functionality enabling the interactive exploration of the data sets. This had a significant part to play in the lack of active use of the GIS held data in the research activity conducted for this report.

Other archaeological projects have used various software packages such as ArcView or GRASS, deployed in Humber wetlands and Welsh Severn intertidal projects (Bell and Neumann 1997; Bell *et al* 2000) as well as numerous archaeological landscape studies such as the of the Berkshire colluvium (Day 1999) and the Avebury and Stonehenge World Heritage Sites (see Batchelor 1997). In any future survey of this intertidal nature, detailed discussions regarding the use and applicability of software packages and their data needs should be considered jointly by those constructing and using the GIS, as well as those providing the archaeological data prior to the fieldwork. The data collection, recording, and the interpretation mechanisms that are to be employed need to be addressed as a whole for the entire project.

The seamless approach: a tested and proposed package
by Michael J Allen

The methodological package used and proposed in this volume was first drafted in 1993, and the revised strategy is presented in Appendix 3. This is essentially that adopted by the English Heritage Rapid Coastal Zone Assessment Surveys (English Heritage 1999). These surveys of relatively large portions of the coast follow a staged programme of desk-based assessment, followed by rapid field assessment. The full, proposed fieldwork strategy for intertidal survey is given in Appendix 3.

Nested survey

The seamless approach, in conceptual terms, must be the way to attempt to tackle these areas; it ensured compatibility of results despite the present-day environment. A planned, nested survey gathered data at relevant and appropriate levels of accuracy and reporting. Only limited, key areas can ever be examined in detail, yet the wider, less time- or location-specific data provide the framework for those detailed records.

Consistency of method

The application of the same methods throughout the survey is beneficial in comparing data which today do not exist in the same environment, but in the past may have. Comparison is facilitated by adoption of a single set of methods; the use of a specific set of techniques underwater, for instance, that differ from those on land, provide areas of contrast more relevant to the methods of recovery and recording, than to the archaeological context.

Time and resources

In intertidal areas the ability to work to time-scales anywhere approaching those on *terra firma* is nigh on impossible, and potentially dangerous, both personally and for the archaeological record. One lesson was the naivety in the two field teams (archaeology and survey) in respect to their comprehension of the needs of each other. The archaeological team, who were familiar with survey, but not at the time GIS, disregarded this element to a certain extent, and the survey team, unfamiliar with the nature of the archaeological record, set off with misconceptions. More importantly and pragmatically, working autonomously has great benefits, but these can only be reaped if there is the availability to provide precise details of the location of all that requires to be surveyed. In some cases this may take longer to describe, sketch map, and to indicate the location, than the time lost by working as a single field team. Communication and liaison in the field even as a 'single' team can be physically difficult.

Underwater survey and work has been a vitally important part of this project and its results are key to the interpretation provided. Such work is, in resource time, considerably more expensive than any land- or intertidal-based operation. It can be six or more times as expensive in time and rescources to record and recover material underwater than on land. Thus appropriate allocation of resources needs to be considered. At Langstone, the HWTMA, Southampton University, and NAS provided an excellent cover, much of which did not fall within the direct budget of the project.

Management of the Langstone intertidal archaeological resource
by Michael J Allen and Julie Gardiner

There are a number of publications dealing with the theory of managing the intertidal and coastal archaeological resource (Firth 1993; 1995) and the combination of *PPG* 16 and *PPG* 20 attempts to provide the legislative framework for such management (see Chapter 1). In Langstone Harbour the management of the archaeological and other resources is undertaken through the Langstone Harbour Board which holds representatives of a number of interested parties, including the RSPB, Hampshire Wildlife Trust etc. It is not appropriate here, therefore, to detail a management plan for the archaeological resources in the study area. The survey project has enabled the isolation of some areas or zones of particularly high archaeological importance and locations where materials, features or deposits are particularly vulnerable to destruction by natural or man-made agencies. The aim here,

therefore, is to outline briefly some of the main areas of high archaeological (and palaeoenvironmental) value and zones or locations where fragility or vulnerability of the archaeological is particularly high. A series of 'perceived' threats are rapidly evaluated in the light of the summary of archaeological potential and vulnerability.

Concerns and issues: the relationship of archaeology to ecology

Within Langstone Harbour the archaeological resource is only one of a number of important cultural and natural resources that exist and require management, protection, and curation. The RSPB provides considerable important management frameworks which include the natural environment and rare habitats for the vast colonies of migrating and roosting wildfowl. It is necessary, for instance, that any archaeological requirements are compatible, or be integrated, with existing management regimes and are modifications to, rather than conflicting proposals for, existing frameworks in the development and conservation offices.

An integrated approach is essential. There is a need to ensure that ecologists and ornithologists have an appreciation of the archaeological resource and its significance as well as having the opportunity to discuss and report with informed archaeologists. There is a need to encourage ways in which research and management issues can be approached, tackled, and reported to the benefit of all interested parties – eg saltmarsh regression and loss of island resources as bird habitats. Likewise, archaeologists also need to appreciate that, in some circumstances, the ecological issues may take precedence over archaeological concerns. In many ways it is conservation and wildlife issues that are providing the main preservational factor for the archaeology (see Present-day harbour: national and international designations, Chapter 1). Hard engineering may protect the diminishing terrestrial land and thus the *in situ* archaeology (as on Farlington Marshes) but may be detrimental to the ecology and habitats required for the wildlife.

Development and perceived threats

In order to gain some idea of the types of natural and man-made threats to the archaeology within the harbour area some of the main, or most obvious, potentially threats are outlined. This list, however, is not exhaustive.

Natural environment

Constant wave attrition: This is creating cliffing and mass movement along the shorelines of the islands, eroding artefacts, and the islands which hold them.

The lowering of foreshores facilitates removal of artefacts out into the submarine channels, and ultimately from the harbour (see An erosion model, Chapter 6). Obviously wave attrition action is exacerbated in storm conditions and thus tends to be seasonally variable.

Erosion is undoubtedly removing the important, yet fragile, archaeological resource; even our own three seasons of fieldwork have observed the loss of some of the clifflines. Even if the artefacts are not totally lost in the short term, the context from which they derive (ie the clays and silts), which also contain important palaeoenvironmental and stratigraphic data, are certainly disappearing.

Spartina *dieback*: This is a common phenomenon along the coast of Britain; it may have its ecological benefits but it is also detrimental to biodiversity and ecological habitat. Its loss engenders sediment instability and increases susceptibility of deposits to wave attack. The loss of sediment induced by *Spartina* dieback has the same consequences as general wave attrition.

Changing current and tidal regimes: see Development threats – Coastal margins, below.

Development threats

Development with the harbour area is likely to take three or four main forms: i) developments on the terrestrial edges of the harbour around Portsea Island, the Havant area, and Hayling Island; ii) along the coastal margins for landings stages, marinas, and marine access; iii) within the harbour such as channel construction, moorings etc; and iv) development across the harbour such as bored pipe corridors.

Harbour-edge development: The destructive nature of building works can be significant and further residential, commercial, recreational, and infrastructure development is likely. The impact on the archaeology is less easily assessed as this research did not examine the normal terrestrial environments on Hayling, Portsea, and Langstone. The presence of former archaeological finds, particularly in the north-west corner of the harbour, across to Langstone and the north-eastern shores of Hayling Island (largely the known extent of the flat cremation cemetery) is reported.

Coastal margins: One of the most significant development threats is along the ribbon of land/sea interface around the edges of the harbour. Threats may include sea defences: the pre-construction work of the Northney sea-wall discovered the late Bronze Age timbers reported by Williams and Soffe (1987) but also destroyed more and lost their structural relationships. A longer term threat is undoubtedly potential increased recreational development – eg marinas, landings, and hard land- and sea-scaping. Some of the 'archaeological' remains are too recent, or 'common', to be considered necessary of protection, curation, or recording. Nevertheless one of the most

common features of the harbour is the numerous wooden structures around the harbour's edge. These include the remains old groins, landing-jetties, piers, and fishtraps; they are a major landscape characteristic of the harbour today. Although detailed study of them has been beyond the scope of this volume, they are an important part of the historic context of Langstone, which has not been fully realised by either our historical or physical surveys.

The marshes around Chalkdock Lake conceal peat-filled channels of palaeoenvironmental importance. They are limited in extent (see Pollen analysis, Chapter 4), so direct impact would be significant. Changing the local drainage and hydrology might have detrimental indirect impact. De-watering and drying of the peats can destroy preserved microfossils, destroying their palaeoenvironmental significance.

All developments along the coastal margins have both direct and indirect impacts. The direct impact is easy to evaluate but indirect impact, such as changes in the local current and sediment movements and, on a large scale, changes to the tidal regime, may have much larger, far-reaching implications that are hard to foresee.

Changes in the local currents and tidal regimes or, more importantly, of the sedimentation and attrition rates, are hard to model from any development proposal; they are rarely accounted for in any engineering proposal, or evaluated during any development control exercise. Nevertheless, such impacts are long-term and may change erosion and attrition rates, accelerating cliffing or sediment deposition. Areas of fragile resources (see below) which may be considered stable, and which may not have eroded for centuries on the basis of historic map evidence, might be subjected to wave attrition. Developments can modify direct wave impact; at Brean Down, in the Bristol Channel, the sea-defence protected the residential land but, inadvertently, the engineered design deflected the full impact of the waves against the base of a sand cliff known to be of archaeological importance (ApSimon *et al* 1961). So great was this effect that considerable erosion occurred which led to large-scale archaeological rescue excavations, followed by construction of a barrier to protect the sand cliff and Scheduled Ancient Monument from further erosion (Bell 1990). In Langstone, even minor changes in the currents and tidal regimes, especially against the islands, may have major and significant effects on the most important and fragile archaeological resources – the islands themselves.

Within the harbour: Moorings, lighting beacons, and individual structures within the harbour have very small footprints and are unlikely to have significant impacts upon the archaeological resource, unless they are directly coincidental with specific sites or monuments, eg Sinah circle structure or a wreck site.

Across the harbour: Development across the harbour for pipes, tunnels etc, are likely to be thrust-bored and surface-impact minimal except at entry, inspection, and exit points where it may be significant. In most locations within the harbour this is likely to be of minimal archaeological importance, excepting at monumental sites (see above). Within the harbour, however, there are buried, deeply incised channels whose floors contain narrow strips of peat (at c –13m OD) and which represent the former land surfaces or river channels at about 9000–7000 BC. These are of palaeoenvironmental significance and, elsewhere (Portsmouth and Southampton Harbours), archaeological artefacts of bone and antler are known to have been recovered from such deposits (Everard 1954a; James 1847; Hooley 1905; Shore and Elwes 1889 – see Palaeo-environmental background, Chapter 1).

Activities: land- and sea-use

Dredging and buoying: Dredging is a common concern, but also a necessity, in the harbour. Dredging is usually restricted to specific channels. It is unlikely that any archaeological site *per se* exists along these courses, excepting wrecks etc but, potentially, artefacts eroded from the islands and foreshores may reside in these locations. Oyster dredging is more widespread, but our survey has shown that the archaeological significance of these areas is low; excepting snags which might represent timber structures or boats etc.

The buoying of monuments to ensure the avoidance of marine craft and dredgers can aid protection, but can also be destructive, Buoys marking the Sinah circle certainly ensured avoidance by all marine craft. They did not, however prevent the buoy chains from damaging the timbers in their tidal course.

Fishing and recreation: There is likely to be minimal direct impact from fishing and most recreational activity within the harbour. The most likely detrimental effects are those of erosion on the fragile islands by visitors (including ornithologists) and removal of artefacts from exposed, but important archaeological contexts or features without appropriate records. The indirect impact of recreation is likely in the infrastructure built to support it, and this is covered in the development threats above.

Areas of high, medium, and low archaeological and palaeoenvironmental potential: fragility, rarity, and loss

Areas of high archaeological and palaeoenvironmental potential

Undoubtedly the main areas of high archaeological potential are the islands in the northern part of Langstone Harbour. What is left of these vestiges of the former land mass (representing less than 2% of the current harbour area) contain *in situ* artefacts rarely found anywhere else in the survey. The shores of all four islands (North Binness Island, Long Island, Baker's Island, and South Binness Island) are strewn with archaeological artefacts (largely flints) from which some of the largest individual prehistoric sherds found by fieldwalking in Hampshire were recovered. The best-preserved prehistoric vessels were recovered eroding from clifflines and the foreshores of the islands, indicating the density and nature of the archaeological resource within them. Archaeologically, Farlington Marshes and the north-west corner of the harbour should be seen as an extension of the islands, as indeed it was formerly part of 'Binners' Island.

Elsewhere in the harbour, other areas are primarily of palaeoenvironmental significance. The first is the submerged peat shelves north of Russell's Lake and at Baker's Rithe; both have been eroded and considerably reduced in size during the survey programme; both are old land surfaces from which archaeological artefacts may be recovered, and both have only been visited once. The peat-filled palaeochannel at Chalkdock Lake, and the deeper, older peat in the base of the buried and incised courses of the Langstone and Broom channels must be considered of high potential. The lower channels have not been investigated, and may contain archaeological artefacts of the earlier Mesolithic.

Areas of medium archaeological and palaeoenvironmental potential

Parts of the mainland, although not investigated in this survey, must have archaeological potential by the artefacts that are recorded eroding from them in this or Bradley and Hooper's (1973) survey. Similarly-poorly investigated areas in this survey are the areas between the islands (North Binness Island–Long Island, and Baker's Island–South Binness) where tidal flow is low. A number of bronze hoards have also been recovered from them as well as the large Creek Field vessel (Fig 50a) which parallels the globular vessel from North Binness (Fig 51).

All of these areas potentially contain *in situ* artefacts and, albeit truncated, features. The large gravel delta outside the mouth of the harbour contains coarse detritus (and artefacts; larger flint tools etc) swept from the harbour. As the sea has sorted this, even dredging from these areas has the potential of finding artefacts, or artefact types, not recovered from previous surveys.

Areas of low archaeological and palaeoenvironmental potential

Most of the areas of accreting muds seem to be largely devoid of archaeological artefacts. This may be a combination of them being obscured and unavailable for recovery by archaeological reconnaissance, but also may reflect areas of lowered foreshores, stripped of artefacts and archaeological features. Much of the harbour coastline (Hayling Island, Portsea Island), is developed by seawalls, pontoons, and other development, destroying the archaeological remains in a ribbon encircling the harbour. The harbour mouth is extensive remodelled, as are the ferry points.

Areas of high risk

The areas of highest risk to loss are the islands which are a diminishing archaeological resource. This loss is gradual long-term attrition. Similarly the peat shelf at Baker's Rithe has been reduced significantly over the past seven years; many of the actual waterlogged trees (which do not float) have eroded away. This is one of the most valuable palaeoenvironmental resources, and potentially a valuable archaeological resource in terms of artefacts recovered, but this was not tested by our survey.

The harbour fringes, most likely to be the subject of planning applications, are other areas of high potential archaeological impact. The find of the late Bronze Age timbers was recovered along the Hayling shoreline.

Recommendations for further research

There is no need for further research on current collections at the present time, but some themes for ongoing and new studies are proposed:

1 Environmental analysis and dating of the known and rapidly diminishing waterlogged submerged forests which are rare relicts of the prehistoric environment. Further, more detailed, pollen work and dating and mapping of the channel sequences is required to provide a stronger environmental picture which can be more directly related chronologically to the artefact scatters and evidence of activity in Langstone. This has to be one of the most significant areas of this project, of which this research has really only highlighted the potential.

   In addition, the recovery of samples (cores) from the deeply buried Mesolithic channel peats undoubtedly warrants further research, with implications for coastal and relative sea-level research of the southern coast of Great Britain.

2 Burial and cemetery – the examination of the nature, date, and extent of this flat cemetery will characterise one of the major later-prehistoric activities of the area. It can be contrasted with contemporaneous burial practices and their location outside the harbour, but within the local region. The significance of the cemetery is outlined in Chapter 7.

3 Erosion transect studies, to record artefact occurrence, redistribution, and loss, the changing microtopography and sediment movement, changing ecology – colonisation (flora and fauna), erosion, wave action. Visits and monitoring at bimonthly intervals over a period of, say, 10 years, in the manner adopted by the RSPB in their two-dimensional erosion study would be desirable. This data will provide some, admittedly short-term, evidence to model local rates of erosion and test the erosion model presented in Chapter 6. This will help evaluate the significance of erosion to the archaeological resource, and to the remains in undisturbed areas.

4 General continued surveillance and reporting of finds and wood etc to isolated material and finds that expand, rather than repeat, the data reported here.

5 Analysis and examination of the large globular Bronze Age vessels (hearth 1702, North Binness Island and Creek Field, Hayling Island), possibly including residue analysis, in an attempt to determine their function or any activity specifically associated with this vessel type.

6 Proper record and dating of the 'harbour' and fishing structures accompanied by a more detailed historic survey to provide the documentary evidence for these activities.

7 Proper historic research into Saxon and medieval activity, especially the Hayling Priory, and archaeological survey to establish the location of any medieval ecclesiastical centre.

8 Historic research of the study area, concentrating on the historic, post-medieval, and recent history to complement the archaeological work.

9 The history of the changes in the relative sea-level that have occurred in the past 2000 years is imperfectly understood. A detailed study of local fluctuations in relative sea-level from the Roman period to the early post-medieval would be of considerable value to the local history and settlements history of the area.

10 This project follows on from that recorded by Bradley and Hooper 25 years ago (1973) and shows the changes in the distributions resulting from erosion removing, uncovering, or burying, artefact scatters. Continued erosion and exposure of new finds ensures that our survey cannot be definitive and that a survey exercise must be repeated at appropriate intervals to map, record, and monitor the changing archaeological resources. Revision of the interpretations made here should then be pursued.

Bibliography

Adam, N, Adams, J, Allen, M J, Draper, S, Fontana, D, Gardiner, J, & Watson, K, 1995 The Langstone Harbour Archaeological Survey Project; second interim report 1994. Unpublished report, Hampshire County Council

Akeroyd, A V, 1966 Changes in relative land and sea levels during the post-glacial in southern Britain with particular reference to the post-Mesolithic period. Unpublished MA thesis, University of London

Akeroyd, A V, 1972 Archaeological and historical evidence for subsidence in southern Britain, *Phil Trans Roy Soc London*, A **272**, 151–71

Allen, J R L, 1987 Late Flandrian shoreline oscillations in the Severn Estuary: the Rumney Formation at its type site (Cardiff area), *Phil Trans Roy Soc London*, B **315**, 157–84

Allen, J R L, 1989 Evolution of salt-marsh cliffs in muddy and sandy systems: a qualitative comparison of British west-coast estuaries, *Earth Surface Processes and Landforms*, **14**, 85–92

Allen, J R L, 1990a Salt-marsh growth and stratification: a numerical model with special reference to the Severn estuary, south-west Britain, *Marine Geology*, **95**, 77–96

Allen, J R L, 1990b The Severn Estuary in southwest Britain; its retreat under marine transgression, and fine-sediment regime, *Sedimentary Geology*, **96**, 13–28

Allen, J R L, 1991 Salt marsh accretion and sea-level movement in the inner Severn estuary: the archaeological and historical contributions, *J Geological Soc London*, **148**, 485–94

Allen, J R L, 1993 Muddy alluvial coasts of Britain: field criteria for shoreline position and movements in the recent past, *Proc Geologists' Assoc*, **104**, 241–52

Allen, J R L, & Fulford, M G, 1986 The Wentlooge Level; a Romano-British saltmarsh reclamation in southeast Wales, *Britannia*, **17**, 91–117

Allen, J R L, & Fulford, M G, 1990 Romano-British wetland reclamations at Longney, Gloucestershire, and evidence for the earlier settlement of the inner Severn Estuary, *Antiq J*, **70**, 288–326

Allen, J R L, & Rae, J E, 1987 Late Flandrian shoreline oscillations in the Severn Estuary: a geomorphological and stratigraphical reconnaissance, *Phil Trans Roy Soc*, B **315**, 185–230

Allen, J R L, & Rae, J E, 1988 Vertical salt-marsh accretion since the Roman period in the Severn Estuary, southwest Britain, *Marine Geology*, **83**, 225–35

Allen, J R L, & Pye, K, 1992 *Saltmarshes; morphodynamics, conservation and engineering significance*. Cambridge: Cambridge University Press

Allen, L G, 1991 *The evolution of the Solent River system during the Pleistocene*. Unpublished PhD thesis, University of Cambridge (Abstract in *Quat Newsl*, **66**, for February 1992)

Allen, L G, & Gibbard, P L, 1994 Pleistocene evolution of the Solent River of southern England, *Quat Sci Rev*, **12**, 503–28

Allen, M J, 1991 Analysing the landscape: a geographical approach to archaeological problems, in A J Schofield (ed) *Interpreting Artefact Scatters; contributions to ploughzone archaeology*, Oxbow Monogr **4**. Oxford: Oxbow, 39–57

Allen, M J, 1992 Products of erosion and the prehistoric land use of the Wessex Chalk, in M G Bell & J Boardman (eds) *Past and Present Soil Erosion*. Oxford: Oxbow, 37–92

Allen, M J, 1994 The landuse history of the southern English chalklands with an evaluation of the Beaker period using environmental data: colluvial deposits as cultural indicators. Unpublished PhD thesis, University of Southampton

Allen, M J, 1995 Land molluscs, in G Wainwright & S Davies *Balksbury Camp Hampshire, excavations 1973 and 1981*, English Heritage Archaeol Rep **4**. London: English Heritage, 92–100

Allen, M J, 1996 Landscape and Land-use: priorities in Hampshire, 500,000 BC to AD 1500, in D A Hinton & M Hughes (eds) *Archaeology in Hampshire: a framework for the Future*. Hampshire County Council, 55–70

Allen, M J, 1997a A medieval wooden harpoon from the south coast of England, *Newswarp*, **12**, 2–6

Allen, M J, 1997b Landscape, land-use and farming, in R J C Smith, F Healy, M J Allen, E L Morris, I Barnes, & P J Woodward *Excavations along the route of the Dorchester by-pass, Dorset, 1986–8*, Wessex Archaeol Rep **11**. Salisbury: Wessex Archaeology, 277–83

Allen, M J, forthcoming High resolution mapping of Neolithic and Bronze Age landscapes and land-use; the combination of multiple palaeo-environmental analysis and topographic modelling, in A S Fairburn (ed) *Plants in Neolithic Britain and beyond: landscape and environment, economy and society*. Neolithic Studies Group, Oxbow Books

Allen, M J, Crockett, A D, Rawlings, M N, & Ritchie, K, 1997 Archaeological fieldwork along the line of the Brean Down Sea Defences; new evidence of landscape change and human activity, *Archaeology in the Severn Estuary 1996: Annual Report of the Severn Estuary Levels Research Committee*, **7**, 31–8

Allen, M J, Fontana, D, Gardiner, J, & Pearson A, 1994 The Langstone Harbour Archaeological Survey Project; the assessment 1993. Unpublished report, Hampshire County Council

Allen, M J, & Gardiner, J, forthcoming a The Mesolithic in Langstone Harbour: terrestrial assemblages in a marine environment, in R Young (ed) *Prehistoric Society Mesolithic Research Day*. Leicester University Press

Allen, M J, & Gardiner, J, forthcoming b The Neolithic of the present day intertidal zone of Langstone Harbour, Hampshire, in F M Haughey & A O'Sullivan (eds) *Neolithic Intertidal Zone Archaeology*. Neolithic Studies Group, Oxbow Books

Allen, M J, Gardiner, J, Fontana, D, & Pearson, A, 1993 Archaeological assessment of Langstone Harbour, Hampshire, *PAST*, **16**, 1–3

Allen, M J, & Pettitt, P B, 1997 A medieval wooden harpoon from the south coast of England, *Medieval Archaeol*, **61**, 236–40

Allen, M J, & Ritchie, K, in press/2000 The stratigraphy and archaeology of Bronze Age and Romano-British deposits below the beach level at Brean Down, Somerset, *Proc Univ Bristol Spelaeol Soc*, **22** (1)

Anderson, F W, 1933 The New Docks excavations, Southampton, *Papers and Proc Hampshire Fld Club*, **12**, 169–76

Andersen, S Th, 1973 The differential pollen productivity of trees and its significance for the interpretation of a pollen diagram from a forested region, in H J B Birks & R G West *Quaternary Plant Ecology*. Oxford: Blackwell, 109–15

Annable, F K, & Simpson, D D A, 1964 *Guide catalogue of the Neolithic and Bronze Age Collections in Devizes Museum*. Devizes: Wiltshire Archaeol Natur Hist Soc

ApSimon, A M, 1961 Kynance Gate and Cornish Prehistory, *The Lizard*, **2** (1), 13–15

ApSimon, A M, & Greenfield, E, 1972 The excavation of Bronze Age and Iron Age settlements at Trevisker, St Eval, Cornwall, *Proc Prehist Soc*, **38**, 302–81

ApSimon, A M, Donovan, D T, & Taylor, H, 1961 The stratigraphy and archaeology of the Late-Glacial and Post-Glacial deposits at Brean Down, Somerset, *Proc Univ Bristol Spelaeol Soc*, **9**, 67–136

Avery, B W, 1990 *Soils of the British Isles*. Wallingford: CAB (Commonwealth Agricultural Bureau) International

Baillie, M G L, 1982 *Tree-Ring Dating and Archaeology*. London: Croom Helm

Balaam, N D, Bell, M G, David, A E U, Levitan, B, Macphail, R I, Robinson, M, & Scaife, R G,

1987 Prehistoric and Romano-British sites at Westward Ho!, Devon: archaeological and palaeo-environmental surveys 1983 and 1984, in N D Balaam, B Levitan, & V Straker (eds) *Studies in palaeoeconomy and environment in South West England*, BAR Brit Ser **181**. Oxford: British Archaeological Reports, 163–264

Bannerman, N, & Jones, C, 1999 Fish-trap types: a component of the maritime cultural landscape, *Int J Naut Archaeol*, **28**, 70–84

Barnes, I, 1993 Second Severn Crossing: English approaches, an interim statement on the 1992/3 fieldwork, *Archaeology in the Severn Estuary 1993: Annual Report of the Severn Levels Estuary Research Committee*, **4**, 5–30

Barrett, J, 1980 The pottery of the later Bronze Age in lowland England, *Proc Prehist Soc*, **46**, 297–319

Barrett, J, & Yonge, C M, 1958 *Collins Pocket Guide to the Sea Shore*. London: Collins (1985 reprint edition)

Batchelor, D, 1997 Mapping the Stonehenge World Heritage Site, in B W Cunliffe & A C Renfrew (eds) *Science and Stonehenge*, Proc Brit Acad **92**. Oxford: Oxford University Press for The British Academy, 61–72

Bass, W M, 1987 *Human Osteology: a laboratory and field manual* (3rd edition). Columbia, Mo: Missouri Archaeol Soc

Becker, B, Krause, R, & Kromer, B, 1989 Zur absoluten Chronologie der frühen Bronzezeit, *Germania*, **67**, 421–42

Beek, G C van, 1983 *Dental Morphology: an illustrated guide*. London: Wright

Bell, M, 1977 Excavations at Bishopstone, *Sussex Archaeol Coll*, **115**. Lewes: Sussex Archaeol Soc

Bell, M G, 1987 The Molluscs, in N D Balaam *et al* 1987, 201–13

Bell, M G, 1990 *Brean Down excavations 1983–1987*, English Heritage Archaeol Rep **15**. London: English Heritage

Bell, M G, & Neumann, H, 1996 Intertidal peat survey in the Welsh Estuary, *Archaeology in the Severn Estuary 1995: Annual Report of the Severn Estuary Levels Research Committee*, **6**, 29–33

Bell, M G, & Neumann, H, 1997 Prehistoric intertidal archaeology and environments in the Severn Estuary, Wales, *World Archaeol*, **29**, 95–113

Bell, M G, Caseldine, A, & Neumann, H, 2000 *Prehistoric Intertidal Archaeology in the Welsh Severn Estuary*, CBA Res Rep **120**. York: Council for British Archaeology

Bellamy, A G, 1995 Extension of the British landmass: evidence from shelf sediment bodies in the English Channel, in R C Preece (ed) *Island Britain: a Quaternary perspective*, Geological Society Special Publication **96**. London: Geological Society, 47–62

Bellamy, P, 1997 Flaked stone assemblages, in R J C Smith, F Healy, M J Allen, E L Morris, I Barnes & P Woodward *Excavations along the Route of the Dorchester Bypass, Dorset, 1986–8*, Wessex Archaeol Rep **11**. Salisbury: Wessex Archaeology, 136–54

Bennett, J P, & Fontana, V J L, 1955 Survey of the littoral fauna of Langstone Harbour. Unpublished survey, Portsmouth Municipal College

Bennett, K D, Whittington, G, & Edwards, K J, 1994 Recent plant nomenclatural changes and pollen morphology in the British Isles, *Quat Newsl*, **73**, 1–6

Bennett, P, & Williams, J, 1997 Monkton, *Current Archaeol*, **151** (vol 13, 7), 258–64

Binford, L R, 1980 Willow smoke and dogs' tails: hunter-gatherer settlement systems and archaeo-logical site formation, *American Antiq*, **45**, 4–20

Bingeman, J M, 1995 Interim Report; Langstone Harbour Prehistory – lecture to the Society of Nautical Research (South), 9 Dec 1995. Unpublished MS

Bird, E C F, & Ranwell, D S, 1964 *Spartina* saltmarsh in southern England IV: the physiography of Poole Harbour, Dorset, *J Ecol*, **52**, 355–66

Birks, H J B, 1989 Holocene isochrone maps and patterns of tree spreading in the British Isles, *J Biogeogr*, **16**, 503–40

Birks, H J B, Deacon, J, & Peglar, S, 1975 Pollen maps for the British Isles 5000 years ago, *Phil Trans Roy Soc*, B **189**, 87–105

Bishop, M J, 1974 The Mollusca of Wicken Fen with some additional records, *Cambridgeshire and Isle of Ely Naturalists Trust Annual Report 1974*, 1–4

Blanchard, V, (ed), undated *City of Portsmouth, Records of the Corporation, 1936–1945*. Portsmouth

Boismier, W, 1980 in P J Fasham *et al* 1980

Borlase, W, 1753 Of the great alterations which the islands of Scilly have undergone since the time of the ancients, *Phil Trans Roy Soc London*, **48**, 57–67

Borlase, W, 1757 An account of some trees discovered underground on the shore at Mount's Bay in Cornwall, *Phil Trans Roy Soc London*, **50**, 51–3

Borlase, W, 1758 *The Natural History of Cornwall*. Oxford

Borlase, W C, 1872 *Naenia Cornubiae*. London

Bradley, R J, 1975 Salt and settlement in the Hampshire-Sussex borderland, in K W de Brisay & K J E Evans (eds) *Salt: the study of an ancient industry*. Colchester: Colchester Archaeology Group, 20–5

Bradley, R J, 1990 *The Passage of Arms*. Cambridge: Cambridge University Press

Bradley, R J, 1992 Roman salt production in Chichester Harbour: rescue excavations at Chidham, West Sussex, *Britannia*, **23**, 27–44

Bradley, R, Entwistle, R, & Raymond, F, 1994 *Prehistoric Land Divisions on Salisbury Plain: The Wessex Linear Ditches Project*, English Heritage Archaeol Rep **2**. London: English Heritage

Bradley, R J, & Fulford, M, 1975 Excavations at Tournerbury, Hayling Island, 1959 and 1971, *Proc Hampshire Fld Club Archaeol Soc*, **32**, 63–70

Bradley, R J, Fulford, M G, & Tyson, H J, 1997 The archaeological resource: regional review, in M Fulford *et al*, 154–78

Bradley, R J, & Hooper, B, 1973 Recent discoveries from Portsmouth and Langstone harbours: Mesolithic to Iron Age, *Proc Hampshire Fld Club Archaeol Soc*, **30**, 17–27

Bradley, R J, & Lewis, E, 1974 A Mesolithic site at Wakeford's Copse, Havant, *Rescue Archaeol Hampshire*, **2**, 5–18

Briard, J, 1984 *L'âge du bronze en France – 3 Les Tumulus d'Armorique*. Paris: Picard

Bray, M J, Carter, D J, & Hooke, J M, 1995 Littoral cell definition and budgets for central southern England, *J Coastal Res*, **11** 381–400

Brooks, S T, 1955 Skeletal age at death: the reliability of cranial and pubic age indicators, *American J Phys Anthropol*, **13**, 567–97

Brothwell, D R, 1972 *Digging up Bones: the excavation, treatment and study of human skeletal remains* (2nd edition). London: British Museum Natural History

Bryant, M, 1967 The flora of Langstone Harbour and Farlington Marshes, *Proc Hampshire Fld Club Archaeol Soc*, **24**, 5–13

Buckley, V, (ed), 1990 *Burnt Offerings: international contributions to burnt mound archaeology*. Dublin: Wordwell

Burrin, P J, & Scaife, R G, 1984 Aspects of Holocene sedimentation and floodplain development in southern England, *Proc Geologists' Assoc*, **85**, 81–96

Butler, J J, 1963 Bronze Age connections across the North Sea, *Palaeohistoria*, **12**

Butot, L J M, & Neuteboom, W H, 1958 Over *Vertigo moulinsiana* (Dupuy) en haar voorkomen in Nederland, *Basteria*, **22**, 52–63

Calkin, J B, 1964 The Bournemouth area in the Middle and Late Bronze Age, with the 'Deverel-Rimbury' problem reconsidered, *Archaeol J*, **119**, 1–65

Cameron, N, & Scaife, R G, 1985 The pollen record, in P Cox, Excavation and survey on Furzey Island, Pollen Harbour, Dorset; 1985, *Proc Dorset Natur Hist Archaeol Soc*, **110**, 65–72

Cameron, R A D, & Morgan-Huws, D I, 1975 Snail faunas in the early stages of a chalk grassland succession, *Biol J Linnean Soc*, **7**, 215–29

Cameron, R A D, & Redfern, M, 1976 *British Land Snails*. London: Academic Press for the Linnean Society of London

Caron, E, 1974 *Smugglers and Revenue Officers in the Portsmouth Area in the Eighteenth Century*, The Portsmouth Papers **22**. Portsmouth

Cartwright, C R, 1982 Field survey of Chichester harbour, 1982, *Sussex Archaeol Coll*, **122**, 23–7

Celik, I, & Rodi, W, 1988 Modelling suspended sediment transport in nonequilibrium situations, *J Hydraulic Eng*, **114**, 1157–89

Chauhan, O S, & Almeida, F, 1988 Geophysical tools as a tool to explore submerged marine archaeological sites, in S R Rao (ed) *Marine Archaeology of Indian Ocean Countries*. Goa: National Institution of Oceanography, 3–5

Christie, P M, 1960 Crig-a-Mennis, a Bronze Age barrow at Liskey, Perranzabuloe, Cornwall, *Proc Prehist Soc*, **26**, 76–97

Churchill, D M, 1965 The displacement of deposits found at sea-level, 6,500 years ago in southern Britain, *Quaternaria*, **7**, 239–47

Clapham, A J, 1999 The characterisation of two mid-Holocene submerged forests. Unpublished PhD thesis, Liverpool, John Moores University

Clapham, A J, Clare, T, & Wilkinson, D, 1997 A plant macrofossil investigation of a submerged forest, in A Sinclair, E Slater & J Gowlett *Archaeological Science 1995*, Oxbow Monogr **64**. Oxford: Oxbow, 265–270

Clark, J G D, Higgs, E S, & Longworth, I H, 1960 Excavations at the Neolithic site at Hurst Fen, Mildenhall, Suffolk, *Proc Prehist Soc*, **26**, 202–45

Clarke, W R, 1838 On the peat bogs and submarine forests of Bournemouth, Hampshire and in the neighbourhood of Poole, Dorsetshire, *Proc Geological Soc*, **2**, 599–601

Cobbett, W, 1830 *Rural Rides* (1909 edition). London: Robert Culley

Cole, H A, 1956 *Oyster Cultivation in Britain. A manual of current practice*. London: HMSO

Collier, P, & Fontana, D, undated, Report for the Royal Society for the Protection of Birds on Environmental Change in Langstone Harbour. Unpublished MS, Department of Geography, University of Portsmouth

Collins, K J, & Mollinson, J J, 1984 Colonisation of the 'Mary Rose' excavation, *Progress in Underwater Science*, **9**, 67–74

Coste, M, 1861 *Voyage d'Exploration sur le Littoral de la France et de l'Italie* (2nd edition). Paris: Imprimerie Imperiale

Cotton, M A, & Gathercole, P W, 1958 *Excavations at Clausentum, Southampton, 1951–1954*. London: HMSO

Coughlan, J, 1976 Marine wood borers in Southampton water, *Proc Hampshire Fld Club Archaeol Soc*, **33**, 5–15

Creeth, W A, 1958 Bronze Age Jar from Kynance Gate, *The Lizard*, **3**, 14–15

Crosby, V, 1993 Havant – former Oak Park School, *Archaeol Hampshire Annu Rep 1993*, 45

Cross, D E, 1965 The salt industry at Lymington, *J Ind Archaeol*, **2**, 86–90

Cundy, A B, & Croudace, I W, 1996 Sediment accretion and recent sea-level rise in the Solent, Southern England: inferences from radiometric and geochemical studies, *Estuarine, Coastal and Shelf Science*, **43**, 449–67

Cunliffe, B W, 1970 A Bronze Age settlement at Chalton Hants (Site 78), *Antiq J*, **50**, 1–13

Cunliffe, B W, 1971 *Excavations at Fishbourne, 1961–1969: Vol 2 The Finds*, Rep Res Comm Soc Antiq London **27**. London: Society of Antiquaries of London

Cunliffe, B W, 1975 *Excavations at Portchester Castle, Vol 1: Roman*, Rep Res Comm Soc Antiq London **32**. London: Society of Antiquaries of London

Cunliffe, B W, 1977 The Romano-British village at Chalton, Hants, *Proc Hampshire Fld Club Archaeol Soc*, **33**, 45–67

Cunliffe, B W, 1991 *Iron Age Communities in Britain* (3rd edition). London: Routledge

Cunliffe, B W, 1993 *Wessex to AD 1000*. London, Longman

Curry, D, Hodson, F, & West, I M, 1968 The Eocene Succession in the Fawley transmission Tunnel, *Proc Geologists' Assoc*, **79**, 179–206

Dacre, M, & Ellison, A, 1981 A Bronze Age urn cemetery at Kimpton, Hampshire, *Proc Prehist Soc*, **47**, 147–203

Day, C A, 1999 Predicting archaeo-colluvium on the Berkshire Downs. Unpublished DPhil thesis, Keble College, University of Oxford

Darwin-Fox, W, 1862 When and how was the Isle of Wight severed from the mainland? *The Geologist*, **5**, 452–4

Davies, P, & van der Noort, R, 1993 The Humber Wetlands Project: archaeological assessment of Humber Basin Lowlands, in J Coles, V Fenwick & G Hutchinson (eds) *Spirit of Enquiry: Essays for Ted Wright*, WARP Occas Pap **7**. Exeter: Wetland Archaeology Research Project, Nautical Archaeology Society, National Maritime Museum, 9–14

DoE, 1993 *Coastal Planning and Management: a review*. London: HMSO

Dean, M, Ferrari, B, Oxley, I, Redknap, M, & Watson, K, (eds), 1992 *Archaeology Underwater – The NAS Guide to Principles and Practice*. Denbigh, Clwyd: Nautical Archaeology Society/Archetype

Devoy, R J N, 1979 Flandrian sea-level changes and vegetation history of the lower Thames Estuary, *Phil Trans Roy Soc London*, B **285**, 355–407

Devoy, R J N, 1982 Analysis of the geological evidence for Holocene sea-level changes and movements in southeast England, *Proc Geologists' Assoc*, **93**, 65–90

Devoy, R J N, 1987a The estuary of the Western Yar, Isle of Wight; sea-level changes in the

Solent region, in K E Barber (ed) *Wessex and the Isle of Wight – Field Guide*. Cambridge: Quaternary Research Association, 115–22

Devoy, R N J, 1987b *Sea surface studies: a global view*. London, New York: Croom Helm

Devoy, R J N, 1990 Controls on coastal and sea-level changes and the application of archaeological-historical records to understanding recent patterns of sea-level movement, in S McGrail (ed) *Maritime Celts, Frisians and Saxons: papers presented to a conference at Oxford in November 1988*, CBA Res Rep **71**. London: Council for British Archaeology, 17–26

Down, A, 1979 *Chichester Excavations 4: The Roman villas at Chilgrove and Upmarden*. Chichester: Phillimore for Chichester Excavation Committee

Downey, R, King, A, & Soffe, G, 1979 *The Hayling Island Temple; third interim report on the excavation of the Iron Age and Roman temple 1976–78*. Privately printed

Douglas, Sir G, (ed) 1908 *The Panmure Papers. Selection of correspondence of Fox Maule, 2nd Baron Panmure, 11th Earl of D'Achousie* (2nd edition) ed G D Ramsay, vol 2, 278

Draper, J, 1990 *Hampshire: the complete guide*. Wimborne: Dovecote Press

Draper, J C, 1951 Stone industries from Rainbow Bar, Hants, *Archaeol Newsl*, **3**, 147–9

Draper, J C, 1958 Hampshire. Survey of islands in Langstone Harbour, *Archaeol Newsl*, **6** (9), 204

Draper, J C, 1961 Upper Palaeolithic type flints from Long Island, Langstone Harbour, Portsmouth, *Proc Hampshire Fld Club Archaeol Soc*, **22**, 105–6

Draper, J C, 1963 Mesolithic distributions in south-east Hampshire, *Proc Hampshire Fld Club Archaeol Soc*, **23**, 110–19

Drewett, P, 1982 *The archaeology of Bullock Down, Eastbourne, East Sussex: the development of a landscape*. Lewes: Sussex Archaeological Society

Dunn, J N, 1972 *A General Survey of Langstone Harbour with particular reference to the effects of sewage*. Hampshire River Authority and Hampshire County Council

Dyer, K R, 1975 The buried channels of the 'Solent River', southern England, *Proc Geologists' Assoc*, **86**, 239–45

Dyer, K R, 1980 Sedimentation and sediment transport, in NERC 1980, 20–4

Earwood, C, 1993 *Domestic Wooden Artefacts in Britain and Ireland from Neolithic to Viking Times*. Exeter: University of Exeter Press

Eckes, R, 1938 Ein Hortfunde der älteren Bronzezeit aus Regensburg, *Germania*, **22**, 7–11

Ellis, A E, 1969 *British Land Snails*. Oxford: Clarendon

Ellison, A B, 1981 Towards a socio-economic model for the middle Bronze Age in southern

England, in I Hodder, G Isaac & N Hammond (eds) *Patterns of the Past: studies in honour of David Clarke*. Cambridge: Cambridge University Press, 413–38

Ely, T, 1904 *Roman Hayling: a contribution to the study of Roman Britain*. 14–15

Ely, T, 1908 *Roman Hayling: a contribution to the study of Roman Britain* (2nd edition).

English Heritage, 1999 *A brief for Rapid Coastal Zone Assessment Surveys, English Heritage and RCHME*. London: English Heritage (draft, release 2, 16 February 1999)

Eogan, G, 1967 The associated finds of gold bar torcs, *J Roy Soc Antiq Ir*, **97**, 129–75

Evans, J G, 1972 *Land Snails in Archaeology*. London: Seminar Press

Evans, J G, 1984 Stonehenge – the environment in the Late Neolithic and Early Bronze Age and a Beaker burial, *Wilts Archaeol Natur Hist Mag*, **78**, 7–30

Evans, J G, Davies, P, Mount, R, & Williams, D, 1992 Mollusc taxocenes from Holocene overbank alluvium in southern central England, in S Needham & M G Macklin (eds) *Alluvial Archaeology in Britain*, Oxbow Monogr **27**. Oxford: Oxbow, 65–74

Everard, C E, 1954a Submerged gravel and peat in Southampton Water, *Proc Hampshire Fld Club*, **18**, 263–85

Everard, C E, 1954b The Solent River: a geomorphological study, *Trans Inst Brit Geogr*, **20**, 41–58

Fabvollière, Favereau de la, D, 1660 Map of Portsmouth, British Library B L Add MS 16371a

Fahnestock, R K, & Haushild, W L, 1962 Flume studies of the transport of pebbles and cobbles on a sand bed, *Geol Soc America Bull*, **73**, 1431–6

Fasham, P J, & Ross, J M, 1978 A Bronze Age flint industry from a barrow site in Micheldever Wood, Hampshire, *Proc Prehist Soc*, **44**, 47–67

Fasham, P J, Schadla-Hall, R T, Shennan, S J, & Bates, P, 1980 *Fieldwalking for Archaeologists*. Hambledon: Hampshire Field Club and Archaeological Society

Ferrari, B, & Adams, J, 1990 Biogenic modifications of marine sediments and their influence on archaeological material, *Int J Naut Archaeol*, **19**, 139–51

Firth, A, 1993 The management of archaeology underwater, in J Hunter & I Ralston (eds) *Archaeological Resource Management in the UK*. Birmingham: Institute of Field Archaeologists, 65–76

Firth, A, 1995 Archaeological and coastal zone management, in A Q Berry & I W Brown (eds) *Managing Ancient Monuments: an integrated approach*. Mold: Clwyd Archaeology Service

Firth, A, in press, Development-led archaeology in coastal environments: investigations at Queenborough, Motney Hill and Gravesend in

Kent, in K Pye & J R L Allen (eds) *Coastal and Estuarine Environments: sedimentology, geomorphology and geoarchaeology*. Geological Society Special Publication, 403–17

Fitzpatrick, A P, 1997 *Archaeological Excavations on the Route of the A27 Westhampnett Bypass, West Sussex, 1992, volume 2: the Cemeteries*, Wessex Archaeol Rep **12**. Salisbury: Wessex Archaeology

Fitzpatrick, A P, Ellis, C, & Allen, M J, 1996a Bronze Age 'jetties' or causeways at Testwood, Hampshire, Great Britain, *PAST*, **24**, 9–10

Fitzpatrick, A P, Ellis, C, & Allen, M J, 1996b Bronze Age 'jetties' or causeways at Testwood, Hampshire, Great Britain, *Newswarp*, **20**, 19–22

Fontana, D, Collier, P, & Inkpen, R, 1999 A GIS approach to interpreting indicators of sea-level change: illustrations from Southern England, *Proceedings of Coast GIS99*, 9–11 September 1999, International Geographical Union Commission on Coastal Systems, IFREMER, Brest, France

Ford, S, 1982 Fieldwork and Excavation on the Berkshire Grims Ditch (a ?territorial boundary of Late Bronze Age date), *Oxoniensia*, **47**, 13–36

Ford, S, Bradley, R J, Hawkes, J, & Fisher, P, 1984 Flintworking in the metal age, *Oxford J Archaeol*, **3** (2), 157–73

Frey, D, 1971 Sub-bottom survey of Porto Longo Harbour, Peleponnesus, Greece, *Int J Naut Archaeol*, **1**, 170–5

Fulford, M G, 1975a *New Forest Roman Pottery*, BAR Brit Ser **17**. Oxford: British Archaeological Reports

Fulford, M G, 1975b The pottery, in B W Cunliffe 1975, 271–367

Fulford, M, Champion, T, & Long, A, (eds) 1997 *England's Coastal Heritage; a survey for English Heritage and the RCHME*, English Heritage Archaeol Rep **15**. London: English Heritage

Futter, G, 1981 Mulberry Harbour, *Airfix Magazine*, June 1981

Futter, G, 1982 Mulberry Harbour, *Airfix Magazine*, September 1982

Gates, W G, (ed) 1928 *City of Portsmouth, Records of the Corporation, 1835–1927*. Portsmouth

Gates, W G, (ed) undated 1 *City of Portsmouth, Records of the Corporation, 1928–1930*. Portsmouth

Gates, W G, (ed) undated 2 *City of Portsmouth, Records of the Corporation, 1931–1935*. Portsmouth

Gao, S, & Collins, M B, 1997 Changes in sediment transport rates caused by wave action and tidal flow time asymmetry, *J Coastal Res*, **13**, 198–201

Gardiner J P, 1987a The occupation 3500–100 bc, and The Neolithic and Bronze Age (discussion), in B W Cunliffe *Hengistbury Head Dorset,*

Volume 1: The Prehistoric and Roman Settlement, 3500 BC – AD 500, Oxford Univ Comm Archaeol Monogr **13**. Oxford: Oxford University Committee for Archaeology, 22–46 & 329–36

Gardiner J P, 1987b Tales of the unexpected: approaches to the assessment and interpretation of museum flint collections, in A G Brown & M R Edmonds (eds) *Lithic Analysis and Later British Prehistory*, BAR Brit Ser **162**. Oxford: British Archaeological Reports, 49–63

Gardiner, J P, 1988 The Composition and Distribution of Neolithic Surface Flint Assemblages in Central-Southern England. Unpublished PhD thesis, University of Reading

Gardiner, J P, 1996 Early farming communities in Hampshire, in D A Hinton & M Hughes (eds) *Archaeology in Hampshire: a framework for the Future*. Hampshire County Council, 6–12

Gardiner, M, & Hamilton, S, 1997 Knapp Farm, Bosham; a significant find of Bronze Age pottery, *Sussex Archaeol Coll*, **135**, 71–91

Gejvall, N G, 1981 Determination of burnt bones from Prehistoric graves, *OSSA LETTERS*, **2**, 1–13

Geraint Jenkins, J, 1974 *Nets and Coracles*. London: David & Charles

Gerloff, S, 1975 *The Early Bronze Daggers in Great Britain and a reconsideration of the Wessex Culture*. Munich: Prähistorische Bronzefunde, VI 2

Gersbach, E, 1974 Ältermittelbronzezeitliche Siedlungskeramik von Esslingen am Neckar, *Fundberichte aus Baden-Württemberg*, **1**, 226–50

Gilkes, O, 1998 The Roman villa at 'Spes Bona', Langstone Avenue, Langstone, Havant, *Hampshire Stud*, **53**, 49–77

Giot, P R, Briard, J, & Pape, L, 1979 *Protohistoire de la Bretagne*. Rennes: Ouest-France

Godbold, S, & Turner, R, 1992 Second Severn Crossing 1991 Welsh Intertidal Zone, *Severn Estuary Levels Research Committee Annual Report 1992*, 45–55

Godwin, H, 1945 A submerged peat bed in Portsmouth harbour. Data for the study of post-glacial history IX, *New Phytologist*, **44**, 152–5

Godwin, H, 1975 *The History of the British Flora* (2nd edition). Cambridge: Cambridge Universty Press

Godwin, H, & Godwin, M E, 1940 Submerged peat at Southampton, data for the study of post-glacial history V, *New Phytologist*, **39**, 303–7

Godwin, H, & Switsur, V R, 1966 Cambridge University Natural Radiocarbon Measurements VIII, *Radiocarbon*, **8**, 390–400

Goodburn, D M, 1991 New light on early ship- and boat building in the London area, in G L Good, R H Jones & M W Ponsford (eds) *Waterfront*

Archaeology, CBA Res Rep **74**. London: Council for British Archaeology, 105–15

Goodman, P J, 1959 Investigations into 'die-back' in *Spartina townsendii* H and J Groves. Unpublished PhD thesis, University of Southampton

Goodman, P J, & Williams, W J, 1961 Investigations into 'die back' in *Spartina townsendii* agg, *J Ecol*, **49**, 391–8

Gornitz, V, 1995 Sea-level rise: a review of recent past and near-future trends, *Earth Surfaces Processes and Landforms* **20**, 7–20

Gray, A J, 1972 The ecology of Morecombe Bay V, the salt marshes of Morecombe Bay, *J Applied Ecol*, **9**, 207–20

Gray, H, 1977 *Anatomy*. New York: Bounty Books

Greig, J, 1982 Past and present lime woods of Europe, in M Bell & S Limbrey (eds) *Archaeological Aspects of Woodland Ecology*, BAR Int Series **146**. Oxford: British Archaeological Reports, 23–55

Hall, M, & Ford, S, 1994 Archaeological excavations at Grange Road, Gosport, 1992, *Proc Hampshire Fld Club Archaeol Soc*, **50**, 5–34

Hamblin, R J O, & Harrison, D J, 1989 *Marine Aggregate Survey Phase 2: South Coast*, British Geological Survey Marine Report 88/31

Hamilton, S, 1984 Earlier first millennium pottery from the excavations at Hollingbury Camp, Sussex, 1967–9, *Sussex Archaeol Coll*, **112**, 55–61

Hampshire County Council, 1982 *Hampshire Treasures: Portsmouth City*. Winchester: Hampshire County Council

Hampshire County Council, 1992 Geotechnical Report: Site Investigations at Portsmouth Sailing Club. L.832, July 1992. Unpublished report, Hampshire County Council Surveyors Department, County Highways Laboratory

Haskins, L E, 1978 The Vegetational History of South-East Dorset. Unpublished PhD thesis, Department of Geography, University of Southampton

Hawkes, J W, 1985 The Roman Pottery, in P J Fasham *The Prehistoric Settlement at Winnall Down, Winchester: Excavations of MARC3 Site R17 in 1976 and 1977*. Hampshire Fld Club Archaeol Soc Monogr **2**. Gloucester: Sutton, 69–76

Hawkes, J W, 1987 The pottery, *A Banjo Enclosure in Micheldever Wood, Hampshire*. Hampshire Fld Club Archaeol Soc Monogr **5**, 27–33

Hawkes, J W, 1989 Later prehistoric pottery, in P J Fasham, D E Farewell & R J B Whinney *The Archaeological Site at Easton Lane, Winchester*. Hampshire Fld Club Archaeol Soc Monogr **6**. Winchester: Hampshire Field Club, 94–9

Hawkes, S C, 1969 Finds from two Middle Bronze Age Pits at Winnall. Winchester, Hampshire, *Proc Hampshire Fld Club Archaeol Soc*, **26**, 5–18

Haynes, F N, & Coulson, M G, 1982 The decline of *Spartina* in Langstone Harbour, Hampshire, *Proc Hampshire Fld Club Archaeol Soc*, **38**, 5–18

Henderson, G, & Webber, N B, 1977 Storm surge in the UK south coast, *Dock and Harbour Authority*, **58**, 21–2

Hencken, H O, 1932 *The archaeology of Cornwall and Scilly*. London: Methuen

Heyworth, A, 1978 Submerged forests around the British Isles; their dating and relevance as indicators of postglacial land and sea-level changes, in J Fletcher (ed) *Dendrochronology in Europe: principles, interpretations and applications to archaeology and history*. Nat Maritime Mus Greenwich Archaeol Ser **4**, Res Lab Archaeol Hist Art Oxford Univ Pub **2**, BAR Int Ser **51**. Oxford: British Archaeological Reports

Heyworth, A, & Kidson, C, 1982 Sea-level changes in south-west England and in Wales, *Proc Geologists' Assoc*, **93**, 91–111

Hillam, J, 1998 *Dendrochronology. Guidelines on producing and interpreting dendrochronological dates*. London: English Heritage

Hillam, J, Morgan, R A, & Tyers, I, 1987 Sapwood estimates and the dating of short ring sequences, in R G W Ward (ed) *Applications of tree-ring studies: current research in dendrochronology and related areas*, BAR Int Ser **333**. Oxford: British Archaeological Reports, 165–85

Hinde, T, (ed) 1985 *The Domesday Book*. London: Guild Publishing

Hjulstrom, F, 1939 Transportation of detritus by moving water. *Recent Marine Sediments: a symposium*. Tulsa: American Association of Petrological Geologists, 5–31

Hodder, I, 1974 The distribution of two types of Romano-British coarse pottery in the West Sussex region, *Sussex Archaeol Coll*, **122,** 86–96

Hodge, W J, 1946 The Mulberry Invasion Harbours – their design, preparation and installation, *The Structural Engineer*, March 1946

Hodgson, J M, 1964 The low-level Pleistocene marine sands and gravels of the West Sussex Coastal Plain, *Proc Geologists' Assoc*, **75**, 547–61

Hodgson, J M, 1967 *Soils of the West Sussex Coastal Plain*, Soil Survey of England and Wales Bull **3**. Harpenden: Rothamsted Experimental Station

Hodson, D, (ed) 1978 *Maps of Portsmouth before 1801*, Portsmouth Record Series. Portsmouth: Portsmouth City Council

Hodson, F, & West, I M, 1972 Holocene deposits of Fawley, Hampshire, the Development of Southampton Water, *Proc Geologists' Assoc*, **83**, 421–41

Holden, J L, Phakey, P P, & Clement, J G, 1995a

Scanning electron microscope observation of incinerated human femoral bone: a case study, *Forensic Sci Int*, **74**, 17–28

Holden, J L, Phakley, P P, & Clement, J G, 1995b Scanning electron microscope observations of heat-treated human bone, *Forensic Sci Int*, **74**, 29–45

Holmes, A G, 1989 A Romano-British site at Shedfield, Hants, *Proc Hampshire Fld Club Archaeol Soc*, **45**, 25–41

Holmes, N J, & Coughlan, J, 1973 The Ascidian fauna of Southampton Water, *Proc Hampshire Fld Club Archaeol Soc*, **30**, 9–15

Hooley, R W, 1905 Excavations on the site of the Electricity Light Works, Southampton, May 1903, *Papers of the Proc Hampshire Fld Club*, **5**, 47–52

Howard, A E, & Bennet, D B, 1979 The substrate preference and burrowing behaviour of juvenile lobsters (*Homarus gammarus*), *J Natur Hist*, **13**, 433–8

Hughes, M, 1974 Iron Age site, Wallington Military Rd, Fareham 1972, *Rescue Archaeol Hampshire*, **2**, 29–97

Hughes, M, 1976 *The small towns of Hampshire: the archaeological and historical implications of development*. Southampton: Hampshire Archaeological Committee

Hughes, M, 1977 Late Neolithic grooved ware from Wallington, *Proc Hampshire Fld Club Archaeol Soc*, **34**, 79

Hughes, M, 1990 The archaeology of D-Day: the remains at Stone Point, Lepe, *Archaeol Hampshire Annu Rep*, 1990, 15–22

Hughes, M, 1982 *Archaeology in Hampshire 1981*. Winchester: Hampshire County Council

Hughes, M, 1992 The archaeology of D-Day: the remains at Stone Point, Lepe, *Fortress* (November 1992)

Hughes, M, & ApSimon, A, 1977 A Mesolithic flintworking site on the south coast motorway (M27) near Fort Wallington, Fareham, Hampshire, 1972, *Proc Hampshire Fld Club Archaeol Soc*, **34**, 23–35

Hundt, H-J, 1951 Eine neue jungneolithische Gruppe im ostliche Bayern (Chamer Gruppe), *Germania*, **29**, 5–17

Hutchinson, G, 1994 *Medieval Ships and Shipping*. Leicester: Leicester University Press

HWMTA, 1997 *Search: annual report 1996/7 of the Hampshire & Wight Trust for Maritime Archaeology*.

Jacobi, R, 1981 The last hunters in Hampshire, in S Shennan & R T Schadla-Hall (eds) *The Archaeology of Hampshire*, Hampshire Fld Club Archaeol Soc Monogr **1**. Hampshire: Hampshire Field Club and Archaeological Society, 10–25

James, H, 1847 On a section exposed by the excavation at the new stream basin in Portsmouth Dockyard, *Quart J Geological Soc London* **3**, 249–51

Jarvis, M G, Allen, R H, Fordham, S J, Hazelden, J, Moffat, A J, & Sturdy, R G, 1984 *Soils and their use in South East England*, Soil Survey of England and Wales Bull **15**. Harpenden: Soil Survey of England and Wales

Jenkins, P, 1986 *Battle over Portsmouth*. Midhurst: Middleton Press

Jockenhövel, A, 1991 Räumliche Mobilitat von Personen in der mittleren Bronzezeit des westlichen Europa, *Germania*, **69** (1), 49–62

Jones, D K C, 1971 The Vale of the Brooks, in R B G Williams (ed) *A Guide to Sussex Excursions*. Inst Brit Geogr Conference (Jan 1971). Falmer, 43–6

Keeble-Shaw, A, 1958 Windmills and watermills in Hampshire, Part 1, Windmills, *Proc Hampshire Fld Club Archaeol Soc*, **15**, 107–10

Kerney, M P, 1999 *Atlas of the Land and Freshwater Molluscs of Britain and Ireland*. Colchester: The Conchological Society of Great Britain and Ireland

Kerney, M P, & Cameron, R A D, 1979 *A Field Guide to the Land Snails of Britain and North-west Europe*. London: Collins

King, A C, 1989 A Bronze Age cremation cemetery at Oliver's Battery, near Winchester, and some related finds, *Proc Hampshire Fld Club Archaeol Soc*, **45**, 13–23

King, A, & Soffe, G, 1994 The Iron Age and Roman temple on Hayling Island, in A P Fitzpatrick & E L Morris (eds) *The Iron Age in Wessex: Recent Work*. Salisbury: Wessex Archaeology, 114–16

King, A, & Soffe, G, 1998 Internal organisation and deposition at the Iron Age temple on Hayling Island, *Hampshire Stud*, **53**, 35–47

Köninger, J, & Schlichtherle, H, 1990 Zur Schnurkeramik und Frühbronzezeit am Bodensee, *Fundberichte aus Baden-Württemberg*, **15**, 149–73

Lane, E W, & Carlson, E J, 1954 Some observations on the effect of particle shape on the movement of coarse sediments, *Trans American Geophysical Union*, **35**, 453–62

Lawson, A J, 1999 The Bronze Age hoards of Hampshire, in A F Harding (ed) *Experiment and Design; archaeological studies in honour of John Coles*. Oxford: Oxbow Books, 94–107

Le Provost, F, Giot, P R, & Onnée, Y, 1972 Prospections sur les collines de Saint-Nicolas-du-Pélem, (Côtes-du-Nord) du Chalcolithique a la Préhistoire, *Annales de Bretagne*, **79**, 39–48

Lloyd, A T, 1967 The Salterns of the Lymington Area, *Proc Hampshire Fld Club Archaeol Soc*, **24**, 86–102

Lobb, H, 1867 *Successful Oyster Culture*. London: William Ridgeway

Locock, M, forthcoming, A Later Bronze Age landscape on the Avon Levels: settlement, shelters and saltmarsh at Cabot Park, in J

Brück (ed) *Landscape and Settlement in Bronze Age Britain.*

Long, A J, 1992 Coastal responses to changes in the East Kent Fens and southeast England, UK over the last 7500 years, *Proc Geologists' Assoc,* **103**, 187–99

Long, A J & Innes, J B, 1993 Holocene sea-level changes and coastal sedimentation in Romney Marsh, southeast England, UK, *Proc Geologists' Assoc,* **104**, 223–37

Long, A J, and Roberts, D H, 1997 Sea-level change, in M Fulford *et al* 1997, 25–49

Long, A J & Scaife, R G, 1996 Pleistocene and Holocene Evolution of Southampton Water and its Tributaries. Unpublished MS, Environmental Research Centre, Department of Geography, University of Durham

Long, A J, Scaife, R G, & Edwards, R J, 1999 Pine pollen in intertidal sediments from Poole Harbour, UK; implications for late-Holocene sediment accretion rates and sea-level rise, *Quat Int,* **55**, 3–16

Long, A J, & Shennan, I, 1993 Holocene relative sea-level and crustal movements in southeast and northeast England, UK, in L A Owen, I Stewart & C Vita Finzi (eds) *Neotectonics: recent advances,* Quaternary Proceedings 3. Cambridge: Quaternary Research Association

Long, A J, & Tooley, M J, 1995 Holocene sea-level and crustal movements in Hampshire and Southeast England, United Kingdom, *J Coastal Res* (Special Issue) **17**, 299–310

Longcroft, C J, 1857 *A Topographical Account of the Hundred of Bosmere.* London

Lou, J, & Ridd, P V, 1997 Modelling of suspended sediment transport in coastal areas under waves and currents, *Estuarine Coastal and Shelf Science,* **45**, 1–16

Louwe Kooijmans, L P, 1993 Wetland exploitation and upland relations of prehistoric communities in the Netherlands, in J P Gardiner (ed) *Flatlands and Wetlands: current themes in East Anglian archaeology.* East Anglian Archaeol Rep **50**. Norwich: Scole Archaeological Committee, 71–116

Lyne, M A B, & Jefferies, R S, 1979 *The Alice Holt / Farnham Roman Pottery Industry,* CBA Res Rep **30**. London: Council for British Archaeology

Macan, T, 1977 *A key to the British fresh- and brackish-water gastropods: with notes on their ecology,* Freshwater Biological Assoc scientific publication **13** (4th edition). Ambleside: Freshwater Biological Association

Magrath, P, 1992 *Fort Cumberland, 1747–1850; key to an island's defence,* The Portsmouth Papers **60**. Portsmouth

MacGregor, A, 1985 *Bone, Antler, Ivory and Horn; the technology of skeletal materials since the Roman period.* London: Croom Helm

McKinley, J I, 1989 Cremations: expectations, methodologies and realities, in C A Roberts, F

Lee & J Bintliff (eds) *Burial Archaeology: current research, methods and developments,* BAR Brit Ser **211**. Oxford: British Archaeological Reports, 65–76

McKinley, J I, 1993 Bone fragment size and weights of bone from modern British cremations and its implications for the interpretation of archaeological cremations, *Int J Osteoarchaeol,* **3**, 283–7

McKinley, J I , 1994a *The Anglo-Saxon Cemetery at Spong Hill, North Elmham Part VIII: the cremations,* East Anglian Archaeol Rep **69**. Dereham: Field Archaeology Division, Norfolk Museums Service

McKinley, J I, 1994b Bone fragment size in British cremation burials and its implications for pyre technology and ritual, *J Archaeol Sci,* **21**, 339–42

McKinley, J I, 1997a Bronze Age 'Barrows' and Funerary Rites and Rituals of Cremation, *Proc Prehist Soc,* **63**, 129–45

McKinley, J I, 1997b The cremated human bone from burial and cremation-related deposits, in A P Fitzpatrick 1997, 55–73

McKisack, M, 1959 *The Fourteenth Century, 1307–1399.* Oxford: Clarendon Press

McMillan, N F, 1968 *British Shells.* London: Frederick Warne & Co

McMinn, R M H, & Hutchings, R T, 1985 *A Colour Atlas of Human Anatomy.* London: Wolfe Medical Publications

Mariette, H, 1961 Une Urne de L'Age du Bronze à Hardelot (Pas-de-Calais), *Helinium,* **1**, 229–32

Marshall, J R, 1962 The morphology of the upper Solway salt marshes, *Scott Geogr Mag,* **78**, 81–99

May, V J, 1969 Reclamation and shoreline change in Poole Harbour, Dorset, *Proc Dorset Natur Hist Soc,* **90**, 141–54

Melville, R V, & Freshney, E C, 1982 *The Hampshire Basin and Adjoining Area* (4th edition). London: HMSO

Menard, H W, 1950 Sediment movement in relation to current velocity, *J Sediment Petrology,* **20**, 148–60

Milne, G, 1995 Foreshore Archaeology, in RCHME, *Thames Gateway; recording historic buildings and landscapes on the Thames Estuary.* Swindon: Royal Commission on the Historical Monuments of England, 23–7

Milne, G, with Bates, M, & Webber, M, 1997 Problems, potential and partial solutions: an archaeological study of the tidal Thames, England, *World Archaeol,* **29**, 130–46

Milne, G, McKewan, C, & Goodburn, D, 1998 *Nautical Archaeology on the Foreshore: Hulk recording on the Medway.* Swindon: Royal Commission on the Historical Monuments of England

Mitchell, V, & Smith, K, 1984 *Branch Line to Hayling.* Midhurst: Middleton Press

Momber, G, 1990 Archaeological, hydrographic and

climatological studies to prove the existence of an ancient fish-trap in Caernarfon Bay. Unpublished MSc thesis, University of Wales

Momber, G, 1991 Gorad Beuno: investigation into an ancient fish trap in Caernarfon Bay, N Wales, *Int J Naut Archaeol*, **20**, 95–109

Mook, W G, 1986 Business meeting: recommendations/resolutions adopted by the twelfth International Radiocarbon Conference, *Radiocarbon*, **28**, 799

Moore, P, 1984 *A Guide to the Industrial Archaeology of Hampshire and the Isle of Wight*. Southampton: Southampton University Industrial Archaeology Group

Moore, P D, 1977 Ancient distribution of lime trees in Britain, *Nature*, **268**, 13–14

Moore, P D, Webb, J A, and Collinson, M E, 1992 *Pollen Analysis* (2nd edition). Oxford: Blackwell Scientific

Morris, E L, 1994 Production and distribution of pottery and salt in Iron Age Britain: a review, *Proc Prehist Soc*, **60**, 371–93

Mottershead, D N, 1976 The Quaternary History of the Portsmouth region, *Portsmouth Geographical Essays*, **2**, 1–21

Muckelroy, K, 1980 Two Bronze Age cargoes in British waters, *Antiquity*, **54**, 100–9

Muckelroy, K 1981 Middle Bronze Age trade between Britain and Europe: a maritime prospective, *Proc Prehist Soc*, **47**, 275–97

Murphy, P, & Wilkinson, T J, 1991 Survey and excavation on the tidal foreshore zone, in J M Coles & D M Goodburn (eds) *Wet Site Excavation and Survey: proceedings of a conference at the Museum of London, October 1990*, WARP Occas Pap **5**. Exeter: Wetland Archaeology Research Project, 10–15

Narthorst, A G, 1873 On the distribution of arctic plants during the post-glacial epoch, *J Botany*, London **2**, 225–8

Nayling, N, 1997 Further fieldwork and post-excavation: Magor Pill, Gwent Levels intertidal zone, *Archaeology in the Severn Estuary 1996: Annual Report of the Severn Estuary Levels Research Committee* **7**, 85–93

NERC, 1980 *The Solent Estuarine System; an assessment of present knowledge*, NERC Pub Ser C, **22**. Swindon: Natural Environment Research Council

Neal, D S, 1980 Bronze Age, Iron Age and Roman settlement sites at Little Somborne and Ashley, Hampshire, *Proc Hampshire Fld Club Archaeol Soc*, **36**, 363–5

Needham, S, 1992 Holocene alluvial and interstratified settlement evidence in the Thames Valley at Runnymede Bridge, in S Needham & M G Macklin (eds) *Alluvial Archaeology in Britain*, Oxbow Monogr **27**. Oxford: Oxbow, 246–60

Needham, S, 1996 Chronology and Periodisation in the British Bronze Age, *Acta Archaeologica*, **67**, Supplementa 1, 121–40

Needham, S, & Dean, M, 1987 La cargaison de Langdon Bay à Douvres (Grande Bretagne) – La signification pour les échanges à travers la Manche, in J-C Blanchet (ed) *Les Relations avec le Continent et les Iles Britanniques à l'Age du Bronze*, Congrés Préhistorique de France, 1984, Actes du Colloque de Bronze de Lille, RAP/SPF, Suppl to Revue Archéologique de Picardie, 119–24

Neumann, H, & Bell, M G, 1997, Intertidal survey in the Welsh Severn Estuary 1996, *Archaeology in the Severn Estuary 1996: Annual Report of the Severn Estuary Levels Research Committee* **7**, 3–20

Nicholls, J, 1987 Two Bronze Age urns from Portsdown, *Proc Hampshire Fld Club Archaeol Soc*, **43**, 15–20

Nicholls, R J, 1987 Evolution of the upper reaches of the Solent River and the formation of Poole and Christchurch Bays, in K E Barber (ed) *Wessex and the Isle of Wight – Field Guide*. Cambridge: Quaternary Research Association, 99–114

Nicholls, R J, & Clark, M J, 1986 Flandrian peat deposits at Hurst Castle Spit, *Proc Hampshire Fld Club Archaeol Soc*, **42**, 15–21

Nyman, J A, Carloss, M, DeLaune, R D, & Partrick Jnr, W H, 1994 Erosion rather than plant dieback as the mechanism of marsh loss in an estuarine marsh, *Earth Surface Processes and Landforms*, **19**, 69–84

Orford, J D, Carter, R W G, McKenna, J, & Jennings, S C, 1995 The relationship between the rate of mesoscale sea-level rise and the rate of retreat of swash-aligned gravel dominated barriers, *Marine Geology*, **124**, 177–86

Parker Pearson, M, 1990 The production and distribution of Bronze Age pottery in south-west Britain, *Cornish Archaeol*, **29**, 5–32

Parker Pearson, M, 1997 Southwestern Bronze Age pottery, in I Kinnes & G Varndell (eds) *'Unbaked urns of rudely shape': essays on British and Irish pottery for Ian Longworth*, Oxbow Monogr **55**. Oxford: Oxbow, 89–101

Paszthory, K, & Mayer, E F, 1998 *Die Äxte und Beile in Bayern*. Munich: Prähistorische Bronzefunde, **IX**, 20

Patterson, A T, 1967 *Palmerston's Folly; the Portsdown and Spithead Forts*, The Portsmouth Papers **3**. Portsmouth

Pearson, G W & Stuiver, M, 1986 High-precision calibration of the radiocarbon timescale, 500–2500 BC, *Radiocarbon*, **28**, 839–62

Perraton, C, 1953 The salt-marshes of the Hampshire-Sussex border, *J Ecol*, **41**, 240–7

Phillips, R A, 1908 *Vertigo moulinsiana*, Dupuy; an addition to the Irish fauna, *Ir Natur*, **17**, 89–93

Philpots, J R, 1890 *Oysters, and all about them* (2 vols). London & Leicester: John Richardson & Co

Pitts, M W, 1980 A gazetteer of Mesolithic sites on the West Sussex coastal plain, *Sussex Archaeol Coll*, **118**, 153–62

Preece, R C, Scourse, J D, Houghton, S D, Knudsen, K L, & Penney, D N, 1990 The Pleistocene sea-level and neotectonic history of the Eastern Solent, southern England, *Phil Trans Roy Soc London*, B **328**, 425–77

Prestwich, J, 1872 On the presence of a raised beach on Portsdown Hill, near Portsmouth and on the occurrence of flint implements on a high level at Downton, *Quart J Geological Soc*, **28**, 38–41

Pycroft, N, 1998 *Hayling An Island of Laughter and Tears*. Hayling Island: N Pycroft.

Quinn, R, 1998 Marine high-resolution reflection seismology: acquisition, processing and applications. Unpublished PhD thesis, University of Southampton

Quinn, R, Bull, J M, & Dix, J K, 1997 Imaging wooden artefacts with Chirp Sources, *Archaeol Prospection*, **4**, 25–35

Quinn, R, Bull, J M, & Dix, J K, 1998 Optimal processing of marine high-resolution seismic reflection (Chirp) data, *Marine Geophysical Res*, **20**, 13–20

Rankine, W F, 1962 A Mesolithic site on the foreshore at Cams, Fareham, Hants, *Proc Hampshire Fld Club Archaeol Soc*, **17**, 140–2

Ranwell, D S, 1964 Spartina salt marshes in Southern England II, Rate and seasonal pattern of accretion, *J Ecol*, **52**, 79–94

Rao, T C S, 1988 Geophysical techniques to locate pre-historic sites and artefacts on the continental shelf, in S R Rao (ed) *Marine Archaeology of Indian Ocean Countries*. Goa: National Institution of Oceanography, 73–7

Redknap, M, 1990 Surveying for underwater archaeological sites: signs in the sands, *Hydrographic J*, **58**, 11–16

Reger, A J C, 1994 A brief history of Hayling Priory and the legend of the lost church. Unpublished MS

Reger, A J C, forthcoming, A brief history of Hayling Priory and the legend of the lost church. Havant Regional Papers **2**

Reid, C, 1892 The Pleistocene deposits of the Sussex Coast and their equivalents in other districts, *Quart J Geological Soc London*, **48**, 344–61

Reid, C, 1893 A fossiliferous Pleistocene deposit at Stone, on the Hampshire coast, *Quart J Geological Soc London*, **49**, 325–9

Reid, C, 1895 On charred pine-wood from Dorset peat mosses, *Proc Dorset Natur Hist Antiquarian Fld Club*, **16**, 14–16

Reid, C, 1896 An early Neolithic kitchen-midden and tufaceous deposit at Blashenwell near Corfe Castle, *Proc Dorset Natur Hist Antiquarian Fld Club*, **17**, 67–75

Reid, C, 1899 *Origin of the British Flora*. London: Dulau & Co

Reid, C, 1902 *The Geology of the Country around Southampton*, Memoirs of the Geological Survey: England and Wales (Sheet 315). London: HMSO

Reid, C, 1903 *The Geology of the Country near Chichester*. Memoirs of the Geological Survey: England and Wales (Sheet 317). London: HMSO

Reid, C, 1913 *Submerged Forests*. Cambridge: Cambridge University Press

Rippon, S, 1996 *Gwent Levels: the evolution of a wetland landscape*, CBA Res Rep **105**. York: Council for British Archaeology

Rippon, S, 1997 *The Severn Estuary: landscape evolution and wetland reclamation*. Leicester: Leicester University Press

Rippon, S, 1999 Fields of corn and flocks of sheep: wetland transformation during the medieval period. Lecture to Geoarchaeology Workshop: Landscape Changes over Archaeological Timescales, University of Reading, 15–17 December 1999

RCHME, 1979 *Long Barrows in Hampshire and the Isle of Wight*. London: HMSO

RCHME, 1992 Catalogue of Archaeological Excavations, Hampshire, National Monuments Record, Archaeological Section. Unpublished database listing

Roberts, M B, and Parfitt, S A, 1999 *Boxgrove: a Middle Pleistocene hominid site at Eartham Quarry, Boxgrove, West Sussex*, English Heritage Archaeol Rep **17**. London: English Heritage

Robinson, M, 1988 Molluscan evidence for pasture and meadowland on the floodplain of the upper Thames basin, in P Murphy & C French (eds) *The Exploitation of the Wetlands*, BAR Brit Ser **186**. Oxford: British Archaeological Reports, 101–12

Rochester, M, undated *Salt in Cheshire*. Cheshire Libraries and Museums

Rowlands, M J, 1976 *The Organisation of Middle Bronze Age Metalworking*, BAR Brit Ser **31**. Oxford: British Archaeological Reports

Rudkin, D J, 1980 *Early Man in Portsmouth and South-East Hampshire*, The Portsmouth Papers **31**. Portsmouth City Council

Salisbury, C R, 1991 Primitive British Fishweirs, in G L Good, R H Jones & M W Ponsford (eds) *Waterfront Archaeology*, CBA Res Rep **74**. London: Council for British Archaeology, 76–87

Saunders, A, 1997 *Channel Defences*. London: Batsford/English Heritage

Scaife, R G, 1980 Late-Devensian and Flandrian palaeoecological studies in the Isle of Wight. Unpublished PhD thesis, University of London, King's College

Scaife, R G, 1982 Late-Devensian and early Flandrian vegetation changes in southern England, in S Limbrey & M Bell (eds) *Archaeological aspects of woodland ecology*, BAR Int Ser **146**. Oxford: British Archaeological Reports, 57–74

Scaife, R G, 1987 The Late-Devensian and Flandrian vegetation of the Isle of Wight, in K E Barber (ed) *Wessex and the Isle of Wight*,

Field Guide. Cambridge: Quaternary Research Association, 156–80

Scaife R G, 1991 Pollen investigation and vegetational history, in P W Cox & C M Hearne *Redeemed from the Heath: the archaeology of the Wytch Farm Oilfield, 1987–1990*, Dorset Natur Hist Archaeol Soc Monogr **9**. Dorchester: Dorset Natural History and Archaeological Society, 180–97

Scaife, R G, & Burrin, P, 1983 Floodplain development and vegetational history of the Sussex High Weald and some archaeological implications, *Sussex Archaeol Coll*, **121**, 1–10

Scaife, R G, and Burrin, P J, 1985 The environmental impact of prehistoric man as recorded in the upper Cuckmere valley at Stream Farm, Chiddingly, *Sussex Archaeol Coll*, **123**, 27–34

Schick, K D, 1986 *Stone Age sites in the making*, BAR Int Ser **319**. Oxford: British Archaeological Reports

Schofield, A J, 1989 Recent finds from Rainbow Bar and some thoughts on site formation, *Lithics*, **10**, 9–15

Scott, E, 1993 *A Gazetteer of Roman Villas in Britain*, Leicester Archaeol Monogr **1**. Leicester: University of Leicester, School of Archaeological Studies

Seager Smith, R H, and Woodward, A, in press, Pottery, in Walker, K E, and Farwell, D E, *Twyford Down, Hampshire; Archaeological Investigations on the M3 Motorway from Bar End to Compton, 1990–1993*. Hampshire Fld Club Archaeol Soc Monogr **9**, 46–78

Sellwood, L, 1984 Tribal boundaries viewed from the perspective of numismatic evidence, in B W Cunliffe & D Miles (eds) *Aspects of the Iron Age in Central Southern Britain*, Oxford Univ Comm Archaeol Monogr **2**. Oxford: Oxford University Committee for Archaeology, Institute of Archaeology, 191–204

Shackley, M, 1978 The behaviour of artefacts as sedimentary particles in a fluviatile environment, *Archaeometry*, **20**, 55–61

Sheldrick, C, Lowe, J J, & Reynier, M J, 1997 Palaeolithic barbed point from Gransmoor, East Yorkshire, England, *Proc Prehist Soc*, **63**, 359–70

Shennan, I, 1989 Holocene crustal movements and sea-level change in Great Britain, *J Quat Sci*, **4**, 77–89

Shore, T W, 1893 Hampshire mudflats and other alluvium, *Papers and Proc Hampshire Fld Club*, **2**, 181–200

Shore, T W, 1905 The origin of Southampton Water, *Papers and Proc Hampshire Fld Club*, **5**, 1–25

Shore, T W, & Elwes, J W, 1889 The new dock extension at Southampton, *Proc Hampshire Fld Club*, **1**, 43–56

Skelton, I, 1826 *Topographical and Historical Account of Hayling Island*. Petersfield: Frank Westwood

Smith, C, & Bonsall, C, 1991 Late Upper Palaeolithic and Mesolithic chronology: points of interest from recent research, in N Barton, A J Roberts & D A Roe (eds) *The Late Glacial in north-west Europe: Human adaptation and environmental change at the end of the Pleistocene*, CBA Res Rep **77**. London: Council for British Archaeology, 208–12

Smith, P, 1994 The Portsmouth Convict Hulks, 1780–1850. Unpublished dissertation for Diploma in Local History, University of Portsmouth

Sparks, F K, 1983 Letter from Portsmouth Town Clerk to the Havant U D C Clerk, Hampshire Records Office, Winchester, IS 1774/DDC/182

Soffe, G, 1980 Note, *Archaeol Hampshire Annu Rep 1980*, 7

Soffe, G, 1981 Recent archaeological discoveries in the Havant and Hayling Island Area, *SHARG Newsl*, **30**, 7–8

Soffe, G, 1995 *The Priory and Parish Church of St Mary the Virgin, Hayling Island; an illustrated guide*. Alresford: Applegraphics Ltd

Soffe, G, forthcoming, Bronze Age burials at Langstone and Hayling Island (quoted in Willams & Soffe 1987)

Soffe, G, Nicholls, J, & Moore, G, 1988 The Roman tilery and aisled building at Crookhorn, Hants, excavations 1974–5, *Proc Hampshire Fld Club Archaeol Soc*, **45**, 43–112

Stace, C, 1991 *New flora of the British Isles*. Cambridge: Cambridge University Press

Stace, C 1997 *New flora of the British Isles* (2nd edition). Cambridge: Cambridge University Press

Stagg, D J, 1980 Archaeological and historical aspects of change in the Solent coastline, in NERC, 1980, 19

Steane, J M, & Foreman, M, 1991 The archaeology of medieval fishing tackle, in G L Good, R H Jones & M W Ponsford (eds) *Waterfront Archaeology*, CBA Res Rep **74**. London: Council for British Archaeology, 88–101

Stone, J F S, 1941 The Deverel-Rimbury settlement on Thorny Down, Winterbourne Gunner, S. Wilts, *Proc Prehist Soc*, **7**, 114–33

Stuart, J D M, & Birbeck, J M, 1936 A Celtic Village on Twyford Down – excavated 1933–1934, *Proc Hampshire Fld Club Archaeol Soc*, **13**, 188–212

Stuiver, M J, & Pearson, G W, 1986 High-precision calibration of the radiocarbon time-scale, AD 1950–6000 BC, *Radiocarbon*, **33**, 35–66

Stuiver, M, & Reimer, P J, 1986 A computer program for radiocarbon age calculation, *Radiocarbon*, **28**, 1022–30

Sutherland, F M J, 1984 Flandrian Sea-level Changes of the South Coast of England. Unpublished MSc thesis, University of Durham

Sydenham, J, 1844 An account of the opening of some Barrows in South Dorsetshire, *Archaeologia*, **30**, 320–38

Taylor, R, 1988, Hoards – the interpretation and analysis of Bronze Age hoards in southern England. Unpublished PhD thesis, University of Reading

Terry, J A, 1987 East Holme Pottery, *Proc Dorset Natur Hist Archaeol Soc*, **109**, 39–46

The Hampshire Telegraph, 1833 *The Hampshire Telegraph*, p4, col 4, 26 August 1833, No 1768

Thomas, I, 1960 The Excavations at Kynance, 1957–60, *The Lizard* (ns), **1** (4), 5–16

Thompson, F H, (ed) 1980 *Archaeology and Coastal Change*, London Occas Pap **1** (ns). London: Society of Antiquaries of London

Tomalin, D J, 1983 British Biconical Urns: their character and chronology and their relationship with indigenous early Bronze Age ceramics. Unpublished PhD thesis, University of Southampton

Tomalin, D J, 1988 Armorican vases à anses and their occurrence in southern Britain, *Proc Prehist Soc*, **54**, 203–21

Tomalin, D J, 1993 Maritime archaeology as a coastal management issue: a Solent case study from the SCOPAC coast, *Proceedings of the 1992 SCOPAC Littlehampton Conference on the role of coastal study groups*. Standing Conference on Problems Associated with the Coastline (SCOPAC). Newport, Isle of Wight: Isle of Wight County Council

Tomalin, D J, 1996 The character and inferred intra-site chronology of the Early Bronze Age Trevisker style pottery, in G Smith, Archaeology and environment of a Bronze Age cairn and prehistoric and Romano-British field system at Chysauster, Gulval, near Penzance, Cornwall, *Proc Prehist Soc*, **62**, 167–219

Tomalin, D J, Loader, R, & Scaife, R G, forthcoming, *Coastal Archaeology in a Dynamic Environment: a Solent case study*, English Heritage Archaeol Rep. London: English Heritage

Tooley, M J, 1990 Sea-level and coastline changes during the last 5000 years, in S McGrail (ed) *Maritime Celts, Frisians and Saxons*, CBA Res Rep **71**. London: Council for British Archaeology, 1–16

Trigg, H R, 1892 *Guide to Hayling Island*.

Tubbs, C R, 1980 Processes and impacts in the Solent, in NERC 1980, 1–5

Tweed, R, 2000 *A History of Langstone Harbour and its Environs in the County of Hampshire*. Winchester: Dido Publications

Tyson, H J, Fulford, M G, & Crutchley, S J, 1997 Survey and recording in the intertidal zone, in M Fulford *et al*, 1997, 74–102

Ullett, M, 1993, Palynological investigation of peat underlying coastal marine deposits at the northern margin of Langstone Harbour. Unpublished BSc dissertation, School of Biological Sciences, University of Portsmouth

University of Portsmouth and Wessex Archaeology, 1993 The Langstone Harbour Project; an integrated research design for the study, mapping and interpretation of the archaeological resource of an intertidal zone. Unpublished MS for Hampshire County Council

van de Noort, R, & Davies, P, 1993 *Wetland Heritage: an archaeological assessment of the Humber Wetlands*. Hull: Humber Wetlands Project, School of Geography and Earth Resources, University of Hull

VCH, 1908 *The Victoria History of Hampshire and the Isle of Wight*, (ed W Page), **3**. London: Constable

VCH, 1912 *The Victoria History of Hampshire and the Isle of Wight*, (ed W Page), **5**. London: Constable

Velegrakis, A F, Dix, J K, & Collins, M B, 1999 Late Pleistocene/Holocene evolution of the upper reaches of the Solent River, Southern England, based upon marine geophysical evidence, *Journ Geol Soc, London* **156**, 73–87

Vine, P, 1965 *London's Lost Route to the Sea*. London: David & Charles

Vine, P A L, 1986 *London's Route to the Sea*. London: David & Charles

Warren, F, 1926–30 Note on a Roman Villa at Havant, *Proc Hampshire Fld Club Archaeol Soc*, **10**, 286–7

Waton, P V, 1982a Man's impact on the chalklands: some new pollen evidence, in M Bell & S Limbrey (eds) *Archaeological Aspects of Woodland Ecology*, BAR Int Series **146**. Oxford: British Archaeological Reports, 75–91

Waton, P V, 1982b A palynological study of the impact of man on the landscape of central southern England, with special reference to the chalklands. Unpublished PhD thesis, Department of Geography, University of Southampton

Webb, P A O, & Suchey, J M, 1985 Epiphyseal union of the anterior iliac crest and medial clavicle in a modern multiracial sample of American males and females, *American J Phys Anthropol*, **68**, 457–66

Webber, N B, 1980 Hydrography and water circulation in the Solent, in NERC, 1980, 25–35

Wessex Archaeology, 1989 W188 East Horton Farm, Hampshire. Unpublished client report

Wessex Archaeology, 1993 *The Southern Rivers Palaeolithic Project*, Report 1. Salisbury: Wessex Archaeology

Wessex Archaeology, 1994a The Langstone Harbour Archaeological Survey Project Archaeological Desk-Based Assessment. Unpublished report for Hampshire County Council

Wessex Archaeology, 1994b *The Southern Rivers Palaeolithic Project*, Report 3. Salisbury: Wessex Archaeology

Wessex Archaeology, 1999 Budds Farm WTW sea defences, Langstone Hampshire. Unpublished client report no 45494, Jan 1999

West, I M, 1980 Geology of the Solent estuarine system, in NERC, 1980, 6–18

West, R G, 1972 Relative land-sea-level changes in southeastern England during the Pleistocene, *Phil Trans Roy Soc London*, A **272**, 87–98

West, R G, Devoy, R J N, Funnell, B M, & Robinson, J E, 1984 Pleistocene deposits at Earnley, Bracklesham Bay, Sussex, *Phil Trans Roy Soc London*, B **306**, 137–57

White, H J O, 1913 *The Geology of the Country near Fareham and Havant*, Memoirs of the Geological Survey: England and Wales (Sheet 316). London: Darling & Son for HMSO

White, W C F, 1971 A gazetteer of brick and tile works in Hampshire, *Proc Hampshire Fld Club Archaeol Soc*, **28**, 81–97

Wilkinson, T J, & Murphy, P, 1986 Archaeological survey of an intertidal zone: the submerged landscape of the Essex Coast, England, *J Fld Archaeol*, **13**, 177–94

Wilkinson, T J, & Murphy, P, 1995 *Archaeology of the Essex Coast. Volume 1: The Hullbridge Survey*. Chelmsford: Essex County Council Archaeology Section with Scole Archaeological Committee

Will, R T, & Clark, J A, 1996 Stone artifact movements on impounded shorelines: a case study from Maine, *American Antiquity*, **61**, 499–519

Williams, P, & Soffe, G, 1987 A Late Bronze Age timber structure on Hayling Island, *Hampshire Fld Club Newsl* (ns), **8**, 23–4

Williams-Freeman, J P, 1919 *Proc Hampshire Fld Club*, **8**, 353

Wilson, W S, & Sully, F W, 1947 The traversing and side launching of heavy craft, *Proceedings of the Conference on Wartime Engineering Problems*, Institute of Civil Engineers (June 1947)

Wimpey (Geo Wimpey & Company), 1962 Report on site investigations for proposed land reclamation scheme in Langstone Harbour. Portsmouth, City Engineer Report, 21–40

Winder, J M, 1991 Marine Mollusca, in P W Cox & C M Hearne *Redeemed from the Heath: the archaeology of the Wytch Farm Oilfield, 1987–1990*, Dorset Natur Hist Archaeol Soc Monogr **9**. Dorchester: Dorset Natural History and Archaeological Society 212–15

Winder, J M, 1992 A study of the variation in oyster shells from archaeological sites and a discussion of oyster exploitation. Unpublished PhD thesis, University of Southampton

Wood, R J 1947, Phoenix, *Proceedings of the Conference on Wartime Engineering Problems*, Institute of Civil Engineers (June 1947)

Wooldridge, S W, & Linton, D L, 1955 *Structure, Surface and Drainage in South-east England*. London: Philip

Woodward, A, & Cane, C, 1991 The Bronze Age pottery, in J A Nowakowski, Trethellan Farm, Newquay, the excavation of a lowland Bronze Age settlement and Iron Age cemetery, *Cornish Archaeol*, **30**, 5–242

Woodworth, P L, 1987 Trends in U K mean sea level, *Marine Geology*, **11**, 57–87

Wymer, J J, 1977 *Gazetteer of Mesolithic Sites in England and Wales*, CBA Res Rep **20**. London: Council for British Archaeology

Wymer, J J, 1999 *The Lower Palaeolithic Occupation of Britain*. Salisbury: Wessex Archaeology

Yonge, C, 1960 *Oysters*. London: Collins

Young, C J, 1977 *Oxfordshire Roman Pottery*, BAR Brit Ser **43**. Oxford: British Archaeological Reports

Young, R, & Humphrey, J, 1999 Flint Use in England after the Bronze Age: Time for a Re-evaluation?, *Proc Prehist Soc*, **65**, 233–44

Unpublished Sources

Abbreviations

Cal Lib Roll:	Calendar of Liberate Rolls
CSPD:	Calendar of State Papers Domestic
CTB&P:	Calendar of Treasury Books and Papers
HRO:	Hampshire Record Office
PCRO:	Portsmouth City Records Office
PRO:	Public Record Office

Sources

Cal Lib Roll 1253; 1254, vol 4, 140, 160

CSPD 1664–1665, 72–73

CTB&P 1660–1667, 38

CTB&P 1706–1707, vol 21, cccxiv

Counsels Brief, 1844 PCRO, G/MN 78 (Traces the history of ownership of the Portsea Salterns)

HRO 15M74/DDC182, Langstone Harbour Development Scheme, 1936–1961

PCRO map 1716, DC/PM2/12

PCRO 1798, CCR, 5–17, 47–49, and 77 (Proceedings of the Portsmouth and Portsea Fishery, 3 June and 6 June 1796)

PCRO DVIF/7/5 (Report of the medical officer of local Government Board on cultivation and storage of oysters and other molluscs, in relation to the occurrence of disease in man)

PRO 1796, T64/233 (Report of survey of several collections of Portsea, Wight Isle and Lymington in Hampshire, and Pool in Dorsetshire, with commissioners remarks thereon – Report for Commissioners of H M Salt Duties, Report No 1 The Portsea Collection. A letter accompanying the report has note 1866 written on it commenting, 'to prove how highly this report must have been valued – the seal has remained unbroken until this time.')

PRO 1854, RAIL 1149/31 (Admiralty Report under 14 and 15 Vict *c* 49 Havant Railway Bill. 16 March 1854)

Appendices

Appendix 1: Langstone Harbour Survey 1993–5
Summary of investigation areas by geographical location

HARBOUR COAST

South-west corner of harbour

Area	location description	purpose and archaeology	features/finds
8	Large area: Covers the south-western corner of the harbour from Fort Cumberland as far north as the pier at Great Salterns, including the Eastney Inlet.	Walkover survey	A small flooded enclosure on the southern shore of Eastney inlet. The remains of wooden jetty on the north shore of the inlet. Remains of a timber landing stage immediately to the north of the inlet.

North-west corner of harbour

Area	location description	purpose and archaeology	features/finds
9	Large area: Covers the north-western corner of the harbour from the pier at Great Salterns up to the head of the Broom Channel and the western edge of Farlington Marshes. Includes Areas 5 and 6.	Walkover survey	Small eroding islands survey in Areas 5 and 6. A group of modern accreting islands noted in the far north-western corner of the harbour.
5	Roughly square area measuring 50 × 50m in size. Covers the remains of a small eroding island in the north-western corner of the harbour and the intertidal zone around it for a distance of 10m. Within Area 9.	Walkover survey	Burnt flint, worked flint, fired clay, and some sherds of flint-tempered pottery. A layer of burnt flint and pottery recorded in the cliff face of the island's coast.
6	Area encloses the southern coast of a small eroding island, joined to the western coast of Farlington Marshes by a bar of mud. The area also includes some of the intertidal zone to the south of the island. Within Area 9.	Walkover survey	Burnt flint, worked flint, flint-tempered and fineware pottery. A layer of burnt flint and pottery was recorded in the island's cliff face.

Hayling Island

Area	location description	purpose and archaeology	features/finds
11	Large area: Encloses the west coast of Hayling Island from the north-eastern corner of the harbour as far south as a headland close to the village of Stoke. Contains Area 2.	Walkover survey	Modern oyster beds. Offshore shingle bar with lines of square and circular sectioned wooden stakes on either side of it. Assumed to be the remains of old oyster beds. A single line of chalk and flint blocks was found on the coast proper at the junction between the intertidal mudflats and the shingle bar. This feature was uninterpreted.
2	Square measuring 50 × 50m, situated on the western coast of Hayling Island, some 200m to the south of some old oyster beds which have now been in-filled. Within Area 11.	Walkover survey	Burnt flint. Possible flint core.

Area	location description	purpose and archaeology	features/finds
12	Large area: Covers a 1.5km long strip of the Hayling Island coastline from the headland at Stoke, southwards to the next headland.	Walkover survey	Lines of chalk and flint blocks radiating out from the Stoke headland. Interpreted as the remains of oyster beds. Two lines of timber stakes found at the midpoint between the two headlands. Interpreted as a fish trap. Two parallel lines of timber stakes some 50m south of the fish trap. Interpreted as jetty remains. A further set of parallel stakes were found at the southern edge of the area.
13	Large area: Encloses the south-eastern quarter of the harbour from the headland at the southern end of Area 12, down to the harbour mouth at Sinah Common.	Walkover survey	Wooden stake 'fish trap' found some 300m south of the northern boundary. Remains of a post-medieval brick kiln some 100m south of the stakes. Further 'fish trap' feature noted 100m south of the kiln. A single sherd of Romano-British pottery found 25m to the east of the above 'fish trap'. A line of substantial wooden stakes found close to the Kench inlet, near the harbour mouth. These are aligned along the top of a gravel bank which runs out into the harbour towards Sinah Lake. Interpreted as the remains of a Victorian railway bridge.

ISLANDS

Area	location description	purpose and archaeology	features/finds
10	Large area: This includes all of the main islands at the northern end of the harbour (Oyster Island, North Binness, Long Island, South Binness, and Baker's Island) along with the northern shoreline of the harbour proper between the eastern coast of Farlington Marshes and Hayling Island Bridge. Includes Areas 1, 3, 4, and 14–26	Walkover survey Feature investigation Total surface collection Sample artefact collection	Oyster Island contained a series of timber post circles, thought to be post-medieval oyster beds along with the remains of an early-20th century brick structure and a linear feature of unknown origin. See individual entries for Areas 14–26 for more details of multiple artefact scatters, pot burials, and assorted features on all other islands.

North Binness Island

Area	location description	purpose and archaeology	features/finds
1	Sub rectangular area measuring 55 × 45m situated on the south-western coast of North Binness Island. Also encloses some of the intertidal zone to the south of the coast. Within Area 10.	Walkover survey Feature investigation Total surface collection	Hearth 1702, ditches 1711 and 113. Flint-tempered pottery, burnt flint, worked flint, modern metalwork, animal bone, and worked bone. Layer of burnt flint and pottery found in cliff section along coast.
4	Rectangular-shaped area measuring 40 × 30m and situated on the south coast of North Binness Island, some 20m to the south of the copse. Within Area 10.	Walkover survey Total surface collection	Burnt flint, worked flint, fired clay and flint-tempered pottery. Layers of burnt flint recorded in coastal cliff section.

Long Island

Area	location description	purpose and archaeology	features/finds
3	Rectangular-shaped area measuring 40 × 32m, situated on the western coast of Long Island. Within Area 10.	Walkover survey Feature investigation Total surface collection	Pot 350 located on the edge of the eroding coast. Contained a soil deposit rich in burnt flint. Also further scatters of burnt flint, worked flint, and some pottery sherds.

Area	location description	purpose and archaeology	features/finds
18	Encloses the north-eastern coast of Long Island. Within Area 10.	Walkover survey	No finds.
19	Area covers the south-western coast of Long Island from the southern edge of Area 3 up to the south-easternmost point of the island. Within Area 10.	Walkover survey Feature investigation and total surface collection	Scatter of worked and burnt flint found in Area 3 was found to extend along the shoreline for a further 370m. Appears to be at its densest some 200m south of Area 3. Feature 305, situated 260m ESE of Area 3. Sub-circular in plan, measuring 0.9m in diameter and 0.2m deep it contained large amounts of burnt flint and some flakes. Interpreted as a hearth. Worked and burnt flint recovered from the eroding topsoil at the far south-eastern tip of Long Island.

South Binness Island

Area	location description	purpose and archaeology	features/finds
7	Area encloses the whole of South Binness Island. Within Area 10.	Walkover survey	Flint scatter 771, charcoal patch and burnt flint 772, burnt flint scatter with carbonised stakes 773. Flint scatter 774, including a pot base containing further burnt flints. Flint scatters 776 and 777. Single flint flake 778.

Baker's Island

Area	location description	purpose and archaeology	features/finds
14	Sub-rectangular area measuring 25 × 10m, covering a small headland 150m to the south-east of the main north-western peninsula on Baker's Island. Within Area 24.	Walkover survey	A layer of burnt flint and some worked flint was observed in the coastal cliff. A spread of flints, along with Romano-British and Bronze Age pottery observed in intertidal zone within 5m of coast.
15	Area enclosing all of the intertidal mudflats between the north-western headland and the main shingle spit which runs out from the south-western coast of Baker's Island. Encloses Areas 22, 23, and 24.	Walkover survey	A large scatter of worked flint around north-western headland. Worked flint noted in a general spread along the south-western coast.
16	Area covering the shoreline and intertidal mudflats to the south of the shingle spit, Baker's Island. Encloses Areas 20–22.	Walkover survey	Large feature noted on southern edge of shingle spit. Appeared to be partially covered by shingle. Scatter of flint-tempered pottery found 5m south of spit. Strip of dark material noted 35m south of spit. Measures 5m wide and 60m long. Contains flint-tempered pottery, worked and burnt flint, along with animal bone. General spread of worked flint across the remaining part of the area.
17	Area covers the whole north-western shoreline of Baker's Island, including a 30m wide strip of the intertidal zone beyond it.	Walkover survey	General scatter of worked flints found along a 100m stretch of the coastline, spreading out some 20m into the intertidal zone. Base of a flint-tempered pot found just off the shore line. Contains traces of soil and burnt bone. Possibly a cremation burial.

20	Area encloses the coastline and 100m of the intertidal mudflat from the south-western point of Baker's Island, northwards, up to 25m south of the shingle bar. Within Area 16.	Walkover survey / Sample artefact collection	Three scatters of worked flints (2025–7) found in the south-western corner of the area. Two timber stakes located on the southern edge of the area. Uninterpreted.
21	Area precisely covers the area occupied by the linear strip of dark material first noted in 1994. Within Area 16.	Walkover survey / Sample artefact collection	Linear feature found to be S-shaped in plan. 4m wide where it meets the coast, narrowing to a point some 50m out into the mudflat. Interpreted as an ancient rivulet. Two total collection squares (2028–9) were marked out within the feature. Very large quantities of burnt flint, some animal bone and a scatter of flint-tempered pottery sherds (5507) were recovered from these squares.
22	Encloses the coastline and 100m of intertidal zone north of Area 21, including the shingle spit and 50m to the north of it. Within Areas 15 and 16 .	Walkover survey / Sample artefact collection	Three scatters of worked flints (2030–2) were located in this area. 2030/1 were found 15 and 5m to the south of the spit respectively. Scatter 2032 was located at the western end of the spit.
23	Sub-rectangular area measuring 80 × 230m, situated to the north of Area 22. Within Area 15.	Walkover survey / Sample artefact collection / Feature investigation	Seven worked flint scatters (2033–9) found within this area, all within 50m of the shore. A single flint-tempered pottery sherd was found on the shoreline 15m from the north-eastern corner of the area. A semicircular feature (2040) was found on the shoreline 5m from the north-eastern corner of the area. Found to be the remains of an eroded headland.
24	Area runs from the northern edge of Area 23 as far as the north-western point of Baker's Island. Within Area 15. Includes Area 14.	Walkover survey / Sample artefact collection	Two scatters of worked flints and pottery sherds found (2044/5). Cliff section investigated in Area 14 found to be a 110m long stretch of material rich in burnt flint with some flint-tempered and Roman pottery mixed in. Scatters 2044/5 are probably formed from material eroded out from this cliff.
25	Area encloses the shingle spit running out from the north-western point of Baker's Island and the intertidal zone 50m each side of it.	Walkover survey / Sample artefact collection	Three scatters of worked flint (2046–8) were found on and around the spit. A single human bone (5008) (not in situ) was found to the north east of the spit. Origin unknown.
26	Area encloses a sub-rectangular zone measuring 240 × 100m, encompassing the coastal and intertidal zones of Baker's Island's north-eastern coast.	Walkover survey / Sample artefact collection	Single scatter 2049 found 40m off the coast, situated on a knoll of firm clay. A series of six small scatters of worked flints (2051–6) were found along the coastline itself.

Appendix 2: Gazetteer of sites and finds in and around Langtstone Harbour

Source: Hampshire Sites and Monuments record, Map sheet SU70SW, SU60SE, (1:2500)

This gazetteer includes the finds and sites recorded in the SMR *within* Langstone Harbour and those on its shoreline. It includes some of the more significant finds to this project outside in the immediately adjacent hinterland (Hayling Island, Langstone village, Havant etc). The authors acknowledge the fact that there are errors and omissions in the Hampshire County SMR, and also that a number of salvage and research sites excavated on Hayling Island, in particular, remain unpublished and for which there is no full excavation account in the public domain. The gazetteer also includes all the major finds from the Langstone Archaeological Survey Project. Each site or location has been given a unique project number, which have been suffixed by two letters indicating their general location; ie NB (North Binness Island), SB (South Binness Island), LI (Long Island), BI (Baker's Island), HI (Hayling Island), FM (Farlington Marshes),PI (Portsea Island), Havant environs (Ha), OI (Oyster Island), and LH (Langstone harbour, ie *within* the harbour), following the system adopted by Gardiner (1988) and the Wootton Quarr project (Tomalin *et al* in press). The information of all the major finds from this project listed in the gazetteer have been given to the SMR and will in due course be fully entered into the Hampshire Sites and Monuments record, and allocated SMR numbers. At the time of going to press this had only just begun for the 53 new entries.

PALAEOLITHIC

Langstone Survey Project Number: LI.1
SMR NUMBER: SU70SW 61

LOCATION: Long Island   **NGR:** SU 7010 0410

Land class: Grassland, nature unknown   **Geology:** Alluvium

Description: Palaeolithic flint implements found in 1969, no further record made (OS card SU70SW1). Also a single Palaeolith found in 1973 in the centre of Long Island which is now in PCM (Acc no 1973.1011). A surface find made at 0m OD.

Langstone Survey Project Number: HI.2
SMR NUMBER: SU70SW 74

LOCATION: Hayling Island   **NGR:** SU 7130 0130

Land class: Intertidal mudflat   **Geology:** Alluvium

Description: 1981 – A Palaeolithic handaxe was found on the foreshore – retained by the finder – Portsmouth City Museum Service SMRSU70SW31

Langstone Survey Project Number: Ha.3
SMR NUMBER: SU60NE 33

LOCATION: Havant   **NGR:** SU 679 075

Land class: Garden, residential   **Geology:** Chalk or Bagshot Beds

Description: Palaeolithic handaxe found in garden at Timber Lane, on surface at 50m OD. Retained by finder. 1984.

MESOLITHIC

Langstone Survey Project Number: HI.4
SMR NUMBER: SU70SW 11

LOCATION: South of Old Oyster Beds   **NGR:** SU 7153 0260

Land class: Reclaimed land   **Geology:** Alluvium

Description: 1969 – Mesolithic flint flakes found on foreshore – origin of artefacts unknown – found and retained by R Bradley (OS card SU70SW16)

Langstone Survey Project Number: LI.5
SMR NUMBER: SU70SW 62

LOCATION: Long Island   **NGR:** SU 7010 0410

Land class: Grassland, nature unknown   **Geology:** Alluvium

Description: A large number of Mesolithic scrapers, blades, flakes and cores found in 1969 and retained by the finder. OS card SU70SW1. surface find made at 0m OD.

Langstone Survey Project Number: SB.6
SMR NUMBER: SU60SE 5
LOCATION: South Binness Island   **NGR:** SU 6995 0297
Land class: Saltmarsh/grassland – nature unknown   **Geology:** Alluvium
Description: Mesolithic flints from S shore in Portsmouth City Museum – some with finder – see Wymer 1977, 115.
– flints from this area found and retained by A J Seagrave in 1975–7
– Mesolithic pick, core and blades found and donated to Portsmouth City Museum acc. no. 115–17/48; SMR Card
SU60SE4

Langstone Survey Project Number: FM.7
SMR NUMBER: SU60SE 7
LOCATION: NW corner Langstone harbour   **NGR:** SU 6796 0432
Land class: Saltmarsh   **Geology:** Alluvium
Description: 1977 – Microlith found on shore E of Eastern Road on Farlington Marshes and retained by C Draper –
site now eroded by sea (1969) – see Wymer 1977, 118 (OS card SU60SE9).

Langstone Survey Project Number: FM.8
SMR NUMBER: SU60SE 17
LOCATION: South of Farlington Marshes   **NGR:** SU 6780 0430
Land class: Intertidal mudflat   **Geology:** Alluvium
Description: 1969 – Mesolithic saw, core and utilised blade found *c* 1965 in mudbank (normally inaccessible) by B
Hooper – pottery, briquetage fragments and post Mesolithic flints also recovered – all with Hooper collection.

Langstone Survey Project Number: PI.9
SMR NUMBER: SU60SE 21
LOCATION: Portsea Island   **NGR:** SU 6600 0370
Land class: Built over. Thoroughfare road and Domestic   **Geology:** Brickearth
garden.
Description: Pebble macehead with hour glass perforation. Now in the British Museum. Wymer 1977, 118.

Langstone Survey Project Number: HI.10
SMR NUMBER: SU60SE 22
LOCATION: West Coast of Hayling Island   **NGR:** SU 7110 0240
Land class: Intertidal mudflat   **Geology:** Alluvium
Description: 1986 – Mesolithic site recovered – ref. Chris Draper. No further information; no record in C. Draper
index. Hampshire County Council Planning Department Arch. Record SU60SE20

Langstone Survey Project Number: FM.11
SMR NUMBER: SU60SE 31
LOCATION: Island SW Farlington Marshes   **NGR:** SU 6790 0420
Land class: Intertidal mudflat/saltmarsh   **Geology:** Alluvium
Description: 1969 – a) Mesolithic core, blades and flakes plus other flint tools collected by C Draper in 1968 from
small island west of Farlington Marshes – no further visits.
b) Mesolithic blades including microlith, saw, pick and other flakes. Found and retained by J C Draper in 1968. See
Wymer 1977, 118 (OS card SU60SE11)

Langstone Survey Project Number: BI.12
SMR NUMBER: SU60SE 47
LOCATION: Baker's Island   **NGR:** SU 69576 0350
Land class: Saltmarsh   **Geology:** Alluvium
Description: 1977 – a) Tranchet axe, axe, pick, core, blade & flake, scraper and other worked pieces of flint all in
Draper Collection – Wymer 1977.
b) End scraper of honey flint 4.75″ long and tranchet axe found by E. Herring, 38 The Thicket, Purbrook now with
Portsmouth City Museum – reg no 115–7/48 – SMR SU60SE2a+4 1969 *Note* C Draper visits over a number of years –
sea encroaches more each year on Island and more material recovered – Island inaccessible at times (OS card
SU60SE2)

Langstone Survey Project Number: NB.13
SMR NUMBER: SU60SE 51
LOCATION: North Binness Island   **NGR:** SU 6935 0465
Land class: Grassland, nature unknown/ Saltmarsh   **Geology:** Alluvium
Description: a) 1958 – Mesolithic cores, blades and flakes, scrapers and other fragments – now in Portsmouth City Museum or Draper Collection – see Wymer 1977.
b) Mesolithic flint tools and 'other finds' from 'other periods' recovered over a number of years by different collectors, especially C Draper and B Hooper *Note* 1955 – C Draper visits over a number of years – sea encroaches more each year on Island and more material recovered – Island inaccessible at times.
c) Mesolithic blades now in Portsmouth City Museum Acc no 115–117/48 SMR SU60SE1

Langstone Survey Project Number: NB.14a
SMR NUMBER:
LOCATION: North Binness Island   **NGR:** centred on SU 6914 0496
Land class: Intertidal foreshore   **Geology:** Alluvium
Description: South coast west, encompassing Area 1, surface artefact scatter, Mesolithic flint assemblage including tranchet adze sharpening flake (and LNEBA assemblage, see NB.14b, and other retouched tools)

Langstone Survey Project Number: LI.15a
SMR NUMBER:
LOCATION: Long Island   **NGR:** centred on SU 6989 0420
Land class: Intertidal foreshore   **Geology:** Alluvium
Description: North-west coast, Area 19, encompassing area 3: surface artefact scatter, a significant Mesolithic assemblage (also LNEBA flintwork LI.15b, Late Bronze Age flints LI.15c and Late Bronze Age vessels 350 LI.15d and 380 LI.15e)

Langstone Survey Project Number: BI.16a
SMR NUMBER:
LOCATION: Baker's Island   **NGR:** centred on SU 6961 0365
Land class: Intertidal foreshore   **Geology:** Alluvium
Description: East shoreline Area 17 and 26, surface artefact scatter, flints, predominantly Mesolithic assemblages associated with small areas of intensive burning, probably hearths, and including large numbers of implements, notably tranchet adzes and sharpening flakes, a pick, hammer stones, and serrated flakes (also some Neolithic flintwork BI.16b, and Bronze Age flint assemblage BI.16c, including Bronze Age vessel BI.16d)

Langstone Survey Project Number: BI.17a
SMR NUMBER:
LOCATION: Baker's Island   **NGR:** centred on SU 6941 0345
Land class: Intertidal foreshore   **Geology:** Alluvium
Description: West shoreline Areas 15 and 16 (encompassing Areas 20–5), surface artefact scatter, some Mesolithic flintwork including a tranchet adze sharpening flake (also a LNEBA flint assemblage BI.17b)

Langstone Survey Project Number: SB.18a
SMR NUMBER:
LOCATION: South Binness Island   **NGR:** centred on SU 6985 0305
Land class: Intertidal foreshore and shingle   **Geology:** Alluvium
Description: South-west shoreline (Areas 771–5), surface artefact scatter, flint assemblages mostly Mesolithic including a tranchet adze – lost (and Neolithic SB.18b, LNEBA and substantial Bronze Age SB.18c flint assemblages, a Bronze Age vessel SB.18d and Roman pottery and hearth SB.18e)

NEOLITHIC

Langstone Survey Project Number: HI.19
SMR NUMBER: SU70SW 6
LOCATION: West Coast of Hayling Island   **NGR:** SU 7179 0355
Land class: **Geology:** Brickearth
Description: Neolithic polished axe in brickearth

Langstone Survey Project Number: Ha.20
SMR NUMBER: SU70SW 47
LOCATION: West of Langstone bridge **NGR:** SU 7140 0470
Land class: Intertidal mudflat **Geology:** Alluvium
Description: Nine Neolithic flints found in 1991 in the NE corner of the harbour, very close to the shore. All flints showed evidence of secondary working with at least two scrapers identified. The flints were found over an area around 0.2 ha in size and were retained by the finder who had had them identified by Hampshire County Museum Service (Enq no 626).

Langstone Survey Project Number: Ll.21
SMR NUMBER: SU70SW 63
LOCATION: Long Island **NGR:** SU 7010 0410
Land class: Grassland, nature unknown **Geology:** Alluvium
Description: A large number of Neolithic flint implements found in 1969, including plano-convex knives, arrowheads and scrapers (OS card SU70SW1). Surface find at 0m OD. No record of exact location made.
Also found: A Neolithic arrowhead 'found to the south of the island'. Presumably this means the intertidal mudflats. Presented to PCM (Acc no 1973.1018).

Langstone Survey Project Number: SB.22
SMR NUMBER: SU60SE 6
LOCATION: South Binness Island **NGR:** SU 6995 0297
Land class: Saltmarsh/grassland, nature unknown **Geology:** Alluvium
Description: a) Neolithic flints, scrapers and flakes found by Portsmouth Museums Society/J C Draper 1958–63 (OS card SU60SE8) – Mesolithic finds also recovered.
b) Flints found by A J Seagrove 1975–7 – PCM SMR card SU60SE16

Langstone Survey Project Number: FM.23
SMR NUMBER: SU60SE 9
LOCATION: On shore opposite North Binness Island **NGR:** SU 6896 0441
Land class: Saltmarsh **Geology:** Alluvium
Description: 1969 – Neolithic flint scraper found and retained by C Draper on shore opposite to N Binness Island, east of Eastern Road (OS card SU60SE10).

Langstone Survey Project Number: HI.24
SMR NUMBER: SU60SE 15
LOCATION: West coast of Hayling Island **NGR:** SU 7160 0285
Land class: Intertidal mudflat **Geology:** Alluvium
Description: 1969 – ?Neolithic flint knife recovered on foreshore, found and retained by B Hooper. (OS card SU60SE16)

Langstone Survey Project Number: FM.25
SMR NUMBER: SU60SE 32
LOCATION: Island SW Farlington Marshes **NGR:** SU 6790 0420
Land class: Saltmarsh **Geology:** Alluvium
Description: 1969 – Neolithic flakes and segment of a leaf-shaped arrowhead including unspecified prehistoric material which may include Neolithic material (SU60SE64) found (1968) on same small island as 31 and retained by C Draper (1969) (OS card SU60SE11).
Finds on all shores of this island but mainly from the south side – sea encroachments produce more material each year.

Langstone Survey Project Number: BI.26
SMR NUMBER: SU60SE 48
LOCATION: Baker's Island **NGR:** SU 6950 0350
Land class: Grassland, nature unknown/Saltmarsh **Geology:** Alluvium
Description: a) 1958 – Neolithic saddle quern in Portsmouth County Museum Acc no 59/58 SMR SU60SE6
b) 1969 – Fragments of another saddle quern also recovered from this site – retained by C Draper (OS card SU60SE2)

Langstone Survey Project Number: NB.27
SMR NUMBER: SU60SE 52

LOCATION: North Binness Island   **NGR:** SU 6935 0465

Land class: Grassland, nature unknown/Saltmarsh   **Geology:** Alluvium

Description: 1958 – Neolithic scrapers recovered *in situ* in association with Roman finds at SU 69580445 – other Neolithic flint finds including scrapers and polished axe and adze fragments recovered from 'an area of the Island'. Note – sea encroaches more each year on Island and more material recovered – Island inaccessible at times.

Langstone Survey Project Number: LI.28a
SMR NUMBER:

LOCATION: Long Island   **NGR:** centred on SU 4702 0405

Land class: Intertidal foreshore   **Geology:** Alluvium

Description: South shoreline (Area 18) and southern peninsular shoreline, surface artefact scatter, Neolithic flint assemblage including 2 leaf-shaped arrowheads (also some Mesolithic, LNEBA LI.28b, and later Bronze Age LI.28c, also late Bronze Age vessel LI.28d)

Langstone Survey Project Number: BI.16b
SMR NUMBER:

LOCATION: Baker's Island   **NGR:** centred on SU 6961 0365

Land class: Intertidal foreshore   **Geology:** Alluvium

Description: East shoreline Area 17 and 26, surface artefact scatter, flints, Neolithic assemblage including 2 leaf-shaped arrowheads (also large Mesolithic assemblage BI.16a, and Bronze Age flint assemblage BI.16c, including Bronze Age vessel BI.16d)

Langstone Survey Project Number: SB.18b
SMR NUMBER:

LOCATION: South Binness Island   **NGR:** centred on SU 6985 0305

Land class: Intertidal foreshore and shingle   **Geology:** Alluvium

Description: South-west shoreline (Areas 771–5), surface artefact scatter, flint assemblages the Neolithic component of which included a leaf-shaped arrowhead (also large Mesolithic SB.18a, and some LNEBA and substantial Bronze Age SB.18c flint assemblages, a Bronze Age vessel SB.18d and Roman pottery and hearth SB.18e)

NEOLITHIC/BRONZE AGE

Langstone Survey Project Number: LH.67
SMR NUMBER:

LOCATION: North of Russell's Lake   **NGR:** SU 6911 0398

Land class: Intertidal mudflats and peat shelf   **Geology:** Alluvium

Description: Peat shelf with branches of oak and Salicaceae; former prehistoric woodland. (3340–2910 cal BC)

Langstone Survey Project Number: LH.68
SMR NUMBER:

LOCATION: Baker's Rithe   **NGR:** SU 6926 0410

Land class: Intertidal mudflats and peat shelf   **Geology:** Alluvium

Description: Peat shelf with *in situ* tree stumps and fallen branches of oak, yew, and alder; former prehistoric woodland. (2310–1950 cal BC)

Langstone Survey Project Number: SB.29
SMR NUMBER: SU70SW 2

LOCATION: South Binness Island   **NGR:** SU 7002 0327

Land class: Intertidal mudflat   **Geology:** Alluvium

Description: Flint implements found in 1955 and recorded on a map from the 1930s. No further details available (OS card SU70SW2). It is not clear whether this was a surface find, although considering its location, just north of the southern tip of South Binness Island, this seems most likely.

Langstone Survey Project Number: FM.30
SMR NUMBER: SU60SE 16

LOCATION: South of Farlington Marshes   **NGR:** SU 6790 0440

Land class: Saltmarsh   **Geology:** Shingle

Description: 1969 – Burnt flints in a hearth, struck flakes and one post-Mesolithic scraper were found by B Hooper *c* 1965 – a small island west of Farlington Marshes now normally inaccessible – finds are in the Hooper collection (OS card SU60SE18).

Langstone Survey Project Number: FM.31
SMR NUMBER: SU60SE 18

LOCATION: South of Farlington Marshes   **NGR:** SU 6780 0430

Land class: Intertidal mudflat   **Geology:** Alluvium

Description: 1969 – Two post-Mesolithic scrapers found on a mudbank (normally inaccessible) by B Hooper *c* 1965. Pottery, fragments of briquetage and Mesolithic flints also found – all with Hooper collection.

Langstone Survey Project Number: FM.32
SMR NUMBER: SU60SE 34

LOCATION: Island SW Farlington Marshes   **NGR:** SU 6790 0420

Land class: Saltmarsh   **Geology:** Alluvium

Description: 1969 – Post-Mesolithic flint – 96 scrapers, 2 borers, 1 core, 1 polished axe flake, 1 awl and waste flakes. Found and retained Hooper 1964–67 (OS card SU60SE11).

Langstone Survey Project Number: FM.33
SMR NUMBER: SU60SE 41

LOCATION: NW corner Langstone harbour   **NGR:** SU 6840 0350

Land class: Intertidal mudflat/saltmarsh   **Geology:** Alluvium

Description: 1986 – A struck flake and a post-Mesolithic utilised flake found with pottery and briquetage by B Hooper *c* 1966. The site is not readily accessible (1969). Present location and conditions of finds not known – 1986.

Langstone Survey Project Number: Ha.34
SMR NUMBER: SU70NW 26

LOCATION: Warblington Bay   **NGR:** SU 7220 0520 –2m OD

Land class: Intertidal mudflat   **Geology:** Brickearth

Description: 1969 – Flint artefacts, mostly struck flints with some scrapers and blades, found on foreshore at Warblington Quay by J S Pile 1967 and retained. Possibly derived from eroding soil overlying the Coombe Rock (OS card SU70NW26). Source of artefacts unknown.

Langstone Survey Project Number: NB.35a
SMR NUMBER:

LOCATION: North Binness Island   **NGR:** centred on SU 6955 0496

Land class: Intertidal foreshore   **Geology:** Alluvium

Description: South coast, east (encompassing Area 4), surface artefact scatter, LNEBA flintwork including a plano-convex knife, debitage and scrapers. (also a few Mesolithic artefacts and a later Bronze Age assemblage, see NB.35b)

Langstone Survey Project Number: NB.14b
SMR NUMBER:

LOCATION: North Binness Island   **NGR:** centred on SU 6914 0496

Land class: Intertidal foreshore   **Geology:** Alluvium

Description: South coast west, encompassing Area 1, surface artefact scatter, LNEBA flint assemblage including a transverse arrowhead (and significant Mesolithic see NB.14a, and other retouched tools)

Langstone Survey Project Number: LI.15b
SMR NUMBER:
LOCATION: Long Island   **NGR:** centred on SU 6989 0420
Land class: Intertidal foreshore   **Geology:** Alluvium
Description: North-west coast, Area 19, encompassing Area 3: surface artefact scatter, a LNEBA assemblage including 3 transverse and an oblique arrowhead and a plano-convex knife (also Mesolithic flintwork LI.15a, Late Bronze Age flints LI.15c and Late Bronze Age vessels 350, LI.15d and 380, LI.15e)

Langstone Survey Project Number: LI.28b
SMR NUMBER:
LOCATION: Long Island   **NGR:** centred on SU 4702 0405
Land class: Intertidal foreshore   **Geology:** Alluvium
Description: South shoreline (including Area 3) and southern peninsular shoreline, surface artefact scatter, LNEBA flint (also some Mesolithic, Neolithic assemblage LI.28a, and Later Bronze Age LI.28c, also Late Bronze Age vessel LI.28d)

Langstone Survey Project Number: BI.17b
SMR NUMBER:
LOCATION: Baker's Island   **NGR:** centred on SU 6941 0345
Land class: Intertidal foreshore   **Geology:** Alluvium
Description: West shoreline Areas 15 and 16 (encompassing Areas 20–5), surface artefact scatter, LNEBA flint assemblage including a polished axe and barb-and-tanged arrowhead (also a Mesolithic flint assemblage BI.17a)

BRONZE AGE

Langstone Survey Project Number: HI.36
SMR NUMBER: SU70SW 1
LOCATION: Creek Field, Hayling Island   **NGR:** SU 7188 0359
Land class: Waste land   **Geology:** Brickearth
Description: 1969. A large LBA/EIA jar 50cm high of a coarse red fabric, with pieced lugs on shoulder – thought by G A Hollyman to be LBA–EIA. Found spring 1955 by H P Pycroft, reported by W G Budden, it stood upright at an angle of 45°, the upper part had collapsed into the lower, restored by PCM Acc no 47/55. Richard Bradley reports that 'as well as the giant MBA pot, this (Creek Field) produced a large domestic assemblage of the same period and the owner told me that there were also traces of at least one building.' NOTE: SMR incorrectly refers to this as 'Crate Field'

Langstone Survey Project Number: HI.37
SMR NUMBER: SU70SW 5
LOCATION: Tye Barn, Hayling Island   **NGR:** SU 7317 0242
Land class: Barn   **Geology:** Brickearth
Description: 1962 Early Bronze Age hour glass perforated mace head, 120mm x 76mm x 35mm, found while digging floor of barn. The type of stone could was not identified, now in PCM

Langstone Survey Project Number: HI.38
SMR NUMBER: SU70SW 7
LOCATION: Shingle bar, 'W of Stoke Common'.   **NGR:** SU 7139 0314
Land class: Reclaimed land, mudflats   **Geology:** Alluvium
Description: 1969 Bronze Age flint scrapers, and other worked flakes found in 1967/8 on a shingle bar 'west of Stoke Common' – artefacts retained by finder in 1969. Found in 1968 by J Fennell. R Bradley has found ?IA briquetage at same spot.

Langstone Survey Project Number: HI.39
SMR NUMBER: SU70SW 20
LOCATION: Old Oyster Beds   **NGR:** SU 7185 0354
Land class: Waste ground on reclaimed land   **Geology:** Brickearth
Description: Bronze Age, 3 inverted cinerary urns found during brickearth digging by Mr Pycroft, now in PCM 1969

Langstone Survey Project Number: HI.40
SMR NUMBER: SU70SW 21

LOCATION: Duckard Point, N Hayling   **NGR:** SU 7261 0427

Land class: Intertidal foreshore   **Geology:** Alluvium

Description: Bronze Age cremation burial. Inverted Bronze Age urn containing cremated bone found in 1968 whilst reclaiming land at Duckard Point, retrieved by M Rule and A Corney and is retained by M Rule.

Langstone Survey Project Number: HI.41
SMR NUMBER: SU70SW 22

LOCATION: South of Old Oyster Beds   **NGR:** SU 7160 0320

Land class: Waste ground.   **Geology:** Alluvium

Description: 1969 – nucleus of burnt flint found on beach – similarities to other sites in area suggest nucleus is remains of late Bronze Age/early Iron Age hearth – since 1969 site has been reclaimed – site found in July 1964 by Richard Bradley (OS card SU70SW21)

Langstone Survey Project Number: HI.42
SMR NUMBER: SU70SW 32

LOCATION: West coast Hayling Island   **NGR:** SU 7179 0361

Land class: Waste ground   **Geology:** Brickearth

Description: Several hearths found during digging of brickearth in 1965, Bronze Age–early Iron Age pottery (probably late Bronze Age)

Langstone Survey Project Number: HI.43
SMR NUMBER: SU70SW 41

LOCATION: North Hayling Island coast   **NGR:** SU 7270 0430

Land class: Intertidal muds   **Geology:** Muds and Brickearth

Description: Remains of a Bronze Age founder's hoard. The cutting edges of two Bronze Age socketed axes and pieces of waste bronze were found on the spoil heap created by the yacht basin by Bari Hooper, and reported by local archaeologist Mr Richard Bradley, but finds retained by M Rule 1969.

Langstone Survey Project Number: Ha.44
SMR NUMBER: SU70SW 53A

LOCATION: Langstone village   **NGR:** SU 7151 0500

Land class: Private garden   **Geology:** Brickearth

Description: 1979 Cremation burial. One middle Bronze Age barrel urn, one inverted containing cremated remains, found in garden in Mill Lane, Langstone. Sherds of 1, possibly 2 other vessels. Finds with HCM Service Acc No A1981 80H (Hughes 1982, 36)

Langstone Survey Project Number: LI.45
SMR NUMBER: SU70SW 54

LOCATION: Long Island   **NGR:** SU 7020 0410

Land class: Grassland, nature unknown   **Geology:** Alluvium

Description: Bronze Age pottery. This consisted of an urn containing cremated remains now in Portsmouth City Museum (PCM) (Acc no 1981.367). Surface find made at 0m OD. Hughes 1982, 36

Langstone Survey Project Number: HI.46
SMR NUMBER: SU70SW 59A

LOCATION: Pound Marsh, N Tournerbury   **NGR:** SU 7324 0059

Land class: **Geology:** Brickearth

Description: Bronze Age round barrow called Windmill Hill 30m diameter × 0.7m high. Remains of medieval mill on barrow. On 'excavation' at 1.8m (5ft 10ins)was a pebble 'pavement' covered by a layer of ashes with a hollowed tree-trunk coffin burial, burnt or decayed. Finds include scrapers and imperfect arrowheads (59B), Trigg, 1892; Williams-Freeman 1919, 353.

Langstone Survey Project Number: LI.47
SMR NUMBER: SU70SW 64

LOCATION: Long Island   **NGR:** SU 7010 0410

Land class: Grassland, nature unknown   **Geology:** Alluvium

Description: Iron Age pottery sherds (probably late Bronze Age) found 'in the 1960s'. Pottery was retained by the finder. OS card SU70SW1. Surface find made at 0m OD.

Langstone Survey Project Number: LI.48
SMR NUMBER: SU70SW 66

LOCATION: Long Island   **NGR:** SU 7010 0410

Land class: Grassland, nature unknown   **Geology:** Alluvium

Description: Large numbers of Bronze Age flint artefacts including arrowheads, a polished axe fragment and knives. All material retained by the finder (OS card SU70SW1). Surface finds made at 0m OD.

Langstone Survey Project Number: HI.49
SMR NUMBER: SU70SW 92

LOCATION: Hayling Island, nr Wadeway   **NGR:** SU 7240 0418

Land class: Alluvium   **Geology:** Alluvium

Description: 1987. Bronze Age post-built structure (Soffe and Williams 1987). Oak timbers and an area of wattle found during building of new sea wall.

Langstone Survey Project Number: PI.50
SMR NUMBER: SU60SE 4

LOCATION: Portsea Island   **NGR:** SU 6700 000

Land class: Site now destroyed – no information given   **Geology:** Alluvium

Description: 1945 – Bronze Age hoard of four solid rings and looped palstave found nr. St James Hospital. Two rings are ornamented with engraved geometric patterns; they are very corroded and light green. Destroyed during enemy action during WWII – record made in 1955.

Langstone Survey Project Number: FM.51
SMR NUMBER: SU60SE 8A

LOCATION: NW corner Langstone harbour   **NGR:** SU 6796 0432

Land class: Saltmarsh   **Geology:** Alluvium

Description: 1977 – Fragments of Bronze Age pottery and flints indicating Bronze Age site east of Eastern Road on shore, found and retained by J C Draper 1958.

Langstone Survey Project Number: FM.52
SMR NUMBER: SU60SE 8B

LOCATION: NW corner Langstone harbour   **NGR:** SU 6796 0432

Land class: Saltmarsh   **Geology:** Alluvium

Description: 1977 – Bronze Age flint implements, scrapers, awl, 60 flakes and pottery fragments east of Eastern Road on shore of Farlington Marshes found and retained by J C Draper (OS card SU60SE9).

Langstone Survey Project Number: FM.53
SMR NUMBER: SU60SE 26A

LOCATION: South of Farlington Marshes   **NGR:** SU 6790 0430

Land class: Saltmarsh   **Geology:** Alluvium

Description: 1979 – 25 pieces of Deverel-Rimbury pottery from 3 pots recovered from a pit exposed at Farlington Marshes. Hampshire County Council Planning Department Arch. Record SU60SE27 – finds now in Draper University Collection July 1979.

Langstone Survey Project Number: FM.54
SMR NUMBER: SU60SE 26B

LOCATION: NW corner Langstone harbour   **NGR:** SU 6790 0430

Land class: Saltmarsh   **Geology:** Alluvium

Description: 1979 – Pit exposed on west side of Farlington Marshes – Pottery (26A) was recovered.

Langstone Survey Project Number: FM.55
SMR NUMBER: SU60SE 33

LOCATION: Island SW Farlington Marshes   **NGR:** SU 67900420

Land class: Saltmarsh   **Geology:** Alluvium

Description: 1969 – Early Bronze Age barbed and tanged arrowhead and scraper found with other unspecified prehistoric material possibly including other Bronze Age items. Hooper 1964–7 (OS card SU60SE11).

Langstone Survey Project Number: FM.56
SMR NUMBER: SU60SE 36

LOCATION: Island SW Farlington Marshes   **NGR:** SU 6790 0420

Land class: Saltmarsh   **Geology:** Alluvium

Description: 1984 – Late Bronze Age and early Iron Age flint (probably all late Bronze Age), tempered red/orange and black pottery sherds found by Hooper 1964–7 (OS card SU60SE11).

Langstone Survey Project Number: FM.57
SMR NUMBER: SU60SE 40

LOCATION: NW corner Langstone harbour   **NGR:** SU 6840 0350

Land class: Intertidal mudflat/saltmarsh   **Geology:** Alluvium

Description: 1986 – One ?Iron Age pot sherd found B Hooper. Flint tools, briquetage, and other pottery also found. The site is not readily accessible (1969). Present location and conditions of finds not known – 1986.

Langstone Survey Project Number: BI.58
SMR NUMBER: SU60SE 49

LOCATION: Baker's Island   **NGR:** SU 6950 0350

Land class: Grassland, nature unknown/Saltmarsh   **Geology:** Alluvium

Description: 1969 – Fragments of Bronze Age pottery and 'other finds' retained by J C Draper *Note* Chris Draper visited over a number of years – sea encroaches more each year on Island and more material recovered – Island inaccessible at times (OS card SU60SE2).

Langstone Survey Project Number: NB.59 (a and b)
SMR NUMBER: SU60SE 53

LOCATION: North Binness Island   **NGR:** SU 6935 0465

Land class: Grassland, nature unknown/Saltmarsh   **Geology:** Alluvium

Description: a) 1958 – Remnant of Bronze Age urn with contents.
b) Bronze Age urn fragment with fingernail decoration – also flint tools – *Note* sea encroaches more each year on Island and more material recovered – Island inaccessible at times (OS card SU60SE1).

Langstone Survey Project Number: NB.60
SMR NUMBER: SU60SE 53B

LOCATION: North Binness Island   **NGR:** SU 6935 0465

Land class: Grassland, nature unknown/Saltmarsh   **Geology:** Alluvium

Description: a) 1969 – Bronze Age flint arrowheads, scrapers, polished adze and axe fragments OS SU60SE1
b) Scrapers, utilised flakes and a pierced awl – either Neolithic or Bronze Age in date – found in 1982 in Portsmouth City Museum Acc no 1982/359 SMR SU60SE25.

Langstone Survey Project Number: Ha.61
SMR NUMBER: SU70NW 75

LOCATION: A27, near Brockhampton   **NGR:** SU 7010 0570 –2m OD

Land class: Grassland, nature unknown   **Geology:** Brickearth

Description: 1971 – Bronze Age pottery found in the locality in areas which appear to be raised shingle beaches, now in Portsmouth City Museum Acc no 29/71 & 48/71. SMR SU70NW60.

Langstone Survey Project Number: NB.62
SMR NUMBER:

LOCATION: North Binness Island   **NGR:** SU 6935 0465

Land class: Grassland, nature unknown/   **Geology:** Alluvium
Saltmarsh

Description: Bronze Age pottery vessel with cremated human bone. This consisted of an urn containing cremated remains found in 1982. Now in Portsmouth City Museum (PCM) (Acc no 1981.367). Surface find made at 0 m OD. 1981: Reported to be found by Chris Draper, but there is some confusion in the SMR and museum archive.

Langstone Survey Project Number: NB.63a
SMR NUMBER:

LOCATION: North Binness Island   **NGR:** SU 6916 0446

Land class: Intertidal foreshore   **Geology:** Alluvium

Description: South coast, west (Area 1), late Bronze Age ditch 1711 (excavated) and two other presumably late Bronze Age ditches, plus a late Bronze Age hearth 1702 with a radiocarbon date of 1410–1060 cal BC, containing pottery see NB.8b.

Langstone Survey Project Number: NB.63b
SMR NUMBER:

LOCATION: North Binness Island   **NGR:** SU 4916 0445

Land class: Intertidal foreshore   **Geology:** Alluvium

Description: Large sherds of coarse flint-tempered handled globular vessel in hearth on the beach. One conjoining sherd found 100m to west. Radiocarbon date indicates a late Bronze Age date (1410–1060 cal BC)

Langstone Survey Project Number: LI.15d
SMR NUMBER:

LOCATION: Long Island   **NGR:** SU 6989 0420

Land class: Intertidal foreshore   **Geology:** Alluvium

Description: Mid to late Bronze Age pottery vessel (350) found sunk into the clays (see also vessel 380, LI.15e)

Langstone Survey Project Number: LI.15e
SMR NUMBER:

LOCATION: Long Island   **NGR:** SU 6991 0420

Land class: Intertidal foreshore   **Geology:** Alluvium

Description: Mid to late Bronze Age pottery vessel (380) found sunk into the clays, only the base few centimetres survived (see also vessel 350, LI.15d)

Langstone Survey Project Number: HI.64
SMR NUMBER:

LOCATION: Elm Close, Hayling Island   **NGR:** SU 7220 9920

Land class: **Geology:**

Description: Fragmentary Bronze Age bucket urn (Rudkin 1980, no 71).

Langstone Survey Project Number: LH.65
SMR NUMBER:

LOCATION: North of Russell's Lake/Leat   **NGR:** about SU 690 040

Land class: Intertidal mudflats and peat shelf   **Geology:** Alluvium

Description: Mid Bronze Age torc recovered in Russell's Leat by local fisherman

Langstone Survey Project Number: NB.35b
SMR NUMBER:

LOCATION: North Binness Island   **NGR:** centred on SU 6955 0496

Land class: Intertidal foreshore   **Geology:** Alluvium

Description: South coast, east (encompassing Area 4), surface artefact scatter, Bronze Age flintwork predominantly debitage and scrapers. Also a few Mesolithic artefacts and a LNEBA assemblage, see NB.35a.

Langstone Survey Project Number: LI.15c
SMR NUMBER:
LOCATION: Long Island   **NGR:** centred on SU 6989 0420
Land class: Intertidal foreshore   **Geology:** Alluvium
Description: North-west coast, Area 19, encompassing Area 3: surface artefact scatter, a late Bronze Age flint assemblage largely comprising debitage, scrapers, borers and knives (also Mesolithic flintwork LI.15a, LNEBA flintwork LI.15b and late Bronze Age vessels 350 LI.15d and 380 LI.15e)

Langstone Survey Project Number: LI.28c
SMR NUMBER:
LOCATION: Long Island   **NGR:** centred on SU 4702 0405
Land class: Intertidal foreshore   **Geology:** Alluvium
Description: South shoreline (including Area 3) and southern peninsular shoreline, surface artefact scatter, later Bronze Age flint with nothing very diagnostic, very few implements, nearly all debitage (also some Mesolithic, Neolithic LI.28a, LNEBA LI.28b, and and also late Bronze Age vessel LI.28d).

Langstone Survey Project Number: LI.28d
SMR NUMBER:
LOCATION: Long Island   **NGR:** SU 7018 0398
Land class: Intertidal foreshore   **Geology:** Alluvium
Description: Mid to late Bronze Age pottery vessel (360) found sunk into the clays, and containing cremated human bone. It was buried inverted. Later Bronze Age flint with nothing very diagnostic, very few implements, nearly all debitage (also some Mesolithic, Neolithic LI.28a, LNEBA LI.28b, later Bronze Age LI.38c flint assemblages).

Langstone Survey Project Number: BI.16c
SMR NUMBER:
LOCATION: Baker's Island   **NGR:** centred on SU 6961 0365
Land class: Intertidal foreshore   **Geology:** Alluvium
Description: East shoreline Area 17 and 26, surface artefact scatter, Bronze Age flint assemblages mainly debitage, nothing very diagnostic (also large Mesolithic assemblages, BI.16a, some Neolithic flintwork BI.16b, and Bronze Age vessel BI.16d).

Langstone Survey Project Number: BI.16d
SMR NUMBER:
LOCATION: Baker's Island   **NGR:** SU 6956 0372
Land class: Intertidal foreshore   **Geology:** Alluvium
Description: East shoreline Area 17 and 26, base of a Bronze Age vessel (521), base only which largely disintegrated on recovery (also surface artefact scatters of Bronze Age flint assemblages BI.16c, large Mesolithic assemblages, BI.16a, and some Neolithic flintwork BI.16b).

Langstone Survey Project Number: SB.18c
SMR NUMBER:
LOCATION: South Binness Island   **NGR:** centred on SU 6985 0305
Land class: Intertidal foreshore and shingle   **Geology:** Alluvium
Description: South-west shoreline (Areas 771–5), surface artefact scatter, flint scatters include a substantial Bronze Age assemblage (a large Mesolithic SB.18a, and some Neolithic SB.18b, LNEBA flint assemblages, a Bronze Age vessel SB.18d and Roman pottery and hearth SB.18e).

Langstone Survey Project Number: SB.18d
SMR NUMBER:
LOCATION: South Binness Island   **NGR:** SU 6985 0305
Land class: Intertidal mudflat/shingle **Geology:** Alluvium
Description: South-west shoreline (Areas 771–775), Bronze Age vessel in foreshore, straight-sided vessel 744/1 (see also (a large Mesolithic SB.18a, and some Neolithic SB.18b, LNEBA and Bronze Age SB.18c flint assemblages, and a Roman pottery and hearth vessel SB.18e).

BRONZE AGE/IRON AGE

Langstone Survey Project Number: HI.66
SMR NUMBER: SU70SW 10

LOCATION: South of Old Oyster Beds   **NGR:** SU 7153 0260

Land class: Reclaimed land   **Geology:** Alluvium

Description: 1969 – Iron Age (possibly late Bronze Age) pottery sherds found on foreshore – pottery origin unknown – found and retained by R Bradley (OS card SU70SW16).

IRON AGE

Langstone Survey Project Number: HI.69
SMR NUMBER: SU70SW 8

LOCATION: Shingle bar, 'west of Stoke Common'.   **NGR:** SU 7139 0314

Land class: Reclaimed land, mudflats   **Geology:** Alluvium

Description: ?Iron Age briquetage found in 1969 on shingle bar west of Stoke Common.

Langstone Survey Project Number: HI.70
SMR NUMBER: SU70SW 9

LOCATION: South of Old Oyster Beds   **NGR:** SU 7152 0246

Land class: Reclaimed land   **Geology:** Alluvium

Description: 1969 – Large quantity of Iron Age pottery sherds with associates patches of burnt clay & calcined flint pieces, sherds extended over 10′ with concentration over northernmost 6′ in section in the shore bank, ?potter's hearth – site quickly eroded by sea – pottery is now in Portsmouth City Museum Acc no H/64/65, A/31/68 (OS card SU70SW20).

Langstone Survey Project Number: HI.71
SMR NUMBER: SU70SW 12

LOCATION: Old Oyster Beds   **NGR:** SU 7158 0348

Land class: Waste ground on reclaimed land   **Geology:** Alluvium

Description: A series of Iron Age hearths was uncovered during topsoil stripping in this area in 1967 as part of the works to construct a bank along the edge of a new refuse tip. The site has since been covered over. Sherds of the pottery recovered are now with a Mr H P Pycroft, who is a local builder and brick maker. The sherds have not been seen by an archaeologist.

Langstone Survey Project Number: HI.72
SMR NUMBER: SU70SW 30

LOCATION: Creek Field   **NGR:** SU 7180 0355

Land class: Waste ground on reclaimed land   **Geology:** Brickearth

Description: Iron Age saltpans at 'Crake Field/ actually Creek Field'. Two U shaped trenches each 20.1m (66ft) long found during brickearth digging in 1966 in Mr Pycroft's brickworks. The trenches or gullys were set at right angles to each other and contained large quantities of burnt flint, Iron Age pottery, and briquetage. On linear gully was 11.3m (37ft) long running SW–NE and terminating in a circular feature 1.68m (5ft 6ins) in diameter and a maximum of 0.55m (1ft 10 ins) thick. It was filled almost entirely with burnt flints with a few bits of charcoal. All of the pottery from this depression was of similar type to straight-sided saucepan pot found at the Trundle. Excavated by Richard Bradley on behalf of M Rule who retains finds and archive, but see Bradley 1992. Note SMR incorrectly refers to this as Crake Field.

Langstone Survey Project Number: NB.73
SMR NUMBER: SU60SE 54

LOCATION: North Binness Island   **NGR:** SU 6935 0465

Land class: Grassland, nature unknown/Saltmarsh   **Geology:** Alluvium

Description: 1969 – Iron Age 'C' pottery and other Iron Age pottery – in possession of C Draper and B Hooper – this is some of the pottery found in association with 54B below, plus 'some Roman finds' – SU60SE1

Langstone Survey Project Number: Ha.74
SMR NUMBER: SU70NW 76

LOCATION: A27, near Brockhampton   **NGR:** SU 7012 0575

Land class: Grassland, nature unknown   **Geology:** Brickearth CBA Rev. 1971 No: 6.22

Description: 1971 – Stripping and reclamation of an area of Storehouse Lake revealed several small hearth areas on the shingle of the old shoreline. Finds include :
Flint flakes (76B), Iron Age pottery sherds (76C) – majority of the pottery is now in Portsmouth City Museum Acc nos 1971/29/48. The density of the scatter was notable, possibly indicating a salt-boiling site.

IRON AGE/ROMANO-BRITISH

Langstone Survey Project Number: HI.75
SMR NUMBER: SU70SW 23

LOCATION: South of Old Oyster Beds   **NGR:** SU 7152 0321

Land class: Waste ground.   **Geology:** Alluvium

Description: 1969 – Iron Age & Romano-British sherds, fragments of briquetage & pot boilers seen in exposed section on point of land at the start of a hard, NW of the former N Hayling railway station.

Langstone Survey Project Number: HI.76
SMR NUMBER: SU70SW 25

LOCATION: South of Old Oyster Beds   **NGR:** SU 7160 0310

Land class: Reclaimed land   **Geology:** Alluvium

Description: 1969 – Pieces of worn briquetage found along beach – seen in 1964 by R Bradley before area was reclaimed for tipping in 1969 (OS card SU70SW23).

Langstone Survey Project Number: HI.77
SMR NUMBER: SU70SW 79

LOCATION: South of Old Oyster Beds   **NGR:** SU 7166 0326

Land class: Waste ground   **Geology:** Alluvium

Description: 1967 – Iron Age pottery sherds and briquetage (derived from a new channel) found and kept by R Bradley (1969).

ROMANO-BRITISH

Langstone Survey Project Number: HI.78
SMR NUMBER: SU70SW 55

LOCATION: West Coast of Hayling Island   **NGR:** SU 7200 0400

Land class: Intertidal mudflat   **Geology:** Alluvium

Description: 1978 – 4 Roman coins found on foreshore SW of Hayling Island road bridge – kept by finder J Edwards, 39 Wisborough Road, Southsea – coin of Constantine I 307–37; one of Constantius – Rev. Gloria Exercius; one possible Constantius.

Langstone Survey Project Number: HI.79
SMR NUMBER: SU70SW 60

LOCATION: South of Old Oyster Beds   **NGR:** SU 7155 0326

Land class: Waste ground on reclaimed land   **Geology:** Alluvium

Description: Fragments of Roman brick or tile found in 1964 by Richard Bradley. Fragments were wasters, probably from a kiln which had been long since submerged below the sea. The site of the find was reclaimed by infilling in 1969.

Langstone Survey Project Number: LI.80
SMR NUMBER: SU70SW 65

LOCATION: Long Island   **NGR:** SU 7010 0410

Land class: Grassland, nature unknown   **Geology:** Alluvium

Description: Romano-British pottery sherds found 'in the 1960s'. Retained by the finder.

Langstone Survey Project Number: HI.81
SMR NUMBER: SU70SW 70

LOCATION: East of Old Oyster Beds | **NGR:** SU 7180 3050

Land class: | **Geology:** Brickearth

Description: A single room 6.1m (20ft) by 3.05m (10ft) of a ?larger building was excavated with a paved stone floor and finds of Roman tiles and wall plaster were made. Ely 1904, 14–15. Later excavated by Downey, King, and Soffe. Late Iron Age and Roman temple.

Langstone Survey Project Number: HI.82
SMR NUMBER: SU70SW 78

LOCATION: South of Old Oyster Beds | **NGR:** SU 7166 0326

Land class: Waste ground on reclaimed land | **Geology:** Alluvium

Description: Romano-British pottery sherds found by Richard Bradley in 1967. Site infilled in 1969 (OS card SU 70SW35).

Langstone Survey Project Number: SB.83
SMR NUMBER: SU60SE 25

LOCATION: South Binness Island | **NGR:** SU 6990 0300

Land class: Intertidal shingle/mudflat | **Geology:** Alluvium

Description: Rim and shoulder of small Rowlands Castle storage jar with batch mark XIII on shoulder recovered in 1978 & donated to Portsmouth City Museum Acc no E/78/18. PCM SMR no: SU60SE17.

Langstone Survey Project Number: FM.84
SMR NUMBER: SU60SE 27

LOCATION: South of Farlington Marshes | **NGR:** SU 6830 0340

Land class: Saltmarsh, intertidal mudflat | **Geology:** Alluvium

Description: 1986 – Abraded Roman 1st–2nd century pottery sherds found, also briquetage, burnt flint and flint tools (OS card SU60SE13) found and retained by B Hooper *c* 1965 – site falls on a small island south of Farlington Marshes which is normally inaccessible.

Langstone Survey Project Number: FM.85
SMR NUMBER: SU60SE 37

LOCATION: Island SW Farlington Marshes | **NGR:** SU 6790 0420

Land class: Saltmarsh | **Geology:** Alluvium

Description: 1984 – 37 abraded 1st/2nd century Roman pottery sherds found by Hooper 1964–7 (OS card SU60SE11).

Langstone Survey Project Number: FM.86
SMR NUMBER: SU60SE 39

LOCATION: NW corner Langstone harbour | **NGR:** SU 6840 0350

Land class: Intertidal mudflat/saltmarsh | **Geology:** Alluvium

Description: 1986 – 9 abraded sherds of 1st/2nd-century Roman pottery found *c* 1966 by B Hooper – also finds of briquetage, flint tools and other pottery. The site is not readily accessible (1969). Present location and condition of finds not known – 1986. (OS card no SU60SE3).

Langstone Survey Project Number: BI.87
SMR NUMBER: SU60SE 50

LOCATION: Baker's Island | **NGR:** SU 6950 0350

Land class: Grassland, nature unknown/Saltmarsh | **Geology:** Alluvium

Description: a) 1969 – Roman pottery recovered from at least 3 locations. 8 × 1st-century sherds (unrolled coarsewares) found with briquetage, *c* 12 sherds of coarsewares recovered nearby. OS card SO60SE2 – 1st-century sherds in Portsmouth County Museum Acc no 5/59 – SMR SU60SE10 (found by D Compton for B Cunliffe).
b) 1969 – briquetage and fired clay strut recovered from digging on the foreshore – now in Portsmouth County Museum Acc no 5/59 (OS card SU60SE2) PCM SMR SU60SE10 – found by D Compton c/o N Grammar School.

Langstone Survey Project Number: NB.88a
SMR NUMBER: SU60SE 55A
LOCATION: North Binness Island   **NGR:** SU 6935 0465
Land class: Grassland, nature unknown/Saltmarsh   **Geology:** Alluvium
Description: Roman brick and tile fragments – possible building site? recovered from southern shore of Island – SU60SE1

Langstone Survey Project Number: NB.88b (a–c)
SMR NUMBER: SU60SE 55B
LOCATION: North Binness Island   **NGR:** SU 6935 0465
Land class: Grassland, nature unknown/Saltmarsh   **Geology:** Alluvium
Description: a) 1955 – Roman pottery recovered from various locations on Island; large number of sherds, including six fragments of storage jars with finger prints, recovered from the site of NB.88a and along the southern shore of the Island; 2nd century pottery also recorded.
b) Concentration of Roman pottery, including samian ware recovered in same location as (a)
c) 11 sherds of Roman coarseware, including one rim of bead rim vessel – now in Portsmouth City Museum Acc no 114/48.

Langstone Survey Project Number: NB.88c
SMR NUMBER: SU60SE 55C
LOCATION: North Binness Island   **NGR:** SU 6935 0465
Land class: Grassland, nature unknown/Saltmarsh   **Geology:** Alluvium
Description: 1986 – Burnt flint recovered from various locations in association with Roman building material (NB.88a) and pottery (NB.88b).

Langstone Survey Project Number: Ha.89a
SMR NUMBER: SU70NW 73
LOCATION: Langstone   **NGR:** SU 7173 0532
Land class: Private garden, built over   **Geology:** Valley gravel
Description: Roman villa in ‘*Spes Bona*’ Langstone Ave, Langstone. Notes by Warren 1926–30, 286–7 and published by Gilkes 1998. Part of western wing of courtyard villa.

Langstone Survey Project Number: Ha.89b
SMR NUMBER: SU70NW 74
LOCATION: Langstone   **NGR:** SU 7170 0530 –5m OD
Land class: Private garden, built over   **Geology:** Valley gravel
Description: 1984 – Two Iron Age Au coins – one a stater – found in garden of ‘*Spes Bona*’ – the site of a Roman villa. Now in Portsmouth City Museum – Acc no 128/47 SMR SU70NW21.
Stater uninscribed Durotrigan Type C Evans type G5–6. AE coin Gallo-Belgic E, Evans type B8.

Langstone Survey Project Number: Ha.90
SMR NUMBER: SU70NW 82
LOCATION: Brockhampton Mill Lake   **NGR:** SU 7050 0550
Land class: Intertidal mudflat   **Geology:** Alluvium
Description: 1983 – Early Roman ceramic flagon neck found on shore line at head of Brockhampton Mill Lake, given to Hampshire County Museum Service Acc no 1982.6. Hughes 1983, *Archaeol in Hampshire Ann Rep* 1982, 52.

Langstone Survey Project Number: NB.91
SMR NUMBER:
LOCATION: North Binness Island   **NGR:** SU 4694 0451
Land class: Intertidal foreshore   **Geology:** Alluvium
Description: Binness Bay, Roman pottery from the foreshore,and stratified in the ‘cliff’ section associated with burnt flint, also briquetage kiln bars found by A Mack, and also previously by both Prof Barry Cunliffe and Bari Hooper

268

Langstone Survey Project Number: SB.18e
SMR NUMBER:
LOCATION: South Binness Island   **NGR:** SU 6985 0305
Land class: Intertidal foreshore and shingle   **Geology:** Alluvium
Description: South-west shoreline (Areas 771–5), surface artefact find of Roman pottery associated with a burnt patch of clay and burnt flint, presumably a hearth (a large Mesolithic SB.18a, and some Neolithic SB.18b, LNEBA and Bronze Age SB.18c flint assemblages, and a Bronze Age vessel SB.18d)

SAXON

Langstone Survey Project Number: HI.92
SMR NUMBER: SU70SW 58
LOCATION: St Mary's Church, Hayling Island   **NGR:** SU 7220 0004
Land class: **Geology:**
Description: Saxon font or lavabo. Saxon inscribed stone, found nr present vicarage of St Mary's in 1850. Carved sandstone, rectangular with a hollowed out rounded bowl and sides decorated with interlace pattern (Green, A R, & Green, P M, 1951 *Saxon architecture and sculpture in Hampshire*, 47–50.

Langstone Survey Project Number: LH.93
SMR NUMBER:
LOCATION: Sinah Lake   **NGR:** *c* SU 701 007
Land class: Intertial muds   **Geology:** alluvium
Description: Circle 6m in diameter of 27 oak timber posts linked with oak wattle panels and surrounding an area of flints, probably an oyster parc. One timber radiocarbon dated to 960–1180 cal AD (980 ± 50 BP, GU-7275).

MEDIEVAL

Langstone Survey Project Number: HI.94
SMR NUMBER: SU70NW 7
LOCATION: Wade Court Farm   **NGR:** SU 7203 0526 –5m OD
Land class: Grassland, nature unknown   **Geology:** Brickearth, valley gravel
Description: 1974 – Medieval pottery sherds including cooking pot rim and fragments of green glazed jug probably 12th/14th century – west of Wade Lane, Portsmouth City Museum SMR SU70NW49. Also Quernstone – 7B.

Langstone Survey Project Number: Ha.95
SMR NUMBER: SU70NW 64
LOCATION: Brockhampton Sewage Works   **NGR:** SU 7090 0560 –2m OD
Land class: Road   **Geology:** Brickearth
Description: 1968 – 3 hearths revealed by road building – medieval pottery bound nearby but could not be said to be associated – *CBA Arch Rev* 1968 – No 3–27.

Langstone Survey Project Number: HI.96
SMR NUMBER: SU70NW 79
LOCATION: Wade Court Farm   **NGR:** SU 7200 0520 –2m OD
Land class: Grassland, nature unknown   **Geology:**
Description: 1955 – Medieval Salterns recorded south of Wade Court – now enclosed by a sea wall with drainage outlets controlled by a sluice (OS card SU70NW 12).

Langstone Survey Project Number: LH.97
Project SMR NUMBER:
LOCATION: Marine: Sweare Deep   **NGR:** SU 730 045
Land class: **Geology:** Alluvium
Description: Wooden harpoon (?yew), dredged from Sweare Deep, dated by AMS (cal AD 1230–1390). Retained by owner. See Allen 1997a; Allen & Pettitt 1997

Langstone Survey Project Number: PI.98
SMR NUMBER:
LOCATION: Portsea Island, Eastney Lake   **NGR:** SS 6771 9939
Land class: Intertidal foreshore   **Geology:** Alluvium
Description: Timber structure: A total of 64 timbers (t4) whose base level heights ranged from 0.627 OD to 1.141 OD. This structure is located on the southern side of Eastney Lake and forms an inverted 'horse shoe' shape which encloses a shingle bank. The original structure was considerably larger extending southwards beneath what is now the Lumsden Road housing estate. Interestingly, the full extent is shown on the 1898 Ordnance Survey map of the area as the tip of a small enclosed area named 'The Glory Hole'. The depth of the enclosed area is not great, probably no deeper than –0.5 to –1 metre OD which would limit its use as a haven. There is a small and rather indistinct linear feature shown in La Fabvollière's (or Charles Manson's) map of around the mid 17th century at this point. Might this suggest that this structure forms the remains of a medieval or Tudor haven?

POST-MEDIEVAL

Langstone Survey Project Number: HI.99
SMR NUMBER: SU70SW 71
LOCATION: Bridge Lake   **NGR:** SU 7184 0427
Land class: Intertidal mudlflat   **Geology:** Alluvium
Description: Post-medieval swing bridge. Built in 1867 for the railway crossing to Hayling Island. Made of wood, the central section could be moved to allow access along Bridge Lake for shipping. The bridge spans are no longer extant but the massive iron columns remain along with the rollers and operating gear.

Langstone Survey Project Number: PI.100
SMR NUMBER: SU60SE 3
LOCATION: Portsea Island   **NGR:** SU 6790 0160
Land class: Grassland, nature unknown/allotment/   **Geology:** Alluvium/plateau gravel
standing water/lake/thoroughfare road/recreational
Description: 1986 – Salterns situated at N side of the creek at Great Salterns representing an ancient salt industry – saltings at Copnor assessed at 8d in the Domesday Book (1086). Saltings sold by auction in 1830 with extensive 'cisterns and buildings for salt works' – brine grounds comprised *c* 70 acres. 18th/19th century – end of Portsea salt industry, finally enclosed by a sea wall and infilled with tipping. Now occupied by allotment gardens, playing fields, and a caravan site – no traces of saltworkings visible in 1955 (OS card SU60SE6). VCH Hants 3, 1908, 194; VCH Hants 5, 1912, 470–1; H Sligh, 1838 *The History of Plymouth*, 13.

Langstone Survey Project Number: PI.101
SMR NUMBER: SU60SE 23
LOCATION: Portsea Island   **NGR:** SU 6600 0370
Land class: Built over/thoroughfare/road   **Geology:** Brickearth
Description: Bastion defences for Portsmouth. Referred to in 1880s on site of an earlier line. Consists of 3 whole and 2 demi-bastions linked by curtain walls and ditch ?9m wide.

Langstone Survey Project Number: Ha.102
SMR NUMBER: SU70NW 49
LOCATION: Warblington Bay   **NGR:** SU 7230 0510
Land class: Marine   **Geology:** Shingle
Description: 1988 – The Wade Way, a causeway which leads south from Langstone High Street and curves SE then S towards Hayling Island – 2m wide – Documents show that Wade is known from 1552 onwards – Minutes from the rights-of-way sub-committee 14.01.88.

Langstone Survey Project Number: BI.103
SMR NUMBER:
LOCATION: Baker's Island NGR: SU 6944 0360
Land class: Saltmarsh **Geology:** Alluvium
Description: A series of five brick-built shelters, each around 1.5m in width and 5m long. The walls of these structures included a regular pattern of gaps in the brickwork. Each building was covered with a flat reinforced concrete roof around 0.30m thick. The origin and function of these buildings is not known for certain, although they are believed to have been used as night bomber decoys during World War II, to lure air attacks away from Portsmouth.
The partially upstanding remains of a flint-walled building were also found on the north-western point of the island. Two 1m long fragments of the north-western and south-eastern walls survive to a height of around 1.6m, while the foundation courses of the rest of the building can still be seen clearly at ground level. From these observations it was possible to estimate the original size of the building at around 8 × 3m. The building's origins are unknown although it is marked on a 19th century map of the island and labelled as 'old walls'.

Langstone Survey Project Number: PI.104
SMR NUMBER:
LOCATION: Portsea Island, Eastney Lake NGR: SU 6789 0000
Land class: **Geology:**
Description: Timber structure: Consists of 196 timbers (t5) whose ground level heights ranged from 0.098m OD to 1.949m OD. The timbers are in three groups. The southern most group are guide posts for the entry to the sea lock entrance to the Portsea section of the Portsmouth and Arundel Canal. These are quite substantial posts, some of which reach to over 8ft in height. These were probably new in 1822 when the canal opened. The canal closed in 1827 and so they are unlikely to have been replacements for the original equipment. The middle group of posts take the form of two parallel lines with two areas projecting south in the middle of the run. It is possible that these are the remnants of a landing jetty. The age of this structure is unknown. However, there is the possibility that it is associated with the Prison Hulks which were moored in Langstone harbour in the early-19th century. The third grouping is to the north and is situated alongside the sea wall. It is possible that this is the landward end of another jetty which extends eastward.

Langstone Survey Project Number: HI.105
SMR NUMBER:
LOCATION: Old Oyster Beds NGR: SU 7143 0296
Land class: Intertidal foreshore **Geology:** Alluvium
Description: Timber structure (t6): 307 timbers heights ranged from –0.654m OD to 0.812m OD. This structure is most likely part of Harry Lobb's oyster farm of the late 1860s. The South of England Oyster Fishery was established in Langstone to develop a 'scientific' oyster farm. These timbers probably form part of the oyster pens. There are two large brick built 'drains' associated with these timbers.

Langstone Survey Project Number: HI.106
SMR NUMBER:
LOCATION: Stoke, nr Knott's Marsh NGR: SU 7143 0248
Land class: Intertidal foreshore **Geology:** Alluvium
Description: Stone row: This is a complex of lines of stones (S1) placed onto the surface of the mud (1m OD) which can be viewed as creating pens. To the outside of these pens there are remains of hurdling down below the surface of the mud. To the seaward end of this structure there are roofing ridge tiles scattered about. These are important because such tiles when stacked into small towers are a recognised means of collecting and nurturing oyster spat. It is possible that these too are associated with the activities of Harry Lobb, although they could be earlier.

Langstone Survey Project Number: HI.107
SMR NUMBER:
LOCATION: Hayling Island NGR: SU 7120 0072
Land class: Intertidal foreshore **Geology:** Alluvium
Description: Brick kiln. The remains of a post-medieval brick-built structure set back against a low cliff were identified at about HWMT (1m OD) on the Hayling Island coast (SU 4712 1007). It was horseshoe-shaped in plan and measured 3m east–west and 2.2m north–south. The front of the structure did not survive above the level of the shingle beach but the back wall stood to *c* 1m. It was built entirely of brick faced with a white, probably lime, wash blackened in places by scorching. Scorched bricks and brick fragments littered the general area. This structure is likely to have been a brick kiln; brickmaking is certainly known from the 19th century (Moore 1984).

Langstone Survey Project Number: OI.108
SMR NUMBER:
LOCATION: Oyster Island   **NGR:** SU 6897 0334
Land class: Intertidal foreshore   **Geology:** Alluvium
Description: Timber structure: timbers (t3) of which 568 were surveyed individually heights ranged from 0.503m OD to 2.077m OD. This structure is situated on a small mound and shingle bar which are locally known as 'Oyster Island'. The shingle bar joins the island to the southern most tip of Farlington Marsh and is covered by most tides. The timber structures here form three distinct areas. Two of these are on the mainland end of the shingle bar and possibly perform a coastal protection function for the small brick and flint built house which once stood here. (Marked on the 1947 Admiralty Chart as 'red roof conspic.') The other, more substantial structure surrounds the southern side of Oyster Island itself. These form three concentric semicircles with 'cells' created by further posts placed radially. There were some posts found on the northern side of the island but these do not conform to the same pattern. The southern area is surrounded by blocks of dressed stone, possibly placed here for reinforcement purposes. To the south-west of the Island (approximately 25m) is a substantial midden of discarded oyster shells.

Langstone Survey Project Number: OI.109
SMR NUMBER:
LOCATION: Oyster Island   **NGR:** SU 690 033
Land class: Intertidal foreshore   **Geology:** Alluvium
Description: WWI searchlight base. The top of the Island has the footings of a searchlight station, possibly originating from the First World War.

WRECKS

Langstone Survey Project Number: LH.111
SMR NUMBER: SU60SE 59
LOCATION: Marine   **NGR:** SU 6928 0057
Land class: **Geology:**
Description: 1993 – Wreck of the 'Irishman' a British tug sunk in Langstone harbour after being mined – wreck appears at v low tides – appears on Air Photo [MO50 48.18.ON 001 0119.OW/Phot/OGB] – sank in 1941.

Langstone Survey Project Number: LH.112
SMR NUMBER: SU60SE 60
LOCATION: Marine   **NGR:** SU 6838 0074
Land class: **Geology:**
Description: Dredger 'Withern' lost 4 cables north of Ferry House in 1926 – wreck is marked with a beacon – v broken and lies on a mud bank [MO 50 48 06.ON 001 01 46.OW/HSA/OGB]

Langstone Survey Project Number: LH.113
SMR NUMBER: SU60SE 61
LOCATION: Marine   **NGR:** SU 6928 0057
Land class: **Geology:**
Description: Dredger 'Percy', English grab Dredger – mined in 1941. IOW SMR

Langstone Survey Project Number: LH.138
SMR NUMBER:
LOCATION: Marine   **NGR:** SU 68550 00575
Land class: **Geology:**
Description: 80 foot Powered barge 'Excelsior'.

UNDATED

Langstone Survey Project Number: HI.114
SMR NUMBER: SU70SW 24
LOCATION: South of Old Oyster Beds   **NGR:** SU 7153 0317
Land class: Waste ground   **Geology:** Alluvium
Description: An unassociated hearth found on beach in July 1964 by Richard Bradley (OS card SO70SW22).

Langstone Survey Project Number: HI.115
SMR NUMBER: SU70SW 34

LOCATION: Old Oyster Beds   **NGR:** SU 7148 0352

Land class: Waste ground on reclaimed land   **Geology:** Alluvium

Description: Burnt flint pot boilers found in a dense scatter in 1964 in what the finder described as a 'mud area over Old Oyster Beds'.

Langstone Survey Project Number: HI.116
SMR NUMBER: SU70SW 35

LOCATION: Old Oyster Beds   **NGR:** SU 7150 0360

Land class: Waste ground on reclaimed land   **Geology:** Alluvium

Description: A dense scatter of burnt flint pot boilers found in 1964. No further details known (OS card no. SU70SW33).

Langstone Survey Project Number: HI.117
SMR NUMBER: SU70SW 36

LOCATION: Old Oyster Beds   **NGR:** SU 71500 390

Land class: Reclaimed land   **Geology:** Alluvium

Description: A dense scatter of burnt flint pot boilers found in 1964 just to the north of the Old Oyster Beds. Note dated (OS card SU70SW33). Surface find made at 0m OD.

Langstone Survey Project Number: HI.118
SMR NUMBER: SU70SW 37

LOCATION: Old Oyster Beds   **NGR:** SU 7170 0341

Land class: Reclaimed land, intertidal mud   **Geology:**

Description: A possible hut circle; a circle of postholes 18.3m (60ft) in diameter with postholes at 6.1m (20ft) intervals containing the pointed, carbonised ends of posts 127mm (5ins) in diameter. Within is a large area of flints with a large ?cooking stone in the centre ?BA–IA, but undated.

Langstone Survey Project Number: FM.119
SMR NUMBER: SU60SE 29

LOCATION: South of Farlington Marshes   **NGR:** SU 6830 0340

Land class: Saltmarsh, intertidal mudflat   **Geology:** Alluvium

Description: 1986 – Burnt flint, pottery, briquetage and flint tools found on island noted in 27 & 28 (OS card SU60SE13).

Langstone Survey Project Number: FM.120
SMR NUMBER: SU60SE 30

LOCATION: NW corner Langstone harbour   **NGR:** SU 6830 0340

Land class: Saltmarsh   **Geology:** Alluvium

Description: 1986 – Scrapers, pottery briquetage and burnt flint recovered on small island south of Farlington Marshes, normally inaccessible (OS card SU60SE13).

Langstone Survey Project Number: FM.121
SMR NUMBER: SU60SE 35

LOCATION: Island SW Farlington Marshes   **NGR:** SU 6790 0420

Land class: Saltmarsh   **Geology:** Alluvium

Description: 1984 – Burnt flint found by Draper 1968.

Langstone Survey Project Number: FM.122
SMR NUMBER: SU60SE 38

LOCATION: Island SW Farlington Marshes   **NGR:** SU 6790 0420

Land class: Saltmarsh   **Geology:** Alluvium

Description: 1969 – 17 fragments of briquetage recovered from small island west of Farlington Marshes – found by Hooper 1964–7 (OS card SU60SE11).

Langstone Survey Project Number: FM.123
SMR NUMBER: SU60SE 42
LOCATION: South of Farlington Marshes   **NGR:** SU 6840 0350
Land class: Intertidal mudflat/saltmarsh   **Geology:** Alluvium
Description: 1986 – 4 fragments of briquetage found in 1966 by B Hooper – pottery and flint tools also found (site is not readily accessible [1969]; present location and condition of finds not known).

Langstone Survey Project Number: NB.124
SMR NUMBER: SU60SE 54B
LOCATION: North Binness Island   **NGR:** SU 6935 0465
Land class: Grassland, nature unknown/Saltmarsh   **Geology:** Alluvium
Description: 1969 – Crouched burial in mud – Iron Age (probably later Bronze Age) pottery found nearby – material with B Hooper.

Langstone Survey Project Number: NB.125
SMR NUMBER: SU60SE 56
LOCATION: North Binness Island   **NGR:** SU 6935 0465
Land class: Grassland, nature unknown/Saltmarsh   **Geology:** Alluvium
Description: 1986 – Mound with protecting earthworks situated at SU 69140464 – mound with earth bank and ditch also situated at SU 69530455 – 1955. Neither Draper or Hooper noted these features which seems odd as they have visited North Binness more than most – do these mounds really exist? (OS card SU60SE1).

Langstone Survey Project Number: NB.126
SMR NUMBER: SU60SE 57
LOCATION: North Binness Island   **NGR:** SU 6935 0465
Land class: Grassland, nature unknown/Saltmarsh   **Geology:** Alluvium
Description: 1969 – Fragments of briquetage, some unabraded (from evaporating parts) also some struts, retained by B Hooper (OS card SU60SE1).

Langstone Survey Project Number: NB.127
SMR NUMBER: SU60SE 58
LOCATION: North Binness Island   **NGR:** SU 6935 0465
Land class: Grassland, nature unknown/Saltmarsh   **Geology:** Alluvium
Description: 1969 – Bronze slag recovered from site near the sea wall – now in Portsmouth City Museum, Acc no 1969/243. SMR SU60SE21.

Langstone Survey Project Number: SB.128
SMR NUMBER:
LOCATION: South Binness Island   **NGR:** centred on SU 701 034
Land class: Intertidal foreshore and shingle   **Geology:** Alluvium
Description: Wadeway to Round Nap Island, (area 776 and 777), large flint assemblage, largely comprising flint debitage of all periods (Mesolithic to Bronze Age).

Langstone Survey Project Number: LH.129
SMR NUMBER:
LOCATION: Langstone harbour, south of Langstone Channel   **NGR:** SU 6983 0137
Land class: Intertidal foreshore   **Geology:** Alluvium
Description: Timber structure: This structure (t2) is formed of 6 remaining timbers. (There may well be more extant beneath the soft mud). Their heights ranged from –0.294m OD to –0.188m OD. This structure was first discovered by Arthur Mack in 1993. It is situated towards the middle of the harbour just to the south of the main Langstone Channel. It sits on top of a mudbank which is covered and uncovered by all tides. It is therefore, fully in the intertidal zone. The timbers themselves are rough-hewn sections of the tree and exhibit sharpening of the point which has been buried in the mud. The condition of the sub-surface timber is good with working marks clearly visible. The function and date of this structure is unclear at this time – though it is possible that it is a fish trap.

Langstone Survey Project Number: HI.130
SMR NUMBER:
LOCATION: Hayling Island   **NGR:** SU 7123 0082
Land class: Intertidal foreshore   **Geology:** Alluvium
Description: Timber structure: 159 timbers (t7) heights ranged from –0.006m OD to 1.065m OD. This is a complex arrangement of stakes placed into the mud. There seem to be some ovoid sub-structures in the middle of the run. It is possibly a fish trap. Its date is unknown.

Langstone Survey Project Number: HI.131
SMR NUMBER:
LOCATION: Hayling Island   **NGR:** SU 7130 0124
Land class: Intertidal foreshore   **Geology:** Alluvium
Description: Timber structure: 132 timbers heights (t8) ranged from 0.105m OD to 1.445m OD. Unknown date, possibly a fish trap.

Langstone Survey Project Number: HI.132
SMR NUMBER:
LOCATION: Hayling Island   **NGR:** SU 7132 0166
Land class: Intertidal foreshore   **Geology:** Alluvium
Description: Timber structure: 233 timbers heights (t10) ranged from –0.266m OD to 1.668m OD. This is a line of timber stakes which project westward from the Hayling Island coast. They are placed more thinly towards the coast and bunched together towards the seaward end.

Langstone Survey Project Number: HI.133
SMR NUMBER:
LOCATION: Hayling Island   **NGR:** SU 7102 0051
Land class: Intertidal foreshore   **Geology:** Alluvium
Description: Timber strcuture: 78 timbers (t12) heights ranged from 0.233m OD to 1.099m OD. The structure is situated adjacent to a small stream outfall and it faces in a south-westerly direction. The structure consists of two lines of round wood stakes driven into the mud which cross each other in the middle of their run to form a shallow and slightly curved X shape. Below the surface the timbers remain in good condition retaining the bark on the outside. As yet it is unclear what the function of the structure is although it may be the remains of a fish trap. Its location would suggest that this is likely as the structure is covered and uncovered by most tides.

Langstone Survey Project Number: HI.134
SMR NUMBER:
LOCATION: Hayling Island   **NGR:** SU 7152 0201
Land class: Intertidal foreshore   **Geology:** Alluvium
Land class: **Geology:**
Description: Timber structure: 385 timbers (t13) heights ranged from 0.228m OD to 1.468m OD. This bears a resemblance to other lines of timber stakes along the coast of Hayling Island although it is a sinuous curve and bifurcates in the middle of its run. It may be another form of fish trap. Its date is unknown.

Langstone Survey Project Number: OI.135
SMR NUMBER:
LOCATION: Oyster Island   **NGR:** SU 689 034
Land class: Intertidal foreshore   **Geology:** Alluvium
Description: Causeway. A submerged causeway between Oyster Island and a shingle bar extending Westward from Baker's Island links Baker's Island to the Mainland. This causeway rarely dries out but is usually walkable in wellington boots at low spring tide. It should be noted that both of the shingle bars, from Farlington Marsh to Oyster Island and from Baker's Island to the causeway are set at right angles to the tidal flow of the water. This flow is quite strong on a falling tide and as a result this may suggest that the existence of these shingle bars is not a result of a natural process. Indeed, the bar between Farlington Marsh and Oyster Island exhibits a significant 'dog-leg' where the flow has caused the bar to migrate southwards which would indicate that it is unlikely to be naturally deposited shingle. It should also be borne in mind that the junction area of the shingle bar with the main part of Baker's Island is an area of significant archaeological deposits.

Langstone Survey Project Number: HI.136
SMR NUMBER:
LOCATION: Hayling Island   **NGR:** SU 7128 0125
Land class: Intertidal foreshore   **Geology:** Alluvium
Description: Timber feature t9: A simple line of only 15 timbers (+0.171 to 0.433m OD) just to the north of this structure t8. It is so close that it could be considered a part of t8. The shoreward end of the strcuture is at 0.43m OD.

Langstone Survey Project Number: HI.137
SMR NUMBER:
LOCATION: Hayling Island   **NGR:** SU 7132 0172
Land class: Intertidal foreshore   **Geology:** Alluvium
Description: Timber feature t11: A line of stakes (HI137) projecting westwards from Hayling Island shore with its shoreward end at 0.84m OD.

Appendix 3: Fieldwork strategy and health and safety issues

Fieldwork strategy

The adoption of a seamless approach is beneficial. Zones of the study area that are currently underwater, in the intertidal zone, or in terrestrial locations are a product of the present landscape. We cannot assume that this landscape bears a direct relationship to the nature of former past landscapes. A seamless approach employs the same methods in all terrains ensuring direct compatibility of results irrespective of the present-day, and therefore somewhat arbitrary, environments.

Physical survey in difficult terrains is made significantly easier using a GPS (or at very least a total station survey). This requires only minimal equipment to be carried through arduous terrains. Only localised and detailed archaeological recording then required more traditional tape measurement. The locations of these surveys are tied into the project survey by GPS or total station survey for the construction of the project base map.

Although much archaeological work is undertaken through individual context sheets in ring binders, the conditions are not conducive to the use of large quantities of paperwork in the field. A traditional well-bound site notebook with graph paper, combining daily records, made sure the fieldwork and the archaeological records (site plans, sample records, etc) were maintained. Relevant and selected elements were transferred to common pro forma 'context' records.

The use of the local knowledge of local collectors and of their recorded finds and find locations is invaluable in reconnaissance of the terrain. Many major intertidal studies (eg Welsh Severn Estuary) have benefitted significantly from the input and involvement of one or more local amateur archaeologists.

On small-scale projects, GIS used as a composite interactive database is not of much greater value than standard archaeological records. On larger-scale projects, however, where the amount of information and number of types of data sets is greater, GIS systems come into their own as a way of storing, collating, and interrogating the study area.

Where GIS is used analytically, to interrogate, model, and predict geographical distributions (archaeological sites, artefacts scatters, sedimentary deposits etc: eg Day 1999), it is an invaluable tool, and the analytical and predictive requirements need to be considered prior to data gathering and selection of the GIS shell.

The recommended, revised staged and nested approach to fieldwork in the intertidal zone is outlined below, and can be compared with the detailed methods given in Chapter 1, and the review of their performance in Chapter 8.

General survey, in particular, is most appropriately conducted by small teams carrying out small scale searches over long periods of time; the complete antithesis to terrestrial excavation which may best be conducted by large teams working intensively over short periods. Intertidal projects are not easily conducted within the time-scale, nor fieldwork frameworks, designed primarily for projects on dry land. Ideally survey should be conducted over an extended period of time, not just short fieldwork seasons, to ensure a more uniform recovery of material that might be temporarily masked. Continuous erosion and modification of many intertidal landscapes ensures that a fieldwork survey should not be considered to be definitive nor entirely representative sample of the study area. Survey should repeat the exercise at suitable intervals (possibly 20–25 years) to re-evaluate the evidence.

Stage 1: Desk based study and assessment and creation of a project base map

- archaeological and palaeoenvironmental desk-based study to synthesise and map all readily available data with which to provide a preliminary assessment of the study area, and recognition of the geographical, archaeological, and historical development of the wider region. Including:
  - examination of records of existing historical archaeological, palaeogeographical, and palaeoenvironmental reports
  - SMR records
  - discussions and interviews with locals such as fishermen, conservation wardens etc
  - evaluation of commercial borehole, albeit crude, data
  - examination of aerial photographs, map, and chart information
  - examination of secondary historical sources
- reassessment of museum and private artefact collections
- topographic mapping/survey
  - creation of the project map by digitisation of aerial photographs or existing maps
- evaluation of the collected data and production of a summary or interim report

Stage 2: Archaeological assessment and data enhancement

- rapid field assessment to locate, define and characterise the archaeological remains:
  - rapid walkover and swimover survey (with representative local artefact collection) to characterise artefact scatters
  - wide scale rapid artefact and site mapping
  - controlled artefact collection of representative samples (small total collection squares) recording of available sections
  - recording of the location and character of archaeological, historical, and underwater sites

- large-scale (hand) auger survey (and underwater) to characterise the sedimentary sequence
- rapid geophysical prospection including *Chirps* etc
- evaluation of the archaeological and palaeo-environmental resource
  - scan of the archaeological artefacts
  - assessment of the assemblage character, location, and distribution
- isolation of specific areas for more detailed archaeological investigation

Stage 3: Site investigation

- detailed site investigation to characterise the study landscape:
  - detailed and controlled collection (total gridded artefact collection units)
  - localised site survey (including underwater)
  - excavation (and underwater if necessary)
  - testpitting
  - targeted augering and power boreholes
  - palaeoenvironmental sampling (from exposed faces and in excavations, and coring)
- assessment of the collected information and selection for analysis, reporting etc

Stage 4: Data analysis and manipulation

- assessment and analysis of selected artefacts and palaeoenvironmental data recovered
- preparation of analytical reports

Stage 5: Synthesis and reporting

- project wide analysis; regression analysis, prediction models etc, as appropriate to the projects aims
- final analysis, interpretation and dissemination
- compilation of relevant report

Health and safety issues

Our precautions for work on mudflats and low intertidal areas were as follows:

Pre-arming

Although no formal training was undertaken, a full fieldwork risk assessment was implemented, and advice actively sought from the Coastguard, the Harbour Master, Langstone Harbour Board, and the Langstone mud-rescue team! An single A4 information sheet with emergency advice and telephone numbers was encapsulated and taken with the field team. We were familiarised with the ground conditions and local tides and guided around the landscape by the RSPB warden and local fishermen as a

team, before undertaking fieldwork. A good working knowledge of the tides, local currents, treacherous muds, and specific hazards was imparted at the onset of the project.

All members of the Wessex Archaeology field team were briefed and given copies of both the fieldwork risk assessment, and guidelines of safety measures specific to the fieldwork in Langstone Harbour.

The archaeological field team were made acutely aware of the boundaries of the nature reserve and of designated areas to which we had permitted access but to which members of the public and bird-watchers did not. All work within these areas was conducted with the sensitivity it deserved, and was coordinated with the life-cycles of the bird and mammals following advice from the RSPB and local wildlife wardens.

The daily fieldwork programme was dictated by tides, and full consultation with both tide charts and local fishermen was made. Fieldwork concentrated in the furthest and most inaccessible locations as low tide made them accessible, and worked shorewards.

Bamboo canes were carried and used as markers of archaeological find spots, section points, and survey areas to be recorded and surveyed at a later time by the survey team. These however, proved very useful as a general probe to check the thickness and consistency of mud and of creeks.

Protocol

i) a minimum team size of 2, preferably 3 people was deployed at all times; never one person alone

ii) at the beginning of each survey mission, the crew always rang in to the office, and rang back to 'sign-off' on return

iii) in the first season of fieldwork, this 'signing-off' procedure was also carried out with the Harbour Master; ie a secure-side person was always notified. Failure to sign-off would instigate enquiries from 'secure-side'

Clothing

iv) good-quality weather-proof clothing and wellingtons, if not waders were worn, or carried, by all teams members in the field

v) although we would always recommend the wearing of fluorescent jackets or tabards, we were requested by the RSPB not to wear fluorescent clothing due to the risk of frightening the bird and wildlife population in this SSSI and Ramsar designated area

Equipment and communication

vi) communication systems. In 1993 and 1994 walkie-talkies were issued to ensure that the team were in communication between themselves at all times – this was a practical, and H&S, feature

vii) a mobile phone was provided for communication beyond the team, and to emergency services, if required

viii) a strong nylon rope was carried at all times (to extricate those stuck in the mud – it was used once)

ix) personal distress flares were carried in a small strong box

Procedures

x) all heavy equipment was delivered to site by boat at high tide and stored in a strong-box, rather than carried across muds at low tide

Dangerous materials

xi) raw sewage outfalls were avoided at all times (see Medical below)

xii) the disturbance of, and contact with, unidentified metallic objects was to be avoided in view of the military use of the area, and known presence of EODs (Explosive Ordnance Devices)

Medical

xiii) encapsulated cards were carried by all staff indicating the risk to the owner of Weil's disease (a water-borne infection carried (*inter alia*) by rat's urine), due to the places of work

xiv) all core field staff of Wessex Archaeology are *required* to have and maintain their tetanus and Hepatitis A injections; non-core staff were recommended to do so

xv) antiseptic cleansing agent (eg Swarfega) was taken in the vehicle to help clean hands, particularly at the end of the day. This is both a practical consideration as intertidal mud can be very difficult to remove, and a health and safety consideration in view of the amount of sewage discharged around the coast (there is one major outlet into Langstone Harbour), as well as the risk of Weil's disease

xvi) basic first-aid kit carried at all times

A useful health and safety checklist is provided in the appendix to *Nautical Archaeology on the Foreshore* (Milne *et al* 1998), and some useful points outlined in *A Brief for Rapid Coastal Zone Assessment Surveys, English Heritage and RCHME* (English Heritage 1999).

General safety guidelines and emergency advice as provided to the Wessex Archaeology field team

General Safety

Take care wherever you are walking as the mud and clay surfaces can be very slippery and may conceal submerged objects. Clean any cuts with clean water and treat with antiseptic as soon as possible.

Avoid running on the mud and hard clay surfaces

Do not pick up unidentified metal objects, they may explode!

Safety on mudflats and islands

Maintain visual contact with each other wherever possible and frequent walkie-talkie contact when you cannot see each other. Beware of narrow creeks into which it is easy to fall. Do not assume the mud in them will be shallow. Enter any with care.

Do not venture into the mud anywhere alone. When walking in the mud it is safer to keep moving. If you stop you tend to stick and sink. Walking in mud which is more than a few inches deep is both slow and extremely tiring. Give yourself plenty of time when working in muddy areas

When working in soft mud carry a rope tied round your waist and attach to another team member.

Do not linger when the tide starts coming in. Beware that the mud can get suddenly softer before you can see the water as the tide comes in; the water seeps in below the mud surface!

In case of emergency

If you are stuck in the mud do not panic. Removing wellingtons/waders might help free you. It may be easier to crawl or 'swim' over the mud. If you cannot get yourself out quickly make sure that the others know you are stuck. Do not struggle.

If someone is stuck in the mud, and you cannot pull them out with a rope (do not wade in and get yourself stuck alongside) – especially if the tide is coming in – do not hesitate to call the emergency services. Other members of the team should retreat to safe ground and maintain visual and walkie-talkie contact with the one who is stuck.

If you get cut-off and stranded, find land above the high-water mark. Ring in to your secure-side contact.

Although issued with personal distress flares these should only be used in a dire emergency; they will be answered by a helicopter.

Index *by Peter Rea*

Page numbers in italics refer to illustrations